CROSSFIRE

CROSSFIRE

The Plot That Killed Kennedy

Revised and Updated Edition

JIM MARRS

BASIC BOOKS
A Member of the Perseus Books Group
New York

First hardcover published by Carroll & Graf in 1989
Previous paperback edition published by Basic Books in 1993

Books published by Basic Books are available at special discounts for bulk purchases in the United States by corporations, institutions, and other organizations. For more information, please contact the Special Markets Department at the Perseus Books Group, 2300 Chestnut Street, Suite 200, Philadelphia, PA 19103, or call (800) 810-4145, ext. 5000, or e-mail special.markets@perseusbooks.com.

Designed by Jeff Williams

Library of Congress Cataloging-in-Publication Data
Marrs, Jim.
  Crossfire : the plot that killed Kennedy / Jim Marrs. -- Revised and updated edition.
     pages cm
  Originally published: New York : Carroll & Graf Publishers, 1989.
  Includes bibliographical references and index.
   ISBN 978-0-465-03180-1 (pbk.) — ISBN 978-0-465-05087-1 (e-book) 1. Kennedy, John F. (John Fitzgerald), 1917-1963—Assassination. I. Title.

E842.9.M36 2013
973.922092—dc23
LSC-C   2013030290
10 9 8 7 6 5

The great masses of the people will more easily
fall victims to a great lie than to a small one . . .
—ADOLF HITLER, *MEIN KAMPF*

CONTENTS

Acknowledgments   xiii
Introduction to the Revised Edition   xv

PART I: THE KILL ZONE

DALLAS—The Stage Is Set 1

The Thirty-fifth President...1

DEALEY PLAZA—November 22, 1963 8

The Motorcade 8

The Crowd..16
    Two Suspicious Men, 29
    The Babushka Lady, 35

The Texas School Book Depository................................39
    The Distracting Seizure, 42
    The Man in the Doorway, 45
    The Oswald Encounter, 51

The Triple Underpass...57
    Smoke on the Grassy Knoll, 58
    The Third Wounded Man, 62

The Grassy Knoll 66
    The Zapruder Film, 66
    The Black Dog Man, 74
    The Badge Man, 80
    A Grassy Knoll Witness, 83

PART II: MEANS, MOTIVES, AND OPPORTUNITIES

LEE HARVEY OSWALD—ASSASSIN OR PATSY? 90

A Mother in History 90

Oswald's Library Card 98

Semper Fidelis 100

Oswald Overseas 101

Oswaldskovich the Marine 106

RUSSIANS (Soviets and Solidarists) 109

Oswald and the U-2 109

Robert E. Webster—Another Oswald? 111

A Phony Defection 112

Comrade Oswald 116

A Whirlwind Romance 119

A Soviet Defector's Story 123

CUBANS (Pro- and Anti-Castro Cubans) 127

Fidel Castro 127

Disaster at the Bay of Pigs 129

544 Camp Street 138

Oswald and the Exiles 140

Oswald's Girlfriend 143

MOBSTERS (Organized Crime) 149

Bootleggers and Boozers 150

Lucky Goes to War 152

Carlos Marcello 154

Santos Trafficante and Cuba 158

The War on Hoffa 160

Momo and His Girlfriends 163

AGENTS (The CIA and Other Intelligence Agencies) 167

The Manchurian Candidates 171

CIA-Mafia Death Plots 173

New Orleans 174

The Saga of Tosh Plumlee 175

Was Oswald a Spy? 179

A Message from Oswald 186

DeMohrenschildt and the Agency 189

The French Connection to the Assassination 192

G-MEN
(J. Edgar Hoover's FBI and the Secret Service) 199

The Top G-man.. 201

Did Oswald Work for the FBI? 210

Cuban Grand Central Station... 219

The Secret Service 224

A Few Drinks at the Cellar 229

REDNECKS AND OILMEN
(Right-wing Extremists and Texas Millionaires) 235

A Bullet for the General... 236

The Miami Prophet 244

Nixon and the JFK Assassination 246

A Killing on Wall Street... 253

Kennedy and Oilmen 256

Oswald's Friends.. 258

All the Way with LBJ... 269

SOLDIERS (The Military) 280

The Military-Industrial Complex 280

Kennedy and Vietnam.. 284

The Man Who Was to Kill Oswald.. 289

Lone Gunmen on the Grassy Knoll 293

PART III: AFTERMATH

DALLAS 303

Mysterious Secret Service Men 309

The Black Car Chase 316

The Account of Roger Craig 318

The Three Tramps 322

The Mafia Man in Dealey Plaza.. 327

The Shooting of J. D. Tippit 330

The Arrest of Oswald 340

The FBI Takes Control... 347

TWO HOSPITALS 351

Jack Ruby at Parkland.. 356

The Switching of Bodies...364

JACK RUBY 370

Jack Ruby—Gangster 375

Jack Ruby—Gunrunner and FBI Informant 379

The Woman Who Foresaw the Assassination 385

Did Ruby and Oswald Know Each Other? 387

The Shooting of Lee Harvey Oswald 398

Jack Ruby's Warnings 400

The Sudden Death of Jack Ruby 410

THE EVIDENCE 415

An Incriminating Palm Print 422

Questionable Backyard Photos...430

Reenactment Problems... 433

THE WARREN COMMISSION 436

The Reluctant Chairman 438

Oswald and the FBI 447

Conflicts in the Testimony 451
The Single-Bullet Theory...458

THE GARRISON INVESTIGATION 466

Clay Shaw and Permindex..469

THE HOUSE SELECT COMMITTEE ON ASSASSINATIONS 485

Blakey at the Helm..491
The Dallas Police Radio Recording 497

THE OLIVER STONE FILM *JFK* 503

Preemptive Attacks...504

THE ASSASSINATIONS RECORDS REVIEW BOARD 506

Douglas Horne's Discoveries 507
The Zapruder Film: Fundamental or Fraud? 509
Hollywood Takes a Look..512

A QUESTION OF OSWALD 515

An Impostor 516
Was Oswald Really Oswald? 521
The Oswald Exhumation 524

CONVENIENT DEATHS 529

Early Deaths 532
Strange Deaths Continue 534

PART IV: CONCLUSIONS

Assassination Coverage 543
A Likely Scenario 547

Sources and Notes 557
Index 581
Photographs follow page 302

ACKNOWLEDGMENTS

When a final "truth" concerning the assassination of President John F. Kennedy is generally accepted by the population of the United States, it will have to be acknowledged that this truth came not from the government, the legal profession, or the news media—rather that truth will have come from the legion of individual citizens who have refused to accept official but superficial and unsupported explanations. At the fiftieth anniversary, this legion of researchers had grown too numerous to cite by name.

Special thanks for this edition of *Crossfire* go to Maritha Gan, Tom Ruffner, Larry Sells, Robert Fullilove, Chip DeNure, Stan Szerszen, Larry Hancock, and Ed Haslem, and to the superb editorial team at Basic Books, including Alex Littlefield, Collin Tracy, Jeff Williams, and Karl Yambert.

Every citizen who gave of their time, effort, and resources to study, assimilate, and disseminate assassination information should come to be regarded as an object lesson on how the individual citizen can make an impact on a system that has proven either unable or unwilling to police itself.

INTRODUCTION TO THE REVISED EDITION

"Will we ever know the truth about the Kennedy assassination?"

This is a question I have been asked many times over the years.

The answer is unequivocally yes. We know the truth today. It has been staring us in the face at least since the public was able to see in the Zapruder film Kennedy's body being thrust to the rear by a frontal shot.

If Lee Harvey Oswald was solely involved, then all information regarding him and the assassination should be available and Oswald should be as forgotten as Charles Guiteau, a disgruntled office seeker who was the lone assassin of President James A. Garfield in 1881. Unlike with Guiteau, because of the ongoing questions and controversy over the JFK assassination, virtually everyone in the educated world knows the name Lee Harvey Oswald.

Fifty years after the event, basic evidence, such as location of wounds, autopsy photographs and X-rays, fingerprints, accuracy of the weapon, even the famous Zapruder film, remain controversial. This is indicative of conspiracy and cover-up.

But, it is argued, if there was a conspiracy, wouldn't someone have spoken out by now? They have. For years now, many books and speakers, along with myriad witnesses and whistle-blowers, have brought forward bits of the truth, only to be ignored, drowned out, and ridiculed by the corporate-controlled mass media, which to this very day has failed to present the full range of assassination information in a comprehensive manner.

Anyone could have shot the president—Castro agents, Mafia hit men, rogue CIA operatives, KGB assassins, even the proverbial lone nut. But only high officials of the federal government and their financial rulers had the power to misdirect an honest investigation and keep the truth of the JFK assassination from the public for half a century.

So, the real question being asked is: "Will there ever be a news conference in which a ranking government official gives us the truth about the assassination?"

The answer to this question is probably no. Too many careers are involved. The Establishment fears the loss of public trust even though their attempts through the years to stifle the truth of many issues have merely resulted in that very loss.

In the case of the JFK assassination, trust has long been part of the problem. When it comes to the assassination of President John F. Kennedy, don't trust any one source. Don't trust this book. Don't trust even the government's basic documentation and pronouncements. Today the evidence of duplicity and fraud is too apparent to ignore.

The assassination today is recognized as a turning point in American history. Beginning on November 22, 1963, American attitudes slowly changed from post–World War II optimism and idealism to cynicism and mistrust of government. This loss of faith in government accelerated in the wake of the Vietnam War, Watergate, the Waco deaths, the Oklahoma City bombing cover-up, and the many unanswered questions about the attacks of September 11, 2001. The wide gulf between the official government version of the Kennedy assassination and the findings of those who have objectively studied the case has prompted cynicism and controversy.

This updated edition of *Crossfire* provides detailed background information on the men and organizations most likely to have been involved in a plot against the president. Also covered are the various attempts by governmental bodies to investigate and resolve what happened in Dallas. Attention is paid to the people behind these investigations, how they arrived at their conclusions, the reliability of the information made available to them, and the possibility of misdirection and deceit.

As an award-winning Texas journalist with more than fifty years of news-gathering experience, I have been in the singular position to learn the true story of the assassination. I have talked with many people involved, including Dallas-area government and law-enforcement officials and news reporters. I spent time with Oswald's wife, Marina, his mother, Marguerite, and Jeanne DeMohrenschildt, who along with her husband, George DeMohrenschildt, was a close friends of Oswald's. I have interviewed assassination witnesses, including James Tague, Jean Hill, Bill and Gayle Newman, Charles Brehm, Malcolm Summers, Phil Willis, and many others. I have interviewed witnesses never questioned by the official investigations, such as Ed Hoffman, Gordon Arnold, Ester Mash, Beverly Oliver, and Madeleine Brown. And I have kept in contact with serious researchers of the assassination, collecting and correlating their work.

Most important, I lived in the Dallas area during the time of the assassination.

As a university journalism major, I met Jack Ruby while visiting his Carousel Club in the fall of 1963. In the fall of 1964, I interviewed Major General Edwin A. Walker, himself a suspect. Within five years of the assassination, I was working as a professional reporter in the Dallas–Fort Worth Metroplex.

A native Texan who grew up in this area, I understand its people, history, and politics. Yet, as a journalist, I have tried to maintain a professional objectivity. I was fortunate to have the time to study the JFK assassination as both a working newsman and a researcher. I have no personal associations or theories to protect.

In 1976 I was invited to teach a course on the JFK assassination at the University of Texas at Arlington. I am told that mine was the first university-level course in the United States to cover the assassination. Through this course, many new leads were developed—such as a witness to a gunman on the Grassy Knoll and the intimidation of Dallas witnesses by Warren Commission staff members and FBI agents. After thirty years, I retired from UTA with my view of the assassination unchanged.

Only by gaining a broad view of the assassination can we begin to detect the outlines of the conspiracy that resulted in the deaths of Kennedy, Officer J. D. Tippit, and the accused assassin, Lee Harvey Oswald. Any one particular issue can be rationalized away as coincidence or happenstance.

Always keep in mind that the United States in 1963 was an entirely different place and time than today. The public had a blind faith in government, which seems hard to believe in light of today's cynical standards. The news media uncritically accepted official pronouncements and police work was conducted in an unsophisticated, even slipshod manner that would shock the highly trained and educated officers of today.

Witnesses tried to distance themselves from the accused assassin. Some, due to either ignorance or a desire to be helpful, or on orders, lied about critical evidence in the case, while the statements of others were misrepresented by investigating officials—for reasons both benign and otherwise. Government agencies were fearful of rumors that might have linked Oswald to them.

Not one single matter of fact in this case can be accepted uncritically. Evidence of deceit, misrepresentation, and manipulation abounds. The very people charged with finding the truth engaged in fabrication, alteration, and suppression of evidence as well as intimidation of witnesses.

So, what is the truth of the assassination?

The front page of the December 1, 1976, edition of the *Fort Worth Star-Telegram* carried my story concerning a new congressional committee tasked with investigating modern American assassinations. My lead paragraph stated:

> The new House Committee on Assassinations may find itself faced with the distinct possibility that a coup d'état occurred in 1963—with the complicity of U.S. Government officials.

Today, nearly forty years after that statement, nothing has been made public that warrants changing that conclusion. With the hindsight of events such as Watergate, Vietnam, the assassinations of Robert Kennedy and Martin Luther King Jr., Ruby Ridge, Waco, the attacks of 9/11, the economic meltdown of 2008, and unfounded wars in the Middle East, Americans have begun to see the lies, corruption, and outright criminal activity within their own government.

Within the probable coup that was the JFK assassination we can find efforts by certain US government officials not only to cover up critical evidence but to block any meaningful investigation. Such attempts at cover-up in a murder case are a serious crime. Obviously, such activity cannot be ascribed to a lone individual or even organized-crime members and certainly not Fidel Castro or Nikita Khrushchev. The plot, though not a conscious action of the government as a whole, nevertheless was homegrown, cultivated within government agencies, especially the military. It was a palace revolt.

Can this be proven? Turn the page and join me in studying the information that collectively reveals the plot that killed Kennedy.

Why seek the truth of this man's death? The answer is simple. Unless we as a nation come to a truthful understanding of what happened to our chief elected official in 1963, we obviously cannot begin to correctly understand the events that are affecting us today or take action to correct past wrongs.

Not only do I seek the killers of President Kennedy, I seek the persons who planned the probable coup against Camelot—those who killed the confidence and faith of the American people in their government and institutions. I seek elementary justice—for both the accused assassin and for the United States of America.

J.M. 2013

Don't let it be forgot
That once there was a spot
For one brief shining moment
That was known as Camelot

—ALAN JAY LERNER

PART I

THE KILL ZONE

Dallas—The Stage Is Set

Although one of the youngest cities in Texas, Dallas has recorded a meteoric rise to greatness and prosperity. Beginning in the days before Texas became a state, Dallas has grown from a small way station for pioneers to a center of corporate business, insurance, banking, and oil and gas. By 1963, Dallas already was the most influential city in the Lone Star State, second only to oil-rich Houston.

However, Dallas also had gained a reputation for being the stronghold of arch-conservatives, if not outright right-wing extremists. It is well-known in Texas police circles that during the 1940s and 1950s—and stretching into the early 1960s—that if a man wanted a job as a Dallas policeman, it helped if he was a member of the Ku Klux Klan, or at least the John Birch Society. The city police and other governmental offices were filled with members of these and other right-wing groups.

But Dallas was instrumental in carrying Texas in a national election. So in late 1963, the city was included on a quick political trip by President John F. Kennedy.

The Thirty-fifth President

John Fitzgerald Kennedy was the first US president born in the twentieth century. He was born on May 29, 1917, in Brookline, Massachusetts, an unpretentious middle-class suburb of Boston. Contrary to later claims that the Kennedys were part of the liberal Eastern Establishment, he was the second oldest son of a family that began their American life with the immigration of Patrick Kennedy from Ireland in 1848. Both grandfathers were prominent Democratic Party ward bosses while a group of Irish leaders ruled the local party but were discriminated against by society's rulers.

At age forty-three, Kennedy became the nation's youngest president, and at the time of his death at age forty-six, he had lived a shorter life than that of any other president.

His brief presidency—1,026 days—stirred the emotions of nearly every American. Hardly anyone was neutral about Kennedy. They either loved him or hated him.

Yet Kennedy seemed oblivious to the controversies surrounding him. Perhaps due to his privileged background, he increasingly appeared more concerned with great historical issues such as civil rights, war, and peace than with the parochial matters of business and politics.

Jack, as the future president was called by his friends, attended only the best schools. At Choate School in Connecticut, though he graduated near the bottom of his class, he nevertheless was selected as the man "most likely to succeed."

A bout with jaundice forced him to drop out of college, but upon recovery, he joined his older brother, Joseph Kennedy Jr., at Harvard. Maintaining only a C average, Kennedy concentrated on sports, particularly football. A somewhat sickly child, Kennedy had continuing bouts with illness compounded by a football injury that aggravated an already-weakened spinal column. For the rest of his life, he suffered recurring back problems.

In an effort to recuperate, Kennedy left school during his junior year to travel in Europe, where his father had been appointed US ambassador to Great Britain after generous contributions to Franklin Roosevelt's election campaign. After war broke out, Ambassador Kennedy was forced to resign because of his undisguised admiration for Germany's Nazi regime.

Young Kennedy returned to write a senior thesis about England's complacent attitudes just before World War II. This thesis was well received at Harvard and later was rewritten to become the best-selling book *Why England Slept*.

He began to show interest in a writing career but was interrupted by joining the US Navy two months before the December 7, 1941, attack on Pearl Harbor by Japan. Early in the war, Kennedy served as an intelligence officer in Washington but was transferred to the South Pacific after J. Edgar Hoover told his father about young Kennedy's love affair with a suspected Nazi agent.

In the summer of 1943, Kennedy was in command of a Navy patrol boat, the PT-109. During a patrol in the Solomon Islands, the boat was struck and broken in half by a Japanese destroyer, the only such incident during the war. He pulled his wounded chief engineer, Patrick McMahon, to a nearby island by swimming for four hours holding McMahon on his back by gripping a strap of the man's life jacket between his teeth. Later, Kennedy arranged for local natives to alert Navy officials to the group's location in enemy-held territory and they soon were rescued. Despite the loss of his command, Kennedy was hailed as a hero.

The story hit the front page of the *New York Times* and Kennedy's name became well-known in Boston. While recovering from his ordeal, Kennedy learned that his older brother, Joseph Jr., had been killed while flying a secret mission over Europe. His father's political aspirations now fell on Jack Kennedy. After the war, a reluctant Kennedy ran for and won a House seat from Massachusetts.

In later years, Joseph Kennedy was quoted as saying, "I told him Joe was dead and it was his responsibility to run for Congress. He didn't want to. But I told him he had to."

With the Kennedy name and Kennedy money behind him, Kennedy easily won two more elections to Congress. Then, in 1952, he defeated Henry Cabot Lodge to become junior senator from Massachusetts.

Despite an uninspiring senatorial career, by 1956 Kennedy's name was brought up as a possible running mate for Democratic presidential hopeful Adlai Stevenson. Although he was edged out as vice presidential candidate by Estes Kefauver, a graceful concession speech caused Kennedy's political stock to rise to new heights.

With an eye toward the 1960 election, Kennedy and his supporters went all out to ensure an impressive victory in his 1958 Senate reelection campaign in Massachusetts. Indeed, he won by the largest margin in the state's history. By 1960, Kennedy was ready for the Democratic presidential nomination, but there were hurdles to overcome. One of these was the fact he was a Catholic and no Catholic had ever been elected president. He overcame this problem by entering—and winning—a series of state primary elections. In West Virginia, with 95 percent Protestant voters, Kennedy beat senator Hubert Humphrey handily, thanks, according to FBI reports, to large organized-crime donations made through Frank Sinatra.

At the 1960 Democratic National Convention in Los Angeles, Kennedy was challenged only by conservative Texas senator Lyndon B. Johnson. Despite a late "draft Adlai Stevenson" movement, Kennedy won on the first ballot by 806 votes to Johnson's 409, thanks primarily to youthful supporters at the precinct level. The pragmatic Kennedy immediately knew that conservative Democrats were needed to win against Republican Richard Nixon, so he forged a temporary coalition by selecting the defeated Johnson as his vice presidential running mate, despite objections from labor and liberals. His selection of Johnson shocked Kennedy's supporters as well as Johnson's.

Years later, Kennedy's secretary Evelyn Lincoln revealed that the FBI director had forced the appointment of Johnson as vice president under threat of revealing Kennedy's sexual affairs. "It was blackmail," she stated. "The malicious rumors were fed to LBJ by J. Edgar Hoover about his [JFK's] womanizing. . . . LBJ and Hoover had boxed him into a hole."

There was no thought of Johnson's qualifications as president should anything happen to Kennedy. It was sheer spur-of-the-moment political tactics.

Nixon and his running mate, Henry Cabot Lodge, tried to raise the issue of experience during the ensuing 1960 election campaign. "Experience Counts" was their slogan, despite the fact that both Nixon and Kennedy had been elected to Congress in 1946 and that Nixon was only four years older than JFK. The slogan mostly was intended to call attention to Nixon's role as vice president under the popular Dwight "Ike" Eisenhower.

Kennedy's Catholicism was attacked by some preachers who regaled their congregations with the specter of a Vatican-dominated White House. The issue prompted Kennedy to tell a meeting of Protestant ministers in Houston, "I believe in an America where separation of church and state is absolute—where no Catholic prelate would tell the president (should he be a Catholic) how to act and no Protestant minister would tell his parishioners for whom to vote."

The real turning point in the 1960 election apparently came in September when Kennedy and Nixon met in the first televised debates in American history. The four debates were viewed by nearly half the nation's population and no one denies that Kennedy emerged the victor. Interestingly enough, however, radio listeners judged Nixon the winner.

The debates were TV show business, anticipating today's slick marketing of candidates. It was all image—Kennedy with a good makeup job appeared robust and self-confident while Nixon, suffering from little makeup and five-o'clock shadow, appeared unsure of himself. Their images aside, there was very little difference in the positions of the two candidates on most issues.

Ironically, when Kennedy called for support of the Cuban exiles in their attempts to regain Cuba from Castro, he was propounding the very program that Nixon had been pushing for many months. However, Nixon felt compelled to attack Kennedy's suggestions as irresponsible since, as he later wrote, "the covert operation [the upcoming Bay of Pigs Invasion] had to be protected at all costs" and, thus, Nixon came out opposing his own plans.

Kennedy won the election, but by one of the slimmest margins in American history. He polled 34,227,096 votes to Nixon's 34,108,546—a margin of 49.9 percent to 49.6 percent. Affluent whites, college graduates, women, Protestants, farmers, senior citizens, and business and professional people mostly voted against this eastern liberal.

Oddly enough, Kennedy's highest ratings in the polls during his term in office came just after the disastrous Bay of Pigs Invasion in April 1961 as Americans rallied to their president. About 82 percent of those polled expressed approval of his handling of the situation, which prompted Kennedy to remark, "My God, it's as bad as Eisenhower. The worse I do, the more popular I get." His popularity soared further in the fall of 1962, when his negotiation with Russian premier Nikita Khrushchev brought an end to the Cuban Missile Crisis, largely perceived in America as a victory over communist expansionism. In reality, it was a quid pro quo deal in which Russia withdrew its missiles from Cuba in return for America's removing its missiles from Turkey plus pledging not to support any further Cuban invasions.

But by the fall of 1963, polls showed Kennedy's popularity had dropped to 59 percent, largely due to his stand on civil rights. His willingness to negotiate with the communist world, his attack on the tax havens of wealthy corporations, and his attempts to regain civilian control over the Pentagon and its intelligence agencies had engendered fear and hatred among the most powerful cliques in the United States.

Newsweek magazine reported that no Democrat in the White House had ever been so disliked in the South. A theater marquee in Georgia advertised the movie *PT-109* with these words on its marquee: "See how the Japs almost got Kennedy."

Kennedy supporters were looking toward the 1964 election, hoping for a mandate that would give Kennedy's ambitious programs much-needed popular support. It never happened.

In the fall of 1963, he went to Texas.

Kennedy had carried Texas by the slimmest of margins in 1960, largely through the efforts of the state's powerful senator, Lyndon Johnson. He needed the state badly in 1964, particularly if his hopes of achieving a large mandate were to be realized. According to Texas governor John Connally, Kennedy first talked of coming to Texas in the summer of 1962. He again mentioned it in the summer of 1963.

According to former senator Ralph Yarborough, he was contacted by Kennedy aides in mid-1963 and was asked what could be done to help the president's image in Texas. Yarborough told this author, "I told them the best thing he could do was to bring Jackie to Texas and let all those women see her. And that's what he did, although I thought it was premature. I didn't think he was going to do that until 1964."

Thus, in an effort to enhance his image and to raise money, Kennedy, along with his wife, made the fateful journey to Texas in November 1963. On November 21, they visited Houston and San Antonio, both cities with heavy defense and space industries. There Kennedy came out strong for defense and NASA expenditures. The crowds loved it. That evening, he flew to Fort Worth, landing at Carswell Air Force Base and driving to the historic Hotel Texas for the night.

In his hotel suite, original paintings by Van Gogh and Monet had been hung on the walls in an effort to impress the Kennedys with Texas sophistication.

The morning of November 22, Kennedy spoke at a breakfast in the hotel sponsored by the Fort Worth Chamber of Commerce. Beforehand, more than 1,000 persons crowded in front of the hotel stood in light drizzling rain, which stopped just as the president made brief remarks. As the presidential party prepared to leave the hotel, vice president Lyndon Johnson arrived to introduce his sister, Lucia Alexander, to Kennedy. Reflecting on the surprisingly warm welcome he had received in Texas, Johnson later was to recall Kennedy as saying, "We're going to carry two states next year if we don't carry any others: Massachusetts and Texas." Johnson wrote in *The Vantage Point* that these were the last words Kennedy spoke to him.

As the rain clouds were breaking up, Kennedy drove back to Carswell for the eight-minute flight to Dallas. Fort Worth and Dallas are so close that even before reaching its full altitude, Air Force One began its descent to Dallas. The flight to Love Field was necessary due to the rivalry between the two cities over Dallas's Love Field (still operating) and Fort Worth's Greater Southwest Airport (relocated and replaced by Dallas–Fort Worth International in 1969). Looking out the plane's window, Kennedy commented to Governor Connally, "Our luck is holding. It looks as if we'll get sunshine."

As Air Force One landed at Love Field, the sky had cleared and a bright sun brought Indian summer weather to north-central Texas. By the noon hour, many people were in their shirtsleeves. The occasional cool breeze from the north was welcomed by Texans weary of the interminable summer heat, which often lasts well into the fall. It was the sort of day that stirs the blood, causing people to seek action outdoors, whether by working in the yard or attending the local football game.

This day there was another reason for wanting to get outside. The president was coming to town. The local media had been full of the news for days. The *Dallas Morning News* carried headlines that morning reading, LOVE FIELD BRACES FOR THOUSANDS and DETAILED SECURITY NET SPREAD FOR KENNEDY. That morning's edition had even run a small map of the president's motorcade route, which would take him from Love Field to the new, modern Trade Mart. However, this map indicated only that the motorcade would travel west on Main Street through the downtown area, through the well-known Triple Underpass, and on to Stemmons Freeway and the Trade Mart, where President Kennedy was scheduled to attend a 12:30 p.m. luncheon.

The city's other daily paper, the *Dallas Times Herald*, had given a more detailed description of the route. A story published the previous Tuesday, headlined YARBOROUGH GETS JFK TABLE SPOT, told how liberal senator Ralph Yarborough had been invited to sit with Kennedy at the head table during Friday's luncheon. It also mentioned that the motorcade would "pass through downtown on Harwood then west on Main, turning back to Elm at Houston and then out Stemmons Freeway to the Trade Mart."

This was one of the only newspaper mentions of the zigzag in the motorcade route, which would violate Secret Service procedures and place the president in a small park named Dealey Plaza, an area surrounded by tall buildings on one side and hillocks with shrubs and trees on the other.

The motorcade had been scheduled to pass through the downtown business section during the noon hour so office workers could watch the parade during lunch. This strategy worked well. Literally thousands of Dallasites turned out in the balmy sixty-eight-degree weather for a view of Kennedy.

Texas politics were in disarray. The state's Democrats had been aghast the previous year when a Republican, former schoolteacher and radio disk jockey John Tower, had been elected to fill Johnson's Senate seat. Tower was the first Republican to win a Texas Senate seat since the War Between the States. With more than seventy Democrats vying for Johnson's seat, the vote had been so split that Republican Tower won, much to the horror of state politicos. The Democratic Party, dominant in the state since Reconstruction, was split between conservatives, headed by senator Lyndon B. Johnson and Governor John B. Connally (a former Johnson campaign manager), and a small but noisy group of so-called liberals, led by Senator Yarborough. The party rift was serious. Yarborough and Connally were hardly speaking to each other. And Texas conservatives were highly vocal against

Kennedy's policies toward Cuba, civil rights, and a nuclear test ban with Russia, not to mention his plan to rescind the 27.5 percent oil depletion allowance, the foundation of Texas oil wealth.

With Texas now a two-party state, unity within the Democratic Party was needed badly. With the 1964 election year approaching, everyone—even his enemies—agreed Kennedy seemed unbeatable. However, he still needed to win over a few key states to acquire the broad mandate he was seeking. Texas was one of them. A presidential visit seemed just the answer.

Houston was the oil capital of the state, while Fort Worth and San Antonio were big defense industry centers. It would be easy to tell those folks what they wanted to hear. Dallas was a problem. At that time, the city was totally controlled by Mayor Earle Cabell, brother of Air Force General Charles Cabell, whom Kennedy had fired as deputy director of the CIA following the failed Bay of Pigs Invasion and who had branded JFK a "traitor." City politics were dominated by the mayor's cohorts on the all-white Citizens Charter Association.

No visit to Texas could ignore Dallas, yet the city had earned a reputation for being both politically bedrock conservative and intolerant of any deviation from that position. A month earlier, US ambassador to the United Nations Adlai Stevenson had been pushed, spat upon, and hit in the head with a picket sign while visiting in Dallas. Just the previous Tuesday, cashiered Army Major General Edwin A. Walker had made the news by shoving a TV cameraman during a Dallas speech by governor George Wallace of Alabama.

Stevenson, along with others close to Kennedy, warned the young president not to journey to Dallas. But in early June, plans for a trip to Texas were finalized during a meeting between Kennedy, Connally, and Johnson in El Paso. In October, a motorcade was added to the plans.

On November 22, apprehension within the Kennedy entourage concerning the trip was still evident, especially in light of a full-page newspaper ad that ran that morning in the *Dallas Morning News* suggesting the president was soft on communism and guilty of traitorous activities. A leaflet handed out along the motorcade route was not as subtle as the newspaper ad. It pictured Kennedy under a headline reading WANTED FOR TREASON.

Yet after landing at Love Field about 11:45 a.m., the Kennedy entourage found the Dallas crowds large, enthusiastic, and friendly, even though a few Confederate flags flew in the background. With horns honking, radios blaring, and the shouts and cheers of the crowd ringing off the sides of the office buildings, the scene was chaotic despite what had been hailed as one of the tightest security efforts in recent memory.

As the motorcade swept toward the central business district, it reached speeds of almost thirty miles per hour. But once the motorcade reached downtown, the crowds became larger, often spilling out into the street, and the pace slowed considerably.

The motorcade was the center of attention.

Dealey Plaza—November 22, 1963

The Motorcade

Leading the presidential motorcade on November 22, 1963, was an enclosed sedan driven by Dallas police chief Jesse Curry. Sitting to Curry's right was Secret Service advance man Winston G. Lawson. In the backseat, behind Curry, sat Dallas County sheriff J. E. "Bill" Decker and to his right was Secret Service special agent in charge Forrest Sorrels.

More than two car lengths behind was the presidential limousine, a specially made long dark-blue Lincoln Continental convertible sedan designated Secret Service Car No. 100-X. Kennedy's Secret Service code name was Lancer, apparently a knockoff of the name Lancelot in the Camelot story.

Driving the limousine was Secret Service agent William Greer, at age fifty-three the oldest man in the White House detail. Next to Greer sat Roy Kellerman, assistant special agent in charge of the Secret Service White House detail.

In the center of the car in fold-down jump seats were Governor Connally, on the right, and Mrs. Connally. In the rear, on a padded seat that could be raised or lowered mechanically, sat Kennedy, wearing a leather back brace. Mrs. Kennedy sat on his left.

Behind the limousine by about a full car length was a follow-up car for Kennedy's Secret Service guards, a 1956 Cadillac convertible touring sedan specially equipped for the Secret Service and designated SS Car No. 679-X.

Following this security car was a 1964 Lincoln four-door open convertible carrying vice president Lyndon Johnson, Mrs. Johnson, and senator Ralph Yarborough. Yarborough told this author that while the crowds on the street were boisterous and friendly, when he looked up at the offices of the big companies and corporations of Dallas, he never saw a smiling face. The driver of his car was Texas state trooper Hurchel Jacks, and Secret Service agent Rufus W. Youngblood rode to the right of him. Their car was trailed by Johnson's Secret Service guards and the rest of the motorcade, consisting of five cars for local dignitaries, three cars for press photographers, one bus for White House staff, and two press buses.

A pilot car, which preceded the motorcade by a quarter of a mile checking for "motor vehicle accidents, fires and obstructions along the route," contained Dallas deputy police chief G. L. Lumpkin, two Dallas homicide detectives, and Lieutenant Colonel George Whitmayer, commander of the local Army Intelligence reserve unit.

Oddly, while a press-pool station wagon had been designated to follow Kennedy's Secret Service follow-up car (it had the number 5 taped on its side), for some unexplained reason it was shoved farther back in the motorcade. This prevented the media representatives from witnessing the assassination or capturing it on film.

Everyone in the presidential limousine appeared to be enjoying the open-air ride and the cheering admiration of the crowd, although Mrs. Kennedy was beginning to feel warm in her pink wool suit and pillbox hat. As the motorcade cruised into the downtown area, apprehensions of the Dallas visit seemed to dissipate as quickly as the morning's overcast.

Bob Hollingsworth, veteran Washington correspondent for the *Times Herald*, had accompanied the Washington press corps to Dallas. He noted, "The amazement over the size of the crowd turned to awe. For those of us who had been with the President since he left the White House for Texas Thursday morning, this was the largest, the most enthusiastic and the best reception he had received in Texas."

Up ahead clear blue sky could be seen past the long, dark corridor of tall buildings as the presidential car entered a small, triangular plaza at the end of Main Street.

The motorcade broke into the open space of Dealey Plaza, named after George Bannerman Dealey, a pioneer Dallas civic leader and founder of the *Dallas Morning News*. The 3.07-acre plaza, the site of the first home in Dallas as well as the first courthouse, post office, store, Masonic lodge, and hotel, has been called the "birthplace of Dallas." It was acquired by the city for the construction of the Triple Underpass, which allows railroad traffic to pass over Commerce, Main, and Elm Streets. The property was christened "Dealey Plaza" in 1935 and placed under the authority of the city's Park Board in 1936 with the official opening of the underpass.

Both incoming and outgoing traffic between downtown Dallas and the major freeway systems to the west is channeled through Dealey Plaza. It is bounded on the east by Houston Street. Turning north from Main Street at the historic red, ornate County Court House, Houston was flanked to the east by the Criminal Courts Building, containing the county jail and the sheriff's office. In the same block to the north was the white Dallas County Records Building. Opposite the records building across Elm Street was the Dal-Tex Building. To its west was the redbrick building that in 1963 contained the Texas School Book Depository.

Bisecting Dealey Plaza is Main Street, with Commerce Street branching off to the south and Elm Street curving in on the north. These three main arteries converge on the west side of the plaza at the railroad bridge known as the Triple Underpass. Facing Houston Street on the west are fountains and monuments to Dealey. On the north and south sides of the plaza are two small arbors or pergolas, flanked on the east by a line of trees and shrubs and on the west by a wooden stockade fence about five feet high.

With a phalanx of Dallas motorcycle police officers clearing the way ahead, the blue Lincoln limousine carrying the Kennedys made a ninety-degree turn from Main onto Houston in front of the Dallas County Sheriff's Office. Almost two dozen deputies and other lawmen stood on the sidewalk watching. All had been ordered not to take part in motorcade security.

The bright sun began warming the car's occupants as they approached the Texas School Book Depository. Atop the building was a large Hertz Rent-A-Car sign containing a digital time and temperature display. In front of the Depository, the limousine slowed to a crawl to make a 120-degree turn onto Elm Street, although turns of more than 90 degrees were prohibited by the Secret Service. The turn was so tight that Greer almost ran the limousine up onto the north curb near the Depository's front door, according to Depository superintendent Roy Truly.

The car continued a slow glide down the incline of Elm deeper into Dealey Plaza, maintaining its position in the center lane of the three-lane street. The crowds thinned out as the Triple Underpass approached, and security men began to relax. About three car lengths ahead of the presidential limousine in the lead car, Agent Lawson, a former Army counterintelligence man now with the Secret Service White House detail, was sitting in the right front seat. He looked at his watch. It was 12:30 p.m. Picking up the car's microphone, he radioed the Trade Mart saying, "We'll be there in about five minutes."

In the presidential limousine, Kennedy was waving to his right at a group of people standing near a large green sign reading STEMMONS FREEWAY. His right arm and hand were extended slightly over the side of the car. Mrs. Kennedy had been waving to her left, but her thoughts were on the Texas heat. Mrs. Kennedy later told the Warren Commission, "And in the motorcade, you know, I usually would be waving mostly to the left side and he was waving mostly to the right, which is one reason you are not looking at each other very much. And it was terribly hot. Just blinding all of us." Sensing her discomfort, Mrs. Connally turned and said, "We'll soon be there."

Mrs. Kennedy recalled seeing the Triple Underpass ahead. "We could see a tunnel in front of us. Everything was really slow then. And I remember thinking it would be so cool under that tunnel."

Mrs. Connally had wanted to mention the warm and enthusiastic welcome for some time, but she had held back. Now she could contain herself no longer. Turning to Kennedy, she said, "Mr. President, you can't say that Dallas doesn't love you." According to Mrs. Kennedy, the president smiled and replied, "No, you certainly can't."

Soon after his remark, Mrs. Connally heard a frightening noise off to her right. She looked in that direction and caught a peripheral glimpse of Kennedy raising both hands to his neck. She heard no sound from the president but noticed a blank, "nothing" expression on his face.

Kellerman, sitting directly in front of Connally and Kennedy, noticed they had just passed a highway sign when he heard a "pop" to his right and immediately looked in that direction, surveying the easternmost slope of the Grassy Knoll. Kellerman told the Warren Commission:

> As I turned my head to the right to view whatever it was . . . I heard a voice from the back seat and I firmly believe it was the President's [saying] "My God, I am hit," and I turned around and he has got his hands up here like this [indicating both hands up near the throat]. . . . [It] was enough for me to verify that the man was hit. So, in the same motion I come right back and grabbed the speaker and said to the driver, "Let's get out of here; we're hit," and grabbed the mike and I said, "Lawson, this is Kellerman . . . we are hit; get us to the hospital immediately." Now in the seconds that I talked just now, a flurry of shells come into the car.

Mrs. Connally testified she heard Kellerman say, "Pull out of the motorcade. Take us to the nearest hospital." The limousine indeed pulled out of the motorcade, accelerated through the Triple Underpass, up the entrance ramp to Stemmons Freeway, and raced toward Parkland Hospital.

Driver Greer said he was busy looking ahead to the railroad overpass and never looked back. This is inconsistent with a film of the assassination that clearly shows Greer looking back over his right shoulder prior to the head shot. Greer then testified he heard a noise he thought was a motorcycle backfire. Then he heard the noise again and caught a glimpse of Connally starting to slump over. He then heard two more noises that seemed to come one on top of the other. Greer said that after the second noise and a glance over his right shoulder at Connally, he stepped on the accelerator. However, film taken that day shows the limousine brake lights remained on until after the fatal head shot to Kennedy.

Mrs. Connally recalled that after the first sound "very soon there was the second shot which hit John [Connally]."

Connally, in testimony consistent both with that of Mrs. Connally and with films made that day, confirmed he was not hit by the first shot. The governor said just after making the turn onto Elm he heard a noise he took to be a shot from a high-powered rifle. He turned to his right because the sound appeared to come from over his right shoulder, but he couldn't see anything. He began to turn to his left when he felt something strike him in the back.

Although critically wounded, Connally was conscious of shots being fired other than the one that struck him. Realizing that he had been hit a second or so after hearing a shot, Connally told the Warren Commission, "There were either two or three people involved or more in this or someone was shooting with an automatic rifle." Connally then heard a final boom and heard the bullet hit home. He later recalled, "It never entered my mind that it ever hit anyone but the President. . . . He never uttered a sound that I heard."

Connally noticed blue brain tissue covering his suit and knew Kennedy was dead. He also noticed blood on the front of his shirt and realized he was hurt badly, perhaps fatally. Crumpling into the arms of his wife, Connally screamed out, "My God, they're going to kill us all!" Connally heard his wife saying over and over, "Be still, you're going to be all right," and he felt the car accelerate. He then lost consciousness.

During the initial phase of the shooting, Mrs. Kennedy did not realize what was happening. She was accustomed to the sounds of motorcycle escorts backfiring and the motorcade had been a cacophony of sirens, racing motors, cheering, and shouting. She did hear Connally shout, "Oh, no, no, no!" She heard "terrible noises" to her right and turned to see Kennedy with his hand at his throat and a "quizzical look on his face." Then the chief executive was struck in the head and fell into her lap. All she could do was cradle him and say, "Oh, my God, they've shot my husband. I love you, Jack."

Over the years a great deal of misinformation has been presented about her next actions. Many persons have stated she tried to climb out of the car in panic or to help

Secret Service agent Clint Hill, who had run to the president's limousine. Actually, she crawled onto the trunk of the limousine and, reaching out, picked up a piece of her husband's head. Mrs. Connally told the Warren Commission she recalled hearing Mrs. Kennedy crying out, "I have got his brains in my hand."

Mrs. Kennedy next climbed back into the limousine under her own power as Hill was desperately clinging to the car's trunk as it accelerated.

When talking to the Warren Commission on June 5, 1964, Mrs. Kennedy did not even recall this activity. But her action was captured in the films taken that day, and later, sitting in Parkland Hospital, she had the object still clutched in her hand. Dr. Marion T. Jenkins encountered a "shell shocked" Mrs. Kennedy in the hospital hallway. "I noticed her hands were cupped in front of her, as if she were cradling something," he recalled. "As she passed by, she nudged me with an elbow and handed me what she had been nursing in her hands—a large chunk of her husband's brain tissues." Perhaps the reason this dramatic incident has been confused in the early years is that if brain matter flew to the rear, this clearly evinces a shot from the front.

In the lead car, which was just about to enter the Triple Underpass when the firing began, Agent Lawson was trying to signal a policeman standing with a group of people on top of the underpass. He didn't like the idea of the president's car passing directly below these people, so he was trying to get the officer to move them to one side. The policeman never noticed him. Lawson may have recalled the security measures in Fort Worth earlier that morning when overpasses were cleared of bystanders and windows facing the president's route were closed by security personnel.

Just then, Lawson heard a loud report to his rear. It sounded more like a bang instead of a crack and Lawson didn't think it was a rifle shot. His first impression was that it was a firecracker. This description was to be repeated by nearly everyone in Dealey Plaza, with some notable exceptions, one being Forrest V. Sorrels, head of the Dallas office of the Secret Service. Like Connally, Sorrels was certain the first sound was a gunshot. After a brief pause, Sorrels heard two more shots coming close together. He shouted to Chief Curry, "Let's get out of here!"

On hearing the first burst of fire, Sheriff Decker glanced back and thought he saw a bullet bouncing off the street pavement. Motorcycle officer James Chaney told newsmen the next day that the first shot missed.

Another Dallas motorcycle officer, Starvis Ellis, in 1978 told the House Select Committee on Assassinations that as he rode alongside the car in which Decker was riding, he, too, saw a bullet hit the pavement. Neither Decker nor Ellis was ever questioned about this extraneous bullet by the Warren Commission.

Curry saw a "commotion" in the presidential limousine. Then a motorcycle officer drew up alongside. "Anybody hurt?" asked Curry. "Yes," replied the officer. Stepping on the accelerator, Curry shouted, "Lead us to the hospital." Both Decker and Curry took the car's radio and ordered their men to rush to the top of the underpass and the adjacent railroad yards where they thought the shots had originated.

Those witnesses deep in the Dealey Plaza believed shots were fired from the

Grassy Knoll, while those farther back in the motorcade—still on Houston and Main Streets—believed shots came from the direction of the Depository.

Motorcycle policeman Marrion L. Baker was riding near one of the press cars. He had just turned onto Houston and his cycle was about to tip over because of a gust of wind and the slow speed. He had just returned from a deer-hunting trip and recognized the first sound as a high-powered rifle shot. He thought the sound came from either the Depository or the Dal-Tex building. Seeing pigeons fluttering off the Depository's roof, he gunned his motor and roared up to the entrance of the building. Within seconds, he and Depository superintendent Roy Truly would encounter Lee Harvey Oswald calmly standing in the second-floor lunchroom of the Depository.

Secret Service agent Paul Landis was riding in the right rear of the Secret Service follow-up car when he heard the report of a high-powered rifle. He saw Kennedy turn to look in the direction of the shot, which Landis believed came from "somewhere towards the front, right-hand side of the road."

With Landis was Secret Service agent Glen Bennett, who thought the sound was a firecracker. But then he looked at the president. In notes he said were made later that day, Bennett wrote, "[I] saw a shot that hit the Boss about four inches down from the right shoulder; a second shoot [sic] followed immediately and hit the right rear high [side] of the Boss's head."

The Secret Service agents assigned to Kennedy all acted with remarkable sluggishness when the firing began. Perhaps it was due to the visit they had paid to a "beatnik" nightspot in Fort Worth, where they drank until early that morning.

The only agent to react quickly was Clint Hill. Interestingly, Hill had not been scheduled to make the Dallas trip, but joined at the last moment only after Mrs. Kennedy made a personal request. Hill also thought the initial sound was a firecracker and began looking to his right for the source of the sound when he saw Kennedy grab at himself and lurch forward slightly. He then realized something was wrong and jumped off the follow-up car. He was racing the few feet to the limousine when he heard more shots. Hill had just secured a grip on a handhold when the car began accelerating. Looking into the backseat of the limousine, Hill saw that the right rear portion of the president's head was missing.

Nearly everyone present recalled a pause of several seconds between the first burst of fire and the final two shots, these coming rapidly, one on top of the other. It was the third and final shot, or volley of shots, that killed President John F. Kennedy. Until then, he had been immobile and quiet, only sagging slightly to his left. Then his head pitched forward violently for a split second only to be pushed hard to the left and rear. A halo of crimson liquid and tissue surrounded his head momentarily and then fell to the rear. The head shot lifted him slightly, then threw him against the car's backseat. He bounced forward and over into his wife's lap.

The two Dallas motorcycle officers riding to the left rear of the limousine, Bobby W. Hargis and B. J. Martin, were splattered by blood and brain matter.

Martin, who had looked to his right after the first shots, later found bloodstains on the left side of his helmet. Hargis, who was riding nearest the limousine about six to eight feet from the left rear fender, saw Kennedy's head explode and was hit by bits of flesh and bone with such impact that he told reporters he initially thought he had been shot.

Presidential assistant David Powers was riding with Secret Service agents in the car directly behind the president. From this vantage point, he described the entire assassination:

> I commented to Ken O'Donnell that it was 12:30 and we would only be about five minutes late when we arrived at the Trade Mart. Shortly thereafter the first shot went off and it sounded to me as if it were a firecracker. I noticed then that the President moved quite far to his left after the shot from the extreme right hand side where he had been sitting. There was a second shot and Governor Connally disappeared from sight and then there was a third shot which took off the top of the President's head and had the sickening sound of a grapefruit splattering against the side of a wall. The total time between the first and third shots was about five or six seconds. My first impression was that the shots came from the right and overhead but I also had a fleeting impression that the noise appeared to come from the front in the area of the Triple Underpass. This may have resulted from my feeling, when I looked forward toward the overpass, that we might have ridden into an ambush.

Several persons in the motorcade smelled gunpowder as the cars swept through the lower end of Dealey Plaza.

Mrs. Earle Cabell, wife of the Dallas mayor, was riding in an open convertible six cars back from the motorcade's lead car. At the opening shots, the car in which she was riding was passing the Depository building. She told the Warren Commission she jerked her head up on hearing the first shot because "I heard the direction from which the shot came." Looking up, she saw an object projecting from one of the top windows of the Depository building. She said,

> I jerked my head up and I saw something in that window and I turned around to say to Earle, "Earle, it is a shot," and before I got the words out . . . the second two shots rang out. . . . I was acutely aware of the odor of gunpowder. I was aware that the motorcade stopped dead still. There was no question about that.

Mrs. Cabell was riding beside congressman Ray Roberts. She said he acknowledged smelling gunpowder too.

Senator Ralph Yarborough also smelled gunpowder as the car carrying him and Lyndon Johnson drove through the plaza. Yarborough, a former Army infantry officer and an avid hunter, also failed to recognize the sound of the first shot. He told this author:

> I thought, "Was that a bomb thrown?" and then the other shots were fired. And the motorcade, which had slowed to a stop, took off. A second or two later, I smelled gunpowder. I always thought that was strange because, being familiar with firearms, I never could see how I could smell the powder from a rifle high in that building.

It does seem strange that people would smell powder from a shot fired more than sixty feet in the air and behind them. However, it's not so strange, if a shot were fired on top of the Grassy Knoll less than twelve feet in elevation with a breeze from the north to carry smoke to street level.

Over the years, an argument has continued over whether the presidential limousine actually stopped. There is no doubt that it slowed, as in the Orville Nix film, the brake lights can been seen coming on after the first shot. Secret Service agent Clint Hill in the follow-up car stepped down and ran for the president's car. He was grabbing for the rear handhold when it began to accelerate.

Witness Jean Hill supported Mrs. Connally by stating the limousine slowed to a stop and even pulled over into the left-hand lane, although the Zapruder film shows no such movement. Based on the reported speed of Zapruder's camera, the Warren Commission determined that the limousine slowed to 11.2 miles per hour and "maintained this average speed . . . immediately preceding the shot which struck the President in the head."

Senator Yarborough may have gotten closest to the truth of the matter when he explained to this author, "Look, you toss a ball into the air. At one point it stops going up and starts coming down. Did it stop?"

One of the strangest omissions in the subsequent investigation by federal authorities concerns a Navy commander who was assigned to film major events involving President Kennedy. In early 1963, Thomas Atkins was assigned as an official photographer for the Kennedy White House. As such, he traveled to Texas with Kennedy and was photographing the motorcade with a quality camera, a 16 mm Arriflex S. He was riding six cars behind Kennedy and filming as the motorcade moved through Dealey Plaza.

In a 1977 article, Atkins said the car he was in had just turned onto Houston Street and was facing the Texas School Book Depository:

> Kennedy's car had just made the left turn heading toward the freeway entrance. Although I did not look up at the building, I could hear everything quite clearly. . . . The shots came from below and off to the right side from where I was [the location of the Grassy Knoll]. . . . I never thought the shots came from above. They did not sound like shots coming from anything higher than street level.

After returning to Washington on Air Force Two, Atkins assembled his footage into a movie he titled *The Last Two Days*. He described the film as "terribly damaging to the Warren Commission finding that Lee Harvey Oswald was the lone assassin." Perhaps this explains why neither Atkins's testimony nor his film was studied by either of the federal panels investigating the assassination. Atkins said in 1977, "It's something I've always wondered about. Why didn't they ask me what I knew? I not only was on the White House staff, I was then, and still am, a photographer with a pretty keen visual sense."

Obviously, the federal authorities didn't want to hear from a man with a "keen visual sense" and strong credentials who might have told them things they did not want to hear.

But if the stories of the motorcade witnesses differed from the later official version of the assassination, it was nothing compared to the stories to come from the crowd of bystanders.

The Crowd

The crowd of witnesses along the motorcade route through Dealey Plaza saw many things that differed from the later official version. Even before the motorcade arrived, men with rifles were seen by people in downtown Dallas.

Shortly before noon, Phillip B. Hathaway and coworker John Lawrence were walking on Akard Street toward Main to get an observation spot for the motorcade when Hathaway saw a man carrying a rifle in a gun case. He described the man as very tall, six-foot-five or more, weighing about 250 pounds and thick in the chest. The man was in his early thirties with "dirty blond hair worn in a crew-cut" and was wearing a gray business suit. Hathaway said the case was made of leather and cloth and was not limp, but obviously contained a rifle. He remarked to Lawrence that it must be a Secret Service man.

This same man may have been seen later that day by Ernest Jay Owens, who told sheriff's officers the afternoon of the assassination that he was driving on Wood Street near Good-Lattimer Expressway when he saw a white male of "heavy build" carrying a "foreign-made rifle" out of a parking lot. Owens said the man was bareheaded and wearing a dark suit.

Once Oswald was captured and proclaimed the assassination suspect, there was no effort to investigate these stories further.

A similar—but even more ominous—incident involved Julia Ann Mercer. Mercer, then twenty-three years old, later told authorities that shortly before 11 a.m. the day of the assassination she was driving a rented white Valiant west on Elm Street just past the point where Kennedy was killed about two hours later. Just after passing through the Triple Underpass, she found her traffic lane blocked by a green Ford pickup truck containing two men..

While waiting for the truck to move, she saw a young man get out of the passenger side of the truck, walk to a long tool compartment along the side, and remove a long paper bag. She could see the outline of a rifle in the bag. The man then walked up on the Grassy Knoll carrying the package and was lost to her sight. She described this man as in his late twenties or early thirties, wearing a gray jacket, brown pants, a plaid shirt, and some sort of wool stocking cap with a tassel on it. Mercer said as she pulled alongside the truck, she locked eyes with the driver, whom she described as heavily built with a round face and light brown hair.

She said during this time, she saw three Dallas policemen standing by a motorcycle on the underpass talking. In Warren Commission Document 205, a policeman did tell of seeing the truck, but believed that it had broken down.

When she was finally able to change lanes, Mercer drove on toward Fort Worth, stopping at the halfway point of the Dallas–Fort Worth Toll Road (now Interstate 30) to have breakfast. While eating, she spoke of her experience, commenting, "The Secret Service is not very secret." As she drove on to Fort Worth, she was pulled over by policemen, who informed her of the assassination and took her back to Dallas for questioning. Apparently persons in the restaurant had informed authorities of her comments and presence at the assassination site. She was held for several hours and questioned by both local and federal authorities, although no one showed her a badge or identified himself.

Early the next morning, FBI men came to her home and took her back to the Dallas County Sheriff's Office, where she was shown some photographs of various men. She picked out two as the men she had seen in the truck the day before. Turning one photo over, she read the name "Jack Ruby." All this transpired prior to Ruby's well-publicized shooting of Lee Oswald the next day.

During the TV coverage of the Oswald shooting, Mercer claims, she again recognized Ruby as the man driving the truck and that Oswald resembled the man carrying the rifle. Oswald's mother also claimed to have been shown a picture of Ruby prior to the Sunday shooting of her son.

Mercer later claimed that her story concerning the truck and its occupants was twisted and changed by both the FBI and the Dallas County Sheriff's Office. For example, according to her sheriff's department statement of November 22, she stated that a sign on the side of the pickup truck carried the words AIR CONDITIONING, a claim she later denied. This one seemingly small change in her testimony sent investigators on a fruitless search for a truck with such a sign and later served to discredit her account. Furthermore, Mercer was able to convince New Orleans district attorney Jim Garrison that her notarized signature on the sheriff's report was forged. After telling her story to Garrison in the late 1960s, Mercer apparently realized how her account disrupted the official lone-nut story and she became inaccessible to the public.

Mercer's experience may have been partly corroborated by another Dallasite, Julius Hardie, who told the *Dallas Morning News* years later that on the morning of November 22, he saw three men on top of the Triple Underpass carrying long arms, although he could not tell if they were rifles or shotguns. Hardie said he reported the incident to the FBI, but no such report has been made public.

As the motorcade arrived in Dealey Plaza, it passed almost twenty sheriff's deputies standing at the intersection of Main and Houston in front of the sheriff's office. They had gathered upon the sheriff's orders earlier that day but Sheriff Decker told them he had received a call from Washington advising him and his men to stand down and not participate in the motorcade's security.

In affidavits, the deputies almost unanimously agreed they thought the shots came from the railroad yards located just behind the Grassy Knoll. They all began running in that direction even before Decker's radio order to "saturate the area of the park, railroad and all buildings" was given.

Deputy L. C. Smith, in a report made that day, told a story that was typical of the deputies' experience:

> I was standing in front of the Sheriff's Office on Main Street and watched the President and his party drive by. Just a few seconds later, I heard the first shot, which I thought was a backfire, then the second shot and third shot rang out. I knew that this was gun shots and everyone else did also. I ran as fast as I could to Elm Street just west of Houston and I heard a woman unknown to me say the President was shot in the head and the shots came from the fence on the north side of Elm. I went at [once] behind the fence and searched also in the parking area. Then came . . . word the shot was thought to have come from the Texas School Book Depository.

Supporting the deputy's stories was W. W. Mabra, then a county bailiff. Mabra, too, was on the corner of Main and Houston,

> so close to the President that I could almost have reached out and touched him. Then I heard the first shot. I thought it was a backfire. People ran toward the knoll. Some said they saw smoke there. I thought at first the shot may have come from there.

Across Main Street from the deputies and Mabra stood Dallas County surveyor Robert H. West, who watched the presidential limousine move slowly toward the Triple Underpass. He heard one small report "similar to a motorcycle backfire," then three like "rifle fire." He said the shots came from the "northwest quadrant of Dealey Plaza [the area of the picket fence on the Grassy Knoll]." West later participated in reconstructions of the assassination for both *Life* magazine and the FBI that convinced him the crime could not have been the work of one man.

Arnold and Barbara Rowland, high school students who had been married the past May, had come to town to see the president. They were standing on Houston Street near a driveway between the County Records Building and the sheriff's office, the west side of which faces Dealey Plaza. Both of the Rowlands believed the shots came from down near the Triple Underpass despite the fact that fifteen minutes before the motorcade arrived they had remarked about seeing two men, one with a rifle and telescopic sight, on the sixth floor of the Texas School Book Depository. Arnold Rowland had assumed the men were part of the Secret Service protection.

He said the man with the rifle was in the far west window of the Depository's sixth floor while the other man, described as an elderly black man with thin hair wearing a plaid shirt, was seen in the easternmost window, the so-called sniper's nest window. Rowland said he lost sight of the man with the rifle as the motorcade approached, but again saw the black man just before Kennedy arrived.

During the excitement of the moment, Rowland said, he neglected to mention the black man when he talked to authorities in the sheriff's office. However, he said the next day FBI agents came to his home and got him to sign a statement. He recalled, "At that time I told them I did see the Negro man there and they told me it didn't have any bearing or such on the case right then. In fact, they just the same as told me to forget it now."

Although the agents "didn't seem interested" in Rowland's story of the two men on the sixth floor, they did attempt to identify the man with the gun by showing Rowland photos of Oswald. However, Rowland said, "I just couldn't identify him . . . because I just didn't have a good enough look at his face." The Warren Commission brushed off Rowland's testimony after FBI agents assured them that Rowland had mentioned nothing about the black man in his earlier statements. Commission attorney David Belin even maneuvered Mrs. Rowland into stating her husband was "prone to exaggerate."

But Rowland's story of seeing two men was corroborated by deputy sheriff Roger D. Craig, who said that Rowland told him about seeing two men pacing in the Depository approximately ten minutes after the assassination. Craig's statements, like Rowland's, were discounted by the Commission when federal agents contradicted their testimony.

However, two men also were seen by Mrs. Carolyn Walther, who worked in a dress factory in the Dal-Tex Building. About noon, she and another employee joined the crowd on the east side of Houston just south of Elm to watch the motorcade. Her account was buried in Warren Commission Exhibit 2086 in 1964 but she repeated her story for CBS television on June 25, 1967:

> I had gone out on the street at about twenty after twelve to get a look at the President when he came by. While I waited, I glanced up at the Depository building. There were two men in the corner window on the fourth or fifth floor. One man was wearing a white shirt and had blond or light brown hair. This man had the window open. His hands were extended outside the window. He held a rifle with the barrel pointed downward. I thought he was some kind of guard. In the same window, right near him, was a man in a brown suit coat. Then the President's car came by. I heard a gunshot. People ran. Like a fool I just stood there. I saw people down. I walked toward them, with the thought they maybe were hurt and I could help them.

People were running toward the Grassy Knoll. A woman cried out, "They shot him!" In all, I heard four shots.

In a 1978 interview with Earl Golz of the *Dallas Morning News,* Carolyn Walther (not to be confused with Deputy Sheriff E. R. "Buddy" Walthers) made these comments:

They (FBI) tried to make me think that what I saw were boxes. Now the boxes are much lighter colored. And this was definitely the shape of a person or part of a person. I never read their report. I talked to them and it seemed like they weren't very interested. They were going to set out to prove me a liar, and I had no intention of arguing with them and being harassed. I felt like I had told them all I knew. And I had relieved myself of the burden of it. And if they didn't want to believe it or had some reason not to, well, then, that was all right with me.

Steelworker Richard Randolph Carr, who was working on the seventh floor of the new Dallas Courthouse, then under construction at the intersection of Commerce and Houston, also reported seeing a man wearing a brown coat. Carr said minutes before the motorcade arrived he saw a heavyset man wearing a hat, horn-rimmed glasses, and tan sport coat standing in a sixth-floor window of the Depository. After the shooting, Carr saw the man walking along Commerce Street.

Ruby Henderson, standing across Elm Street from the Depository, also saw two men on an upper floor of the building. While she was uncertain whether it was the sixth floor, she saw no one above the pair. She described the shorter of the men as having a dark complexion, possibly even African American, and wearing a white shirt. The shorter man was wearing a dark shirt. This pair may have been Depository employees James Jarman and Harold Norman, who watched the motorcade from the fifth-floor window just below the so-called sniper's nest.

Today, such stories of two men on the sixth floor of the Depository moments before the shooting has since been bolstered by two films made that day. One, an 8 mm home movie made by Robert Hughes, who was standing at the intersection of Main and Houston, shows the front of the Depository just as Kennedy's limousine passes the building turning onto Elm. The film shows movement in both the corner window of the sixth floor and the window next to it. Deep within the Warren Commission exhibits is an FBI report acknowledging receipt of Hughes's film. In another FBI document, it is claimed that the figure in the second window from the corner was simply a stack of boxes. No reference is made to movement.

In 1975, CBS television asked Itek Corporation to look again at the Hughes film. The company concluded that there were no moving images in the double window next to the sixth-floor corner window, a conclusion that is still disputed by various photographic experts.

But in late 1978, a second movie surfaced that supports the two-man allegation.

This film, taken by Charles L. Bronson, who was standing only a few feet west of Hughes, also shows the sixth-floor corner windows of the Depository just moments before the Kennedy motorcade passed. Bronson's film was viewed in 1963 by an FBI agent who reported that it "failed to show the building from which the shots were fired," thus relegating the film to obscurity. It was rediscovered in 1978 when the film was mentioned in declassified FBI documents and was obtained by the *Dallas Morning News*.

The newspaper commissioned Robert Groden, who served as staff consultant on photographic evidence for the House Select Committee on Assassinations, to study the film. Groden told the newspaper:

> There is no question that there is movement. And, I'm sure, given time and money, a computer could probably clarify the images a bit more. . . . You can actually see one figure walking back and forth hurriedly. I think what was happening there is the sniper's nest was actually being completed just prior to the shots being fired.

The House committee studied the Bronson film further and, while acknowledging movement in the second window, stated it was "more likely . . . a random photographic artifact than human movement." However, the committee did recommend that the film be analyzed further. There is no evidence such further study was conducted.

Another witness to the pair of men in the Depository was an inmate of the Dallas County Jail, located just across the street to the east of the Depository. Several prisoners were in a sixth-floor cell on a level with the sixth-floor Depository window.

Oddly, none of the jail inmates was ever identified or sought by federal investigators despite their excellent vantage point. However, one of the inmates, John L. Powell, who was in a sixth-floor cell opposite the Book Depository, told the *Dallas Morning News* in 1978 that the prisoners saw two men, one with a rifle, in the sixth-floor window of the Depository prior to the motorcade's arrival. Powell even stated he could see them so clearly he saw one "fooling with the scope" on the gun. "Quite a few of us saw 'em. Everybody was trying to watch the parade and all that. We were looking across the street because it was directly straight across. The first thing I thought is, it was security guards. . . . I remember the guys," he said, adding the pair were wearing "kind of brownish looking or duller clothes . . . like work clothes." He also stated "maybe more than half" of the forty inmates in his holding cell were looking across to the Book Depository.

In June 1964, Stanley M. Kaufman, one of Jack Ruby's attorneys, mentioned to Warren Commission assistant counsel Leon D. Hubert, "It might be helpful to the commission to know that there were people in jail who saw the actual killing." Yet, three months later, the Commission closed shop and nothing was done. "I remember that that did occur and it sort of concerned me at the time as to why—if they were trying to find out all these facts—why they didn't go up there and talk to all those prisoners," Kaufman told Dallas reporter Earl Golz in 1978.

Confirmation of the presence of two men on the sixth floor also might have come from Canadian journalist Norman Similas, who was in Dallas for a bottlers' convention. It was a trip he would not soon forget. On November 21, Similas photographed and spoke with vice president Lyndon Johnson, who had addressed the convention. Later that evening, Similas visited the Carousel Club and spent more than an hour talking with its owner, Jack Ruby. The next day, Similas strolled over to Dealey Plaza to photograph President Kennedy's motorcade. He stood on the south side of Elm not ten feet from Kennedy's car at the time of the first shots. In a report published in the Canadian magazine *Liberty*, Similas said:

> The Presidential limousine had passed me and slowed down slightly. My camera was directly angled toward the Texas School Book Depository in the background. The picture I took on the curb of Elm Street was trained momentarily on an open, sixth-floor window. The camera lens recorded what I could not possibly have seen at that moment—a rifle barrel extended over the windowsill. When the film was developed later, it showed two figures hovering over it.

Were there two people in Similas's photo? No one will ever know for sure. In that same article, he added:

> Upon my return to Toronto, I submitted my developed negatives to a daily newspaper. When they were not used on Monday, November 25, I phoned and asked that they be returned. Later I received a fat cheque in the mail, but the one negative which clearly showed what I believe to be two figures in the window of the assassin's nest was missing. When I pressed for it, I was told that this negative had somehow become lost. It has never been returned to me.

Ronald B. Fischer, an auditor for Dallas County, and another county worker, Robert E. Edwards, were standing on the southwest corner of Elm and Houston, directly across the street from the Depository. Less than ten minutes before the motorcade arrived, Edwards commented, "Look at that guy there in that window." Looking up, Fischer saw the head and shoulders of a man wearing a white T-shirt or possibly a light sport shirt in a southeast corner window. The man was surrounded by boxes and was staring "transfixed," not toward the approaching motorcade, but in the direction of the Triple Underpass. Less than a minute later the motorcade passed their position and both Fischer and Edwards shifted their attention to the motorcade. Then Fischer heard what he thought was a firecracker followed by sounds he knew to be shots. They seemed to be coming from "just west of the School Book Depository building [the location of the Grassy Knoll]." They both ran toward the Grassy Knoll and forgot the man in the window.

Hugh W. Betzner Jr. was twenty-two years old on November 22, 1963, and was taking pictures with an old camera near the intersection of Houston and Elm. After taking Kennedy's picture as he turned in front of the Depository, Betzner ran west into Dealey Plaza following the presidential limousine. In a sheriff's report that day, Betzner stated:

> I started to wind my film again and I heard a loud noise. I thought this noise was either a firecracker or a car had backfired. I looked up and it seemed like there was another loud noise in a matter of a few seconds. I looked down the street and I could see the President's car and another one and they looked like the cars were stopped.

Betzner said he then heard at least two more shots fired and saw the impact in the limousine. The motorcade then sped up and Betzner joined spectators running up the Grassy Knoll toward the wooden picket fence from where he assumed the shots had emanated. Minutes later, he looked across Elm Street and saw "police officers and some men in plain clothes . . . digging around in the dirt as if they were looking for a bullet."

Near Betzner was another photographer, Phillip Willis, a World War II veteran, who took a series of pictures considered by many as the most important photos taken of the assassination other than the Zapruder film.

Willis, along with his wife and two young daughters, was in Dealey Plaza to get pictures of the president and Lyndon Johnson, whom Willis said he knew personally. As the presidential limousine turned onto Elm in front of the Depository, Willis snapped a photo, then ran farther west on Elm. He told the Warren Commission, "Then my next shot . . . in fact, the shot caused me to squeeze the camera shutter, and I got a picture of the President as he was hit with the first shot. So instantaneous, in fact, that the crowd hadn't had time to react." Willis said he did not see the effects of the next shots because his two daughters, Linda and Rosemary, were running along Elm and he became concerned for their safety.

As a retired Air Force major, Willis said he had absolutely no doubt that the shots were from a high-powered rifle and were coming from the direction of the Texas School Book Depository. (An interesting note: Willis was in Hawaii during the attack on Pearl Harbor and captured the sole surviving member of a Japanese midget submarine, thus becoming the first American to take a Japanese prisoner during World War II.)

Willis's younger daughter, Rosemary, ran back to her father, saying, "Oh, Daddy, they have shot our president. His whole head blew up and it looked like a red halo."

Willis said he took more photographs as "the party [the motorcade] had come to a temporary halt before proceeding on to the underpass."

In later years, this author interviewed Willis, who refuted two of the theories to come from federal investigations of the assassination. One, the single-bullet theory of the Warren Commission, states that one shot, identified by the Commission as the first shot, struck both Kennedy and Connally. Willis said, "There is no damn way that one bullet hit both men. That is the most stupid thing they ever stuck to—that one-bullet theory."

The House Select Committee on Assassinations, also attempting to deal with the wounds in Kennedy's back and throat, which do not support a conclusion of one shot from the high rear, theorized that Kennedy may have bent over momentarily while out of the Zapruder camera view and thus received a back wound lower than the throat wound. Willis retorted, "That is not right. I got the nearest, best shot while JFK was behind the [Stemmons Freeway] sign. He was upright and waving to the crowd. A split second later, he was grabbing at his throat."

Willis also had a comment after telling of Kennedy falling to the left rear after the fatal head shot: "As many deer as I have shot, I've never known one to fall towards me."

Although the Warren Commission quoted Willis as saying that he heard three shots, all from the Depository, Willis said:

I always thought there had to be another shot from somewhere. I have always gone against the one-gunman theory. I always thought there had to have been some help. I saw blood going to the rear and left [of Kennedy]. That doesn't happen if that bullet came from the Depository [which was behind him].

Willis added:

I also got a photo, taken immediately after [the shooting stopped] that shows Ruby standing in front of the Depository building. He was the only person there wearing dark glasses. He was identified by people who knew him and no one else has been able to say it was someone else. Ruby made a big effort to show he was in the *Dallas Morning News* at the time, but it wouldn't take five minutes to walk from the *News* [to Dealey Plaza].

Interestingly, in publishing Willis's photo the Warren Commission cropped the picture right through the face of the man Willis claimed was Jack Ruby. In recent years archivist Richard Trask argued that the man in Willis's photo is not Ruby. However, he failed to mention that Willis knew Ruby before the assassination and recognized him in his photo.

Linda Willis, who was running along Elm Street with her sister, Rosemary, told this author in 1978, "I very much agree that shots came from somewhere other than the Depository. And where we were standing, we had a good view. So many of the people who have decided they know what happened there weren't even there. I was, and that's what makes the difference." Neither Willis nor his daughters believed the Warren Commission or the later House committee were seriously trying to find out the truth of the assassination.

Behind Willis, sitting on a concrete retaining wall across the street from the Depository, was forty-five-year-old Howard Leslie Brennan, who was to become the star witness for the Warren Commission. Brennan, who had been working as a pipe fitter on a construction project behind the Depository, had eaten lunch and then taken this position to view the motorcade. It was determined that Brennan was 120 feet from the sixth-floor window. He said he saw a man in an upper floor of the Depository shortly before the motorcade arrived. He described the man as a slender white male in his early thirties wearing "light-colored clothing." Brennan told the Warren Commission:

> I heard what I thought was a backfire. It ran in my mind that it might be someone throwing firecrackers out of the window of the red brick building [the Depository] and I looked up at the building. I then saw this man I have described in the window and he was taking aim with a high-powered rifle. I could see all of the barrel of the gun. I do not know if it had a scope on it or not. I was looking at the man in this window at the time of the last explosion. Then this man let the gun down to his side and stepped out of sight. He did not seem to be in any hurry. . . . I believe I could identify this man if I ever saw him again.

Brennan, who immediately rushed into the Depository to tell a policeman what he had seen, apparently was one of the only witnesses to have actually seen a gunman fire from the Depository. However, later that evening Brennan was unable to pick Lee Harvey Oswald out of a police lineup. Much later, it was determined that Brennan had poor eyesight and, in fact, a close examination of the Zapruder film shows that Brennan was not looking up at the time of the shooting but, as expected, was looking toward the president's car.

Brennan's job foreman, Sandy Speaker, told this author:

> They took [Brennan] off for about three weeks. I don't know if they were Secret Service or FBI, but they were federal people. He came back a nervous wreck and within a year his hair had turned snow white. He wouldn't talk about [the assassination] after that. He was scared to death. They made him say what they wanted him to say.

It is noteworthy that the Warren Commission so lacked confidence in Brennan's testimony that they called him back the same day of his appearance and asked, "Have you ever worked for the Union Terminal Company in Dallas?" and "Did you ever state to anyone that you heard shots from opposite the Texas School Book Depository and saw smoke and paper wadding come out of boxes on a slope below the railroad trestle at the time of the assassination?" When Brennan answered no to both questions, and after going off the record, the Commission lawyer dismissed him.

However, Brennan's story of a man firing from the sixth-floor window was supported by a statement to sheriff's deputies that day by fifteen-year-old Amos Lee

Euins. Euins, a schoolboy, was standing near Brennan on the south side of the Elm and Houston Street intersection when he heard a shot. He stated:

> I started looking around and then I looked up in the red brick building. I saw a man in a window with a gun and I saw him shoot twice. He then stepped back behind some boxes. I could tell the gun was a rifle and it sounded like an automatic rifle the way he was shooting.

Euins then ran west of the Depository, where he found a policeman. He led the cop back to the Depository and told him of seeing a figure with a "bald spot" firing from an upper window.

Another witness who saw a gunman in the Depository was L. R. Terry, who was standing across Elm Street near Brennan and Euins. In 1978, Terry told this author:

> I was right across from that book store when Kennedy was shot. I saw a gun come out of there just after I saw Kennedy and Connally go by. I could only see a hand, but I couldn't tell if [the man] was right-handed or left-handed. He did not have on a white shirt. The parade stopped right in front of the building. There was a man with him. They [investigators] could find out that the man who killed Kennedy had somebody with him. But I don't know who it is. . . . I just saw the gun barrel and the hand.

Across the street from Brennan, Euins, and Terry were Texas School Book Depository superintendent Roy Truly and Depository vice president Ochus V. Campbell.

They had started to go off to lunch about 12:15 p.m. when they saw the crowds and decided to wait and see the presidential motorcade. As the motorcade approached, they were having difficulty seeing over the heads of the crowd, so the two men moved closer to Elm Street and a bit farther west into the plaza. Here they were joined by Mrs. Robert A. Reid, the Depository's clerical supervisor.

The presidential limousine made such a tight turn onto Elm (nearly 120 degrees) that Truly stated he thought the right front tire came close to striking the abutment between Elm and the street in front of the Depository. The car nearly stopped, then straightened and moved into the center of three lanes to begin its downward glide into the plaza, they heard an "explosion . . . from west of the building [the Depository]." Truly thought it was a firecracker or toy cannon. He also said he saw the limousine stop for a second or two.

When Mrs. Reid turned to Campbell and said, "Oh my goodness, I'm afraid those came from our building," he replied, "Oh, Mrs. Reid, no, it came from the grassy area down this way."

Danny G. Arce, who worked in the Depository, also was standing near Truly and Campbell. He told the Warren Commission shots "came from the railroad tracks to the west of the Texas School Book Depository." Truly said after the initial explosion, everything seemed frozen. Then there were two more explosions, and he realized that shots were being fired. He saw the president's car come to a stop.

Another Depository employee saw a bullet hit the street at the time of the first shot. Virgie Rachley (by the time of her Warren Commission testimony she had married and was Mrs. Donald Baker) was a bookkeeper at the Depository. She and other workers were standing near Truly and Campbell in front of the Depository facing Elm Street. She told the Warren Commission:

> After he passed us, then we heard a noise and I thought it was firecrackers because I saw a shot or something hit the pavement. . . . It looked just like you could see the sparks from it and I just thought it was a firecracker and I was thinking that . . . somebody was fixing to get in a lot of trouble and we thought the kids or whoever threw it were down below or standing near the underpass or back up here by the sign.

Mrs. Baker told Commission attorney Wesley Liebeler that the stray bullet struck the middle of the southernmost lane on Elm Street just behind the presidential limousine.

Truly said the crowd around him began to surge backward in panic. He became separated from Campbell and quickly found himself back on the steps of the Depository. Moments later a motorcycle policeman pushed past him and ran into the Depository. Truly caught up with him in the lobby and they moved toward their encounter with a Depository employee—Lee Harvey Oswald.

Campbell ran with many others to where he believed the shots had come from, "near the railroad tracks located over the viaduct on Elm Street."

Mary E. Woodward, a staff writer for the *Dallas Morning News*, had gone to Dealey Plaza with four coworkers to get a look at the president while they ate lunch. As the limousine passed, she and another writer who had seen Kennedy during the final weeks of the 1960 campaign commented on how relaxed and robust he appeared. Standing near the Stemmons Freeway sign located down the slope to the west of the Depository, Woodward heard a "horrible, ear-shattering noise" coming from behind them and to their right [the Grassy Knoll]. She thought it was some sort of joke, a car backfiring perhaps.

She saw both the president and Mrs. Kennedy look around as if they, too, had heard the sound. The presidential limousine came to a halt. Then Woodward heard two more shots, coming close together, and the president slumped down in the car. A woman nearby began weeping and cried, "They've shot him!" Woodward was never questioned by the Warren Commission.

Gloria Calvery and Karen Westbrook, both employees of a publishing firm with offices in the Depository building, had gone out during lunch to see the president. They were standing with others almost halfway between the corner of Elm and Houston and the Triple Underpass. Both heard the first blast and saw Kennedy struck by a bullet just as the presidential limousine got directly in front of their position. Yet, in their March 1964 statements to the FBI, neither was simply asked about the origin of the shots nor were they asked to testify to the Warren Commission.

A. J. Millican, a coworker of Howard Brennan's, had no difficulty in determining where the shots came from. Millican told authorities that day he was standing on the north side of Elm Street about halfway between Houston and the Triple Underpass, which was between the Depository and the Grassy Knoll. He said he noticed "a truck from Honest Joe's Pawn Shop" park near the Depository, then drive off about five or ten minutes before the president arrived. He told sheriff's deputies:

> Just after the President's car passed, I heard three shots from up toward Elm right by the Book Depository Building, and then immediately I heard two more shots come from the arcade between the Book Store and the Underpass, then three more shots came from the same direction only sounded further back. It sounded approximately like a .45 automatic, or a high-powered rifle.

Millican, who provided perhaps one of the clearest descriptions of the firing sequence and the location of the shots, was never interviewed by or called to testify to the Warren Commission or the House Select Committee on Assassinations. He died in 1986, apparently having never been questioned by anyone. His only testament was a sheriff's deposition made that day.

However, his supervisor, Sandy Speaker, said his entire work crew was there and they all corroborated Millican's story. In an interview with this author, Speaker said:

> I was the superintendent of construction for the Republic Bank project at the time. Millican and also Howard Brennan were working for me. We were fabricating plumbing piping for the Republic Bank Building under construction at the west end of Pacific Street [north of the Texas School Book Depository]. Millican and the whole crew had knocked off for lunch and were by the Depository building to watch the parade. I hadn't gotten there when [the motorcade] passed. I was less than a half-block away and heard the shots. I heard at least five shots and they came from different locations. I was a combat Marine with the First Marine Division in World War II, hand-to-hand combat, missions behind enemy lines, and I know what I am talking about. I've said for years there were more than three shots fired.

John A. Chism, along with his wife and three-year-old son, were near Millican, standing directly in front of the Stemmons Freeway sign. They said the first shots were fired just as the president got in front of them. They saw Kennedy slump to the left and into his wife's arms. Mrs. Chism told Dallas authorities that day, "And then there was a second shot that I heard, after the President's wife had pulled him down in the seat. It came from what I thought was behind us [the Grassy Knoll] and I looked but I couldn't see anything."

Chism also looked behind him at the sound of the shots, then saw "the motorcade beginning to speed up."

Jean Newman was a twenty-one-year-old manufacturing company employee who came to view the motorcade in Dealey Plaza. She told sheriff's deputies she was standing between the Stemmons Freeway sign and the Book Depository when the shots were fired. She stated, "The first impression I had was that the shots came from my right." To her right was the Grassy Knoll.

Also near the Stemmons Freeway sign were two of the most suspicious characters in Dealey Plaza that day. Despite their activities and the fact that both were captured in several photographs made at the time, this pair was never mentioned publicly until the House Select Committee on Assassinations investigation in the late 1970s.

Two Suspicious Men

About the time that Kennedy was first hit by a bullet, two men standing near each other on the north sidewalk of Elm Street acted most strangely—one began pumping a black umbrella while the other waved his right arm high in the air. These and subsequent actions by this pair aroused the suspicions of researchers over the years, yet the initial federal investigation ignored both men. Their activities are known only through analysis of assassination photographs.

As Kennedy's limousine began the gentle descent into Dealey Plaza, a man can be seen standing near the street-side edge of the Stemmons Freeway sign holding an open umbrella. He holds the umbrella in a normal fashion and the top of the umbrella almost reaches the bottom of the sign.

In photos taken minutes before Kennedy's arrival, the umbrella is closed and, immediately after the shooting, pictures show the umbrella was closed again. The man's umbrella was open only during the shooting sequence. Furthermore, as seen in the Zapruder film, once Kennedy is exactly opposite the man with the umbrella, it was pumped almost two feet into the air, twirled, and then lowered.

At the same time, the second man—in photos he appears to be dark complected, perhaps black or Hispanic—raised his right hand into the air, possibly making a fist. This man was located on the outer edge of the Elm Street sidewalk opposite the umbrella man, who was on the inner edge.

The man with the open umbrella was the only person in Dealey Plaza with an open umbrella. Under the warm Texas sun, there was no reason to carry an open umbrella at that time.

Two prominent theories have emerged concerning the "umbrella man" and his activities that day. Assassination researcher Robert Cutler long maintained that the umbrella may have been a sophisticated weapon that fired a dart or "flechette" filled with a paralyzing agent. Cutler's theory is supported by the 1975 testimony of a CIA weapons developer who told the Senate Intelligence Committee that just such an umbrella weapon was in the hands of the spy agency in 1963.

Charles Senseney, who developed weaponry for the CIA at Fort Detrick, Maryland, described a dart-firing weapon he developed as looking like an umbrella. He said the dart gun was silent in operation and fired through the webbing when the umbrella was open. Senseney said the CIA had ordered about fifty such dart weapons and that they were operational in 1963.

In his 1970 book, Cutler theorized that the umbrella was used to fire a paralyzing dart into Kennedy immobilizing him for marksmen with rifles. He claims this theory accounts for the small puncture wound in Kennedy's throat described by Dallas doctors, but which was altered by the time of the Bethesda autopsy. According to Cutler, this dart explains Kennedy's lack of motion during the shooting sequence. Since such a weapon existed and since the actions of both Kennedy and the "umbrella man" were consistent with the operation of such a weapon, Cutler's theory cannot be summarily dismissed. However, the use of such an exotic and questionably effective weapon in such a momentous event stretches credulity.

Most assassination researchers prefer the alternative theory that both of these suspicious men may have been providing visual signals to hidden gunmen. This theory suggests that Kennedy was killed by a crossfire coordinated by radiomen. The two men, who were among the closest bystanders to the president when he was first struck, gave signals indicating that he was not fatally hit and therefore more shots were required.

A fascinating twist on this latter theory came from researcher Gary Shaw, who said the two men may have been providing Kennedy with a last-second sight of who was responsible for his death. Shaw recalled that throughout the planning of the Bay of Pigs Invasion, CIA officers had promised an "umbrella" of air protection of the Cuban invaders. This "umbrella" failed to materialize because Kennedy refused to authorize further US military support for the invasion. According to Shaw's theory, the man with the open umbrella symbolized the promise of an air-support "umbrella" while the dark-complected man may have been one of the anti-Castro Cuban leaders known to Kennedy. Thus, in the last seconds of his life, Kennedy may have seen the open umbrella and the face of a Cuban he knew was involved in the Bay of Pigs and realized who was participating in his death.

But this is all speculation. The existence of the "umbrella man" and the dark-complected man is fact. Even their activities after the assassination bear study. While virtually everyone in Dealey Plaza was moved to action by the assassination—either falling to the ground for cover or moving toward the Grassy Knoll—these two men sat down beside each other on the north sidewalk of Elm Street.

Here the dark-complected man appears to put a walkie-talkie to his mouth. In a photograph taken by Jim Towner, what seems to be an antenna can be seen jutting out from behind the man's head while his right hand holds some object to his face.

Several photos taken in the seconds following the assassination show both of these men sitting together on the Elm Street sidewalk. Moments later, the man with the umbrella gets up, takes one last look toward the motorcade still passing under the Triple Underpass, and begins walking east in the direction of the Depository. The dark-complected man saunters toward the Triple Underpass passing people rushing up the Grassy Knoll. He can be seen stuffing some object—the walkie-talkie?—into the back of his pants.

Despite the suspicious actions of these two men, there is no evidence that the FBI or the Warren Commission made any effort to identify or locate them. Officially they did not exist. Yet over the years, this pair became the focal point of criticism by private researchers. Researchers claimed the lack of investigation of these men indicated the shallowness of the government probes into the assassination.

Once the House Select Committee on Assassinations was formed in the mid-1970s, researchers urged an investigation of both men. The committee finally released a photograph of the "umbrella man" to the news media and urged anyone with knowledge of the man to come forward.

Coincidentally—if it was a coincidence—the "umbrella man" suddenly was identified a few weeks after this national appeal. In August 1978, an anonymous telephone caller told researcher Penn Jones Jr. that the man with the umbrella was a former Dallas insurance salesman named Louis Steven Witt. Jones contacted some local newsmen, including this author, and together they confronted Witt, who then was working as a warehouse manager. Witt refused to talk with newsmen but acknowledged that he was in Dealey Plaza on the day Kennedy was killed.

Jones later wrote, "I felt the man had been coached. He would answer no questions and pointedly invited us to leave. His only positive statement, which seemed to come very quickly, was that if subpoenaed, he was willing to appear before the House Select Committee on Assassinations in Washington."

Witt indeed appeared before the committee during its public testimony. His story was comic relief compared to the intense scrutiny of witnesses like Marina Oswald and Warren Commission critics. His story was facile and improbable and when the umbrella that Witt claimed was the same one he had had in Dealey Plaza in 1963 was displayed, it suddenly turned wrong-side out, prompting one committee member to quip, "I hope that's not a weapon."

Witt told the committee that on the spur of the moment, he grabbed a large black umbrella and went to Dealey Plaza to heckle Kennedy. He claimed that someone had told him that an open umbrella would rile Kennedy. While Witt offered no further explanation of how his umbrella could heckle the president, committee members speculated that the umbrella in some way referred to the pro-German sympathies of Kennedy's father while serving as US ambassador to Britain just prior to World War II. They said the umbrella may have symbolized the appeasement policies of British Prime Minister Neville Chamberlain, who always carried an umbrella.

According to Witt:

> I think I went sort of maybe halfway up the grassy area [on the north side of Elm Street], somewhere in that vicinity. I am pretty sure I sat down . . . [when the motorcade approached] I think I got up and started fiddling with that umbrella trying to get it open, and at the same time I was walking

forward, walking toward the street. . . . Whereas other people I understand saw the President shot and his movements; I did not see this because of this thing [the umbrella] in front of me. . . . My view of the car during that length of time was blocked by the umbrella's being open.

Based on the available photographs made that day, none of Witt's statements were an accurate account of the actions of the "umbrella man" who stood waiting for the motorcade with his umbrella in the normal over-the-head position and then pumped it in the air as Kennedy passed, affording him a full view of the limousine.

Witt's bizarre story—unsubstantiated and totally at odds with the actions of the man in the photographs—resulted in few researchers accepting Louis Steven Witt as the true "umbrella man."

And there continues to be no official accounting for the dark-complected man who appears to have been talking on a radio moments after the assassination. The House committee failed to identify or locate this man and Witt claimed he had no recollection of such a person, despite photographs that seem to show the "umbrella man" talking with the dark man. Witt claimed only to recall that a "Negro man" sat down near him and kept repeating, "They done shot them folks."

Interestingly, one of the committee attorneys asked Witt specifically if he recalled seeing the man with a walkie-talkie, although officially no one has ever admitted the possibility of radios in use in Dealey Plaza.

These two men remain among the mystery people of Dealey Plaza.

Meanwhile, others in the crowd continued to give accounts that differed with the later government pronouncements. Dolores Kounas was a clerk-typist with McGraw-Hill Publishing Company, which had offices on the third floor of the Depository building. She, along with two other McGraw-Hill employees, was standing just west of the Depository across Elm Street from Millican and the Chisms. She, too, thought the first shot was a firecracker, but after hearing a second shot and seeing people fall to the ground, she realized they were shots. She later told the FBI:

Although I was across the street from the Depository building and was looking in the direction of the building as the motorcade passed and following the shots, I did not look up at the building as I had thought the shots came from a westerly direction in the vicinity of the viaduct.

Forty-four-year-old James Altgens, a photographer for the Associated Press in Dallas, arrived in Dealey Plaza early. He had been assigned to get a picture of Kennedy as he passed through downtown Dallas and decided the west end of Dealey Plaza would provide an excellent opportunity to catch the president with the downtown buildings in the background. However, when Altgens tried to station himself on the Triple Underpass, he was shooed away by a Dallas policeman, who told him it was railroad property and only railroad employees were allowed there.

So Altgens walked around by the Depository, then on to the intersection of Main and Houston, where he took a photo as the president passed. He then ran farther into the plaza, where he made several photographs from the south curb of Elm as the motorcade approached from Houston.

In the May 24, 1964, issue of the *New York Herald Tribune* magazine section, there was an article regarding Altgens's photograph. This article raised a pertinent question:

> Isn't it odd that J. W. Altgens, a veteran Associated Press photographer in Dallas, who took a picture of the Kennedy assassination—one of the witnesses close enough to see the President shot and able to describe second-by-second what happened—has been questioned neither by the FBI nor the Warren Commission?

With this question now public, the federal government went to work. On June 2, 1964, with the Warren Commission's investigation winding down, Altgens was finally interviewed by FBI agents. The agents reported, "He recalled that at about the instant he snapped the picture, he heard a burst of noise which he thought was firecrackers . . . he then turned the film in his camera . . . when he heard another report which he recognized as a gunshot."

Altgens elaborated:

> I made one picture at the time I heard a noise that sounded like a firecracker. . . . I figured it was nothing more than a firecracker because from my position down here the sound was not of such volume that it would indicate to me it was a high-velocity rifle. . . . It sounded like it was coming up from behind the car . . . who counts fireworks explosions? I wasn't keeping track of the number of pops that took place, but I could vouch for No. 1 and I can vouch for the last shot, but I cannot tell you how many shots were in between. There was not another shot fired after the President was struck in the head. That was the last shot—that much I will say with a great degree of certainty.

Despite his vantage point and his photographic background, Altgens was never called to testify to the Warren Commission, which was satisfied to merely cite from his FBI interrogation. Even then, they argued with his statement that he snapped his camera's shutter at the sound of the first shot, stating in their report that he took the picture "later than the point at which the President was shot in the neck."

Another of Altgens's photos was taken just seconds after the first shots were fired and showed a slender man standing in the doorway of the Depository. Many people, including his mother, have claimed the man was Lee Harvey Oswald. More on that later.

Near Altgens on the grassy triangle in the lower part of Dealey Plaza were a handful of people, all the closest witnesses to the actual assassination.

Charles Brehm, along with his five-year-old son, had watched the presidential motorcade turn onto Houston from near the front of the Depository building. Holding his son, Brehm ran across Elm and stationed himself halfway between Houston and the Triple Underpass on the grassy triangle south of Elm. In a 1966 film documentary, Brehm stated:

> I very definitely saw the effect of the second bullet that struck the President. That which appeared to be a portion of the President's skull went flying slightly to the rear of the President's car and directly to its left. It did fly over toward the curb to the left and to the rear.

Brehm said the piece of skull landed in the grass not far from his location. He told the FBI some days later that "it seemed quite apparent to him that the shots came from one of two buildings back at the corner of Elm and Houston Streets." He added he was not certain but "it seemed to him that the automobile almost came to a halt after the first shot."

Brehm, an ex-serviceman with experience in bolt-action rifles, was probably the closest witness to the fatal head shot. He was not called to testify to the Warren Commission. But he continued to tell his story over the years, even appearing at Dallas events concerning the assassination.

Two significant home movies were made of the assassination, one by Maria Muchmore, who had moved from a position near Main and Houston to the center of the grassy triangle behind Brehm. She caught on film the final and fatal head shot to Kennedy and the disappearance of the limousine into the Triple Underpass.

Further behind Muchmore, across Main Street, Orville Nix captured the entire assassination sequence. It is the Nix film that most clearly shows the presidential limousine coming to a brief halt with its brake lights on prior to the fatal head shot. Also in the Nix film are suspicious flashes of light on the Grassy Knoll, which is in the background. Are these muzzle flashes from rifles? To date, no sophisticated analysis has been conducted.

Nix was interviewed by an assassination researcher some years later and asked about the direction of the shots. He stated, "I thought it [shots] came from a fence between the Book Depository and the railroad tracks."

Nix also said that he later talked about the assassination with a friend, Forrest V. Sorrels, then head of the Dallas Secret Service office. He said at the time of the assassination, Sorrels, too, believed shots had come from the picket fence on the Grassy Knoll.

The Warren Commission never called Nix to testify, although he indicated he was willing to do so to the FBI, nor did the Commission have his film adequately analyzed. Only after some researchers claimed that photographs of a gunman on the Grassy Knoll were visible in the Nix film was it closely studied. In late 1966, Itek Corporation, which handles government contracts and is closely tied to the CIA, studied the film on the request of United Press International. Itek scientists concluded that the gunman figure was actually shadows from a tree branch.

It might be noted that even this conclusion is not totally accepted by suspicious researchers since, moments later, Nix panned back over the same area and the "shadow" figure is no longer visible. If the figure was merely shadows, it would seem that they should still be there in the later frames. When asked if the film the government returned to him was his original, Nix later responded, "I would say no . . . some of the frames were missing . . . some were ruined."

Only a couple of the witnesses from the center grassy area testified to the Warren Commission, and one of the best witnesses was never identified until years later when she was interviewed by an assassination researcher.

Also taking films on the south side of Elm Street was a woman who stood filming right behind Brehm and his son. From this vantage point, her movie would show not only the Grassy Knoll in the background, but also the Texas School Book Depository at the time of the shooting.

Despite the most intensive FBI investigation in history, federal authorities officially were unable to locate the woman and, for years, she was known to researchers only as the "babushka lady" because of a triangular kerchief she wore on her head that day.

The Babushka Lady

Perhaps the reason the federal authorities were unable to identify or locate the "babushka lady" is the explosive story she had to tell.

Located many years later by researcher Gary Shaw, Beverly Oliver, by then married to an evangelist and a "reborn" Christian, said she was nineteen years old at the time of the assassination and worked as a singer for the Colony Club, a strip-show club located next door to Jack Ruby's Carousel Club.

On November 22, she took a prototype Super-8 Yashica movie camera to Dealey Plaza and ended up just behind Charles Brehm on the grassy triangle just south of Elm Street. The camera was a gift from a friend who had access to new camera technology.

Photos taken that day show that Oliver filmed the entire assassination as the motorcade moved down Elm. Undoubtedly her film would have included the windows of the Texas School Book Depository as shots were fired, clear pictures of the "umbrella man" and the "dark-complected man" on the north side of Elm, and the Grassy Knoll area at the time of the fatal head shot.

Oliver said that on Monday following the assassination, she was approached by two men as she neared the Colony Club. She believed they were either FBI or Secret

Service agents. They said they knew she had taken film in Dealey Plaza and wanted to develop it for use as evidence. Oliver was told her film would be returned to her within ten days. She complied.

She never saw her film again. There was no mention of either her or her film in the Warren Report.

Years later, when shown photographs of FBI agents involved in the assassination, Oliver identified Regis Kennedy as one of the men who took her film. Kennedy played a key role in the New Orleans aspect of the assassination investigation and came under suspicion in later years because of his insistence that New Orleans Mafia boss Carlos Marcello was merely a "tomato salesman."

Not long after the assassination, Oliver married George McGann, a Dallas underworld character whose best man was Russell D. Matthews. Matthews, a close friend of Jack Ruby, was described by the House Select Committee on Assassinations as "actively engaged in criminal activity since the 1940s."

The committee also developed evidence connecting Matthews with associates of Florida Mafia chieftain Santos Trafficante. Further, Matthews was a father figure to another Dallas thug, convicted murderer-for-hire Charles V. Harrelson, the father of film star Woody Harrelson.

Oliver revealed that during the presidential campaign of 1968, she and McGann had a two-hour conversation with candidate Richard Nixon in a Miami hotel. Why former president Nixon would meet with a well-known criminal is unclear, but in light of information that has been made public since the Watergate affair linking Nixon to organized-crime figures, this story no longer seems so far-fetched.

In 1970, McGann was killed in a gangland-style slaying in west Texas.

Oliver also said that two weeks prior to the Kennedy assassination, she was visiting in Ruby's club. There she met a man Ruby introduced as "Lee Oswald of the CIA." She later recognized Oswald when his picture was broadcast following the assassination. She also met David Ferrie in Ruby's club in late 1963. "In fact, he was there so often, I mistook him as the assistant manager of the Carousel Club," she told this author.

A friend of Oliver's also knew of Oswald's being in Ruby's club and spoke openly about it. According to Oliver, her friend disappeared and she "decided it would be in her best interests not to say anything." She remained quiet until the mid-1970s, when she was located and interviewed by Shaw and, later, by Texas newsmen.

Although Beverly Oliver was the object of a secret briefing by Commission attorney Robert Tannenbaum on March 17, 1977, and a transcript of this briefing was accidentally leaked to the news media, there is no mention of her or her film in the committee's report.

Obviously it is highly suspicious to researchers that one of the closest witnesses to the assassination and a witness who claimed to have been with both Ruby and Oswald prior to November 22, 1963, was never located or identified by federal authorities. Not to mention that when a report was prepared, it was not released to the public.

Oliver continued to share her story through 2013. The details were published in her 1994 book, *Nightmare in Dallas*. Largely due to her hesitation in going public for so many years, a concerted effort appeared to have been mounted to discredit her. Other than simply voicing disbelief, most accusations were based on flimsy arguments, such as one that claimed the shoes depicted on the person in the Dealey Plaza photographs appeared too small to fit the older and larger Oliver. However, until someone with better credentials and a convincing story comes forth, most researchers accept Beverly Oliver as the "babushka lady."

A few feet to the west of Oliver on the center grassy slope were two important witnesses: Mary Moorman, who took a photograph at the moment of the fatal head shot that may have pictured the gunman on the Grassy Knoll, and her friend Jean Hill, who, like Willis, claimed to have seen Jack Ruby in front of the Texas School Book Depository at the time of the shooting.

Ironically, neither Moorman nor Hill, probably the closest witnesses to the fatal head shot other than Brehm, were there simply to see Kennedy. Both women had come to Dealey Plaza to take pictures of Dallas police motorcycle officers they fancied. Hill had just moved to Dallas from Oklahoma and Moorman was showing her the city, as well as trying to get her a date with one of the policemen escorting the motorcade.

The women were stopped by a policeman at the corner of Elm and Houston and initially prevented from entering the grassy triangle in the center of the plaza. However, after some flirting, the officer allowed them through and they took up a position on the south side of Elm midway between Houston and the Triple Underpass.

Hill, who said she was getting in a "cops and robbers frame of mind" hoping to date the policeman, noticed that a van with writing on it saying UNCLE JOE'S PAWN SHOP was allowed through the police lines and drove in front of the Depository and behind the concrete pergola on top of the Grassy Knoll. She thought this was suspicious since no one else had been allowed into that short street in front of the Depository. She jokingly said to Moorman, "Do you suppose there are murderers in that van?"

As the presidential motorcade turned onto Elm, Moorman began taking snapshots with a Polaroid camera and handing the photos to Hill, who applied fixative and put them in the pocket of her red-cloth raincoat.

Hill said Kennedy was smiling and waving to a crowd of people on the north side of Elm. She told this author:

> I knew he'd never look our way because all the people were on the other side of the street, so I jumped out into the street and yelled, "Hey, Mr. President, look this way. We want to take your picture." As he began turning toward us, he was hit. Then a bullet hit his head and took the top off. Mary fell to the ground and shouted, "Get down, they're shooting!" But being young

and dumb, I kept standing for a minute trying to see where the shots came from. It was eerie. Everything seemed frozen. I saw a man fire from behind the wooden fence. I saw a puff of smoke and some sort of movement on the Grassy Knoll where he was. [She later pinpointed this location as about fifteen feet north of the eastern corner of the wooden picket fence—the exact location of a figure discovered in Moorman's photograph.] Then I saw a man walking briskly in front of the Texas School Book Depository. He was the only person moving. Everybody else seemed to be frozen with shock. Because of my earlier thoughts, I became suspicious of this man and thought he might be connected with that truck I saw.

Hill said she heard between four and six shots altogether and then ran across the street in an effort to locate the men she had seen. She didn't find them, but she claimed that on the following Sunday morning she recognized TV photos of Jack Ruby as the man she had seen in front of the Depository. Minutes after the shooting, Hill said she was standing just west of the Depository when she was taken into custody by two men who identified themselves as Secret Service agents.

Meanwhile, a Dallas reporter had talked with Moorman and taken her to the sheriff's office. Here she was later joined by Hill, who said their photographs had been taken by federal authorities.

Directly across Elm from Hill and Moorman was the Newman family. Bill Newman, his wife, Gayle, and their two small children were standing west of the Stemmons Freeway sign directly below the Grassy Knoll. Newman told sheriff's officers:

We were standing at the edge of the curb looking at the [president's] car as it was coming toward us and all of a sudden there was a noise, apparently a gunshot. . . . By [the] time he was directly in front of us . . . he was hit in the side of the head. . . . Then we fell down on the grass as it seemed that we were in direct path of fire. . . . I thought the shot had come from the garden directly behind me, that was an elevation from where I was as I was right on the curb. I do not recall looking toward the Texas School Book Depository. I looked back in the vicinity of the garden.

Later that day during a local television interview, Newman was apparently the first person to publicly speak of the Grassy Knoll. When asked where the shots had come from, Newman responded, "Back up on the, uh, knoll . . . what you call it." UPI reporter Merriman Smith, in a dispatch sent only twenty-five minutes following the shooting, noted, "Some of the Secret Service agents thought the gunfire was from an automatic weapon fired to the right rear of the president's car, probably from a grassy knoll to which police rushed."

Another witness, far above the crowd in Dealey Plaza, had a bird's-eye view of the assassination. Jesse C. Price was the building engineer for the Union Terminal Annex, which is the southern counterpart of the Texas School Book Depository. The building stands at the corner of Houston and Commerce. Price said he went up on the roof to get "a better view of the caravan." While sitting on the edge of the building's roof overlooking the plaza, Price heard shots "from by the . . . Triple Underpass."

In an affidavit signed that day, Price stated, "There was a volley of shots, I think five and then much later . . . another one." He said the shots seemed to come from "just behind the picket fence where it joins the underpass."

Price also said he saw a man, described as young, wearing a white dress shirt, no tie, and khaki-colored pants, running behind the wooden picket fence "towards the passenger cars on the railroad siding" with something in his hand that "could have been a gun."

Price was never called to testify to the Warren Commission. In fact, it should be noted that many of the closest and most critical witnesses were never queried by the Warren Commission. And those who were can be forgiven for not providing any useful information. For example, on April 3, 1964, statements given to the FBI by seventy-three Depository employees were given to the Warren Commission by FBI director J. Edgar Hoover. These statements were all given in late March 1964, a time in which every citizen had been conditioned for nearly four months to the idea that Lee Harvey Oswald was the lone assassin and that only three shots came from the sixth floor of the Depository. Adding to this predetermination by both government and mass media were rumors already circulating in Dallas that it might be unhealthy to contradict the official government position on the assassination. Incredibly, virtually none of the witnesses were questioned as to their opinion of the origin of the shots or even how many shots were fired. In fact, for the most part, they read like pre-prepared statements simply signed by the participants, none of whom were willing to challenge federal authorities.

Even in the face of contradictions in evidence and testimony by those in Dealey Plaza, one fact seems inescapable—most of the witnesses in the crowd believed shots came from the Grassy Knoll area.

However, it is also certain that at least one or more shots were fired from the direction of the redbrick building at the northwest corner of Elm and Houston—the Texas School Book Depository.

The Texas School Book Depository

Overlooking Dealey Plaza at its northeast corner is the seven-story redbrick building that in 1963 housed the Texas School Book Depository. It had little to do with Texas public schools.

The Depository was a private company that acted as an agent for a number of book publishers, furnishing office space and providing warehousing, inventorying, and shipping.

School systems would place orders with the publishers for textbooks and the publishers would send the orders along to the Depository, where about a half dozen young men acted as order fillers—locating and collecting the books as per each order.

On November 22, 1963, one of these order fillers was Lee Harvey Oswald.

Oswald and his wife, Marina, had separated at the time he left for New Orleans in the spring of 1963. They reunited in that Louisiana city, but in September, it was decided that since Marina was about to have a baby, she would return to Texas with a friend, Ruth Paine, while Oswald continued his activities—which reportedly included a trip to Mexico City.

When Oswald arrived back in Dallas on October 3, Marina was living in Irving, a suburban city west of Dallas. She was staying in the home of Michael and Ruth Paine—they, too, were separated at the time—and over the weekend of October 12–13, Oswald had arrived there to visit. During this weekend, Mrs. Paine said she gave Oswald, who had no driver's license, a driving lesson in her car.

About a week before, Oswald allegedly had returned from his trip to Mexico City. However, there continues to be much controversy concerning this journey.

On Monday, October 14, Mrs. Paine drove Oswald to Dallas, where he rented a room at 1026 N. Beckley Avenue from Mrs. A. C. Johnson for $8 a week. Oswald had filled out applications at the Texas Employment Commission and reportedly was looking for work.

That same day, Mrs. Paine mentioned Oswald—and the fact that he needed work because his wife was about to have another baby—to neighbors, including Mrs. Linnie Mae Randle. Mrs. Randle mentioned that Wesley Frazier, a younger brother who lived with her, worked at the Texas School Book Depository and that a job might be available there. Marina Oswald, who was present at this gathering, reportedly urged Mrs. Paine to check into the job possibility. Mrs. Paine agreed and called Depository superintendent Roy Truly that very day.

Before the Warren Commission, Truly recalled getting a call from a woman in Irving who said she knew a man whose wife was going to have a baby and needed a job. Truly agreed to talk with the man.

Mrs. Paine mentioned her call to Oswald later that evening and the next day, October 15, Oswald interviewed with Truly for the job. Oswald began working as temporary help the next day. Truly said the fall was their busiest time of year. Plus more hands were needed as the flooring on the sixth floor was being torn up and replaced. Truly told the commission:

> Actually, [it was] the end of our fall rush—if it hadn't existed a week or two longer [than usual], or if we had not been using some of our regular boys putting down this plywood, we would not have had any need for Lee Oswald at that time, which is a tragic thing for me to think about.

Oswald was paid $1.25 an hour to fill book orders. Once shown the procedures, he worked on his own. Truly described Oswald as "a bit above average" as an employee. Coworkers said Oswald was pleasant enough but kept mostly to himself.

During his first week at work, Oswald got acquainted with Frazier and soon asked Frazier to drive him to Irving to visit his family. Frazier, who had only started working at the Depository the month before, said he was eager to make friends in Dallas. So Frazier agreed and, in fact, gave Oswald a ride to Irving every weekend prior to the assassination—except one when Oswald told Frazier he was staying in Dallas to take a driving test.

On Sunday, November 17, Marina Oswald had Mrs. Paine call a Dallas telephone number Oswald had given her. When she asked for Lee Oswald, Mrs. Paine was told there was nobody there by that name. The next day, Oswald called the Paine home and angrily told Marina he was using a fictitious name at the Beckley Avenue address and not to call him there.

On Thursday morning, November 21, Oswald reportedly asked Frazier to drive him to Irving after work because he wanted to get some curtain rods to put in his Beckley Avenue apartment. According to this curtain rod story—only Frazier and his sister claimed to have seen Oswald with a package and their descriptions were inconsistent and vague—the next morning Frazier's sister saw Oswald place a paper-wrapped package in Frazier's car and Frazier noticed the packet as the pair drove to work. Frazier later said Oswald told him it was the curtain rods. Oswald also said he would not be riding back to Irving as usual, but he gave no explanation. Frazier said once at the Depository, Oswald got out of the car and walked ahead into the building carrying his package with one end cupped in his right hand and the other tucked under his right arm, parallel to his body. Most researchers who have studied the Mannlicher-Carcano (technically merely a Carcano carbine) state that, even disassembled, the barrel is too long to carry in this position.

When Frazier entered the building, he could not see Oswald and never knew what became of the package. Many researchers believe the curtain rod story was concocted by authorities later in an attempt to explain how Oswald got a rifle into the Depository. Some researchers suspect Frazier, who could have been charged with being an accessory to the assassination, was susceptible to being coached by authorities. Furthermore, photographs made of Oswald's Beckley Avenue room that weekend clearly show curtains in place, obviating any need for curtain rods. When questioned by the authorities on what he had taken into the Depository, Oswald denied the curtain rod story, saying he only carried his lunch to work.

Jack Dougherty, another Depository employee whose Warren Commission testimony appears somewhat incoherent, nevertheless said, "Yes, I saw [Oswald] when he first came in the door." Commission attorney Joseph Ball asked, "Did he have anything in his hands or arms?" "Well, not that I could see of," was the response.

Many Depository employees saw Oswald that morning. He appeared to be carrying on normal work duties, particularly on the sixth floor, where he was assigned that day.

Frazier said he never saw Oswald after noon. He told the Warren Commission that as the presidential motorcade approached, he joined other Depository employees who were standing on the steps of the building facing Elm.

Minutes before the presidential motorcade arrived, an odd incident occurred that has puzzled researchers for years.

The Distracting Seizure

About 12:15 p.m., a young man described as wearing green Army fatigues collapsed at 100 N. Houston, near the front door of the Texas School Book Depository. He apparently suffered some sort of seizure. Dallas policeman D. V. Harkness radioed the police dispatcher to send an ambulance to that location at 12:18 p.m. Radio logs showed that the ambulance, after picking up the victim, radioed, "We are en route to Parkland." However, Parkland never recorded a patient registering at this time, and the entire incident seemed forgotten.

Despite the suspicious timing and proximity to the assassination, there is no mention of this incident in the Warren Commission Report and the FBI didn't get around to investigating it until May 1964.

And this investigation took place only after a former employee of O'Neal Funeral Home, apparently more curious about the incident than the FBI, called the bureau's Dallas office to report the incident, adding the patient "disappeared" after arriving at Parkland. The O'Neal caller stated he "felt it possible that this incident may have been planned to distract attention from the shooting that was to follow."

The FBI detailed their investigation of the matter in Commission Document 1245, which was not included in the Warren Report or its twenty-six volumes.

Agents contacted the ambulance driver, Aubrey Rike, who said he had picked up a man "who was conscious and only slightly injured with a facial laceration." Rike added that in the confusion at Parkland, this man had simply walked off. Rike also said a Secret Service agent at Parkland told him to remain there "because they might need [his ambulance] to move the President to another location." It was Rike who later helped load the president's body into his ambulance for the sad return to Love Field.

On May 26, Bureau agents located the "victim" after finding his name in O'Neal records. Jerry B. Belknap had paid his $12.50 ambulance charge back on December 2, 1963. Based on a later FBI report and an interview with Belknap by assassination researcher Jerry D. Rose, the following story came to light: Belknap said he had suffered from seizures since being struck by a car while getting off a school bus as a child. He was standing near the Depository when he stepped back from the crowd and lost consciousness. He said the next thing he knew, a policeman was standing over him.

Once at Parkland, he was sitting on a small table and, after asking for attention, was told to lie down. He said that a short time later there was a great rush of people who went into a different section of the emergency room. This was the Kennedy party with the stricken president.

Belknap said a male attendant finally brought him some water and an aspirin but that, after realizing that he was not going to get immediate treatment, he walked out without registering. Amazingly, his exit was accomplished under the noses of security agents who were locking down the hospital. Outside, Belknap caught a bus back downtown, where he first learned of the assassination.

Intriguingly, Belknap told Rose that he had been interviewed by both Dallas police and the FBI within days of the assassination, months before the FBI's reported investigation in May 1964. He commented that the two police agencies apparently distrusted each other and both asked him the same questions. Asked about the June 1964 FBI report concerning him, Belknap offered the explanation that perhaps an agent had called him on the phone and simply confirmed the results of the earlier interview. Belknap also stated in 1983 that an investigator from "some committee in Washington" had contacted him within the past few years. However, if this investigator was with the House Select Committee on Assassinations, there is no reference to him in its report or attendant volumes.

Belknap died in 1986.

The entire "seizure" episode is strange and full of contradictions and coincidence—Belknap even reported seeing Jack Ruby once "acting like a big shot." Belknap also said he lost consciousness at the scene, while the FBI report said he didn't.

Researchers view the incident as either a strangely convenient coincidence or as some as-yet-undiscovered plot to distract police and bystanders while assassins moved into position just prior to Kennedy's arrival in Dealey Plaza.

Ambulance driver Rike, who died in April 2010, told this author he felt the incident was suspicious because he personally had been summoned to that same location on false calls several times in the days leading up to the assassination. In fact, there may have been more than a dozen such fake calls, a fact not immediately noticed as they were spaced over separate shifts of drivers. All requested an ambulance be sent to the corner of Elm and Houston. "We would get these calls for service and I would run up there to the area by the School Book Depository but there would be no one there. This happened up to twelve times in the two weeks preceding the assassination," said Rike. "It seemed like someone was timing how long it took for an ambulance to get there." Rike pointed out that the Kennedy motorcade was running about five minutes late, which meant if it had been on time, it would have arrived at Elm and Houston simultaneously with his ambulance. Speculation was that this would have congested the intersection, causing the Kennedy limousine to stop, making the president a stationary target.

Researchers agree the incident deserves further investigation, particularly in light of the fact that Rike and Dennis McGuire, the ambulance drivers who took Belknap to Parkland, remained there to load Kennedy's body for the return trip to Love Field that fateful afternoon.

One Depository employee who felt strongly that shots had originated from within the building was Geneva L. Hine, who operated the Depository's credit desk on the second floor. She told the Warren Commission she had seen President Kennedy before and offered to answer the telephones while some of the office women could go outside to view the motorcade. By herself, Hine watched the president's car turn from Houston onto Elm. Suddenly, she said, she heard three shots that "sounded like cannon shots, they were so terrific." They caused the building to shake and appeared to come from within the building, she said.

But the most curious aspect to Hine's statement was the cause of her leaving the telephones and venturing to the window. "I was alone until the lights all went out and the phones became dead because the motorcade was coming near us and no one was calling so I got up and thought I could see it from the east window in our office."

The lights all went out and the phones went dead just as Kennedy's motorcade approached the Depository? There was no other blackout in any other part of Dallas. This most suspicious happenstance did not prompt any follow-up questions from Commission attorneys Joseph A. Ball and Samuel A. Stern, who merely went on to ask Hine what she saw out the window.

At the time of the shooting, most persons within the Depository believed the shots came from elsewhere.

Steven F. Wilson was vice president of a school textbook–publishing company and had an office on the third floor of the Depository. Wilson told the FBI he watched the motorcade go by from a closed third-floor window but lost sight of the president when he "became obscured by some trees which are on Elm Street." He further stated:

> In a matter of ten seconds or less . . . I heard three shots . . . there was a greater space of time between the second and third shots than between the first and second. The three shots were fired within a matter of less than five seconds. The shots sounded to me like rifle shots. At that time, it seemed like the shots came from the west end of the building or from the colonnade located on Elm Street across from the west end of our building [the pergola on the Grassy Knoll]. The shots really did not sound like they came from above me.

Elsie Dorman, who worked for Scott-Foresman Co., was in her fourth-floor office filming the presidential motorcade as it moved toward her on Houston. The only film made from the Depository, hers was of poor quality and did not capture the assassination. With her were fellow workers Dorothy Ann Garner, Victoria Adams, and Sandra Styles. Garner told the FBI, "I thought at the time the shots or reports came from a point to the west of the building." Adams told the Warren Commission:

> We heard a shot, and it was a pause, and then a second shot, and then a third shot. It sounded like a firecracker or a cannon at a football game, it seems as if it came from the right below [the area of the Grassy Knoll] rather than from the left above [the sixth-floor window].

Styles told Bureau agents she could not tell where the shots came from, but that she and Adams immediately "left the office at this time, went down the back stairs, and left the building at the back door." Wesley Frazier, who had driven Oswald to work that morning, was on the front steps of the Depository. He told the Warren Commission of his experience:

Right after he [Kennedy] went by . . . I heard a sound and if you have ever been around motorcycles you know how they backfire, and so I thought one of them motorcycles backfired because right before his car came down, now there were several of these motorcycle policemen, and they took off down toward the underpass down there. . . . I heard two more of the same type, you know, sounds, and by that time people were running everywhere and falling down and screaming. . . . I figured it was somebody shooting at President Kennedy . . . and from where I was standing it sounded like it was coming from down [at the] railroad tracks there. . . . So, we started back into the building and it wasn't but just a few minutes that there were a lot of police officers and so forth all over the building there.

Frazier said one of the Depository employees with him on the steps of the building as Kennedy passed by was Billy Nolan Lovelady, who was to become well-known to researchers as "the man in the doorway."

The Man in the Doorway

Associated Press photographer James Altgens snapped a picture seconds after Kennedy was first struck by a bullet. In the background of this photo a man can be seen standing in the west corner of the Texas School Book Depository's front doorway.

Soon after the assassination, many people—including his mother—suggested the man in the doorway looked amazingly like Lee Harvey Oswald. Obviously, if the man in the photo was Oswald, he could not have been firing a rifle on the sixth floor. Controversy over this issue has continued to roil since the time of the assassination. In 2012 a group of researchers, including McKnight University professor emeritus James H. Fetzer, retired University of Wisconsin–Stevens Point history professor David Wrone, and health specialist Ralph C. Cinque, began an "Oswald Innocence Campaign" based primarily on the photo of the man in the doorway, who they said "clearly evident upon close examination" was Lee Oswald.

The Warren Commission, based primarily on testimony from Depository employees, concluded the man in the doorway was Billy Lovelady. After being interviewed at length by the FBI, Lovelady identified the man in the photo as himself.

Lovelady, who had worked at the Depository since 1961, was one of the men assigned to lay plywood flooring on the sixth floor that day. He said that about 11:50 a.m. he and other employees stopped work so they could clean up before taking their lunch break. Lovelady said the workers took both of the Depository's two elevators and were racing each other down to ground level. He recalled hearing Oswald shout to them to wait or to send an elevator back for him.

After buying a soft drink, Lovelady told the Warren Commission, he went out the main door and sat on the steps of the Depository to eat his lunch with some coworkers. Lovelady said he remained there as the motorcade passed by, and then heard some noises. "I thought it was firecrackers or somebody celebrating the arrival of the President. It didn't occur to me at first what had happened until this

Gloria [Calvery] came running up to us and told us the President had been shot," he recalled.

Asked where he thought the shots came from, Lovelady replied, "Right there around that concrete little deal on that knoll." Lovelady, along with fellow Depository employees, joined the throng of people rushing toward the Grassy Knoll, but said a short time later he returned to the Depository, entering through a back door unchallenged.

William Shelley, Depository manager and Oswald's immediate supervisor, acknowledged that Lovelady was on the steps of the building when Kennedy passed by. He told the Warren Commission he heard "something sounded like it was a firecracker and a slight pause and then two more a little bit closer together." He too said the shots sounded like they came from west of the Depository.

Additionally, Wesley Frazier and a Depository clerk, Sarah Stanton, both signed statements averring they were with Shelley and Lovelady on the Depository steps at the time of the shooting.

That should have been the end of questions concerning the identity of the man in the doorway. However, on February 29, 1964, the FBI interviewed Lovelady and photographed him wearing a short-sleeved shirt with vertical stripes, totally unlike the dark, mottled long-sleeved shirt worn by the man in the Altgens picture.

Later Lovelady explained the discrepancies in the shirts by telling CBS News, "Well, when the FBI took [my picture] in the shirt, I told them it wasn't the same shirt."

The shirt Lovelady was wearing that day—and subsequently tried to sell for a large sum of money—was a broad plaid, which he said was buttoned at the neck. The man in the doorway photo appears to be wearing a dark mottled shirt open to the navel with a white T-shirt underneath, exactly what Oswald was wearing when arrested less than an hour and a half later.

And even Dallas police chief Jesse Curry seemed to continue to question the identity of the man in the doorway. In his 1969 book, Curry compared photos of the doorway man with Oswald and merely commented, "The Warren Commission attempted to prove that the man was Billy N. Lovelady who worked at the depository."

The House Select Committee on Assassinations (HSCA) considered this issue in depth. They had anthropologists study the features of the man in the photograph and the committee received photographic analyses of the man's shirt. The committee concluded "that it is highly improbable that the man in the doorway was Oswald and highly probable that he was Lovelady." But this probability did not end the controversy. Skeptics noted that the HSCA Report never mentioned that the man in the doorway wore his shirt open to the navel. Pictures of Lovelady taken that day showed his shirt buttoned to the neck.

Most researchers today accept that Lovelady was the man in the doorway. Museum curator and archivist Richard B. Trask, in his monumental 1994 book on assassination photographic evidence, *Pictures of the Pain*, wrote about reenactment photos of Lovelady shot on the Depository steps in 1971. He noted, "At a distance of eight years from the original event, it was still readily evident that Lovelady was one and the same in both the 1963 and 1971 photos."

But the controversy continued when in 2013 researchers with the Oswald Innocence Campaign claimed the Altgens photo, particularly the area within the Depository doorway, had been altered. As will be seen, this is not the only allegation of photographic alteration in the assassination case. However, these researchers focus primarily on the clothing worn by both Oswald and Lovelady. David Wrone pointed out that the collars of the two shirts "furl" differently, with Oswald's assuming the look of a false lapel. They said by proving that the man in the doorway could not be Lovelady, it appeared by default that it was Oswald.

Adding to the controversy, in 2007 the Assassination Records Review Board released handwritten notes by Dallas Police homicide captain Will Fritz made during his initial interrogation of Oswald on the day of the assassination. Fritz noted Oswald told him he had gone "to 1st floor [and] had lunch" and then was "out with Bill Shelley in front." Oswald said it was Shelley, his immediate boss, who told him to go home, as there would be no more work that day, although Shelley denied even seeing Oswald any time after the shooting. Most Depository employees indeed had left the building by about 2 p.m. after being told there would be no more work that day. Shelley also made it clear that after the shooting he and Lovelady moved toward the railroad tracks and finally reentered the Depository through the rear door. So if Oswald did indeed encounter Shelley, it would have had to be prior to or during the assassination and not afterward.

"The 'Doorman' was Oswald, and there is no doubt about it," argued Ralph Cinque, administrator of the Oswald Innocence Campaign website. "He is wearing Oswald's clothes—to a tee. He has got Oswald's build and even Oswald's mannerisms. And the whole case for Lovelady never made a lick of sense, relying as it does on phony pictures, phony movies, and, in a word: lies."

Since Lovelady said he was sitting on the steps and the man in the photo is standing, peering around the edge of the front-door alcove, and since the FBI did such a dismal job of proving it was Lovelady, coupled with claims of alterations to the Altgens photo, suspicion still lingers about the identity of the man in the doorway.

While many researchers today are ready to concede that the man may have been Lovelady, there is a growing resistance to this admission. And the stakes are high. If it can ever be conclusively demonstrated that the man in the Depository doorway is Lee Oswald, the case for his committing the crime six floors above completely falls apart.

But if the man in the doorway was not Oswald, then where was he? Was he on the sixth floor firing the Carcano, just as two federal panels have concluded?

Despite the years of confident statements by federal authorities, no one has unquestionably placed Oswald on the sixth floor at the time of the shooting.

In later years Dallas police chief Jesse Curry admitted to newsmen, "We don't have any proof that Oswald fired the rifle, and never did. Nobody's yet been able to put him in that building with a gun in his hand."

When asked where he was at the time of the shooting, Oswald told Dallas police he was eating lunch on the first floor of the Depository in what was called the "domino room" at the time of the assassination, and there is some evidence to back up his statement.

Bonnie Ray Williams was one of the Depository workers who were laying plywood flooring on the sixth floor that day. During the elevator race to the first floor a few minutes before noon, Williams said, he heard Oswald call, "Guys, how about an elevator?" from either the fifth or sixth floor. Oswald also apparently asked them to send an elevator back up to him.

Williams told the Warren Commission he thought the others planned to gather on the sixth floor to watch the motorcade, so he returned there with his lunch, consisting of chicken, bread, and a bag of chips in a brown paper sack along with a soft drink. Williams said he sat on some boxes near a window facing out onto Elm Street and ate his lunch. He said he saw no one else on the sixth floor, which was one large open area. However, he noted stacks of book cartons here and there. Becoming impatient because no other workers had joined him, Williams threw down the remains of his lunch and left the sixth floor at "approximately 12:20." Since the presidential motorcade was running approximately five minutes late, this means there was no one in the sixth-floor window at the time Kennedy should have arrived in the street below. In a January 14, 1964, FBI report, agents quoted Williams as saying he left the sixth floor after about three minutes. However, Williams denied ever saying that and it is reasonable that he couldn't have eaten his lunch in only three minutes.

At the time, the news media made a great deal of comment about the chicken bones and lunch sack found on the sixth floor. Many people thought this proved that a cold and calculating assassin had patiently eaten his lunch while waiting for Kennedy to arrive.

Going down one of the elevators, Williams saw two other workers, Harold Norman and James Jarman, on the fifth floor and joined them to watch the motorcade. Williams and Norman were captured in a photograph taken that day as they leaned out of the fifth-floor window directly below the famous sixth-floor "sniper's" window to view the president.

Williams told the Warren Commission:

> After the President's car had passed my window . . . [there] was a loud shot—first I thought they were saluting the President, somebody—even maybe a motorcycle backfire. The first shot—[then] there was two shots rather close together. The second and the third shot was closer together then the first shot . . . well, the first shot—I really did not pay any attention to it, because I did not know what was happening. The second shot, it sounded like it was right in the building . . . it even shook the building,

the side we were on. Cement fell on my head. . . . Harold was sitting next to me and he said it came from right over our head. . . . My exact words were, "No bullshit?" And we jumped up. . . . I think Jarman, he—I think he moved before any of us. He moved towards us, and he said, "Man, someone is shooting at the President." And I think I said again, "No bullshit?" . . . Then we all kind of got excited. . . . But, we all decided we would run down to the west side of the building. . . . We saw policemen and people running, scared, running—there are some tracks on the west side of the building, railroad tracks. They were running towards that way. And we thought . . . we know the shots came from practically over our head. But . . . we assumed maybe somebody was down there.

Norman said he and Jarman had eaten lunch in the domino room on the first floor, then walked out the front door where they saw other Depository employees, including Lovelady, sitting on the steps.

As the motorcade approached, they took an elevator to the fifth floor and got seated in a southeast corner window, where they were joined by Williams moments later. Norman said he heard three loud shots and "I could also hear something sounded like shell hulls hitting the floor." Later he said he even heard the sound of the bolt working on a rifle above them.

After the three men ran to the west window and saw police combing the railroad yards, Norman said, he and Jarman tried to leave the Depository but were turned back by police officers.

Jarman told the same story but said he didn't hear the shells hit the floor or hear the sound of the rifle bolt. He did say that when the three men ran to the Depository's west window, "I saw policemen and the secret agents, the FBI men, searching the boxcar yard and the passenger train and things like that."

One thing that has always puzzled assassination researchers is Williams's statement of being on the sixth floor until "approximately 12:20," then Norman's claim of hearing ejecting shell casings and the working of the rifle bolt.

It has been established that the plywood floor in the Depository was thin and full of cracks, which could account for the plaster dust that fell on Williams's head. It could also account for Norman's hearing shell casings hit the floor and even the working of the rifle bolt—except that apparently none of the three men on the floor below heard anyone moving above them.

How could they have heard shells dropping and a rifle bolt operating and not heard movement above them in the minutes before the shooting? As confirmed by photographs taken at the time and the testimony of witnesses below, someone constructed a "sniper's nest" of book cartons in the minutes preceding the shooting.

Yet Williams, Norman, and Jarman heard nothing?

Obviously someone was on the sixth floor, but was it Oswald?

The 56-year-old janitor at the Depository, Eddie Piper, told authorities he saw Oswald on the first floor about noon. Oswald, who reportedly never left the sixth floor, told police he had followed the workers down to the first floor and had eaten lunch in the domino room on the Depository's first floor.

Oswald told interrogators he recalled two black employees walking through the room while he was there. He said he thought one was named "Junior" and the other was short.

Jarman's nickname was "Junior" and Norman was indeed short. Norman, in Commission testimony, said he ate his lunch in the domino room, adding, "I can't remember who ate in the . . . domino room with me. . . . I think there was somebody else in there." But, as happens so often in these interviews, there was no follow-up question as to who else might have been in the domino room.

Jarman told of helping Oswald correct a book order earlier that morning, then talking with him again on the first floor. Then at lunchtime, Jarman said, he bought a soft drink and returned to where he had been sitting by a first-floor window "where Oswald and I was talking." His testimony is confusing and appears incomplete. It was not helped by any clarifying questions from the Warren Commission attorney. It must be understood that in 1963 Dallas, black citizens were highly suspicious and defensive toward authorities. When confronted by police, not to mention federal officers, they were inclined to tell them whatever they wanted to hear and were easily led in their testimony.

This presents a significant question that could have been asked by any competent defense attorney if Oswald had ever gotten a fair trial. If Oswald was not in the first-floor domino room as he said, how could he have noted the presence of two men and accurately described Norman and Jarman?

Bill Shelley, Oswald's supervisor, told the Commission he saw Oswald near a telephone on the first floor about ten minutes till noon.

Carolyn Arnold, secretary to the Depository's vice president, was quoted in an FBI report saying "she thought she caught a fleeting glimpse of Lee Harvey Oswald standing in the [first-floor] hallway" as she left the building to watch the motorcade at about 12:20 p.m. In 1978, Arnold told the *Dallas Morning News* she saw and recognized Lee Oswald in the second-floor lunchroom as she was leaving the building to watch the motorcade at 12:25 p.m. The Warren Commission claimed no Depository employee saw Oswald after 11:55 a.m. Arnold stated:

> I do not recall that he (Oswald) was doing anything. I just recall that he was sitting there . . . in one of the booth seats on the right hand side of the room as you go in. He was alone as usual and appeared to be having lunch. I did not speak to him but I recognized him clearly.

Arnold said she knew Oswald because he would come to her desk on the second floor occasionally and ask for change. He never accepted pennies but only nickels and dimes. The FBI mangled her testimony, reporting only that after she left the depository and stood about thirty feet in front of the building to watch the motorcade, she "thought she caught a fleeting glimpse of Lee Harvey Oswald standing in the hallway" on the first floor. In 1978, after reading over her statements of 1963, she stated she had been misquoted by the FBI. She said:

> That is completely foreign to me. [The FBI account] would have forced me to have been turning back around to the building when, in fact, I was trying to watch the parade. Why would I be looking back inside the building? That doesn't make any sense to me.

In later years, Arnold, who married and became Mrs. Carolyn Johnston, was surprised to learn the FBI had made no mention of her sighting Oswald in the lunchroom.

While it is still possible that Oswald could have raced upstairs in time to be in the "sniper's" window by 12:30 p.m., recall that newlyweds Arnold and Barbara Rowland saw two men in the sixth-floor window, one with a rifle, at 12:15. This time can be fixed with confidence because Arnold Rowland reported seeing the man with the gun just as a nearby police radio announced that the presidential motorcade was approaching Cedar Springs Road. Police dispatcher's records showed the motorcade passed Cedar Springs between 12:15 and 12:16 p.m.

The Warren Commission concluded that Oswald stayed on the sixth floor after he was seen by the elevator racers about 11:55 a.m. and remained there to commit the assassination.

As can be seen, there is quite credible evidence that he was exactly where he said he was—in the first-floor break or domino room—at the time of the shooting. The domino room was one short flight of steps to the Depository's front door, where the Oswald figure was photographed by Altgens.

Oswald then apparently walked to the Depository's second-floor lunchroom to buy a soft drink. It was there that a Dallas policeman encountered Oswald less than ninety seconds after the final shot was fired in the assassination.

The Oswald Encounter

Since at 12:30 p.m. November 22, 1963, the presidential motorcade was running approximately five minutes behind schedule—probably due to the two unscheduled stops along the way to greet the crowd ordered by Kennedy—it is unbelievable that an assassin would leisurely wait in the Depository domino room until 12:15 to make his move to the sixth floor.

Understand that the first floor of the Texas School Book Depository is slightly above ground level. One entered the building by walking up a flight of outside steps, then an additional flight of stairs at the rear of the building led to the second floor. Here was located an employees' lunchroom containing vending machines and was reserved exclusively for the white-collar employees of the Depository. Warehouse personnel and order fillers (usually ethnic minorities) were relegated to the first-floor domino room although they were allowed to use the vending machines.

Dallas motorcycle patrolman Marrion Baker rushed to the Depository after seeing pigeons fly off the building's roof at the sound of the first shots. In a later reenactment for the Warren Commission, it took Baker only fifteen seconds to park his cycle and race up the front steps of the Depository.

Baker told the Warren Commission, "I had it in mind that the shots came from the top of this building." He continued:

> As I entered this lobby there were people going in as I entered. And I asked . . . where the stairs or elevator was, and this man, Mr. Truly, spoke up and says to me . . . "I'm the building manager. Follow me, officer, and I will show you." So we immediately went out through the second set of doors, and we ran into the swinging door.

Depository superintendent Roy Truly had followed Baker into the building. Both men tried the elevators near the front entrance but found them inoperable, perhaps due to the electrical outage mentioned by Geneva Hine of the Depository's credit desk. They quickly went to the building's elevators on the northwest corner of the first floor but could not bring them down since someone had left them locked in position on an upper floor. Truly told the Commission:

> Those elevators . . . were both on the fifth floor, they were both even. And I tried to get one of them . . . it would have been impossible for [Oswald] to have come down either one of those elevators after the assassination. He had to use the stairway as his only way of getting down—since we did see the elevators in those positions.

Truly yelled, "Bring that elevator down here!" to no avail and Baker said, "Let's take the stairs." Moving up the stairs behind Truly, Baker said he noticed a man walking away from him through a glass window in a door near the rear second-floor landing. With drawn pistol, Baker confronted the man and ordered him to come to him. In a handwritten report to the FBI on November 23, Baker stated, "On the second floor where the lunchroom is located, I saw a man standing in the lunchroom drinking a Coke." However, the words "drinking a Coke" were scratched out in this initial report and there was no reference to the Coke in his Warren Commission testimony.

Truly said the man he recognized as Oswald "didn't seem to be excited or overly afraid." He told the Warren Commission he noticed nothing in Oswald's hands, but this was months later, after many discussions with federal authorities.

Baker turned to Truly and asked if the man was an employee and Truly replied he was. Baker then turned and continued his race for the roof.

Oswald apparently simply sauntered down the steps and out the front door of the Depository.

Mrs. Robert Reid, clerical supervisor at the Depository, was standing with Depository officials in front of the building at the time shots were fired. She then turned and ran into the building to her second-floor office. She told the Warren Commission:

> I looked up and Oswald was coming in the back door to the office. I met him by the time I passed my desk several feet and I told him, "Oh, the President's been shot, but maybe they didn't hit him." He mumbled something to me, I kept walking, he did too. I didn't pay any attention to what he said because I had no thoughts of anything of him having any connection with it at all because he was very calm. He had gotten a Coke and was holding it in his hands. . . . The only time I had seen him in the office was to come and get change and he already had a Coke in his hand so he didn't come for change.

Like Baker, Mrs. Reid reenacted her movements for the Warren Commission on March 20, 1964. She said it took approximately two minutes to move the distance from where she heard the final shot to the point she met Oswald.

As can be seen, the issue of the Coke becomes critical here.

It strains one's imagination to believe that anyone could fire on the president of the United States, then run to the opposite corner of the sixth floor—where the rifle was discovered a short time later—stash the weapon, race down five flights of stairs with heavy fire doors on each floor, and show no sign of exertion or anxiety when confronted by a policeman with a drawn pistol.

This scenario becomes absurd if the purchase of a Coke from a vending machine with its attendant fumbling for pocket change is thrown into the time frame.

Baker told the FBI the next day that Oswald was "drinking a Coke" when he saw him but then deleted any reference to the drink in his Warren Commission testimony. Truly, months later, said he did not notice anything in Oswald's hands. But Reid said Oswald was holding a Coke when she saw him seconds after his encounter with Baker.

Even the accused assassin had something to say about the soft drink. In Appendix XI of the Warren Report, Dallas homicide captain Will Fritz reported on his first interview with Oswald about an hour after his arrest at the Texas Theater. Joining Fritz shortly after 3 p.m. were FBI agents James P. Hosty and James W. Bookhout. Fritz quickly got to the point, asking Oswald where he was when the president was shot. According to Fritz:

> He said that he was having his lunch about that time on the first floor. . . .
> I asked Oswald where he was when the police officer stopped him. He said he was on the second floor drinking a Coca-Cola when the officer came in.

In their FBI report, Hosty and Bookhout confirm this conversation by noting:

Oswald stated that he went to lunch at approximately noon and he claimed he ate his lunch on the first floor in the lunchroom; however he went to the second floor where the Coca-Cola machine was located and obtained a bottle of Coca-Cola for his lunch.

On November 25, Agent Bookhout filed a report reiterating this account:

Oswald stated that on November 22, 1963, at the time of the search of the Texas School Book Depository building by Dallas police officers, he was on the second floor of said building, having just purchased a Coca-Cola from the soft drink machine, at which time a police officer came into the room with pistol drawn and asked him if he worked there.

It also should be noted that Captain Fritz's notes of his interrogation of Oswald, released only in the 1990s, said that Oswald "claims 2nd floor Coke when off[icer] came in."

In light of all this information, it seems clear that Oswald indeed was holding a soft drink when confronted by Officer Baker, which leaves a run across the sixth floor to stash the rifle and a stampede down the wooden stairs in time to purchase a drink almost outside the realm of possibility. The Coke question may seem a small one, but it also indicates the loopholes riddling the official story of the assassination and the lengths the federal government took to obscure certain issues.

The problem of Oswald's documented presence in the Depository's second-floor lunchroom, with or without a Coke, is compounded by accounts of someone seen on the sixth floor long after Oswald should have been gone. Clerk Lillian Mooneyham of the 95th District Court told the FBI that she watched the motorcade move west on Main from windows in the Dallas Criminal Courts Building, then ran with two others to the west side of the building. She heard an initial shot, which she took to be a firecracker, followed by a "slight pause and then two more shots were discharged, the second and third shots sounding closer together." According to an FBI report of January 10, 1964, Mooneyham said, "I left Judge [Henry] King's courtroom and went to the office of Judge Julian C. Hyer . . . where I continued to observe the happenings from Judge Hyer's window."

The FBI report continued:

Mrs. Mooneyham estimated that it was about four and a half to five minutes following the shots fired by the assassin, that she looked up towards the sixth floor of the TSBD and observed the figure of a man standing in the sixth floor window behind some cardboard boxes. This man appeared to

Mrs. Mooneyham to be looking out of the window; however, the man was not close up to the window but was standing slightly back from it, so that Mrs. Mooneyham could not make out his features.

Adding support to Mooneyham's account of a man standing in the "sniper's nest" window minutes after the shooting are photographs taken about that time by military intelligence agent James Powell and news photographer Tom Dillard.

Dillard, who was riding in the motorcade, said he took a picture of the Depository facade seconds after the last shot was fired. Powell estimated his picture was made about thirty seconds after the final shot.

A comparison with photos taken just prior to the shooting led photographic experts of the House Select Committee on Assassinations to conclude, "There is an apparent rearranging of boxes within two minutes after the last shot was fired at President Kennedy." Obviously, Oswald could not have been in the Depository lunchroom meeting Baker and Truly while at the same time arranging boxes on the sixth floor.

Needless to say, Mooneyham was never called as a witness before the Warren Commission. Her credible testimony remains buried in the Commission's twenty-six volumes.

A further point here is that several Depository employees, including Billy Lovelady and William Shelley, were on or near the back stairway of the building just after the assassination. No one heard footsteps or saw Oswald racing down the five flights of stairs for his encounter with Baker and Truly.

Recall that Victoria Adams and Sandra Styles, who worked for Scott-Foresman and Company in the Depository, told the FBI they both ran from the building down the back stairway after viewing the assassination from their fourth-floor office window. Neither encountered Oswald on the stairway or remarked of hearing footsteps on the old wooden stairs moments after the shooting. These were the same creaky stairs that Oswald would have had to rapidly descend in time for his meeting with Officer Baker.

Adams told the Warren Commission that upon arriving on the first floor she saw fellow Depository employees Bill Shelley and Billy Lovelady. The authors of the Commission's report tried to dismiss the time frame of Adams's testimony by stating, "If Miss Adams accurately recalled meeting Shelley and Lovelady when she reached the bottom of the stairs, then her estimate of the time when she descended from the fourth floor is incorrect, and she actually came down the stairs several minutes after Oswald and after Truly and Baker as well."

In 2011, author Barry Ernest interviewed Garner, the office supervisor over Adams, Elsie Dorman, and Styles, in 1963. She confirmed that Adams and Styles both left the fourth-floor window immediately following the shooting. "I remember them being there and the next thing I knew, they were gone," she recalled. "They left very quickly . . . within a matter of moments." Garner said she followed the women and stood at a vantage point where she could see the back stairs. She heard Adams and Styles moving down the stairs. Asked if she saw Oswald on the stairs, Garner laughed and told Ernest she "felt sure she would have remembered it if she had seen Oswald anywhere earlier that day, based on his later notoriety and the fact it would have made an impression on her mind."

Of great importance, however, Garner said she did recall a policeman on the stairs, who could only have been Officer Baker. Garner's recollection was supported by a letter accompanying Adams's signed deposition to the Warren Commission sent by assistant US attorney Martha Joe Stroud on June 2, 1964. The last paragraph stated, "Miss Garner, Miss Adams' supervisor, stated this morning that after Miss Adams went downstairs she (Miss Garner) saw Mr. Truly and the policeman come up."

Could Oswald have indeed fired the fatal shots, then stopped to rearrange his box supports, then raced to the opposite end of the Depository's sixth floor, where he reportedly stashed his rifle, then raced silently down five flights of creaky stairs unnoticed by the office workers only to be discovered calmly standing by a soft drink machine by Baker and Truly less than two minutes later?

Or was it someone else who fired, then arranged a "sniper's nest" before quietly slipping out of the Depository about the time Oswald was encountering Baker and Truly in the second-floor lunchroom?

Also standing on the steps of the Depository was Joe R. Molina, the company's credit manager. Like most everyone else, Molina thought the shots came from west of the building.

In 1964, Molina specifically requested to testify to the Warren Commission because of what happened to him after the assassination. Molina said about 1:30 a.m. on the Saturday following the assassination, he and his family were awakened by Dallas police, who began searching his home. Molina told the commission, "They were looking for something . . . they sort of wanted to tie me up with this case in some way or another and they thought that I was implicated."

He said he was questioned about his membership in G.I. Forum, a predominantly Hispanic group actively working to help veterans, and was told to report to Dallas police headquarters later that day. Molina was kept waiting at the police station most of the day, then learned that his name had been given to the news media by Chief Curry, who described Molina as someone associated with "persons of subversive background." Unable to get a retraction from the Dallas police, Molina asked to testify to the Warren Commission in an attempt to clear his name. But the damage had already been done.

On December 13, twenty-one days after the assassination, Molina was told that the Depository's credit system was to be automated and that he was to be replaced. He said the action came as no real surprise because the company had been receiving hate mail and phone calls accusing it of hiring communists.

Despite assurances from Depository officials that Molina's firing was not connected to the events of the assassination, it appears obvious that Joe Molina, too, became one of its victims.

Many Depository employees went outside to view the motorcade. Several, such as Bonnie Richey, Sharon Nelson, Stella Mae Jacob, and Gloria Jeanne Holt, were prevented from entering the Depository when police sealed the building. They did not return for work that day. Most Depository employees signed reports to the FBI during March 1964. Oddly, the reports were all worded alike and agents apparently never asked critical questions such as "Where did shots come from?" "How many shots?" or "Did you see the effect of any shot?" Most apparently were simply asked, "Did you know Lee Harvey Oswald?" and "Did you see any strangers in the building that day?"

As the evidence quickly piled up against Oswald and the Depository became the center of the investigation, the authorities, news media, and public soon forgot the initial focus of attention in Dealey Plaza—the Triple Underpass.

The Triple Underpass

On the west side of Dealey Plaza is a large railroad bridge that spans the three main downtown Dallas traffic arteries of Commerce, Main, and Elm Streets.

Since all three streets converge under this concrete bridge, it quickly became known as the Triple Underpass. To the east of the underpass is Dealey Plaza and downtown Dallas, while on the west there are several roads leading to freeway systems and an industrial area.

Atop the east side of the Triple Underpass is a panoramic view of Dealey Plaza from a position about fifteen feet in the air.

This was the position of about a dozen men on November 22, 1963, as they stood along the eastern edge of the underpass to watch the presidential motorcade approach and pass beneath them.

Dallas policeman J. W. Foster was one of two police officers assigned as security guards atop the Triple Underpass. His orders were to prevent any "unauthorized" personnel from standing on the railroad bridge under which Kennedy passed.

Foster had allowed some railroad workers, who had been repairing rails, to remain on the underpass after checking their identities. Since the bridge actually was railroad property and it was railway workers who walked over to the eastern banister to view the motorcade, he did not believe they fell into the "unauthorized" category.

He told the Warren Commission he earlier had prevented some people from standing on the bridge—one of these was AP photographer James Altgens.

Foster said as the motorcade approached he was standing just behind the line of railway workers, about ten or eleven of them, when he heard what sounded like a large firecracker. He moved up to the concrete railing to get a better view. He said he saw "the President slump over in the car, and his head looked just like it blew up."

From his vantage point—above and directly in front of the car—this trained and experienced police officer may have been one of the best witnesses to what actually happened at the time of the shooting. However, neither in his report of December 4, 1963, nor in his April 9, 1964, testimony to the Warren Commission was he asked to describe in detail what he saw.

Warren Commission lawyer Joseph Ball did ask Foster his opinion as to the source of the shots and Foster replied, "It came from back in toward the corner of Elm and Houston Streets [the location of the Texas School Book Depository]."

Foster said he ran from the underpass toward the Depository building, where he watched the rear exits until a sergeant came and told him to check out railroad cars in the nearby switching yard. However, Foster said he went instead to the front of the Depository and told a supervisor where he was when shots were fired, then "moved to—down the roadway there, down to see if I could find where any of the shots hit."

He was successful, telling the Commission he "found where one shot had hit the turf."

Foster said he found where a bullet had struck the earth just beside a manhole cover on the south side of Elm Street. Foster remained at this location for a time until the evidence was taken away by a man in a suit, later identified by the Dallas police chief as an FBI agent.

The spot where Foster found a tear in the grass was near where witness Jean Hill was standing at the time of the assassination. Shortly after the shooting, she was questioned by Secret Service agents, one of whom asked her if she saw a bullet land near her feet.

Foster's counterpart on the west side of the Triple Underpass was Officer J. C. White. White said he was approximately in the middle of the underpass when the motorcade passed below, but that he didn't see or hear anything because a "big long freight train" was moving north between him and Dealey Plaza. Oddly, close scrutiny of films and photographs taken that day show no such freight train moving at that time.

But if the stories of the two Dallas policemen on top of the underpass seem strangely incomplete and sketchy, this was not the case of the railroad workers standing over the motorcade. These workers not only heard shots from their left, the direction of the infamous Grassy Knoll, but also saw smoke drift out from under the trees lining the knoll.

Smoke on the Grassy Knoll

About forty witnesses on or around the infamous Grassy Knoll said they heard shots or saw smoke in that area. Most were ignored by the Warren Commission.

Sam M. Holland, a track and signal supervisor for the Union Terminal Railroad Company, told the Warren Commission he went to the top of the Triple Underpass about 11:45 a.m. that day. He said there were two Dallas policemen and "a plain-clothes detective, or FBI agent or something like that" there and that he helped identify the railroad employees. He said by the time the motorcade arrived, other people were lining the Triple Underpass, but that the police were checking identification and sending them away.

By the time the presidential limousine was approaching the underpass, Holland was standing just in front of Officer Foster. He told the commission:

> And the motorcade was coming down in this fashion, and the President was waving to the people on this [north] side [of Elm]. . . . The first report that I heard . . . was pretty loud . . . and the car traveled a few yards and Governor Connally turned in this fashion, like that, with his hand out and . . . another report rang out and he slumped down in his seat . . . [then Kennedy] was hit again along . . . in here. . . . I observed it. It knocked him completely down on the floor . . . just slumped completely over. . . . I heard a third report and I counted four shots. . . . There was a shot, a report. I don't know whether it was a shot. I can't say that. And a puff of smoke came out about six or eight feet above the ground right out from under those trees.

Holland said the first two or three shots seemed to come from "the upper part of the street," followed by others of "different sounds, different reports." In a 1966 filmed interview, Holland was even more specific:

> I looked over to where I thought the shot came from and I saw a puff of smoke still lingering under the trees in front of the wooden fence. The report sounded like it came from behind the wooden fence. . . . I know where the third shot came from—behind the picket fence. There's no doubt whatsoever in my mind.

Due to Holland's credibility and clear description of what he saw, the Warren Commission Report accurately stated, "According to S. M. Holland, there were four shots which sounded as though they came from the trees on the north side of Elm Street where he saw a puff of smoke."

Having mentioned the smoke in the trees, the report went on to conclude, "In contrast to the testimony of the witnesses who heard and observed shots fired from the Depository, the Commission's investigation has disclosed no credible evidence that any shots were fired from anywhere else."

The clear implication by the Warren Report is that Holland was mistaken in believing shots came from behind the wooden picket fence. However, the testimony of the other railroad workers on the Triple Underpass—Richard C. Dodd, James L. Simmons, and Thomas J. Murphy, none of whom were asked to testify to the Warren Commission—corroborated Holland's version of the assassination. The only account of what they saw is in FBI reports made during March 1964. These reports are sketchy and seem very incomplete in view of the questions that these men should obviously have been asked.

Simmons, a Union Terminal car inspector, was in the group on the Triple Underpass. In his FBI report, it merely states:

> When the President's car started down Elm Street he heard three shots ring out. President Kennedy slumped down in his seat and appeared to have been hit by a bullet. . . . Simmons said he thought he saw exhaust fumes of smoke near the embankment in front of the Texas School Book Depository building.

During a 1966 filmed interview, Simmons's account is much clearer:

> As the President's limousine rounded the curve on Elm Street, there was a loud explosion. . . . It sounded like it came from the left and in front of us, towards the wooden fence. And there was a puff of smoke that came from underneath the trees on the embankment directly in front of the wooden fence. . . . I was talking to Patrolman Foster at the time and as soon as we heard the shots, we ran around to [behind] the picket fence. . . . There was no one there but there were footprints in the mud around the fence and footprints on the two-by-four railing on the fence.

Railroad workers who also saw smoke off to their left included Nolan H. Potter, Richard C. Dodd, and Clemon E. Johnson.

Simmons was quoted in his FBI report as seeing smoke near the Depository, yet he plainly stated later that it was in front of the Grassy Knoll fence. There is no mention of smoke in Dodd's FBI report, yet in a later filmed interview, he said, "Smoke came from behind the hedge on the north side of the plaza."

In 1966 interviews in Dallas, both Walter L. Winborn and Thomas J. Murphy—who were among the railroad workers on the Triple Underpass—confirmed seeing smoke in the trees on the Grassy Knoll.

It would be most interesting to talk to the other people who stood on the Triple Underpass that day. Perhaps they, too, saw the smoke, but such sighting was left out of their reports—if any report was made.

Further corroboration of the smoke came well into the 1980s, when a frame from TV news film was analyzed by assassination researchers. NBC photographer Dave Weigman was riding in the seventh car in the motorcade. Hearing shots, Weigman started filming even before the firing stopped. He then jumped out of the convertible and ran up the Grassy Knoll with his camera still operating. Because of all this motion, his blurred and jerky film was overlooked as assassination evidence until recently. However, in one clear frame, which depicts the presidential limousine just entering the Triple Underpass, a puff of smoke is clearly visible hanging in front of trees on the knoll—exactly where Holland and the other railroad workers placed it.

It has been well established that there was no other natural source of smoke in that area that day. FBI reports attempted to show that it might have come from police motorcycles but none were on the knoll at the time.

Warren Commission apologists for years have tried to argue that modern rifles do not smoke. This is an error, since a recently oiled rifle or defective ammunition certainly can cause white smoke during firing. This was made clear to this author in the summer of 1978 when the House Select Committee on Assassinations fired rifles in Dealey Plaza in connection with their acoustical studies. Visible puffs of smoke were common.

And considering the slightly gusting breeze from the north that day, the idea that smoke drifted over Elm Street from the knoll is highly plausible. It is now obvious that many people that day saw this puff of smoke drifting down from the knoll—also recall those witnesses who said they smelled gunpowder in the lower end of Dealey Plaza. However, it is equally obvious that the authorities, particularly the FBI and the Warren Commission, did not want to hear about it.

Dallas policeman Earle Brown also smelled gunpowder although he was far from the Depository. Brown was standing on the catwalk of a railroad bridge crossing over Stemmons Freeway located just north of the Triple Underpass. Because of his location, Brown said he was unable to get a clear view of the motorcade. Brown said the first indication to him that something was wrong was when a large flock of pigeons suddenly flew up from a grassy low area between him and the underpass. He said, "They heard the shots before we did because I saw them flying up . . . then I heard these shots and then I smelled this gunpowder. . . . It come on . . . maybe a couple of minutes later."

Brown said the gunpowder smell seemed to come from the direction of the Depository. However, the Grassy Knoll was almost in a direct line between the officer and the Depository.

Another railroad worker, Royce G. Skelton, supported the statements of Sheriff Decker and others who saw one of the first bullets strike the pavement near Kennedy's car.

In an affidavit signed the day of the assassination, Skelton stated:

> I was standing on top of the train trestle where it crosses Elm Street with Austin Miller. We saw the motorcade come around the corner and I heard something which I thought was fireworks. I saw something hit the pavement at the left rear of the [President's] car, then the car got in the right-hand lane and I heard two more shots. I heard a woman [say] "Oh no" or something and grab a man inside the car. I then heard another shot and saw the bullet hit the pavement. The concrete was knocked to the south away from the car. It hit the pavement in the left or center lane.

Austin Miller, standing next to Skelton on the Triple Underpass, also mentioned this errant bullet in his affidavit that day. Miller stated:

> I saw a convertible automobile turn west on Elm off Houston Street. It had [proceeded] about halfway from Houston Street to the Underpass when I heard what sounded like a shot [then in] a short second two more sharp reports. . . . One shot apparently hit the street past the car. I saw something which I thought was smoke or steam coming from a group of trees north of Elm off the railroad tracks.

If a bullet hit the street pavement, it certainly could not have been the one that passed through Kennedy and Connally as described by the Warren Commission and it was not the bullet that struck the Main Street curb wounding a bystander. But more than three shots would mean more than one assassin.

The one assassination witness who singlehandedly caused more concern than anyone else within the 1963–1964 federal investigation was Jim Tague, the third man wounded in Dealey Plaza on November 22, 1963.

The Third Wounded Man

James Thomas Tague, like Jean Hill and Mary Moorman, was not planning to see Kennedy. Shortly after noon that day, he had driven downtown to take a girlfriend (later his wife) to lunch.

As Tague drove his car east on Commerce Street, he found himself stopped in the traffic that was halted at Houston Street due to the arrival of the presidential motorcade. The hood of his car was just poking out the east side of the Triple Underpass. Tague got out of his car and stood by the underpass on a small concrete median separating Commerce and Main to watch the motorcade.

In an interview with this author, Tague said when the shots were fired, he immediately thought, "Who's the nut throwing firecrackers?" However, after hearing more shots, he realized what was happening and ducked behind the corner of the underpass. He said the shots were coming from the area of the Grassy Knoll "behind the concrete monument."

Tague was watching a policeman run up the Grassy Knoll with a drawn pistol when another policeman came up to him asking, "What happened?" "I don't know," mumbled the shocked Tague.

Dallas motorcycle patrolman Clyde A. Haygood had been riding back in the motorcade on Main Street approaching Main when he heard a shot, then a pause followed by two shots close together. He gunned his three-wheeled motorcycle up on Houston and turned on Elm in time to see people pointing toward the Grassy Knoll and the railroad yards.

Haygood said he got off his cycle on Elm Street just below the Grassy Knoll and went up into the railroad yards but saw nothing suspicious despite quite a number of people in the area. He said he returned to his motorcycle after speaking to a man he believed to be a railroad detective.

Haygood told the Warren Commission:

> At that time some people came up and started talking to me as to the shooting. . . . One came up . . . and said he had gotten hit by a piece of concrete or something, and he did have a slight cut on his right cheek, upper portion of his cheek just to the right of his nose.

Haygood said just then another witness came up and told him the first shot had come from the Texas School Book Depository. Using the call number 142, Haygood radioed the police dispatcher and asked that the Depository be sealed off. He also mentioned a man who had been wounded by flying concrete.

Tague and the policeman walked into the plaza a bit and encountered a man, who was sobbing, "His head exploded!" This man apparently was Charles Brehm.

Moments later deputy sheriff Eddy R. Walthers arrived and, pointing to Tague, said, "You've got blood on your face."

In his report that day, Walthers, who was standing with the other deputies in front of the sheriff's office, stated:

> I immediately went to the Triple Underpass on Elm Street in an effort to locate possible marks left by stray bullets. While I was looking for possible marks, some unknown person stated to me that something had hit his face while he was parked on Main Street. . . . Upon examining the curb and pavement in this vicinity I found where a bullet had splattered on the top edge of the curb on Main Street. . . . Due to the fact that the projectile struck so near the underpass, it was, in my opinion, probably the last shot that was fired and had apparently went high and above the President's car.

Tague said he called the Dallas FBI office later that afternoon, to tell them about the bullet striking the curb, but "they didn't want my testimony about the stray bullet." Apparently no one else wanted to hear about the extraneous bullet either. There was no mention of the incident in the news accounts at the time nor was there any investigation of the bullet mark on the curb until the summer of 1964.

During late 1963 and early 1964, it was widely reported that the first shot struck Kennedy in the back, the second bullet hit Governor Connally, and the third was the fatal head shot. This was a consistent theory of three bullets. Tague's story of yet another bullet was totally inconsistent with the lone-assassin/three-shot theory being formulated by the Warren Commission, which initially seemed prepared to ignore both Tague and the bullet mark on the curb.

In fact, there may have been an effort to eliminate the evidence. In late May 1964, about a month before the Warren Commission finally talked to Tague, the car salesman took a camera to Dealey Plaza to photograph the mark on the curb. He was surprised to find that it was not there. Only faint traces of the bullet mark were found. Tague said it looked as if someone had tried to repair the curb.

Apparently it was a letter from an assistant US attorney in Dallas that finally prompted the Warren Commission to confront the Tague wounding. Martha Joe Stroud mailed a letter to Commission general counsel J. Lee Rankin on June 9, 1964. In the letter was the comment:

> I am enclosing a photograph made by Tom Dillard of the *Dallas Morning News*. It is a shot of the curb which was taken shortly after the assassination on November 22, 1963. When I talked to Mr. Dillard yesterday he indicated he did not know whether the photograph was material. He did say, however, that he examined the curb when the photo was taken and that it looked like a piece of lead had struck it.

Faced with this notification of the curb shot by a government official, the Commission was stirred to action. On July 7, 1964, the Warren Commission asked the FBI to look into the matter. In an FBI document dated July 17, the FBI stated, "The area on the curb [where the bullet or fragment hit] was carefully checked and it was ascertained there was no nick in the curb in the checked area, nor was any mark observed."

This FBI document attempted to explain the disappearance of a mark that had been plainly seen eight months earlier. It stated:

> It should be noted that, since this mark was observed on November 22, 1963, there have been numerous rains, which could have possibly washed away such a mark and also that the area is cleaned by a street cleaning machine about once a week, which could also wash away any such mark.

But if the FBI could ignore the mark, the Commission could not. Since both a Dallas policeman and a sheriff's deputy had mentioned Tague in their reports, although not by name, and after the arrival of Assistant US Attorney Stroud's letter, his story could no longer be ignored.

On July 23, 1964, Tague finally was deposed in Dallas by Commission attorney Wesley Liebeler.

Following Tague's testimony, the Commission again asked the bureau to investigate the matter. This time the FBI suddenly found the mark, removed the piece of curb in question and took it to Washington for analysis. In an August 12, 1964, report signed by J. Edgar Hoover, it was stated:

> Small foreign metal smears were found adhering to the curbing section within the area of the mark. These metal smears were spectrographically determined to be essentially lead with a trace of antimony. No copper was found. The lead could have originated from the lead core of a mutilated metal-jacketed bullet such as the type of bullet loaded into 6.5 milli-

meter Mannlicher-Carcano cartridges or from some other source having the same composition. . . . The absence of copper precludes the possibility that the mark on the curbing section was made by an unmutilated military-type full metal-jacketed bullet. . . . Further, the damage to the curbing would have been much more extensive if a rifle bullet had struck the curbing without first having struck some other object. Therefore, this mark could not have been made by the first impact of a high-velocity bullet.

So the FBI, which at first had stated no bullet hit the curb, now said the mark had to have been made by a rifle bullet but not on first impact. If the FBI is correct—and keep in mind the many instances of misinformation and omission by the bureau regarding assassination evidence—the mark on the curb could only have been made by the lead fragment of a bullet.

Yet the only one that could have lost such an amount of lead is the final head shot and that was at a location more than two hundred feet away, a considerable distance for a small fragment to travel and still impact the curb as described.

If the bullet mark on the curb was a miss, it was an incredible miss. If the shot that struck the Main Street curb came from the Texas School Book Depository's sixth floor, it must have missed Kennedy by thirty-three feet in the air and twenty-one feet to the right. Such a miss is hardly compatible with the claim that Oswald was able to hit home with two out of three shots with a misaligned scope on his inefficient rifle aiming at a target moving laterally and away from him at a distance of more than 265 feet.

Another possibility, never considered by the Warren Commission, was that the mark was made by a lead bullet without copper jacketing. But of course, this would indicate different ammunition and perhaps a different rifle from the one allegedly used by Oswald. Or perhaps the curb was hit by a large fragment of bullet that had already struck the street (recall the witnesses who saw one do just that) and had separated from the copper jacket.

Whatever the truth of the curb bullet and despite the attempt to ignore this evidence, the matter of the wounding of Tague was finally acknowledged and the Warren Commission was compelled to construct a scenario of the assassination that included the "single-bullet theory," which postulates that one bullet caused seven wounds to Kennedy and Connally. This theory has not been accepted by a majority of Americans. More on that later.

Despite immediate attempts to establish the Texas School Book Depository as the sole location from which shots were fired, public attention, both in 1963 and even today, continued to be drawn to the wooded hillock to the west of the Depository that has become known as the Grassy Knoll.

The Grassy Knoll

Probably no small section of land in the United States has been the object of more controversy than that small northern portion of Dealey Plaza known as the Grassy Knoll.

While Elm Street and two large grassy areas of Dealey Plaza dip down approximately 24 feet as one travels the 495 feet from Houston Street on the east, the Grassy Knoll remains at ground level.

There actually are two grassy knolls on both the north and south sides of the west end of the plaza, but during the assassination of President John F. Kennedy, it was the north knoll that drew public attention.

Located between the Texas School Book Depository and the Triple Underpass, the Grassy Knoll provided an ideal ambush site. Running along the top of the knoll was a wooden picket fence about five feet high. In front of this fence were shrubs and evergreen trees that, even in late November, provided a leafy canopy over the fence. The fence ran east approximately seventy-five feet from the north edge of the Triple Underpass, then turned north for about fifty feet, ending in a parking area behind a concrete pergola located to the west of the Depository.

It was from a vantage point atop a low concrete wall on the south end of this pergola that the most famous home movie of all time was made—the Abraham Zapruder film.

The Zapruder Film

A 26.6-second, 8 mm film made on November 22, 1963, became the cornerstone of investigations, both public and private, in the years after the Kennedy assassination. It has been long regarded as the most objective, and thus most important, piece of evidence in the attempts to unravel what actually happened to President Kennedy. And it almost didn't happen.

Abraham Zapruder, a native of Russia and a thirty-third-degree Freemason, in 1963 was a ladies' dress manufacturer with offices in the Dal-Tex Building at 501 Elm Street in downtown Dallas near Jack Ruby's nightclub and across the street from the Texas School Book Depository. He had a new camera but had not intended to film that day. What with his work and the morning rains, Zapruder thought "I wouldn't have a chance even to see the President." But his secretary, Lillian Rogers, urged him to make use of his new camera—a Bell & Howell 8mm camera with a telephoto lens. So Zapruder made a fourteen-mile round-trip drive to his home to pick up his camera. By the time he returned, crowds were already gathering to watch the motorcade.

After trying several different locations—none of which proved suitable for viewing the president without obstructions—Zapruder finally climbed onto a four-foot-high concrete block at the end of two steps leading to the pergola on the north Grassy Knoll. He almost lost his balance while testing his camera on some nearby office workers, so he asked one in the group, his receptionist Marilyn Sitzman, to join him and provide steady support. From this excellent vantage point, Zapruder and Sitzman watched the motorcade approach Elm Street. Having set the camera's speed control on "run" and his lens on "telephoto," Zapruder proceeded to film the entire assassination sequence.

The film must be seen run in its entirety for a viewer to actually receive its maximum impact. But, in synopsis, the film shows:

> The motorcade curves onto Elm and begins moving slowly toward the camera. President Kennedy and his wife are smiling and waving to opposite sides of the street. Then the presidential limousine disappears for a brief second behind a freeway sign and when it emerges, Kennedy is already reacting to a shot. He clenches his fists and brings both up to his throat. He does not appear to say anything, but only remains stiff and upright, sagging slightly to his left. Connally turns to his right, apparently trying to see behind him, then begins to turn back to his left when he freezes. His hair flies up and his mouth opens. He is obviously struck by a bullet. Mrs. Kennedy meanwhile has placed her hand on her husband's arm and is looking at him horrified as he continues to sag toward her. A few seconds pass and, by now, Kennedy is bent slightly forward. Suddenly, after an almost imperceptible forward motion of his head, the entire right side of his skull explodes in a halo of blood and brain matter. Kennedy is slammed violently backward to the left rear where he rebounds off the back of the seat and falls toward the car's floor. Mrs. Kennedy climbs onto the trunk of the limousine in an effort to grab something while a Secret Service agent leaps onto the rear of the car, which finally begins to accelerate.

On July 22, 1964, Zapruder told the Warren Commission, "I heard the first shot and I saw the President lean over and grab himself like this [holding his left chest area]."

His testimony is very pertinent because the Warren Commission, in its attempt to prove a lone assassin fired from the sixth floor of the Depository, stated:

> The evidence indicated that the President was not hit until at least frame 210 and that he was probably hit by frame 225. The possibility of variations in reaction time in addition to the obstruction of Zapruder's view by the sign precluded a more specific determination than that the President was probably shot through the neck between frames 210 and 225.

By placing the moment of the first shot at the point where Kennedy was out of Zapruder's sight behind the sign, the Commission moved the shot closer to the visual effect of a strike on Connally, buttressing the "single bullet" theory. By moving the time of the shot forward, the Commission also abolished the worrisome problem of how an assassin in the sixth-floor window could have accurately fired through obscuring tree branches.

The problem with the Commission's scenario of a hit between frame 210 and 225, of course, is that Zapruder claims he saw Kennedy react to the first shot, which had to have happened before he disappeared from camera view.

Zapruder went on to tell the Commission that following the shooting, he saw some motorcycle policemen "running right behind me . . . in the line of the shooting." He said, "I guess they thought it came from right behind me." When asked where he thought the shots came from, Zapruder replied, "I also thought it came from back of me."

In fact, Zapruder stated on four separate occasions in his testimony that he thought shots came from behind him in the direction of the picket fence on the Grassy Knoll.

But when Commission attorney Wesley J. Liebeler asked Zapruder, "But you didn't form any opinion at that time as to what direction the shots did come from actually?" Zapruder—who by this time was fully familiar with the public position that Oswald had fired three shots from the Depository—was confused and replied, "No." This response has been seized upon by some debunkers who claimed Zapruder did not know from which direction the shots came.

Zapruder, who was very shaken by the assassination, noted that there was considerable reverberation in Dealey Plaza at the time. He said he did not remember jumping down from the cement block and crouching for cover inside the white pergola with Sitzman as determined by photographs taken at the time or going back to his office. He recalled only walking back up Elm Street in a daze, yelling, "They shot him, they shot him, they shot him."

His secretary called authorities and soon Dallas Secret Service agent in charge Forrest Sorrels and *Dallas Morning News* reporter Harry McCormack came to take his film for processing.

The day after the assassination, select frames from Zapruder's film had been sold to *Life* magazine. In charge of the sale was *Life*'s publisher, C. D. Jackson, who later claimed he was so horrified by the film that he wanted to lock it away. However, in later years, Jackson was shown to have been closely associated with CIA officials and ranking globalists such as Allen Dulles, John J. McCloy, and Joseph Alsop, the latter being instrumental in establishing the Warren Commission. As revealed in British Security Coordination (BSC) files declassified in 1998, Dulles, who represented prewar Nazis and later served as CIA director, was recruited as a British agent in 1940. When the first CIA director, Walter Bedell Smith, wanted prominent Americans as members of the shadowy and elitist Bilderberger organization, he said he "turned the matter over to C. D. Jackson and things really got going."

The sale of the Zapruder film to *Life* might be the only instance of a private company purchasing critical evidence in a major crime prior to any court trials. Asked about the sale by Liebeler, Zapruder said, "Well, I just wonder whether I should answer it or not because it involves a lot of things and it's not one price—it's a question of how they are going to use it, are they going to use it or are they not going to use it."

He finally said, "I received $25,000, as you know, and I have given that to the Firemen's and Policemen's Benevolence with a suggestion, [to use the money] for Mrs. Tippit [wife of the Dallas policeman slain the afternoon of the assassination]."

Later in his testimony, Zapruder told of giving his camera to Bell & Howell for its archives. He said, in return, he asked the company to donate a sound projector to the "Golden Age Group." He told Liebeler, "I didn't want anything for myself. . . . I don't like to talk about it too much."

After the trauma of the assassination, the American public was gratified to learn from the media that Zapruder had received only $25,000 for his film and that the money was to have gone to the widow of the slain Officer Tippit. Like so much of the Warren Commission testimony, Zapruder's statement was less than truthful.

A copy of his contract with *Life* made public much later revealed that his film brought him more than $150,000. This would be close to $1 million in today's money. He also received 50 percent of Time-Life profits from rights to the film. Why so much for one film? Perhaps it has something to do with the fact that no member of the American public saw the Zapruder film run as a movie while it was in the sole possession of Time-Life Corp.

While few, if any, of the Warren Commission members viewed the film, single frames from this important piece of evidence were printed in Volume XVIII. But an odd thing happened. No one who has viewed the Zapruder film has been unaffected by the final, gory head shot followed instantaneously by Kennedy's violent fall rearward. Most researchers consider this moment in the film as obvious evidence of a shot from Kennedy's right front, the location of the Grassy Knoll.

Yet when published by the Warren Commission, the critical frames that depict the rearward motion of Kennedy's head were transposed to indicate a forward motion. In 1965 FBI director J. Edgar Hoover explained this reversing of the Zapruder frames as a "printing error."

Further twisting of what was depicted in the film came soon after the assassination. In its December 6, 1963, issue, *Life* magazine reported the fact that the Dallas doctors regarded a small wound in Kennedy's throat as an entrance wound, a real problem considering that the Texas School Book Depository was to his rear at all times. So a *Life* writer simply threw out the explanation:

> But [Zapruder's] 8mm film shows the President turning his body far around to the right as he waves to someone in the crowd. His throat is exposed—toward the sniper's nest—just before he clutches it.

This account is patently wrong, as anyone who has seen the film can attest. The reason for such wrongful information at such a critical time will probably never be known, as the author of this statement, Paul Mandel, died shortly afterward.

Then there is the story of news anchor Dan Rather, which has been known to assassination researchers for years. Rather, then a CBS newsman, was the only reporter present at a private screening of the Zapruder film the day after the assassination. He described what was in the film over nationwide radio and was fairly accurate until he described the fatal head shot.

Rather stated Kennedy's head "went forward with considerable violence," the exact opposite of what is in the film. In his 1987 book, *The Camera Never Blinks*, Rather ironically attempted to explain this misstatement by claiming he must have blinked at that moment in the film. Several months later, Rather was promoted to White House correspondent for CBS and by the 1980s, he was chief news anchorman.

Another questionable statement by Rather involves his location at the time of the assassination. In his book, Rather wrote how he was waiting to pick up news film from a CBS cameraman in the presidential motorcade. He wrote he was standing on the west side of the Triple Underpass and missed witnessing the assassination by only a few yards.

However, recently discovered film footage of the west side of the underpass has now become public. This film plus some still photographs show the Kennedy limousine speeding through the underpass and onto Stemmons Freeway—but no sign of Dan Rather.

The American public finally got the opportunity to view the Zapruder film only because of the Clay Shaw trial in New Orleans during 1967–1969. During that turbulent trial, New Orleans district attorney Jim Garrison attempted to prove there was a conspiracy to kill President Kennedy and that New Orleans Trade Mart director Clay Shaw was a member of that conspiracy.

As part of Garrison's attempt to prove the existence of a conspiracy, he subpoenaed the Zapruder film from Time-Life Corp. Time-Life fought this subpoena all the way to the Supreme Court, which finally ruled that the corporation had to comply with the legal subpoena.

Time-Life grudgingly turned over to Garrison a somewhat blurry copy of the film—but that was enough. Soon, thanks to the copying efforts of Garrison's staff, bootleg Zapruder films were in the hands of several assassination researchers.

Finally in March 1975, a copy of the film was aired nationally about midnight on ABC's *Goodnight America* thanks to guests Robert Groden and comedian Dick Gregory. At long last, the American public was able to see for themselves the assassination of the thirty-fifth president. Within a few years clearer copies of the Zapruder film became available to the public.

From the beginning, researchers have used the Zapruder film as the cornerstone of assassination evidence—a virtual time clock of the events in Dealey Plaza, based on the known average camera speed of 18.3 frames per second.

Today the Zapruder film itself has been called into question. In 1971, author David Lifton was permitted to view an exceptionally good-quality copy of the Zapruder film in Time-Life's Los Angeles office. He said the rear of Kennedy's head in the critical moments following the head shot appeared to have been "blacked out" and he discovered "splices on the film which had never been mentioned by Time-Life."

His suspicion that the film may have been tampered with by persons with access to sophisticated photographic equipment was heightened in 1976 with the release of

CIA Item 450. This group of documents, pried from the agency by a Freedom of Information Act suit, indicated the Zapruder film was at the CIA's National Photo Interpretation Center possibly on the night of the assassination and "certainly within days of the assassination." One of the documents tells of the existence of either a negative or a master positive of the film and calls for the production of four prints— one "test print" and three duplicates. Interestingly, that number of prints is exactly what existed in Dallas the day after the assassination—one original and three copies.

Lifton wrote:

> In my view, previously unreported CIA possession of the Zapruder film compromised the film's value as evidence: (1) the forward motion of Kennedy's head, for one frame preceding frame 313, might be the result of an altered film, and if that was so, it made the theory of a forward high-angle shot . . . completely unnecessary; (2) an altered film might also explain why the occipital area [of Kennedy's head], where the Dallas doctors saw a wound, appears suspiciously dark, whereas a large wound appears on the forward, right-hand side of the head, where the Dallas doctors saw no wound at all.

The late Jack White, a photographic analyst and researcher who testified to the House Select Committee on Assassinations, concurred with Lifton, stating he detected evidence of photographic retouching in some Zapruder frames. Interception and alteration of the Z film prior to its delivery to Time-Life has now been confirmed by documents, witness testimony, and the scrutiny of Hollywood experts, as will be detailed later.

Long considered one of the best pieces of evidence, if the CIA indeed tampered with the Zapruder film after the assassination, it becomes problematic in evaluating what really happened in Dealey Plaza.

And like so much else in the assassination case, the suppression, alteration, and deception surrounding the Zapruder film may eventually reveal more than the film itself.

In April 1975, for $1 Time-Life sold the Zapruder film back to the heirs of Zapruder, who died in 1970. The film was placed in cold storage within the National Archives for safekeeping. With the passage of the JFK Act in 1992, the Zapruder family, fearful that the film could be taken as an assassination record, tried to retrieve it but was rebuffed by the National Archives and Records Administration. Their fear was justified, as the Assassination Records Review Board designated the film as a JFK record belonging to the government. In 1998, the film was digitally replicated under license of the Zapruder family and distributed under the title *Image of an Assassination: A New Look at the Zapruder Film*. The government kept the film but compensated the Zapruder family with $16 million of taxpayer money.

In December 1999, the original film was donated to the Sixth Floor Museum in Dallas, where it resides today.

Just down the slope of the Grassy Knoll from Zapruder was the Bill Newman family. They not only noticed Zapruder with his camera, but in later years, Newman told this author, "At first I thought he shot the president."

Bill and Gayle Newman, along with their two young sons, had gone to Love Field to see Kennedy. But when they didn't get a good view, they rushed downtown and situated themselves on Elm Street just below the concrete cupola on the Grassy Knoll. Newman recalled for this author:

> We hadn't been there five minutes when the President turned onto Elm Street. As he was coming straight toward us there was a boom, boom, real close together. I thought someone was throwing firecrackers. He got this bewildered look on his face and was sort of slowly moving back and forth. Then he got nearer to us and, bam, a shot took the right side of his head off. His ear flew off. I heard Mrs. Kennedy say, "Oh, my God, no, they shot Jack!" He was knocked violently back against the seat, almost as if he had been hit by a baseball bat. At that time I was looking right at the president and I thought the shots were coming from directly behind us. I said, "That's it! Get on the ground!" The car momentarily stopped and the driver seemed to have a radio or phone up to his ear and he seemed to be waiting on some word. Some Secret Service men reached into their car and came out with some sort of machine gun. Then the cars roared off. Very soon after this a man asked us what happened and we told him and he took us to Channel 8 [WFAA-TV] studios.

Newman said some sheriff's deputies were waiting for them after the TV interview and took them to the sheriff's office, where they joined other Dealey Plaza witnesses who were held for about six hours.

He said that on Sunday, November 24, some FBI agents came to their home and "took down what we said." That was the last contact the Newmans had with federal authorities. He said:

> I was a little disappointed that I didn't get called to testify to the Warren Commission. Someone told me that the reason I wasn't asked to testify was that I was talking about shots from someplace other than the Depository building. . . . I've already been corrected several times that I was wrong about several things and that there are experts who know more about it than I do. But it's real hard for me to believe that it was the act of one lone individual. I've gotten the feeling over the years that people in Washington know what really happened but it's never been divulged. But then I have no evidence to that.

Near the Newmans was Cheryl McKinnon, who later became a reporter for the *San Diego Star News*. In 1983, she wrote of her experience:

On Nov. 22, 1963, I stood, along with hundreds of others, on the Grassy Knoll in Dealey Plaza, waiting for just one thing—a chance to see, even just for a moment, that magical person, the President, John F. Kennedy. . . . As a journalism major in school, my plans were to write about my experiences as a class project. . . . As we stood watching the motorcade turn onto Elm Street, I tried to grasp every tiny detail of both President Kennedy and Mrs. Kennedy. "How happy they look," I thought. Suddenly three shots in rapid succession rang out. Myself and dozens of others standing nearby turned in horror toward the back of the Grassy Knoll where it seemed the sounds had originated. Puffs of white smoke still hung in the air in small patches. But no one was visible. . . . I tried to maintain the faith with my government. I have read the Warren Commission Report in its entirety and dozens of other books as well. I am sorry to say that the only thing I am absolutely sure of today is that at least two of the shots fired that day in Dealey Plaza came from behind where I stood on the Knoll, not from the book Depository. . . . I have never quite had the same faith and trust in those that lead us as I did before.

Sitting on the steps leading to the top of the Grassy Knoll at the time of the assassination was Emmett J. Hudson, one of the groundskeepers of Dealey Plaza. With Hudson were two other men; neither apparently was ever identified by the federal investigations. In his Warren Commission testimony, Hudson recalled:

Well, there was a young fellow, oh, I would judge his age about in his late twenties. He said he had been looking for a place to park . . . he finally [had] just taken a place over there in one of them parking lots, and he came on down there and said he worked over there on Industrial and me and him both just sat down there on those steps. When the motorcade turned off of Houston onto Elm, we got up and stood up, me and him both . . . and so the first shot rung out and, of course, I didn't realize it was a shot . . . the motorcade had done got further on down Elm. . . . I happened to be looking right at him when that bullet hit him—the second shot. . . . It looked like it hit him somewhere along about a little bit behind the ear and a little above the ear [on the right-hand side of his head]. . . . This young fellow that was . . . standing there with me . . . he says, "Lay down, mister, somebody is shooting the President." . . . He kept on repeating, "Lay down," so he was already laying down one way on the sidewalk, so I just laid down over on the ground and resting my arm on the ground . . . when that third shot rung out. . . . You could tell the shot was coming from above and kind of behind.

In his testimony, Hudson plainly tried to tell Commission attorney Liebeler that the shots came "from above and kind of behind" him, the location of the picket fence on the Grassy Knoll. Liebeler led Hudson, saying, "And that would fit in with the Texas School Book Depository, wouldn't it?"

"Yes," replied an agreeable Hudson. Liebeler then asked Hudson if he saw anyone standing in the area with a rifle "on a grassy spot up there near where you were standing or on the overpass or any place else?"

Hudson replied, "I never seen anyone with a gun up there except the patrols."

Asked Liebeler, "The policemen?"

"Yes, sir," replied Hudson.

In an affidavit signed the day of the assassination, Hudson was even more specific as to where shots came from. He stated, "The shots that I heard definitely came from behind and above me."

Sitting near the midway point of the steps leading to the top of the Grassy Knoll, a location "behind and above" would be the exact position of the easternmost leg of the wooden picket fence.

Hudson said he did not know the young man who sat with him and, apparently, the federal authorities were never able to locate him.

The third man appears behind Hudson in photographs taken in the seconds during which the head shot occurs. He, too, has been unidentified but, perhaps, is the explanation for one of the enduring assassination mysteries.

The Black Dog Man

In at least two photographs taken during the assassination by separate photographers, a human figure is visible behind a low retaining wall to the south of the Grassy Knoll pergola just behind Zapruder's position. In photos made seconds later, this figure has disappeared, leading many assassination researchers to suspect that this figure may have been an assassin. This suspicion was heightened when the House Select Committee on Assassinations had photographs of the figure computer enhanced and concluded that it indeed was that of a person, who appeared to be holding a long object.

With no known identity, this person was dubbed the "black dog man" by researchers and committee staffers because in a photo taken by Phil Willis the figure resembles a black dog sitting on its haunches atop the wall. Closer examination of the photos, however, indicates the figure is most likely farther back from the retaining wall. And this may provide a partial answer to the figure's identity.

In photos of the assassination, a third man can be seen joining Hudson and his companion on the steps of the Grassy Knoll just as the presidential limousine arrives opposite them on Elm Street. Within scant seconds of the fatal head shot, the third man lifts his left foot and within seconds has disappeared back up the steps.

Life magazine, in its November 24, 1967, issue, displays the photographs of Hugh Betzner and Phil Willis and comments:

> A dark shape is seen in both pictures on the slope—which has become famous as the "Grassy Knoll"—to the left of the Stemmons Freeway sign

and half hidden by a concrete wall. By photogrammetry Itek has verified it as the figure of a man. Previously published photographs, taken at the moment of the fatal head shot, show that by then he had joined two men seen in Willis' picture standing behind a lamppost at left. There is no evidence to indicate he was anything more than an onlooker.

So the riddle of the "black dog man" appeared solved. It was the figure of a man seen from waist up as he stood or walked on the sidewalk behind the retaining wall approaching the top of the steps. Yet today many assassination researchers still deny it was the man who joined Hudson.

Seconds later—as determined in photographs—the unidentified man joined Hudson and companion, who were apparently unaware of the man behind them, then turned and ran back up the steps immediately after the head shot.

However, this explanation does not exonerate the third man as simply an "onlooker." Who was he? Where did he come from? What did he see both before and after he joined the two men on the steps? And why did he turn and race back up the steps (he was gone within seconds) at a time when everyone else in Dealey Plaza was stationary with shock?

The federal investigations could provide no answers to these questions, so in the minds of some researchers, the "black dog man" joins the ranks of suspicious persons in Dealey Plaza.

Almost immediately after the final shot was fired, many people—including policemen, sheriff's deputies, and spectators—began rushing toward the Grassy Knoll.

Dallas motorcycle officer Bobby Hargis thought the shots had come from the Triple Underpass because "I had got splattered, with blood [and] I was just a little back and left of Mrs. Kennedy, but I didn't know."

Hargis stopped his motorcycle on the south side of Elm and ran up the Grassy Knoll to where the concrete wall of the Triple Underpass connected with the wooden picket fence on the knoll. Peering over the wall, Hargis looked at the crowd standing on the Underpass. Asked if he saw anything out of the ordinary, Hargis told the Warren Commission, "No, I didn't. That is what got me."

Hargis returned to his still-running motorcycle and rode through the Triple Underpass. He told the commission, "I couldn't see anything that was of a suspicious nature, so I came back to the Texas School Book Depository. At that time it seemed like the activity was centered around the . . . Depository."

Seymour Weitzman was a college graduate serving as a deputy constable of Dallas County. He had been standing with deputy constable Bill Hutton at the corner of Main and Houston when the motorcade passed. The pair had turned to walk to a nearby courthouse when Weitzman heard three shots, "first one, then . . . a little period in between . . . [then] the second two seemed to be simultaneously." He told the Warren Commission:

I immediately ran toward the President's car. Of course, it was speeding away and somebody said the shots or firecrackers . . . we still didn't know the President was shot . . . came from the wall. I immediately scaled the wall. . . . Apparently, my hands grabbed steam pipes. I burned them. [In the railroad yards behind the picket fence.] We noticed numerous kinds of footprints that did not make sense because they were going different directions . . . [with Weitzman at the time were] other officers, Secret Service as well.

Behind Weitzman came Dallas policeman Joe M. Smith, who had been handling traffic at the intersection of Elm and Houston in front of the Depository. Smith had helped at the scene of the strange seizure incident minutes before the motorcade arrived and had returned to his position in the middle of Elm where barricades had been placed to halt traffic.

Moments after the president's car passed him, Smith heard shots, but he couldn't tell from which direction they came. He told the Warren Commission a hysterical woman ran up to him, crying, "They are shooting the president from the bushes!"

Smith said he immediately went up the short street that branches off of Elm in front of the Depository and entered the parking lot behind the wooden picket fence. He told the Commission:

I looked into all the cars and checked around the bushes. Of course, I wasn't alone. There was some deputy sheriff [Weitzman] with me, and I believe one Secret Service man when I got there. I got to make this statement, too. I felt awfully silly, but after the shot and this woman, [I] pulled my pistol from my holster, and I thought, this is silly, I don't know who I am looking for, and put it back. Just as I did, he showed me that he was a Secret Service agent. . . . He saw me coming with my pistol and right away he showed me who he was.

In 1978, Smith told author Anthony Summers that "around the hedges [lining the parking lot], there was the smell, the lingering smell of gunpowder."

Smith then moved toward the Triple Underpass because "it sounded to me like they [shots] may have come from this vicinity here." In his testimony, Smith said he saw "two other officers there," but it is unclear if he was speaking about behind the fence or the Triple Underpass. After fifteen or twenty minutes, Smith said he returned to the front of the Depository, where he helped other officers seal the building.

For some unexplained reason, at the end of his testimony Commission attorney Wesley Liebeler suddenly asked Smith if there was any reason why the presidential motorcade could not have gone straight down Main Street and turned onto Stemmons Freeway on its way to the Trade Mart. "As far as I know, there is no reason," replied Smith. This was a question that has been asked by several security-conscious researchers over the years. Although not the normal flow of traffic, a straight run down Main would have made the dogleg turns on Houston and Elm Streets unnecessary and might have prevented the assassination.

One witness who was in a position to observe the area behind the picket fence was Lee Bowers, a railroad supervisor who was stationed in a tower just north of the Grassy Knoll. Bowers told a fascinating story of suspicious cars moving in the sealed-off railroad yards minutes before the motorcade arrived and of seeing strange men behind the picket fence. Incredibly, his testimony takes less than six pages of the Warren Commission volumes.

Bowers, an ex-Navy man who had studied religion at Southern Methodist University in Dallas, was working for the Union Terminal Company, controlling the movement of trains in the railroad yards from a tower about fourteen feet off the ground. The tower is located about fifty yards northwest of the back of the Texas School Book Depository. A block-long street breaks off from Elm and passes in front of the Depository, ending in a parking lot bordered on the south by the wooden picket fence atop the Grassy Knoll. It was the only paved artery in or out of the parking area.

Bowers told the Warren Commission:

> The area had been covered by police for some two hours. Since approximately 10 o'clock in the morning [of the assassination], traffic had been cut off into the area so that anyone moving around could actually be observed. Since I had worked there for a number of years, I was familiar with most of the people who came in and out of the area. . . . There were three cars that came in during the time from around noon until the time of the shooting. They came into the vicinity of the tower, which was at the extension of Elm Street . . . which there is no way out. It is not a through street to anywhere.

Bowers said he noticed the first car about 12:10 p.m. It was a blue-and-white 1959 Oldsmobile station wagon with out-of-state license plates and some bumper stickers, "one of which was a Goldwater sticker." The station wagon circled in front of the railroad tower "as if he was searching for a way out, or was checking the area, and then proceeded back through the only way he could, the same outlet he came into."

About 12:20 p.m., a black 1957 Ford with Texas license plates came into the area. Inside was "one male . . . that seemed to have a mike or telephone or something. . . . He was holding something up to his mouth with one hand and he was driving with the other." Bowers said this car left after three or four minutes, driving back in front of the Depository. "He did probe a little further into the area than the first car," he added.

Minutes before the assassination, Bowers said a third car—this one a white 1961 or 1962 Chevrolet four-door Impala—entered the area. Bowers said:

> [It] showed signs of being on the road. . . . It was muddy up to the windows, bore a similar out-of-state license to the first car I observed [and

was] also occupied by one white male. He spent a little more time in the area. . . . He circled the area and probed one spot right at the tower . . . and was forced to back out some considerable distance, and slowly cruised down back towards the front of the School Depository Building. . . . The last I saw of him, he was pausing just about in—just above the assassination site. . . . Whether it continued on . . . or whether it pulled up only a short distance, I couldn't tell. I was busy.

Bowers said about eight minutes later, he caught sight of the presidential limousine as it turned onto Elm Street. He stated:

I heard three shots. One, then a slight pause, then two very close together. Also, reverberation from the shots. . . . The sounds came either from up against the School Depository Building or near the mouth of the Triple Underpass.

Bowers said he saw two men standing directly between his vantage point and the Triple Underpass, but they "gave no appearance of being together" although they were only ten or fifteen feet from each other. He described this pair:

One man, middle-aged, or slightly older, fairly heavyset, in a white shirt, fairly dark trousers. Another younger man, about mid-twenties, in either a plaid shirt or plaid coat or jacket. . . . They were facing and looking up toward Main and Houston and following the caravan as it came down.

Bowers also saw the railroad employees and the two Dallas policemen standing on the Triple Underpass. Toward the eastern end of the parking lot, Bowers saw two other men. He said, "Each had uniforms similar to those custodians at the courthouse." Bowers then described what he saw following the shots:

At the time of the shooting there seemed to be some commotion, and immediately following there was a motorcycle policeman who shot nearly all of the way to the top of the incline. . . . He was part of the motorcade and had left it for some reason, which I did not know. . . . He came up into the area where there are some trees and where I had described the two men were in the general vicinity of this . . . one of them was [still there]. The other one, I could not say. The darker-dressed man was too hard to distinguish from the trees. The one in the white shirt, yes, I think he was.

Asked by Commission attorney Joseph Ball to describe the "commotion" that attracted his attention, Bowers said:

I just am unable to describe rather than it was something out of the ordinary . . . but something occurred in this particular spot which was out of the ordinary, which attracted my eye for some reason, which I could not identify. . . . Nothing that I could pinpoint as having happened that—

Ball interrupted. "Afterwards did a good many people come up there on this high ground at the tower?" he asked, before Bowers could tell what caught his attention on the knoll.

In a later filmed interview, Bowers did describe what caught his eye. He stated:

> At the time of the shooting, in the vicinity of where the two men I have described were, there was a flash of light or . . . something I could not identify . . . some unusual occurrence—a flash of light or smoke or something which caused me to feel that something out of the ordinary had occurred there.

Bowers said after the shooting, "a large number of people" converged on the parking lot behind the picket fence, including "between fifty and a hundred policemen within a maximum of five minutes." He added, "[Police] sealed off the area and I held off the trains until they could be examined, and there were some transients taken [off] at least one train."

One witness who may have encountered one or more of the men Bowers saw behind the picket fence was Gordon Arnold, who never testified to either of the federal panels investigating the assassination. On the day of the assassination, Arnold was a twenty-two-year-old soldier who had just arrived back in Dallas after Army training. He went downtown to have lunch when he decided to take movies of the president. Parking his car near Bowers's railroad tower, Arnold took his movie camera and walked toward the Triple Underpass. He told this author:

> I was walking along behind this picket fence when a man in a light-colored suit came up to me and said I shouldn't be up there. I was young and cocky and I said, "Why not?" And he showed me a badge and said he was with the Secret Service and that he didn't want anyone up there. I said all right and started walking back along the fence. I could feel that he was following me and we had a few more words. I walked around to the front of the fence and found a little mound of dirt to stand on to see the motorcade. . . . Just after the car turned onto Elm and started toward me, a shot went off from over my left shoulder. I felt the bullet, rather than heard it, and it went right past my left ear. . . . I had just gotten out of basic training. In my mind live ammunition was being fired. It was being fired over my head. And I hit the dirt. I buried my head in the ground and I heard several other shots, but I couldn't see anything because I had my face in the dirt. [His prone position under the trees on the knoll may explain why Arnold did not appear in photographs taken of the knoll at that time.] I heard two shots and then there was a blend. For a single-bolt action [rifle], he had to have been firing darn good because I don't think anybody could fire that rapid a bolt action. . . . The next thing I knew, someone was kicking my butt and telling me to get up. It was a policeman. And I told him to go jump in the river.

And then this other guy—a policeman—comes up with a gun. I don't recall if it was a shotgun or what. And he was crying and that thing was waving back and forth. I felt threatened. One of them asked me if I had taken any film and I said yes. He told me to give him my film, so I tossed him my camera. I said you can have everything, just point that gun somewhere else. He opened it, pulled out the film, and then threw the camera back to me. All I wanted to do was get out of there. The gun and the guy crying was enough to unnerve me.

Arnold ran straight back to his car and drove out of the parking area unchallenged. Two days later, Arnold reported to duty at Fort Wainwright in Alaska and he did not return for several years.

Arnold's presence on the Grassy Knoll has been questioned by some researchers because he doesn't appear in photographs taken that day. His position well under the overhanging trees on the knoll left him in deep shadow. He was seen, however, by at least one person in the presidential motorcade. Former senator Ralph Yarborough, who was riding in the same car as Vice President Johnson, confirmed Arnold's position in 1978 when he told the *Dallas Morning News*:

Immediately on the firing of the first shot I saw the man you interviewed [Arnold] throw himself on the ground. He was down within a second of the time the shot was fired and I thought to myself, "There's a combat veteran who knows how to act when weapons start firing."

Arnold, later an investigator for the Dallas Department of Consumer Affairs, did not give his name to authorities and was never questioned by either the Warren Commission or the House Select Committee on Assassinations, although his account of the assassination appeared in the July 27, 1978, edition of the *Dallas Morning News*.

Corroboration of Arnold's story may have come in 1982 with discovery of a figure in the background of a snapshot made at the instant of the fatal head shot to Kennedy by a woman standing on the south curb on Elm Street.

The Badge Man

Mary Moorman took a now well-known Polaroid picture just as Kennedy was struck in the head. She sold her rights to the photo that day to United Press International for $600. The photo was never examined or printed by the Warren Commission, but it was published widely in newspapers and magazines after the assassination.

For years, researchers pored over the Moorman picture looking for evidence of a Grassy Knoll gunman. Despite some tantalizingly blurry objects discovered along the top of the west leg of the picket fence, no credible photo of a gunman was found.

The House Select Committee on Assassinations did study the picture, but found it had badly faded and "was of quite poor quality." However, because of acoustical evidence indicating a shot from the Grassy Knoll, the committee recommended "this particular photograph should be reexamined."

Then, in 1982, Texas researchers Gary Mack, now curator of the Sixth Floor Museum in Dallas, and Jack White, who died in 2012, began studying the Moorman photo in light of Gordon Arnold's experience. After obtaining a clear slide made from an original, good-quality copy of Moorman's photo, they began studying the bushy area east from the corner of the fence. It was here they discovered what appeared to be two figures. Interestingly, the figures appear in the same general area that the House committee's acoustical tests indicated shots were fired from, though the sound experts located a shot west of the corner of the fence, while the figures are north of the corner.

When blown up, the figures are detectable even by untrained observers. One police official even commented that one man seemed to be wearing "shooter's glasses." The main figure has been dubbed "badge man" because he appears to be wearing a dark shirt with a semicircular patch on the left shoulder and a bright shiny object on his left chest—the exact configuration of a Dallas police uniform.

Although the "badge man's" hairline, eyes, left ear, and jaw are visible, his mouth and neck are obscured by a bright spot—apparently the smoke or muzzle flash from a rifle he is holding in the classic rifle-firing position.

After analyzing the photographic blowup as well as making reenactment photos in Dealey Plaza, Mack and White felt the "badge man" and perhaps even a companion were standing behind the wooden picket fence about fifteen feet north from the corner. This places the figure just to the left of Gordon Arnold's position and to the right and rear of Abraham Zapruder.

In the 1980s, Mack and White tried unsuccessfully to interest a major news organization in financing a scientific analysis of the "badge man" photo. Finally, a national tabloid agreed to have the blowup studied. White and a representative from the newsmagazine flew to the Massachusetts Institute of Technology, where the photo was subjected to sophisticated computer enhancement. They were told that, without question, the photo showed a man firing a rifle.

The next day, however, the chairman of the MIT department involved suddenly gave all materials back to them and, with no explanation, told them the school would no longer participate in any study of the photo.

The "badge man" blowup was included in *The Men Who Killed Kennedy*, a British television documentary by Nigel Turner produced in 1988. In this program, "badge man" was identified as a professional Corsican assassin named Lucien Sarti. This documentary, which was nominated for awards in Britain and shown to millions of people around the world, was not aired in the United States until the early 1990s when it was purchased by the Arts & Entertainment Company and shown on its History Channel after being broken into a series of programs slated to be shown each November until the fiftieth anniversary in 2013.

One of these programs, aired in 2003, "The Guilty Men," implicated Lyndon B. Johnson in the JFK assassination and was thus roundly criticized by surviving

Johnson associates, including his wife, Lady Bird Johnson, who died in 2007. Also among the critics was the last surviving member of the Warren Commission and the only appointed US president, Gerald R. Ford. After this group threatened legal action, the History Channel had three historians review the offending program. These eminent Establishment historians included Robert Dallek, a retired history professor at Boston University who since 1996 was a visiting professor at the LBJ School of Public Affairs at the University of Texas at Austin; Stanley Kutler, a Guggenheim Fellow and history professor best known for his lawsuit against the National Archives that resulted in the release of President Nixon's Watergate tapes; and Thomas Surgue, a graduate of Columbia University and King's College, Cambridge, receiving grants from the Guggenheim Foundation, the Brookings Institution, and the American Philosophical Society, among others. Although some of the persons interviewed for the programs in question said they and their material had never been questioned, this Establishment panel concluded the offending program was not credible and should not have been aired. After offering a public apology, the History Channel withdrew the program from distribution.

Also withdrawn without any explanation were two other programs, the one on Corsican assassin Lucien Sarti and the other dealing with Judyth Vary Baker, who claimed to have been with Lee Oswald in New Orleans, both working for elements within the US government.

The "badge man" has been largely ignored in assassination literature and documentaries. In a 2008 documentary on the Discovery Channel titled *JFK: Inside the Target Car*, Gary Mack stated there was no one behind the wooden picket fence, apparently forgetting that he was instrumental in making public the "badge man" analysis. He also misdirected the audience to the long stretch of fence rather than the shorter one, the location of the figure in the photograph.

But the cumulative evidence indicating that the "badge man" may indeed have been the Grassy Knoll gunman is supported by the following accounts:

—Gordon Arnold's story of hearing a shot come from his left rear.

—Zapruder's testimony that shots came from his right rear.

—Bowers's testimony that he saw a flash of light and smoke near two men wearing uniforms near the east end of the fence.

—The House Select Committee on Assassinations, which placed at least one shot within ten feet of the fence corner (although on the west leg).

—Jean Hill, who said she saw smoke and movement north of the fence corner at the moment of the head shot.

—Sam Holland and others who told of finding muddy footprints, cigarette butts, and mud on a car bumper behind the picket fence minutes after the shots were fired.

—Numerous witnesses who ran behind the fence but said they saw only railroad workers and policemen there.

—The testimony of Emmett Hudson, Constable Weitzman, and Officer

Smith, all of whom saw policemen on the knoll when there were none officially accounted for in that area.

All in all, the photographic blowup of these figures on the knoll may be the most important evidence yet confirming the existence of assassins on the Grassy Knoll. In any other case, if there was a photograph of a shooter behind the fence, two separate acoustical studies confirming at least one shot from behind the fence and a large number of witnesses who said a shot came from behind the fence, anyone arguing that no shots were fired from behind the fence would be considered an idiot. But this is the Kennedy assassination and some continue to say the deed was committed only by Lee Oswald firing from the sixth floor of the Depository.

Curiously, no official government agency or major news organization has been willing to either make a serious study of the Moorman photo or present the photo to the general public. Further evidence of what went on behind the picket fence at the moment of the assassination can be found in the little-known story of a crucial witness.

A Grassy Knoll Witness

It is strange irony that the one person who apparently witnessed men with guns behind the wooden picket fence on the Grassy Knoll at the time of the Kennedy assassination was unable to tell anyone what he saw. Ed Hoffman of Dallas was deaf since birth and, as is common with that disability, he cannot speak. However, this did not prevent him from attempting to alert authorities to what he saw behind that fence.

Although Hoffman told his family and friends what he saw at the time and later reported it to the FBI, his story remained unpublicized over the years. Finally, in the summer of 1985, he told his story to this author. It was later substantially confirmed by FBI documents. Ed Hoffman died on March 24, 2010.

Virgil Edward Hoffman was twenty-six years old on November 22, 1963, and at noontime was driving toward downtown Dallas on the Stemmons Freeway when he noticed numerous people lining the freeway. He suddenly realized that President Kennedy was to motorcade through the city that day, so he stopped his car just north of a railroad bridge across Stemmons and joined the spectators.

It should be noted that, since all news coverage of the motorcade stopped after the shooting in Dealey Plaza, only someone who was there that day could have known that many people were lining Stemmons to get a glimpse of the president.

After waiting for a time, Hoffman decided to walk along the shoulder of the freeway to a point where it crossed over Elm Street in hopes of getting a view into Dealey Plaza. From this vantage point, Hoffman was approximately two hundred yards west of the parking lot behind the picket fence at an elevation of about the height of the first floor of the Texas School Book Depository.

Being unable to hear, he was not aware that Kennedy's motorcade was passing through the plaza. However, he was aware of movement on the north side of the picket fence. He became aware of a man running west along the back side of the fence wearing a dark suit and a tie. The man was carrying a rifle in his hands. As the man reached a metal-pipe railing at the west end of the fence, he tossed the rifle to a second man standing on the west side of the pipe near the railroad tracks that went south over the Triple Underpass. The second man was wearing light coveralls and a railroad worker's hat.

The second man caught the rifle, ducked behind a large railroad switch box—one of two at that site—and knelt down. The man disassembled the rifle, placed it in a soft brown bag (Hoffman's description matches that of the traditional railroad brakeman's tool bag), then walked nonchalantly north into the rail yards in the general direction of the railroad tower containing Lee Bowers.

The man in the suit, meanwhile, had turned and run back along the picket fence until midway, when he stopped and began walking calmly toward the corner of the fence. Hoffman could not see the corner due to cars and overhanging tree branches.

Unable to hear, Hoffman was at a loss to understand what was happening as he watched these men.

However, moments later Kennedy's car came into sight out of the west side of the Triple Underpass. Hoffman saw the president lying on the seat of the blood-splattered car and realized something terrible had occurred.

As the presidential limousine turned onto the Stemmons access ramp just below his position, Hoffman tried to alert the Secret Service agents to what he had witnessed. He ran down the grassy incline waving his arms and trying to make them understand that he had seen something, when one of the agents in the president's follow-up car produced a "machine gun," which he leveled at him. Hoffman stopped and threw up his hands and could only watch helplessly as the motorcade rushed past him onto Stemmons in the mad rush to Parkland Hospital.

There was no mention at the time of any Secret Service man with a machine gun, yet Hoffman was emphatic that it was an automatic weapon with a pistol grip, carrying handle, and clip. It is now known that Secret Service agent George W. Hickey Jr. in the follow-up car did display an AR-15, the civilian model of the M-16 automatic rifle, further corroborating Hoffman's story.

Upset over what he had seen, Hoffman looked around for help. He saw a Dallas policeman standing on the railroad bridge crossing Stemmons and he walked toward him waving his arms in an attempt to communicate what he had seen. However, the policeman, unable to understand, simply waved him off. This part of Hoffman's story also is partially corroborated, since policeman Earle Brown filed a report stating that he was on the Stemmons railroad bridge at the time of the assassination. However, questioned recently about these events, Brown said he has no recollection of seeing Hoffman.

Unable to get help, Hoffman walked back to his car and drove behind the Texas School Book Depository for several minutes trying to locate the man with the rifle in the brown bag. He was unsuccessful. However, this indicates the total lack of security around the Depository in the chaotic minutes following the assassination.

Hoffman was able to drive around in the rail yards behind the Depository for some time and then leave without being stopped or questioned by authorities.

He then drove to the Dallas FBI office but found no one there except a receptionist. He left his name and address with the FBI. The FBI never responded.

At the time, Hoffman had a relative at the Dallas police station, and he drove there next, hoping to find some help. However, the station was sealed off and the officer on the door refused to allow him to enter.

Thwarted in his attempts to tell authorities what he had seen, Hoffman finally went home, where his parents, also deaf and mute, urged him not to become involved.

Hoffman said nothing until Thanksgiving 1963, when he met his policeman relative at a family function. Despite his parents' warnings, he told his story to Dallas policeman Robert Hoffman, who assured him that the federal authorities were investigating the case and that, in fact, the assassin had already been caught. Robert Hoffman later explained:

> I know that Eddie's a very bright person and always has been, and can't think of any reason why he would make up something like this. . . . His father was very, very concerned that Eddie knew anything about the assassination at all. It was time when suspicions were running high and he was worried about Eddie getting involved in any way. . . . It just wasn't a time for loose statements that couldn't be proved or backed up with any evidence.

Confident that he had done his civic duty and that the case was closed, Ed Hoffman said he didn't consider telling his story to anyone else.

However, as the years went by, Hoffman became more and more aware of the official version of the assassination and knew that the theory that one man had fired from the sixth floor of the Depository did not agree with what he had seen.

Finally on June 28, 1967, at the urging of coworkers, Hoffman visited the Dallas FBI once again. Apparently Hoffman had difficulty in communicating with the agents or they purposely distorted his story, because the FBI report of that day states:

> Hoffman said he observed two white males, clutching something dark to their chests with both hands, running from the rear of the Texas School Book Depository building. The men were running north on the railroad, then turned east, and Hoffman lost sight of both of the men.

The report added:

> Approximately two hours after the above interview with Hoffman, he returned to the Dallas office of the FBI and advised he had just returned from the spot on Stemmons Freeway where he had parked his automobile and had decided he could not have seen the men running because of a fence

west of the Texas School Book Depository building. He said it was possible that he saw these two men on the fence or something else [*sic*].

Whether or not the FBI agents were able to understand Hoffman correctly, they did talk to his father and brother on July 5, 1967. Both said Hoffman loved President Kennedy and had told his story to them just after the assassination. However, they also said Hoffman "has in the past distorted facts of events observed by him." Of course, it was his father who had urged him not to become involved in the case at all, so there was motivation to downplay his son's story.

Officially, this was the end of any investigation into Hoffman's story at that time. Unofficially, Hoffman said one FBI agent told him to keep quiet about what he had seen or "you might get killed."

Despite this not-so-subtle attempt to silence Hoffman, he continued to tell his story to fellow workers at the Dallas electronics firm where he was employed since before the assassination. Hoffman retired in the late 1990s and died in March 2010.

On March 25, 1977, one of Hoffman's supervisors who understood sign language contacted the Dallas FBI office. He said he felt that the FBI did not fully understand what Hoffman was trying to tell them during the 1967 interview and that Hoffman deserved to be heard.

At this urging, FBI agents again talked with Hoffman on March 28, 1977, and even accompanied him to the site on Stemmons Freeway. This time, with his supervisor acting as translator, Hoffman was able to give more details. He said he thought he saw a puff of smoke near where the men were standing, and essentially his story was the same as the one he told in 1985 except he said he saw both men run north into the rail yards.

Although this time the FBI took photographs of the area based on Hoffman's testimony, they again showed little interest in pursuing his story.

On the cover sheet of their report to the FBI director, the Dallas agents wrote:

On Pages 71–76 of the *Report of the President's Commission on the Assassination of President John F. Kennedy*, the witnesses at the Triple Underpass are discussed, but the Warren Commission's investigation has disclosed no credible evidence that any shots were fired from anywhere other than the Texas School Book Depository building. In view of the above, the Dallas Office is conducting no additional investigation.

In other words, since the federal government concluded Oswald was the lone assassin, Hoffman must have been mistaken. The agents were careful to include in their report his father's opinion: "The father of Virgil Hoffman stated that he did not believe that his son has seen anything of value and doubted he had observed any men running from the Texas School Book Depository."

Such dismissiveness might account for the fact that there was no mention of

Hoffman or his testimony by the US government until researchers obtained reports on him through the Freedom of Information Act in 1985.

Since Hoffman, despite his hearing disability, appears to be a most credible witness and since his story only reinforces those of others who told of gunmen on the knoll, it deserves serious consideration. However, as late as 2007, some were still sniping at Hoffman's account. M. Duke Lane argued that surely the policemen on or near Stemmons Freeway would have reported Hoffman's attempts to gain their attention. Despite the fact that everyone, including witnesses in Dealey Plaza, did not realize what had happened for several minutes and police there had already released traffic stopped for the motorcade, Lane wrote:

> During this time, because of their proximity to the Triple Underpass, the officers were undoubtedly on the lookout for anything that might have seemed suspicious in any way, or even just out of the ordinary: after all, the President had just been "hit" and was on his way to the hospital; the shooter or shooters might still be in the area. The police were not taking chances. . . . While it may be somehow possible that Ed saw and approached none of them, it is implausible that none of *them* saw *him*, made no moves to detain him at any time, and simply let him speed away in his car. . . . We're left with the inescapable conclusion that the Ed Hoffman tale . . . is nothing more than a tale, a figment of the imagination of a humble and otherwise unassuming man who, for whatever reason, got caught up in a story possibly not of his own making, but which nevertheless created and sustained that "fifteen minutes of fame" all men are said to be entitled to.

Such an ad hominem attack would seem ill supported since many of the details in Hoffman's story have been independently corroborated—the crowds on Stemmons, the automatic rifle, the cop on the railroad bridge, and the testimony of Jesse Price, who saw a man running behind the picket fence from the roof of the Union Terminal Annex. His account may be the best version to date of what happened behind the picket fence. Hoffman's experience also serves as a vivid commentary on the FBI's failure to follow serious leads, the bureau's attempts to intimidate witnesses into silence. and the unremitting attacks on anyone who would dare challenge the official government version of assassination events.

In reviewing the experiences of the people in Dealey Plaza the day Kennedy died, it is apparent that not one single person saw the assassination as it was described by the government's investigations.

In the motorcade, Governor Connally's testimony—totally corroborated by the Zapruder film—indicated that both he and Kennedy could not have been struck by the same bullet.

Many people, including Sheriff Decker, Royce Skelton, and Austin Miller, saw one bullet strike Elm Street. Others, like Policeman Foster, saw a bullet hit the grass on the south side of Elm.

Some heard shots coming from at least two separate locations, while those on the Triple Underpass even saw smoke drift out from under the trees on the Grassy Knoll. Still others reported a bullet strike on the Stemmons Freeway sign. Motorcade riders heard shots from separate locations, but the majority believed shots came from the direction of the Triple Underpass. Both Sheriff Decker and Police Chief Curry ordered their men to rush to the railroad yards behind the Grassy Knoll.

Despite great efforts on the part of authorities to establish the Depository as the source of all shots, public attention—both in 1963 and today—kept returning to the infamous Grassy Knoll.

PART II

MEANS, MOTIVES, AND OPPORTUNITIES

The assassination of president John F. Kennedy was not an isolated event. It occurred within a complex matrix of national and international events and issues. Therefore, for any truthful understanding, the assassination must be placed within a context of the times.

As president, Kennedy daily was juggling a wide variety of responsibilities on many different fronts—foreign policy, civil rights, agriculture, finance, politics, crime-busting, and defense considerations.

Likewise, Lee Harvey Oswald—the man identified by two government panels as Kennedy's assassin—did not live isolated from the world of his time. During his brief twenty-four years of life, Oswald came into contact with an incredible array of groups and individuals, all of whom had reason to wish for the elimination of Kennedy. Beginning with an uncle connected to organized crime, young Oswald moved through a shadowy world of soldiers, intelligence agents from both sides of the Cold War, Russian communists and anticommunists, pro-and anti-Castro Cubans, FBI men, and right-wing extremists. To place the events of November 22, 1963, in proper perspective, it is necessary to become familiar with these groups and with their relationships to Oswald and each other.

After all, every good detective begins a murder investigation by determining who had the means, motive, and opportunity to commit the act. The obvious starting place is with the one man universally acknowledged as the person most closely connected to the assassination—Lee Harvey Oswald.

Lee Harvey Oswald—Assassin or Patsy?

Prior to his enlistment in the Marines and with the possible exception of the early death of his father, Lee Harvey Oswald's boyhood was little different from that of millions of other Americans.

Oswald was born in New Orleans, Louisiana, on October 18, 1939, two months after the death of his father, Robert E. Lee Oswald, a collector of insurance premiums. While this unfortunate event must have had some effect on young Oswald, it was a fate endured by thousands of other young Americans, none of whom have felt compelled to murder national leaders.

In 1945, Oswald's mother married for a third time, but three years later the marriage ended in divorce. From that point on, Oswald and his brother, Robert, were brought up by their mother, Marguerite.

A Mother in History

The House Select Committee on Assassinations in 1979 concluded that President Kennedy was "probably assassinated as the result of a conspiracy." However, they maintained that Lee Harvey Oswald was the actual killer and that another gunman—whose presence was established by two separate scientific tests based on a Dallas police recording of the gunfire in Dealey Plaza—escaped and remains unidentified.

This finding was a milestone to the many Americans who had come to disbelieve the lone-assassin theory of the Warren Commission.

Typically, however, this reversal of official American history was still not enough for the mother of the accused assassin, Marguerite Oswald. She told news reporters:

> The committee members have made a first step in the right direction. It's up to us to do the rest. . . . I hope and know the future will vindicate my son entirely. It took us 15 years to come this far. It may take another 15 years or longer. I probably won't be around, but the world will know that Lee Harvey Oswald was innocent of the charges against him.

This was the statement of a woman who was much more than merely a supportive mother. It came from a woman who faced more public hostility than most murderers—a woman who faced the autumn of her years alone and in poverty. And all because of a child she bore.

Marguerite Claverie was born in New Orleans in 1907, of French and German descent. Her mother died a few years after her birth, leaving young Marguerite and her five siblings in the care of her father, a streetcar conductor. According to relatives, the Claverie family was poor but happy.

At the age of seventeen, Marguerite completed one year of high school. She then dropped out to become a law-firm receptionist. In August 1929, she married Edward John Pic Jr., a clerk. However, the marriage was not successful and the couple divorced in 1931, several months after the birth of her first son, John Edward Pic.

In 1933, she married Robert Edward Lee Oswald, himself recently divorced. She described her marriage to Oswald as the "only happy part" of her life. Out of this union came a second son, Robert. Then her happiness came to an end. Two months before the birth of Lee Harvey Oswald in October 1939, her husband died of a sudden heart attack. Making her way alone, she saw an opportunity to establish a family once again by remarrying in 1945. Sending the two elder sons off to boarding school, she and her new husband, Edwin A. Ekdahl, took six-year-old Lee and moved to Benbrook, Texas, a small town south of Fort Worth.

However, soon there were arguments over money and charges of infidelity against Ekdahl. A divorce was granted in 1948 and she was allowed to use her former name of Oswald. It is interesting to note that Ekdahl's divorce attorney was Fred Korth, who in the fall of 1963 was fired as secretary of the Navy by President Kennedy amid charges that Korth may have been involved along with Lyndon Johnson in a scandal over the General Dynamics TFX airplane contracts.

John Pic and Robert Oswald rejoined their mother, but both soon left home to join the military. Marguerite was left with only young Lee. Some accounts say Marguerite overly mothered Lee, while others claim she neglected the boy. However, the former seems to be closer to the truth in light of the fact that she became a practical nurse charged with babysitting the children of prominent Texans such as Amon Carter Jr. and former Texas representative Tom Vandergriff. Despite much conjecture, there is little evidence that Lee's childhood was any better or any worse than many others.

Lee dropped out of school to join the Marines. But in 1959, he received a sudden discharge and returned to Fort Worth for a two-day visit with his mother. Lee said he was off to New Orleans to work for an import-export firm, but several weeks later Mrs. Oswald read in the newspapers that her twenty-year-old son had turned up in Russia, where he told US officials he wanted to defect.

Instead of branding her son a traitor, she told reporters, "I feel very strongly that as an individual, he has the right to make his own decision. Lee has definite ideas. I believe God gives us a conscience and the ability to know right and I feel he has the right to make his own decision."

Despite this motherly support, Lee seemed to make every effort to avoid Marguerite after his return from the Soviet Union in 1962. At one point he moved his Russian bride and their infant daughter from Fort Worth to Dallas without leaving his mother a forwarding address.

The family was reunited only briefly during those dark days of November 1963.

Mrs. Oswald was on her way to work on November 22 when she heard over the car radio that Kennedy had been shot while riding in a motorcade in downtown Dallas. She also learned that a young ex-Marine named Lee Harvey Oswald was being held by police as the suspected assassin.

Concerned by the broadcasts and apparently with no friends to turn to, she contacted the local newspaper, the *Fort Worth Star-Telegram*, and asked if someone would take her to Dallas. She told reporter Bob Shieffer, who drove her to the Dallas police station, "I want to hear him tell me that he did it."

Mrs. Oswald also told them that she had been persecuted since her son's journey to Russia and knew the meaning of suffering. She described being fired by her last employer, *Star-Telegram* publisher Amon Carter Jr. She said she had been acting as a day nurse for the Carters' children until about two weeks prior to the Kennedy assassination. The Carters suddenly let her go after arriving back from a weekend trip to Las Vegas.

She once told this author, "You don't know what it's like to have someone look at you and say, 'You've done a good job, but we no longer need your services.'" She also noted this was the same weekend Jack Ruby was reported visiting in Las Vegas.

Following the assassination in Dallas, Mrs. Oswald was unable to hear the confession she sought from her son—she was not allowed to talk with him. And Oswald steadfastly maintained his innocence. He shouted to news reporters gathered in the police station hallway, "No, sir, I didn't kill anybody. I'm just a patsy!"

After Oswald's murder by Jack Ruby two days later, his mother's tone changed to one of suspicion and accusation, blaming the Dallas police and federal authorities for her son's death. She asked bitterly, "Why would [Jack Ruby] be allowed within a few feet of a prisoner—any prisoner—when I could not even see my own son?"

To compound her suspicions, she maintained until her death that the FBI had shown her a photo of Ruby the night before her son was slain. She said about 6:30 p.m. on November 23, the night after the assassination, an FBI agent and another man knocked on the door of the hotel where she and Lee's wife were being kept by the authorities. After being told that her daughter-in-law was tired and couldn't talk with the men, the FBI agent asked Marguerite a question. She recalled the incident to news reporters a week later:

> He had a picture coupled [*sic*] inside his hand and asked me if I had ever seen that man before. I told him, "No sir, believe me, I never have." Then he left. A few days later, I walked into the room where I was staying and, in front of my son Robert and a lot of witnesses, I picked up a paper and when I turned it over I said, "This is the picture of the man that FBI agent showed me." I did not even know at the time he was the man who shot my son. I was told that the picture was [of] Mr. Jack Ruby.

FBI officials, when informed of her statement, speculated that she must have been confused as to the date she was shown the photograph.

On July 10, 1964, FBI agent Bardwell D. Odum signed an affidavit with the Warren Commission stating that he had shown the picture to Mrs. Oswald. He said the photo was furnished by FBI superiors, who obtained it from the CIA. The FBI said they included the photo as a Warren Commission exhibit. It was reportedly supplied by the CIA, which was secretly photographing visitors to the Soviet embassy in Mexico City.

This incident was the beginning of Mrs. Oswald's lifelong suspicion of federal authorities. To the end of her life, she maintained that Lee had been working as some sort of agent for the US government and that unnamed "high officials" were part of the plot to kill Kennedy and blame her son. After Watergate she told a local newspaper, "If you called in all the FBI men involved in Lee Harvey Oswald's life and questioned them, one thing would lead to another and it would probably break the assassination case."

Just after the assassination, Mrs. Oswald said, "They [the public] all turned their backs on me before [when Oswald appeared in Russia] and they will turn their backs on me again, but my faith will see me through." And faith was truly about the only thing left for Mrs. Oswald.

With the exception of a couple of mysterious "benefactors" who kept her supplied with publications concerning the assassination, Marguerite Oswald was forced to live through the next two decades on less than $500 a month in Social Security payments. In the bicentennial summer of 1976, she was without a refrigerator for almost two months because she could not afford repairs. The loneliness and poverty of her life, however, failed to crush her fighting spirit. She continued to assail the official version of the assassination and to strike out at media presentations of the event.

In 1978, after viewing a CBS "docudrama" titled *Ruby and Oswald*, she told the local newspaper:

> I have every right to be upset over that program as well as many other things because they are talking about my son and my family. They sit there and tell the gullible American public that their program is the truth and based on documentation. Well, I'm sitting here with things you've never heard of. I can tear that CBS program apart like I did the Warren Commission.

Her thoughts on the Warren Commission, whose conclusions were taken as gospel at the time but gradually lost the confidence of the majority of Americans, are summed up in a letter Mrs. Oswald wrote to several congressmen in 1973 at the height of the Watergate crisis:

> On Nov. 29, 1963, the then President of the United States, Lyndon B. Johnson, created a commission to evaluate all the facts and circumstances surrounding the assassination of President John F. Kennedy and the subsequent killing of the alleged assassin and to report its findings and conclusions to him. . . . President Johnson selected Earl Warren, Chief Justice of the United States, as its chairman. Because I was critical of the commission, I was asked, "Mrs. Oswald, are you implying that the Chief Justice would whitewash evidence or hide information so that the American people, as

well as the whole world, would never learn the truth?" I answered, yes, in the name of security, men of integrity and who are the most esteemed, most respected and honored, who have the welfare of the country at heart, would be most likely to do what the White House wanted and thought necessary. The Watergate affair has followed this pattern. Those we believe are above reproach, those who have reached the pinnacle or are near it, those who are guiding our nation's destiny are found to have manipulated events to accomplish certain things they think were for the good of the country. Those who have a deep sense of patriotism and loyalty are most likely to twist events to accomplish their purposes. . . . The Watergate affair only strengthens my convictions and proves my theory. [In 1963, the] suspect was my son and seven such respected men branded a dead man who was neither tried nor convicted, assassin.

Through the years, Mrs. Oswald, who always claimed to be a "mother in history," was quick to point out that her defense of her son went beyond simple motherly love. She once told this author, "If he was truly guilty, I can accept that. But whether it's my son or someone else's son, I want the proof and the proof is just not there."

In her last years, Mrs. Oswald was virtually a recluse in her modest but well-kept brick home on the west side of Fort Worth. An occasional visitor—usually a journalist—and her small dog, Fritz, were her only company.

Neither her other sons nor Lee's wife, Marina, ever spoke to her again after November 1963. When money problems pressed too hard, she would sell a book or a letter from her mammoth collection of assassination materials. It was such money problems that helped create the belief that Mrs. Oswald would talk only for profit. However, as several Fort Worth news reporters can confirm, she never hesitated to pick up her telephone and call the media when a particular news item rankled her. She once explained the charge of talk-for-cash this way:

Well, here I am without money, wondering where my next meal is coming from and these writers come to my house wanting an interview. Then they go out and write some piece—some of them don't even talk to me more than fifteen minutes or so—and they get all this money for their work. That's not fair!

In January 1981, Mrs. Oswald quietly entered a Fort Worth hospital. Rumors circulated that she had cancer. By the end of that month, Marguerite Claverie Oswald was dead. Her memorial service was private. She was buried next to Lee in east Fort Worth's Rose Hill Memorial Burial Park. But her cause lives on. In one of her last letters to this author she wrote but one simple sentence: "Again—The charges against my late son Lee Harvey Oswald are false."

Oswald's early life is shrouded in innuendo and misinformation, much of it stemming from the passionate attitudes following the assassination.

Anyone who had had any contact with Oswald was hunted down and interviewed by news reporters and many were deposed by the Warren Commission.

And no one, including some family members, had anything good to say about the man accused of killing one of this nation's most popular presidents.

Some examples of misinformation include the Warren Commission's statement that Marguerite placed Lee in an "orphan's home." While in one respect this is true, a closer look shows that Mrs. Oswald had to work to earn a living for their fatherless family. Keep in mind there were no daycare centers in 1942.

Mrs. Oswald explained to news reporters years later that she placed Robert and Lee in the Bethlehem Children's Home, operated by the Lutheran Church. Admittedly it was also an orphanage, but more precisely, it was the forerunner of a daycare center. Relatives looked in on the boys and Marguerite saw them on weekends and holidays.

Lee's oldest brother, John Pic, told the Warren Commission that Lee slept with his mother until almost eleven years old, thus supplying much fodder for later psychological speculation. Mrs. Oswald's version sounds more mundane:

> [While] I was married . . . Lee had his own bed, of course, all the while. After I divorced this man [Ekdahl], all I got from this divorce was $1,500 and I paid $1,000 down on a home. Well, I had to buy furniture. I bought used furniture, and one of the boys slept on an army cot, and the other on a twin bed, and, because of the circumstances, Lee slept with me; which was a short time because then his brother joined the service and when he did, Lee took his bed. But it just implies that all through his life he slept with his mother, which isn't the case, you see. It's quite a difference.

Robert Oswald supported his mother's version of this issue by writing, "If this [sleeping arrangement] had a bad effect on Lee, I'm sure mother didn't realize it. She was simply making use of all the space she had."

Much was made of Oswald's truancy in New York during 1953–1954, as well as the psychological testing resulting from this infraction.

In the summer of 1952, shortly before Lee's thirteenth birthday, he and his mother had gone to live with his half-brother, John Pic, and his wife in New York City, where Pic was stationed with the Coast Guard. There were reports of fights and divisions within the family and by the start of the school year, Lee and his mother had moved into their own apartment in the Bronx.

This whole scenario is problematic, as there appears to have been a Lee Oswald attending school in both New York and New Orleans at this same time. The Lee in New York was teased in junior high school because he wore jeans and spoke with a Texas accent, so he began staying away. However, unlike most truants who ended up in pools halls or street gangs, Lee continued his education on his own, frequenting the local library and the zoo. Finally caught, the youngster was handed over for psychiatric observation to an institution called Youth House. Here he stayed from April 16 until May 7, 1953. Mrs. Oswald said it was only after having both her gifts and her person searched for cigarettes and narcotics that she realized Youth House was one step short of jail. She said her son implored her, "Mother, I want to get out of here. There are children in here who have killed people and smoke. I want to get out."

While under the care of the state, Oswald was given psychiatric tests. The results were essentially inconclusive. They showed him to be a bright and inquisitive young man who was somewhat tense, withdrawn, and hesitant to talk about himself or his feelings.

Even the Warren Report, which generally tried to depict Oswald in the worst possible light, conceded:

> Contrary to reports that appeared after the assassination, the psychiatric examination did not indicate that Lee Oswald was a potential assassin, potentially dangerous, that "his outlook on life had strongly paranoid overtones," or that he should be institutionalized.

Yet this innocuous event was used against Oswald in a widely publicized 1993 book by Gerald Posner titled *Case Closed*. Posner quoted Youth House staff psychiatrist Dr. Renatus Hartogs as declaring young Oswald "to have definite traits of dangerousness." Posner said Hartogs "vividly remembered Oswald eleven years later when he testified to the Warren Commission." However, Hartogs, who came to the United States from Germany just before World War II and became a citizen in 1945, actually told the Commission he only "vaguely" remembered Oswald but found him "polite" and "in full contact with reality." When asked if he had any independent recollection of the Oswald interview, Hartogs replied, "I was able to reconstruct the picture of the boy." Contradicting the Warren Report, Hartogs told Posner he recommended Oswald be institutionalized. But then he also failed to recall young Oswald until well after the assassination when a *New York Times* reporter came to him and asked if he had examined young Lee. "I said that I did not know for sure, but it is possible. . . . Then very soon the FBI came in here and said you were the doctor who examined Oswald and from then on I knew for sure that it was me."

According to the official history, after his experience in Youth House there were no further truancy problems with young Lee. In January 1954, Lee and his mother returned to New Orleans, where he finished the ninth grade and began the tenth. Upon arriving in New Orleans, the Oswalds lived initially with Mrs. Oswald's sister and her husband, Lillian and Charles "Dutz" Murret, before finding an apartment of their own.

Everyone who knew Oswald as a youth agrees that he was somewhat introverted and was what could be best described as a "bookworm." His interests were varied, including animals, astronomy, classic literature, and eventually, politics. Reading comic books and listening to radio and TV were also among his favorite pastimes.

Robert Oswald later recalled:

One of his favorite [TV] programs was "I Led Three Lives," the story of Herbert Philbrick, the FBI informant who posed as a communist spy. In the early 1950's Lee watched that show every week without fail. When I left home to join the Marines, he was still watching the reruns.

There can be little doubt that the well-read but lonely young Oswald spent much of his time daydreaming, fantasizing about being an important person someday.

Oswald appears to have been drawn at an early age to the epic and intense ideological struggle between communism and democratic capitalism. He claimed his first contact with communist ideology came with a pamphlet handed to him on a New York street corner. In a Moscow interview shortly after arriving in Russia, Oswald told newspaper reporter Aline Mosby, "I'm a Marxist. . . . I became interested about the age of 15. From an ideological viewpoint. An old lady handed me a pamphlet about saving the Rosenbergs. . . . I looked at that paper and I still remember it for some reason, I don't know why."

Julius and Ethel Rosenberg had been convicted of passing atomic bomb secrets to the Russians in a celebrated—and still controversial—case beginning in 1950, when Oswald was only twelve. They were executed on June 19, 1953.

However, this story of early interest in communism must be taken with a large grain of salt. After all, this is simply what Oswald told a reporter at a time he was trying hard to prove he was a devout communist supporter so he would be accepted into Russia.

But this one obscure statement to one reporter on one occasion was turned into a realistic scene cemented in the public's mind by celebrated author Don Delillo in his 1988 book *Libra*, a top contender for the National Book Award. It illustrates how an unsubstantiated fact can be impressed on the public, much like the many depictions of an Oswald character perched in the sixth-floor window with a rifle.

His brother Robert also expressed puzzlement over this story, writing:

If Lee was deeply interested in Marxism in the summer of 1955, he said nothing about it to me. During my brief visit with him in New Orleans, I never saw any books on the subject in the apartment on Exchange Place. Never, in my presence, did he read anything that I recognized as communist literature. I was totally surprised when the information about his interest in Marxism came out, at the time of his defection to Russia.

In New Orleans, Oswald's study of communism intensified, according to the Warren Commission. Strangely enough, at the same time he made a patriotic move—joining the Civil Air Patrol (CAP).

Marguerite Oswald told this author about another fascinating incident. She said one day after junior high school, Lee arrived home in the company of a military officer who said Lee was a self-starter, an independent sort but bright—just the sort of young man the military was looking for. Could Oswald's recruitment into military intelligence—or at least his becoming a person of interest to them—have begun that early in his life?

But it was in New Orleans that young Oswald made one of the most intriguing connections of his life. And it may have been in the Civil Air Patrol that his procommunism posturing was truly born.

Oswald's Library Card

It has been established that Oswald's CAP leader was a mysterious character named David W. Ferrie. Ferrie, an airline pilot, private investigator, and outspoken right-winger, went on to have connections with reputed Mafia boss Carlos Marcello, anti-Castro Cuban groups, former FBI agent Guy Banister and his anti-Castro activities, and the CIA. For years, supporters of the lone-assassin theory argued fervently against any connection between Ferrie and Oswald despite the fact that the House Select Committee on Assassinations interviewed the former recruit instructor for Oswald's Lakefront CAP unit, Jerry Paradis, who told them, "Oswald and Ferrie were in the unit together. I know they were there because I was there. . . . I'm not saying that they may have been together. I'm saying it is a certainty."

This argument abruptly ended when a PBS documentary broadcast a photograph of the pair together at a CAP function. Ferrie will be discussed at length in other sections of this book.

Could Ferrie, who reportedly used his CAP position to establish homosexual contacts with young boys, have influenced the fifteen-year-old Oswald to begin making a procommunist "cover" for himself with an eye toward becoming a US agent?

Did Ferrie seek to take advantage of the impressionable young Oswald with stories of using his intelligence contacts to help Oswald enter the exciting world of espionage? Considering Ferrie's known homosexuality and intelligence connections, this speculation is not far-fetched.

We may never know, however, since in 1967 Ferrie was found dead in his New Orleans apartment the day after being released from protective custody by District Attorney Jim Garrison, who named Ferrie as his chief suspect in a plot to assassinate President Kennedy and described him as "one of history's most important individuals."

One particularly puzzling incident involved David Ferrie's library card, which provided tantalizing evidence that the connection between the two continued up to the assassination.

Within hours of Kennedy's assassination, an employee of former FBI agent Guy Banister contacted New Orleans authorities and said both Banister and Ferrie had been in touch with Oswald. Oswald used the same address—554 Camp Street—as Banister's office on some of his Fair Play for Cuba material. Banister also was a supporter of right-wing causes and had been assisting anti-Castro Cubans through his New Orleans private detective agency.

Authorities could not immediately locate Ferrie. Sometime later, Ferrie told New Orleans police he had driven to Texas the night of the assassination to go goose hunting. However, subsequent investigation of Ferrie's companions revealed that they had decided not to hunt geese but, instead, had gone to a Houston skating rink where Ferrie spent two hours at a pay telephone making and receiving calls.

One of Ferrie's friends told New Orleans police that shortly after Kennedy's assassination, an attorney named C. Wray Gill had come to Ferrie's home and mentioned that when Oswald was arrested in Dallas, he was carrying a library card with Ferrie's name on it.

Gill, an attorney for Carlos Marcello, promised to act on Ferrie's behalf upon his return to New Orleans. On the evening of the Sunday that Jack Ruby killed Oswald, Ferrie contacted Gill, who then accompanied Ferrie to the authorities the next day. Ferrie denied knowing anything about Oswald or the assassination and was released.

However, one of Oswald's former neighbors in New Orleans, Doris Eames, and Ferrie's former building manager, Mrs. Jesse Garner, later recalled Ferrie visiting them both after the assassination asking about a library card. And Oswald's former landlady said Ferrie came to her asking about the library card just hours after the assassination and *before* the bizarre Texas trip. After all the furor over the library card, there is nothing in the official record indicating such a card was ever found in Oswald's possession. Yet when they questioned Ferrie, the Secret Service reportedly asked if he had loaned his library card to Oswald.

Could such a library card have disappeared from Oswald's belongings while in Dallas police custody? It certainly would not be the only such incident—an incriminating photograph of Oswald was discovered after nearly fifteen years among the possessions of a retired Dallas policeman. And if such a card existed, it would have been strong evidence that a relationship between Oswald and Ferrie continued long after young Oswald moved away from New Orleans.

In the fall of 1955, Oswald began the tenth grade at Warren Easton High School in New Orleans but dropped out soon after his birthday in October. He had his mother sign a false affidavit stating he was seventeen and he tried to join the Marine Corps. Undoubtedly he was looking forward to Marine training in San Diego. His brother Robert, who had joined the Marines three years earlier, had given Lee his training manual. His mother later recalled, "He knew it by heart."

His desire to join the Marines was decidedly odd if we are supposed to believe, as the Warren Commission did, that he was a full-blown Marxist by this time. It makes more sense to believe that Oswald eagerly looked forward to serving in the military because he already knew that plans were being made for his service in intelligence. But his hopes were dashed when the recruiting authorities failed to believe the affidavit. Oswald had to wait another year for his chance at the Marines. His mother noted, "Lee lived for the time that he would become seventeen years old to join the Marines—that whole year." Yet, during that time, he continued to build an identity as a communist sympathizer.

During a meeting of the New Orleans Amateur Astronomy Association, he began expounding on the virtues of communism, saying communism was the only way of life for the workers and that he was looking for a communist cell to join but couldn't find one. Another time, he was kicked out of the home of a friend after the friend's father overheard him praising the communist system.

Some have interpreted this penchant for communism as sincere and as evidence of how deeply disturbed Oswald had become. However, when viewed from another side, there is the real possibility that—believing the promises of Captain Ferrie that the adventuresome world of spies lay ahead of him and visualizing himself as another Herbert Philbrick—Oswald was already concocting a procommunist cover. After all, to catch a communist, you had to play like one.

Up until his meeting with Ferrie his interest in politics and ideology had been no different from that of any other bright kid. And his family had a tradition of honorable military service. The questions over Oswald's regard for communism intensified after he entered the Marine Corps.

Semper Fidelis

Six days after his seventeenth birthday, Oswald was sworn into the US Marines, whose motto is Semper Fidelis, Latin for "always faithful."

On October 26, 1956, Oswald arrived at the Marine Corps Recruit Depot in San Diego, California. Here he completed basic training with no apparent problems, although his marksmanship on the rifle range was less than what was desired by his fellow Marines. He failed to qualify on his first test.

Former Marine Sherman Cooley recalled that Oswald was given the name "Shitbird" because on his first test he couldn't qualify on the M-1 rifle. Cooley said, "It was a disgrace not to qualify and we gave him holy hell." More than fifty Marines who served with Oswald were interviewed by author Henry Hurt in the early 1980s and all said Oswald's proficiency with a rifle was laughable. In a later interview, Cooley was even more explicit: "If I had to pick one man in the whole United States to shoot me, I'd pick Oswald. I saw the man shoot. There's no way he could have ever learned to shoot well enough to do what they accused him of doing in Dallas."

Another Marine buddy, Nelson Delgado, also has publicly spoken of Oswald's ineptness with a rifle. After the assassination, Delgado told investigators that during his initial Marine training, Oswald was often "gigged" for having a dirty rifle and that when the unit went to the rifle range, Oswald got "Maggie's drawers"—a red flag signifying that he hadn't even hit the target, much less the bull's eye.

However, when Delgado tried to tell this to the FBI after the assassination, he claimed, "They attacked my competence to judge his character and shooting ability and criticized my efforts to teach him Spanish." Hounded and fearful, Delgado finally moved his family to England because "the conspirators may think I know more than I do."

In a second round of testing, Oswald managed to qualify as a "sharpshooter" by only two points in December. Sharpshooter is the second of three grades of marksmanship. He did not do nearly so well when he tested a third time for the record shortly before leaving the Marines. Then, he barely made "marksman," the lowest grade.

On January 20, 1957, he completed basic training and went on to Camp Pendleton, California, where he completed advanced infantry training. While learning combat skills, Oswald reportedly continued to speak favorably of communism—an odd circumstance for the Marines in the 1950s unless he was still trying to establish a procommunist cover. Odder still is that at no time did any of Oswald's Marine superiors note for the record his displays of procommunist sentiment.

During this time, despite his procommunist provocations, Oswald apparently was liked well enough by his fellow Marines, who called him "Ozzie Rabbit" after a TV cartoon character "Oswald the Rabbit."

In March 1957, Oswald reported to the Naval Air Technical Training Center in Jacksonville, Florida, although other evidence indicated an Oswald remained at Camp Pendleton until May. The Oswald in Florida studied to be a radar air controller, a job given only to men with higher-than-average intelligence. This job also required a security clearance of "Confidential," which Oswald obtained at the time he was promoted to private first class.

Daniel Patrick Powers, who was with the Oswald in Jacksonville, recalled that Oswald used almost all his weekend passes to go to New Orleans, presumably to visit his mother. However, Mrs. Oswald was in Texas at the time and relatives in New Orleans could recall only one phone call from Oswald.

Could he have been gaining more advice from Captain Ferrie or someone else on how to concoct a procommunist cover in preparation for becoming a spy?

According to military records, Oswald graduated May 3 and was sent to Keesler Air Force Base in Mississippi, where he completed an Aircraft Control and Warning Operator Course.

After finishing seventh in a class of fifty, Oswald was given a Military Occupational Specialty (MOS) of Aviation Electronics Operator and, after a brief leave, was sent to the Marine Corps Air Station at El Toro, California. He stayed there until shipped to Japan aboard the USS *Bexar* on August 22. Shipmates noticed that Oswald read *Leaves of Grass* by Walt Whitman, and other "good type of literature."

Oswald Overseas

Upon arriving in Japan, the young Marine was sent about twenty-five miles southwest of Tokyo to the air base at Atsugi, home of the First Marine Aircraft Wing—and one of two bases where the then top-secret U-2 spy plane flights were originating. Also at Atsugi was an innocuous group of buildings housing what was known only as the "Joint Technical Advisory Group." In reality, this was the CIA main operational base in the Far East and speculation has arisen that this was where the young Oswald entered the real world of spying.

During his duty hours, Oswald sat in a hot, crowded, semicircular radar control room known as the "bubble" and intently watched his radarscope for signs of Russian or Chinese aircraft crossing into Allied airspace. The job's monotony was broken only by an occasional unidentified aircraft and the strange plane code-named "Race Car."

The radar operators would overhear Race Car asking for wind information at 90,000 feet. They at first thought this was some sort of joke, since the world altitude record at that time was only slightly more than 65,000 and the radar height-finding antenna read only up to 45,000.

However, slowly the men of Oswald's unit, Marine Air Control Squadron No. 1, realized that they were overhearing conversations from the strange-looking aircraft that they would see wheeled out of a large nearby hangar and scream into the air. When asked about the craft, the officers would say only that it was a "utility plane." The men didn't know this utility plane, or U-2, was being used to penetrate Soviet and Chinese airspace to photograph military and industrial targets.

Oswald seemed to show particular interest in Race Car and other "secrets" of Atsugi. One Marine recalled seeing Oswald taking photographs of the base and he showed special interest during unit briefings on classified material.

Just as he had gone off alone to New Orleans, Oswald began making two-day visits to Tokyo. Years later, Oswald reportedly confided that he made contact with a small group of Japanese communists in Tokyo while in the Marines. Even Warren Commission lawyers W. David Slawson and William T. Coleman Jr. stated in a report that was classified for a time, "There is the possibility that Oswald came into contact with communist agents at that time."

Oswald told a friend at the time that he was having an affair with a Japanese girl who worked as a hostess in a Tokyo nightclub called the Queen Bee.

This was an intriguing connection indeed, for the Queen Bee was one of the three most expensive nightspots in Tokyo. An evening at the Queen Bee could cost up to $100. It catered especially to officers and pilots—including U-2 pilots, according to author Edward Jay Epstein. It was believed that the hostesses of the Queen Bee, one hundred of the most beautiful women in Tokyo, were using their charms to gain information from American servicemen.

It was a decidedly odd meeting place for Oswald, who was making less than $85 a month, with much of that being sent back to help support his mother.

Was the poor Marine private Oswald being used to gather intelligence or was Oswald testing his intelligence abilities to infiltrate communist agents in the Queen Bee? The answer to this question may have come when author/researcher Mark Lane interviewed one of Oswald's former Marine pals from Atsugi.

David Bucknell, who was never interviewed by the Warren Commission, told of an incident in which he and Oswald went for beers at a bar near Santa Ana, California, where they were both stationed in 1959. While sitting there, the two Marines were approached by two women who engaged them in conversation. According to Bucknell, later that day Oswald said this incident reminded him of a similar experience at Atsugi. According to Oswald's story, he was sitting alone in a Japanese bar when an attractive woman joined him and began asking questions regarding his work at Atsugi. Since his work involved the highly secret U-2 plane, Oswald reported this meeting to his superior officer. Soon this officer arranged a meeting between Oswald and a man in civilian clothes. Oswald told Bucknell the man explained that Oswald could do his country a great service by giving false information to the woman, a known KGB agent. Oswald agreed and thus became an intelligence operative. Oswald said he had been encouraged to continue meeting the woman and was given money to spend at the Queen Bee.

While no US intelligence agency has admitted it, there is further evidence to suggest that he was indeed used as an agent. Sergeant Gerry Patrick Hemming, who served in Japan with Oswald and later joined anti-Castro Cubans, said he was recruited into the CIA while in Japan and, while Oswald never said so, based on conversations between the two, he believed the same thing happened to Oswald.

A former CIA finance officer, James Wilcott, testified to the House Select Committee on Assassinations that colleagues told him that Oswald was a secret operative for the spy agency in Japan. Wilcott, who served in the CIA from 1957 through 1966, said after Kennedy's assassination he had several conversations with CIA personnel involved in covert operations. He said, based on these conversations and his experience of paying CIA funds to secret operations through the use of code names, or "cryptos," he became convinced that Oswald was brought into the CIA while serving as a radar operator in Japan and later was sent to infiltrate Russia as a spy.

When CIA officials denied these charges—one went so far as to suggest that Oswald was actually recruited by the Soviet KGB while in Japan—the committee decided not to believe Wilcott.

Another tantalizing piece of evidence that Oswald was involved in intelligence work while stationed in Japan comes from his Marine Corps medical records. Those records show that on September 16, 1958, Oswald was treated for "urethritis, acute, due to gonococcus." Gonorrhea is a venereal disease condemned loudly by the military. For servicemen, a case of gonorrhea often results in disciplinary measures. However, Oswald's medical record states, "Origin: In line of duty, not due to own misconduct." The fact that Oswald was absolved of any responsibility in contracting gonorrhea astounds service veterans and is strong evidence that his extracurricular activities had the blessings of the military, if not of the CIA.

Another small but eye-opening revelation came from secret meetings of the Warren Commission. General counsel J. Lee Rankin—armed with initial reports from the military—told Commission members two months after the assassination, "We are trying to run that down, to find out what he studied at the Monterey School of the Army in the way of languages." The Monterey School, now called the Defense Language Institute, is one of the government schools for giving sophisticated and rapid language courses. Rankin's remark, made public only after a Freedom of Information

Act suit, seems to imply that the Commission had knowledge of Oswald's attending courses at Monterey.

And it is certainly easier to believe that Oswald got a crash course in the Russian language in the military than to believe that this high-school dropout learned one of the world's most difficult languages by reading books and listening to records, as implied by the Warren Commission. Fellow Marines testified they could not recall Oswald listening to any language records.

It is possible that undercover work was behind a strange shooting incident that took place just as his unit was scheduled to be transferred to the Philippines in late 1957. On October 27, Oswald was gathering gear from his locker when reportedly a .22-caliber derringer fell onto the floor and discharged, grazing his left elbow. As nearby Marines rushed into his room, all Oswald would say was, "I believe I shot myself."

Before the incident, Oswald had told a friend, George Wilkins, that he had bought the derringer from a mail-order firm in the United States. At least two of the Marines present, Thomas Bagshaw and Pete Connor, now claim the bullet missed Oswald altogether. Others at the time had the impression that Oswald shot himself in an attempt to prevent being transferred to the Philippines. If that was the case, it failed. Although absent almost three weeks for medical treatment, he was returned to duty just in time to ship out with his unit on November 20.

The maneuvers of Oswald's unit in the Philippines and South China Sea were largely uneventful. While the unit was on Corregidor Island, actor John Wayne stopped in briefly and a photograph was taken of him. In a background doorway stands Marine Oswald, who was serving his third straight month on mess duty.

His lengthy hospital stay following the derringer incident and the amount of time he spent pulling KP (kitchen police) may indicate time away from his regular unit spent in intelligence training. According to witnesses, his elbow wound was very minor, yet Oswald spent nearly three weeks in a hospital. More time gaps in his military career were to come.

Back at Atsugi, Oswald was court-martialed for possessing an unregistered weapon—the derringer. On April 11, 1958, he was found guilty and sentenced to twenty days at hard labor, forfeiture of $50 in pay, and reduced back to the rank of private. His confinement was suspended for six months on the condition that he stay out of trouble.

It was about this time that Oswald put in for a hardship discharge. As this application was being processed, there apparently was a need for more time away from his unit for additional intelligence training. This may have been accomplished by an incident that began in the Enlisted Men's Club at Atsugi. Oswald, who heretofore had not been known as violent, tried to pick a fight with Technical Sergeant Miguel Rodriguez, allegedly the man who had assigned him to so much KP duty. Rodriguez failed to rise to the bait.

On June 20, Oswald sought out Rodriguez at the Bluebird Club in Yamato and again tried to fight with the sergeant. After Oswald poured a drink on Rodriguez, military police intervened, and the next day, Rodriguez signed a complaint against Oswald. At the court-martial, Oswald acted as his own defense, claiming he was drunk and spilled the drink on Rodriguez accidentally. Rodriguez said then—and after the assassination—that Oswald had not been drunk and had poured the drink on him deliberately.

The judge ruled that Oswald was guilty of using "provoking words" to a noncommissioned officer and sentenced him to twenty-eight days in the brig and forfeiture of $55. Furthermore, his previous suspension of sentence was revoked and Oswald supposedly went to the brig until August 13, a period of more than forty-five days. Only one Marine who was in the Atsugi brig during this time recalled seeing Oswald and he said during this brief encounter Oswald was wearing civilian clothes.

After his release, several Marines commented that Oswald seemed different. Joseph D. Macedo said he found him "a completely changed person." Others said that where "Ozzie Rabbit" had been extroverted and fun-filled, this new Oswald was cold and withdrawn. It may well be right here that a new Oswald—an entirely different man—was substituted for the New Orleans–born Marine. See the section "Was Oswald Really Oswald?"

Meanwhile, a previously granted extension of overseas duty was canceled and it appeared that Oswald would soon be on his way home. However, in September 1958, the Chinese communists began making moves against the Nationalist Chinese islands of Quemoy and Matsu and there was a general mobilization. Oswald accompanied his unit to Formosa (now Taiwan). Not long after their arrival on the island, Oswald was assigned guard duty. About midnight, the officer of the guard, Lieutenant Charles R. Rhodes, heard several shots. Running to the scene, Rhodes found Oswald slumped against a tree holding his M-1 rifle in his lap. Rhodes recalled, "When I got to him, he was shaking and crying. He said he had seen men in the woods and that he challenged them and then started shooting. . . . He kept saying he couldn't bear being on guard duty."

Almost immediately, Oswald was shipped back to Atsugi, arriving on October 5, 1958, according to official reports. Years later, Rhodes said he still believed that Oswald planned the shooting incident as a ploy to get himself transferred back to Japan. Rhodes never received any explanation for the willingness of the Marine Corps to go along with this "ploy" except that Oswald was being returned for "medical treatment."

Recall the medical records concerning Oswald's gonorrhea contracted "in line of duty." However, this record is dated September 16, 1958, two days *after* Oswald officially left with his unit for Formosa.

This, as well as several other discrepancies in Oswald's military service records, has caused some assassination researchers to believe that more than one man was using the name Oswald during this time. Perhaps more time was needed to prepare Oswald for upcoming intelligence missions.

Back at Atsugi and with his unit gone, Oswald was temporarily assigned to a Marine squadron at Iwakuni, an air base about 430 miles southwest of Tokyo. Here, quite by accident, he came into contact with Owen Dejanovich, a Marine who had attended radar school with him. Dejanovich tried to renew the acquaintanceship but was rebuffed by Oswald, who avoided the one man who had known him previously. Dejanovich also found Oswald changed. He said Oswald kept referring to the Marines as "you Americans" and raving about "American imperialism" and "exploitation." He also noticed that Oswald was keeping company with locals again, this time with a "round-eyed Russian girlfriend."

Oswaldskovich the Marine

On November 2, 1958, Oswald boarded the USS *Barrett* for the two-week trip to San Francisco. On November 19, he took a thirty-day leave, traveling by bus to Fort Worth, where he stayed with his mother, but he spent most of his time hunting squirrels and rabbits.

On December 22, he was assigned to Marine Air Control Squadron No. 9 at El Toro, California. Here he was one of seven enlisted men and three officers who formed a radar crew. According to the Warren Report, "This work probably gave him access to certain kinds of classified material, some of which, such as aircraft call signs and radio frequencies, was changed after his [attempted] defection to Russia."

It was here that Oswald's public embracing of communism reached new heights. He would answer questions with *da* or *nyet* and address fellow Marines as "Comrade." When playing chess, he always wanted the red pieces, which he referred to as the "victorious Red Army." His Marine companions began calling him "Oswaldskovich."

One of his fellow Marines, Kerry Thornley, was so impressed by this "eightball" that he later wrote a novel using a character based on Oswald. He noted:

> What causes me to have second thoughts about his commitment to communism is his enthusiasm for a book unpopular with the few self-admitted communists I have known, for obvious reasons. The book is George Orwell's *1984*, a severe criticism in fiction form of socialist totalitarianism. . . .
> I read *1984* and for a while decided Oswald was not truly in sympathy with Marxism. It had to be a joke, I concluded.

Marine Nelson Delgado also got along well with Oswald. Delgado, a Puerto Rican, said Oswald "treated him like an equal." Oswald and Delgado talked at length about Cuba and Fidel Castro's coming to power. After a while, Oswald began asking Delgado how he could get in touch with some Cubans.

Delgado said one day he handed Oswald a note saying he should write the Cuban embassy in Washington, DC. Not long after that, Delgado noticed that Oswald, who previously received few letters, began receiving mail several times a week and that at least some of this mail came from the Cuban consulate.

If Oswald was a genuine Marine communist, it beggars the imagination to think that his officers took no notice. In fact, Thornley told of an incident in which a young lieutenant did notice that Oswald was receiving a Russian newspaper in the mail. According to this story:

> The lieutenant grew very excited over his discovery and possibly made an open issue of Oswald's probable sympathy to the communist cause. Most of the troops . . . were very much amused at the lieutenant's having "pushed the panic button." Oswald, of course, didn't think it was so funny. But apparently the lieutenant's warnings were ignored by the command.

Were these warnings ignored or were higher-ups more knowledgeable about Oswald's activities?

Another hint as to Oswald's true allegiances may be found in an odd incident involving his friend Thornley, with whom Oswald spent many hours in ideological and philosophical discussions.

Thornley told the Warren Commission that one day while he and Oswald were preparing for a military parade and were remarking about the stupidity of the thing, Oswald said it made him angry. Thornley then said:

> "Well, come the revolution you will change all that" . . . at which time [Oswald] looked at me like a betrayed Caesar and screamed, "Not you, too, Thornley!" And I remember his voice cracked as he said this. He was definitely disturbed at what I had said and I didn't really think I had said that much. . . . I never said anything to him again and he never said anything to me again.

This sounds more like a person deeply hurt that a good friend would seriously believe him to be a communist than like a communist sympathizer angered over an innocuous jibe.

James Botelho, today a California judge, was a roommate of Oswald's during his stay at El Toro. Botelho even once took Oswald home to meet his parents. He has never bought the idea that Oswald turned communist. In an interview with author/researcher Mark Lane, Botelho stated, "I'm very conservative now and I was at least as conservative at that time. Oswald was not a communist or a Marxist. If he was I would have taken violent action against him and so would many of the other Marines in the unit."

Whatever his true beliefs about communism, Oswald at this time knew bigger things were looming on his horizon.

In the spring of 1959, he had applied to study philosophy at the Albert Schweitzer College in Switzerland and had been accepted. In a cryptic letter to his brother, he wrote, "Pretty soon I'll be getting out of the Corps and I know what I want to be and how I'm going to be it."

Years later, Marine Bucknell told Mark Lane that during 1959 he, Oswald, and other Marines at the El Toro base were ordered to report to the military Criminal

Investigation Division (CID). There a civilian tried to recruit those present for an intelligence operation against "communists" in Cuba.

Oswald was selected to make several more trips to CID and later told Bucknell that the civilian was the same man who had been his intelligence contact at Atsugi. Sometime later, Oswald confided to Bucknell that he was to be discharged from the Marines and go to Russia. Oswald said he was being sent there by American intelligence and that he would return to America in 1961 as a hero.

Judge Botelho, Oswald's former roommate, told of his reaction to Oswald's trip to Russia:

> Well, when Oswald's presence in the Soviet Union was made public, it was the talk of everyone who knew him at the base. First of all, I was aware of the fact that the radio codes and other codes were not changed and that Oswald knew all of them. That made me suspicious. I knew Oswald was not a communist and was, in fact, anti-Soviet. Then, when no real investigation about Oswald occurred at the base, I was sure that Oswald was on an intelligence assignment in Russia. . . . Two civilians dropped in [at El Toro], asked a few questions, took no written statements, and recorded no interviews with witnesses. It was the most casual of investigations. It was a cover-investigation so that it could be said that there had been an investigation. . . . Oswald, it was said, was the only Marine ever to defect from his country to another country, a communist country, during peacetime. That was a major event. When the Marine Corps and American intelligence decided not to probe the reasons for the "defection," I knew then what I know now: Oswald was on an assignment in Russia for American intelligence.

Plans for a trip to Russia apparently had been made for Oswald and the Marines, a branch of the US Navy Department, seemed oddly obliging.

On August 17, 1959, Oswald applied for a dependency discharge on the grounds that his mother needed his support. This application was accompanied by affidavits from his mother, an attorney, a doctor, and two friends—all supplied by his mother—stating she had been injured at work in December 1958 and was unable to support herself. Later investigation showed a candy box had fallen on her nose and that she had not even bothered to see a doctor until well after the incident. Nevertheless, within two weeks, to the surprise of his fellow Marines, Oswald's request was approved and he was released from service on September 11.

On September 4, Oswald applied for a passport, plainly stating that he might travel to various countries including Russia and Cuba. This, of course, was in opposition to his claim that he was going home to care for his injured mother. His passport was "routinely" issued six days later, just in time for his exit from the Marines.

After a brief stopover in Texas with his mother, Oswald withdrew $203 from his only known bank account and continued on to New Orleans, where he purchased a ticket for Le Havre, France, on the freighter *Marion Lykes* for $220.75.

He had told his mother he was going to New Orleans to work for an import-export firm, but in a letter mailed just before he sailed, he wrote:

I have booked passage on a ship to Europe. I would have had to sooner or later and I think its best I go now. Just remember above all else that my values are different from Robert's or yours. It is difficult to tell you how I feel. Just remember, this is what I must do. I did not tell you about my plans because you could hardly be expected to understand.

Until the day she died, Oswald's mother maintained her son was an agent of the US government.

On September 20, 1959, Oswald left on the first leg of a journey that would take him to his destiny—via Russia.

Russians

In the summer of 1959, Soviet premier Nikita Khrushchev visited the United States. Both Khrushchev and his Western counterpart, US president Dwight Eisenhower, seemed sincere in wanting to ease the tensions between their two countries.

A summit meeting was scheduled for mid-May 1960. It might have produced a limited nuclear-test-ban treaty, already foreseen as the first major accord of the Cold War.

But it was not to be. On May 1, traditionally celebrated in Russia as May Day, CIA pilot Francis Gary Powers was captured alive after his U-2 spy plane crashed in the Soviet Union following an explosion.

Khrushchev was furious, yet he tried to give Eisenhower latitude in disclaiming any knowledge of the incident. He stated that the U-2 flight may have been the work of "American aggressive circles" trying to "torpedo the Paris summit, or, at any rate, prevent an agreement for which the whole world is waiting."

After days of half-truths and evasions, Eisenhower finally admitted that the spy plane was acting on his orders and took responsibility for the fiasco, just as John Kennedy would take responsibility for the disastrous Bay of Pigs Invasion a year later. It has been reported that Eisenhower actually had ordered the U-2 overflights halted but this order was thwarted within his own command structure.

And questions still surround the U-2 incident, especially with students of history. For example, in *The People's Almanac* David Wallechinsky and Irving Wallace note, "It is possible that certain US military leaders deployed Powers purposely to sabotage the peace talks which Eisenhower himself acutely desired."

Oswald and the U-2

Francis Gary Powers and his ill-fated U-2 spy plane were brought down six months after a former Marine named Lee Harvey Oswald arrived in Moscow and told an

American embassy official he planned to give the Soviets classified information he had gained as a radar operator in the Marine Corps.

Richard E. Snyder, a CIA intelligence operative serving as senior consular officer at the Moscow embassy, recalled that Oswald went so far as to state that he knew something that would be of "special interest" to Soviet intelligence.

What "special interest" information did Oswald have? The Russians had known about the U-2 program for some time and their antiaircraft missiles were capable of shooting down the high-flying craft. What the Soviets lacked was detailed altitude information on the U-2 that would have allowed them to accurately control their missiles at great altitudes. Oswald, who served as a radar operator at Atsugi, Japan, one of the staging bases for the U-2 flights, had that information.

After being swapped for a Soviet spy, Powers returned to the United States and wrote a book about his ordeal titled *Operation Overflight*. He pointed out Oswald's claim that he had information for the Soviets and implied that if indeed Oswald gave information pertaining to U-2 operational altitudes and radar techniques used during its flight, the Russians may have learned enough to enable them to shoot down the U-2. Powers also said his Soviet interrogators seemed to have special knowledge about the Atsugi base, although Powers maintained he had never been stationed there.

For years the Warren Commission withheld from the American public files detailing Oswald's connection with the U-2 flights.

Some people familiar with the U-2 incident believe the plane may have been downed due to sabotage. In 1977, Powers was killed when his helicopter, used to report news for a Los Angeles television station, ran out of gas and crashed. His death was ironic in that fuel consumption was of critical importance to U-2 pilots.

There are two tantalizing clues that Oswald may have indeed had some connection with the U-2 incident. In a letter to his brother, Oswald wrote regarding Powers, "He seemed to be a nice bright American-type fellow when I saw him in Moscow." There is no explanation of how or when Oswald might have seen Powers, particularly since officially Oswald never returned to Moscow after being sent to Minsk in 1960.

After his return to the United States, Oswald told former Army security employee Dennis Ofstein, a fellow worker at Jaggers-Childs-Stovall, the Dallas graphic arts firm with government contracts where Oswald worked in the fall of 1962, that he had viewed Russian jets in Moscow on May Day. Of Oswald's three May Days spent in Russia, the only one unaccounted for is May 1, 1960—the day the U-2 was captured.

Because of the U-2 flights during this time, Soviet intelligence was extremely interested in American defectors, because of both the knowledge they might have and the suspicion that most, if not all, were spies trying to infiltrate the country.

Apparently American intelligence was equally curious to learn about the Soviets. According to author Anthony Summers, who studied documents from both the

State Department and the House Select Committee on Assassinations, only two US enlisted men defected to Russia between 1945 and 1959. Yet in the eighteen months prior to January 1960, no fewer than nine defected, five of them US Army men from West Germany and two Navy men.

All these defectors, including at least three civilians, had backgrounds in the military or in sensitive defense work. It is known that, like Oswald, at least four of these returned to the United States after a few years.

Robert E. Webster—Another Oswald?

The case of Robert E. Webster, an American who told officials he was defecting to Russia less than two weeks before Oswald, is worth considering since there appear to be similarities between the two.

Webster, a former Navy man, was a young plastics expert who simply failed to return home with colleagues after working at an American trade exhibition in Moscow. He had been an employee of the Rand Development Corporation, one of the first US companies to sell technical products to Russia.

Although Rand Development was thought to be separate from the more notorious Rand Corporation—the CIA think-tank front where Daniel Ellsberg copied the Pentagon Papers—there is some evidence of connections between the two. The firms were at one time located across the street from each other in New York City; Rand Development held several CIA contracts; and several top officials of Rand Development—president Henry Rand, George Bookbinder, and Christopher Bird—were later connected with the CIA.

While in Russia, Webster took a Soviet girl as common-law wife (he was already married to a woman in the United States) and the couple had a child.

Like Oswald, Webster claimed to have become disenchanted with Soviet life and he returned to the United States about the same time as Oswald. But now the story turns even stranger. Although Webster is said to have told American officials he never had any contact with Lee Harvey Oswald, when Oswald was arranging his return to the United States in 1961, he "asked [US Embassy officials] about the fate of a young man named Webster who had come to the Soviet Union shortly before he did."

And there are some intriguing connections between Webster and Oswald's wife, Marina. Years later in America, Marina told an acquaintance that her husband had defected after working at an American exhibition in Moscow. This, of course, reflects Webster's story, not Oswald's. After the assassination, when American intelligence was looking into Marina's background, they discovered an address in her address book was that of Webster's Leningrad apartment.

Were Webster and Oswald two of several fake defectors being sent into Russia during 1958 and 1959? The parallels of their stories are striking. Author Summers talked with former CIA officer Victor Marchetti, who analyzed Soviet military activities during the time Oswald went to Russia, and was told:

At the time, in 1959, the United States was having real difficulty in acquiring information out of the Soviet Union; the technical systems had, of course, not developed to the point that they are at today, and we were resorting to all sorts of activities. One of these activities was an ONI [Office of Naval Intelligence] program which involved three dozen, maybe forty, young men who were made to appear disenchanted, poor, American youths who had become turned off and wanted to see what communism was all about. They were sent into the Soviet Union or into Eastern Europe, with the specific intention the Soviets would pick them up and "double" them if they suspected them of being US agents, or recruit them as KGB agents. They were trained at various naval installations both here and abroad, but the operation was being run out of Nag's Head, North Carolina.

This is particularly interesting because this Navy program sounds exactly like Oswald's experience.

While Oswald was in Russia, the State Department was engaged in studying US defectors to Russia. Otto Otepka, the official in charge of the study, said one of its goals was to determine which defectors were genuine and which may have been US intelligence operatives.

In June 1963, five months prior to the Kennedy assassination, Otepka said he was ousted from his job and, in fact, barred from access to his study material on defectors, one of whom was Lee Harvey Oswald.

Asked by a researcher in 1971 whether Oswald was a real or fake defector, Otepka replied, "We had not made up our minds when . . . we were thrown out of the office."

This incident is especially troubling, for if the shutdown of the State Department investigation was because of Oswald, this is strong evidence that someone within the US government had prior knowledge of Oswald's role in the upcoming assassination.

A Phony Defection

Oswald's attempted defection to Russia was as fabricated as many other aspects of his life.

The *Marion Lykes* arrived in Le Havre, France, on October 8, 1959. Oswald arrived in Southampton, England, October 9 and, according to the Warren Commission, set off for Helsinki, Finland, arriving and checking into the Torni Hotel that same day.

However, in Oswald's passport, the British immigration stamp reads, "Embarked 10 Oct. 1959."

This presents a real problem, since the only direct flight from London to Helsinki that day did not arrive in time for Oswald to have checked into the Torni Hotel at the hour shown in the hotel's register.

The discrepancy in times has led some researchers to believe that Oswald got to Finland by some means other than public transportation—perhaps in US military aircraft. But this possibility, of course, smacks of intelligence work and was not officially investigated.

Another oddity: Throughout his life, Oswald was tight with money, usually staying in cheap rooming houses and apartments. However, once in Helsinki, he registered in the Torni Hotel, then moved the next day into the Klaus Kurki Hotel, two of the city's most expensive and luxurious lodgings.

The Warren Commission claimed Oswald then visited the Soviet consulate in Helsinki and obtained a visa in two days, which must have been some sort of record, as the Commission also determined that the shortest normal time for obtaining a visa was one week.

Oswald's visa was issued October 14 and the Commission said Oswald left by train the next day for Moscow, arriving on October 16.

However, the leading Swedish newspaper *Dagens Nyheters* reported three days after the assassination that Oswald failed to get his Soviet visa in Helsinki—information that since then has been confirmed by Swedish intelligence. The paper said Oswald instead went to Stockholm, where he obtained a visa at the Russian embassy after two days. Curiously, neither the Warren Commission nor the House Select Committee on Assassinations mentioned this side trip.

Whatever the facts, the speed and ease with which Oswald journeyed to Moscow gives the impression that more was motivating this young man than the simple desire to experience a communist state.

Arriving in Moscow by train, Oswald was taken in tow by a representative of Intourist, the official state tourist agency, who placed him in the Hotel Berlin, where he registered as a student. The next day Oswald went sightseeing with his Intourist guide, a young woman named Rima Shirokova, and promptly informed her he wanted to defect.

Despite his proclamation that he was a "communist" wanting to live in Russia, after several contacts with Soviet authorities Oswald was informed on October 21 that his visa had expired and he had two hours to leave Moscow. Faced with deportation, Oswald reportedly cut his left wrist in a suicide attempt. Conveniently, this was done just before a meeting with his Intourist guide. She found him in his hotel room and took him to a hospital. This act accomplished the same end result of the Marine shooting incident—he was out of sight in the hospital for eleven days.

He was released on October 28 and, accompanied by Shirokova, checked out of the Hotel Berlin and into the Metropole. The Warren Commission concluded, "The government undoubtedly directed him to make the change." Oswald had indeed been in touch with Soviet government officials from the Pass and Registration Office.

He remained in his hotel room three days, apparently awaiting orders from someone. He told Shirokova he was impatient, but didn't say why.

By Saturday, October 31, 1959, Oswald was ready to make his move. Striding past the Marine guards at the US embassy, he plopped his passport down in front of a receptionist and declared he had come to "dissolve his American citizenship."

He was directed to Richard E. Snyder, the second secretary and senior consular official, who tried to dissuade the young ex-Marine from his planned course of action. Oswald handed Snyder an undated, handwritten note that displayed a sophisticated knowledge of the legal subtleties concerning the revocation of citizenship. It reflected the same type of knowledge that apparently had allowed Oswald to make his journey to Moscow in a most unorthodox manner.

The note stated:

> I, Lee Harvey Oswald, do hereby request that my present citizenship in the United States of America, be revoked. . . . I take these steps for political reasons. My request for the revoking of my American citizenship is made only after the longest and most serious considerations. I affirm that my allegiance is to the Union of Soviet Socialist Republics.

Present with Snyder was John McVickar, another senior consular officer. In later years, McVickar said he felt Oswald

> was following a pattern of behavior in which he had been tutored by a person or persons unknown . . . seemed to be using words he had learned but did not fully understand. . . . In short, it seemed to me there was the possibility that he had been in contact with others before or during his Marine Corps tour who had guided him and encouraged him in his actions.

In later years Snyder himself came under suspicion of aiding Oswald in an intelligence mission when it was revealed that he had worked for the CIA—although the agency claimed it was only for a brief time in 1949.

When the House Select Committee on Assassinations looked into the matter, investigators found that Snyder's CIA file was unavailable "[as] a matter of cover." The committee found this revelation "extremely troubling."

According to the Warren Commission, Snyder did not permit Oswald to renounce his citizenship. Since it was a Saturday, Snyder explained that Oswald would have to return on a normal business day to fill out the necessary paperwork. Oswald never returned and, therefore, technically never renounced his citizenship. On November 3, Oswald sent the embassy a letter protesting its refusal to accept his renunciation of citizenship. However, he never showed up in person to pursue that act. And when embassy personnel attempted to contact Oswald, he refused to see them.

His widely publicized defection never happened.

Could the three-day wait in his hotel room have been because he had been coached not to defect unless it was on a Saturday? How could a high school dropout know all of these legalistic subtleties without being briefed by more knowledgeable persons?

Even American newswoman Priscilla Johnson, who interviewed Oswald a few days later in his hotel room, thought he "may have purposely not carried through his original intent to renounce [citizenship] in order to leave a crack open."

During this time, Oswald granted two newspaper interviews, one to Aline Mosby of UPI and the other to Johnson, who said she represented the North American Newspaper Alliance syndicate. Oswald harangued both reporters with his fervent support of Marxism and its ideals and both dutifully reported his comments in newspaper articles that appeared back in the United States.

Johnson (now Priscilla Johnson McMillan) would later write the book *Marina and Lee*, which supposedly "reveals the innermost secrets of [Marina's] life with the man who shot JFK." McMillan once was an assistant to Senator John F. Kennedy and went on to become an acknowledged expert on Soviet affairs. It is McMillan who has been primarily responsible for much of the information concerning Oswald's personal life shortly before the assassination.

There has been much speculation over the years that McMillan was operating on behalf of US intelligence when she was in contact with Oswald. She has testified that she never worked for the CIA. However, the House Select Committee on Assassinations reported that she had applied to work for the CIA in 1952, had been "debriefed" by that agency after a trip to Russia in 1962, and in fact had provided the CIA with "cultural and literary" information.

Suspicion about her increased with the release of an FBI memorandum dated November 23, 1963, in which a State Department security officer informed the FBI, "One Priscilla Johnston [*sic*] and Mrs. G. Stanley Brown also had contact with Oswald in Russia. Both these women were formerly State Department employees at the American Embassy and their contact with Oswald was official business."

By December 1959, Oswald had dropped from sight in the Soviet Union and was not heard from again for more than a year. During that time, most of what is known about Oswald's activities comes from his "Historic Diary," supposedly a day-to-day account of his life in Russia. *Life* magazine had obtained a copy of the so-called diary from *Dallas Morning News* reporter Hugh Aynesworth. Some accused Aynesworth of pilfering the document from Oswald's belongings while others thought someone passed it to the reporter to solidify Oswald's procommunist background. Aynesworth, who earlier had tried to join the CIA, has refused to reveal the diary's origin. The diary appeared to have been written long after the events described.

Even the Warren Commission had trouble with Oswald's diary, noting, "It is not an accurate guide to the details of Oswald's activities. Oswald seems not to have been concerned about the accuracy of dates and names and apparently made many of his entries subsequent to the date the events occurred."

For instance, Oswald notes in his entry for October 31, 1959—the day he visited the American embassy—that John McVickar had taken Richard Snyder's place as "head consul." This change did not take place until two years after that date, at a time Oswald was preparing to leave Russia.

In later years, experts hired by the House Select Committee on Assassinations concluded the "diary" was written entirely on the same paper and was most probably written in one or two sittings.

This fact further fuels the charge that Oswald, even while in the Soviet Union, was acting on orders from someone else. This charge was even voiced by Warren Commission general counsel J. Lee Rankin, who told Commission members in executive session, "That entire period is just full of possibilities for training, for working with the Soviets, and its agents."

Aside from the "diary," there is precious little documentation about Oswald's stay in Russia. But in early 1964, the Soviet government did provide the Warren Commission with fifteen pages of documents, including copies of Oswald's passport, a job application from a Minsk radio factory, some hospital records, and a supervisor's report from the factory.

Comrade Oswald

Although much about Oswald's life in Russia is unknown, several tantalizing pieces of information tell a decidedly different story of his sojourn there from the one previously told.

After spending New Year's Day 1960 in Moscow, Oswald reportedly was then sent to Minsk with 5,000 rubles. The money supposedly came from the Red Cross, although Oswald himself wrote that the money actually came from the Soviet MVD (the Soviet secret police) after he "denounced" the United States. He reported that he was greeted in Minsk on January 8 by no less than the mayor of the city, who promised him a rent-free apartment.

And what an apartment it was—a spacious flat with a separate living room, tile floors, and modern furniture, accommodations far beyond the means of the average Russian worker. Two private balconies overlooked a picturesque bend in the Svisloch River.

It was here that Oswald entertained his newfound Russian friends, such as Pavel Golovachev. The son of General P. Y. Golovachev, a "hero of the Soviet Union" and a man who reportedly traveled in Minsk's highest social circles, Golovachev was pictured in some of the snapshots Oswald made in his Minsk home.

Oswald was assigned duties as a "metal worker" in the Byelorussian Radio and Television factory. Here, between his wages and the continuing "Red Cross" allowance, Oswald reportedly was making more money than the factory's director.

Oswald wrote about affairs with at least five local girls, whom he would take to nearby movies, theaters, and opera. As he wrote in his "diary," he was "living big."

On a darker side, it should be noted that Minsk, along with being a somewhat cosmopolitan city by Russian standards, also was the site of an espionage training school made known to the CIA as far back as 1947. It provided a convenient red herring for those hoping to distract from Oswald's homegrown intelligence connections.

In testimony to the Warren Commission on May 14, 1964, FBI director J. Edgar Hoover said:

Just the day before yesterday information came to me indicating that there is an espionage training school outside of Minsk—I don't know whether it is true—and that he [Oswald] was trained at that school to come back to this country to become what they call a "sleeper," that is a man who will remain dormant for three or four years and in case of international hostilities rise up and be used.

Almost adjacent to this spy school is the Foreign Language Institute. In a manuscript about his life in Minsk, Oswald admitted, "I was in the Foreign Language Institute." Perhaps realizing his slip, Oswald edited this remark to read, "I was visiting friends in the Foreign Language Institute."

In addition to his money and lavish apartment, there is other evidence to suggest that Oswald was living a privileged life with his Soviet hosts. Although officially he never left Minsk and he pointed out how most Soviet citizens were prohibited from traveling far from their home, Oswald apparently traveled extensively in Russia.

Jeanne DeMohrenschildt, who along with her husband, George, befriended Oswald after his return to the United States, said he was quite interested in photography. She said he had photographs of various locations in Russia that he showed her with great pride. He also told her about his enjoyable weekends hunting. And found among his possessions was a Soviet hunting license showing he had been a member of the Belorussian Society of Hunters and Fishermen, which carried with it the privilege of owning a 16-gauge shotgun, another feat impossible for the average Russian.

About the only fact that can be stated without question concerning Oswald's life in Russia is that he lived well beyond the means of the ordinary Soviet citizen. To most researchers, this abundant life indicates some sort of special relationship with Soviet officials. The exact nature of this relationship is still unknown. However, many assassination students believe two things: one, that Oswald's fake defection to Russia may have had something to do with the downing of the U-2 spy plane on May 1, 1960, and second, whatever the purposes of his intelligence mission to Russia, it had nothing to do with the subsequent assassination of President Kennedy except to paint Oswald as a communist operative and force the Soviets into covering up any connection with the accused assassin.

Although Oswald was not heard from in Russia between December 1959 and February 1961, the wheels of the US bureaucracy were turning.

As early as November 10, 1959, the FBI, upon learning of Oswald's attempted defection, placed a "flash" notice on his fingerprint card. This served to alert bureau officials should Oswald's fingerprints turn up in any FBI investigation. It also placed his name on a watch list used in monitoring overseas communications.

By the summer of 1960, the FBI was fully alert to Oswald and to the possibility that some sort of espionage game was being played out, even to the extent of someone posing as Oswald. On June 3, 1960, FBI director Hoover wrote to the State

Department's Office of Security, warning, "Since there is a possibility that an imposter is using Oswald's birth certificate, any current information the Department of State may have concerning subject will be appreciated."

About this same time, the Marine Corps, informed that Oswald had offered to tell military secrets to the Soviets, took action. After failing to reach Oswald with certified letters, the Marine Corps officially changed Oswald's "honorable discharge" to "dishonorable" on September 13, 1960.

But it was Oswald's mother who seemed to get the swiftest reaction from queries about her son. After phone calls to the FBI and letters to her congressmen failed to turn up information about her son, Mrs. Oswald spent her small savings on a train ticket to Washington. Arriving on January 28, 1961, she called the White House wanting to speak to President Kennedy, who had been inaugurated only eight days before.

Failing to reach the president, she asked to speak to Secretary of State Dean Rusk. Instead, she was granted an immediate interview with Eugene Boster, White House Soviet affairs officer. Although she had not heard from her son in more than a year and his trip to Russia allegedly was made entirely on his own, Mrs. Oswald quoted Boster as saying, "Oh, yes, Mrs. Oswald, I'm familiar with the case." As before, she charged that her son was working for the US government and demanded that the government locate him in Russia.

On February 1, 1961, less than a week after Mrs. Oswald's Washington visit, the State Department sent a "Welfare-Whereabouts" memo to Moscow. On February 13, 1961, the US embassy in Moscow received a letter from Oswald dated February 5, stating, "I desire to return to the United States, that is if we could come to some agreement concerning the dropping of any legal proceedings against me."

Secretary Snyder was understandably astonished that Oswald should write to him just after he had been asked to locate the ex-Marine. Mrs. Oswald saw the rapidity of the response from her son as an indication the US government was in contact with her son while in Russia.

The Warren Commission attributed Oswald's sudden reappearance to mere coincidence, in light of the fact that routine queries about Oswald had not yet been initiated by the American embassy.

In his letter, Oswald again showed unusual knowledge of the legalities of citizenship. He pointed out that he had never "taken Russian citizenship" and added, "If I could show [the Soviets] my American passport, I am of the opinion they would give me an exit visa."

Perhaps recalling Hoover's memo of the previous summer, the State Department informed Snyder that Oswald's passport was to be delivered in person.

On May 16, 1961, after some written sparring with the embassy, Oswald further complicated the entire matter by writing:

Since my last letter I have gotten married. . . . My wife is Russian, born in Leningrad, she has no parents living and is quite willing to leave the Soviet

Union with me and live in the United States. . . . I would not leave here without my wife so arrangements would have to be made for her to leave at the same time I do.

Oswald was ready to return to the United States, but only with his new bride.

A Whirlwind Romance

A little more than a month after telling the American embassy that he wished to return home, Oswald met the Russian woman who would become his wife and a chief witness against him after the assassination.

Around March 17, 1961—nobody seems to be certain of the date, including Marina—Oswald attended a trade union dance at the Palace of Culture in Minsk. Here he met nineteen-year-old Marina Nikolaevna Prusakova, who was the hit of the party in a red brocade dress and hairstyle "à la Brigitte Bardot." Oswald was introduced to her as "Alik" and soon they were dancing.

Marina said they spoke Russian and she believed "Alik" to be a Soviet citizen, but from the Baltic area—Estonia, Latvia, or Lithuania—based on his accent. She was greatly surprised to learn this man was really an American named Lee Harvey Oswald.

After the dance, Oswald and Marina visited in the home of friends, where Oswald spoke up in defense of the United States, saying that while there were defects such as unemployment and discrimination, there still was "more democracy."

Oswald wrote in his "diary," We are going steady, and I decide I must have her, she puts me off, so on April 15 I propose, she accepts."

They married on April 30, less than six weeks after first meeting.

In later years, Marina exhibited a strange memory loss about many aspects of their meeting, whirlwind romance, and wedding. She told varying stories as to who first introduced her to Oswald, and then finally stated she just couldn't remember. She also told the House Select Committee on Assassinations that Oswald had proposed to her "a month and a half" before their wedding. This would mean Oswald proposed the first night they met. However, this was by no means the only inconsistency in Marina's recollections.

Marina claimed to be born on July 17, 1941, in the northern seaside town of Molotovsk. A war baby, she never knew who her father was and took her mother's name. In the book *Marina and Lee*, she suddenly revealed that she had found out that her father was a Soviet traitor named Nikolai Didenko. This may be a small matter, but it was never revealed to the Warren Commission. Her mother left her as an infant with elderly relatives in Arkhangelsk, where she grew up until rejoining her mother at age seven. By then her mother had married an electrical worker named Alexander Medvedev and by 1952, the family was living in Leningrad. Here Marina attended a pharmacist school.

Upon graduation in June 1959, she was assigned a job in a pharmaceutical warehouse, but quit after only one day and spent the rest of the summer on vacation. At the end of the summer, she went to Minsk to live with her maternal uncle, Colonel Ilya Vasilyevich Prusakov, a ranking officer in the MVD (the Soviet Ministry of Internal Affairs, portions of which functioned as secret police), a leading citizen in Minsk, and a Communist Party member.

It was at her uncle's urging that she attended the dance where she met Oswald. Marina's uncle apparently never protested her marriage, although his position could have allowed him to study Oswald's KGB file, which must have shown that Oswald had written to the American embassy about returning to the United States, since it is now known that the KGB was keeping him under surveillance.

Within a matter of days after their marriage, Oswald told Marina he wanted to return to the United States. Soon Marina began to apply for the documents necessary to leave the Soviet Union. Her exit visas appear to have been expedited even though there were several problems with her background information. She stated her name as "Marina Nikolaevna," which indicated her father's name was Nikolai. She insisted, however, that she never knew the name of her father. Her birth certificate identified her birthplace as Severodvinsk. This was the name given to Molotovsk, but not until 1957. Furthermore, since being a member of the Communist Party might cause problems in leaving Russia, she denied any membership. Actually, she was a member of the Komsomol, the Communist Party's youth movement.

These discrepancies did not escape the notice of the CIA. Shortly after the assassination, a CIA memorandum noted:

> At the time [the agency] was becoming increasingly interested in watching develop a pattern that we had discovered in the course of our bio[graphical] and research work: the number of Soviet women marrying foreigners, being permitted to leave the USSR, then eventually divorcing their spouses and settling down abroad without returning "home." . . . We eventually turned up something like two dozen similar cases.

Noting that the birth certificate Marina brought to the United States was issued July 19, 1961, and that she had to have one to obtain a marriage license, author Edward Epstein concluded, "It thus seemed that new documents—and possibly a new identity—were furnished to Marina after it was decided that she would accompany Oswald to the United States."

On July 8, 1961, Oswald had flown to Moscow to retrieve his passport at the American embassy. Since he had never technically defected, his passport was promptly returned, although the State Department cautioned the embassy to proceed carefully in Oswald's "involved case" and to make sure "that the person in communication with the Embassy is . . . Lee Harvey Oswald."

Accounts of Oswald's time during this period are filled with inconsistencies. For example, in his diary he claims to have returned to Minsk from Moscow on July 14. However, on August 1, Rita Naman and two other tourists reported meeting a young American in Moscow and snapping his picture. Two photos made by these tourists were displayed by the House Select Committee on Assassinations, which concluded the young American was Oswald.

With all their applications made, the Oswalds settled down to wait for approval to leave Russia.

To further complicate the situation, a baby girl—June Lee Oswald—was born to Marina on February 15, 1962. On May 10, the Oswalds heard from the American embassy that everything was in order and that they should come to Moscow to sign the final papers.

It was during this time that Marina noted a cooling in Oswald's attitude toward her. He became reclusive and irritable. This coolness was to increase after they left Russia. "Lee changed," Marina told the Warren Commission. "I did not know him as such a man in Russia." It was almost as if he had made up the story of his love and instead was simply following some sort of orders in his courtship. Afterward, with his assignment completed, he didn't bother to act like his love was real.

On May 24, 1962, the Oswalds again were in Moscow to attend to the final details of their departure from Russia. On June 1, Oswald signed a promissory note at the American embassy for a repatriation loan of $435.71, the money needed for his return, and the couple boarded a train that same evening.

Their trip home also has nagging indications of intelligence handling. The Warren Commission said the couple crossed out of communist territory at Brest. Yet Marina's passport was stamped at Helmstedt, one of the major checkpoints on the East German border. Intriguingly, Oswald's passport shows no Helmstedt stamp at all, raising the possibility that he somehow traveled a different route from Marina.

Arriving in Amsterdam, the Oswalds stayed not in a hotel, but in a private establishment recommended by someone in the American embassy in Moscow, according to Marina. She described this place variously as a "private apartment" and as a "boardinghouse." While the official record shows they stayed here only one night, after the assassination Marina recalled a three-day stay and she reacted with confusion when questioned about this by the House Select Committee on Assassinations. She did note that advance arrangements had been made at this place and that their hosts spoke English.

Many researchers suspect that Oswald, and perhaps Marina, were "debriefed" by US intelligence during their Dutch stopover. Even the chief counsel of the Warren Commission called the episode "unexplained."

Furthermore, in a statement to the Secret Service just after the assassination, Marina gave a version of their trip from Russia that was totally different from that given in the Warren Report. She claimed they "then arrived in New York by air . . . stayed in some hotel in New York City for one day and then went by train to Texas."

The Warren Commission, backed by tickets, documents, and Marina's later testimony, stated that the couple arrived in Hoboken, New Jersey, on June 13, 1962, aboard the ship SS *Maasdam*. There they were met by Spas T. Raikin, a representative of the Traveler's Aid Society, which had been notified of the Oswalds' arrival by the State Department. Raikin helped whisk the Oswalds through customs and then found them a place to stay in New York. He later arranged contact with Lee's brother, Robert, who sent the couple $200 for plane fare to Fort Worth, Texas.

According to BBC researcher and author Anthony Summers, Raikin was also an official with an anticommunist émigré group with links to both the FBI and US military intelligence as well as anticommunist groups in New Orleans "headquartered in the very building [544 Camp Street] where, in months to come, Oswald's name was to be linked with CIA-backed anti-Castro activists."

The Department of Health, Education and Welfare (HEW) had approved the financial aid to Oswald upon urging from the State Department. In Dallas HEW records, it states that Oswald went to Russia "with State Department approval," an allegation later repeated by Oswald himself on a New Orleans radio program.

When the Oswalds arrived in New York, they had seven suitcases. When they left by plane, they had only five. Asked about the dwindling number, Oswald stated he had sent them ahead by rail. However, when the couple arrived in Fort Worth, Robert stated they had only two suitcases.

The lost baggage may have something to do with their flight to Texas, which, although many direct flights were available, went by way of Atlanta. Atlanta was the home of Natasha Davison, the mother of Captain Davison, the US attaché with intelligence connections who had met with the Oswalds in Moscow.

Yet, with all this evidence suggesting that Marina may have been part of some unrevealed intelligence program, she was accepted publicly by the Warren Commission as "a simple, devoted housewife." Privately, Commission members thought differently. At one point, they voiced the fear that she might be a KGB agent. Commission member Senator Richard Russell commented, "That will blow the lid if she testifies to that." One Warren Commission lawyer described Marina as "a very different person [from her public image] . . . cold, calculating, avaricious."

Some believe that Marina lied in many instances during her testimony to the Warren Commission. But keep in mind that the testimony of Oswald's wife would not have been admissible had Oswald come to trial.

Despite all this, some of Marina's testimony proved very damaging to Oswald. In the hours after the assassination, Marina was quoted as saying, "Lee good man. Lee not shoot anyone." But after she was held for weeks by the federal authorities, her statements began to change. Instead of describing what a good husband Oswald had been, she began saying he was violent to her. After initially being unable to identify the Carcano rifle as her husband's, she later described it as "the fateful rifle of Lee Harvey Oswald." She also began to tell stories of other attempts at assassination by Oswald—one against Richard Nixon and another against General Edwin Walker.

Today Marina has reversed her statements of 1963–1964. More mature, with a good command of English, she has publicly made several astounding admissions, including:

—How federal authorities forced her Warren Commission testimony by threatening deportation and ordered her not to read or listen to anything pertaining to the assassination.

—That today she believes a conspiracy resulted in Kennedy's death.

—Lee Harvey Oswald was an agent who "worked for the American government" and was "caught between two powers—the government and organized crime."

—Oswald was "killed to keep his mouth shut."

—That someone impersonated Oswald to incriminate him and "that's no joke."

—Lee Harvey Oswald "adored" President Kennedy.

In a 1988 interview published in *Ladies' Home Journal*, Marina said:

When I was questioned by the Warren Commission, I was a blind kitten. Their questioning left me only one way to go: guilty. I made Lee guilty. He never had a fair chance. . . . But I was only 22 then, and I've matured since; I think differently.

By 1979, Marina had begun to doubt the official explanation of the assassination and even joined in efforts to have Oswald's body exhumed due to serious questions concerning its identity. More on that later.

Considering the background of both Lee and Marina and the length of time Oswald spent in Russia, it seems inconceivable that they were not interrogated by US intelligence after their return. Yet the official story is that no US intelligence agency had any interest in this ex-Marine.

Considering the Marine career of Oswald and the military information available to him as a radar operator, it is equally unbelievable that the Soviets did not interrogate Oswald at great length, especially if they found out about his connections with the U-2 flights from Atsugi.

Yet, this is precisely what the Soviets claimed in what has to be one of the most bizarre aspects of the Kennedy assassination—an aspect kept from the American public by the Warren Commission.

A Soviet Defector's Story

The strange story of Yuri Nosenko began on January 20, 1964, just two months after the events in Dallas.

Nosenko, an officer in the American Division of the KGB, had contacted the CIA initially on June 3, 1962, just two days after Oswald left Russia for the United States. Nosenko offered to spy for the Americans. However, nothing further had been heard from him and US analysts were highly suspicious of his offer.

Then on January 20, 1964, Nosenko landed in Geneva as part of a Soviet disarmament delegation. He soon made his way to a telephone and renewed his offer to American intelligence, but with a difference—this time he wanted to defect. His defection set in motion a chain of events that would lead to bitter divisions between the CIA and FBI as well as within the CIA itself.

Once he was in American hands, CIA officials were shocked to learn that Nosenko claimed to have been the KGB official who had personally handled the case of Lee Harvey Oswald during his stay in Russia. Nosenko said—based on two mental examinations made of Oswald—the KGB found the would-be defector not very bright and even "mentally unstable." and that the KGB had never debriefed Oswald about his military background or ever considered recruiting him as an agent.

That was exactly what many people in the CIA and on the Warren Commission wanted to hear. However, others in the agency were immediately suspicious of this man. After all, it appeared Nosenko had forever left a ranking position and his family simply to assure the US government that the man accused of killing the president was not a Soviet agent.

CIA counterintelligence chief James Jesus Angleton was particularly wary of Nosenko. He observed that most of the information Nosenko provided revealing Soviet agents and operations was already known to the CIA prior to his defection. Furthermore, shortly after bringing Nosenko to the United States, CIA interrogators began to find errors and gaps in his testimony.

To make matters worse, Nosenko's story was corroborated by one of the FBI's deepest secrets—their own Soviet KGB defector referred to only by his code name, Fedora. Thus, if Nosenko was lying, then Fedora, too, became suspect.

In a remarkable attempt to resolve the issue, Nosenko underwent "hostile interrogation," nothing new since 9/11 but shocking back then. He was kept in solitary confinement for 1,277 days under intense physical and psychological pressure. He was put on a diet of weak tea, macaroni, and porridge, he was given nothing to read, a light was left burning in his unheated cell twenty-four hours a day, and his guards were forbidden to speak with him or even smile. Toward the end of this ordeal, Nosenko was given at least two lie detector tests by the CIA. He failed both. But Nosenko did not crack.

The believers of Nosenko, headed by the CIA's Richard Helms and J. Edgar Hoover, took his intransigence to mean that he was telling the truth about the KGB's having no interest in Oswald. But doubts remained. So at the CIA's request, the Warren Commission obligingly made no reference to Nosenko.

The counterintelligence faction, led by Angleton, still believed that the KGB contrived Nosenko's defection for two purposes: to allay suspicions that the Soviets had anything to do with the JFK assassination and to cover for Soviet "moles," or agents deep within US intelligence.

Through the 1980s, Nosenko continued to be an adviser on Soviet intelligence to the CIA and the FBI at a salary of more than $35,000 a year. He has been given a new identity as well as more than $150,000 as payment for his ordeal.

There appears to be evidence that Oswald continued to keep in touch with Soviet officials almost up until the time of Kennedy's assassination. According to CIA documents, Oswald visited the Soviet embassy in Mexico City on September 23, 1963, and met with Valery Vladimirovich Kostikov, who was described as a consul in the Soviet embassy. However, a CIA memorandum added, "[Kostikov] is also known to be a staff officer of the KGB. He is connected with the Thirteenth, or 'liquid affairs' department, whose responsibilities include assassination and sabotage."

Of course, Oswald's contact with this man, who was operating as a normal member of the Soviet embassy, may have been coincidental. However, it is significant that the Warren Commission, aware of the implication of this contact, failed to pursue the matter or include this information in its report, though this contact subsequently was used to paint Oswald as a would-be Soviet assassin.

Years later, FBI agent James Hosty, who was connected to Oswald prior to the assassination, said he was unhappy with the revelation about Kostikov's KGB ties and that, had he been made aware of this connection by the CIA, he would have placed Oswald's name on the bureau's "Security Index" of individuals to monitor.

Two theories have emerged:

One, Oswald was recruited by the KGB while serving in Japan and was encouraged to defect to Russia, then sent back to the United States to kill President Kennedy. This theory is rejected by most students of the subject, including author Edward Jay Epstein, whose book *Legend* studied the Oswald-Soviet connections in detail. Epstein reasoned, "I think that the fact that Oswald traces so clearly back to the Russians makes it extremely unlikely that they would have recruited him as an assassin."

Second, Oswald, whether genuine or substitute, was recruited into US intelligence as a spy and sent to Russia. There, the KGB attempted to turn him into their agent and sent him back to the United States, unaware that he would be blamed for Kennedy's death. This would explain the extraordinary lengths by the Soviets to disavow any connection with Oswald.

In the overall view, Oswald obviously was mixed up in some sort of intelligence work. And while it is likely that the Soviets would attempt to recruit this lowly Marine and would-be defector, it is highly unlikely that they would consider using him in something so dangerous as assassinating the US president. In murdering Kennedy, the Soviets would have been risking all. World War III would be the likely result should a Soviet assassination plot be uncovered. And what would they have gained by killing Kennedy? Virtually nothing, except promoting Lyndon Johnson to be president. Johnson had far stronger anticommunist credentials than Kennedy with much closer ties to the military-industrial complex most feared by the Soviets.

Such thinking was confirmed in later years when it was learned that on the day after the assassination Nikolai T. Fedorenko of the Soviet Union Mission to the United Nations met with all Russian diplomatic personnel at the Soviet Mission. Fedorenko stated that Kennedy's death had caused considerable shock in Soviet government circles and was very much regretted by the Soviet Union.

According to documents obtained by the Assassinations Records Review Board, by the fall of 1965, Colonel Boris Ivanov, chief of the Soviet Committee for State Security, told Soviet KGB personnel in New York City that the KGB was in possession of data purporting to indicate President Johnson was responsible for Kennedy's assassination. He ordered all operatives to obtain all the information available on Johnson, his background and associates.

In 1979, the House Select Committee on Assassinations, even after hearing the Nosenko story, concluded, "The committee believes, on the basis of the evidence available to it, that the Soviet Government was not involved in the assassination of President Kennedy."

But perhaps the best argument against Soviet involvement comes from the memoirs of the highest-ranking Soviet official ever to defect to the West. In his 1985 book, *Breaking with Moscow*, Arkady N. Shevchenko wrote:

> Our leaders would not have been so upset by the assassination if they had planned it and the KGB would not have taken upon itself to venture such a move without Politburo approval. . . . Moscow firmly believed that Kennedy's assassination was a scheme by "reactionary forces" within the United States seeking to damage the new trend in relations. The Kremlin ridiculed the Warren Commission's conclusion that Oswald had acted on his own as the sole assassin. There was in fact widespread speculation among Soviet diplomats that Lyndon Johnson, along with the CIA and the Mafia, had masterminded the plot. Perhaps one of the most potent reasons why the U.S.S.R. wished Kennedy well was that Johnson was anathema to Khrushchev. Because he was a southerner, Moscow considered him a racist (the stereotype of any American politician from below the Mason-Dixon line), an anti-Soviet and anti-communist to the core. Further, since Johnson was from Texas, a center of the most reactionary forces in the United States, according to the Soviets, he was associated with the big-time capitalism of the oil industry, also known to be anti-Soviet.

A final argument against Soviet involvement is that while it is conceivable that the Russians somehow contrived Kennedy's death and that high-level US government officials were forced to cover this up to prevent a devastating world war, it makes no sense that these facts would not have been leaked slowly to the American public in the late 1960s and early 1970s in an effort to gain support for the anticommunist war in Vietnam and to blunt the growing antiwar movement.

The fact that Russian assassination plans didn't surface goes far to prove that hard evidence of Soviet involvement in Kennedy's death is nonexistent. But if the Russians had nothing to do with the assassination, what about their protégés on the island of Cuba?

Cubans

In a 1952 military coup, former Cuban army sergeant Fulgencio Batista seized control of Cuba, which had been under US trusteeship since the Spanish-American War of 1898. A dictator and a despot, Batista nevertheless was supported by the United States and worked closely with many American groups, especially organized criminals.

By the late 1950s, Cuba was a mecca for American gamblers, tourists, investors, and offshore banking speculators.

Only one man seemed determined to overthrow Batista—a young attorney named Fidel Castro.

Fidel Castro

Born the son of a Spanish-born plantation owner on August 13, 1926, Fidel Alejandro Castro Ruz had an active boyhood in rural eastern Cuba. He once threatened to burn the house down if his parents didn't send him to school.

In 1952, he ran for Parliament but was stymied when the dictator Batista canceled the elections. From that time on, Castro devoted himself to ousting Batista.

Gathering some followers, Castro made his first assault on Batista on July 26, 1953, attacking the dictator's Moncada Barracks. The attack was a military disaster. Captured and tried, the youthful Castro proclaimed, "Condemn me. It does not matter. History will absolve me."

Sentenced to fifteen years in prison, Castro was released after twenty-two months. He then fled to Mexico, where he began reorganizing his guerrilla fighters. He used the brutality displayed by Batista at the Moncada Barracks as a rallying point and named his revolution the "26th of July Movement" after the disastrous attack. Since 1959, this date has been celebrated as Cuban Independence Day.

In 1956, Castro swam the Rio Grande and entered the United States to arrange the purchase of a dilapidated yacht named the *Granma*. Returning to Mexico, he began planning the next stage of his revolution—the invasion of his homeland. Confident that he would rapidly gain followers, Castro even made his invasion plans public.

On December 2, 1956, when he and eighty-two guerrillas waded ashore on the swampy coast of his native Oriente Province, Batista's soldiers were waiting in ambush. Only twelve guerrillas, including Castro, survived and escaped into the Sierra Maestra mountains.

After Batista proclaimed his death, Castro invited a reporter for the *New York Times* to his camp to show he was very much alive, and he predicted that final victory would be his.

After several years of basic survival in the mountains—during this time, Castro grew his now-famous beard—the young revolutionary and his followers began to take the initiative. By the summer of 1958, his guerrilla band had grown to more than eight hundred, and later that year a detachment led by Ernesto "Che" Guevara captured the provincial capital of Santa Clara in central Cuba.

Although backed by an army of some 30,000, Batista panicked and decided to quit the island. Taking bags of cash, Batista fled to the Dominican Republic in the first few hours of 1959.

Castro's fantasy revolution had suddenly become a dream come true. For two weeks, Castro slowly moved toward Havana. The excitement and passions of the moment were almost overpowering. Veteran news correspondents could not recall a more jubilant scene since the liberation of Paris in World War II. For a period of weeks, the jubilation continued, but then became subdued in the wake of trials and executions of prerevolution "war criminals."

With the defeat of Batista, Castro became the undisputed leader of Cuba, even proclaiming himself "Jefe Maximo" (maximum leader). And he began making drastic changes in the island.

Castro closed down the gambling casinos and houses of prostitution that had been the source of an estimated $100 million a year for organized crime in the United States. He nationalized the sugar industry, the backbone of Cuba's economy, and by the summer of 1960, he had seized more than $700 million in US property, including banks that had been accused of laundering money for American interests. (Even his parents' plantation was nationalized, angering his own mother and prompting his younger sister Juanita to leave Cuba and become an anti-Castroite.)

Some social gains were made on the island. Within a few years, illiteracy had been reduced from 24 percent to 4 percent. But Castro also proclaimed that he was the leader of socialist revolution in South America, although he strongly maintained that he was not a communist. American interests were quick to respond. The US government abruptly restricted sugar imports and began encouraging its allies not to trade with Castro.

With his trade restricted and hearing rumors that the United States might invade the island at any time, Castro turned to the Soviet Union for support. He began selling sugar to Russia in 1960 and soon Soviet technicians and advisers began to arrive on the island. This confirmed the suspicions of American interests, who began to brand Castro a communist who subverted the status quo in Central and South America.

As Castro's social, economic, and agricultural reforms continued, often with brutal effectiveness, Cubans began to split into two factions—the Fidelistas (supporters of Castro) and the anti-Castroites, many of whom fled Cuba. By the end of the first year of Castro's takeover, more than 100,000 Cubans were living in the United States.

As the United States stepped up its program of isolating Cuba—first with cutting off the island's sugar markets and oil supplies, then through diplomatic maneuvers with other South American countries, and finally by introducing arms and saboteurs into Cuba—Castro grew more and more fearful of an armed invasion by the United States.

On January 3, 1961, the United States ended diplomatic relations with Cuba after Castro demanded the US embassy staff be cut to only eleven persons. Castro charged that 80 percent of the staff was "FBI and Pentagon spies." In 1961 most Americans had never heard of the CIA, a then little-known and super-secret organization, much like the National Security Agency today. Two weeks later, the United States forbade its citizens to travel to Cuba. In the same month, the month that John F. Kennedy took office as president, Castro placed his militia on twenty-four-hour alert, proclaiming that the "Yankee invasion" was imminent.

In February, Soviet deputy prime minister Andrei Gromyko arrived in Cuba to arrange large-scale economic and military assistance to Castro.

And on April 17, 1961, less than three months after Kennedy became president, Castro's fears were realized. A force of anti-Castro Cubans backed by the United States landed at the Bay of Pigs.

Disaster at the Bay of Pigs

The plans to destroy Castro and regain control of Cuba began while Eisenhower was in office, more than a year before Kennedy became president.

By early 1960, the thousands of Cuban refugees in the United States had begun forming small groups dedicated to regaining their homeland, each claiming to be the one true voice of the exiles. To bring order to this situation, the CIA in May 1960 helped create a Cuban coalition that came to be known as the Cuban Revolutionary Council. Early on, this task was handled by CIA officer E. Howard Hunt—later to be involved in the Watergate affair and to be accused of being in Dallas the day Kennedy was killed.

Secrecy was the prime concern of everyone involved. Even CIA director Allen Dulles did not know many details of the plan. He had simply turned the whole project over to a deputy director, Richard M. Bissell Jr. Bissell, in turn, handed the project to the former CIA station chief in Caracas, who recruited various CIA personnel, such as Hunt, Tracy Barnes, and David Atlee Phillips.

Many of the CIA officers involved in the Bay of Pigs had participated in the 1954 overthrow of the popularly elected government of Jacobo Arbenz in Guatemala, and their intent was to stage a similar low-key coup in Cuba.

Unknown to these CIA officers who began to create a Cuban-refugee fighting force, Bissell was working on a concurrent project—the assassination of Fidel Castro.

Bissell's idea began to work its way through the CIA bureaucracy with unintended

humorous results. Plans were conceived to poison Castro's cigar, to slip him a depila-
tory so his famous beard would fall out, or administer an LSD-type chemical so that
the Cuban leader would hallucinate. These schemes took on a more sinister aspect,
however, with the suggestion that American gangsters be hired to do the job.

President Dwight Eisenhower knew none of this. All he knew was that on March
17, 1960, at the urging of a top-secret committee for covert operations—known as
the 5412 Committee because it was authorized by National Security Council Directive 5412/2—he had authorized a CIA plan titled "A Program of Covert Action
Against the Castro Regime." This plan offered a four-point program: (1) creating a
Cuban government in exile, (2) constructing a "powerful" propaganda offensive, (3)
creating a "covert intelligence and action organization" inside Cuba, and (4) developing "a paramilitary force outside of Cuba for future guerrilla action."

This "paramilitary force" was to evolve into Brigade 2506, a Cuban-exile expedi-
tionary force supported by US air and sea power.

One man who did understand what all this might mean was Eisenhower's vice
president, White House action officer, and head of the 5412 Committee—Richard
M. Nixon. Nixon had several reasons for supporting action against Castro. A year
earlier, the anticommunist Nixon had met with Castro and concluded, "Castro is
either incredibly naïve about communism or is under communist discipline." As
one of the congressmen who passed the legislation creating the CIA, Nixon undoubtedly wanted to support the men who through the years had passed along
information politically helpful to him. Then, too, the November election was approaching and Nixon was eager to have the Republican administration get the
credit for ending Castro's reign. His close ties to organized-crime figures also may
have played a role.

Whatever his reasons, Nixon kept exhorting his executive assistant for national
security affairs, General Robert E. Cushman Jr., to press the CIA officers for action.

Meanwhile, Hunt and an associate, Bernard L. Barker (who later participated
in the Watergate break-in under Hunt's guidance), were wheeling and dealing in
the Miami Cuban exile community, sometimes carrying as much as $115,000 in a
briefcase to secure agents. Training camps were located, arms secured, and Cubans
recruited. The plan was advancing into broader and grander stages and still the low-
er-level operators were in charge.

On July 23, 1960, presidential candidate John F. Kennedy was first briefed by
Dulles about the Cuban operation. At that time only guerrilla infiltration and air
drops were contemplated; Kennedy did not learn of the full invasion plan until after
his election, a key point to remember.

Shortly after the election, Dulles—along with Bissell—again briefed Kennedy
on the Cuban plan. This briefing, too, was long on vague generalities and short on
details.

It was not until near the end of 1960 that anyone outside of the CIA officers in
charge were told that the plan had been expanded to include an invasion with air
support. Even military brass, who were being asked for material assistance, were

sworn to secrecy. Most of those ranking military officers brought into the plan thought the whole thing sounded "impractical."

The invasion was indeed impractical, because first, it was predicated on a massive revolt against Castro by the Cuban people, a concept loudly advanced by the CIA analysts but doubted by most others involved. Second, it was apparent that to succeed, the invasion had to have the support of US naval and air power, a contingency both Eisenhower and Kennedy had opposed.

By mid-March 1961—with the invasion only a month away—Kennedy was having second thoughts. The Trinidad Plan, an invasion proposal hastily put together by the Pentagon, was rejected by the new president as "too spectacular," with its amphibious assault, air strikes, and the landing of a provisional government. Kennedy wanted something quiet, something that would not reveal US involvement.

A week before the invasion, Kennedy left no doubt as to his position on using US military forces to help the Cuban exiles. The *New York Times* carried a two-column headline reading: PRESIDENT BARS USING US FORCE TO OUST CASTRO. The Cuban exiles were aghast, but their CIA officers quietly assured them that no one would stand by and watch them die. Miscommunication was rampant up and down the chain of command.

Kennedy, advised that the invasion had been approved by the previous administration, was faced with a fait accompli. Reluctantly he gave his approval and on Saturday, April 15, 1961, less than three months after Kennedy took office, a force of six B-26 bombers left a secret airfield in Nicaragua for Cuba. It was to have been sixteen, but Kennedy ordered a reduction to "minimum" scale.

This weekend air strike was a partial success. Castro's tiny air force was caught on the ground. Only three T-33 jets—considered good only as trainers—along with two B-26 bombers and a few decrepit British Sea Furies escaped the bombing raid. But it was enough.

On Monday, April 17, the Cuban Brigade landed at Bahia de Cochinos or Bay of Pigs (named after the wild boars that inhabited this desolate area of Cuba) under the code name Zapata. Ironically, Castro knew the area intimately since it was his favorite hunting spot. It was a good location for a landing, with only two main road arteries leading past swamps and dense undergrowth. But this same attribute also made it a formidable trap should Castro's forces arrive quickly and in force.

A second air strike had been planned and, by most accounts, would have completed the destruction of Castro's air force. However, the CIA planners had failed to reckon with John F. Kennedy. Kennedy hesitated, growing more and more concerned that the entire world was realizing that the United States was supporting this invasion of another country. His concern was a far cry from Washington's policies of today. Today, it is known that failure to order in the second strike actually came from Air Force General Charles Cabell, who as deputy director of the CIA helped organize the invasion. It has been suggested that cancellation of the second air strike actually was part of a plan to discredit Kennedy and force him into more conciliation with the military intelligence communities.

United Nations ambassador Adlai Stevenson, who had been lied to by the CIA about US involvement, was also discredited after telling the General Assembly that the United States had nothing to do with the invasion.

Although the Cuban Brigade already was running into trouble on the beaches—one of their ships, the *Houston*, was set afire by Castro's planes while an escorting ship, the *Barbara*, was fired upon by its own side for failing to pick up *Houston* survivors. Researchers have pondered over the fact that George H. W. Bush, married to a Barbara, has been accused of using his Houston oil firm, Zapata Petroleum Corp., as a front for the anti-Castro Cubans prior to the Bay of Pigs Invasion. In addition, his father, Connecticut senator Prescott Bush, was instrumental in creating the CIA.

Secretary of state Dean Rusk was concerned that the "international noise level" had risen to an intolerable degree. Rusk argued that no further air strikes be attempted until it could be made to look like the planes came from captured Cuban airfields. Kennedy concurred. Castro's surviving planes were able to disrupt the landing, allowing his troops to bottle up the beaches. The Bay of Pigs had become a death trap for the Cuban Brigade.

Kennedy authorized US Navy ships sitting offshore to help evacuate the Brigade, but the Cuban commanders didn't want evacuation. They wanted the ammunition, naval support, and "umbrella" of air cover that had been promised to them. It never came. As the remnants of the Brigade called for help from the beaches, US military men could only stand silent by their weapons and watch as the gallant Cuban Brigade was torn to bits.

As news of the debacle spread, everybody concerned was furious.

Kennedy felt betrayed. He believed he had been led down a primrose path by overly optimistic CIA officials. The CIA planners felt betrayed in that the actual invasion had been scaled down on Kennedy's orders. The military felt betrayed because they had not been allowed to help plan the invasion. And the Cuban exiles felt betrayed most of all because they had been led to believe they had the full support of the US government. Thanks to gossip from their superiors and CIA advisers, many believed—and still do—that Kennedy was totally responsible for the failure of the invasion.

In Guatemala City, staging area for the Brigade, the CIA officers were devastated. Many were getting drunk. CIA station chief Robert Davis described them this way: "If someone had gotten close to Kennedy, he'd have killed him. Oh, they hated him!"

Of the men of the Cuban Brigade, 114 were killed, 1,202 were captured by Castro's forces, and 150 either never landed or made their way back to safety. The captured Brigade was finally freed on December 23, 1962, after the United States agreed to exchange them for $53 million worth of food and drugs.

Infuriated by this disastrous defeat, Kennedy nevertheless took the burden of blame. He told reporters, "There's an old saying that victory has a hundred fathers and defeat is an orphan. What mattered was only one fact: I am the responsible officer of government."

No one—especially in the CIA, the military, organized crime, or in the Cuban exile community—would forget this acceptance of responsibility.

Following a shake-up in US intelligence over the Bay of Pigs disaster—Kennedy fired Dulles and Cabell—attorney general Robert Kennedy took over responsibility for Cuban affairs.

Soon another war—this one much darker and more secret—was being waged against Castro under the code name "JM/WAVE." This program operated on the campus of the University of Miami under the cover of an electronics firm called Zenith Technological Services. On November 3, 1961, JM/WAVE came under Operation Mongoose, the ongoing covert mission against Castro also known as the "Cuban Project." It was headed by Air Force General Edward Lansdale, already acknowledged as an expert on nation building due to his fighting communists in the Philippines following World War II. He advocated action in the social, economic, and political aspects of a country as well as aggressive military operations. A 1958 book titled *The Ugly American* was a thinly disguised account of the experiences of Lansdale and others in Southeast Asia.

By mid-1962, Operation Mongoose involved nearly 600 CIA case officers, as many as 3,000 contract agents, and numerous fronts such as boat shops, detective and travel agencies, and gun stores. With nearly a quarter million Cuban refugees living in the United States, it was easy to find those with a burning passion to liberate their island and return home.

The operation out of the JM/WAVE station was inconsistent from the start. President Kennedy stated "all actions should be kept at a low key," while his brother Robert told CIA officials "no time, money, effort—or manpower—should be spared."

The near-nightly raids on Cuba—landing saboteurs, dropping propaganda leaflets, and conducting occasional military-style raids—actually achieved very little except to confirm Castro's accusations that the United States was guilty of aggression.

Today several of the military and intelligence officials who were dealing with President Kennedy during this period say they believed that the assassination of Castro was to be a part of this "Cuban crusade." However, there is no supporting documentation, and in fact the only documentation available indicates quite the opposite.

Early in 1962, Robert Kennedy was trying to prosecute a top Mafia boss named Sam Giancana, when he found the CIA interceding on Giancana's behalf. Pursuing the matter, Kennedy was finally told about the earlier deals between the CIA and Mafia to kill Castro. According to CIA attorney Lawrence Houston, the attorney general ordered a halt to dealings with the Mafia. The younger Kennedy later told aides, "I stopped it. . . . I found out that some people were going to try an attempt on Castro's life and I turned it off."

However, the lethal partnership between the agency and the crime syndicate didn't stop until well after President Kennedy was assassinated, indicating the CIA continued to operate out of control even after the agency shake-up following the Bay of Pigs disaster.

Whatever the Kennedys' role in Castro assassination plots, they got nowhere. Castro outlived both Kennedys and there is now some evidence to suggest that the CIA-Mafia plots may have been nothing more than a "scam" on the part of organized crime to gain leverage over the government.

The ongoing tension with Cuba took on a more serious and urgent tone when on October 22, 1962, Kennedy announced that US reconnaissance aircraft—the same U-2 spy plane that had ended Eisenhower's hopes for the 1960 summit meeting—had photographed offensive missile sites with nuclear capability being constructed in Cuba.

President Kennedy called for emergency meetings of the United Nations Security Council and the Organization of American States. He also ordered a "quarantine" of Cuba and vowed full retaliation against Russia if a nuclear warhead was launched from Cuba.

As Soviet ships carrying missiles approached the US naval blockade of Cuba, the world watched and trembled. Nuclear holocaust seemed imminent. Then Americans were told that the Soviets blinked. Their freighters turned back and everyone breathed a sigh of relief. Only much later did the American people learn that Kennedy had accepted a proposal from Soviet premier Nikita Khrushchev that included a pledge from the United States to remove its missiles from Turkey and never to invade or support any invasion of Cuba, in exchange for Russia's withdrawal of the Cuban missiles.

But Kennedy's diplomacy in ending the missile crisis, perhaps unknown to the lower ranks, earned him further rebuke by military and CIA officers who believed the presence of missiles justified a US invasion of Cuba and the elimination of the Castro regime. These suspicions only made the military and intelligence officers, along with their Cuban protégés, more convinced that Kennedy was "soft on communism."

In March 1962, General Lyman Lemnitzer, chairman of the Joint Chiefs of Staff, recommended, and the Joint Chiefs approved, a plan to turn public opinion against Castro called Operation Northwoods. These plans called for conducting "false-flag" operations in the United States—hijacking American airliners and ships, setting off bombs in American cities, and even assassinations. All this was to be blamed on Castro's Cuba.

President Kennedy rejected Operation Northwoods and demoted Lemnitzer, and senior military officers ordered the documents destroyed. But someone slipped up and ironically the papers were discovered in the early 1990s by the Assassination Records Review Board, created to gather documents related to Kennedy's assassination.

Beginning in 1963, the Cubans found US government support for their continuing efforts against Castro to be nonexistent. In fact, moves were under way to stop exile action against Cuba.

The clamp-down on exile activity, whether sincere or official window dressing, marked the beginning of a new relationship with both Cuba and the Soviet Union—and a change of tactics by JFK.

Kennedy used Jean Daniel, a journalist with the French newspaper *L'Express*, as an unofficial contact with Castro. On October 24, 1963, Kennedy met with Daniel and urged him to pass along his good intentions to the Cuban premier during a scheduled interview in Havana. Daniel did meet with Castro and reported that the Cuban leader said:

> I believe Kennedy is sincere. I consider him responsible for everything, but I will say this . . . in the last analysis, I'm convinced that anyone else would be worse. . . . You can tell him that I'm willing to declare [Sen. Barry] Goldwater my friend if it will guarantee Kennedy's reelection!

Ironically, Daniel was with Castro on November 22, when the Cuban leader received word of Kennedy's assassination. *"Es una mala noticia* [This is bad news]," Castro said three times, adding, "All will have to be rethought. I'll tell you one thing; at least Kennedy was an enemy to whom we had become accustomed. You watch and see . . . I know that they will try to put the blame on us for this thing."

Castro was correct. From the day of the assassination, there was an effort to lay the blame on him.

But the attempt to reconcile relations with Castro had not been strictly unofficial. On September 17, 1963, ambassador Seydou Diallo of Guinea in West Africa brought word to William Attwood, then a special adviser to the US delegation to the United Nations and a former US ambassador to Guinea, that Castro wanted to reach some sort of understanding with the Kennedy administration. According to Diallo, Castro was unhappy at being forced to align closely with the Soviet Union and wanted to normalize relations with the United States. Attwood reported Diallo's conversation to his superior, UN ambassador Adlai Stevenson, who telephoned President Kennedy. Kennedy directed Stevenson to have Attwood meet with Cuban UN delegate Carlos Lechuga. This led to discreet meetings between Attwood and Lechuga, where they decided that Attwood would travel to Cuba for direct meetings with Castro.

Although these unprecedented approaches to Cuba were strictly secret, it is almost certain that people within US intelligence were aware of the rapprochement. Attorney general Robert Kennedy himself told Attwood the secret maneuvering was "bound to leak."

Three days after Kennedy's assassination, Attwood was formally notified that Havana was ready to proceed with a meeting. President Lyndon Johnson was briefed on the situation, but he turned a cold shoulder. Attwood sadly told author Anthony Summers, "The word came back that this was to be put on ice for the time being, and the time being has been ever since."

Besides Miami, the next largest operational area for militant anti-Castro Cubans was the city of New Orleans, Lee Harvey Oswald's birthplace. It was there that numerous leads have been developed linking the CIA, the FBI, anti-Castro Cubans, and military intelligence with Oswald.

Oswald's interest in Cuba went back to his Marine days, when he and Marine buddy Nelson Delgado toyed with the idea of traveling to Cuba and assisting Castro in his war against Batista. There was nothing unusual here. That same idea had crossed the minds of thousands of daydreaming American schoolboys.

But in Oswald's case, this dream may have taken on some reality. According to Delgado, the Marine Oswald began receiving letters plainly stamped with the seal of the Cuban consulate in Los Angeles. Oswald once traveled to Los Angeles with Delgado, saying his purpose was to "visit the Cuban consulate." There also were reports of Oswald's meeting with mysterious strangers, whom Delgado believed had to do with "the Cuban business."

Gerry Patrick Hemming, a Marine with Oswald who was recruited into the CIA, has told of meeting Oswald in the Cuban consulate. Hemming, himself working for naval intelligence, said Oswald seemed to be "an informant or some type of agent working for somebody."

On April 24, 1963, less than a year after arriving back in Fort Worth from Russia, Oswald packed a bag and bought a bus ticket for New Orleans, telling Marina and friends that he couldn't find a job in Texas.

Shortly before leaving for New Orleans, he had written a letter to the Fair Play for Cuba Committee (FPCC), a pro-Castro organization headquartered in New York City and the object of intense scrutiny by various US intelligence agencies, including the FBI and Army intelligence. Oswald praised Castro and asked for FPCC pamphlets, membership applications, and advice on tactics. He also mentioned he "was thinking about renting a small office at my own expense."

The FPCC director, V. T. Lee, promptly answered, saying the committee faced serious opposition and warned Oswald against provoking "unnecessary incidents which frighten away prospective supporters." It was advice that Oswald would totally ignore.

Staying with relatives in New Orleans, Oswald managed to get a job at the William B. Reily Co., a coffee manufacturer. The company's owner, William Reily, was a financial backer of the Crusade to Free Cuba Committee, one of the many front groups raising money for the Cuban Revolutionary Council. Oswald actually may have been placed within Reily as an operative. His job apparently was to distinguish which of the Cuban exiles at both the firm and in New Orleans were genuine anti-Castroites and which were Castro spies.

Through the spring and summer of 1963, Oswald, an avid reader, checked out twenty-seven books from the New Orleans Library. His reading ran from Ian Fleming's James Bond novels to Aldous Huxley and science fiction. Library records show Oswald also read two books about John F. Kennedy, *Profiles in Courage* and *Portrait of a President*. Oswald checked out nothing about Cuba.

In fact, it was during this time that a strange incident occurred that throws further doubt on Oswald's sincerity as a communist sympathizer. In July 1963, Oswald accompanied his uncle, Charles "Dutz" Murret, to a Jesuit seminary in Mobile, Alabama, where a cousin was enrolled. Here Oswald made what audience members thought was a well-constructed speech against Soviet-style communism. He took the opposite position from his procommunist public posturing over the previous few months in New Orleans—further evidence that Oswald was living some sort of dual life.

Back in New Orleans, this duplicity continued. Although Oswald handed out leaflets for the FPCC and continued to write to the national organization, his New Orleans chapter was a complete fraud. He even had his wife sign the name "Hidell" as president of his New Orleans chapter of the FPCC.

While there has been no documented evidence—a few letters to the FPCC aside—that Oswald was in contact with any pro-Castro group, he definitely was in touch with anti-Castro Cubans. On August 5, 1963, Oswald entered a store owned by Cuban militant Carlos Bringuier, a man with connections to both the Cuban Revolutionary Council and the CIA. Oswald told Bringuier and friends that he was a Marine veteran with experience in guerrilla warfare and offered to train Cuban exiles. Pushing his point, Oswald returned the next day with a Marine training manual, which he left with Bringuier. He again said he wanted to join the fight against Castro.

Bringuier already was on guard. In his Warren Commission testimony, he said that some time earlier he had been interviewed by FBI agent Warren De Brueys, who had told him the bureau might try to infiltrate his anti-Castro organization.

Three days later, Bringuier was shocked when a friend rushed into his store and said that the same man who had wanted to train exiles was on the New Orleans streets passing out pro-Castro literature. Bringuier and others sought out Oswald and confronted him. A crowd gathered as Bringuier railed against this "communist" who had tried to infiltrate the exiles. Losing his temper, Bringuier cursed Oswald, threw his leaflets into the air, then drew back his fist as if to strike. Oswald, who kept smiling throughout this episode, said, "Okay, Carlos, if you want to hit me, hit me."

But there was no fight. Police arrived and took Oswald, Bringuier, and two others into custody. All were charged with disturbing the peace. Oswald tried to contact his uncle for the $25 bail but failed. His uncle's daughter, however, contacted a family friend, New Orleans gambler Emile Bruneau, who put up the money.

However, before leaving the New Orleans police station, oddly Oswald asked to speak to an FBI agent. Despite being outside normal business hours, agent John Quigley soon arrived and spent more than an hour with Oswald. His report gave every detail of Oswald's travels and stay in New Orleans and appeared more like a debriefing to the bureau by Oswald than the ramblings of an anti-American.

It is interesting to note the impression of Oswald by the New Orleans police. Speaking of the Bringuier episode, Lieutenant Francis Martello later said, "He seemed to have them set up to create an incident," while Sergeant Horace Austin recalled, "[Oswald] appeared as though he is being used by these people."

After this brush with the law, Oswald's pro-Castro stance became even more public. He was soon on New Orleans radio and television telling his pro-Castro story to a wider audience. Tipped off to Oswald by Bringuier, radio reporter William Stuckey allowed Oswald to expound on his thoughts on Cuba and South America. This radio interview is significant in that it was widely used after the assassination to "prove" his procommunist credentials.

A few days later, armed with information obtained from the FBI and the House Un-American Activities Committee, Stuckey and right-wing broadcaster Ed Butler verbally ambushed Oswald in another radio interview. This interview may have provided an accidental peek at Oswald's real allegiance. Oswald was suddenly confronted with his attempted defection to Russia. The pro-Castro Oswald, self-proclaimed secretary of the New Orleans chapter of the FPCC, was suddenly revealed to have been a communist sympathizer who had tried to renounce his American citizenship. Caught off guard, Oswald stammered, "I was under the protection of the . . . uh . . . that is to say, I was not under the protection of the American government . . . but I was at all times considered an American citizen."

It has been documented that both the CIA and the FBI at that time were making efforts not only to penetrate the FPCC but also to discredit the pro-Castro organization. Was revealing Oswald's Soviet life part of this program?

But the most intriguing aspect of Oswald's stay in New Orleans centered around 544 Camp Street.

544 Camp Street

It was at 544 Camp Street in an old, three-story office building that the paths of Lee Harvey Oswald, the FBI, the CIA, anti-Castro Cubans, and organized-crime figures all crossed.

Until a few months prior to Oswald's arrival in New Orleans, the aging building housed the offices of the Cuban Revolutionary Council (CRC), the umbrella anti-Castro organization created by CIA officer E. Howard Hunt.

CRC members included Carlos Bringuier, the man who had the much-publicized street encounter with Oswald; Sergio Archaca-Smith, a CRC top official with close documented ties to CIA operative and pilot David Ferrie; and Carlos Prio Socarras, former president of Cuba before Batista and one of the leading Cuban exiles close to CIA agents E. Howard Hunt, Bernard Barker, and Frank Sturgis (all of later Watergate fame).

Prio—who had paid for the yacht *Granma* Castro used to land his revolutionaries on Cuba—had turned on Castro and become a leading anti-Castroite. It is alleged that Prio was to have become the new president of Cuba following the ill-fated Bay of Pigs Invasion.

Prio once was arrested in a gunrunning conspiracy along with a man named Robert McKeown. According to evidence developed by the Warren Commission,

McKeown had been involved in a deal "running jeeps to Cuba" and other smuggling operations with Jack Ruby, the man who killed Oswald.

In April 1977, before he was scheduled to testify for the House Select Committee on Assassinations, Prio was found shot in the chest in his Miami Beach garage. The wound was ruled self-inflicted.

Although the CRC had left 544 Camp Street by the time Oswald was seen there in the summer of 1963, there were still plenty of Cuban connections. A side entrance to 544 Camp Street was 531 Lafayette Street, the address of Guy Banister Associates, a private detective agency. Banister, who the *New Orleans States-Item* paper in 1967 claimed helped supply munitions to the Bay of Pigs invaders, was a former FBI man with connections reaching into the bureau, the CIA, and organized crime as well as the Cuban exiles.

In 1978 his secretary, Delphine Roberts, told the *Dallas Morning News* that Oswald had worked for Banister as "an undercover agent" in the summer of 1963. During that same time, another of Banister's employees was Oswald's former Civil Air Patrol leader, David Ferrie, who worked for both the CIA and the New Orleans mob.

In the Warren Commission exhibits are some of Oswald's Fair Play for Cuba Committee leaflets. They are stamped:

FPCC
544 CAMP STREET
NEW ORLEANS, LA.

Another intriguing contact point between Oswald, 544 Camp Street, and the Cubans was Ernesto Rodriguez. Recall that in the summer of 1963 Oswald wrote the Fair Play for Cuba Committee stating he was going to get a small office. During this same time period, the owner of the 544 Camp Street building, Sam Newman, said he was approached by a Hispanic man who asked about renting an office and said he was an electrician by day and wanted to teach Spanish at night.

Shortly after the assassination and acting on a tip, authorities talked with Rodriguez, who did teach Spanish and whose father was in the electrical business.

Rodriguez admitted that he had met Oswald, who apparently wanted to learn Spanish. Rodriguez also said that Oswald had offered to train anti-Castro exiles and, in fact, it was Rodriguez who had sent Oswald to meet Carlos Bringuier.

There was plenty of undercover activity going on at 544 Camp Street in the summer of 1963. The location may have had something to do with it. The building was located close to the New Orleans offices of both the FBI and the CIA, it was near the Crescent City Garage where Oswald was seen in the company of FBI agents, and it was just around the corner from the William B. Reily Coffee Company, Oswald's employer.

New Orleans district attorney Jim Garrison believed it was at 544 Camp Street that plans were set in motion that culminated in Dealey Plaza.

The CIA reported to the Warren Commission that Oswald's pro-Castro activities included an attempt to secure a visa to visit Cuba during a trip to Mexico City in late September 1963. The agency apparently went to great lengths to prove that Oswald was in Mexico City at this time, but the effort was not entirely successful. Photographs of a man entering the Soviet embassy and a tape recording made at the time were shown to be of someone other than Oswald.

To document Oswald's visit to the Cuban embassy, the CIA relied on the testimony of a Mexican who worked at the embassy, Silvia Tirado de Duran. Duran, however, is a dubious witness at best since it is now known that the twenty-six-year-old woman was arrested twice following the assassination on orders from the CIA and may have been coerced into giving false testimony.

But again, it is the connections between the assassination and anti-Castro groups that have always turned up the most intriguing evidence—evidence that has largely been ignored by US authorities, particularly the Warren Commission.

Oswald and the Exiles

One of several incidents often cited to connect Lee Harvey Oswald with the anti-Castro Cubans involves one of the most violent of the exile groups, Alpha 66, and its founder, Antonio Veciana Blanch.

Veciana, a former Cuban bank accountant who turned against Castro, was helping to conduct raids against the island during the missile crisis and has consistently maintained that he was working for the CIA.

In the spring of 1963, Kennedy publicly criticized the hit-and-run raids of Alpha 66, to which Veciana replied publicly, "We are going to attack again and again." The militant Cuban leader has claimed to have worked for a CIA officer known to him as "Maurice Bishop." According to Veciana, he met with Bishop more than a hundred times and the CIA officer helped guide the activities of Alpha 66, including plans to assassinate Castro. Veciana said his relationship with the agency did not end until 1973, when Bishop paid him $253,000 as back pay for his services.

But Veciana's most astounding claim is that during a visit to Dallas in late August or early September 1963, he saw his CIA case officer in conversation with a man he later recognized as Lee Harvey Oswald.

Although the House Select Committee on Assassinations failed to "credit" Veciana's story of the Oswald-Bishop meeting, it nevertheless went to great lengths to try to locate the mysterious Bishop, including sending an artist's sketch of Bishop to US newspapers. The committee also scoured CIA files to try to identify Bishop. Unsurprisingly, the agency denied ever assigning a case officer to Veciana.

Veciana also told the committee that shortly after the assassination, Bishop contacted him and reminded him that he had a relative working for Cuban intelligence living in Mexico. According to Veciana, Bishop wanted Veciana to offer his relative a "large sum of money" to say that the relative and his wife met Oswald during his Mexico City trip. Veciana said he agreed to this scheme but was unable to contact his relative.

The House committee later developed information that Bishop may have been none other than David Atlee Phillips, former chief of the Western Hemisphere Division's Directorate of Operations in the CIA. Phillips denied being Bishop and a suddenly fearful Veciana agreed. However, after arranging a meeting between Veciana and Phillips, the committee staff reported it "suspected that Veciana was lying when he denied that the retired CIA officer was Bishop." Its report added, "Further, a former CIA case officer who was assigned from September 1960 to November 1962 to the JM/WAVE station in Miami told the committee that the retired officer [Phillips] had in fact used the alias, Maurice Bishop."

Though the controversy continues today, most JFK researchers believe Phillips and Bishop were one and the same.

David Atlee Phillips died of cancer on July 7, 1988. In an unpublished novel concerning a CIA officer who lived in Mexico City, Phillips had his character lament:

> I was one of those officers who handled Lee Harvey Oswald. . . . We gave him the mission of killing Fidel Castro in Cuba. . . . I don't know why he killed Kennedy. But I do know he used precisely the plan we had devised against Castro. Thus the CIA did not anticipate the president's assassination, but it was responsible for it. I share that guilt.

A prime example of the interference with investigations into links between anti-Castro Cubans and the assassination came just days after Kennedy was killed. The Chicago field office of the Secret Service reported to superiors that it had heard from an informant that a Chicago group "may have [had] a connection with the JFK assassination." The informant reported that on the day before the assassination, a Cuban militant named Homer S. Echevarria had stated that he had "plenty of money" for an illegal arms deal and would proceed with the plan "as soon as we take care of Kennedy."

The Secret Service checked on Echevarria and discovered he was an associate of the military director of the Cuban Student Directorate (the New Orleans chapter of the CSD was headed by Carlos Bringuier, who had squabbled with Oswald on the streets of that city) and that the munitions deal was financed by "hoodlum elements . . . not restricted to Chicago."

Although the Secret Service wanted to pursue the matter, the FBI—which on November 29, 1963, President Johnson designated to control the assassination investigation—"made clear that it wanted the Secret Service to terminate its investigation" of the Echevarria report. The case was closed.

One anti-Castro-Cuban-Oswald story that was not so easy to brush off is that of Cuban exile Silvia Odio. She and her sister Annie came from a distinguished and wealthy Cuban family. The sisters had been forced to flee Cuba after their parents were imprisoned by the Castro government. Their father, who initially had supported Castro's revolution, had turned against the bearded leader and was arrested for concealing a man named Reinaldo Gonzalez, who was involved in a plot to kill

Castro. Interestingly, Gonzalez's co-conspirator was Antonio Veciana, the leader of Alpha 66 who operated under the instructions of Maurice Bishop.

Shortly before moving to Dallas, Silvia Odio had joined with other anti-Castro Cubans in Puerto Rico and formed Junta Revolucionaria (the Cuban Revolutionary Junta) or JURE.

One night in late September 1963—they believe it was the 26th or 27th—three men came to Odio's Dallas apartment. There were two Hispanics and one Caucasian, described as weary, unkempt, and unshaved.

The leader of the trio identified himself as "Leopoldo" and introduced the other Hispanic man as "Angel" or "Angelo." He introduced the American as "Leon Oswald."

The men said they had just arrived from New Orleans, were members of JURE, and were working with the Cuban Revolutionary Council (CRC). They knew her father's underground name and many details of anti-Castro activities in Cuba, including recent plots to kill Castro. They told Silvia Odio that they were trying to raise funds for anti-Castro operations and wanted her help in translating solicitation letters to American businessmen. Something about the men, however, made Odio uneasy and she sent them away after warning them that she did not want to be involved in a campaign of violence. During their brief stay, her sister Annie also got a good look at the trio.

Within forty-eight hours, "Leopoldo" called Silvia Odio and asked for her thoughts on their American companion. She said the man then made a series of comments, saying:

> Well, you know he's a Marine, an ex-Marine, and an expert marksman. He would be a tremendous asset to anyone, except that you never know how to take him. . . . He's kind of loco, kind of nuts. He could go any way. He could do anything—like getting underground in Cuba, like killing Castro. . . . The American says we Cubans don't have any guts. He says we should have shot President Kennedy after the Bay of Pigs. He says we should do something like that.

Apparently, that was all "Leopoldo" had to say, for he quickly hung up and Odio never heard from him again. She later told author Anthony Summers, "Immediately, I suspected there was some sort of scheme or plot."

Although the Odio sisters wrote of the incident to their father and told the story to friends well *before* Kennedy's assassination, they did not tell authorities of the strange visitors. Both sisters were shocked and frightened to see photographs of Lee Harvey Oswald since, then and now, they both believe him to be "Leon Oswald."

After the assassination, word of the Odio visit reached the FBI, which investigated the matter for the Warren Commission. The Commission, having already accepted FBI and CIA evidence that Oswald was on his way to or in Mexico City at the time of the Odio visit, stated, "While the FBI had not yet completed its investigation into this matter at the time the report went to press, the Commission has concluded that Lee Harvey Oswald was not at Mrs. Odio's apartment in September 1963."

No one seemed to even consider whether someone might have been posing as Oswald.

The Odio story caused great problems with the Warren Commission Report. If Oswald was in Dallas, he couldn't have been traveling by bus to Mexico at the same time. And if the Oswald in Odio's apartment was not the real Oswald, then it is clear that someone was impersonating him with an eye toward implicating Oswald in the assassination. Small wonder the Commission decided to let the matter rest.

Oswald's Girlfriend

Recent revelations by Judyth Vary Baker may go a long way in untangling the morass of characters and agendas involving Lee Harvey Oswald in New Orleans during the summer of 1963.

Baker, who in 2013 was living outside the United States after claiming death threats, told her life story in the 2010 book *Me & Lee*. Although Baker's story has suffered attacks from all sides, her story is nevertheless internally consistent and well supported by known facts and documentation.

As a precocious teenager Baker vowed to find a cure for cancer after losing her grandmother to that disease. Still in high school, she came to the attention of military and medical authorities for her work in cancer research as well as a project on how to acquire magnesium from sea water. The magnesium project brought the attention of Florida leaders, including the powerful senator George Smathers, both a personal friend of President Kennedy's and a staunch supporter of the anti-Castro Cubans. Smathers helped bring her cancer studies to the attention of Drs. Harold Diehl and Alton Ochsner, both high-ranking officers of the American Cancer Society.

They were desperately looking for a cure for cancer because they knew that the polio vaccines developed by Jonas Salk and Albert Sabin in the 1950s had been made from monkey glands, which also carried a cancer-causing DNA virus called Simian Virus (SV) 40. While the vaccines may have checked the spread of polio, the contamination brought on an epidemic of cancer, some not becoming apparent for many years. Simian Immunodeficiency Virus, found in drugs from monkey glands, is thought by some to be a forerunner of Acquired Immunodeficiency Syndrome (AIDS).

Baker said that in late April 1963 she arrived in New Orleans to continue her cancer research. She was enticed by promises of a scholarship to Tulane University and the privilege of working with renowned cancer researcher Dr. Mary Sherman, director of the bone pathology laboratory at the Ochsner Clinic there.

To Baker's consternation, she was never given a scholarship or allowed to work in the clinic. Instead, she was put in touch with David Ferrie, who told her he was running a clandestine but government-backed cancer lab trying to find a cure. Ferrie's apartment was filled with cages for white mice and an assistant knowledgeable in cancer research was needed. Judyth Baker fit the bill.

But even before she could meet with Dr. Ochsner, Baker came across a young man in the post office who spoke to her in Russian. Having studied some Russian, Baker was instantly drawn to this new friend—Lee Harvey Oswald.

During the ensuing weeks, Baker claimed to have developed a love for Lee, despite the fact that both were already married. This, of course, made their rendezvous secretive and not likely to have been documented. This lack of proof has caused much disbelief in her story. It was also convenient to the romance that Oswald's wife was in Texas and Baker's husband was only home infrequently, as he worked on oil rigs in the Gulf of Mexico.

David Lewis was in the thick of the New Orleans scene in the summer of 1963. He was an acquaintance of Ferrie's and Oswald's as well as an employee of Guy Banister's. His wife, Anna Lewis, said she and her husband once were introduced by Oswald to Mafia boss Carlos Marcello in his 500 Club. Several times the Lewises met with Lee and Judyth. In a taped interview Anna Lewis was asked to describe their relationship. "I would say they were lovers," she responded. She apparently was not lying to support Judyth's story, because judging by her other comments, Anna Lewis obviously did not care for Baker.

What is documented is that both Lee Oswald and Judyth Baker went to work at the Reily Coffee Company on the same date—Friday, May 10, 1963. This was five days before Baker's twentieth birthday. Oswald was twenty-three. Only three days before, both Lee and Judyth had met with Dr. Ochsner, a well-known supporter of anti-Castro activities. Realizing from the conversation that Ochsner obviously had known Oswald previously, Baker then knew their meeting in the post office had not been an accident.

Baker soon understood that both she and Lee were working for clandestine yet powerful backers. She knew Oswald had connections to Carlos Marcello, a Dallas nightclub owner named Jack Rubenstein, and local businessman Clay Shaw, but she also suspected ties to the CIA as well. Once when she asked Oswald about the source of his money (other than his Reily paycheck), he put his finger to his lips and said, "I can't tell you. But I can guarantee that the money isn't coming from Uncle Fidel."

Baker explained, "I gave up trying to follow the players, techniques, and motives in Lee's complex covert world."

Her days became increasingly harried. She covered for Oswald at the coffee company by clocking him out each day while he was at Ferrie's apartment, running errands, and meeting with Guy Banister. After work she would go to Ferrie's apartment to do research and write reports on their progress. She said she and Lee also were tasked with trying to ferret out any Castro supporters from among the many

Cubans employed at the Reily Coffee Company. She explained that Oswald's distributing of pro-Castro literature was part of this same agenda.

Due to his many roles, Oswald frequently was missing from his job. This was confirmed by Charles Le Blanc, the Reily employee who "broke Oswald in on the job." After the assassination, LeBlanc told the FBI, "Oswald was not attentive to his job and wandered about the building considerably and was usually gone when he was needed." He said when he asked Oswald where he had been, Oswald would just shrug his shoulders and say, "Just been around."

In his travels to and from the coffee company, Oswald would stop frequently at the nearby Crescent City Garage, where, as will be described later, he was seen in the company of federal agents.

Further support for Baker's story comes from the fact that Oswald was fired from his job at the Reily Coffee Company on July 19, 1963. Three weeks later, Oswald was arrested for the street incident with Carlos Bringuier and his name appeared in the newspaper. That same day, Baker, who had accompanied Oswald to his meeting with Bringuier, also was fired from Reily. The Cuban spy-hunt phase had come to an end but the cancer project continued.

In Ferrie's informal lab, Oswald would clean the mice cages while Baker would accept new mice from Cuban couriers who brought them from a breeding laboratory in a nearby house, test for the most virulent tumors in the injected mice, and then grind up the tumors in a blender to produce what they called the "product," which was delivered to Dr. Mary Sherman for analysis.

Very soon, Baker began to realize their work was carrying them into the realm of cancer-causing agents as biological weapons more than attempting to find a cure. She said she and Oswald as well as Dr. Sherman became concerned.

Their fears were well founded, for in late August a "volunteer" inmate was brought from Louisiana's Angola State Prison to the Jackson State Mental Hospital in Jackson, Louisiana, where he was injected with the latest "product." Baker's story explains an incident in nearby Clinton, Louisiana, involving Oswald, Ferrie, and a man later identified as Clay Shaw, an incident that still puzzles assassination researchers. What would Shaw, Ferrie, and Oswald be doing in Clinton? One suggestion has been that the trio was somehow involved in the FBI's Counterintelligence Program (COINTELPRO). It is now well established that COINTELPRO was a ruthless long-term bureau program Hoover designed to disrupt and discredit political groups he opposed. The notorious wiretapping of Dr. Martin Luther King Jr. is just one example of this program.

But Baker offered another explanation. So as not to draw attention to themselves in the small town of Jackson, the Oswald group parked near the courthouse in Clinton to await a phone call notifying them that the prisoner was on the way.

Located about ninety miles northwest of New Orleans and twelve miles east of Jackson, Clinton was a small community of about 1,500 people in 1963. While the town was larger than Jackson, it was still difficult to keep the townspeople from knowing just about everything that went on there—especially if it involved strangers.

In 1963, the civil rights program was gaining strength throughout the South. That summer would become known as "civil rights summer" and tiny Clinton was one of the communities targeted for a black voter registration drive by the Congress of Racial Equality. Tensions in Clinton were high. Earlier in the summer, several blacks were arrested there simply for writing appeals to the mayor and district attorney.

One morning, between August 22 and September 17—a time when Oswald's whereabouts remain officially unaccounted for—a long line of blacks waited to undergo the then-tedious process of registering to vote. Local police stood nearby, watchful for any breach of the peace. The incident that morning—pieced together from several witnesses—began with the arrival of a large, black Cadillac carrying three men. After the car parked near the registrar's office, one of the men—a slightly built white man—got out and joined the line of blacks. Later, witnesses were unanimous in identifying the man as Lee Harvey Oswald.

The registrar, Henry Palmer, had more to go on than just looks. He later recounted, "I asked him for his identification and he pulled out a US Navy I.D. card. . . . I looked at the name on it and it was Lee H. Oswald with a New Orleans address." Palmer said Oswald told him he wanted to get a job at nearby East Louisiana State Hospital and thought he would have a better chance if he was a registered voter. Oswald was told he had not lived in the area long enough to qualify as a voter and, after thanking Palmer, he returned to the Cadillac. Baker explained that Oswald, becoming bored and very interested in the civil rights movement, made a bet that he could register to vote without the problems some of the blacks faced.

Meanwhile, Town Marshal John Manchester had approached the car, but left after speaking to the driver, whom he later described as "a big man, gray-haired, with ruddy complexion."

New Orleans district attorney Jim Garrison later attempted to prove that the driver was Clay Shaw, the defendant in Garrison's JFK assassination-plot trial in 1967. Many researchers argued that the driver was Guy Banister. Baker's assertion that it was Shaw was given weight by Registrar Palmer, who in later years told this author that he had known Guy Banister in the Army and that the man driving the Cadillac in Clinton was definitely not Banister, thus providing strong support to Garrison's charge that the man was indeed Clay Shaw.

The tragic outcome of this visit was that the prisoner eventually arrived at the hospital, was injected with the cancer agent, and died soon after. It was only then that Baker said she learned that the man she thought had volunteered to help find a cancer cure because he already was dying from the disease actually was a perfectly healthy Cuban prisoner chosen because he was approximately the same size and weight as Castro. She finally saw the ultimate goal of the cancer-cure project—developing a cancer-causing agent for use on Cuba's leader.

Horrified, Baker left a note for Ochsner stating, "Injecting disease-causing materials into an unwitting subject who does not have a disease is unethical." Her note set off a firestorm. Ferrie warned her, "He's your enemy now. He told me that you and Lee are expendable."

Realizing the gravity of her situation, Baker moved out of New Orleans and returned to Florida to live with her husband, Robert Baker. Oswald made a mysterious trip to Mexico. According to Baker, Oswald was to have passed the cancer-causing "product" to a contact in Mexico City for transmittal to Cuba. But the scheme fell apart, according to what Oswald was told, because of Hurricane Flora in late September 1963. It was among the deadliest hurricanes in history, causing more than 7,000 deaths. In its path across Cuba, it destroyed safe houses, disrupted communications, and caused Oswald's contact to miss the rendezvous in Mexico.

Still in communication via a complicated telephone arrangement through Ferrie, who had access to illegal and untraceable sports betting lines, Baker said, she and Oswald began to realize that the attempt on Castro might have masked a bigger, darker agenda—a move against President Kennedy.

On Wednesday night, November 20, only two days before the assassination, Baker had her last phone conversation with Oswald. It was highly emotional as Baker begged him to get out of the plot. But Oswald said he was trying to foil the plot and added, "If I stay, there will be one less bullet fired at Kennedy." Oswald also repeated the name David Atlee Phillips, saying this was the man he believed was organizing the assassination. It was Phillips, aka Maurice Bishop, seen meeting with Oswald by the CIA-backed anti-Castroite Antonio Veciana. Phillips also worked with David Morales in the JM/WAVE operation. Morales was named by E. Howard Hunt in a 2007 deathbed statement as a major link between CIA Covert Action Officer Cord Meyer and William Harvey, head of the ZR/RIFLE CIA-Mafia assassination team, and the real shooters in the assassination conspiracy.

Following the assassination, Baker was shocked to witness the televised murder of Oswald by Jack Ruby, a man she had met in New Orleans through Lee Oswald. She soon received a phone call from David Ferrie advising her to become a "vanilla girl," that is, to lay low, blend in, and forget about her career in science. He said if she was lucky, she might live.

Baker learned that Dr. Sherman had been murdered in July 1964 and that Jack Ruby, David Ferrie, and one of Ferrie's associates had all died in early 1967 under questionable circumstances at the beginning of the Garrison investigation. Baker took Ferrie's advice. She did not speak of her experiences in New Orleans or her connection to Lee Oswald until December 1998, when she rented a copy of Oliver Stone's film *JFK*. Her experiences all came flooding back. With her children grown and her husband now deceased, she decided to go public with her story. Also, she said, "I realized Lee had been murdered by a friend [Jack Ruby]. . . . My eyes were opened to the corruption that rules our nation." Baker came to realize that her lover Lee Oswald was involved in intelligence work for the US government, just as his mother always claimed, and had infiltrated a group bent on assassinating the president but was set up as a patsy and murdered in public to protect the real assassins by silencing him.

One of Baker's staunchest supporters has been Florida advertising executive Edward T. Haslam, a native of New Orleans and author of the 2007 book *Dr. Mary's Monkey*, which documents the polio vaccine adulteration, the cancer lab, and the work by Drs. Sherman and Ochsner, David Ferrie, and Oswald. In his first edition, Haslam wrote it would be vital to the story if a living witness could be found. He was astounded to learn of and meet Judyth Vary Baker. But this brought up a bizarre and unexplained circumstance.

In 1972 while attending Tulane University in New Orleans, Haslam was invited to a party, the hostess of which was introduced as Judyth Vary Baker. This Baker got Haslam off into the kitchen and began to question him about his interest in the Kennedy assassination. Although, like many college students, Haslam had spoken out about the many questions regarding the assassination, he felt uncomfortable about this questioning by Baker and, making excuses, he soon left, never to return to that apartment. Imagine his astonishment when in the year 2000 he was introduced to Judyth Vary Baker in Florida and quickly realized this was not the same woman he had met in 1972 New Orleans. Adding to the mystery was the fact that the real Judyth Baker fled New Orleans in the fall of 1963 and never returned. Who knew enough about the work in New Orleans to organize an impersonation of Judyth Baker in 1972? And to what purpose was someone scouring Tulane University and its environs to learn who may have known about Oswald and his activities there? This incidence lends strong support to the idea that a very dangerous secret was being preserved through cover-up and misdirection. Some people believe the adulteration of the polio vaccine and the subsequent rise in cancer deaths may even be a bigger secret than who was responsible for JFK's death.

While many people, particularly those close to US intelligence and military sources, still claim that Kennedy may have been killed on orders from Castro as a reprisal for the CIA-Mafia-Cuban plots against him, the evidence points more toward the anti-Castro Cubans under the tutelage of the CIA.

Former senator Robert Morgan, a member of the Senate Intelligence Committee that in 1976 looked into CIA-Mafia plots, continued to maintain that Kennedy brought about his own death. Differing from the conclusions of his own committee, Morgan stated flatly, "There is no doubt in my mind that John Fitzgerald Kennedy was assassinated by Fidel Castro, or someone under his influence, in retaliation for our efforts to assassinate him."

But one anti-Castro leader, John Martino, spelled out the assassination plan to a Texas business friend in 1975. In a startling telephone conversation with Fred Claasen, repeated by author Anthony Summers, Martino admitted to serving as a CIA contract agent. He told Claasen:

> The anti-Castro people put Oswald together. Oswald didn't know who he was working for—he was just ignorant of who was really putting him together. Oswald was to meet his contact at the Texas Theater. They were to meet Oswald in the theater, and get him out of the country, then eliminate him. Oswald made a mistake. . . . There was no way we could get to him. They had Ruby kill him.

Most researchers today doubt Castro had a hand in Kennedy's death. Even the accused assassin couldn't buy it. During interrogation on the Sunday morning he was killed by Jack Ruby, Oswald was asked if his beliefs regarding Cuba played a role in the assassination. Asked by Secret Service inspector Thomas J. Kelley if Kennedy's assassination would have any effect on the US policy toward Cuba, Oswald replied, "Will Cuba be better off with the President dead? Someone will take his place, Lyndon Johnson, no doubt, and he will probably follow the same policy."

Also, while Castro eventually did learn of the plots against him, there is no firm evidence that he knew of these schemes in time to have launched a retaliatory strike by November 1963. There seems no serious motive for Castro to have Kennedy killed outside of simple revenge—and every motive against the idea.

In a 1977 interview with Bill Moyers broadcast on CBS, Castro denied any thought of trying to kill the US president:

> It would have been absolute insanity by Cuba. . . . It would have been a provocation. Needless to say, it would have been to run the risk that our country would have been destroyed by the United States. Nobody who's not insane could have thought about [killing Kennedy in retaliation].

The day after the assassination CIA director John McCone received a memo from his Mexico City station stating that Oswald had been in contact with Valery Kostikov, a KGB officer there thought to be an expert on assassination. Prophetically, the memo added, "If Oswald was part of a foreign conspiracy, he might be killed before he could reveal it to US authorities." This information immediately was passed to President Johnson, who probably knew better than to subscribe to a foreign plot. However, here was the excuse to proclaim fear of a Soviet plot and World War III and to curtail any potentially dangerous investigations.

Johnson had his aide Cliff Carter notify Dallas County district attorney Henry Wade to not mention any conspiracy and he ordered all intelligence agents in Mexico to stop investigating any leads involving conspiracy. This was the initial step that blocked the plans to blame Castro for the assassination.

But if the evidence of Castro's involvement in the assassination is meager, it is more than made up for by the abundance of evidence of anti-Castro Cuban involvement, as we have seen in this chapter.

And behind the anti-Castro Cubans always lurked the shadowy hands of US intelligence and the even darker specter of organized crime.

Mobsters

Immigrants to the United States in the late 1800s and early 1900s, trapped by their inability to speak English, lack of education, and class and cultural differences, found themselves crammed into inner-city ghettos spawning a multitude of street gangs. They carried names like the Whyos, the Dead Rabbits, the Bowery Boys, the Tenth Avenue Gang, the Gas House Gang, and the Midnight Terrors. Despite their colorful names, these gangs were anything but funny. Young toughs would rob and beat their victims in broad daylight, with little to fear from the police—as long as they confined their illegal activities to the ghetto and its cowed population.

In the various ethnic communities some people had belonged to the secret societies of other countries—the Mafia of Sicily, the Camorra of Italy, and the Tongs of China. They brought the learned terror and intimidation of these societies to their new home, where it found fertile soil.

As America entered the twentieth century, the city gangs were becoming more adept at their profession and expanding operations to include gambling, prostitution, and lotteries. They also were the bankers for the poor, charging exorbitant interest rates from those who could borrow money nowhere else.

The Irish brought a new dimension of power to the gangs. Unhampered by a language barrier and experienced in politics in their homeland, the Irish gangs gained advantages by allying themselves with political figures. Initially it was the politicians who used the gangsters. Ballot boxes were stuffed, voters intimidated, and opposition rallies broken up. But as the gang leaders grew more wealthy, and thus more powerful, soon the politicians came seeking favors. Through the years that Tammany Hall controlled New York City, Irish gangsters provided the enforcement muscle.

Bootleggers and Boozers

For more than fifty years prior to 1920, American groups such as the Women's Christian Temperance Union and the Anti-Saloon League had lobbied Congress and state legislatures to prohibit the manufacture and sale of distilled spirits. Finally, with many male voters off serving in the military and with the emotional exhaustion and moral primness following World War I, their dream became reality. In December 1917, Congress passed the Eighteenth Amendment to the Constitution, prohibiting the sale of intoxicating beverages, and by January 1919, the necessary thirty-six of the forty-eight states had ratified it.

In October 1919—overriding the veto of President Woodrow Wilson— Congress passed the Volstead Act, which created the government bureaucracy needed to enforce the Eighteenth Amendment. At midnight January 16, 1920, Prohibition became the law of the land.

Less than an hour after midnight, six masked men drove a truck into a Chicago railroad switchyard, broke into two freight cars, and made off with $100,000 worth of whiskey marked FOR MEDICINAL USE ONLY. Bootleggers bought a quart of quality Scotch at sea for $4, then diluted it into three quarts selling for as much as $40 a bottle.

That was just the beginning of an era that witnessed rapid decay of public morality, disrespect for law, and the rise of a gigantic criminal empire that remains with us today. In addition to the growing power of this criminal empire, Americans saw law-enforcement powers slowly shift from local officials to the national government.

New power bases arose, such as the fledgling Federal Bureau of Investigation, begun in 1909, and a variety of Prohibition agencies, which were to evolve into such modern forms as the Bureau of Narcotics and Dangerous Drugs (forerunner of the Drug Enforcement Agency) and the Alcohol, Tobacco, and Firearms agency (now the Justice Department's Bureau of Alcohol, Tobacco, and Firearms and Explosives).

Illegal booze was smuggled into the United States in every conceivable manner and from every conceivable point—across the Mexican and Canadian borders and offloaded from ships to small powerboats that moved out of remote bays almost at will.

One erstwhile honest businessman who turned to bootlegging may have been Joseph P. Kennedy, patriarch of the Kennedy clan. Although no conclusive evidence of Kennedy's bootlegging is available—his business papers are still kept locked away in Boston's John F. Kennedy Library—it has been widely rumored that the elder Kennedy got started on the road to riches by importing illegal booze. This allegation is supported by the fact that as soon as Prohibition ended, Kennedy immediately was in the Scotch, gin, and rum business through a firm he founded called Somerset Importers.

Unlike today's War on Drugs, even Prohibition's most ardent supporters were forced to concede that it simply didn't work. If enough people want a commodity, others will find a way to get it to them—for a price.

The price of alcohol prohibition—the massive corruption of the political and legal system, the enormous power wielded by the criminal gangs, and the deaths and maiming from toxic hooch and gangland wars—was too steep. On December 5, 1933, Prohibition was repealed. After national Prohibition ended, each state created its own liquor authority, opening up new avenues for bribery and payoffs.

As America's fortunes soared between 1910 and 1929, so did those of the gangs, particularly those with farsighted leadership. A Jewish gangster from New York, Arnold Rothstein, became an example of the successful underworld leader. Nicknamed "The Brain," Rothstein grew from a small-time gambler into one of the most powerful men in the city. He reportedly even fixed the 1919 World Series. Though he initially refrained from bootlegging, Rothstein eventually became the largest supplier of illegal booze in the East. He began to move in respectable circles, rubbing elbows with city and state officials.

Rothstein was considered a wealthy front man for New York's real Mafia leaders, which by the late 1920s involved two large families run by Giuseppe Masseria and Salvatore Maranzano. These families were locked in a protracted blood feud known as the Castellammorese War (from Maranzano's Sicilian hometown of Castellammore del Golfo).

Eventually gangsters from both New York and Chicago were drawn into the war. By 1931, the war was going against Masseria when one of his lieutenants, Charles "Lucky" Luciano (real name: Salvatore Lucania), decided to arrange a "peace" by having Masseria murdered on April 15, 1931, in a Coney Island restaurant.

Luciano immediately called a meeting with Maranzano ending the war. Luciano was now the preeminent leader of the criminal mobs. Wisely, Luciano declined the title of *capo di tutti capi* (boss of all bosses). Instead he created a commission of bosses and organized the old Mafia families into a national crime syndicate, finally realizing the dream of merging the criminal gangs.

Luciano began to move control of crime away from the traditional Italian and Sicilian families. New faces were beginning to show up in the crime syndicate. The Jewish math wizard Meyer Lansky, Legs Diamond, Dutch Schultz, and Benjamin "Bugsy" Siegel were among those slowly being admitted to policy meetings. But Luciano was still the man in charge. After extensive investigation, Tennessee senator Estes Kefauver wrote, "The Mafia is the cement that binds organized crime and the man who perfected the cement was Luciano."

Lucky Goes to War

Next to Prohibition, one of the most far-reaching events in the history of organized crime came during World War II when Lucky Luciano became partners with the US government.

Luciano never gave up his original means of making money—prostitution—and it proved his undoing.

In 1936, under special New York County prosecutor Thomas E. Dewey, Luciano was tried and convicted of compulsory prostitution, ending up in Clinton State Prison at Dannemora in upstate New York. It appeared Luciano was safely put away. But then came World War II.

The war produced undreamed-of wealth for the mobs wherever they were. The friendly bootleggers of yesterday became the friendly black marketers of today, supplying nylons, new cars, gasoline coupons, tires, food ration stamps, and even military commissions and discharges.

It was unnecessary to counterfeit ration coupons. Gangsters simply obtained real ones from corrupt officials within the Office of Price Administration, a semi-volunteer organization that counted among its young lawyers an aspiring politician from California, Richard M. Nixon. One man who dealt with the Office of Price Administration and became rich in the automobile-tire business during the war was Charles G. "Bebe" Rebozo, who remained close friends with Nixon through the years.

Toward the end of 1942, the first year of war for the United States, things were not going well for the US Navy. In March of that year alone, twenty-four American ships had been sunk by German U-boats and on November 9, 1942, the former French liner *Normandie* caught fire and rolled over in its North River moorings in Manhattan while being refitted as a troop carrier. It was plainly an act of sabotage—and later was attributed to mobster Vito Genovese, who returned to Italy during the war and supported dictator Benito Mussolini. Furthermore, naval intelligence was convinced that information about ship convoys was being transmitted to the Axis by longshoremen of German and Italian extraction.

In a desperate attempt to compensate for years of neglect in the intelligence field, US military officers decided to contact the mob for help. Navy Secretary Frank Knox created a special intelligence unit for the Third Naval District, including the Port of New York, which handled nearly half of all US foreign shipping. This unit was headed by Lieutenant Commander Charles Radcliffe Haffenden, who quickly opened an unobtrusive office in Manhattan's Astor Hotel, where he met with mob figures.

The Navy appealed to Manhattan district attorney Thomas E. Dewey to put them in touch with Mafia leaders. A Dewey investigator, Murray Gurfein, contacted Mafia boss Joseph "Socks" Lanza as a first step. Lanza immediately went to gangster Meyer Lansky, who had helped guide Luciano in organizing the national crime syndicate. Lansky, sensing an opportunity to increase his prestige with the syndicate, met with Commander Haffenden and promised to get Luciano's support. Years later, Lansky told biographers, "Sure, I'm the one who put Lucky and Naval Intelligence together. . . . The reason I cooperated was because of strong personal feelings. I wanted the Nazis beaten. . . . I was a Jew and I felt for those Jews in Europe who were suffering. They were my brothers."

Although officially no deals were made with Lansky and Luciano—they supposedly cooperated out of sheer patriotism—soon Luciano was transferred from the "Siberia" of Dannemora to the more genial surroundings of Great Meadow Prison near Comstock, New York. The alliance proved effective.

Union strikes and sabotage were practically nonexistent on the New York docks during the war. And when US forces landed in Sicily, Mafia men were waiting to show them the location of German positions and safe routes through minefields.

During this final phase of the war, the Mafia-military cooperation—known as Operation Underworld—moved from the Navy to the Office of Strategic Services, forerunner of the CIA.

On January 3, 1946, Dewey—by then governor of New York—forwarded to the state legislature an executive clemency for Luciano that noted his "aid" to the war effort. Luciano was freed from prison but promptly deported. He had never bothered to become an American citizen. He sailed for Italy aboard the SS *Laura Keene* on February 3, 1946. Once ensconced in Italy, Luciano didn't accept retirement. He began to bring his formidable organizational abilities to worldwide crime. Later that year, he turned up in Havana, Cuba, where Lansky was busy consolidating the gambling and prostitution business. However, American authorities warned the Cubans that medical supplies would be shut off if Luciano was allowed to remain. He soon departed.

Returning to Italy, Luciano began to organize an international narcotics syndicate that remains in operation today.

Official awareness of organized crime dates back to a conference of law-enforcement officials called together by US attorney general J. Howard McGrath in 1950. Officials from New Orleans, Dallas, and other cities testified to the brutal takeover of crime in their areas. One dissenter was Otto Kerner, the US attorney from Chicago, who maintained there was "no organized gambling in the city of Chicago." In 1973, Kerner was convicted of accepting $150,000 in bribes from horse-racing interests.

One of the results of the 1950 conference was the creation of a Select Senate Committee to probe organized crime under the sponsorship of senator Estes Kefauver of Tennessee. The Kefauver Committee hearings lasted well into 1951 and provided much more public knowledge about the national crime syndicate. While Kerner and McGrath—along with FBI director J. Edgar Hoover—had maintained that no crime syndicate existed, Kefauver and his committee provided the evidence that it did. The committee found that organized, professional gambling and bookmaking was widespread throughout the nation, that the narcotics industry was a "highly organized crime," and that the mob had infiltrated legitimate businesses ranging from advertising to transportation.

It also showed the amount of official corruption the syndicate needed to flourish. The committee's final report quoted a mobster named John Roselli, who later became embroiled in the CIA-Mafia assassination schemes, saying, "The wire service, the handbooks, the slot machines, and the other rackets which have thrived in the city of Chicago cannot operate without local corruption; if the handbooks are open, the conclusion is inescapable that the police are being paid off."

The Kefauver Committee also found that organized crime had spread from New York and Chicago to new markets in places like Kansas City, New Orleans, and Dallas.

After visiting New Orleans, the committee described it as "one of America's largest concentrations of gambling houses." One of these houses, the Beverly Club, was found to be owned by Phil Kastel, Frank Costello, Jake Lansky (Meyer's brother), and a local Mafia leader, Carlos Marcello.

Carlos Marcello

Carlos Marcello (real name: Calogero Minacore) was born in 1910, the child of Sicilian parents living in Tunisia. That same year the family came to New Orleans. At that time, the leader of the Mafia in New Orleans was Charles Montranga.

In 1922, Montranga was succeeded by one of his lieutenants, Sam Carolla. Carolla became a bootlegger during Prohibition and consolidated the mob's control of New Orleans. In 1932, Carolla was convicted of shooting a federal agent and was sent to prison, where he continued to run his crime organization. That same year, New York mayor-elect Fiorello LaGuardia was clamping down on mob operations there, so Frank Costello moved his slot machine business to New Orleans with Carolla's permission. Carolla even supplied a young associate to run the new gambling operation—Carlos Marcello.

By 1947, Carolla and Marcello—with the aid of Costello and Meyer Lansky—had expanded their gambling operations to include a racetrack, wire service, and several plush casinos. That year, Carolla was deported to Sicily and despite two illegal trips back, his control over New Orleans passed to Marcello.

By 1963, the New Orleans Metropolitan Crime Commission estimated Marcello's empire to range into the hundreds of millions of dollars, although Marcello claimed he made only about $1,600 a month as a tomato salesman. Much of Marcello's earnings had been put under the names of close relatives, hiding his true worth.

Marcello's national crime contacts included Costello, Joe Civello of Dallas, Sam Yaras of Chicago, Mickey Cohen of Los Angeles, and Santos Trafficante Sr., identified by the Kefauver Committee as Tampa's leading mobster.

Since the Kefauver Committee hearings, the US government had tried unsuccessfully to deport Marcello, who held only a Guatemalan passport obtained allegedly by bribes.

In the spring of 1961, Marcello found he was facing a new, and much tougher, government opponent than in the past. Entering the offices of the Immigration and Naturalization Services in New Orleans for his quarterly appointment to report as an alien, Marcello found himself handcuffed and driven to Moisant International Airport on direct orders from the new US attorney general, Robert F. Kennedy.

He was flown 1,200 miles to Guatemala City, where he was dumped without luggage and with little cash. Forced to leave Guatemala because of the ensuing political uproar, Marcello somehow found his way back to Miami. House Select Committee on Assassinations chief counsel G. Robert Blakey claimed wiretaps showed Marcello was flown back to the United States by a Dominican Republic Air Force plane; however, others claim he was flown back by pilot David Ferrie.

Although still fighting deportation, Marcello managed to remain in the United States. But his Sicilian pride must have been greatly injured at Kennedy's unceremonious actions. It was not long afterward that Marcello reportedly made threats against the attorney general.

Edward Becker, a Las Vegas promoter and corporate "investigator," told the House Select Committee on Assassinations that he was present at a meeting in September 1962, at Marcello's estate just outside New Orleans, Churchill Farms. Becker said at the mention of Kennedy's name, Marcello became angry and stated, "Don't worry about that little Bobby son-of-a-bitch. He's going to be taken care of." According to Becker, Marcello then uttered a Sicilian curse:

Livarsi na petra di la scarpa. (Take the stone out of my shoes.)

Marcello described President Kennedy as a dog and Bobby Kennedy as the tail. He then gave a startlingly accurate prophesy of what was to come. He said the dog will keep biting you if you only cut off its tail, but cut off the head and the dog will die, tail and all. The analogy was clear—with John Kennedy out of the way, his brother and attorney general Bobby Kennedy's war on crime would come to an end.

Becker said Marcello even had a plan. Marcello said he would use a "nut" for the job, someone who could be manipulated so that the killing could not be traced back to Marcello.

The House Select Committee on Assassinations determined that there were many connections between Marcello and the JFK assassination—Marcello's associate in Dallas, Joe Civello, was close with Jack Ruby; a Marcello employee, David Ferrie, was Oswald's Civil Air Patrol leader and said to have been in contact with Oswald during the summer of 1963; and Oswald's uncle, Charles "Dutz" Murret, was acquainted with Marcello through his personal driver as well as other associates.

It was just a few months after Marcello's reported threat that Lee Harvey Oswald arrived in New Orleans.

In the early 1980s, Marcello was convicted in a sting known as Operation Brilab. While operating under cover, one of the FBI agents involved, Michael F. Wacks, had grown close to Marcello. Wacks said despite the distance in time, Marcello could not hide his hatred for the Kennedys. "Historians don't understand the loyalty mob bosses felt politicians owed them," Wacks told this author. "They thought they were on the same level. If they put someone into power and he didn't do their bidding, their solution was to take him out."

Debilitated by strokes as well as advancing Alzheimer's, Marcello died in March 1993.

Conflict over who would lead the American crime syndicate was resolved on October 25, 1957, when two gunmen shot Albert Anastasia out of a barber's chair in New York. Earlier that year, Frank Costello, Luciano's successor, was shot while entering his Manhattan apartment. He lived but was charged with tax evasion after a note was found on him listing receipts from the recently built Tropicana Hotel in developing Las Vegas. Costello retired from the rackets.

Three weeks after Anastasia's death, Vito Genovese called a mob conference, held at the country estate of a Mafia lieutenant near the small town of Apalachin in upstate New York. On hand was a collection of almost every leader of the crime syndicate. The purpose of the meeting, according to later testimony of some of those present, was to demand that Genovese be named "boss of all bosses" after he justified the attacks on Costello and Anastasia. One argument presented was that Anastasia had tried to move in on the Cuban gambling operations of Santos Trafficante Jr. of Florida.

But before business could be settled, the police arrived, tipped off by an alert New York State Police sergeant who had become suspicious of all the big black cars with out-of-state license plates. Police roadblocks and searches of surrounding woods netted fifty-nine of the crime leaders, most of whom claimed they had come to visit a sick friend. These included Joe Bonanno, Joseph Magliocco, Carlo Gambino, Carmine Lombardozzi, John Bonventre, and Joseph Profaci from New York; Anthony Magaddino from Niagara Falls; Vito Genovese, Gerardo Catena, Joseph Ida, and Frank Majuri from New Jersey; Frank DeSimone from California; Joe Civello from

Dallas; and Trafficante. Carlos Marcello had wisely sent a surrogate while others, such as Sam Giancana of Chicago, escaped.

It was the first public look at organized crime since the Kefauver Committee hearings in the early 1950s. One of those aware of the serious threat posed by the mob's syndicate was young attorney Robert Kennedy, who after making a nation-wide fact-finding tour in 1956 and 1957 became most concerned with the mob's takeover of labor unions.

On January 30, 1957, the US Senate unanimously created the Senate Select Committee on Improper Activities in the Labor or Management Field—which became known as the McClellan Committee after its chairman, senator John L. McClellan of Arkansas. The committee's chief counsel was Robert F. Kennedy. One member of the McClellan Committee was a young senator from Boston, John F. Kennedy. Kennedy later said his brother wanted him on the committee to keep it from being overloaded with conservative, antilabor people.

Both Kennedys were highly active in the committee's work, which first took on the corrupt leader of the International Brotherhood of Teamsters, Dave Beck. Following the committee's investigation, Beck was convicted in a state court of larceny and then convicted of tax evasion in federal court. Beck went to prison in 1957. President Gerald Ford granted him a full pardon in May 1975.

With Beck gone, the presidency of the Teamsters Union went to Jimmy Hoffa. Even before Hoffa could be brought before the McClellan Committee, he was indicted for attempting to bribe commission attorney John Cye Cheasty.

At his trial, the FBI showed a film of the men conversing and Hoffa being arrested right after the money was exchanged. However, the jury of eight blacks and four whites was more impressed with Hoffa's defense attorney, Edward Bennett Williams (owner of the Washington Redskins), as well as World Heavyweight Champion boxer Joe Louis, who embraced Hoffa while visiting the court.

Hoffa went free to testify before the McClellan Committee. But Hoffa said he had a faulty memory when it came to most questions concerning his association with underworld characters, such as Paul Dorfman. Dorfman was described by the McClellan Committee as "an associate of Chicago mobsters and the head of a local of the Waste Material Handlers Union." Dorfman also was connected to a young Jack Ruby, the man who silenced Lee Harvey Oswald.

Dorfman's stepson, Allen Dorfman, was to play a major role in Hoffa loans to the underworld using the Teamsters' Central States Health and Welfare Fund as well as the Pension Fund. Today these are collectively known as the Central States Funds.

In 1951, Hoffa persuaded the welfare fund's two trustees—one of whom was Hoffa's successor, Frank Fitzsimmons—to place the fund with a newly formed branch of Union Casualty Agency. Union Casualty was owned by Paul Dorfman's stepson, Allen, and the elder Dorfman's wife, Rose.

Later Hoffa also sent the Central States Pension Fund to the Dorfman-controlled agency. These two funds made up 90 percent of the company's contracts, according to author Dan Moldea.

Veteran mob observers have established the close ties between Hoffa and two other underworld chieftains—Carlos Marcello and Santos Trafficante Jr.

Santos Trafficante and Cuba

During the mid-1950s, with gunfire punctuating internal mob leadership disputes in New York and various government panels revealing the extent of organized crime in the United States, crime bosses began to look south for relief.

As early as 1933, the mob's financial wizard, Meyer Lansky, had obtained gambling concessions in Cuba, located just ninety miles off the Florida coast. Lansky had originally visited Cuba seeking molasses to make rum but discovered a suitable political climate for gambling operations. Befriending the self-proclaimed dictator of Cuba, Fulgencio Batista, Lansky soon opened several casinos. But World War II brought a halt to his plans for turning the island into a haven for gamblers. There simply weren't enough planes and boats available to make the project profitable.

In 1944, the Cuban economy was sagging and Batista was forced to make concessions to his political opponents, which included procommunists. According to investigative reporter Howard Kohn, the Office of Naval Intelligence—already in contact with Lucky Luciano through Lansky—asked Lansky to pressure Batista into stepping down. On Lansky's urging, Batista called an election, was defeated, and left Cuba for an eight-year exile in Florida.

On March 10, 1952, Batista returned to Cuba and seized power in a bloodless military coup. Reportedly, it was large amounts of money Lansky placed in numbered Swiss bank accounts that convinced Cuban President Carlos Prio Socarras not to resist Batista's comeback.

Under Lansky's manipulation, Batista's government agreed to match investments in Cuba dollar for dollar plus grant a gambling license to any establishment worth more than $1 million. Soon the island's economy was booming as hotels and casinos were quickly built. Lansky built the Hotel Nacional, whose pit boss was his brother, Jake. He and other associates had interest in the Sevilla Biltmore and the Havana Hilton. Lansky himself built the $14 million Hotel Havana Riviera, which was run by Dino and Eddie Cellini, organized-crime figures from Ohio.

But Lansky, a Jew, still was not considered an official member of the Italian Mafia–dominated American crime syndicate. Organized-crime authority G. Robert Blakey wrote, "The undisputed Mafia gambling boss in Havana was Santos Trafficante, Jr."

When Trafficante Sr. died in 1954, his family crime business—mostly narcotics trafficking and gambling—went to his namesake. By the late 1950s, Trafficante Jr. was well situated in Cuba, owning substantial interest in the Sans Souci, a renowned nightspot partly managed by a Trafficante associate, John Roselli, later a central figure in the CIA-Mafia plots against Castro.

Both Trafficante and Lansky also were part owners of the Tropicana Casino in

Havana, which was managed by former Dallas gambler Lewis McWillie, the "idol" of Jack Ruby.

In Cuba, Meyer Lansky and associate Bugsy Siegel used the same tactics they had used successfully in 1945 when they turned a dusty parcel of Nevada desert into the Las Vegas strip—flying in high rollers to stay at their hotel-casinos. In reviewing the Havana operations during those years, Blakey wrote, "Havana, in short, was a full-service vice capital, owned and operated by the Mob."

Other men who had gambling interests in Cuba during this time were connected to Teamster boss Jimmy Hoffa. Two New York underworld figures allied with the Tommy Lucchese family, Salvatore Granello and James Plumeri, were part owners of a Havana racetrack and a large casino. Granello and Plumeri also helped Teamster officials get Miami Local 320 of the International Brotherhood of Teamsters started, according to Dan Moldea, author of *The Hoffa Wars*. Moldea also wrote that at the time Granello and Plumeri were splitting kickbacks with Hoffa on loans made through the Central States Pension Fund.

One high-placed guest in Cuba at the time was Congressman Richard Nixon, who made frequent trips to the island, visiting both President Batista and the casinos. According to Nixon biographer Earl Mazo, Nixon visited Cuba as early as 1940 to consider "the possibilities of establishing law or business connections in Havana."

But the glamorous nightlife of Havana came to an abrupt end on New Year's Day 1959, when Fidel Castro entered the city and proclaimed a new Cuban revolution. Both Batista and Lansky fled Cuba that same day. Lansky later lamented that he caught one of the last planes leaving Havana and was forced to leave behind $17 million in cash that had been earmarked for his various partners via Swiss bank accounts.

Jake Lansky, left behind to hold together his brother's gambling and narcotics operations, was jailed by Castro along with Santos Trafficante. Castro loudly proclaimed, "I'm going to run all these fascist mobsters, all these American gangsters, out of Cuba. I'm going to nationalize everything. Cuba for Cubans!"

By 1960, Castro had made good on his threat. He had deported all syndicate members, closed the whorehouses and casinos, and shut down the drug labs.

Both the crime syndicate and some American government officials were appalled at this turn of events. The CIA particularly wanted something done since, according to agency sources quoted by journalist Howard Kohn, the agency had used the underworld's Havana casinos to hide payments to the crime figures it sometimes employed. Thus the idea of invading Cuba may have been born. A murky alliance developed between the CIA, the crime syndicate, the US military, and anti-Castro Cuban exiles, and this alliance produced the ill-fated Bay of Pigs Invasion.

Four ex–casino bosses—including Hoffa associates Salvatore Granello and James Plumeri—even supplied the CIA with intelligence reports gathered from trusted Cuban contacts.

Along with the plans to invade Cuba, there were concurrent schemes to assassinate Castro. Involved in these plots were Trafficante, Frank Sturgis, Robert Maheu (the ex-FBI man who was liaison between the CIA and the Mafia and later became manager of the Howard Hughes empire), and two Mafia chiefs, John Roselli and Sam "Momo" Giancana.

With the failure of the invasion, the mob joined with the CIA, the military, and the Cuban exiles in placing the blame squarely on President John F. Kennedy.

Although mob gambling activity quickly shifted to Las Vegas and the Bahamas, crime leaders did not forget who had cost them their Havana "vice capital."

According to evidence gathered by House Select Committee on Assassinations, Trafficante was in touch with a wealthy Cuban exile living in Miami named Jose Aleman. Trafficante had offered to arrange a million-dollar loan for Aleman from the Teamsters Union and had "already been cleared by Jimmy Hoffa himself." Aleman said he met with Trafficante at Miami's Scott-Bryant Hotel in September 1962, and the talk turned to Hoffa. According to Aleman, Trafficante brought the conversation around to President Kennedy, saying, "Mark my words, this man Kennedy is in trouble and he will get what is coming to him."

Aleman said when he disagreed, saying Kennedy was doing a good job and probably would be reelected, Trafficante replied, "You don't understand me. Kennedy's not going to make it to the election. He's going to be hit." Later Aleman said Trafficante "made it clear" he was not guessing and even gave "the distinct impression that Hoffa was to be principally involved in the elimination of Kennedy."

Unknown to Trafficante, Aleman was an informant for the FBI at the time of this alleged conversation. He promptly reported what he had heard to the bureau but said FBI officials would not listen or take him seriously. In 1978, long after JFK's successful assassination when Aleman testified before the House Select Committee on Assassinations, his story became vague. He said perhaps Trafficante meant Kennedy was going to be "hit" by a lot of Republican votes in 1964. Aleman also admitted he was "very much concerned about my safety."

Jimmy Hoffa survived the McClellan Committee hearings. But it was the start of a personal war between two of the nation's most powerful men—Bobby Kennedy and the Teamster leader.

The War on Hoffa

James Riddle Hoffa was born on February 14, 1913, in Brazil, Indiana. After the death of his father when he was seven, young Hoffa moved to Detroit with his mother, brother, and two sisters.

By 1932, Hoffa was already involved in the union movement. Angered over low pay and working conditions at the Kroger Food Company, Hoffa helped organize a work stoppage. After several days of negotiation, the company signed a one-page contract. It was the start of a one-company union and was affiliated with the American Federation of Labor. By the mid-1930s, Hoffa's fledgling union was absorbed by bigger organizations. After being fired by Kroger, he joined Detroit Teamsters Joint Council 43 as an organizer and negotiator.

In the early 1930s, Hoffa had a love affair with Sylvia Pigano, a woman with family connections to organized-crime figures. This was Hoffa's introduction to the underworld, which over the years became an invaluable source of support. From that point on Hoffa's rise to the presidency of the International Brotherhood of Teamsters continued unabated. He walked a thin line, maintaining contacts with mobsters on one hand and presenting the image of a respectable labor leader on the other.

In 1957, fresh from his victory in exposing Teamster president Dave Beck's embezzlement of union money, McClellan Committee chief counsel Robert Kennedy turned his sights on Beck's successor, Jimmy Hoffa. After the committee hearings, Hoffa was acquitted on charges of wiretapping and perjury. He was living a charmed life, but his hatred for Kennedy was increasing.

And the feeling was mutual. Robert Kennedy voiced concern over blackmail by organized crime. If the mob so desired, it could have pressured Hoffa into calling a nationwide Teamsters strike that could have disrupted the entire country. For the Kennedys, this was an intolerable situation.

When the election year of 1960 arrived, Hoffa knew which side he had to be on. He and the Teamsters threw their support behind Richard Nixon. In fact, Edward Partin, a Louisiana Teamster official and later a government informant, revealed that Hoffa met with Carlos Marcello to raise money for Nixon.

But money wasn't enough. Nixon lost and Robert Kennedy became attorney general. After the election, Hoffa was quoted as saying, "Nobody had to tell me that he was really going to go after my scalp now."

In 1958, US attorney general William P. Rogers had formed a special group on organized crime to investigate Vito Genevese's Appalachian meeting of mob bosses. Following that precedent, Attorney General Kennedy organized a special unit within the Organized Crime and Racketeering Section to investigate the Teamsters Union. Headed by Walter Sheridan, who had been an investigator for the McClellan Committee, the unit became known as the "Get Hoffa Squad." The squad managed to bring 201 indictments and 126 convictions against Teamster officials.

On May 18, 1962, Hoffa was indicted for receiving $1 million in illegal payments through the Test Fleet Corporation, a trucking company set up under his wife's name. His trial ended in a hung jury, but Hoffa was indicted along with five others for jury tampering on May 9, 1963. On June 4, 1963, Hoffa was indicted for fraudulently obtaining $20 million in loans from the Teamsters' Central States Pension Fund.

Earlier, in September 1962—about the same time that Marcello and Trafficante had hinted that President Kennedy was going to be assassinated—Ed Partin, the Teamster official–turned–informant, went to Louisiana law-enforcement officials about a threat by Hoffa. Partin believed that Hoffa thought Partin was closely associated with Marcello since he lived in Louisiana and spoke openly with him. Visiting in Hoffa's Washington office in August 1962, Partin said Hoffa began talking about plans to kill Robert Kennedy. Thinking out loud, Hoffa discussed two schemes. One involved firebombing Hickory Hill, Kennedy's Virginia estate. The second involved shooting Kennedy with a rifle while he rode in an open car.

Partin's story was passed along to Kennedy aides, who were highly skeptical until an FBI lie detector test indicated Partin was telling the truth and had actually obtained explosives to deliver to Hoffa.

It was in the middle of Hoffa's jury-tampering case that President Kennedy was shot in Dallas. Upon learning that the flags were flying at half-mast at Teamster headquarters in Washington, Hoffa admonished officials there, shouting, "Why the hell did you do that for him? Who the hell is he?" On the day Ruby murdered Oswald, Hoffa told a Nashville reporter, "Bobby Kennedy is just another lawyer now."

In the jury-tampering and the fraudulent-loan cases Hoffa was convicted, fined, and imprisoned. He received executive clemency from President Richard Nixon on December 23, 1971, without the customary consultation with the sentencing judge. However, the clemency contained a provision prohibiting Hoffa from seeking office in the union. Hoffa filed suit to have the restriction nullified and began making overtures to Teamster rank and file. Ironically, he pledged that if elected Teamster president in 1976, he would purge the union of all mob influence.

On July 30, 1975, Hoffa was to meet Anthony "Tony Pro" Provenzano, a New Jersey Teamster official and reputed member of the crime syndicate. Hoffa disappeared from a Detroit restaurant parking lot and was finally declared dead in 1982. To this date, neither his body nor his killer has been found.

One of the biggest boosts to Robert Kennedy's anticrime campaign began in June 1962, when an underworld tough serving a prison term in Atlanta for narcotics murdered a fellow inmate with an iron pipe. The convict's name was Joseph Valachi and he killed the man, believing him to be an assassin sent by his longtime boss and cellmate, Vito Genovese. Genovese had slipped back into the United States after World War II to resume his narcotics operations.

Imprisoned, Genovese had heard rumors—apparently false—that Valachi was cooperating with authorities and had given his veteran soldier the "kiss of death." Soon after, there were three attempts on Valachi's life. Valachi didn't want to wait for the fourth. So, believing a man in the prison courtyard was a Genovese killer, Valachi beat him to death. He picked the wrong man.

With both the government and the mob seeking his life, Valachi decided he had nothing to lose by cooperating with authorities. Over the next year, he provided federal agents with a bonanza of information on the national crime organization known variously as the Mafia, La Cosa Nostra (Our Thing), the Outfit, the Arm, the Syndicate, and so on.

On September 25, 1963, Valachi took his story to the public, testifying before McClellan's Senate committee. He presented a wealth of detail about the organization of the mob, its codes, rules, and regulations, and its most important members, including those who sat on the "Commissione," the board of directors.

Valachi's testimony was a great embarrassment to FBI director J. Edgar Hoover, who it was later learned was meeting with mob bosses at the time. These revelations forced Hoover to grudgingly admit that such a thing as a crime syndicate must exist.

In his ever-increasing war against organized crime, Kennedy made use of the Treasury Department's Internal Revenue Service to go after mob members. John H. Davis, a Kennedy relative and author of *The Kennedys*, wrote, "Given another five years in office, the Kennedys could conceivably have exterminated the Cosa Nostra entirely, or at least crippled it beyond repair."

Crime bosses wanted something done about the Kennedys, especially since they felt double-crossed by the two brothers.

After all, the connections between crime and the Kennedys reportedly went back a long way. In 1927, a shipment of bootleg whiskey on its way from Ireland to Boston was hijacked in southern New England. Almost the entire guard was killed in the resulting shootout. The hijackers were part of the Luciano-Lansky mob, and it was rumored that Joseph P. Kennedy was involved in the shipment. Kennedy reputedly lost a fortune on the deal and was besieged by widows of the guards seeking financial assistance. Lansky later told biographers he was convinced that Kennedy held a grudge against him personally from that time on and, in fact, had passed the hostility on to his sons.

But the crime contacts didn't stop with Prohibition. According to crime author Ovid Damaris, Kennedy would likely have lost the state of Illinois—and possibly the 1960 presidential election—except for overlarge voting in Cook County, home of Chicago mayor Richard Daley. Following the election, Illinois Republicans made an unofficial check of 699 paper ballot precincts in Cook County and turned up enough irregular votes to shift the victory to Richard Nixon. However, demands for an official recount were blocked by Daley's political machine. And behind that machine was the real power in Chicago at that time—Sam Giancana.

Momo and His Girlfriends

Sam Giancana (real name: Momo Salvatore Guingano) was born May 24, 1908, to poor Sicilian immigrants living in Chicago. He grew up in the ghettos and was streetwise at an early age.

A member of a gang called the 42s, Giancana was first convicted of car theft in 1925. Before he was twenty, he was arrested in connection with three murders, including the slaying of Octavious Granady, a black man who sought election as a committeeman.

In 1932, Giancana came to the attention of Paul "The Waiter" Ricca (real name: Felice DeLucia), who worked for the notorious Genna brothers. Giancana became the personal driver for Ricca, who took over the Chicago syndicate after the suicide of Frank Nitti in 1943. In 1944, Ricca went to prison for extortion and Anthony Accardo took over as Chicago's syndicate boss. Giancana became his chauffeur. Giancana helped Accardo consolidate the rackets and gambling operations in Chicago. In 1957, Giancana was one of those who escaped from Vito Genevese's ill-fated Appalachian meeting.

In 1960, when Accardo retired after an income tax–evasion indictment, Giancana took over the syndicate. By 1963, Giancana had been arrested sixty times and had served time for burglary, auto theft, and moonshining. He also was one of the wealthiest and most powerful men in Chicago and in the syndicate.

After the death of his wife, Angeline, in 1954, Giancana became well-known as a ladies' man. While visiting Las Vegas in 1960, Giancana met Phyllis McGuire, the youngest of the McGuire Sisters singing group. According to G. Robert Blakey, chief counsel of the House Select Committee on Assassinations, McGuire had run up gambling debts of more than $100,000. Giancana—who along with Accardo secretly owned interest in the Desert Inn and the Stardust casinos in Las Vegas although both were nominally owned by Morris "Moe" Dalitz—made good McGuire's debt. Soon afterward, Giancana made his Las Vegas headquarters at the nearby Green Gables Ranch, leased by McGuire.

During the 1960 election, Giancana and other mob leaders apparently thought they had bought some relief from growing government awareness and prosecution of the syndicate, especially considering the close ties between FBI director Hoover, who continued to deny the existence of the Mafia, and mob figures such as Roy Cohn and Frank Costello.

In addition to meeting mob leader Joseph Bonanno in the winter of 1959, Kennedy reportedly received campaign contributions from the syndicate channeled to his father by singer Frank Sinatra. Yet another conduit for these funds may have been a woman with connections to both Kennedy and Giancana. Ironically, evidence of these contributions to Kennedy were picked up by FBI phone taps that were part of an electronic surveillance program initiated by Attorney General Robert Kennedy's war on crime.

Giancana believed he had a strong hold on Kennedy in the form of a beautiful dark-eyed brunette named Judith Exner. Going then as Judy Campbell, Exner said she was introduced to John F. Kennedy on February 7, 1960, by Frank Sinatra, whom she had been dating. In her 1977 book, *My Story*, she wrote that both John Kennedy and his brother Edward were sitting with Sinatra in the lounge of the Sands Hotel in Las Vegas. She said she and John Kennedy met again a month later, this time alone and in the Plaza Hotel in New York where, according to Exner, they shared a bed.

From that point on, Kennedy saw Exner regularly. The pair exchanged telephone calls frequently, including some to the White House, which were noted by the FBI. Why the FBI? The bureau had been monitoring Exner's activities because of the other man in her life—Chicago mob boss Giancana. Exner claimed she was introduced to Giancana, again by Sinatra, a month after she had become Kennedy's lover. When Giancana discovered she was seeing the Democratic presidential candidate, he took an immediate and continuing interest in her. Soon Giancana was bedding the paramour of the soon-to-be president.

In later years, Exner said, "I feel like I was set up to be the courier. I was a perfect choice because I could come and go without notice, and if noticed, no one would've believed it anyway."

What passed between Kennedy and Giancana in this extraordinary triangle is not known, but in 1988, Exner revealed that she had acted as a courier carrying sealed envelopes for the two men on at least ten occasions. Citing ill health, Exner said she wanted to set the record straight. She said she did not tell about the envelopes during 1975 testimony to the Senate Intelligence Committee because she feared for her life. She also claimed that she never opened the envelopes or knew their contents. Most of her courier activities took place during the tough 1960 campaign and Exner speculated that her actions may have been connected with attempts to influence the critical West Virginia Democratic primary.

Once, after being questioned by FBI agents, Exner complained to Kennedy, who by then was president. She claimed Kennedy assured her, "Don't worry. They won't do anything to you. And don't worry about Sam. You know he works for us."

Kennedy continued to see Exner until a meeting with J. Edgar Hoover on March 22, 1962. On that date Hoover revealed to the president the extent of Exner's ties with organized crime and the obvious fact that he knew about Kennedy's liaison with her. Shortly after Hoover left the White House, there was one more call to Judith Exner. No more were ever logged. Kennedy also broke off his friendship with Sinatra, perhaps suspecting that the singer had set him up. Exner died of cancer in 1999.

But the worst was yet to come. Although still seeing Exner, Giancana became suspicious that Phyllis McGuire was seeing comedian Dan Rowan. Giancana asked his contact with the CIA, Robert Maheu, to place a wiretap on Rowan's telephone, but a maid discovered the tap and told Rowan, who brought it to the attention of the federal government. The Justice Department initiated proceedings against Maheu for illegal wiretapping.

In May 1962, a month after the Kennedy-Hoover meeting apparently ended the president's relationship with Exner, CIA officials asked Robert Kennedy not to prosecute Maheu for fear that Giancana's role in the incident would become known. They reminded Kennedy that Giancana had played a role in the clandestine effort against Castro's government.

Thinking the plots against Castro had been stopped back in 1961, Robert Kennedy was adamant about pressing charges. Then on May 7, CIA general counsel Lawrence Houston finally told Kennedy the whole ugly truth—that the agency had contracted with Giancana and John Roselli to murder Fidel Castro. According to Houston, Kennedy fixed him with a cold look and said, "I trust that if you ever try to do business with organized crime again—with gangsters—you will let the attorney general know."

From that moment on, both Kennedys must have feared what Sam Giancana might reveal if he chose—the CIA-Mafia murder plots and Giancana's girl in bed with the president. However, this fear did not stop the younger Kennedy from prosecuting his war against targeted Mafia big shots, including Giancana.

The FBI haunted Giancana day and night, watching his home and trailing his car. It was most effective. Crime associates wouldn't come near and Giancana couldn't go where he pleased. He was isolated.

In June 1963, Giancana caused chins to drop throughout the underworld by becoming the first mobster ever to go to court seeking an injunction against FBI surveillance. Gaining the injunction required Giancana to swear in court that he was an honest businessman, which in turn would expose him to government cross-examination—an unprecedented hazard for a crime boss. Giancana must have felt confident that the government would not question him too closely. And he was right. To a stunned courtroom, the US attorney announced that the government waived the right to cross-examination. The decision not to question Giancana had come straight from the attorney general.

But his luck did not hold. Following Kennedy's assassination, Giancana was deposed as a Mafia boss and went into exile in Mexico. However, the Mexican authorities arrested and deported Giancana back to the United States in mid-1974. Back in Chicago, he became a witness against organized crime. On June 19, 1975, just before he was to testify to a Senate committee about CIA and Mafia assassination plots, his police protection was suddenly called away while someone slipped into his home and shot him in the back, rolled the body over, and shot him six times in the face and throat, a time-honored underworld warning against stool pigeons.

Back in 1963, even when the opportunity to get Giancana was dropped, the Kennedy Justice Department's all-out war against the underworld continued. The top crime bosses were incensed. Hadn't they contributed to Kennedy's election? Hadn't they helped steal critical votes? Hadn't Kennedy dabbled with one of their women? It undoubtedly looked like double-cross to the mob chieftains. And in the underworld the only solution for a double-crosser is elimination—a "hit."

On November 22, 1963, Attorney General Kennedy met with about forty of his Organized Crime and Racketeering Section staff. They had been meeting regularly for the past two and a half years.

One of the young crime busters was G. Robert Blakey, who years later would become chief counsel of the House Select Committee on Assassinations, created to investigate the murders of John and Robert Kennedy.

Just before they broke for lunch, the last topic of discussion was Sam Giancana and political corruption in Chicago. The attorney general had just finished lunch at his McLean, Virginia, home when J. Edgar Hoover called to inform him, "The president's been shot." Hoover went on to give a fairly full account of Lee Harvey Oswald and his background at a time when the Dallas authorities were not even certain of their suspect's identity.

Kennedy never met with the Organized Crime and Racketeering Section again. With John F. Kennedy's death, the war on crime was lost. Organized crime was ecstatic, but on FBI wiretaps, older and wiser mob leaders urged caution in speaking about the assassination. One was overheard explaining, "Police spies will be watching carefully to see what we . . . think and say about this." Such caution was certainly justified. In the years since the assassination, more and more attention has been drawn to the mob as one of the most likely suspects.

Beginning with Jack Ruby right on through to David Ferrie and Jim Braden, crime figures keep cropping up throughout the assassination case. There is no question that organized crime had the means, motive, and the opportunity to murder the president. But could the crime bosses have effectively covered their tracks without the help of federal government officials?

It now appears that the vocal wishes of the crime bosses to eliminate the Kennedys were echoed by certain powerful men in government, finance, and corporate business. In the subtitle of his book *The Plot to Kill the President*, G. Robert Blakey stated bluntly, *"Organized Crime Assassinated J.F.K."* Blakey once told this author:

> One reason no one realized organized crime's involvement [for many years] was that people never saw before . . . what was going on in Cuba. They failed to see the significance of men like [mobster and "mentor" to Jack Ruby] Lewis McWillie and Russell Matthews [a Dallas gambler friend of Ruby's who was best man at the wedding of "babushka lady" Beverly Oliver and gangster George McGann] because they did not understand these men's connections.

Asked if the fact that organized crime has been connected with the assassination only in recent years might suggest some control within the government on the part of the mob, Blakey replied, "That's conceivable. . . . I would find that troubling, but no more so than the fact that they killed the man and got away with it."

Following his brother's death, Robert Kennedy appeared to lose interest in prosecuting the mob and the Justice Department staff followed suit. While there must have been motivation to protect his brother's loving-husband image, the cooling of the attorney general's passion for fighting the mob likely was due more to the potential revelations of CIA-Mafia assassination plots.

In fighting what the Kennedys had perceived as a great internal evil, they had once again found themselves confronted by the CIA.

Agents

Since the first conflicts of man, there has been a need for intelligence, or information on the activities and purposes of a perceived enemy. In modern America the growth of myriad intelligence organizations over the years has spawned an intelligence industry. Under acronyms such as CIA, DIA, NSA, ONI, NRO, AFOSI, DEA, and NGA, these intelligence power bases have grown far beyond their original charters. Today many thoughtful persons are concerned that these disparate agencies, with the exception of the military, are now bundled together within the Department of Homeland Security.

The most publicized of these is the Central Intelligence Agency, whose history reveals a government organization that does much more than merely collect and interpret intelligence. In less than ten years after its creation in 1947, this coordinating agency grew to oversee military operations, destabilization efforts in foreign countries, and the assassination of national leaders—aided by an unholy alliance with organized crime.

At the end of World War II, information on a wide variety of issues and activities was being handled by as many as a dozen various intelligence organizations, including those within the military. President Harry S. Truman and others perceived a need for a coordinating intelligence unit. This need was further reinforced by the Congressional Joint Committee on the Pearl Harbor Attack, which concluded that the fragmentation of US intelligence prior to 1941 resulted in the Japanese taking this nation by surprise. The committee recommended a unified intelligence service. Creating such a hybrid would not be easy. None of the existing intelligence units wanted to relinquish power or authority.

During World War II, one of the organizations that proved most effective against the Axis powers was the Office of Strategic Services (OSS), headed by the colorful General William "Wild Bill" Donovan. The OSS not only gathered a remarkable amount of information on the enemy, but also engaged in various covert activities. It was a rough-and-tumble wartime operation that provided the factual background for many a fictional spy novel and movie.

The OSS was closed down at the end of the war, and on January 22, 1946, just four months later, President Truman signed a directive creating the National Intelligence Authority (NIA), composed of the secretaries of state, war, and navy as well as the president's personal representative. The operating arm of the NIA was the Central Intelligence Group (CIG), made up of veteran intelligence officers from the participating departments. These men were managed by a director appointed by the president. To limit the CIG, Truman specifically prohibited any clandestine or paramilitary activities. The CIG was to have "no police, law-enforcement or internal-security functions" or conduct "investigations inside the . . . United States."

The veteran spies and operatives of the old OSS were soon transferred to this new organization, operating under the designation of the Office of Special Operations (OSO). And these men of action soon wanted more elbow room in their restricted world of intelligence gathering.

By 1947, the CIG's staff had grown to nearly 2,000, with about one-third operating overseas. But it continued to be only one of several intelligence organizations. This changed on September 15, 1947, when Truman signed the National Security Act, creating the national Security Council (NSC), the Air Force as a separate branch of the services, and renaming the War Department the Department of Defense, uniting the Departments of the Army, Navy, and Air Force. With little notice, this act also created the Central Intelligence Agency (CIA), giving the United States its first full-blown peacetime intelligence service.

In later years, Truman stated:

> I never had any thought . . . when I set up the CIA, that it would be injected
> into peacetime cloak-and-dagger operations. Some of the complications

and embarrassment that I think we have experienced are in a part attributable to the fact that this quiet intelligence arm of the President has been so removed from its intended role.

Under the National Security Act—passed in the heat of the growing anticommunist hysteria sweeping the United States and just two months after a still-controversial crash at Roswell Army Air Field in New Mexico—the CIA was responsible only to the National Security Council, which was headed by the president, effectively giving the president absolute control over the new agency.

The CIA had its own budget, much of this off the books and handled through the little-known Exchange Stabilization Fund of the Treasury Department, and was authorized to hire and train its own personnel. Yet the same restrictions of the old CIG remained—no clandestine or paramilitary operations and no internal spying.

However, a catch-all phrase had been included in the CIA's charter that stated the agency could perform "such other functions and duties related to intelligence affecting the national security as the NSC may from time to time direct."

Utilizing this phrase—and with the blessings of the National Security Council—the CIA in 1948 became active in suppressing communist influence in the national elections in Italy. This marked the beginning of the agency's career of meddling in the affairs of other nations.

In 1949, the Central Intelligence Act was passed, exempting the CIA from all laws requiring the disclosure of "functions, names, official titles, salaries and number of personnel employed by the Agency" and allowing the director to spend money from its secret budget simply by signing vouchers.

Now operating with secret funds and with the vague authority of "other such functions and duties related to intelligence," the CIA began to flex its muscles. Victor Marchetti, a former executive assistant to the CIA's deputy director, wrote:

> From those few innocuous words the CIA has been able, over the years, to develop a secret charter based on NSC directives and presidential executive orders, a charter almost completely at variance with the apparent intent of the law which established the Agency. This vague phrase has provided the CIA with freedom to engage in covert action, the right to intervene secretly in the internal affairs of other nations. It has done so usually with the express approval of the White House, but almost always without the consent of Congress, and virtually never with the knowledge of the American people.

In 1948, the Office of Policy Coordination (OPC) was created by the National Security Council as a covert psychological and paramilitary operations unit under Frank Wisner. By 1951, the OPC had run afoul of so many US laws and policies it was merged into the CIA and was known thereafter as the CIA's Department of Plans. However, any attempt at curtailing such activities was thwarted by the appointment of Allen Dulles as the new director.

By 1955, the CIA contained more than 15,000 employees, not including thousands of foreign assets and contract agents. In addition to its enormous secret budget—often disguised as portions of other US government budgets—the CIA created a number of wholly or partly owned properties, or "fronts," to provide cover for clandestine operations.

These fronts included airlines, import-export companies, "high-tech" firms, advertising agencies, foundations, and many others. And these were not dummy businesses. In most ways they operated normally, generating additional money to fund agency operations. Using these fronts, the CIA channeled money to academic, labor, youth, and cultural organizations.

Many foreign leaders—such as King Hussein of Jordan, Archbishop Makarios of Cypress, Luis Echeverria of Mexico, and Willy Brandt of West Germany—have been named as recipients of CIA funds over the years.

It has been charged that the CIA, whose leaders have been drawn from the highest circles of business and wealth in the United States, often has been merely a security force for big business, more concerned with American corporate investments than with true national security issues. For example, in 1953 the popularly elected prime minister of Iran, Dr. Mohammed Mossadegh, whose government had nationalized the oil industry, was overthrown in a coup initiated by the CIA. The CIA man in charge of that operation was Kermit Roosevelt, who later became vice president of Gulf Oil. Gulf Oil benefited greatly from the new Iranian political situation.

On June 18, 1954, a CIA-financed right-wing coup in Guatemala overthrew the popularly elected government of Jacobo Arbenz, which had nationalized the property of United Fruit Company. Secretary of state John Foster Dulles's law firm had written the United Fruit contracts with Guatemala in the 1930s. John Moors Cabot, assistant secretary of state for inter-American affairs, was a major United Fruit stockholder. And CIA director Allen Dulles had been president of United Fruit, while his predecessor as CIA director, General Walter Bedell Smith, soon would become a United Fruit vice president.

One reason the CIA succeeded in becoming a world-class force was the relationship of its longtime director, Allen Dulles, with his brother John Foster Dulles, the secretary of state. David Wise and Thomas B. Ross, authors of *The Invisible Government*, wrote:

> Uniquely, they embodied the dualism—and indeed the moral dilemma—of United States foreign policy since World War II. . . . Foster Dulles reflected the American ethic; the world as we would like it to be. While he took this position, his brother was free to deal with nastier realities, to overturn governments and engage in backstage political maneuvers all over the globe with the CIA's almost unlimited funds. He was, as Allen Dulles once put it, able to "fight fire with fire." . . . It was under Allen Dulles's stewardship that the CIA enjoyed its greatest expansion, particularly in the field of government-shaking secret operations overseas.

And during the time the agency was expanding and initiating its activities across the globe, few Americans had ever heard of the organization. The agency's anonymity was largely the product of a timid news media. Former CIA director William Colby wrote, "The press, by and large, willingly accorded the CIA a privileged position among government agencies and refrained from inquiring into and reporting on its activities as a self-imposed act of patriotism."

"Patriotism" and "national security" were the watchwords of the CIA and other intelligence organizations and were used effectively to keep secret a multitude of sins and questionable activities. Some CIA activities clearly violated both the agency's charter and US laws. One agency endeavor—the search for effective brainwashing and behavior-modification methods—is especially chilling.

The Manchurian Candidates

The fact that German rocket scientists were brought to the United States after World War II under Project Paperclip to become the leaders of the US space program is well documented. Not so well known is how German experimentation with mind control also was continued in America after the war.

Although US judges at the Nuremberg war crimes trials sentenced seven German scientists to death for their part in human experimentation in the concentration camps, their research material was forwarded to the OSS and their work was continued. With the creation of the CIA, this work became part of the agency's behavior-modification program, first called BLUEBIRD, then later changed to ARTICHOKE.

By 1954, the ARTICHOKE program was part of the CIA's Technical Services Staff (TSS), which also provided the agency with weaponry, disguises, gadgets, forged documents, and codes. ARTICHOKE teams usually consisted of a psychiatrist, a drug expert, a technician, and a hypnotist, who sometimes posed as a polygraph operator.

Such programs to alter minds formed the basis of a 1959 book by Richard Condon titled *The Manchurian Candidate*. Later a movie that reportedly was one of John F. Kennedy's favorites, the book concerns an American soldier captured in Korea who is brainwashed into becoming a remote-controlled killer for the purpose of assassinating a US presidential candidate.

On April 13, 1953, the CIA mind-control program—including "covert use of biological and chemical materials" proposed by Richard Helms and managed by Dr. Sidney Gottlieb—was authorized by Director Dulles under the overall name MK-ULTRA. Under MK-ULTRA, the CIA went beyond mind-control experimentation to develop deadly toxins capable of killing without leaving a trace. One such toxin was later used in pills agency officials gave to a mobster in the CIA-Mafia plots to assassinate Fidel Castro.

Interestingly, one of the two CIA field stations that were involved in MK-ULTRA and had quantities of both LSD (lysergic acid diethylamide) and other chemical mind-altering agents was at Atsugi in Japan, the same station where Lee Harvey

Oswald served as a Marine radar operator and apparently was involved in under-cover operations.

Since the CIA has admitted that its most convenient source of mind-control guinea pigs were "individuals of dubious loyalty, suspected agents or plants, subjects having known reason for deception, etc.," one must wonder whether Oswald may have been part of a mind-altering program of the agency—if in fact there was one. In an article published in *Rolling Stone*, the authors claim to have contacted a Marine from Oswald's unit who said he participated in some of the LSD experiments.

In the summer of 1963, Oswald entered the office of New Orleans assistant district attorney Edward Gillin. He was asked to take a seat but instead choose to stand in front of Gillin's desk. Oswald proceeded to question Gillin about a new drug called LSD. After spending almost an hour extolling the virtues of the drug as one that would affect the social and economic history of the world for the next two hundred years, Oswald said he wanted to try some and wished to know if it was legal (which it was at that time). Thinking his visitor was a bit crazy, Gillin suggested Oswald visit the police chemist with his query but advised he take nothing without consulting a doctor first. Gillin never saw Oswald again until recognizing him on TV accused of killing the president.

The exact nature of Oswald's relation to any CIA mind-control program likely will never be known. According to John Marks, author of *The Search for the "Manchurian Candidate,"* Gottlieb, upon retiring from the agency in 1973 and with the agreement of Helms, destroyed what they thought were the last remaining documents on MK-ULTRA.

Since Oswald may have taken a mind-altering drug; since his killer, Jack Ruby, told Dallas police he had no recollection of shooting Oswald; since Sirhan Sirhan, the presumed assassin of Robert Kennedy, still claims he can't remember what happened in the Ambassador Hotel; and since a San Quentin psychologist, Dr. Eduard Simson, proclaimed that Sirhan had been "programmed" by drugs, hypnosis, or both, the possibility of mind control in the JFK assassination—while admittedly unlikely—cannot be ruled out.

But the techniques of using someone under mind control by drugs and hypnosis as an assassin or decoy in an assassination had not yet been perfected in 1963. It is more likely that conspirators at that time would have resorted to a less sophisticated method—they would simply have hired professional assassins from the mob, the CIA, or the military and thrown a scapegoat to the public.

For all the myths that have arisen about CIA prowess, the actual history of the agency reveals as many glaring errors as victories.

Agency analysts failed to foresee the 1967 Arab-Israeli War, the 1968 Tet Offensive in South Vietnam, the collapse of communism, or the terrorist attacks of September 11, 2001.

One CIA officer deeply involved in the Cuban operations, including the Bay of Pigs, was William Harvey, who established and managed the CIA's infamous "Executive Action" program of calculated assassinations code-named ZR-RIFLE. Referring to Harvey's program, president Lyndon Johnson once commented, "We were running a damn Murder, Inc. in the Caribbean."

It is in this area—assassination plots—that the US intelligence community in general, and the CIA in particular, have created serious suspicions in the minds of researchers regarding possible complicity in the death of President Kennedy.

CIA-Mafia Death Plots

In September 1963, CIA officers again tried to hatch an assassination plot against Castro—this time using a Cuban government official named Dr. Rolando Cubela. His CIA code name was AM/LASH.

An unofficial Cuban minister, Cubela had contacted the CIA some two years earlier and offered to defect. The agency had persuaded him to remain in place as a valuable conduit of inside information.

This time, meeting in a São Paulo, Brazil, safe house, Cubela startled his CIA contacts by offering to assassinate Castro if he had the support of the US government. This offer was sent to Desmond FitzGerald, a personal friend of Robert Kennedy and one of the CIA officials in charge of Operation Mongoose, that covert operation to bring down Cuba's communist government.

Despite cautions from CIA counterintelligence that Cubela might be a Castro agent testing US government intentions, FitzGerald ordered that Cubela be told that his offer to eliminate Castro was under consideration at the "highest levels." This strange story has been related in both *Legend: The Secret World of Lee Harvey Oswald* by Edward Jay Epstein and *The Kennedys* by John H. Davis.

Toward the end of October Cubela made an extraordinary demand. He wanted personal assurance that the Kennedy administration actively supported his plan to kill Castro. On October 29, again against the advice of counterintelligence, Fitz-Gerald personally met with Cubela and assured him that once Castro was gone, the Kennedy administration would support a new Cuban government. But when Cubela asked for a rifle with telescopic sights and the means to deliver poison, FitzGerald declined to discuss such specifics. Another meeting with Cubela was set and on that day, the CIA case officer supplied Cubela with a poison ballpoint pen. Cubela was told the rifle and some explosives would be delivered to him soon. Ironically, Cubela received his assassination tools from the CIA on November 22, 1963.

Although no documentation of the AM/LASH plot has survived, some senior CIA officials now claim that the plot did have the support of both Robert Kennedy and his brother. Since both are now dead, there's no real way to know, plus the animosity of certain CIA officers toward the Kennedys should be kept in mind when evaluating this charge.

It was the knowledge of AM/LASH, however, that caused consternation among CIA officials when Castro made certain public statements concerning assassination plots. While attending a reception in the Brazilian embassy in Havana, Castro told an Associated Press reporter, "Kennedy is the Batista of our time and the most opportunistic president of all time." Castro went on to warn against "terrorist plans to eliminate Cuban leaders," adding, "United States leaders should think that if they assist in terrorist plans to eliminate Cuban leaders, they themselves will not be safe." This warning has for years been used to support the theory that somehow Castro had learned of the CIA plots against him and, in retaliation, sent assassins after Kennedy. But since Castro didn't catch Cubela until 1966, it is unlikely that AM/LASH was the impetus of his 1963 remarks.

While the CIA's Mongoose program continued in Florida, similar operations were being conducted in New Orleans, long a hotbed of Cuban exile–CIA activity. One of the centers of this activity was the shabby three-story office building at 544 Camp Street, a connecting point for the CIA, the FBI, anti-Castro Cubans, and Lee Harvey Oswald.

New Orleans

Within days of Kennedy's assassination, the FBI in New Orleans questioned David Ferrie, who denied any knowledge of the assassination. The FBI agents let him go, apparently unaware of Ferrie's Civil Air Patrol connection to accused assassin Lee Harvey Oswald or to New Orleans crime boss Carlos Marcello. Neither apparently did the agents know that Ferrie had been working for Detective Guy Banister in the summer of 1963.

Whatever information Ferrie gave the FBI will never be known, since the interview was classified and locked away on orders of J. Edgar Hoover and in 1976, the National Archives reported that Ferrie's original statement was missing from its collection of assassination documents.

Both Ferrie and Banister were well connected with the Cuban exiles living in New Orleans. As a contract agent for the CIA, Ferrie claimed to have flown on hazardous missions into Cuba, including landing there on the night of the ill-fated Bay of Pigs Invasion.

Ferrie's role as CIA agent was confirmed in 1975 when Victor Marchetti, former executive assistant to the CIA's deputy director, stated that during high-level CIA meetings in 1969, CIA director Richard Helms disclosed that Ferrie and other figures in the Garrison investigation had indeed worked for the agency in aiding the anti-Castro Cubans.

Banister investigator Jack Martin and others have told investigators through the years of contact between CIA contract agent Ferrie and Oswald during 1963. Martin said he suspected that Ferrie "had taught Oswald how to purchase a foreign-made firearm."

According to Beverly Oliver, the "babushka lady," Oswald and Ferrie were even seen together in Jack Ruby's Carousel Club shortly before the assassination.

Delphine Roberts also claims that Oswald and Ferrie were associates. She said that on one occasion Ferrie even took Oswald to an anti-Castro guerrilla training camp outside New Orleans "to train with rifles." Once she saw Oswald handing out pro-Castro literature on a New Orleans street. Her boss, the rabid anticommunist Banister, reassured her, "Don't worry about him. . . . He's associated with the office." Roberts later said, "I knew there were such things as counterspies, spies and counterspies, and the importance of such things. So I just didn't question them."

The day after Kennedy's assassination, Secret Service agents went to 544 Camp Street after seeing the address on some of Oswald's pamphlets. Guy Banister's office was closed. They learned that "Cuban revolutionaries" had had an office there. The agents brushed the whole thing off by reporting that they hadn't found a trace of the Fair Play for Cuba Committee at 544 Camp Street.

The Saga of Tosh Plumlee

One man whose amazing travels for US intelligence and the military led him through the Cuban revolution and the Bay of Pigs Invasion on into the Kennedy assassination and even further into the Iran-Contra scandal of the Reagan administration was William Robert Plumlee.

Tosh, as he likes to be called, was born in 1937. After nearly becoming a juvenile delinquent, he joined the US Army in April 1954 and was assigned to the Texas 49th Armored Division. Later he was transferred to Dallas, where he joined the 4th Army Reserve Military Intelligence Unit. While working as an aircraft mechanic at Dallas's Love Field, Tosh earned his pilot's license in 1956 and was soon recruited by the CIA.

Working under such CIA officials as William Harvey, Tracy Barnes, and Rip Robertson, Tosh flew arms to Castro just prior to his 1959 revolution. After the United States turned against Castro, Tosh flew a reconnaissance mission over Cuba but crashed just before the Bay of Pigs Invasion. Making his escape back to the United States, Tosh continued his work for the agency. As a pilot operating out of the JM/WAVE station in Miami, he ferried agents and materials all around the Gulf of Mexico. He was shocked in later years to learn that one of his passengers, a military officer known to him as Colonel Rawlston was actually the Mafia chieftain John Roselli. His shock deepened when he recalled a secret flight he made on November 21, 1963.

In 2004 Plumlee gave this "true account" of that flight:

> Beginning November 20, 1963, I was assigned to be a copilot on a top-secret flight, which was attached to a military intelligence unit and supported by the CIA. Our mission, we were told, was to abort a pending attempt on the president's life which was to take place in Dallas. We were contracted as "cut-outs," a system used to shield a secret operation from public exposure. Our team was based out of south Florida. My pilot for this operation was Emanuel Rojas. We had flown together before. I was the copilot for this

operation. The first leg of the flight would be from Lantana, Florida (about five miles south of West Palm Beach), to Tampa, Florida. The aircraft used for the first phase of this trip was a D-18 Twin Beech aircraft. We took off before daybreak on November 21, 1963, expecting to arrive in Tampa about sunup. We were to pick up other personnel at Tampa. One of these people was John Roselli, whom I knew.

I had known John Roselli before this flight. I had flown Roselli and others to places like Cuba, Bimini, Galveston, Las Vegas, and California. He was also known to me as "Colonel Rawlston" or just "the Colonel." We (Rojas and I) were to pick up "the Colonel" at Tampa's Congress Inn that morning. We changed aircraft at Tampa to a waiting DC-3 that was registered to "Atlantic Richfield," and continued our trip to New Orleans, where a couple of people, who I did not know, got off and a few others got on. The Colonel stayed on board the DC-3. We continued our trip leaving New Orleans and continuing to Houston International Airport, where we spent the night at the Shamrock Hilton, not far from the airport.

The next morning, November 22, 1963, between 4:30–5 a.m., our weather briefing was not favorable for a VFR [visual flight rules] flight into Dallas's Red Bird airport. We selected Garland as an alternate in case the weather had not improved by the time we arrived near Dallas air space. We did not file a flight plan nor intended to file IFR [instrument flight rules]. This would have left a record of our flight with air traffic control. We continued to Garland, in northeast Dallas, instead of Redbird Airport in Oak Cliff, a suburb of Dallas. We made this decision because of possible bad weather southwest of Dallas that had not cleared as yet.

We arrived in Garland near daybreak. There had been so many threats against the president's life that we didn't have a great sense of urgency about this particular one. While waiting out the bad weather in Garland, and about thirty minutes after landing three of the passengers were picked up by car, including Roselli. There are three documented corroborations of my presence at Garland airport that morning. After the weather had cleared sufficiently for the plane to continue via VFR flight rules to Redbird Airport in Dallas, we left Garland for the ten-minute flight to Redbird. We landed at Redbird around 9:30 or 10:30 a.m., perhaps as late as 11 a.m., where everybody got off and went their own way.

The pre-mission briefing was held at Loxahatchee, Florida, on the evening of November 20th, but since I was not "field operational" at that time, except as a "contract pilot," I was not directly addressed at the briefing, other than routing and weather reports pertaining to flying the team into position. . . . I only began to learn the full scope of the operation from my pilot Rojas and a field operative friend of mine named Sergio. Most of the details of this operation were told to me only after we had become airborne. I would learn more operational details upon reaching Redbird Airport.

I learned that it had been discussed by the abort team where to go, how to abort, and what to look for. I had not at first paid much attention to any of these details as bits and pieces unfolded. I was told that the abort team, for whom I was only the pilot at that time, would probably be looking for a minimum of 19 or 20 people that would be in the plaza. Most of the team members felt that this was another false alarm, there had been many during the past few weeks.

Although my specific assigned function was only as a pilot, upon arriving at Redbird Airport, Sergio asked me if I wanted to come along and see the president. I could also act as a spotter for him and his team, which he said were assigned to the south side of the plaza. I was told other members of the team would be patrolling the north side and the overpass. I understood we would be looking for a type of triangulated ambush. I gladly accepted Sergio's offer. It seemed like an adventure I didn't want to miss. We were driven from Redbird Airport to a place not far from the Oak Cliff Country Club, then driven to Dealey Plaza, where we (Sergio and I) checked various areas and attempted to spot potential members of an attack team from the position on the South Knoll.

While on the South Knoll, Sergio and I were attempting to evaluate the most logical places where shooters might be located, but everything was confused, the timing was off; team members were late getting into position. They were not where they were supposed to be and the limited radio contacts that we had with them were not working or spotty at best. It was soon after our arrival that the motorcade arrived. When the shots rang out, I had the impression of 4 or 5 shots, with one being fired from behind and to my left on the South Knoll, near the underpass and south parking lot. While leaving via the south side of the underpass near the train tracks, Sergio and I smelled gunpowder. I never saw Roselli in Dealey Plaza that day.

We were picked up on the back side of the underpass, southwest side, by a person who had previously been at the country club. After driving away, and on the way back to Redbird we stopped in the parking lot of Ed McLemore's Sportatorium, where Sergio changed out of the clothes he had muddied when he fell down the slippery west side of the railroad tracks. We stopped by the house in Oak Cliff, then returned to Redbird Airport. We waited for a few of the operatives who had been on our flight into Dallas to return. We waited as long as we could before departing without Roselli and some of the others. At approximately 2 o'clock in the afternoon, we took off from Redbird without filing a flight plan. Our original flight out of Dallas called for us to fly to Sheppard Air Force Base in Wichita Falls, Texas. But because of the assassination that routing was changed at the last minute by Rojas. We would head for Houston and back to south Florida.

On the plane, besides myself, were Rojas, Sergio, a person who I knew as

Gator from the Loxahatchee camp, and two other individuals that I didn't know. Gator had identifying characteristics of an unusually large Adam's apple and a missing finger, which had supposedly been bitten off at an alligator farm.

The people on the flight out of Dallas were very quiet. I interpreted their silence as dejection at the mission's failure to abort the assassination of the president. I believed that if these men had been the shooters or assassins themselves, they would have been very excited because they had carried it off. That's why to this day I take issue with the idea, which I have been asked to speculate on many times, that the attack on the president was in behalf of the CIA, Mafia, or military intelligence, and I had unknowingly flown an attack team in which had assassinated the president.

Shortly after this flight, Tosh was arrested and extradited to Colorado, where he was prosecuted for passing bad checks. Only one check in the amount of $51.25 was produced and Tosh tried to explain that the CIA had failed to deposit his pay for January 1962. He was jailed, which kept him out of the public eye during the time of the Warren Commission. Released in 1964, Tosh got married and tried to forget his life as a "black ops" pilot. But it didn't work.

During the Reagan administration, Tosh was a pilot in the Iran-Contra scandal, in which illegal arms were shipped to Iran in hopes of freeing American hostages. Profits from these arms sales were then used to fund anticommunists, or Contras, in Nicaragua. Tosh said arms were flown to the Contras and their cocaine was flown back to the United States.

In 1977, Plumlee testified behind closed doors before Idaho senator Frank Church's Select Committee to Study Governmental Operations with Respect to Intelligence Activities, better known as the Church Committee. This panel probed illegal and clandestine activities of the FBI and CIA. He also testified before the Senate Foreign Relations Committee in 1990 and 1991 concerning his knowledge of the Iran-Contra missions. Despite his testimony and box loads of government documents pertaining to Plumlee and the operations he has disclosed, Tosh remains a controversial figure in the assassination research community, with many claiming he has failed to corroborate his various stories, as if his detractors expect illicit government operations to be thoroughly documented.

In 1991, this author accompanied Tosh on a driving trip to Florida where he pointed out various anti-Castro safe houses and aircraft still sitting on runways that were used in anti-Castro activities, and was warmly greeted in Alpha 66 headquarters, one of the Cuban exile organizations.

One of the aspects of Tosh's story that has struck researchers as bizarre is his claim that he and other "black ops" operatives were quartered in the Loxahatchee Work Prison, which was next to a landing strip they used to fly in and out on missions. Yet, in 1991, the old prison was still there, as was the adjacent landing strip. And in a telephone conversation with this author, Alton Chaney, the retired warden of the prison, confirmed that in the 1960s the county had a contract with the federal government to house some federal prisoners. He said he was never told anything about the inmates but they seemed to have been involved in some sort of witness protection program and he knew the names he was given for them were false. "It was kinda funny," recalled Chaney. "Some of those prisoners just kinda came and went." A prison record would indeed seem to be the perfect alibi. One could claim he had never been at the scene of the crime, as he was in jail at the time. But none of this will ever be proven, as the stockade commander, O. C. Reynolds, said when he took over the prison in the early 1970s he was surprised to find no records were available for past years.

Returning to Dallas, Tosh was able to describe and locate with precision Cuban safe houses, including the garage apartment behind Oswald's Beckley Street rented room and Oswald's 1962 apartment at 602 Elsbeth, which he was able to describe accurately as determined in a later visit by this author.

There was also an odd connection between Tosh's story of the assassination and that of James Files, who in later years claimed to be the Grassy Knoll gunman. Both men, apparently unknown to each other, were told the people who went into Dealey Plaza that day were "abort" teams sent to stop an assassination attempt. Both also started their careers in the US military. Files even said that he was told by John Roselli that the gangster was flown into Dallas on a "military flight."

Considering the accounts of Plumlee, Ferrie, Martin, and Roberts, as well as Oswald's bizarre military record and his trip to Russia, one must seriously consider that the ex-Marine was working in intelligence, just as his mother claimed.

Was Oswald a Spy?

After reviewing all available evidence, the answer to the above question seems to be an unequivocal yes.

The following is a quick look at some of the evidence pointing to Oswald's involvement with spy work:

—His childhood—as a bright loner who read a wide range of books and was drawn to unpopular ideas, attracted by spy stories (the TV show *I Led Three Lives* and Ian Fleming's James Bond novels were among his favorites)—perfectly fits the profile of people most desired for intelligence work.

—Oswald's Marine career is checkered with inconsistencies and unexplained absences suggesting secret intelligence training.

—He was assigned to Atsugi base in Japan, which housed a large CIA facility.

—Oswald had an incredible ability with the Russian language. Several Russians, including his wife, said he spoke like a native, yet this high-school dropout reportedly taught himself Russian from books.

—The fact that several people—including a former CIA paymaster,

Oswald's Marine roommate James Botelho, and fellow Marine Gerry Patrick Hemming—have stated that Oswald worked for US intelligence.

—The manner in which Oswald traveled so easily in and out of Russia as well as the unaccounted-for funds he used suggests intelligence guidance.

—The ability of this American "defector" to leave the Soviet Union with his Russian-born wife at a time when most Russians were being denied exit permits.

—The ease with which this would-be defector obtained passports in both 1959 and 1963.

—The fact that Oswald wrote a lengthy report on his activities in Russia and, later, made a detailed report to the FBI concerning his Fair Play for Cuba Committee activities in New Orleans.

—Oswald's notebook contained the word "microdots," a common spy technique of photographically reducing information to a small dot.

—Oswald's nonbinding "defection" to Russia fit perfectly the profile of an Office of Naval Intelligence program to infiltrate American servicemen into the Soviet Union during the late 1950s.

—One of Oswald's closest contacts, George DeMohrenschildt, was himself an intelligence operative, first for the Nazis and later for the CIA.

One of the strongest pieces of evidence proving Oswald's spy work concerns a small Minox camera found among his effects by Dallas police. Information developed by the *Dallas Morning News* in 1978 revealed the camera was not available to the public in 1963. It may have been spy equipment issued to Oswald. This evidence was so explosive that the FBI tried to get Dallas detectives to change their reports regarding the camera and for nearly fifteen years kept hidden photos taken by Oswald.

Dallas detectives Guy Rose and R. S. Stovall reported finding the Minox camera loaded with film in Oswald's Marine sea bag in the Irving home of Michael and Ruth Paine hours after the assassination. The three-inch-long German-made camera was famous for being used by spies on both sides during World War II. An inventory of Oswald's property taken from the Paine home was made on November 26, 1963. Listed under item 375 was "one Minox camera." This inventory list was witnessed by agent Warren De Brueys, the FBI man in New Orleans who had been assigned to monitor Oswald during the spring and summer of 1963. Later, however, the FBI property inventory listed item 375 as a "Minox light meter." Detective Rose told the *Dallas Morning News*, "[The FBI] were calling it a light meter, I know that. But I know a camera when I see it . . . . The thing we got at Irving out of Oswald's sea bag was a Minox camera. No question about it. They tried to get me to change the records because it wasn't a light meter. I don't know why they wanted it changed, but they must have had some motive for it."

The motive may have been that the existence of the camera pointed to Oswald's intelligence connections.

Dallas Morning News reporter Earl Golz contacted Minox Corporation and spoke to Kurt Lohn, formerly in charge of Minox distribution in New York City. According to Lohn, the serial number of the camera found in Oswald's belongings—number 27259—did not exist among any Minox cameras distributed for commercial sale in the United States. Lohn said all Minox cameras distributed in the United States carried six-digit serial numbers beginning with 135000. Number 27259 was "not a registered number . . . not a valid number," said Lohn. Golz also determined that Minox did not sell a light meter in the United States in 1963.

A later FBI report stated that a Minox III camera was obtained on January 31, 1964, from Ruth Paine and that it belonged to her husband, who worked for Bell Helicopter. However, Mrs. Paine told Golz she did not remember being asked to turn over such a camera. Michael Paine reportedly also had a Minox camera but it was damaged and "unworkable."

In 1979, acting on a Freedom of Information Act request by an assassination researcher, the FBI, which had denied the existence of any Minox camera, released about twenty-five photographs taken with a Minox camera belonging to Oswald. Michael Paine was unable to recall taking any pictures such as the ones the FBI released.

On page 113 of a book published by Dallas police chief Jesse Curry in 1969 is a photograph of Oswald's property taken from the Paine home. Clearly pictured is the camera along with various Minox camera equipment, including a binocular-type telephoto lens.

Who issued Oswald an unregistered Minox "spy" camera? More important, why did the FBI attempt to have Dallas police change their reports to indicate a light meter was found rather than a camera?

In 1976, a CIA document was released that showed that the agency indeed had considered Oswald for recruitment. This contradicted the sworn Warren Commission testimony of CIA official Richard Helms, who stated the agency had never had "or even contemplated" any contact with Oswald. This document, written by an unidentified CIA officer three days after Kennedy's assassination, states "we showed intelligence interest" in Oswald and "discussed . . . the laying on of interviews."

Harry J. Dean, who said he participated in undercover operations against Castro as well as the infiltration of such organizations as the Fair Play for Cuba Committee, the Minutemen, and the John Birch Society for the CIA, claimed Oswald shot no one in Dallas, but was set up to take the blame for the assassination by a conspiracy headed by US congressman John Rousselot and General Edwin Walker. Dean also explained that "Oswald wasn't in the Security Index because the FBI officials knew that he was working to preserve security, not hinder it."

An internal CIA cable dated October 16, 1963, indicated that more than a month prior to the assassination at least six senior CIA officials were apprised by a "usually reliable and extremely sensitive source" that a Lee Oswald had visited the Soviet embassy in Mexico City in September. The memo stated this Oswald was "probably identical" to a "Lee Henry Oswald," a Marine radar operator who had renounced his

US citizenship in Russia. A later CIA message on October 22 corrected the name to Lee Harvey Oswald.

"The CIA would have kept the names of these highly-regarded officers—Tom Karamessines, Bill Hood, John Whitten ('John Scelso'), Jane Roman, and Betty Egeter—secret for thirty years," wrote Jefferson Morley, a former editor at the *Washington Post*, in 2012. "Why? Because the officers most knowledgeable about Oswald reported to two of the most powerful men in the CIA: Deputy Director Richard Helms and Counterintelligence Chief James Angleton."

Morley added, "We can't do much about the JFK tragedy at this late date, but we can acknowledge that CIA negligence led directly to the president's death. The officers who obscured information about Oswald should be stripped of any medals or commendations they received for their job performance in 1963. Fifty years later, it's time for accountability."

But others saw much more than negligence involved in this obfuscation of Oswald's records prior to the assassination. There are the questions concerning a CIA "201" file on Oswald discovered only in 1977. The existence of this file came to light after a Freedom of Information Act request by assassination researchers. Many persons knowledgeable about the agency equate a 201 file with a personnel file, implying Oswald had worked for the CIA. Agency officials told the House Select Committee on Assassinations that the file on Oswald was nothing unusual and reflected merely that Oswald had "potential intelligence or counterintelligence significance." However, at least three former CIA officers have stated publicly that the mere existence of a 201 file on Oswald indicated a relationship between the ex-Marine and the agency.

Victor Marchetti, formerly an executive assistant to the CIA's deputy director, said, "Basically, if Oswald had a 201 file, he was an agent."

Bradley E. Ayers, a CIA officer who trained anti-Castro Cubans, added, "[A 201 file meant Oswald was] either a contract agent, working for them full time, or he was on some kind of assignment for the CIA."

Former CIA agent Patrick McGarvey, said, "If a guy has a 201 file, that means he's a professional staff employee of the organization."

The CIA went to great lengths to convince the House Committee that possessing a 201 file on Oswald—and that keeping this information secret for nearly fifteen years—was in no way suspicious.

The committee, however, found many problems with the 201 file. For example, Oswald's file reportedly was opened on December 9, 1960, yet a confidential State Department telegram reporting Oswald's attempted defection to Russia—cause enough to open a file on him—was sent to the CIA back on October 31, 1959.

Other problems with the Oswald file are that a former official with the CIA's Directorate of Operations records explained an "AG" code on the file that varied from the official agency explanation that this pertained to American defectors. Also, the 201 file was under the name "Lee Henry Oswald," leading the committee to wonder whether dual files were kept (a suspicion the CIA denied). One CIA memo indicated as many as thirty-seven documents were missing from the Oswald file, although agency officials later claimed they were missing only at the time the memo was written.

Further, a recently obtained CIA document states that Oswald's 201 file filled "two four-drawer safes," yet the House committee was given a virtually empty folder.

Oswald's role with the CIA was cemented in 1995 with the publication of *Oswald and the CIA* by the respected military historian John M. Newman, who discovered by analyzing internal CIA messages that Oswald, knowingly or unknowingly, was being used operationally by the agency prior to the JFK assassination. This shocking information—that Oswald was being used by the CIA prior to the assassination—apparently was not considered newsworthy by the corporate mass media, which failed to widely report on this development.

Another minor but intriguing fact indicating Oswald's spy work is that at the time of his arrest, he was carrying a three-by-two-inch top of a department-store box labeled "Cox's Ft. Worth." Intelligence agents have been known to carry such innocuous but unusual items, called bona fides, to identify themselves to other agents. The box top's significance is enhanced by the fact that it was not included in the Warren Commission exhibits, which presented thousands of less relevant items.

However, the whole question of Oswald's connection to US intelligence is so full of claims and counterclaims, deceit and misinformation, it is unlikely the whole truth of the matter will ever be resolved.

What is known—or at least believed by most people who have studied the issue at any depth—is that the weight of the evidence proves Oswald was in some way connected with US intelligence work, exactly as his mother always claimed.

While at the time of the JFK assassination the official story was that no US government agency had been interested in Oswald or knew of his whereabouts, it is now known that both the CIA and the FBI were keeping a close watch on the ex-Marine's activities. Oswald's alleged trip to Mexico City between September 26 and October 3, 1963, is a case in point. According to the Warren Commission, Oswald was in Mexico City to visit the Soviet and Cuban embassies. Proof of these visits came from the statements of a Cuban embassy employee, Silvia Duran, and from CIA operatives monitoring the Soviet embassy.

On October 10, 1963, yet another CIA teletype went to the State Department, the FBI, immigration authorities, and the Department of the Navy regarding the "possible presence of Subject [Oswald] in Mexico City":

> On October 1, 1963, a reliable and sensitive source in Mexico reported that an American male, who identified himself as Lee Oswald, contacted the Soviet Embassy in Mexico City. . . . The American was described as approximately 35 years old, with an athletic build, about six feet tall, with a receding hairline. . . . It is believed that Oswald may be identical to Lee Harvey Oswald, born on 18 October 1939 in New Orleans, Louisiana.

Obviously this description did not match that of the twenty-three-year-old, five-foot-nine, slender Oswald in Dallas.

The Warren Commission, seriously concerned about the ties between Oswald and the Soviets and Cubans in Mexico City, asked the CIA for documentation of Oswald's activities. After months of foot-dragging, the agency could provide only the unsupported statement of Duran as proof that Oswald had been at the Cuban embassy.

Not shown to the Warren Commission was a cable the director of the CIA sent to its station in Mexico City urging the secret arrest of Silvia Duran on the day after the assassination. Duran, a twenty-six-year-old Mexican national, had been employed at the Cuban embassy only one month before Oswald allegedly arrived in Mexico. Her predecessor had been killed in an automobile accident. The CIA cable regarding Duran's arrest, declassified only in recent years, stated:

> Arrest of Silvia Duran is extremely serious matter which could prejudice US freedom of action on entire question of Cuban responsibility. . . . With full regard for Mexican interests, request you ensure that her arrest is kept absolutely secret, that no information from her is published or leaked, that all such info is cabled to us, and that fact of her arrest and her statements are not spread to leftist or disloyal circles in the Mexican government.

In a 1978 article, Mark Lane concluded:

> This almost incredible cable reveals the extent of CIA control over Mexican police officials, many of whom had been trained by the CIA, and many of whom were engaged by the CIA while they ostensibly worked for the Mexican government. The CIA's willingness to order Mexican police officials to make false statements to their own superiors and to mislead the "circles in the Mexican government" provides an insight into the CIA's desperation to secure some evidence to prove . . . that Oswald had gone to the Cuban Embassy.

Apparently the statements that Duran gave to the Mexican authorities were not to their liking. She was not released for several days and only then after she had identified Oswald as the man who visited the embassy.

Once free, Duran began to speak of her experience. This prompted yet another CIA cable, which ordered CIA personnel to have Duran rearrested, but to conceal who was behind the action. A portion of this cable stated, "To be certain that there is no misunderstanding between us, we want to insure that Silvia Duran gets no impression that Americans are behind her re-arrest. In other words we want Mexican authorities to take responsibility for the whole affair."

Duran was rearrested and would not speak of her experiences afterward. She was never interviewed or called as a witness by the Warren Commission, which never learned of her two arrests.

Since the Oswald in the Cuban embassy apparently made quite a scene when told he could not get a visa to Cuba in three days—he shouted and called the embassy personnel "bureaucrats"—he should have been well remembered by Duran and others there. But in 1978, Cuban consul Eusebio Azcue told the House Select Committee on Assassinations that he was convinced the man who visited the embassy in 1963 was not the Oswald arrested in Dallas. After viewing photos of Oswald, Azcue stated, "My belief is that this gentleman was not, is not, the person or the individual who went to the consulate."

Silvia Duran—perhaps due to her experience in the hands of the police—has maintained over the years that the man was Oswald. However, in 1979, author Anthony Summers arranged for her to watch films of Lee Harvey Oswald. Duran, who admitted that her identification of Oswald was more from the name than from the fuzzy newspaper photos printed at the time, watched the Oswald films and concluded, "I was not sure if it was Oswald or not. . . . The man on the film is not like the man I saw here in Mexico City." To add to Duran's confusion, she recalled the man who visited the consulate was short, no more than five feet six inches in height—far shorter than the five-foot-nine Lee Oswald.

While the CIA stated that both the Cuban and Soviet embassies were under photographic surveillance during Oswald's visits, they could offer no proof. Lamely, CIA officials explained to the Warren Commission that the camera at the Soviet embassy was turned off on Saturdays (the day Oswald supposedly visited) and that the camera at the Cuban embassy just happened to break down the day Oswald was there. However, the day of the assassination, CIA officials sent photos taken outside the Soviet embassy in Mexico City to the FBI, claiming they were of Oswald. They are obviously of someone else. This someone appears to be about thirty-five years old, six feet tall, with an athletic build. CIA officials admitted there had been a "mix-up" on the photos.

The absence of any valid photos of Oswald at the embassies raises suspicion that an impostor was posing as Oswald during these embassy visits. Further evidence of this comes from an episode involving tape recordings. In 1976, at the onset of the House assassinations investigation, CIA officer David Atlee Phillips, stationed in Mexico City at the time of Oswald's alleged visit, told the House committee's general counsel that the CIA had tape-recorded conversations between Oswald and the Soviet embassy but had not told the Warren Commission. When pressed on why the tapes, clear proof of Oswald's Mexican visits, had not been given to the Commission, Phillips said they had been routinely destroyed about a week after Oswald's visit since prior to the assassination Oswald was not considered important.

It should be noted that in its report on Oswald's Mexico City visit, the House committee concluded that the CIA station there did not report all information on Oswald "in an accurate and expeditious manner prior to the assassination" to CIA headquarters.

Phillips's testimony was thrown into doubt when, long after his 1976 testimony, a five-page FBI document dated November 23, 1963, became public. According to this document, which was not seen by the Warren Commission, FBI agents who were questioning Oswald in Dallas were informed by CIA officers that Oswald had contacted the Soviet embassy in Mexico City. The report went on to state, "Special agents of this Bureau, who have conversed with Oswald in Dallas, Texas, have observed photographs of the individual referred to above and have listened to a recording of his voice. These special agents are of the opinion that the above-referred-to individual was not Lee Harvey Oswald."

If this FBI report is correct, then the CIA wiretap tape of Oswald was not destroyed in October but was available to bureau agents the day after the assassination. When, then, was this evidence destroyed and by whom?

One disturbing aspect of all this is that either the CIA notified other agencies in October that Oswald was in Mexico City, not knowing the man was an impostor, then failed to follow up on their mistake later. Or, more ominously, the agency knowingly participated in a scheme to place Oswald in Mexico City at that time— nearly two months *before* the assassination. Was this an attempt to link Oswald with the Soviets and Cuba? Or was another Oswald in Mexico City intent on delivering the cancer-causing agent, prompting the need for an impostor to divert attention from the cancer plot?

It is equally disturbing that the House Select Committee on Assassinations made a three hundred–page report on these mysterious happenings in Mexico City, then failed to put it into its published report claiming the information was withheld to protect the CIA's "sensitive sources and methods."

Another Mexico incident, which has been misreported for years, concerns a note from Oswald to a "Mr. Hunt."

A Message from Oswald

In August 1975, Texas JFK researcher Penn Jones Jr. received a typewritten letter in Spanish from Mexico City signed only with the initials "P.S." Translated, the letter read:

> Dear Sir:
>
> At the end of last year I gave Mr. [Clarence] Kelly, the director of the FBI, a letter from Lee Oswald. To my understanding it could have brought out the circumstances to the assassination of President Kennedy.
>
> Since Mr. Kelly hasn't responded to that letter, I've got the right to believe something bad might happen to me, and that is why I see myself obligated to keep myself away for a short time.
>
> Convinced of the importance of that letter mentioned and knowing that you have been doing some investigation independently of the assassination, I'm sending you a copy of the same letter.

Accompanying this typed letter was a copy of a handwritten note in English dated November 8, 1963, that reads:

Dear Mr. Hunt,

I would like information concer[n]ing my position.

I am asking only for information. I am suggesting that we discuss the matter fully before any steps are taken by me or anyone else.

Thank you,

Lee Harvey Oswald

Jones, too, sent this information to the FBI and he, too, received no reply.

Earl Golz, a reporter for the *Dallas Morning News*, later obtained a copy of the Oswald note from Jones. He had three handwriting experts in Dallas compare the note to known examples of Oswald's handwriting. The experts all agreed that the handwriting was the same. The *Dallas Morning News* carried an accurate account of the strange note and asked whether "Mr. Hunt" might refer to Dallas oilman H. L. Hunt. However, handwriting experts for both the FBI and the House Select Committee on Assassinations were suspicious of the letter's legitimacy. Joseph P. McNally, a former NYPD crime lab commander and a veteran examiner of questioned documents, told the committee that because the Oswald letter was a photo reproduction and that some oddities in Oswald's signature were found, experts were unable to reach a conclusion as to the letter's authenticity, "although the writing pattern or the overall letter designs are consistent with those as written on the other documents."

In 1983, it was learned that the FBI studied the note with the idea it may have been intended for Hunt's son, Nelson Bunker Hunt. The results of the FBI probe, however, have never been made public.

Jones pointed out that the note came from Mexico City and that allegedly CIA officer E. Howard Hunt, who was in charge of anti-Castro Cubans at the time, was stationed there along with David Atlee Phillips during Oswald's reported visit.

Jones told this author, "To me, knowing Hunt's background with the Cuban Revolutionary Committee and the CIA, it makes more sense that the note is addressed to E. Howard Hunt."

But since neither the FBI nor the two official government investigations appears to have taken an interest in the note, there the matter rests.

The fact of the Oswald note and its accompanying letter leads some assassination researchers to believe that Oswald's brief and mysterious visit to Mexico City might provide clues that US government agents were behind the assassination.

Yet another contact with the CIA that has become known only in recent years involves a man who "coincidentally" obtained the Mexican travel permit number just before Oswald's—William George Gaudet.

When applying for a new passport in June 1963, Oswald did not try to hide his past or his intentions. On the application, he acknowledged he might travel to

Russia and other European countries later that year. He also noted that his previous passport had been canceled. Despite these admissions—coupled with the fact that the State Department, which loaned him money to return from the Soviet Union, knew of his attempted defection and threat to give military secrets to the Soviets— Oswald received a new passport within twenty-four hours.

On September 17, a week after the alleged meeting between Oswald and CIA case officer "Maurice Bishop," Oswald visited the Mexican consulate in New Orleans and applied for a tourist card. He was issued card number 24085, which was valid for fifteen days.

After the assassination, the FBI, with the help of Mexican authorities, identified every person who had applied for Mexican entry papers on September 17—all but one. The FBI reported they could not locate the record of the card holder immediately preceding Oswald, No. 24084. However, in 1975, apparently due to a bureaucratic mix-up in declassifying FBI documents, it was learned that card holder No. 24084 was William George Gaudet, who had worked for the CIA for more than twenty years.

Gaudet claimed that sheer coincidence placed his name just ahead of Oswald's on the Mexican tourist card application sheet. Gaudet, who worked in the area of Latin America for the agency, operated the *Latin American Newsletter* for a number of years. Shortly after the assassination, Gaudet said, he was interviewed by FBI agents, but only after obtaining the approval of his CIA boss in New Orleans. No record of that interview has been made public.

In a 1978 interview with author Anthony Summers, Gaudet admitted he had known Oswald in New Orleans, but then qualified this by saying he had only observed Oswald handing out leaflets. "He was a strange man, an unusual man," was Gaudet's description of Oswald. Gaudet did firmly state that while in New Orleans, Oswald was in contact with known CIA and FBI agents. Gaudet told Summers, "I do know that I saw him one time with a former FBI agent by the name of Guy Banister." He also mentioned David Ferrie, saying, "He was with Oswald."

Gaudet said he did not accompany Oswald on a bus to Mexico, but went by air. He now claims he cannot remember whether his 1963 Mexican trip involved intelligence activity. He also said that due to his experience with the CIA, he is not surprised that little information concerning Oswald's intelligence activities has been forthcoming: "[CIA officials] told me frankly when I did things for them that if something went awry they would never recognize me or admit who I was. If I made a mistake, that was just tough, and I knew it." The former CIA operative went on to say he finds it "extremely possible" that Oswald was working for some American intelligence agency and added, "I think he was a patsy. . . . I think he was set up on purpose." Gaudet also agreed with many assassination researchers who believe that the anti-Castro Cubans were involved in a plot to kill Kennedy. But when asked if he thought the Cubans could have carried out an assassination alone, he replied, "No, I don't think so."

But if Gaudet did not actually accompany Oswald to Mexico, one very suspicious man did—Albert Osborne. Although the passenger list for Continental Trailways bus No. 5133, which allegedly carried Oswald to Mexico City, is missing, the FBI managed to locate some of the travelers, including two Australian girls who told of a conversation with a man who told them of his experiences in the Marines and in Russia. These girls told the FBI that the man also had sat next to and talked at length with an older man.

FBI agents tried to locate a man named John Howard Bowen who had been on Oswald's bus. However, they found only Albert Osborne, but Osborne seemed to know a lot about Bowen. After three visits from the FBI, Osborne finally admitted that he was the man they were seeking, having used the alias "John Bowen" for many years. He denied ever having met Oswald. Even the Warren Commission didn't buy that, stating "his denial cannot be credited."

Osborne claimed to be a missionary who traveled extensively all over the world, although he never said how these travels were financed. Also, no confirmation of his story could be found by checking border records in the countries he claimed to have visited. Despite his lies to the FBI regarding his name, no charges were ever brought against Osborne.

In recent years, several assassination researchers have claimed that Osborne worked for the CIA, but no hard evidence of this has been established. It is interesting to note, however, that when Oswald ordered Fair Play for Cuba Committee materials printed in New Orleans, he used the name "Osborne."

Other intriguing connections between the CIA and the JFK assassination concern George DeMohrenschildt and the Carcano rifle found in the Texas School Book Depository.

DeMohrenschildt and the Agency

George DeMohrenschildt and his wife, Jeanne, were identified by the Warren Commission as the people closest to Lee Harvey Oswald just before the assassination. DeMohrenschildt's son-in-law, Gary Taylor, even told the Warren Commission, "If there was any assistance [to Oswald] or plotters in the assassination they were, in my opinion, most probably the DeMohrenschildts."

DeMohrenschildt undoubtedly is one of the most colorful and suspicious of all the persons connected to Oswald. He even wrote to Lyndon Johnson in April 1963, at a time he was in contact with Lee Oswald, and was told by LBJ aide Walter Jenkins a meeting with the vice president might be arranged. Based on CIA memos now available, thanks to Freedom of Information Act suits, it is known that DeMohrenschildt had a relationship with the agency dating back to OSS days. One memo by former CIA director Richard Helms states that DeMohrenschildt applied to work for the government as early as 1942 but was rejected "because he was alleged to be a Nazi espionage agent."

The charge had some substance. After a trip to Yugoslavia with his wife in 1957 (they were shot at by guards of Marshal Tito), DeMohrenschildt provided the CIA with "foreign intelligence which was promptly disseminated to other federal agencies in 10 separate reports," according to the Helms memo. Another agency memo indicated DeMohrenschildt also furnished lengthy reports on travels he made through Mexico and Panama at the time of the Bay of Pigs Invasion.

Asked by a Warren Commission attorney if he believed the DeMohrenschildts may have been spying on the invasion preparations, Taylor replied, "Yes."

In fact, at the time DeMohrenschildt was befriending Lee Harvey Oswald, one of his close friends in Dallas was J. Walton Moore with the CIA's Domestic Contacts Division. DeMohrenschildt publicly stated that before becoming involved with Oswald, he had checked with Moore. Moore, according to DeMohrenschildt, said unhesitatingly, "Yes, he's okay. He's just a harmless lunatic."

In a CIA memorandum written not long after Oswald returned from Russia, the CIA author wrote, "Don't push too hard to get the information we need, because this individual [Oswald] looks odd."

Much later it was learned how the CIA was to further "debrief" Oswald—by using the genial George DeMohrenschildt. Author Edward Epstein interviewed DeMohrenschildt on the morning of March 29, 1977. That same morning, an investigator from the House Select Committee on Assassinations had attempted to contact DeMohrenschildt. Three hours later DeMohrenschildt was dead from a shotgun blast to the head. His death was ruled a suicide although the detective in charge of his investigation expressed some reservations about this verdict.

According to Epstein, DeMohrenschildt said Moore encouraged him to see Oswald and that, in fact, he was to question Oswald "unwittingly" about his stay in Russia. DeMohrenschildt said that after his first meeting with the ex-Marine, Oswald gave him a lengthy memo covering his activities in Russia.

DeMohrenschildt, a petroleum engineer, and Moore had offices in the same Dallas bank building and often ate lunch together, according to Jeanne DeMohrenschildt.

The CIA memos, Moore's closeness, and DeMohrenschildt's own testimony all confirm that a certain relationship existed between the CIA and the man closest to Oswald in early 1963. While this does not necessarily involve the agency in a plot to kill Kennedy, it raises questions about what agency officials might have known regarding such a plot.

In a related issue that belies the idea set forth in 1963 that the CIA was neither aware of Oswald nor interested in him, it is now known that the agency was opening Oswald's mail while he was in Russia. In letters to his mother, Marguerite Oswald, in 1976, former CIA legislative counsel George L. Cary admitted that the agency had opened mail from her to her son while he was in Russia. Cary said the admission was a result of an investigation into the CIA's mail intercept program—known as HT-Lingual—by the Government Information and Individual Rights Subcommittee of the House Government Operations Committee.

Another possible connection between the CIA and the JFK assassination concerns a former CIA operative named Robert D. Morrow. In his book *Betrayal*, Morrow tells how he purchased four 6.5 mm Carcano rifles on orders from a CIA superior. Morrow remains convinced that at least one of these rifles ended up in the hands of Dallas police on November 22, 1963.

Morrow even presented a plausible, though unproven, account of the assassination:

> Oswald, who went to Russia for the CIA and was an FBI informant by the summer of 1963, was brought into an assassination plot led by CIA consultant Clay Shaw, using right-wing CIA operatives and anti-Castro Cubans headed by Jack Ruby in Dallas and Guy Banister in New Orleans. This group, operating outside Agency control, manipulated events to insure Oswald being named as the assassin. They also used an Oswald look-alike to incriminate the ex-Marine by firing shots from the Texas School Book Depository. Dallas policeman J. D. Tippit was killed by this Oswald substitute when he failed to go along with the group's scheme to have Tippit kill the real Oswald in the Texas Theater. With the capture of Oswald, Ruby was compelled to stalk and finally kill the accused assassin.

The Mannlicher-Carcano ammunition also raised questions about CIA involvement. According to an FBI document, the 6.5 mm ammunition found in the Texas School Book Depository was part of a batch manufactured on a US government contract by Western Cartridge Corporation of East Alton, Illinois, which is now a part of Winchester-Western Division of Olin Industries.

In the mid-1950s, the Marine Corps purchased four million rounds of this ammunition, prompting the author of one FBI document to state, "The interesting thing about this order is that it is for ammunition which does not fit and cannot be fired in any of the United States Marine Corps weapons. This gives rise to the obvious speculation that it is a contract for ammunition placed by the CIA with Western Cartridge Corporation under a USMC cover for concealment purposes."

It is well-known that the CIA had used "sanitized" weapons—that is, weapons that cannot be traced directly back to the agency or the United States—in various missions around the world.

Most of the information available suggesting links between the assassination and the CIA is circumstantial—which is hardly surprising. After all, agency officials could hardly be expected to reveal information possibly connecting them to the president's death. However, at this time there can be little doubt that many persons connected to Oswald—David Ferrie, Guy Banister, Carlos Bringuier, and other anti-Castro Cubans—were also connected to the CIA, although some knowledgeable persons, such as former CIA operative Morrow and others, claim they were operating outside of agency control.

One strange incident involved an intelligence operative named Gary Underhill, who had served in World War II and was considered one of the top US experts on unconventional warfare. At the time of the assassination, Underhill performed "special assignments" for the CIA and was on close terms with officials of both the agency and the Pentagon. Several days after the assassination, Underhill visited friends in New Jersey. He was badly shaken and fearful. He said that President Kennedy had been killed by a small group within the CIA and that he believed his life was in danger. A short time later, Underhill was found fatally shot in his Washington apartment. His death was ruled a suicide although he was shot in the left side of his head and a pistol was found in his left hand—and it was well-known that Underhill was right-handed.

There is also the very real possibility that the assassins who killed Kennedy may have had no direct link at all with Oswald and his Cuban contacts. This intriguing possibility—which could go far in explaining why none of the trails leading backward from Oswald's acquaintances in New Orleans seem to connect firmly with the shooting in Dealey Plaza—became apparent several years ago with the revelation of a French connection to the assassination.

The French Connection to the Assassination

In 1979 the House Select Committee on Assassinations concluded that many Dealey Plaza witnesses were correct in stating that at least one gunman fired on Kennedy from the Grassy Knoll.

While the committee said it could not identify the Grassy Knoll gunman, the second gunman may have been a premier French assassin with close contacts to the CIA, organized crime, and even an oblique connection with Jack Ruby. According to evidence revealed in the late 1970s, more than one French assassin may have been operating in Dealey Plaza.

Central to this possibility is CIA Document No. 632–796, which the agency released in 1977 along with more than 3,000 other documents. Dated April 1, 1964, and carrying the handwritten title "Jean Soutre's Expulsion from US," the half-page document stated:

> 8. Jean SOUTRE aka [also known as] Michel Roux aka Michael Mertz— On March 5, [1964] the FBI advised that the French had [withheld] the Legal Attaché in Paris and also the [withheld] had queried the Bureau in New York City concerning subject, stating that he had been expelled from the US at Fort Worth or Dallas 18 hours after the assassination. He was in Fort Worth on the morning of 22 November and in Dallas in the afternoon. The French believe that he was expelled to either Mexico or Canada. In January he received mail from a dentist named Alderson. . . . Subject is believed to be identical with a Captain who is a deserter from the French Army and an activist in the OAS [a right-wing French militant group]. The French are concerned because of De-Gaulle's planned visit to Mexico. They would like to know the reason for his expulsion from the US and his

destination. Bureau files are negative and they are checking in Texas and with the INS [Immigration and Naturalization Service].

And the government did check, first with the dentist, who was still practicing in Houston, Texas, in the 1980s. Dr. Lawrence M. Alderson told researchers that FBI agents began watching him in early 1964. He said agents finally contacted him and said they were trying to find the Frenchman "under any circumstances under any conditions."

Alderson said, "They felt that Jean knew who, or he himself had, assassinated Kennedy. And they wanted to know who in Washington had had him flown out of Dallas. And, to my knowledge, nobody ever found out or nobody knew."

Alderson said he had not seen the Frenchman since serving as a security officer with him shortly after World War II. He confided that he was working for the CIA at the time. The dentist gave the following information about the Frenchman, Jean Soutre (pronounced "sweatra"):

> He's a career soldier. From what I can gather, he was in the French under-ground movement in Algiers. I do know he left the French Air Force. . . . I believe he was in the Fourth French Air Force Headquarters in France. He was a very prominent and upcoming French security officer. When I knew him, he was a lieutenant. . . . I lived with him so I knew him quite well. He was very well educated, very outgoing, forward, dynamic. He came from a very poor family. In France, you don't have a thing if you're from a poor family unless you have a military career behind you. So, he was very interested in his career and this is why I never did really understand why he left it. But, he very definitely left, I presume, his wife. I have not heard from her in many years. She was a well-to-do, beautiful woman from a Southern France wine family. The last I heard from her, she was the one who told me that he had left the French Army and had gone underground trying to save Algeria. So, evidently, he was rather committed, or felt committed, to leave his career, which was the only career he had. The next time I heard of him, quite truthfully, was when the CIA, or the FBI rather, had me tailed for about two months following the assassination. . . . The last contact I had with the CIA was in France when I was working for him. So, the only contact I had in this country was with the FBI.

After providing a snapshot of his French friend, Alderson said Soutre in the early 1950s was about twenty-five years old and spoke English, Spanish, and German without a trace of an accent.

An FBI report stated that three persons named John Mertz, Irma Rio Mertz, and Sara Mertz flew from Houston to Mexico City on November 23, 1963, according to records of Pan American World Airways. The FBI report concluded, "These records contain no further identifying data regarding these individuals."

Although Soutre could have flown out of the country by private or even military aircraft, it is interesting to note the coincidental departure of the Mertzes at a time corresponding to that in the CIA document. After all, even the FBI report noted that Soutre also was known as Michel Roux and Michael Mertz.

Today it is known that Roux and Mertz are the names of two real individuals, both of whom were connected to the shadowy world of intelligence work.

The name "Mertz" crops up in the 1974 Pulitzer Prize–winning investigative book *The Heroin Trail*, compiled by the staff of *Newsday*. According to this book, Michael Victor Mertz was a World War II French Resistance hero and a captain in the French secret service after the war. Mertz operated in Germany, Turkey, and Morocco under the cover of his military title. In April 1961, Mertz was ordered to penetrate the terrorist group Organisation de l'armée secrète (OAS), the secret group fighting to keep Algeria a French possession. Reflecting the methods of Lee Oswald, Mertz posed as an OAS sympathizer and was arrested later in 1961 for distributing pro-OAS leaflets. He was sent to an internment camp. There he worked his way into the highest levels of the OAS and was able to break up a bomb plot against Charles de Gaulle.

However, security work was not the only activity in which Mertz became involved. Even before saving de Gaulle, Mertz had become one of France's biggest heroin smugglers, according to *Newsday*, which cites numerous French police and court records. It is known in intelligence circles that de Gaulle often turned his back on drug smuggling, particularly if it involved people he was indebted to for their work against either the Nazis or the OAS.

One of Mertz's contacts in both heroin smuggling and the French secret service was a man named Christian David, a petty hoodlum who had escaped a French prison and later was recruited into French intelligence for use against the OAS. According to *Newsday* and other knowledgeable sources, David was one of the men involved in the 1965 murder of Moroccan opposition leader Mehdi Ben Barka.

In 1972, Barka's murder—which is still officially unsolved—was brought up when David was arrested in Brazil and charged with being a member of a smuggling ring that had imported more than 1,000 pounds of heroin into the United States over a three-year period.

After his arrest in Brazil, David was extradited to the United States and sentenced to twenty years in prison for heroin smuggling. He didn't stay there long. In 1975, when the Senate Intelligence Committee began looking into the CIA's "Executive Action" program, David was ordered extradited back to France and was taken out of the country.

The committee was especially concerned with the agency's Executive Action program because it was established to commit assassinations. The program was part of the operational arm of the CIA's Technical Services Division and was code-named ZR/RIFLE.

Former CIA director Richard Helms spoke at length about ZR/RIFLE to the committee. Two members of the ZR/RIFLE team were identified by Helms only by their CIA cryptonyms—WI/ROGUE and QJ/WIN. According to evidence gathered by the committee, WI/ROGUE was a French Corsican, a stateless soldier of fortune and a criminal. This man approached QJ/WIN and attempted to recruit him into the CIA's assassination program. Although it was never learned whether this recruitment effort was successful, there is evidence that it was.

Declassified CIA notes concerning the ZR/RIFLE project state:

4. Operational assets:

(1.) Personnel: QJ/WIN is under written contract as a principal agent, with the primary task of spotting agent candidates. QJ/WIN was first contacted in [deleted by CIA], in conjunction with an illegal narcotics operation into the United States. For a period of a year and a half, he was contacted sporadically by CIS Lucien Conein [who later became chief of foreign intelligence for the Drug Enforcement Agency] on behalf of the Bureau of Narcotics. Files of this bureau reflect an excellent performance by QJ/WIN.

Helms said this about QJ/WIN, "If you needed somebody to carry out murder, I guess you had a man who might be prepared to carry it out."

Until the Senate hearings, the ZR/RIFLE program and its agents, WI/ROGUE and QJ/WIN, were among the CIA's most closely guarded secrets. Several separate sources familiar with both intelligence operations and drug smuggling claim that WI/ROGUE and Christian David are one and the same. This claim is further supported by David's own admission of intelligence associations and by his convenient extradition to France in 1985.

The association of David and Mertz, coupled with their descriptions and backgrounds, which match those of the CIA agents, suggests that QJ/WIN was Michael Victor Mertz, who also used the name Jean Soutre.

If all this isn't complicated enough, QJ/WIN even had a tenuous connection with Jack Ruby—in the person of Thomas Eli Davis III.

Tom Howard, Ruby's first attorney, asked his client if there were anyone the prosecution might produce who could damage Ruby's defense of momentary insanity. Ruby hesitantly came up with the name "Davis." Ruby said Davis had first approached him about using some of Ruby's strippers in pornographic movies, but that later the two had become involved in gunrunning activities.

The FBI told the Warren Commission they could not locate such a person. However, the CIA did—and still does—have a classified file on Thomas Eli Davis III.

Veteran newsman Seth Kantor details Ruby's connection to Davis in his book *Who Was Jack Ruby?* Born to a respectable Texas rancher couple on August 27, 1936, Davis was discharged from the Army in 1958 and attended the University of Michigan until he was asked to leave because of low grades.

In June 1958, Davis entered a Detroit bank and handed a teller a note that threatened her life if she didn't give him money. According to the teller, Davis then said,

"I can't do it. I can't do it," then threw his thousand-dollar take on the floor. He fled from the bank only to be caught by police a block away. Due to his family's good reputation and his lack of a criminal record, Davis received five years of probation.

While on probation, Davis obtained passport No. D236764, issued by the State Department on January 31, 1963, in New Orleans, a feat almost impossible for a convicted felon without highly placed and powerful help.

Davis's ensuing activities took him into the murky world of anti-Castro gunrunning, and it was here Davis met Ruby. Ruby told his attorney that Davis had come to one of his nightclubs and that he had intended to go into the gunrunning business with Davis on a regular basis. However, apparently Davis's activities were not limited to dealing with Cuban gunrunners.

At the time of the Kennedy assassination, Davis was in North Africa, allegedly setting up a deal to supply arms to the OAS. Less than a month later, he was jailed in Tangiers in connection with the assassination.

His wife told authorities that her husband was a soldier of fortune who had operated in such diverse countries as Indonesia, Algeria, and Cuba, and in the months prior to his arrest they had traveled through London, Paris, and Madrid.

According to correspondence between J. Edgar Hoover and the State Department, Moroccan security police detained Davis "because of a letter in his handwriting which referred in passing to Oswald and the Kennedy assassination."

Kantor wrote that evidence showed Davis was freed from jail through the efforts of QJ/WIN, "the code name given by the CIA to an unsavory foreign agent with a network of Mafia contacts." Here could be the connection not only between Davis and the CIA, but between Davis and Mertz (if indeed Mertz was QJ/WIN).

Through early 1963, Davis had contact with the anti-Castro Cubans, as confirmed by his wife and family. And he not only was in New Orleans at the same time as Oswald in the summer of 1963, but once admitted to reporter George Carter that he had used the name Oswald while in North Africa.

Based on the two men's similar statures, ages, and features, many researchers today believe that Davis may have posed as Oswald in the months leading up to the assassination. Neither the Warren Commission nor the House Select Committee on Assassinations chose to investigate the Davis story. Whatever information Davis had was carried to his grave.

Former Wise County, Texas, sheriff Eldon Moyers said that in September 1973 Davis was attempting to steal copper wire from a construction site there when he cut into a 7,000-volt power line and was fatally electrocuted.

Through his connection to QJ/WIN, Davis certainly was in the right circles to be involved in assassination attempts. According to testimony given to the Senate Intelligence Committee, QJ/WIN's boss on the ZR/RIFLE team was the CIA's William Harvey. Harvey's specialty was anti-Castro activities in general and the attempts to assassinate Castro in particular. Harvey, of course, was in contact with John Roselli and Florida Mafia chief Santos Trafficante Jr.

A reporter from Dallas once queried the FBI about Jean Soutre and his presence in Dallas in 1963 and was told that man was not Soutre, but another Frenchman named Michel Roux, whose name just happened to coincide with one of Soutre's aliases.

However, the bureau, which could find nothing concerning Soutre/Mertz/Roux in 1964, could not offer any substantiating documents to support its story about the Soutre namesake.

At the heart of this labyrinth of intelligence and mob intrigue is QJ/ WIN, who appears to have been Michael Victor Mertz.

Soutre today has been located, working as the public-relations director for a French casino. He denied any inside knowledge of the assassination. Soutre did suggest that Mertz, an old enemy, may have been in Dallas using his name.

Virgil Bailey, an inspector for the Immigration and Naturalization Service, has told Texas researchers he remembered being ordered to pick up a Frenchman in Dallas at the time of the assassination. Bailey complied but in later years could not recall the man's name. However, Bailey described the Frenchman to researcher Gary Shaw as a man about forty-five years old with thin, graying hair. In 1963, Soutre was about thirty-five years old and Roux was about twenty-five. Mertz, the agent connected to both intelligence and worldwide organized crime, was about forty-five years old.

The answers to questions raised by the French connection to the Kennedy assassination lie in locked files in Washington. But some assassination researchers feel the other gunman in Dealey Plaza just might have been the Frenchman known to the FBI as Michel Roux, to the French authorities as Jean Soutre, to the CIA as QJ/ WIN, and to the international crime syndicate as Michael Victor Mertz.

Further evidence of the French connection to the assassination came in 1988 when Los Angeles author Steve J. Rivele claimed that after several years of investigative work he had learned the names of three French gangsters who killed Kennedy. He cited one source for his information as the imprisoned Christian David. Rivele said David claimed to have been offered a contract to kill JFK by the chief of the Marseilles Mafia, Meme Guérini. Years later Rivele stated, "My own conviction at this point is that the contract probably originated with Carlos Marcello of New Orleans who placed it in Marseilles through his colleague Santo Trafficante Jr., who had the closest relations with [Meme's brother] Antoine Guérini."

The three alleged hit men were Sauveur Pironti, who in 1988 was living in Marseilles and denied any connection with the assassination; Lucien Sarti, who was killed in Mexico in 1972; and a man named Bocognoni, who is believed to be living in Central or South America.

According to Rivele's sources, Sarti wore a police uniform and fired from behind the wooden picket fence on the Grassy Knoll. Pironti and Bocognoni reportedly fired on Kennedy from a nearby building—either the old Dal-Tex Building or perhaps the Dallas County Records Building.

Pironti, questioned by European news reporters after Rivele's book *The Murderers of John F. Kennedy* was published in France in 1988, denied any involvement. His denial was supported by French military authorities who said Pironti was serving at a sea post at the time of the assassination. However, later investigation failed to substantiate this alibi.

According to Rivele, David and another mobster, Michel Nicoli, claimed that Lee Harvey Oswald played no part in the assassination. Allegedly the three assassins—Pironti, Sarti, and Bocognoni—were hired to kill Kennedy by the French Union Corse, the European branch of the international crime syndicate, on orders from organized-crime figures in America. The trio of hit men flew to Mexico, where they were met at the Texas border by some Chicago mobsters who drove them to Dallas. After the assassination, the trio remained in a safe house for more than a week and then were flown out of the country.

Interestingly enough, when Rivele approached US government officials with David's story, he was put in touch with Lucien Conein—the same man who was working with QJ/WIN, the shadowy CIA "asset." Conein, known in Vietnam as "Black Luigi," often bragged about his connections with the Union Corse. Conein claimed he was made an honorary member of this branch of the Sicilian Mafia after serving with Corsican partisans as an officer in the OSS and the French Foreign Legion.

It was Conein who, at the urging of Nixon aide Charles Colson, implicated President Kennedy in the assassination of Vietnam's Diem, telling news reporters that Kennedy knew in advance of the plot to overthrow the Vietnamese president.

Asked to comment on the French connection to Kennedy's death, James H. Lesar, vice president of the Assassination Archives and Research Center in Washington, DC, said, "I think that it's sufficiently serious that the Department of Justice and the US Secret Service should investigate it further."

Today it appears that no such investigation has been forthcoming, the US media has paid little attention to Christian David's admissions, and Rivele reportedly went into hiding after receiving death threats. Today he blogs on the Internet.

The agency's suspicious activities in Mexico City; the memos of October 1963; Morrow's purchase of Mannlicher-Carcano rifles; and the ZR/RIFLE program, which may have included the French criminal Christian David, suggest foreknowledge of the assassination within the CIA.

In an October 3, 1963, story in the *New York Times*, Richard Starnes of the Scripps-Howard newspapers quoted a "high United States source" in Vietnam as comparing the CIA's growth to a "malignancy," which Starnes's high-level source was not certain even the White House could still control. The official added, "If the United States ever experiences [an attempt at a coup to overthrow the government] it will come from the CIA and not the Pentagon [as the agency] represents a tremendous power and total unaccountability to anyone."

Even Kennedy's successor once voiced suspicion of the spy agency. According to the *Washington Post*, Marvin Watson of President Johnson's White House staff in 1967 confided to an FBI official who wrote that "[Johnson] was now convinced there was a plot in connection with the assassination. Watson stated the President felt that CIA had had something to do with this plot."

Naturally, the CIA long has maintained innocence in the assassination and the House Select Committee on Assassinations concluded that while the agency was "deficient in its collection and sharing of information both prior to and subsequent to the assassination," the CIA was not involved.

Many researchers today are not as certain as the House committee, although, most agree that the CIA—as a government agency—probably did not plan or authorize Kennedy's death.

G-Men
(J. Edgar Hoover's FBI and the Secret Service)

Anyone making a serious study of the JFK assassination must take a long, hard look at the FBI and the Secret Service. The former—as we now know—monopolized the investigation of the tragedy while the latter failed to prevent it.

The contacts between accused assassin Lee Harvey Oswald and the FBI are many and troubling. No fewer than seven FBI agents were associated with the twenty-four-year-old Oswald during the year and a half between his return from Russia and the assassination.

While the bureau has been especially sensitive about the JFK assassination, it also has been unintentionally helpful. During the past five decades, more than 5 million pages of documents regarding the assassination have been released by the government, often forced by Freedom of Information Act suits. The occasional nuggets of information buried in the raw ore of these documents, most from the FBI, have helped piece together aspects of the case.

Increasingly the bureau has been called to task for its handling of the JFK assassination. At least two government panels have chided the bureau for inadequacies in its assassination investigation. The House Select Committee on Assassinations concluded that the bureau "failed to investigate the possibility of a conspiracy to assassinate the President." Likewise, the Senate Intelligence Committee chastised the bureau for shoddy work in the assassination investigation. Although the Warren Commission spent several pages of its report suggesting ways to improve the performance of the Secret Service, no criticism was leveled at the FBI. This was not surprising since the Commission's whole investigation was based on J. Edgar Hoover's initial findings.

Ironically, it was government corruption that prompted the creation of the FBI in the first place. Just after the turn of the twentieth century, there was a growing demand in Washington to combat the "public-be-damned" attitude of the giant trusts—later to become multinational corporations—and corruption within a number of federal agencies. Such abuses were the province of the Department of Justice, which Congress had never seen fit to equip with investigators. When investigations were required, treasury agents were called in on a temporary basis.

In 1907, despite objections in Congress, attorney general Charles J. Bonaparte went ahead with plans to create an investigative force, stating, "A Department of Justice with no force of permanent police in any form under its control is assuredly not fully equipped for its work." With the approval of president Theodore Roosevelt, Bonaparte issued an order dated July 26, 1908, creating an investigative agency within the Justice Department. Less than one year later, Bonaparte's successor, Attorney General George W. Wickersham, gave the new agency a permanent position and a name—the Bureau of Investigation.

But the new bureau could enforce only federal crimes and—outside of counterfeiting—there were hardly any federal crimes at that time. The bureau had little to do.

But in 1910 Congress, pressured by a public that was shocked and outraged by press accounts of worldwide prostitution, or "white slave" rings, unanimously passed the White Slave Traffic Act. This law became known as the Mann Act after its sponsor, representative James Robert Mann of Illinois. The law gave federal agents authority in any case in which a woman was taken across state or national boundaries for immoral purposes.

The Mann Act was loosely written, applying to female criminals as well as innocent sex "slaves." In effect, it gave the fledgling bureau an excuse to intervene in any case in which a woman involved in criminal activity crossed state lines.

World War I boosted the bureau into national prominence. During 1914 and 1915 explosions, fires, and other acts of sabotage occurred at several war plants. American public opinion slowly began shifting from neutrality to animosity toward Germany. The pace of this shift quickened in January 1917, when Germany resumed unrestricted submarine warfare on American shipping. Congress declared war against the Central Powers, led by Germany, on April 6 and president Woodrow Wilson ordered the bureau to address wartime issues.

Wisely noting that all Americans of German descent could not be interned for the duration of the war, Wilson nevertheless required more than one million "enemy aliens" to register. The bureau, which had only three hundred agents by then, was expected to enforce this presidential edict.

The nation suddenly became aware of the danger of spies, and a full-blown spy scare swept across the land—much of the suspicion directed at labor unions and anarchists. Aided by a group of private vigilantes called the American Protective League, which eventually numbered more than a quarter million members, the bureau began to expand but quickly dropped association with the league, which was accused of overzealous activities and intimidating labor unions.

The next year a bomb exploded at the home of the new attorney general, A. Mitchell Palmer, killing the two bombers. Palmer was incensed and immediately took action. He replaced bureau director Alexander Bielaski with William J. Flynn, a former chief of the Secret Service. Palmer also created a General Intelligence Division under the command of his twenty-four-year-old special assistant who had come to the bureau fresh out of the George Washington University Law School two years before—J. Edgar Hoover.

The Top G-man

No one man has held so much power for so long in the history of the United States as John Edgar Hoover.

In the 1950s, Hoover was an honors-encrusted hero, hailed as the foremost defender of American freedom and democracy. By the 1970s, he was being likened to Heinrich Himmler, Hitler's dreaded SS commander.

By the 1980s, knowledge of FBI abuses under Hoover's leadership had become widespread, although the major news media—perhaps recalling the veneration it had lavished on Hoover for so long—seemed reluctant to spotlight his darker activities.

The truth of Hoover's place in the still-untold history of modern-day America lies in the man's background and motivations. One reason so little is known about him is that for so long everything printed about Hoover was either a product of FBI public relations or, at least, was approved by Hoover or a subordinate. To get any cooperation from the Bureau—a necessity for obtaining any information involving a federal investigation—news reporters were forced to stay on Hoover's good side. Any story criticizing the director was an excuse to place the writer on the bureau's list of people to be ignored.

Hoover was born on January 1, 1895, five years before the twentieth century began. He was the youngest of four children. Born in Washington, DC, Hoover rarely left the city in his entire life. Until her death in 1938, he lived with his mother in the family home at 413 Seward Square. Afterward he continued living there with his constant companion and the FBI's associate director, Clyde Tolson.

His father, Dickerson N. Hoover, was a minor bureaucrat who served as chief of the Coast and Geodetic Survey's printing division. His mother, Annie M. Scheitlin Hoover, was a plump housewife who faithfully instilled American middle-class virtues and Lutheran Christianity in her children.

As a schoolboy delivering groceries, young Hoover discovered the quicker he delivered, the more trips he could make, which meant more money. He soon was given the nickname "Speed." Active in athletics, Hoover was once hit in the nose by a baseball—the basis of his bulldog-like appearance. After graduating from Washington's Central High School, Hoover got a job as a clerk in the Library of Congress. At night he began attending George Washington University Law School, where he obtained his law degree in 1916 and a master of law in 1917.

With the world at war, there was frantic activity in the Department of Justice. Jobs were opening up every day. On July 26, 1917, Hoover joined the department and was placed in the enemy alien registration section. Earning a reputation as a diligent and efficient worker, Hoover soon became an assistant to the attorney general, who placed him in charge of the General Intelligence Division. Soon after taking charge of the division, Hoover was instructed by Attorney General A. Mitchell Palmer to study subversive groups within the United States. Hoover went at the project with zeal.

As Hoover studied the background of communism, he came to a studied conclusion that in 1919 was used to deport about 3,000 American citizens:

American communists supported the Third International which was run by Soviet communists who advocated the violent overthrow of the US Government. Therefore American communists were advocating the violent overthrow of the government and could be deported as "enemy aliens."

This marked the beginning of the infamous "Palmer raids," in which Hoover prepared the legal cases. Early in 1920, at the orders of Attorney General Palmer, the bureau launched a series of raids on communist meeting places in thirty-three cities, rounding up more than 2,500 aliens. These raids drew both praise and condemnation. Through the years, Hoover continually used the communist threat to great personal advantage, even putting his name on the popular book *Masters of Deceit*, which helped fan the fires of the 1950s communist scare.

Was there any real threat from American communists? In his resignation letter to Hoover, William C. Sullivan, at one time third-ranking official at the FBI, wrote:

> In the mid-Forties when the membership of the Party was about 80,000 and it had many front organizations, you publicized this widely month in and month out. In fact it was far too widely publicized to the point where you caused a communist scare in the nation which was entirely unwarranted. . . . I am just as opposed to communism as you but I knew then and I know now that it was not the danger you claimed it was and that it never warranted the huge amounts of the taxpayer's dollars spent upon it. . . . What happened when the Communist Party went into a rapid decline? You kept the scare campaign going just the same for some years. However, when the membership figures kept dropping lower and lower you instructed us not to give them to the public any more and not even to the Justice Department. . . . At the time of my leaving the Bureau [1971] . . . the membership figures of the Communist Party are down to an amazing 2,800 in a nation of over 200 million people and you still conceal this from the people.

It has been said that of the small number of members of the Communist Party in those days, almost half were FBI informers. But Hoover never let the facts stand in the way of his campaign to eradicate communism, even if it meant neglecting one of the true menaces to America—organized crime.

In the forty-eight years that Hoover controlled the United States' only national police organization, he served eight presidents and outlasted more than a dozen attorneys general. Hoover also was close to leaders of the Nazi-dominated International Criminal Police Organization (Interpol) prior to World War II and was named vice president of Interpol in 1946.

Organized-crime investigator Peter Maas has reported that prior to Robert Kennedy's becoming attorney general, only four FBI agents in the New York office were assigned to organized crime and they were kept busy with in-office "bookkeeping" duties. Yet about four hundred agents were on the streets of the city searching out communists.

As late as January 1962, Hoover was on record as saying, "No single individual or coalition of racketeers dominates organized crime across the nation." As with the communist threat, Hoover was not telling the truth.

Shortly after the aborted mob conference at Apalachin in 1957, Sullivan and other top FBI officials prepared a monograph on the Mafia that was sent to the top twenty-five government officials concerned with law enforcement. Learning of this, an angry Hoover recalled all twenty-five copies and had them destroyed. He denounced the monograph as "baloney," and this report was never heard of again.

After Mafia thug Joe Valachi was brought to Washington by attorney general Robert Kennedy's Justice Department for testimony before a Senate committee, Hoover was forced to grudgingly admit to the existence of an organized-crime structure in this nation. Why did Hoover act like there was no such thing as the Mafia when there was so much evidence to the contrary?

In his book *The Bureau*, Sullivan wrote:

> [Hoover] didn't want to tackle organized crime. He preferred his agents to spend their time on quick, easy cases—he wanted results, predictable results which produced the statistics Hoover thrived on. . . . Investigating the Mafia promised to be more difficult than rounding up juvenile auto thieves. Organized crime is far more complicated: the Mafia runs legitimate businesses as a front for their illegal operations. Mafioso are rich and can afford the best lawyers, while we have to use government lawyers, some of whom are excellent, some of whom aren't worth a damn. And the Mafia is powerful, so powerful that entire police forces and even a mayor's office can be under Mafia control. That's why Hoover was afraid to let us tackle it. He was afraid we'd show up poorly.

There were also other considerations. Most people now accept that Hoover's lack of interest in organized crime was a result of the blackmail threat due to his homosexuality. According to Don Fulsome, who covered the Nixon White House for United Press International, "J. Edgar Hoover was in the hip pocket of America's godfathers, reputedly because they had pictorial proof of his homosexuality." This referred to persistent rumors that the mob had photographs of Hoover in compromising situations with Tolson as well as wearing a pink ballerina's tutu.

Hoover was well-known for his ingratiating attitude toward Washington politicians. The more powerful the politician, the more Hoover tried to befriend him—and control him, thanks to the voluminous files Hoover had accumulated through the years.

One thing is certain: by the time of World War II, the FBI's vast power was centered solely in J. Edgar Hoover.

But if blame must be assigned for this situation, it may, as argued by Tom Wicker, associate editor of the *New York Times*, be laid on the American public. Wicker wrote:

> The public—gulled, it is true, by the Bureau's incessant propaganda—until recent years loved it all; and what considerable percentage of voters Washington

believed were still devoted to J. Edgar Hoover at his death was suggested by the President's funeral oration and by Congress's decision that his body should lie in state, where Lincoln and Kennedy had lain. There was little or no out-cry when the Director, guardian of liberty, spoke up for Joe McCarthy, called Martin Luther King a liar and for years singlehandedly held up congressional passage of a consular treaty with the Soviet Union. There was always a radio audience for "The FBI in Peace and War" and the G-man movies to which the Director invariably lent "technical assistance" and his seal of approval—as long as they pictured his men on the side of the angels. For decades, his turgid and moralistic articles appeared with the regularity of the seasons in "Read-er's Digest" and "American" magazines, and publishers took turns presenting his self-aggrandizing books to the waiting public. If J. Edgar Hoover passed eventually beyond the normal restraints of office, the American public seemed to view this process happily, and with a sense of gratitude.

Public criticism, however, grew over the Palmer raids of communist meeting places. Federal agents were charged with unconstitutional searches and seizures, individual rights violations, and even using agents provocateur.

After hearing testimony of warrantless arrests and prisoners being held incom-municado, one federal judge declared, "It may . . . be observed that a mob is a mob, whether made up of government officials acting under instructions from the Depart-ment of Justice, or of criminals, loafers, and the vicious classes." Later a Senate com-mittee looked into the raids, but divided on its views of the operation and failed to reach a consensus. It was the first—and last—congressional investigation of the FBI.

Chastised by the complaints over the Palmer raids, the Justice Department saw its morale go from bad to worse. In an effort to demonstrate leadership in this moral crisis, newly elected president Calvin Coolidge appointed Harlan Fiske Stone, a former dean of the Columbia University Law School, attorney general. Soon after taking control of what had become known as the "Department of Easy Virtue," Stone named twenty-nine-year-old Hoover acting director of the bureau.

Hoover moved rapidly to restore respect for the bureau, which was in real danger of being disbanded due to the years of problems and criticism. His actions produced immediate results. Asked whether one of his agents would investigate the activities of a senator's son, Hoover once stated, "This Bureau cannot be used for partisan purposes."

Backed solidly by Stone, Hoover rehabilitated the bureau's image.

Over the next fifteen years, Hoover moved the bureau from a few hundred un-armed investigators to a full-fledged national police agency. And all the while, he kept an eye open for favorable public relations opportunities. By the early 1930s, Prohibition had propelled crime into the national spotlight and Hoover was there to share the glory. During the heyday of Bonnie and Clyde and the Ma Barker Gang, hardly a day passed that Hoover wasn't being quoted in the nation's press. His legend grew.

In the early 1930s, Hoover, a staunch Republican, was very cautious about his moves within Franklin Roosevelt's Democratic administration.

By 1933, kidnapping was added to the list of crimes under the jurisdiction of the FBI due to the public clamor over the abduction of aviation pioneer Charles Lindbergh's infant son. This list grew longer the next year, with the addition of killing or assaulting a federal officer, fleeing across state lines, and extortion involving interstate commerce. By 1935, bureau agents had the power to go beyond investigation. They were allowed to serve warrants and subpoenas, to make seizures and arrests, and to carry arms. The bureau had become the very thing that Hoover had often spoken against—a national police force. Also that year, the word "federal" was added to the bureau's name, and soon the initials FBI were well-known all over the world.

By the beginning of World War II, the FBI boasted an Identification Division with thousands of fingerprint records, a complete and up-to-date laboratory, and a National Police Academy for training state and local law-enforcement officers. Even today it is considered the peak of a lawman's career to be selected for training at the FBI Academy at Quantico, Virginia. And Hoover made use of this, too. According to former assistant director Sullivan, "Hoover felt that the alumni of the FBI training course were his men. Thanks to this network of FBI-trained police officers, we had a private and frequently helpful line to most city and state police organizations throughout the country."

Hoover also used the FBI Academy's prestige against perceived enemies. On the day of the JFK assassination, a shocked Dallas FBI agent named James Hosty told Dallas police lieutenant Jack Revill that Lee Harvey Oswald was a communist known to the FBI, and that the bureau had information that Oswald was capable of committing the assassination. Since all government agencies were saying they had no knowledge of Oswald, this story was a bombshell.

As a result of this conversation, Dallas police chief Jesse Curry told TV news reporters that the FBI was aware of Oswald but had not informed the Dallas police. When challenged to prove his charge by the head of the Dallas FBI office, Curry qualified his statement by saying he had no personal knowledge of the issue. But the damage had been done.

Until Curry's retirement in 1966, Hoover conducted a vendetta against the Dallas police, according to FBI documents released in 1980. The documents show that under orders from Hoover, FBI officials were prohibited from conducting training courses for Dallas police, and policemen from that city were not invited to attend the FBI Academy, claiming lack of manpower.

In January 1966 Dallas mayor Erik Jonsson visited Hoover in Washington. After hearing Hoover's complaints against Curry, Jonsson told the petulant director he would "immediately instruct the city manager to have a stern talk" with the police chief. Curry resigned less than a month after the Jonsson-Hoover meeting and within weeks, Dallas police were again receiving FBI training.

Hoover did not gain such immense power overnight. After turning his bureau into an anticrime force, he began to look into other areas. Beginning with secret meetings between President Roosevelt and Hoover in the summer of 1936, the bureau began moving quietly into intelligence gathering. In 1939, on the eve of World War II, the bureau was directed to investigate espionage, sabotage, and violations of neutrality regulations. It also apprehended draft evaders and enemy aliens. It should be noted that Hoover was one of the few government officials who opposed the relocation and incarceration of Japanese Americans as a violation of their civil rights.

This new authority marked the beginning of this nation's multiagency intelligence establishment and marked a period of extraordinary growth for the bureau. The FBI, which boasted only 391 agents in 1933, counted nearly 5,000 by the end of the war.

During the war, the FBI was called upon to gather intelligence on activities detrimental to US interests in South America. And while this activity was ordered terminated with the creation of the Central Intelligence Agency in 1947, the FBI even today retains large offices in Mexico City, Brasilia, Ottawa, Vienna, Berlin, Tokyo, Bangkok, and Baghdad, among many other cities.

Also during the war, Hoover's path crossed that of a young naval intelligence officer with unexpected and long-term repercussions. The FBI had been snooping after a suspected Nazi agent, a beautiful woman named Inga Arvad who had attended the wedding of Germany's Field Marshal Hermann Goering and met with Adolf Hitler. A former Miss Denmark, she had no trouble attracting young men in wartime Washington. One of these men was naval Ensign John F. Kennedy.

Hoover's FBI wiretapped an apartment shared by Kennedy and "Inga binga," as he called his paramour, and picked up the sounds of sexual play. They also picked up a few remarks by Kennedy concerning sensitive security matters. After both the Navy and his father had been alerted to the danger presented by Kennedy's involvement with a suspected agent, young Kennedy was quickly transferred to the South Pacific. It was there, of course, that Kennedy led the survivors of PT-109 back to safety, thus becoming a war hero and helping to launch his political career—all thanks to the diligent J. Edgar Hoover. It could thus be argued—with great irony—that it was Hoover who actually set young Kennedy on the course that ended in Dallas.

After World War II, FBI intelligence activities increased, thanks to the anticommunist hysteria of the Cold War years. In fact, it was the FBI that launched senator Joseph McCarthy on his ill-fated anticommunist crusade. In 1950, a one-hundred-page FBI document alleging communist infiltration of the US government was leaked to a military intelligence officer with instructions to pass it along to the Jewish American League Against Communism. The league offered the document to McCarthy, who was further encouraged to fight communism by Father Edmund A. Walsh, vice president of Georgetown University and an anticommunist author.

Assistant FBI Director Sullivan wrote, "We gave McCarthy all we had, but all we had were fragments, nothing could prove his allegations."

While Hoover always claimed that information the bureau collected was never to be released to unauthorized persons, it was a rule that he bent for friends. In 1948, when New York governor Thomas Dewey ran for president against Harry Truman, Hoover secretly agreed to put the bureau's resources at his disposal, hoping that he would be made attorney general upon Dewey's election. Dewey lost.

In 1954, vice president Richard Nixon was able to obtain information in FBI files to use in his attack against representative Robert L. Condon of California.

It is well-known now that Hoover deliberately leaked derogatory material on Dr. Martin Luther King Jr. during the 1960s as a part of COINTELPRO, Hoover's secret counterintelligence program.

It was this ability, first to gather information and then to control it, that gave Hoover his extraordinary power. Former assistant FBI director Sullivan wrote:

> Hoover was always gathering damaging material on Jack Kennedy, which the President, with his active social life, seemed more than willing to provide. We never put any technical surveillance on JFK, but whatever came up was automatically funneled directly to Hoover. I was sure he was saving every-thing he had on Kennedy, and on Martin Luther King, Jr., too, until he could unload it all and destroy them both. He kept this kind of explosive material in his personal files, which filled four rooms on the fifth floor of headquarters.

Perhaps the presence of these files, which still held information on Kennedy and Inga Arvad, explains why reappointing Hoover was one of JFK's first actions after becoming president.

It has been reported that Hoover's personal and confidential files were destroyed soon after his death by Tolson and Hoover's faithful secretary, Helen Gandy.

Hoover's reappointment by Kennedy certainly wasn't due to Hoover's politics. A Republican who liked to boast that he had never voted, Hoover had quietly helped Nixon as much as possible during the 1960 campaign. According to Sullivan, Hoover did his best to keep the news media supplied with anti-Kennedy stories.

Hoover's methods of ingratiating himself both to presidents and attorneys general he served have been well documented. He would send them letters marked "Top Secret, Eyes Only" filled with juicy tidbits of gossip about congressmen and political enemies. Most presidents disdained this practice, but two—Lyndon B. Johnson and Richard Nixon—seemed to enjoy the unusual channel of information.

Nixon and Hoover were GOP allies from the days when Nixon was a representative from California. Sullivan noted, "I spent many days preparing material based on research taken from FBI files that I knew was going straight from Hoover to congressman Nixon, material which Nixon used in speeches, articles and investigations."

Nixon had been rejected as an FBI agent in 1937—Hoover later told him that the bureau wasn't hiring at the time, but the agent who rejected him reported that Nixon was "lacking in aggression." Despite this, Nixon and Hoover remained close friends. Hoover was a regular dinner guest at the Nixon White House in later years.

Following the assassination, Lyndon Johnson had a strong right-hand man in Hoover. According to Sullivan, Johnson—worried that Robert Kennedy might make a grab for the Democratic presidential nomination in 1964—asked Hoover for a special security team of FBI men, headed by Cartha D. DeLoach. Sullivan wrote, "Ostensibly, the agents would be there to guard against threats to the President, but this security force was actually a surveillance team, a continuation of the FBI's surveillance on Martin Luther King in Atlantic City. By keeping track of King, LBJ could also keep track of RFK."

Johnson and Hoover had much in common, according to Sullivan. He wrote, "Johnson and Hoover had their mutual fear and hatred of the Kennedys in common—and more. As neighbors in Washington since the days when Johnson was a senator from Texas, they had been frequent dinner guests in each other's homes."

Johnson cemented his friendship with—and perhaps his power—over Hoover in January 1964, less than two months after Kennedy's assassination. In a ceremony conducted in the White House Rose Garden, Johnson praised his friend Hoover as "a hero to millions of decent citizens, and an anathema to evil men."

After noting Hoover's accomplishments through the years, Johnson said:

> Edgar, the law says that you must retire next January when you reach your 70th birthday, and I know you wouldn't want to break the law. But the nation cannot afford to lose you. Therefore, by virtue of and pursuant to the authority vested in the President, I have today signed an Executive Order exempting you from compulsory retirement for an indefinite period of time.

Although this order was renewed each year, it was tantamount to installing Hoover as FBI director for life since it would have required a subsequent executive order to rescind this action. Such action put an end to pre-assassination rumors in DC that Kennedy would use the mandatory retirement limit to remove Hoover after the 1964 election.

This extraordinary action coupled with the timing—with both the Warren Commission and the FBI's assassination investigation just getting into full swing—has led more suspicious assassination researchers to suspect that this presidential exemption was a partial payment to Hoover for his lack of a penetrating probe into Kennedy's death.

Shortly after this event, Hoover replaced Courtney Evans as the bureau's White House liaison with Cartha DeLoach, who had been quite intimate with Johnson since his early days in the Senate. DeLoach figured prominently in the assassination investigation and revealed in the 1970s that Johnson had begun to suspect that the CIA had something to do with Kennedy's death, ignoring the malfeasance of the FBI.

According to Sullivan, once Johnson assumed the powers of the presidency, his relationship with the trusty Hoover began to change. He wrote:

> The Director was over 65 by that time, past retirement age for federal employees, and he stayed in office only because of a special waiver which re-

quired the President's signature each year. That waiver put Hoover right in Johnson's pocket. With that leverage, Johnson began to take advantage of Hoover, using the Bureau as his personal investigative arm. His never-ending requests were usually political, and sometimes illegal. . . . And Hoover hot-footed it to Johnson's demands . . . he found himself very much in the back seat, almost a captive of the President.

In addressing the relationship between Hoover and Johnson, biographer Richard Gid Powers wrote, "Because of the extraordinary rapport between them, there was no service Hoover would refuse Johnson, no matter how far removed it might be from his law enforcement or domestic intelligence responsibilities."

Some researchers have darkly hinted that LBJ may have had more leverage on Hoover than simply securing his job as director—that it may have had something to do with the JFK assassination.

There can be no doubt that Hoover had an abiding and intense hatred for both John and Robert Kennedy, because of their politics, their associates, their personal lives, and their style. Sullivan recalled hearing Clyde Tolson, Hoover's associate director, confidant, and roommate, once say, "Goddamn the Kennedys. First there was Jack, now there is Bobby, and then Teddy. We'll have them on our necks until the year 2000." Hoover reportedly nodded in agreement.

This hatred for the Kennedys makes the bureau's numerous contacts with Lee Harvey Oswald all the more suspicious. The FBI was involved with Oswald starting when he went to Russia. Then there was Hoover's 1960 memo to the State Department, warning "there is a possibility that an impostor is using Oswald's birth certificate." Very much aware of Oswald and even suspecting that someone may have been posing as the ex-Marine, the FBI attempted to keep tabs on Oswald after his attempted defection to Russia.

On April 27, 1960, John W. Fain, a resident FBI agent in Fort Worth, interviewed Robert Oswald concerning his brother's activities in the Soviet Union. The older Oswald said his whole family was shocked at his brother's behavior and that Lee had never had any sympathy for or connection with communism before his trip to Russia. Fain also interviewed Marguerite Oswald the next day concerning a $25 money order she had tried to send to her son.

Apparently the FBI was not the only US agency with an active interest in Oswald. On July 3, 1961, more than a year before Oswald arrived back home from Russia, Fain prepared another report on Oswald. This report is rich in detail of Oswald's life history as well as his activities in the Soviet Union. According to this document, much of the information on Oswald came from the district office of naval intelligence in New Orleans.

Armed with this naval intelligence information, Fain and FBI special agent Tom Carter requested a meeting with Oswald at the Fort Worth FBI office on June 25, 1962, less than two weeks after the Oswalds arrived back in Fort Worth from Russia. According to their report, Oswald told of flying home with Marina and their child, but he failed to mention the stopover in Atlanta. He also told of borrowing $435 to get home, but he declined to talk about why he went to Russia, saying only that he didn't want to relive the past.

The agents said Oswald "exhibited an impatient and arrogant attitude" during the interview. He also denied that he had attempted to renounce his American citizenship and that he had offered the Russians any military information.

Interestingly, Oswald did assure the FBI agents that "in the event he is contacted by Soviet Intelligence under suspicious circumstances or otherwise, he will promptly communicate with the FBI." Could this agreement have been the beginning of a special relationship between Oswald and the bureau?

Oswald's next recorded contact with the bureau was on August 16, 1962, when Fain and Special Agent Arnold Brown approached him near his home at 2703 Mercedes Street in Fort Worth, where he and Marina had lived for about a month. Believing that Oswald had been "evasive" during his first interview, Fain had decided to contact him again, only this time the agents sat with Oswald in a parked car near his home. Fain explained that they didn't want to embarrass Oswald in front of his wife, so they declined his offer to come into the house.

The more suspicious researchers view this unusual meeting in a car as a time when the FBI may have begun to recruit Oswald as an informant. But according to the agents, Oswald once again denied any misconduct in Russia, denied that he had tried to defect, and denied that any Soviet intelligence personnel had ever tried to contact him or offer any "deals." Once again, Oswald agreed to contact the FBI if anyone connected with Soviet intelligence tried to meet with him.

After satisfying themselves that Oswald was not a member of the American Communist Party, Fain and Brown marked the Oswald file closed. Fain retired from the bureau on October 29, 1962.

However, that was not to be the last contact between Oswald and the bureau. After arriving in New Orleans in the spring of 1963, Oswald became the object of yet another security investigation by the FBI. This time the special agent in charge of Oswald's file was Milton R. Kaack, who prepared a detailed report dated October 31, 1963, on Oswald, his background, and his New Orleans activities.

But the strangest contact between Oswald and the bureau came on August 10, 1963, the day after his arrest for disturbing the peace while handing out Fair Play for Cuba Committee leaflets on a New Orleans street corner.

Did Oswald Work for the FBI?

If Oswald indeed participated in spy work, particularly for the United States, it was most likely known to the FBI. What better prospect to recruit as an informant than an experienced American agent with a procommunist background or "cover"?

It is telling to note that following his arrest in New Orleans, Oswald, styled as a malcontent loner who tried to defect to Russia, should ask to meet with an FBI agent rather than a lawyer.

The day after Oswald's arrest in New Orleans for disturbing the peace was a Saturday. The weekend is hardly a time for a quick FBI response to the request of a police prisoner jailed for creating a disturbance, a minor infraction. Yet special agent John Quigley soon arrived at the New Orleans police station and met with Oswald for an hour and a half.

The five-page report of that meeting written by Quigley reads like a comprehensive report on the Fair Play for Cuba Committee. Oswald gave the agent background information on himself, then detailed his activities since coming to New Orleans, including his attempt to form a Fair Play for Cuba Committee chapter and the squabble between Oswald and anti-Castro Cubans.

Quigley, who told the Warren Commission he had never heard of Oswald until that Saturday, had a faulty memory. He later admitted that on April 18, 1961, he had reviewed Oswald's Navy file at the nearby US Naval Air Station in Algiers, Louisiana, at the request of the Dallas FBI office.

Quigley could give the Commission no reason why Oswald had wanted to see an FBI agent in 1963, but an FBI document released in 1977 may give a clue. There Quigley reports being contacted by a New Orleans police intelligence officer who "said that Oswald was desirous of seeing an agent and supplying to him information with regard to his activities with the FPCC in New Orleans." Again this statement, along with the detailed description Oswald gave of his activities, seems to indicate that Oswald was trying to make some sort of report. In this "report," Oswald continually mentions the fictitious head of the New Orleans FPCC, A. J. Hidell, saying that he had talked with Hidell several times by telephone but had never met him. Asked for Hidell's number, Oswald said he couldn't remember it.

In all, at least ten FBI agents filed affidavits with the Warren Commission stating unequivocally that Lee Harvey Oswald was never an informant for the bureau. Could they have said the same for "Harvey Lee Oswald," or "A. J. Hidell"? During his Warren Commission testimony, Quigley made an odd slip of the tongue, referring to Oswald as "Harvey Lee Oswald" until corrected by assistant counsel Samuel Stern. It is well-known that FBI informants, and even agents themselves, often use code, or cover names.

It is interesting to note that J. Gordon Shanklin and Kyle G. Clark, the FBI supervisors in the Dallas office, mentioned only that no payment was made to Oswald for information in their affidavits. They did not specifically deny knowledge of Oswald as an informant, as had the other agents in their affidavits.

Other circumstances of Oswald's New Orleans stay also indicate the possibility of a relationship with the FBI. In 1975, a New Orleans bar owner, Orest Pena, claimed to have seen Oswald in his Habana Bar in the company of both Cubans and FBI agent Warren De Brueys.

Pena, himself an FBI informant and a Cuban exile associated with the CIA-backed Cuban Revolutionary Council, said he remembered Oswald as a man who came into his bar with a Cuban and ordered a lemonade, then vomited it up. He said he saw Oswald together with De Brueys and other "government agents" on several occasions.

Pena also said that about ten days before he was to testify before the Warren Commission, De Brueys threatened him, saying, "If you ever talk anything about me, I will get rid—I'll get rid of your ass."

Pena added that Commission staff counsel Wesley J. Liebeler did not let him speak freely, so he decided to keep his mouth shut. Agent De Brueys denied both allegations and the House Select Committee on Assassinations chose to believe him.

Then there is the strange story of William S. Walter, who served as a security clerk for the New Orleans FBI office in 1963. Like CIA paymaster James Wilcott, Walter was a minor functionary who claimed to have seen the wrong things. When he tried to tell what he knew, he found himself facing an official stone wall. Testifying to the House Select Committee on Assassinations, Walter said he was on duty the day that Quigley interviewed Oswald in the New Orleans police station. In response to Quigley's request for a file check on Oswald that day, he said he found that the New Orleans FBI office maintained both a security and an informant file on Oswald. However, Quigley told the committee that there was no informant file on Oswald, only the security file.

Walter's story apparently was echoed by Dallas FBI agent Will Hayden Griffin. According to a 1964 FBI memorandum, Griffin reportedly told people that Oswald was definitely an FBI informant and that files in Washington would prove it. Griffin later denied making any such comment.

But Walter had other information for the committee. He claimed that while he was serving night duty in the FBI office on November 17, 1963, the New Orleans FBI office received a teletype from FBI headquarters warning against a possible assassination attempt on Kennedy during the coming trip to Dallas on November 22. Walter said he was alone in the New Orleans FBI office in the early morning hours when the teletype came through. He said it was headed "urgent," marked to the attention of all special agents, and signed "Director."

The thrust of the teletype was that the bureau had received information that a "militant revolutionary group" might attempt to assassinate Kennedy on his proposed trip to Dallas. It went on to say that all receiving offices should "immediately contact all CI's [confidential or criminal informants], PCI's [potential confidential or criminal informants], local racial and hate-group informants and determine if any basis for threat. Bureau should be kept advised of all developments by teletype."

Walter said he telephoned the special agent in charge, Harry Maynard, who ordered Walter to call special agents with CIs and PCIs. Walter said he did this, writing the names of five agents contacted on the face of the teletype. By 8 a.m., Maynard had arrived for work and Walter went home.

Five days later, on November 22, 1963, Walter said, he was in a barber shop when he heard about Kennedy's assassination. Rushing back to the FBI office, he showed the teletype to various agents and asked, "How could this have happened? We had five days' notice!" Later that day, Walter said, he typed a copy of the teletype and wrote the five agents' names on the copy, which he took home.

Walter said soon after the assassination, Director Hoover ordered all agents in the New Orleans office who had written reports dealing with the case to review those reports. The object was to make sure there was nothing in them that might "embarrass the Bureau." Originals of the reports were to be destroyed.

Checking the relevant file later, Walter discovered the teletype was missing. In 1975, Walter told his story and showed his copy of the teletype to senator Richard Schweiker of Pennsylvania. Later the House Select Committee on Assassinations looked into the matter. The committee checked with New Orleans agents, supervisor Maynard, and even Walter's ex-wife, who also worked for the FBI. All claimed to know nothing about a teletype. The committee, declaring that it "declined to believe that that many employees of the FBI would have remained silent for such a long time," concluded that Walter's story was "unfounded."

Unfounded or not, there were other stories in New Orleans that were even harder to dismiss—take, for example, Adrian Thomas Alba, operator of the Crescent City Garage. The Crescent City Garage was located next door to the William Reily Coffee Company, Oswald's employer while in New Orleans. Alba, a quiet man who has not sought publicity, was both operator and part owner of the garage. Alba said the garage had a contract to maintain a number of cars for the nearby Secret Service and FBI offices.

Alba said Oswald made frequent visits to his garage during the summer of 1963 and he got to know the ex-Marine quite well. They talked about firearms and Alba would loan Oswald his gun magazines. He claimed to have helped Oswald fix the sling on his rifle.

But Alba's best story concerns a visit in early summer 1963. He said a man he believed to be an "FBI agent visiting New Orleans from Washington" came to his garage and took a green Studebaker from the car pool, after showing his credentials. The next day Alba said he saw the same car parked by Oswald's workplace about thirty yards away. According to Alba, "Lee Oswald went across the sidewalk. He bent down as if to look in the window and was handed what appeared to be a good-sized white envelope. He turned and bent as if to hold the envelope to his abdomen, and I think he put it under his shirt. Oswald went back into the building and the car drove off."

Years later, Alba said he saw the same thing happen the next day, but was farther away and could not see what was passed to Oswald. He said he did not tell the Warren Commission about these incidents because he did not recall them until 1970 when he was reminded of them by a TV commercial depicting a man running to and from a taxi.

The House Select Committee on Assassinations checked garage records and found that two Studebakers had been signed out during that time in 1963, but by Secret Service agents.

Alba recalled seeing Oswald after he was fired from the coffee company, allegedly for malingering. Alba said Oswald seemed pleased with the turn of events and said he expected to soon be working at the National Aeronautics and Space Administration (NASA) plant near New Orleans. Alba quoted Oswald as saying, "I have found my pot of gold at the end of the rainbow." Of course, this was not to be. Oswald's destiny lay in Dallas.

But oddly enough, five Reily Coffee employees, all of whom were in contact with Oswald, did join the NASA facility shortly after Oswald's departure. Former New Orleans district attorney Jim Garrison came across these intriguing employment shifts during his ill-fated JFK assassination probe. Oswald left the coffee company on July 19, 1963, just a few weeks before he began his public show of handing out FPCC material. According to Garrison, Alfred Claude, the man who hired Oswald at Reily, went to work for Chrysler Aerospace Division at NASA's New Orleans facility. Emmett Barbee, Oswald's immediate superior at Reily, followed Claude to the NASA center in a few days. And within a few weeks they were joined by John D. Branyon and Dante Marachini, both of whom worked with Oswald. Branyon and Marachini also began aerospace careers at the New Orleans NASA center. Marachini, who had gone to work for Reily the same day as Oswald, also was a friend of CIA-Mafia agent David Ferrie.

To compound these oddities, Garrison found that two of Ferrie's friends also went to work for the NASA center about this same time. James Lewallen, a friend of Ferrie's who lived in the same apartment house as Marachini, went to work for Boeing, located in the NASA complex. Melvin Coffee, who had accompanied Ferrie on his strange Texas odyssey the night of the assassination, was hired by NASA at Cape Kennedy in Florida.

Was all this coincidence or was there some connecting link between these occurrences? Garrison claimed these men were lured into government-connected jobs so as to make them unavailable during the subsequent assassination investigation. And in fact, none of these men were called to testify before the Warren Commission. Garrison wrote in *A Heritage of Stone*, "The fact that these transfers were being made not in direct support of the assassination, but looking far beyond that, in order to complicate further investigations which might afterward occur, serves to give some idea of the scope and professional nature of the entire operation."

Other Dallas FBI agents swore under oath that Oswald was never an FBI informant. However, the truthfulness of their statements has come under severe question in light of the saga of Dallas FBI agent James P. Hosty Jr., who was assigned to check on Oswald prior to the assassination. Although Hosty claims to never have met Oswald in person, his name, address, telephone number, and car license number appeared in Oswald's personal notebook—a fact omitted from a December 23, 1963, FBI report to the Warren Commission.

In testimony to the Commission, Director Hoover explained that the omission was due to the fact that the report was not originally intended for the Commission. He said that the information on Hosty in Oswald's notebook was presented to the Commission in a February 11, 1964, report. Of course, by that time, the Commission was already very much aware of the connection between Hosty and Oswald.

Hoover also explained that it was not unusual for agents to leave their name, address, and telephone number for persons they were attempting to contact. He said

Oswald's wife, Marina, probably jotted down Hosty's license number for her husband. Hosty, however, claimed he had parked his car some distance from the house where Marina was staying to avoid drawing attention to his visit.

On January 22, 1964, Texas attorney general Waggoner Carr called Warren Commission general counsel J. Lee Rankin to report that he had information that Oswald had been recruited as an informant for the FBI in September 1962. He further stated that Oswald was being paid $200 a month and assigned Informant Number S-179 or S-172. Carr cited Dallas County district attorney Henry Wade, a former FBI man, as the source of this information. The number designation was not in accordance with normal FBI informant identification but because of the uncertainty of the numbers, it obviously was mistranslated during communication to Wade and the letter "S" was used to signify "security" matters, which would have fitted with Oswald's background.

This led to the question of Oswald's cashing money orders and checks. One such incident involved Western Union Telegraph Company night manager C. A. Hamblen, who just a few days after the assassination got into a brief conversation with Bob Fenley, a reporter for the *Dallas Times Herald*. Hamblin told Fenley he recalled Oswald, or a man who looked just like him, causing trouble in the Western Union office while trying to cash money orders in small amounts and once sending a telegram to the secretary of the Navy. Hamblen said he was certain it was Oswald who on more than once occasion was disagreeable to the office girls to the point that Hamblen himself would serve him. Fenley had the newspaper's police reporter, George Carter, talk to Hamblen to verify his account. Carter did and then wrote a story for the paper that subsequently brought the matter to the attention of the Warren Commission. Federal authorities ordered Western Union officials to search for records confirming the transactions but none were found. By the time the Commission questioned Hamblen, July 23, 1964, he had become less certain of the disagreeable man's identity. The Warren Commission reported that Hamblen's superiors at Western Union had concluded the whole thing was a figment of Hamblen's imagination. They added, "And the commission accepts this assessment."

Less easy to dismiss were others' statements reporting that Oswald had attempted to cash checks or money orders. Leonard E. Hutchinson, proprietor of Hutch's Market in Irving, Texas, recalled that shortly before the assassination a man who looked like Oswald would stop in to purchase milk and cinnamon rolls. One time this man was accompanied by an elderly woman and a younger woman who spoke a foreign language. On another occasion the Oswald character left without a word when Hutchinson refused to cash a two-party check for $189, as a matter of store policy, which limited check cashing to less than $25. Since Oswald was usually at the Irving home of Ruth Paine only on weekends and in "the absence of any other sign that Oswald ever possessed a personal check for $189," the Commission decided he had never had such a check.

Anyone who has worked for the government knows that officials are very diligent about withdrawing taxes. It is interesting to note that if Oswald was being paid $200 a month as an FBI informant, his take-home pay would have been about $189.

The specter of Oswald as an FBI informant prompted a special executive session of the Warren Commission the same day as Carr's call. The minutes of that meeting were classified "top secret" until March 1975. At this meeting Commissioners were tense. What could they do with this report that Oswald, already designated as JFK's assassin, was working for the FBI?

Commission general counsel J. Lee Rankin said, "When the Chief Justice and I were just briefly reflecting on [the Oswald–FBI informant rumor], we said if that was true and it ever came out, could be established, then you would have people think that there was a conspiracy to accomplish this assassination that nothing the Commission did or anybody could dissipate."

Representative Hale Boggs of Louisiana mused, "Its implications are . . . are fantastic."

Referring to the fact that the Commission had no independent investigators and was forced to rely on the FBI for its information, Rankin complained, "[The FBI] would like us to fold up and quit. . . . They found the man. There is nothing more to do. The Commission supports their conclusions, and we can go on home and that is the end of it."

Boggs remarked, "I don't even like to see this being taken down." Former CIA director and Commission member Allen Dulles agreed: "Yes, I think this record ought to be destroyed. Do you think we need a record of this?"

On January 27, the commissioners met again to consider this information. It is obvious from the transcripts that they feared approaching Hoover with the matter. Turning to former CIA director Dulles, Boggs asked how the FBI could disprove that Oswald was an informant. Dulles replied, "That is a hard thing to disprove, you know. . . . I never knew how to disprove it. . . . The record may not be on paper. But on paper you would have hieroglyphics that only two people know what they meant, and nobody outside of the agency would know; and you could say this meant the agent and somebody else could say it meant another agent."

"The man who recruited [the agent] would know, wouldn't he?" asked Boggs. "Yes, but he wouldn't tell," replied Dulles. "Wouldn't tell under oath?" asked an incredulous Earl Warren, chief justice of the US Supreme Court and chair of the Commission. Dulles replied, "I wouldn't think he would tell under oath, no. . . . He ought not tell it under oath. . . . What I was getting at, I think, under any circumstances. I think Mr. Hoover would say certainly he didn't have anything to do with this fellow."

Exasperated, Boggs exclaimed, "What you do is . . . make our problem utterly impossible because you say this rumor can't be dissipated under any circumstances."

During this same meeting Rankin revealed that he had received the same Oswald-informant information from yet another source—the Secret Service. He said the Secret Service named a Dallas deputy sheriff, Allan Sweatt, as its source.

It was here that the commissioners decided to just drop the entire matter. The

FBI was informing them that Oswald was never an informant, and they could never prove or disprove it.

Furthermore, although it would be several weeks before the Commission began hearing witnesses and taking testimony, it now appears the verdict already was in. In the same Commission minutes, Georgia senator Richard Russell commented, "They [the FBI] have tried the case and reached a verdict on every aspect."

If Oswald was working for the FBI, it could explain many things. It could explain his mysterious movements and associations in New Orleans, where he tried to join both pro- and anti-Castro groups. It could explain why he asked for Agent Quigley after his arrest. It could explain his light sentence after being found guilty of disturbing the peace. It could explain the remarks—later denied—by Agent Hosty in Dallas that the FBI knew about Oswald. It also could explain why the FBI did not pass along its security file on Oswald to the Dallas police and it could explain why Dallas FBI chief Shanklin demanded that Hosty be allowed to question Oswald while in police custody.

It also might explain a well-documented instance of the FBI destroying evidence after the assassination. In August 1975, the *Dallas Times Herald* reported it had recently learned that two weeks before the JFK assassination, Oswald had delivered a note to the Dallas FBI office and that the note had been destroyed after the assassination. This story prompted an investigation by the Justice Department and eventually became the center of hearings before a subcommittee of the House Judiciary Committee.

It is now certain that two to three weeks prior to the assassination, Oswald came to the Dallas FBI office and asked a receptionist to see Agent Hosty. When told Hosty was not in, Oswald left a note. The receptionist, Nancy Fenner, noted that Oswald asked for "S.A. [Special Agent] Hosty . . . [in] exactly those words." It's surprising that Oswald would be so familiar with bureau jargon. Years later Fenner recalled the note as some type of warning, something like, "Let this be a warning. I will blow up the FBI and the Dallas Police Department if you don't stop bothering my wife—Lee Harvey Oswald."

Hosty, who said he was told not to mention the note at the time of the assassination, said the note was not violent in tone and that it said something more like, "If you have anything you want to learn about me, come talk to me directly. If you don't cease bothering my wife, I will take appropriate action and report this to the proper authorities."

Hosty also said the note was folded and expressed doubts that Fenner had read it properly.

He said that within hours after the assassination, he was called into the office of the special agent in charge, J. Gordon Shanklin. Hosty said Shanklin was visibly "agitated and upset" and wanted to know about the Oswald note. After Oswald had been killed, Shanklin again called in Hosty. Hosty said Shanklin produced the Oswald note from his desk drawer and said, "Oswald's dead now. There can be no trial. Here, get rid of this." As Hosty tore up the note, Shanklin cried, "No! Get it out of here. I don't even want it in this office. Get rid of it!" Hosty said he took the pieces of the note to a nearby restroom and "flushed it down the drain."

Another Dallas agent, Kenneth Howe, also testified he showed Shanklin the Oswald note the weekend of the assassination. Existence of the note also was talked about among some members of the Dallas Police Department. Ruth Paine even mentioned in her testimony to the Warren Commission in 1964 that Oswald had dropped off a note to the FBI. She told the Commission, "[Oswald] told me he had stopped at the downtown office of the FBI and tried to see the agents and left a note."

The House Select Committee on Assassinations said the incident concerning the note was a "serious impeachment of Shanklin's and Hosty's credibility," and that with the note's destruction, "it was not possible to establish with confidence what its contents were."

To the House committee Shanklin denied any knowledge of the Oswald note. But assistant FBI director William Sullivan said Shanklin had discussed an "internal problem" concerning a message from Oswald with him and that the presence of the note was common knowledge at FBI headquarters, thus adding the crime of perjury to destruction of evidence.

Why did the bureau acknowledge the existence of the note only after media reports in 1975? It seems unbelievable that the FBI would knowingly destroy evidence, especially if it would have proven Oswald prone to violence. Some researchers say a more plausible explanation is that Oswald, as an FBI informant, tried to warn the bureau about the coming assassination. This could explain the receptionist's insistence that the note contained threatening words. It also could explain why the FBI was so concerned and fearful of the note that it was ordered destroyed. Such a warning would corroborate Judyth Vary Baker's claim that Oswald tried to stop the assassination.

Incidentally, Hosty was one of seventeen FBI agents reprimanded for the way they handled the assassination case. He was suspended for thirty days without pay and transferred to Kansas City. However, after the Oswald-note matter was investigated by the House Select Committee on Assassinations and despite the contradictions between Hosty's testimony and that of his superior, Shanklin, Hosty was given more than $1,000 in repayment for the Hoover-imposed suspension. "Rather than come out and admit [that I was wronged in 1963] . . . [the FBI] just gave me my money back," commented Hosty.

In light of the FBI's meticulously worded denials that Oswald had ever been paid as an FBI informant, it should be noted that not all informants work for money. It is common practice for the FBI to gain information from people who have something to fear from the bureau, perhaps the possibility of being charged with a past crime or even possible deportation. Oswald's wife had never become a US citizen and therefore was subject to deportation at the government's pleasure. She even mentioned this to the Warren Commission, saying, "Sometimes the FBI agents asked me questions which had no bearing or relationship [to the assassination], and if I didn't want to answer, they told me that if I wanted to live in this country, I would have to help in this matter."

According to Dallas police captain Will Fritz, Oswald became angry when Agent Hosty confronted him. According to Fritz, Oswald "beat on the desk and went into a kind of tantrum," telling Hosty, "I know you. You accosted my wife on two occasions." Asked by Fritz what he meant by "accosted," Oswald replied, "Well, he threatened her. . . . He practically told her she would have to go back to Russia." Perhaps Oswald was recruited not with the promise of money, but with the threat of Marina's deportation.

While this may never be proven, this author learned years ago that the Dallas police received a letter about two weeks before the assassination warning that an attack on Kennedy would take place in their city. It was signed by A. J. Hidell, Oswald's alias. With nothing else to support this warning, the letter was merely filed away. In the days following that fateful Friday, federal agents combed through the police department—even searching the saddlebags on police motorcycles—and took everything that might deal with the assassination. Needless to say, the Hidell warning letter has never been seen again. Did Oswald try to alert both the FBI and the Dallas police to the coming assassination?

Finally, while it cannot be established with any certainty that Oswald was working for the FBI, it is now known that his killer definitely was. In early 1959, at a time when Jack Ruby may have been involved in smuggling activities with Cubans, he contacted the FBI and said he wanted to provide the bureau with information. Accordingly, agent Charles W. Flynn opened a potential confidential or criminal informant (PCI) file on Ruby.

The relationship between Ruby and the bureau was mentioned in a letter from Hoover to the Warren Commission dated June 9, 1964. However, this information was kept classified until 1975.

In the 1964 letter, Hoover stated that Ruby "furnished no information whatsoever and further contacts with him were discontinued." This disclaimer is difficult to swallow, since records show that agents met with Ruby on at least eight occasions between April and October 1959.

Since Ruby was an FBI informant, and considering the massive circumstantial evidence now available concerning Oswald's relationship to the bureau, the possibility of Lee Harvey Oswald's having worked for the bureau appears to be probable.

And if by the spring of 1963, when Oswald arrived in New Orleans, he was indeed working with the FBI, it could explain his contacts with the characters at 544 Camp Street.

Cuban Grand Central Station

By the summer of 1963 the faded three-story Newman Building at the corner of Camp and Lafayette Streets in New Orleans had become known as the "Cuban Grand Central Station."

Previously housed here was the CIA-backed Cuban Revolutionary Council, which counted Carlos Bringuier as a member, as well as Sergio Archaca-Smith's Crusade to Free Cuba, both virulently anti-Castro groups. Also in the same building was the private detective firm of Guy Banister. In the summer of 1963, Banister's employees included Jack Martin and David Ferrie, Oswald's former Civil Air Patrol leader, and reportedly Oswald himself.

During the 1940s Banister was the special agent in charge of the FBI office in Chicago, Jack Ruby's hometown. One of his FBI associates at that time was Robert Maheu, who left the bureau in the 1950s and later became the chief go-between in the CIA-Mafia assassination plots against Castro.

According to Banister's family, he was also involved with naval intelligence during the war and maintained contacts with that group throughout his life.

Banister left the bureau and came to New Orleans in the 1950s at the request of the mayor to become chief of police. However, in 1957, he was forced to retire after an incident in the Old Absinthe House, where Banister allegedly threatened a waiter with a gun. He then formed Guy Banister Associates, which occupied a ground-floor office in the Newman Building with the address of 531 Lafayette Street, the side entrance to 544 Camp Street. This office was within walking distance of the New Orleans FBI office, the Office of Naval Intelligence, and other government agencies.

A member of the John Birch Society, Banister also was a member of the Minutemen and the Louisiana Committee on Un-American Activities, and was the publisher of a racist publication titled *Louisiana Intelligence Digest*. Reportedly an alcoholic, Banister was later described as "a tragic case" by a member of the New Orleans Crime Commission.

With the rise of Fidel Castro, Banister threw himself into the anti-Castro Cuban activity in New Orleans. He helped organize such anti-Castro groups as the Cuban Revolutionary Democratic Front and Friends of a Democratic Cuba. According to an April 25, 1967, story in the *New Orleans States-Item*, Banister even served as a munitions supplier during the planning stages of the Bay of Pigs Invasion. In fact, Banister employees have said that as late as 1963, guns of every type littered Banister's office.

Banister also ran a network of young informants on the campuses of Tulane and Louisiana State Universities, collecting what he hailed as the largest file of anticommunist intelligence in the South.

Jerry Milton Brooks, a former Minuteman who worked for Banister, said he would regularly take Banister's updated files to the New Orleans FBI office, where they were integrated into the bureau's files. Brooks also said Maurice B. Gatlin, another Banister employee who regarded the younger Brooks as a protégé, once said, "Stick with me—I'll give you a license to kill."

Although Banister's files were scattered after his sudden death in June 1964—he reportedly died of a heart attack before authorities could question him about his contacts with Oswald and the assassination—some idea of their scope can be found in indexed titles made public by Louisiana lawmen. "Central Intelligence Agency," "Ammunition and Arms," "Civil Rights Program of JFK," and significantly, "Fair Play for Cuba Committee" and "International Trade Mart" are just a few of these titles. Banister's operation was right in the thick of New Orleans intelligence activities, located near government offices and just around the corner from the Reily Coffee Company, Oswald's employer and a supporter of anti-Castro Cuban exiles.

Banister's secretary, Delphine Roberts, recalled Oswald at 544 Camp Street, and said he filled out one of Banister's "agent" application forms. She later told author Anthony Summers, "Oswald came back a number of times. He seemed to be on familiar terms with Banister and with the office."

Roberts's daughter, also Delphine, had a photography studio at 544 Camp Street and she, too, recalled Oswald:

> I knew he had his pamphlets and books and everything in a room along from where we were with our photographic equipment. He was quiet and mostly kept to himself, didn't associate with too many people. He would just tell us "hello" or "good-bye" when we saw him. I never saw him talking to Guy Banister, but I knew he worked in his office. I knew they were associated. I saw some other men who looked like Americans coming and going occasionally from the room Oswald used. . . . I got the impression Oswald was doing something to make people believe he was something he wasn't. I am sure Guy Banister knew what Oswald was doing.

It appears that by late summer 1963, Oswald was playing a dangerous game—caught up in a mixture of CIA- and FBI-related agents who were in touch with both anti-Castro Cubans and organized-crime figures.

———

Despite the contacts between Oswald and both current and former FBI agents—plus the evidence of advance warnings of the assassination to the bureau—the Dallas tragedy still occurred.

While no unquestionable case for FBI involvement in the assassination itself can be made, there is now no doubt that the bureau manipulated the subsequent investigation.

For starters, top FBI officials took total control of all evidence the very day of the assassination and held it, with no chain of evidence, for three full days before the bureau was officially called into the case, as will be discussed later.

About noon on Tuesday, November 26, following several morning conferences with top aides and the district attorney, police chief Jesse Curry announced to reporters that it had been decided to call in the FBI for assistance with the assassination case. The transfer of evidence from city police to federal control was completed four hours later.

So now the FBI was officially on the case and officially in charge of the evidence.

But what could have happened during the two days while the evidence was unofficially in their hands? Fabrication, substitution, elimination, alteration—with no effective chain of responsibility, anything could have happened.

Today the FBI has been accused of poor management of evidence at best and downright falsification of evidence at worst. For example, an FBI document released to the public in 1968, File No. DL 89-43, signed by special agent Vincent Drain and dated November 29, 1963, reports that wrapping paper available at the School Book Depository was "found to have the same observable characteristics as the brown paper bag shaped like a gun case which was found near the scene of the shooting on the sixth floor." This is incriminating evidence against Oswald. However, in 1980 among many FBI documents released by the bureau was another File No. 89-43, signed by Agent Drain and dated November 29, 1963. This one states the wrapping paper from the Depository was "found not to be identical with the paper gun case found at the scene of the shooting." When asked about this discrepancy, an FBI spokesman simply said the latter document was a phony. This prompted researchers to wonder how many other "phony" documents rested in FBI files.

Such discrepancies should prove to any objective researcher that severe questions remain concerning the validity of the government's evidence in the assassination.

Under Hoover's iron control, it would have been easy for ranking bureau officials to do with the evidence whatever they pleased. The fact that federal authorities had all the assassination evidence under covert control for two days could go far in explaining the contradictions and questionable conclusions of the official investigation. Apparently at least one person understood the gravity of this issue, as there was an attempt to obscure it in the Warren Commission materials.

In 1992, the "confidential" deposition of FBI fingerprint expert James C. Cadigan was made public by the National Archives. The deposition was clearly altered with edits in pencil intended to obscure statements regarding the early unofficial handling of the assassination evidence.

While the assassination evidence is often ambiguous and contradictory and will certainly be in controversy for years to come, the handling of the evidence clearly points to manipulation and obstruction at the highest levels of federal authority, providing a clear view of who was responsible for at least the demonstrable cover-up, if not the assassination itself.

In fact, FBI activities after the assassination fall well within the realm of criminal behavior. Consider:

Suppression of evidence: Examples include the loss of Beverly Oliver's assassination film, which she claimed was taken by an FBI agent; the disappearance of an assassination bullet taken from under the noses of a police guard by an FBI agent; the suppression of testimony, such as Ed Hoffman's, which failed to support the lone-assassin theory; and the bureau's failure to follow important leads, even when requested to do so by the Warren Commission.

Destruction of evidence: Examples include the destruction of an Oswald note by FBI Agent Hosty; the destruction of a license-plate number on a photograph of General Edwin Walker's home found intact among Oswald's possessions; and the immediate cleaning of the presidential limousine, which effectively destroyed vital ballistic evidence.

Intimidation of witnesses: Examples include Richard Carr, who saw two men run from the Texas School Book Depository but later was told by FBI agents, "If you didn't see Lee Harvey Oswald in the School Book Depository with a rifle, you didn't witness it"; Ed Hoffman, who was told by a bureau agent, "You'd better keep quiet; you could get killed"; and Jean Hill, who said she was hounded by bureau agents until she stopped giving media interviews.

In any normal criminal case, such behavior would constitute a jailable offense, but this was not an ordinary case, and the culprits were not ordinary citizens but FBI agents. If a local police agency proves to be corrupt, the FBI can be brought in to investigate. But in the case of the bureau, who investigates the investigators?

Since there can be no question that in 1963 the FBI was personified by J. Edgar Hoover, the questions of means, motive, and opportunity must fall on his shoulders. Did Hoover have the means of committing the assassination? Surrounded by countless informers, agents, and former employees—many of whom were in contact with Lee Harvey Oswald—Hoover's means were limitless.

Hoover's motives are obvious. First, his hatred of the Kennedys was notorious, and second, he was afraid that upon reelection John Kennedy would not allow him to continue as FBI director. This fear was well founded. Rumors in Washington were plentiful that Hoover would be forced to retire as FBI director after Kennedy's reelection in 1964.

William Hundley, former head of the Justice Department's organized-crime section, is quoted in *The Director* as saying that what finally destroyed the fragile relationship between Hoover and attorney general Robert Kennedy was "that Bobby mentioned to too many people who complained to him about Hoover that, 'Look, just wait,' and we all got the message that they were going to retire him after Jack got re-elected and Hoover hit seventy. And it got back to him."

Presidential aide David Powers stated he believes that the question of Hoover's retirement was the subject of one of the very few private meetings between Kennedy and the bureau chief: "[Hoover] had a long lunch with the President and Bobby [on October 31, 1963] and, as you know, three weeks later we went to Dallas."

But did Hoover have the opportunity? Hoover built his immense power base by currying favor with men more powerful than himself. It is extremely unlikely that Hoover, a consummate bureaucrat, would have assumed the responsibility for initiating the assassination.

It is, however, certainly plausible that Hoover—after having discovered the assassination plot through his network of agents and informers—caused it to happen simply by not preventing it. Of course this is tantamount to criminal complicity and would have required substantial manipulation of testimony and evidence to prevent discovery of the bureau's role.

Hoover would have needed help. And help he had, in the form of the new president, his former neighbor and dinner friend Lyndon B. Johnson—another man about to lose his job thanks to the Kennedys.

But what about protection of the president? Could his official protection be circumvented? Could a plot to assassinate a US president succeed without in some way neutralizing or involving the Secret Service?

The Secret Service

On the day of his inauguration, Thomas Jefferson walked from the Washington boardinghouse where he was staying to the Capitol without benefit of any protection.

It was symptomatic of the young Republic that presidents had not yet acquired the mantle of royalty and thus did not require protection. This naïveté began to change after an assassination attempt on president Andrew Jackson on January 10, 1835. In August 1842, a drunken painter threw some rocks at President John Tyler, who was walking on the White House grounds. Congress soon passed an act creating an auxiliary watch of the Washington Metropolitan Police for the protection of public and private property consisting of a captain and fifteen men. Although the act was aimed primarily at protecting property—particularly the White House—it was the crude beginning of presidential protection.

Even after Abraham Lincoln was fatally shot by actor John Wilkes Booth in Ford's Theater on April 14, 1865, there was no clamor to create official protection for the president. Americans thought his death was just an accident of the war.

The Secret Service, which was organized as a division of the Treasury Department the year Lincoln was killed, originally was meant only to pursue counterfeiters. It was not until after the assassination of president James A. Garfield in 1881 that a serious attempt was made to protect presidents. While the number of White House policemen grew to twenty-seven after mail threats increased against president Grover Cleveland, it was not until 1894 that Secret Service agents were informally assigned to the president.

Throughout the Spanish-American War, a small detail of Secret Service men were stationed at the White House. However, Secret Service protection of president William McKinley did not prevent his assassination on September 6, 1901. McKinley was attending a public reception at the Pan American Exposition in Buffalo, New York, when self-professed anarchist Leon F. Czolgosz fired two bullets into him despite the proximity of four Buffalo detectives, four soldiers, and three Secret Service agents. McKinley died eight days later and Czolgosz was executed.

The McKinley assassination finally provoked a response from Congress, which in 1902 ordered the Secret Service to assume full-time protection of the president. Two agents were permanently assigned to the White House. By World War II, the White House detail of the Secret Service had grown to thirty-seven men.

Following an unsuccessful attack on president Harry S. Truman by Puerto Rican nationalists in 1951, legislation was passed permanently authorizing the Secret Service to protect not only the president, but also his immediate family, the president-elect, and the vice president.

By 1963, the Secret Service remained a small and specialized group restricted by law. Nevertheless, the Secret Service had an average strength of more than five hundred and ran sixty-five field offices throughout the country.

Protecting president John F. Kennedy was no easy matter, as Kennedy was quite active in both his public and personal life.

Kennedy assistant Kenneth O'Donnell was in charge of the White House staff and, as such, had control over the Secret Service. However, O'Donnell left security measures up to the special agent-in-charge of the White House detail, Gerald Behn. Sizing up the problems of protecting an active president such as Kennedy, O'Donnell once told Behn, "Politics and protection don't mix."

During his fateful trip to Texas, Kennedy was assigned no fewer than seventy Secret Service agents plus eight clerks. This was about 14 percent of the entire Secret Service force. Yet glaring deficiencies in the president's protection are now known.

Although apparently at least three assassination attempts were planned against Kennedy in the fall of 1963, information on them was not forwarded to either the agent in charge of Kennedy's protection or the special agent-in-charge of the Dallas Secret Service office.

In Chicago the Secret Service arrested an ex-Marine named Thomas Arthur Vallee, who was a member of the right-wing John Birch Society and a vocal Kennedy critic. Vallee was discovered to have an M-1 rifle, a handgun, and 3,000 rounds of ammunition in his car. It was also learned that Vallee had asked for time off from his job on November 2, the date Kennedy was to visit Chicago. Despite the weapons found, Vallee was released from custody on the evening of November 2 and was still considered a threat. Yet no word of the Vallee matter was transmitted to Dallas.

One of the most telling stories to come out of the Secret Service at this time, however, concerned the first black man to serve on the Service's White House detail. Abraham Bolden was personally selected by Kennedy, apparently in an attempt to integrate the previously all-white Secret Service detail.

Born in poverty, Bolden had been a police officer with an outstanding record before joining the Service. However, Bolden criticized the White House detail for laxity and was transferred to the Chicago office.

According to Bolden, the Chicago Secret Service office received a teletype from the FBI shortly before Kennedy's November 2 visit warning that an assassination attempt would be carried out in that city by a four-man Cuban hit squad armed with high-powered rifles. Bolden said the entire office was involved in this matter but that it was kept top secret.

Years later, Bolden could not identify Vallee as a participant in this threat, and the belief among researchers is that Vallee played no part in the second assassination plan.

Kennedy's Chicago trip was canceled, although the House Select Committee on Assassinations could not determine why.

Three weeks after Kennedy's death, Bolden discovered that information on the Chicago threat was to be kept from the Warren Commission and he made a trip to Washington to tell what he knew. However, he was quickly taken back to Chicago, where he was later charged with discussing a bribe with two known counterfeiters. Brought to trial, Bolden was convicted of accepting a bribe—even after one of the two counterfeiters admitted to perjury—and was sentenced to a lengthy prison term after his motion for a retrial was denied.

While the Secret Service has admitted the Chicago threat occurred, it has repeatedly refused to clarify the matter. Bolden was released from prison and in 2012 continued to gain signatures requesting the president to "expunge, pardon or take other executive action that will clear the record of conviction of Abraham W. Bolden, Sr." He claimed he was framed and convicted to silence him regarding the Kennedy threat. Bolden has since learned that the information on the incident in Chicago came from an informant named "Lee," naturally leading to speculation that it may have been informant Lee Oswald. Whatever the Chicago threat may have been, the information again was not passed along to Dallas.

Likewise, the Service failed to follow up on another threat, this time from the volatile Miami area. Here a wealthy right-wing extremist named Joseph A. Milteer accurately predicted what was to happen to Kennedy in Dallas almost three weeks before the event. Again, while this information was forwarded to the Service's Protective Research Section (PRS) in Washington, it was never relayed to Winston G. Lawson, the advance agent in Dallas, or to Forrest V. Sorrels, the special agent in charge in Dallas.

And neither Lawson nor Sorrels got a preview of the zigzag turn that placed Kennedy below the Texas School Book Depository windows on November 22.

The journey through Dealey Plaza itself was made necessary because of the selection of the Dallas Trade Mart as the site of the noon luncheon for the Kennedy entourage. And according to White House aide and advance man Jerry Bruno, this decision was made by Texas Governor John Connally after some questionable manipulations.

After reviewing possible luncheon sites, the Secret Service and White House advance men settled on two locations—the new Dallas Trade Mart on Stemmons Expressway and the Women's Building in Fair Park, home of the Texas State Fair, located south of the downtown area.

The Secret Service and the Kennedy people decided the Women's Building would be a preferable location because it presented fewer security problems and could accommodate more people. However, Democrats headed by Lyndon Johnson and John Connally wanted the Trade Mart because it was more modern and would be more acceptable to Dallas's wealthy elite.

Bruno wrote, "There was another point about the Women's Building site that didn't seem important to anyone at the time. If Kennedy had been going there instead of to the Trade Mart, he would have been traveling two blocks farther away from the Texas School Book Depository—and at a much faster rate of speed."

The struggle over the luncheon site continued until November 18, when Bruno got a call from White House aide Kenneth O'Donnell. Bruno quoted O'Donnell as saying, "We're going to let Dallas go, Jerry. We're going to let Connally have the Trade Mart site."

Bruno was flabbergasted. Despite the recommendations of the Secret Service, the Kennedy White House, and himself, Connally had managed to swing the decision to the Trade Mart. Bruno said he later learned that the Johnson-Connally people had held up selling tickets to the fund-raising luncheon in an effort to force the site-location selection their way.

Bruno wrote that upon learning of Kennedy's death, "I was angry, furious, at Connally and his demands to control the trip, where Kennedy should go, and now the President had been shot because we went here instead of there."

But if the Secret Service had no control over the luncheon site, they certainly were in control of the motorcade. And several strange things happened there.

Police Chief Curry originally had asked that the presidential limousine be flanked by eight motorcycle policemen, four on each side of the car. However, Curry told the Warren Commission that Secret Service Agent Lawson ordered the number of cycles reduced to four, two on each side, and that the cycles were told to stay by the rear fender of the limousine. This order seems unusual to those familiar with motorcade security, since the purpose of motorcycle outriders is to form a screen for the limousine rider in the event of trouble.

Curry was puzzled, too, over this apparent lack of concern for security as well as the fact that Dallas authorities were kept in the dark about Oswald. Years later, he wrote:

> In retrospect, the physical security arrangements provided by the Dallas Police Force for the Secret Service were carried out exactly as they had requested. In my opinion all police officers involved gave their complete and wholehearted cooperation. Yet the Dallas Police Department was never given any information or asked to cooperate with the FBI or Secret Service in any attempt to locate possible conspirators. The Dallas Police Department was never informed of the presence of Lee Harvey Oswald in Dallas, of his connections with the Communist Party, or the fact that he "was capable of committing the assassination of President Kennedy."

Curry also had planned to have a car containing police captain Will Fritz and other Dallas detectives immediately following the presidential limousine, a traditional practice during similar motorcades in the past. However, again Lawson vetoed this plan "so Fritz and his men were not in the motorcade."

And certainly the Dallas detectives could not have moved any slower than Kennedy's Secret Service protectors when the shots were fired in Dealey Plaza.

Photos taken several seconds after the first shots show almost a total lack of response by the agents riding in a backup car behind the presidential limousine. While Kennedy is clutching at his throat, two of his guards have begun looking toward the rear while the others are looking directly at the president. The only agent to react with speed was Clint Hill, who was not even supposed to be on the Dallas trip. Assigned to protect Jackie Kennedy, Hill had been brought along at the last minute due to a specific request by the First Lady.

But the one aspect of the Secret Service protection that raises the disturbing possibility of complicity concerns the actions of presidential limousine driver William Greer.

At age fifty-four, Greer was one of the oldest members of the White House detail. He had driven both president Harry Truman and president Dwight Eisenhower. On the evening of November 22, 1963, Greer drove Kennedy's body from Air Force One to Bethesda Naval Hospital for autopsy.

Greer testified to the Warren Commission that as the limousine cruised down the incline of Elm Street through Dealey Plaza, he heard a noise that he thought was a motorcycle backfire. Shortly he heard a second similar noise and glanced over his right shoulder long enough to see Governor Connally begin to slump to his left. Greer said he never caught sight of Kennedy.

He said the presidential limousine was moving at between twelve and fifteen miles per hour the entire time.

However, based on films made during the assassination and eyewitness testimony, it is now known that immediately after the first shot, the brake lights on the limousine came on and the big Lincoln slowed to almost a complete standstill, causing the Secret Service follow-up car to move up and almost touch the rear bumper. Contrary to his testimony, films show Greer looking over his right shoulder in Kennedy's direction for several seconds—in fact, until after the fatal head shot is delivered.

This discrepancy between Greer's testimony and reality has caused the more suspicious-minded researchers to suspect that some individuals within the Secret Service may have played a role in placing an underprotected president under the guns in Dealey Plaza. Some even still accept the rumor that Greer himself shot Kennedy.

By comparing the Zapruder film with the Orville Nix film, it is clear that when shots were first fired at the president, Greer braked the limousine to almost a complete stop, and only after the fatal head shot do the brake lights go off and the car accelerates. All this violates Secret Service regulations, which state at the first sign of trouble, accelerate and drive out of danger. It is also clear that Greer turns his head and looks back at Kennedy at the time of the fatal head shot, which is at odds with his Warren Commission testimony, in which he claimed he never looked back and did not even know the assassination had taken place until Roy Kellerman next to him said, "Let's get out of here, we're hit!"

However, a lingering theory that the driver shot Kennedy is not true. If Greer had shot JFK, someone in the crowd, some less than ten feet away, would have said something. Other Secret Service agents and others in the know would have whispered about this for years. Rumors would have floated around Washington and Nellie Connally would have talked, at least as gossip. But none of this happened.

This issue didn't come up until the mid-1980s, when conspiracy author William Cooper latched onto a hypothesis of researcher Lars Hanson of California, who, upon viewing a bad fourth- or fifth-generation copy of the Zapruder film, speculated that the driver turned and shot Kennedy. Upon careful inspection of the film and further reflection, Hanson denounced his own theory but this did not stop Cooper from selling bad copies (some so bad there was no color) of the Zapruder film and continuing to assert the driver had shot JFK even though Hanson and several other JFK researchers, this author included, warned him it was a false claim. Cooper continued to sell his story to other credulous researchers until he was killed after shooting at local deputies who came to serve him a warrant in 2001. In addition to his claim that Greer shot JFK, Cooper also claimed that all the nearest witnesses to the JFK head shot were dead within a few years of the assassination, a demonstrably false claim.

So what exactly do you see in the Zapruder film? It is true that Greer turns to his right and looks back at JFK at the time of the head shot, a somewhat suspicious circumstance, as Greer claimed he never looked back. Greer then faces front and the car accelerates. In those days it was customary for men to wear hair grease and Kellerman's hair was especially slicked down. Sunlight glinted off the top of his head. In viewing the Zapruder film in slow motion, one notices that the "pistol" moves simultaneously with Kellerman's head. Also, a few frames earlier when the sunlight gleams off the tops of both Kellerman's head and Greer's, the brightness of the highlight is the same. As Greer turns to his right, Kellerman bends forward slightly and the sun fully catches the top of his head, resulting in a bright highlight, which is a horizontal "L" shape and could be misidentified as a gun, especially if one has been preconditioned to think of it in that way. But as Kellerman's head moves, so does the shape. The brief flash seen is simply the sunlight reflecting off the metal rim of the frame for the privacy window, used when the top was on the car. That day, the top was down and the privacy window rolled down but the frame remained. While it may be questionable as to why Greer turned and looked back at Kennedy and then could not recall that fact for the Warren Commission, at no time did his two hands leave the steering wheel of the limousine.

Greer's testimony, like that of all government officials presented to the Warren Commission, was taken at face value and there was no real attempt at cross-examination. Likewise, testimony that indicated why the reaction of the Secret Service agents that day was so sluggish was not examined closely by the Warren Commission.

A Few Drinks at the Cellar

Within days of the assassination, it was common knowledge in the Fort Worth–Dallas area that Kennedy's Secret Service agents were drinking well into the morning hours of November 22 at a notorious Fort Worth club, the Cellar.

The story eventually spread nationwide when columnist Drew Pearson wrote about the incident, adding editorially, "Obviously men who have been drinking until nearly 3 a.m. are in no condition to be trigger-alert or in the best physical shape to protect anyone."

The stories set off an investigation within the Secret Service. Chief James J. Rowley, a former FBI man who had been with the Secret Service since 1938, obtained statements from the ten agents involved, plus some Fort Worth news reporters and Pat Kirkwood, the club's owner and an acquaintance of Jack Ruby.

Everyone, including Kirkwood, stressed that the Cellar had no license to sell alcoholic drinks. Rowley told the Warren Commission, "This is a place that does not serve alcoholic beverages."

Why the concern about alcohol? The Warren Commission cited Section 10 of the Secret Service Manual:

> 10. Liquor, use of—a. Employees are strictly enjoined to refrain from the use of intoxicating liquor during the hours they are officially employed at their post of duty, or when they may reasonably expect that they may be called upon to perform an official duty. *During entire periods of travel status, the special agent is officially employed and should not use liquor, until the completion of all of his official duties for the day. . . . However, all members of the White House Detail and Special Agents cooperating with them on Presidential and similar protective assignments are considered to be subject to call for official duty at any time while in travel status. Therefore, the use of intoxicating liquor of any kind, including beer and wine, by members of the White House Detail . . . while they are in travel status, is prohibited.*

The regulations further stated, "Violation or slight disregard of the above paragraphs . . . will be cause for removal from the Service."

Several of the agents involved, including four who were riding in the Secret Service follow-up car behind Kennedy, admitted drinking, but no more than two beers. Of those who went to the Cellar, most said they had one or two drinks called a "Salty Dick," described as grapefruit juice and soda. Again, everyone concerned stressed that the Cellar did not sell alcohol, although alcohol brought in by a patron was allowed.

At least three agents guarding Kennedy's hotel suite took their "coffee break" at the Cellar, leaving two Fort Worth firemen behind to guard the president.

Since all the agents turned out at seven that morning "sober, alert and ready for the performance of their duties," Rowley told the Warren Commission he did not punish them for violating regulations.

According to the Warren Commission:

> Chief Rowley testified that under ordinary circumstances he would have taken disciplinary action against those agents who had been drinking in clear violation of the regulation. However, he felt that any disciplinary ac-

tion might have given rise to an inference that the violation of the regulation had contributed to the tragic events of November 22. Since he was convinced that this was not the case, he believed that it would be unfair to the agents and their families to take explicit disciplinary measures.

Obviously, Rowley and others in the government were very much concerned that the public might recall that President Lincoln was killed when his guard left his post to have a drink next door and might attach some significance to the fact that Kennedy's agents were keeping late hours in a "beatnik" club owned by an associate of Jack Ruby.

The entire affair was toned down and quietly forgotten—except by Cellar owner Kirkwood. During the intervening years, Kirkwood has admitted that while the Cellar had no license to sell liquor, nothing prevented him from giving it away. And give it away he did. In a 1984 article in the *Fort Worth Star-Telegram* recalling the wild days of the Cellar, Kirkwood recalled, "We had strange rules. We'd give drinks to doctors, lawyers, politicians, stag girls, policemen, anybody we thought we might need if something broke out."

Kirkwood's mother recalled that sometimes her son would "give away five hundred dollars' worth of whiskey in a month." This author, even though underage, was served alcohol in the Cellar when accompanied by older news reporters. In the newspaper article, Kirkwood mentioned the Secret Service incident:

> After midnight the night before [the assassination], some reporters called me from the Press Club [of Fort Worth], which didn't have a license to sell drinks after midnight. [They] said they had about 17 members of the Secret Service and asked if they could bring them to my place. I said sure. About 3:30 [a.m.], these Secret Service men were sitting around giggling about how the firemen were guarding the President over at the Hotel Texas. That night got the Cellar mentioned in the Warren Report.

Jimmy Hill, who managed the Cellar for eleven years, was even more to the point in that same article:

> After the agents were there, we got a call from the White House asking us not to say anything about them drinking because their image had suffered enough as it was. We didn't say anything, but those guys were bombed. They were drinking pure Everclear [190 proof alcohol].

It might be noted that no one saw the agents in a drunken revelry—although at least one unmarried female reporter tagged along with them for company. In fact, according to most present, the agents sat by themselves quietly talking and drinking. However, the fatigue of the multi-stop Texas trip coupled with the alcohol and lack of sleep obviously left the agents in less-than-optimal condition to perform their duties.

During the wild ride to Parkland Hospital, presidential aide Kenneth O'Donnell thought about the interval between the final shots. Years later, he wrote:

> If there was an interval of at least five seconds between the second and third shots, as it seemed, that was long enough for a man to run 50 yards. If the Secret Service men in the front had reacted quicker to the first two shots at the President's car, if the driver had stepped on the gas before instead of after the fatal third shot was fired, would President Kennedy be alive today?

Former senator Ralph Yarborough echoed O'Donnell's concern when he wrote the Warren Commission:

> All of the Secret Service men seemed to me to respond very slowly, with no more than a puzzled look. Knowing something of the training that combat infantrymen and Marines receive, I am amazed at the lack of instantaneous response by the Secret Service when the rifle fire began.

The reaction-impairment issue aside, conspiracy-minded researchers, noting that throughout history a great man's bodyguards usually have been the key to a successful coup d'état, have suggested that Kennedy's guards may have been aware of the coming events in Dealey Plaza and were under too much stress to get a quiet night's sleep.

Interestingly, none of Vice President Johnson's Secret Service guards were in the entourage that drank at the Press Club and then moved on to the Cellar.

Aside from the sluggish reaction of the Secret Service agents in Dealey Plaza, other oddities occurred in the motorcade during the assassination.

One agent, John D. Ready, did start to react by jumping off the follow-up car (a 1956 Cadillac touring sedan convertible). However, he was recalled by special agent in charge Emory Roberts.

This was reminiscent of an earlier incident as the motorcade left Love Field. Captured on film by ABC's Dallas affiliate WFAA, agent Henry J. Rybka can be seen being waved off Kennedy's limousine by Roberts. He then throws his hands several times to reflect his confusion over this unusual and unexplained order.

Then there is the much-publicized story of agent Rufus Youngblood, who reportedly threw himself valiantly on top of Vice President Johnson after the shooting began in Dealey Plaza. Youngblood was considered the hero of the hour. In his report of that day, Youngblood wrote that upon hearing the first shot, "I quickly looked all around again and could see nothing to shoot at, so I stepped over into the back seat and sat on top of the vice President."

In a statement to the Warren Commission, Johnson mentioned the incident:

I was startled by a sharp report or explosion, but I had no time to speculate as to its origin because Agent Youngblood turned in a flash, immediately after the first explosion, hitting me on the shoulder, and shouted
to all of us in the back seat to get down. I was pushed down by Agent
Youngblood. Almost in the same moment in which he hit or pushed me,
he vaulted over the back seat and sat on me. I was bent over under the
weight of Agent Youngblood's body, toward Mrs. Johnson and Senator
Yarborough.

Years later in his book, *The Vantage Point*, Johnson elaborated:

It is apparent that there were many reactions to the first shot. . . . I did
not know what it was. Agent Youngblood spun around, shoved me on the
shoulder to push me down and shouted to all of us, "Get down!" Almost
in the same movement, he vaulted over the seat, pushed me to the floor,
and sat on my right shoulder to keep me down and to protect me. Agent
Youngblood's quick reaction was as brave an act as I have ever seen anyone
perform. When a man, without a moment's thought or hesitation, places
himself between you and a possible assassin's bullet, you know you have
seen courage. And you never forget it.

However, former Texas senator Ralph Yarborough, who was sitting beside Johnson that day, told this author, "It just didn't happen. . . . It was a small car, Johnson
was a big man, tall. His knees were up against his chin as it was. There was no room
for that to happen."

Yarborough recalled that both Johnson and Youngblood ducked down as the
shooting began and that Youngblood never left the front seat. Yarborough said
Youngblood held a small walkie-talkie over the back of the car's seat and that he and
Johnson both put their ears to the device. He added, "They had it turned down real
low. I couldn't hear what they were listening to."

It would be most interesting to learn what the men listened to, since Dallas police
radio channel 1 designated for the presidential party was blocked from radio traffic
for about eight minutes beginning at 12:26 p.m., about four minutes before the
shooting, by a transmitter stuck open. It may have been that Johnson and Youngblood were listening to a channel reserved for inter-vehicle radio traffic, but no transcripts of this channel have been made public.

Obviously, either Yarborough or Johnson and his Secret Service agents did not
tell the truth of what happened in the motorcade.

In reviewing the Secret Service activity in the course of Kennedy's Dallas trip,
even the gullible Warren Commission concluded that while "the detailed security measures taken at Love Field and the Trade Mart were thorough and well-
executed, in other respects . . . the advance preparations for the President's trip were
deficient."

The House Select Committee on Assassinations was even harsher, stating:

> In summary, the committee concluded that the Secret Service did in fact possess information that was not properly analyzed and put to use with respect to a protective investigation in advance of President Kennedy's trip to Dallas. Further, it was the committee's opinion that Secret Service agents in the Presidential motorcade in Dallas were not adequately prepared for an attack by a concealed sniper. Finally, the committee found that the investigation by the Secret Service of a possible assassination conspiracy was terminated prematurely when President Johnson ordered that the FBI assume primary investigative responsibility.

There is cause for suspicion over the mystery of men encountered by several people in Dealey Plaza—including at least one policeman—who claimed to be Secret Service agents and even displayed credentials. Officially, all agents were in the motorcade or already at the Trade Mart. No government panel has ever adequately investigated this matter to determine whether these men were bogus or real agents.

Whether laxity, negligence, violations of regulations, or even malice, all the accusations against the Secret Service pale when compared to the 1992 nonfiction book *Mortal Error*, in which author Bonar Menninger claims that Secret Service agent George Hickey, riding the backup car, attempted to return fire at Oswald in the sixth floor, but bumbled and accidently shot Kennedy in the back of his head with an AR-15, the civilian model of the Army's M-16 rifle. Menninger, then a reporter for the *Kansas City Business Journal*, obtained most of his theory from Howard Donahue, a retired ballistics expert from Towson, Maryland. In 1995, Agent Hickey sued publisher St. Martin's Press over this claim but the suit was dropped in 1997 due to arguments that too much time had passed since the book was published. In 1998 a settlement for an undisclosed sum was reached between Hickey and St. Martin's. While warmly embraced and publicized by the Establishment media at the time, Menninger's thesis was largely dismissed by the JFK research community, primarily on the basis that films of the assassination showed no such shooting by Hickey was possible. However, it is true that Hickey brandished an AR-15 after the motorcade left Dealey Plaza, as was seen and described by Ed Hoffman and others along the route to Parkland.

While the president's guards certainly had the opportunity to achieve Kennedy's death—either through direct action or through inaction—no motive has been established. And since the Service is a small agency within the federal government with relatively little power or influence, no one seriously believes that the Secret Service initiated or orchestrated the assassination.

However, there remains a real possibility that certain individuals within the Secret Service may have been working for someone other than John Kennedy on November 22, 1963.

Rednecks and Oilmen

By the fall of 1963, President John F. Kennedy had acquired more domestic enemies than just irate anti-Castro Cubans, vengeful mob bosses, and disgruntled intelligence operatives.

Both big business and supporters of states' rights felt threatened by the new Kennedy brand of federalism—the wielding of total power from Washington.

Hatred of Kennedy also was being fomented among those people opposed to the growing civil rights movement, particularly in the old Confederate states, which included Texas.

Into this cauldron of century-old passions stepped Kennedy the politician, hoping to find a middle ground between the radical activists—on both sides.

Kennedy friend Theodore Sorensen wrote, "Jack Kennedy . . . knew comparatively little and cared little about the problems of civil rights and civil liberties."

However, during the presidential campaign of 1960, Kennedy found it expedient to chastise the Eisenhower administration for not doing more to end segregation, despite the fact that two civil rights bills were passed during that time, the first such major legislation since the Emancipation Proclamation of 1863.

In his 1961 inaugural address, Kennedy spurred on the expectations of millions of black Americans when he said:

> Let the word go forth from this time and place, to friend and foe alike, that the torch has been passed to a new generation of Americans . . . one unwilling to witness or permit the slow undoing of those human rights to which this nation has always been committed and to which we are committed today at home and around the world.

Such rhetoric was effective for Kennedy. During the 1960 election, blacks responded to Dr. Martin Luther King's support of Kennedy. They turned out a hefty 78 percent vote for the Massachusetts senator.

By 1962, polls showed Kennedy ranked behind only King himself in popularity among black Americans despite the fact that immediate action by Kennedy on civil rights was limited. Although Kennedy had promised to end segregation in federal housing, it was nearly two years after taking office, with violent racial incidents increasing across the nation, before he took action. Kennedy dawdled until June 1963, before sending his own civil rights bill to Congress and even this did not pass until after his death, when the measure was adroitly maneuvered through Congress by President Lyndon Johnson.

By September 1961, following a summer of tension, violence, and bus "Freedom Rides," the Interstate Commerce Commission, acting on a request by President Kennedy, banned segregation on buses and in terminals.

While the Kennedys certainly did not invent the problem and, in fact, joined the push for civil rights belatedly and reluctantly, they nevertheless were the first major

American leaders to fully address the problem and appeal for wisdom and restraint from both blacks and whites.

And despite its faint beginnings, some of the most dramatic accomplishments of the Kennedy administration were in the area of civil rights. For the first time blacks were appointed to major government jobs as well as judgeships; civil rights laws aimed at ending voter discrimination and public segregation were vigorously enforced by the Kennedy Justice Department despite a recalcitrant J. Edgar Hoover, and an executive order was issued creating a Committee on Equal Employment Opportunity headed by Vice President Johnson.

But racial problems continued. The day after Kennedy's inaugural address, a black Air Force veteran named James Meredith applied for enrollment to the segregated University of Mississippi but was rejected. In his fourth attempt to enroll, Meredith arrived in Oxford, Mississippi, on September 30 accompanied by three hundred US marshals. He was met by a crowd of about 2,500 segregationists and students who turned Meredith and his supporters away with bricks and bottles. The marshals responded with tear gas, and a bloody night-long riot ensued—leaving two people dead and more than 375 injured, including 166 federal officers.

The violence was quelled by the arrival of 3,000 Army and National Guard troops and Meredith was enrolled on October 1 under the protection of marshals who remained with him until his graduation in August 1963. One of those involved in that bloody incident was a former Army general named Edwin A. Walker who later would be connected with Lee Harvey Oswald.

A Bullet for the General

About 9:10 p.m. on April 10, 1963, Major General Edwin A. Walker was narrowly missed by a rifle bullet that crashed through a first-floor window and slammed into a wall of his fashionable Dallas home.

Seventeen months later the Warren Commission concluded that Walker's assailant was none other than Kennedy's alleged assassin, Lee Harvey Oswald. This conclusion has increasingly been called into question as more information about the event has become known.

By the fall of 1963, Walker was notorious in conservative Dallas. A native Texan born in 1909, Major General Walker was commander of the US Army's 24th Division, stationed in West Germany, where he used his position to indoctrinate his troops with right-wing propaganda, including the assertion that both the US government and the military had come under "communist control." The Korean War hero once declared, "We must throw out the traitors, and if that's not possible, we must organize armed resistance to defeat the designs of the usurpers and contribute to the return of a constitutional government."

Ordered to stop this practice, Walker instead resigned from the Army in 1961 and returned to the United States, where he began making political speaking tours. He even made an unsuccessful bid for governor of Texas in 1962, losing to John Connally.

On September 30, 1962, Walker was in Oxford, Mississippi, aligned with those who were trying to prevent the university enrollment of James Meredith. After Walker was charged with being a ringleader of the violent Oxford mob, Attorney General Robert Kennedy ordered that he be held temporarily in a mental institution.

By 1963, Walker was back in Dallas and had become a prominent figure in right-wing political activity there, particularly in the John Birch Society. In a 1964 interview with this author, Walker outlined his beliefs:

> The United Nations charter, which is only eight pages, should have been placed before [the American public] to study. Very few . . . have even seen the Fulbright Memorandum or the Walter Reuther Memorandum submitted to Attorney General Kennedy upon his request. . . . Very few had even seen these papers or the UN declaration on racial discrimination, the UN term for integration. This paper declares that the whole world will integrate. I do not know where such authority comes from or who it represents. I can realistically predict that no one living today will see 600 million Chinese integrated with 100 million Japanese, Turks integrated with Greeks, or Mohammedans with Israelis. . . . A cause for America first and last and always is essential to our existence. All organizations which are implementing such a cause are in the best interest of the country and are needed. The Birch Society is doing a great job in educating people and exposing such memoranda as I have referred to previously.

Walker's connections in the months preceding the assassination are both convoluted and intriguing.

A driver and aide to Walker in the fall of 1963 was the brother of Larrie Schmidt, who along with Bernard Weissman authored the infamous "Welcome Mr. Kennedy to Dallas . . ." ad that ran in the *Dallas Morning News* the morning of November 22. The ad, which carried a heavy black border, asked twelve loaded questions of Kennedy ending with "Why have you scrapped the Monroe Doctrine in favor of the 'Spirit of Moscow'?" Financial contributors to this anti-Kennedy ad included oilman H. L. Hunt's son, Nelson Bunker Hunt; Joseph Grinnan, volunteer coordinator for the local John Birch Society; and H. R. "Bum" Bright, former owner of the Dallas Cowboys. The ad was signed "The American Fact-Finding Committee," but Weissman admitted to the Warren Commission that the group was "formed strictly for the purpose of having a name to put in the paper."

Another Walker aide, Robert Allan Surrey, produced the "Wanted for Treason" leaflets that were distributed along the Kennedy motorcade route. Surrey later revealed to researcher Penn Jones that one of his close bridge-playing friends was none other than James Hosty, the FBI agent who, on orders, destroyed a note to the bureau from Lee Harvey Oswald after the assassination.

But perhaps the most significant connections between Walker and other assassination-connected characters were his contacts with anti-Castro Cubans and New Orleans.

Carlos Bringuier, the anti-Castro Cuban who was arrested with Lee Harvey

Oswald in New Orleans, was with Walker on the faculty of Christian Crusade Anti-communist Youth University. According to researcher Gary Shaw, the CIA retained Walker to arm and train Cuban exiles sometime after the Bay of Pigs Invasion.

One member of the militant Cuban exile group Alpha 66 was Filipe Vidal Santiago, who was frequently seen with Walker. Santiago was known to drive a 1957 Chevrolet. Such a car figured prominently in several aspects of the assassination case.

About an hour after the slaying of Dallas patrolman J. D. Tippit, police dispatchers broadcast a pickup order for a 1957 Chevrolet last seen at the intersection where Tippit was killed. The charge was: "Investigation of carrying a concealed weapon." The license number given by police registered to a Dallas man who told researchers he sold the car prior to September 1963, indicating the license plate reported on November 22 may have been stolen. This—and other instances of cars with illegitimate license plates around the Tippit slaying and Oswald's rooming house—were never adequately investigated.

Among the evidence that led the Warren Commission to conclude that it was Oswald who shot at General Walker were three photographs made of Walker's Dallas home found in Oswald's belongings. Commission photo experts said backgrounds of the pictures indicated they were made no later than March 10, one month before the attack on Walker and two days before mail orders were sent off for Oswald's pistol and the Carcano rifle.

In one of the photographs is a 1957 Chevrolet in Walker's driveway. This photo—as shown in Warren Commission Exhibit 5—has a hole in it obliterating the car's license number.

In FBI reports, R. B. Stovall, one of the Dallas detectives who confiscated Oswald's belongings from the Paine home in Irving, is quoted as saying:

> At the time he observed this photograph [the detective] surmised that Oswald had evidently taken the license plate number area out of the photograph to keep anyone from identifying the owner of that automobile. He advised he is positive the photograph was mutilated as shown in Commission Exhibit 5 at the time they recovered it at the Paine residence.

According to the bureau, Stovall's partner, Guy Rose, commented:

> He had noted that someone had torn out a section on the automobile, which area contains the license plate for the 1957 Chevrolet. . . . He stated . . . that it had been mutilated at the time they had recovered the box containing the photographs.

However, during her Warren Commission testimony, Marina Oswald made it clear that the hole was not there when she was shown the photo by the FBI.

She told Commission attorney Wesley Liebeler:

When the FBI first showed me this photograph, I remember that the license plate, the number of the license plate was on this car, on this photograph. It had the white and black numbers. There was no black spot that I see on it now. When Lee showed me this photograph there was the number on the license plate on this picture. . . . This black spot is so striking I would have remembered it if it were on the photograph that Lee showed me or the FBI. . . . There was no hole in the original when they showed it to me—I'm positive of it.

Someone is lying. If the license number was obliterated while in the hands of the FBI, as stated by Marina Oswald, this is clear evidence of official destruction of evidence.

The truth of the matter came in 1969 with the publication of Dallas police chief Jesse Curry's *JFK Assassination File*. On page 113 is a police photograph of Oswald's belongings and in the foreground is the Walker photograph with the Chevrolet's license-plate number intact. This piece of evidence was altered while in the hands of the authorities.

Apparently this criminal action disturbed at least one Warren Commission staff member. In 1966, two years after the Warren Commission had concluded its work, attorney Liebeler wrote a letter to Charles Klihr, a volunteer worker for General Walker, stating:

The [Oswald] picture was mutilated by someone in such a manner that the license plate is no longer visible. When we noticed this during the investigation we asked the FBI to determine whose car it was. They asked [Walker aide] Surrey about it and he told them he thought it was your car. I find no indication that FBI agents talked with you about the matter, however. . . . I would appreciate it very much if you would let me know whether or not the FBI did interview you about this and if you were able to identify the car as your own.

There is no record as to Klihr's response to Liebeler's letter.

All of these strange connections take on more sinister tones when viewed with the possibility that General Walker may have even been in contact with Oswald, his assassin Jack Ruby, or both.

A tenuous tie may be a St. Paul, Minnesota, man named John Martin, who was an acquaintance of General Walker's and filmed him in his Dallas home in the late summer of 1963. Incredibly, Martin journeyed on to New Orleans, where on September 9 he photographed Lee Harvey Oswald handing out Fair Play for Cuba Committee material on the same roll of film.

Walker's connections in New Orleans were many and substantial, ranging from anti-Castro Cubans in touch with David Ferrie and Guy Banister to Louisiana political leaders. According to Louisiana State Police files, Walker was involved in several hurried and secret meetings in New Orleans during the two days prior to the assassination, including a conference with Judge Leander Perez, one of the state's most powerful men.

In fact, Walker was on a Braniff flight from New Orleans when Kennedy was assassinated. He reportedly became upset when word of the assassination was broadcast over the plane's loudspeaker and roamed up and down the aisle telling fellow passengers to remember that he was on that flight at the time of Kennedy's death.

According to *Farewell America*, a book by French intelligence agents, Walker later joined oilman H. L. Hunt in a secret hideaway in Mexico where "they remained for a month, protected by personal guards, under the impassive eyes of the FBI."

Also in this book, the authors state that in late summer of 1963 David Ferrie introduced Oswald to both General Walker and Clay Shaw, the director of the International Trade Mart later prosecuted by district attorney Jim Garrison.

Author Anthony Summers reported that Walker gave a talk in Dallas that may have been attended by Lee Harvey Oswald. He quotes another member of the audience who claimed Oswald sat at the back of the room during a meeting of the Directorio Revolucionario Estudiantil, an anti-Castro Cuban group. Oswald reportedly said nothing during the fund-raising meeting.

Then there are disconcerting reports that Walker knew Oswald's killer, Dallas nightclub owner Jack Ruby. Researcher Penn Jones has stated that Ruby made no secret of his admiration for the resigned general and that he once stated that Walker was "100 percent right" in his belief that Cuba should be taken back from Castro. More significant are the statements of former Walker employee William McEwan Duff. According to Warren Commission Document 1316-B, Duff claimed that Ruby visited Walker's home on a monthly basis between December 1962 and March 1963, shortly before Walker was fired upon.

Many researchers feel it is also significant that General Walker's name and telephone number were found in Oswald's address book. They believe this may indicate a possible connection between the two. However, Walker maintained he never met Oswald, and the Warren Commission concluded, "Although Oswald's notebook contained Walker's name and telephone number there is no evidence that they knew each other. It is claimed that this information was inserted at the time Oswald was planning his attack on Walker."

Yet another odd connection between Walker and the assassination involved car salesman Warren Reynolds. Reynolds chased the murderer of Patrolman Tippit but initially was unable to identify Oswald as the killer. Two months later, Reynolds was shot from ambush and after recovering was befriended by General Walker. After consulting with Walker, Reynolds was able to identify Oswald to the Warren Commission in July 1964.

The Warren Commission concluded, without even bothering to talk to Walker, that his assailant had been Oswald. The evidence used to reach this conclusion was the testimony of Marina Oswald, a note discovered at the Paine home, photographs

Oswald reportedly took of the Walker home, and identification of a bullet found at the crime scene.

Marina Oswald's testimony has been called into question in a number of matters, and her stories of murder attempts by Oswald on Walker and Richard Nixon are fraught with inconsistencies and omissions. It is also curious that her first statement that Oswald tried to kill Walker came on December 3, 1963, about a week after a West German newspaper reported there might be a connection between the Walker shooting and the assassination. The Warren Commission reported that the German news story was "fabricated by the editor," but then advanced the same allegation.

The note in question turned up only after the Kennedy assassination, when Secret Service agents showed the note to Ruth Paine and asked her to identify it. The undated note, written in Russian, reportedly had been left in a Russian volume titled *Book of Useful Advice* and was only discovered nearly two weeks after the assassination when it fell out of the book's pages. Government handwriting experts declared that Oswald wrote the message, and Marina conveniently told investigators she thought she saw it shortly after the Walker shooting.

However, Ruth Paine told the Warren Commission about the Dallas police search of her home mentioning, "Before I left they were leafing through books to see if anything fell out but that is all I saw." Mrs. Paine's testimony fuels the suspicion that authorities may have planted the note.

In it, Oswald detailed instructions to his wife on what to do in his absence. He told her where to find the mailbox key, that the current bills had been paid, and even said she could "throw out or give my clothing, etc. away." Two noteworthy passages stated:

> Send the information as to what has happened to me to the Embassy [undoubtedly the Russian embassy, which Oswald had been contacting periodically] and include newspaper clippings—should there be anything about me in the newspapers. I believe that the Embassy will come quickly to your assistance on learning everything.
>
> If I am alive and taken prisoner, the city jail is located at the end of the bridge through which we always passed on going to the city (right in the beginning of the city after crossing the bridge).

These two sections raise troublesome questions for the official version of the Walker shooting.

Since Marina reportedly knew nothing of her husband's attack on Walker in advance, how could she be expected to watch for stories on Oswald in the newspapers, since any such account would report only that an unknown sniper had fired on the general? Also, why would a supposed American defector to Russia who returned home expect assistance for his family from the Soviet embassy if he were charged with the attempted murder of a prominent right-wing Dallasite?

Warren Commission critic Sylvia Meagher wrote, "I suggest that Oswald wrote the undated letter in relation to a project other than the attack on General Walker—one that also involved risk of arrest or death—and that Marina was informed about her husband's plans in advance."

As noted by the Warren Commission, Oswald's letter "appeared to be the work of a man expecting to be killed, or imprisoned, or to disappear." Yet at the time of the Walker incident, he had no money, no passport, and no reasonable expectation of escape.

The bullet found in Walker's home also presents problems. Contemporary news stories of the April 10 incident quote Dallas police as saying the recovered bullet was "identified as a 30.06," not a 6.5-millimeter Mannlicher-Carcano.

In 1975, researcher George Michael Evica received FBI spectrographic analyses of a bullet (CE 399) and bullet fragments reportedly recovered in the assassination investigation. According to Evica, these scientific reports, termed "inconclusive" by Director Hoover when reporting to the Warren Commission, revealed:

> The bullet recovered in the assassination attempt on General Walker does not match either CE 399 or two fragments recovered from President Kennedy's limousine; the Warren Commission's linking of Lee Harvey Oswald to the General Walker assassination attempt is seriously weakened.

Further confusion over the bullet has been raised by Walker himself, who claimed the bullet exhibited by the House Select Committee on Assassinations is not the same bullet recovered from his home in 1963. He said the original slug was so mangled as to be hardly recognizable as a bullet.

After studying the government's evidence carefully, author Meagher concluded, "Despite the [Warren] Commission's reliance on the testimony of Marina Oswald, compelling evidence virtually excludes the use of the Carcano rifle in the attempt on the life of General Walker."

And even if Oswald were responsible for the Walker shooting, there is evidence that he did not act alone.

Walter Kirk Coleman, who in 1963 was a fourteen-year-old neighbor to Walker, told police he heard the shot and, peeking over a fence, saw some men speeding down the alley in a light green or light blue Ford, either a 1959 or 1960 model. Coleman also said he saw another car, a 1958 black Chevrolet with white down the side, in a church parking lot adjacent to Walker's house. The car door was open and a man was bending over the backseat as though he was placing something on the floor of the car. At the time of the Warren Commission, Coleman was not called to testify and in fact told Walker that authorities had ordered him not to discuss the incident.

Just prior to the Walker shooting, two of the general's aides saw suspicious activity around his home. Walker aide Robert Surrey said on April 6 he saw two men prowling around the house, peeking in windows. Surrey said the pair were driving a 1963 dark purple or brown Ford with no license plates.

And Walker aide Max Claunch told researcher Gary Shaw that a few nights before the shooting incident he noticed a "Cuban or dark-complected man in a 1957 Chevrolet" cruise around Walker's home several times.

The problems with the official version of the Walker shooting as well as the many unfollowed leads in this area are troubling to assassination researchers.

On January 14, 1963, George Wallace was sworn in as governor of Alabama, pledging, "Segregation now, segregation tomorrow, and segregation forever."

In August, following further unrest and violence in the South, Dr. Martin Luther King Jr. led some 250,000 people in a Freedom March on Washington. Here he proclaimed, "There will be neither rest nor tranquility in America until the Negro is granted his citizenship rights."

The march took place less than three months after President Kennedy had finally submitted his own civil rights bill in Congress. Resistance to Kennedy's plans was widespread although a June 1963 Gallup poll indicated 59 percent of the population approved of the president and his programs.

On June 12, 1963, Georgia senator Richard B. Russell promised other southern senators, "To me, the President's legislative proposals are clearly destructive of the American system and the constitutional rights of American citizens. I shall oppose them with every means and resource at my command."

Within six months, Russell was sitting as a member of the Warren Commission, charged with finding the truth of Kennedy's death.

One government employee who watched the famous Washington monuments become surrounded by demonstrators was FBI director J. Edgar Hoover. The strange and obsessed Hoover was particularly anxious over King and his civil rights movement. The aging director not only saw his essentially southern way of life threatened but was convinced that King's organization was being directed by communists.

William Sullivan, at the time Hoover's man in charge of intelligence operations for the bureau, wrote:

> Hoover told me that he felt that King was, or could become, a serious threat to the security of the country. He pointed out that King was an instrument of the Communist Party, and he wanted it proved that King had a relationship with the Soviet bloc. Hoover also made it clear that he wanted evidence developed that would prove that King was embezzling or misusing large sums of money contributed to him and his organization.

According to Sullivan, FBI agents jumped to please the director. He noted, "We gave him what he wanted—under the threat of being out on the street if we didn't agree."

Hoover's vendetta continued against King until the black leader was himself cut down by an assassin's bullet in 1968. Behind this vendetta was COINTELPRO, Hoover's secret counterintelligence program, created in part "to expose, disrupt, misdirect, or otherwise neutralize" King and his Southern Christian Leadership Conference. Suspicions that Hoover's FBI or some other part of the federal government played a role in King's death were heightened in 1999 when a Memphis jury found Memphis restaurant owner Loyd Jowers guilty of arranging an assassination plot also involving governmental agencies. In the wake of the verdict, King's widow, Coretta Scott King, echoed allegations in the Kennedy assassination by stating:

> There is abundant evidence of a major high-level conspiracy in the assassination of my husband, Martin Luther King, Jr. . . . The conspiracy of the Mafia, local, state and federal government agencies, were deeply involved in the assassination of my husband. The jury also affirmed overwhelming evidence that identified someone else, not James Earl Ray, as the shooter, and that Mr. Ray was set up to take the blame.

Also secretly targeted for careful scrutiny under this program were President Kennedy and Hoover's own boss, attorney general Robert Kennedy.

According to Sullivan, "Hoover was desperately trying to catch Bobby red-handed at anything . . . and was always gathering damaging material on Jack Kennedy, which the President, with his active social life, seemed more than willing to provide."

Both Kennedy brothers eventually supported King and the civil rights program as they came to realize that its adoption as official policy was inevitable. As Kennedy biographer John H. Davis pointed out, "The most potentially dangerous enemy to emerge from Kennedy's civil rights policy was the FBI and its director."

From the ranks of angered segregationists came one man with a prophetic vision of Kennedy's death.

The Miami Prophet

On November 9, 1963, a Miami police informant named William Somersett met with Joseph A. Milteer, a wealthy right-wing extremist who promptly began to outline the assassination of President Kennedy.

Milteer was a leader of the archconservative National States Rights Party as well as a member of other groups such as the Congress of Freedom and the White Citizens' Council of Atlanta. Somersett had infiltrated the States Rights' Party and secretly recorded Milteer's conversation.

The tape, later turned over to Miami police, recorded Milteer stating during Kennedy's impending visit to Miami, "You can bet your bottom dollar he is going to have a lot to say about the Cubans, there are so many of them here. . . . The more bodyguards he has, the easier it is to get him . . . from an office building with a high-powered rifle. . . . He knows he's a marked man."

Somersett said, "They are really going to try to kill him?" Milteer responded, "Oh, yeah, it's in the works. . . . (An investigation) wouldn't leave any stone unturned there, no way. They will pick up somebody within hours afterward . . . just to throw the public off." Captain Charles Sapp, head of Miami's Police Intelligence Bureau, was concerned enough with Milteer's remarks to alert both the FBI and the Secret Service.

Again, apparently no word of this right-wing plot reached Secret Service agents involved in Kennedy's Dallas trip. In later years, however, Sapp recalled that plans for a Miami motorcade were scrapped and the president instead flew to a scheduled speech by helicopter.

On the day of the assassination, Milteer telephoned Somersett, saying he was in Dallas and that Kennedy was due there shortly. Milteer commented that Kennedy would never be seen in Miami again.

While the House Select Committee on Assassinations was unable to confirm Milteer's presence in Dallas during the assassination, it also failed to prove he was elsewhere. Texas researcher Jack White claimed to have located a photograph of a man bearing a striking resemblance to Milteer standing in the crowd near the Texas School Book Depository.

Back in Miami after the assassination, Milteer again met with Somersett and said, "Everything ran true to form. I guess you thought I was kidding you when I said he would be killed from a window with a high-powered rifle. . . . I don't do any guessing." Milteer said not to worry about the capture of Oswald, "because he doesn't know anything." "The right-wing is in the clear," added Milteer. "The patriots have outsmarted the communist group in order that the communists would carry out the plan without the right wing becoming involved."

The FBI questioned Milteer on November 27 and he denied making any such statements. And while some information of the Milteer incident was belatedly turned over to the Warren Commission, there is no mention of Milteer in its report or twenty-six volumes. Before the prophetic Milteer could be questioned further about his apparent foreknowledge of Kennedy's assassination, he died after receiving burns when a heater exploded in a vacation cabin.

The Milteer episode raises a number of questions, not the least of which is why his specific knowledge of a threat against the president—tape-recorded by a police agency—was not passed along to FBI and Secret Service personnel in Dallas.

But the racial unrest that rocked the United States in the 1960s was not President Kennedy's only domestic problem. He was being verbally attacked not only by poor minorities with rising expectations, but also by wealthy businessmen who felt threatened by his announced social reforms.

Big business was already leery of Kennedy, who as a senator had opposed the Taft-Hartley law, aimed at curbing the power of labor unions, and who as president had failed to consult the business world before making certain appointments. The fears of big business increased in the spring of 1962 when Kennedy used the power of the presidency to force US steel manufacturers to roll back recent price increases.

Kennedy already had served notice on the giant steel companies in September

1961, when he sent a letter to industry leaders warning them against any price increases. In his letter, Kennedy rationalized:

> The steel industry, in short, can look forward to good profits without an increase in prices. Since 1947, iron and steel common stocks prices have risen 397 percent; this is a much better performance than common stock prices in general.

On April 6, 1962, at the request of the federal government, the Steelworkers Union agreed to limit its wage demands to a ten-cent hourly increase beginning that summer. Then on April 11, US Steel and five other major steel companies announced a 3.5 percent hike in the cost of steel. Incensed, Kennedy told the news media:

> The American people will find it hard, as I do, to accept a situation in which a tiny handful of steel executives, whose pursuit of private power and profit exceeds their sense of public responsibility, can show such utter contempt for the interest of 185 million Americans.

Administration officials suggested an FBI investigation and on April 13, the Defense Department awarded a $5 million contract to a smaller steel firm that had not raised prices. The next day, the six major firms announced their price increase had been rescinded.

Kennedy's denunciation of the steel executives sent shock waves through the business community. He had demonstrated that a proactive president could influence major corporate decisions. A *US News and World Report* editor wrote, "What happened is frightening not only to steel people but to industry generally. . . . President Kennedy had the public interest at heart in acting as he did, but the results may not in the long run be what he intended them to be."

Other results of the Kennedy administration were infuriating corporate executives. Mergers were becoming widespread in the business world and Attorney General Kennedy and his trust busters were taking a dim view of them.

During 1963, the Justice Department's Antitrust Division won forty-five of forty-six cases; asked a federal court to force General Motors Corporation to dispose of its locomotive business while charging the firm with monopolizing the manufacture and sale of intercity buses; and ordered General Dynamics to drop a division dealing with industrial gases.

Business and political leaders began to regret that the winner of the 1960 presidential election had not been Richard M. Nixon.

Nixon and the JFK Assassination

Most Americans remember Richard Milhous Nixon as the only US president to resign his office under the threat of certain impeachment.

Few know of or recall Nixon's connection with the Kennedy assassination, including that Nixon was in Dallas the day Kennedy died but couldn't recall that fact when interviewed by the FBI on February 28, 1964. United Press International reported the day after the assassination, "Richard Nixon, the former vice president who lost the presidential election to President Kennedy in 1960, is shown Friday after he arrived at Idlewild Airport [now John F. Kennedy International] in New York following a flight from Dallas, Tex., where he had been on a business trip."

Born January 9, 1913, in Yorba Linda, California, Nixon was a self-made man who reached the pinnacles of power after struggling up from a background of meager financial circumstances.

Nixon wanted to attend Harvard like young Kennedy, but was forced to settle for California's Whittier College, where he honed his skills as a debater. He went on to graduate from Duke University Law School in Durham, North Carolina, then unsuccessfully tried to join the FBI.

Shortly after Pearl Harbor, Nixon took a job with the tire-rationing department of the Office of Price Administration in Washington. It is interesting that Nixon's lifelong friend, Florida entrepreneur Charles "Bebe" Rebozo, began his profitable career selling recapped tires. Although Nixon claimed he did not meet Rebozo until 1948 while vacationing in Florida after the Alger Hiss spy case, some researchers say the pair were in contact during the war.

Later in the war, Nixon enlisted in the Navy and served in the South Pacific, where on one island he built a small shack used for high-stakes gambling and drinking.

In 1946, Nixon successfully ran for Congress after labeling his opponent, incumbent congressman Jerry Voorhis, a "friend of the communists." With his anticommunist credentials, Nixon was immediately named to the House Un-American Activities Committee, where his name became nationally known due to his part in the case of Alger Hiss, a government official accused of being a Soviet spy.

By 1950, the ambitious Nixon was ready to run for a Senate seat. His opponent was a liberal former Hollywood actress named Helen Douglas. Nixon painted Douglas as a friend of communism and dubbed her the "pink lady." He accused her of voting with a "notorious communist-line congressman" from New York, failing to mention that Nixon himself had voted with this same congressman 112 times. Such campaign tactics earned Nixon the epithet "Tricky Dick." But they also proved effective. Nixon beat Douglas by nearly 700,000 votes.

The man most responsible for Nixon's smear tactics was his close friend and campaign manager Murray Chotiner, a lawyer who represented ranking mobsters and who had connections leading back to reputed New Orleans Mafia chief Carlos Marcello and Teamsters leader Jimmy Hoffa.

In 1952, after only six years in politics, Nixon became vice president under Dwight Eisenhower, thanks to the support of his political mentor, former New York governor Thomas Dewey, and his undermining of the favorite-son candidacy of fellow Californian Earl Warren.

Throughout the Eisenhower years, the war-hero president snubbed Nixon both politically and socially. In 1960, when Eisenhower was asked what major decisions Nixon had participated in, he caustically replied, "If you give me a week, I might think of one."

But Nixon was busy building up his own power base with men of dubious backgrounds.

In his memoirs, mobster Mickey Cohen wrote that he gave Chotiner $5,000 for Nixon's 1946 congressional campaign and raised $75,000 from Las Vegas gamblers for Nixon's 1950 Senate race.

Furthermore, Ed Partin, a former aide to Jimmy Hoffa turned government informant, detailed a meeting between Hoffa and New Orleans mob boss Carlos Marcello at the height of the 1960 presidential campaign: "I was right there, listening to the conversation. Marcello had a suitcase filled with $500,000 cash which was going to Nixon. It was a half-million-dollar contribution. The other half [of a promised $1 million] was coming from the mob boys in New Jersey and Florida."

Nixon's organized-crime contacts apparently continued even after he resigned the presidency in disgrace. During a 1975 golf tournament at La Costa Country Club in California, Nixon's golfing companions included Allen Dorfman, a mob-Teamster financial coordinator, and Tony Provenzano, a former Teamster official and convicted Mafia killer.

Investigative authors Carl Oglesby, Howard Kohn, David Scheim, and others have revealed that Nixon was a frequent visitor to Cuba during the early 1950s and was in contact with confederates of organized-crime financial wizard Meyer Lansky.

When Fidel Castro gained power in Cuba, Lansky was one of those mob chieftains who wanted him overthrown. An attempt with CIA officers to plan an invasion of Cuba was initiated by Eisenhower's White House political action officer, Richard Nixon. In his book *Six Crises*, Nixon wrote, "The covert training of Cuban exiles by the CIA was due in substantial part, at least, to my efforts. This had been adopted as a policy as a result of my direct support."

Before the invasion could be launched, a serious snag occurred for Nixon and his backers—he lost the 1960 election to John F. Kennedy.

Rather than bide his time waiting for the next presidential election, Nixon ran against Pat Brown for the California governorship in 1962. He was handily defeated, especially after news broke of a secret $200,000 loan from billionaire Howard Hughes to Nixon's brother.

Within two years, Nixon was back on the political stage, campaigning for Republican candidates. GOP stalwarts repaid this activity by again nominating Richard Nixon for president in August 1968. By then, of course, both John and Robert Kennedy were dead.

During the Nixon years, his friends in organized crime were not forgotten. The Nixon administration intervened in at least twenty trials of crime figures, ostensibly to protect "intelligence sources and methods." In 1973, Nixon's attorney general, Richard Kleindienst, denied an FBI request to continue an electronic surveillance operation that was beginning to penetrate connections between the Mafia and the Teamsters. Neither did Nixon forget his friend Jimmy Hoffa, whom he pardoned in 1971 despite recommendations against such action.

But of all Nixon's possible crime connections, the most intriguing involves Jack Ruby, the killer of Lee Harvey Oswald. In 1975, Trowbridge Ford, a political science associate professor at College of the Holy Cross in Worcester, Massachusetts, was poring over a stack of recently released FBI documents. Ford was astonished to discover a memorandum written by a bureau staff assistant to a government panel looking into organized-crime activity in 1947. The memo stated:

> It is my sworn statement that one Jack Rubenstein of Chicago, noted as a potential witness for hearings of the House Committee on Un-American Activities, is performing information functions for the staff of congressman Richard Nixon, Republican of California. It is requested Rubenstein not be called for open testimony in the aforementioned hearings.

Later in 1947, Chicago's Rubenstein moved to Dallas and shortened his name to Jack Ruby.

The idea that Jack Ruby had worked for Nixon should have set off the national news media. Instead, FBI officials told Ford that the document he discovered was a fake and the story was quickly dropped. Here once again we see an FBI statement admitting that fake or phony documents reside in its files.

By the early 1980s, Ford told this author he had studied literally thousands of genuine FBI documents and had slowly come to the conclusion that the Nixon-Ruby memo was probably legitimate. Regardless, the matter raises even more suspicion when viewed with Nixon's presence in Dallas the day Kennedy died.

On November 20, 1963, Nixon arrived in Dallas, where a convention of the American Bottlers of Carbonated Beverages was being held. A newsman from the *Dallas Times Herald* interviewed Nixon and wrote:

> The former Vice President arrived in Dallas Wednesday night to attend a board meeting of Pepsi-Cola Company, which is represented by his New York law partnership. He plans to leave Dallas Friday morning a few hours before the arrival of President Kennedy. Mr. Nixon said that although he planned to talk by telephone to several Dallas Republican leaders, he had no plans for a formal meeting with them.

Interestingly, researcher Richard Sprague examined Pepsi-Cola corporate records and found no board meeting was held in Dallas in 1963.

The connections and politics of Pepsi-Cola deserve serious attention from assassination researchers. The soft-drink company's advertising was handled by J. Walter Thompson, the giant public relations firm that also worked to sell the Pentagon's brand of "peace."

Nixon was longtime friends with Pepsi-Cola president Don Kendall and, later as US president, it was Nixon who opened the lucrative Soviet soft-drink market to Pepsi. A Justice Department investigation into this transaction revealed that a "high government official had all the red tape done away with so Pepsico could obtain the Soviet franchise without any competition."

Pepsi went on to help those who had helped the company. In 1973, Kendall formed the Save the Presidency Committee, which sought to protect Nixon from the wrath of Watergate investigations.

It is especially interesting to note that Cartha DeLoach, the FBI official who was chief liaison between Director Hoover and President Lyndon Johnson, later joined Pepsi-Cola.

With Nixon in Dallas was Pepsi-Cola heiress and actress Joan Crawford. Both Nixon and Crawford made comments in the Dallas newspapers to the effect that they, unlike the president, didn't need Secret Service protection, and they intimated that the nation was upset with Kennedy's policies. It has been suggested that this taunting may have been responsible for Kennedy's critical decision not to have the Plexiglas top placed on his limousine on November 22.

Nixon also caused a stir in Dallas when he suggested that Lyndon Johnson would be dropped from the 1964 Democratic national ticket. Quoted in the November 22, 1963, *Dallas Morning News*, Nixon stated, "We must remember that President Kennedy and his advisers are practical politicians. . . . Lyndon was chosen in 1960 because he could help the ticket in the South. Now he is becoming a political liability in the South, just as he is in the North."

On the morning of November 22, Nixon was driven to Love Field in Dallas, where he boarded American Airlines Flight 82 for New York. Less than two hours after Nixon left, Air Force One landed at Love Field with the doomed Kennedy.

Three months later, the Warren Commission asked the FBI to investigate Marina Oswald's allegation that her husband had tried to kill Nixon during a visit to Dallas. The FBI report dealing with Nixon's interview stated:

> On February 28, 1964, the Honorable Richard M. Nixon, former Vice President of the US, was contacted by Assistant Director in charge of the New York Office, John F. Malone, and furnished the following information:
>
> Mr. Nixon advised that the only time he was in Dallas, Texas, during 1963 was two days prior to the assassination of President John F. Kennedy.

The question of whether Nixon was merely forgetful or dissembling in his comment to the FBI might have been cleared up by yet another bureau report, "Letter of FBI of June 29, 1964, concerning Richard Nixon." However, this document was reported missing from the National Archives in 1976.

Nixon's recollection improved during a 1967 interview with journalist Jules Witcover. Speaking about the assassination, Nixon said:

I was in a taxicab when I got the news. I had been in Dallas attending a meeting. I flew back to New York the next morning. It must have happened just as my plane was landing. My cab stopped for a light in Queens and a guy ran over and said, "Have you got a radio? The President's been wounded." I thought, "Oh, my God, it must have been one of the nuts." A half hour later I got to my apartment and the doorman told me he was dead. I called J. Edgar Hoover and asked him, "What happened? Was it one of the nuts?" Hoover said, "No, it was a communist."

The supposed attack on Nixon by Oswald undoubtedly is one of the more ludicrous incidents of the Warren Commission investigation—and it is a prime example of the unreliability of Marina Oswald's testimony.

In early February 1964, when Marina Oswald first testified to the Commission, she failed to mention the incident when asked if her husband had expressed any hostility toward any official of the United States. In June, her memory jogged by an FBI report from Oswald's brother Robert, she said that just a few days before Oswald left for New Orleans on April 24, 1963, he had put on a good suit after reading a morning newspaper. She told the Commission:

I saw that he took a pistol. I asked him where he was going and why he was getting dressed. He answered, "Nixon is coming. I want to go and have a look." . . . I called him into the bathroom and I closed the door and I wanted to prevent him and then I started to cry. And I told him that he shouldn't do this, and that he had promised me.

She told the Commission she locked him in the bathroom to prevent him from trying to shoot Nixon. However, as confirmed by an FBI investigation, the bathroom—like all others—locked from the inside. Accordingly, in a subsequent interview with the Commission, Marina amended her story by saying she held the bathroom door for hours to prevent Oswald from leaving.

The Commission, upon learning that Nixon was not even in Dallas at any time near this incident, decided that Marina may have been mistaken and that the target of Oswald's pistol may have been Vice President Johnson, who had visited Dallas on April 23.

In an Oval Office meeting on June 23, 1972—just five days after the Nixon-connected burglars were caught in the Watergate office complex—Nixon spoke with his chief of staff, H. R. Haldeman, saying, "Of course, this Hunt [Watergate burglar and CIA liaison with the anti-Castro Cubans E. Howard Hunt], that will uncover a lot of things. You open that scab, there's a hell of a lot of things, and we feel that it would be very detrimental to have this thing go any further. . . . The President believes that it is going to open the whole Bay of Pigs thing up again."

After telling Nixon that the FBI was aware of CIA operatives' involvement in the Watergate affair, Haldeman told his chief, "The problem is it tracks back to the Bay of Pigs and it tracks back to some other, the leads run out to people who had no involvement in this, except by contracts and connection, but it gets into areas that are liable to be realized."

What could Nixon and Haldeman have been talking about? The "whole Bay of Pigs thing" had been over for more than ten years. Nixon was out of office when the actual invasion began and the assault's disastrous consequences were a matter of historical record. Could they have been circuitously referring to the interlocking connections between CIA agents, anti-Castro Cubans, and mobsters that likely resulted in the Kennedy assassination? Did they themselves have some sort of insider knowledge of this event?

Haldeman appeared to answer these questions a year later in his 1994 book, *The Haldeman Diaries: Inside the Nixon White House*. He wrote, "It seems that in all of those Nixon references to the Bay of Pigs, he was actually referring to the Kennedy assassination."

It also is significant to recall that when Hunt later demanded $2 million to keep quiet about what he knew, Nixon agreed and the money was raised. Some of this money was being ferried by Hunt's first wife, Dorothy, when she died in the crash of United Airlines Flight 553 in December 1972.

It may also be significant to consider the number of people connected with the Warren Commission who were hired or considered for employment by Nixon's circle during Watergate.

Nixon White House counsel John Dean's lawyer was Commission administrative aide Charles N. Shaffer; Nixon counsel John Ehrlichman hired Commission senior counsel Joseph Ball as his lawyer; Nixon initially wanted Commission general counsel J. Lee Rankin as Watergate prosecutor, then wanted Commission member John McCloy but later accepted Commission special counsel Leon Jaworski (who represented Texas Attorney General Waggoner Carr); Nixon named Rankin to "edit" White House tapes; Nixon accepted Commission senior counsel Albert E. Jenner as chief minority counsel for the House Judiciary Committee considering Nixon's impeachment; and Nixon asked Commission counsel Arlen Specter to help with his defense.

Specter, the former senator from Pennsylvania, was the chief architect of the controversial "single-bullet theory" for the Warren Commission. He was a protégé of Nixon's attorney general, John Mitchell, and had served as co-chairman of the Pennsylvania division of the Committee to Re-Elect the President (CREEP) in 1972.

Commission attorney David Belin—long its most ardent supporter—headed Lawyers for Nixon.

In the final days of Watergate, organized-crime investigator Dan E. Moldea revealed that military authorities, including Nixon's chief of staff, General Alexander Haig, began to connect their chief with several mobsters, including Florida's Santos Trafficante, believed responsible for setting up heroin routes from Vietnam and making payoffs to Nixon associates.

Moldea quoted a Justice Department official as saying:

The whole goddamn thing is too frightening to think about. We're talking about the President of the United States . . . a man who pardoned organized crime figures after millions were spent by the government putting them away, a guy who's had these connections since he was a congressman in the 1940s. I guess the real shame is that we'll never know the whole story, it'll never come out.

In a final nose-thumbing to the American people, Nixon appointed former Warren Commission member Gerald R. Ford as vice president after Spiro Agnew resigned in 1973 under tax evasion charges.

One of Ford's first public actions was to pardon Nixon of any crimes—past, present, or future.

If there was a plot to assassinate Kennedy, wouldn't someone have become aware of it?

There are many indications that in the fall of 1963, certain persons did.

We already have learned of persons seemingly aware of Kennedy's impending death, such as racist J. A. Milteer. It appears that some corporate leaders also may have been aware of Kennedy's fate.

A Killing on Wall Street

In the thirty minutes following Kennedy's assassination in Dallas, the Dow Jones average fell more than 21.16 points. An estimated 6 million shares of stock changed hands, wiping out about $15 billion in paper values on the New York Stock Exchange alone. It was the greatest stock market panic since 1929. The panic and confusion was such that the Securities and Exchange Commission closed the stock exchange shortly after 2 p.m., more than eighty minutes before normal closing time. It was the first emergency shutdown of the stock market since August 1933.

A few sharp investors—or perhaps individuals with knowledge of what was to come—had taken "short" positions in scattered areas of the market. That is, some stocks unaccountably were sold before the market dropped, indicating some people may have had advance word that something momentous was about to happen and that stock values would drop.

When the stock market reopened on November 26, 1963—just four days after the assassination—the New York Stock Exchange made a record $21 billion advance, more than regaining the losses incurred the day Kennedy died. It was the biggest single-day rise in the history of the stock market. More huge profits were made. No one has publicly identified the men who made their own private killing in the stock market, but it has been estimated that the profits made on November 22 alone totaled more than $500 million.

At least one author has suggested that the immense amount of money that changed hands on November 22, 1963, was the motivation behind Kennedy's death. And while most researchers reject this idea, many do believe that certain individuals—using insider information on the impending assassination—could not resist the temptation to profit from the tragedy.

Another overlooked aspect of Kennedy's attempt to reform American society involves money.

At the time of the War Between the States, president Abraham Lincoln found the big banks demanded high interest rates, from 24 to 36 percent, to fund the war. Rather than saddle the nation with unredeemable debt, he ordered the US Treasury to issue new legal tender—United States notes. Previously, demand notes had been issued. They were simply promissory paper redeemable for gold or silver. United States notes, the longest serving paper money in US history, were fiat notes, money issued through the treasury backed only by faith in the federal government. Under Lincoln's orders, these new notes, popularly known as greenbacks, replaced demand notes. The greenback currency worked so well that political struggles and court cases continued into the late 1870s, when silver certificates again began to be issued.

Kennedy understood, as did Lincoln, that by returning to the Constitution, which states that only Congress shall coin and regulate money, the soaring national debt could be reduced by not paying interest to the bankers of the Federal Reserve System, who print paper money, then loan it to the government at interest. He moved in this area on June 4, 1963, by signing Executive Order (EO) 11110 authorizing the Treasury Department to start printing and issuing silver certificates based on the remaining silver in the US Treasury and the Commodity Credit Corporation. Gold-backed currency in the United States had ended in 1933.

Kennedy's executive order stated:

> The authority vested in the President by paragraph (b) of section 43 of the Act of May 12, 1933, as amended (31 USC. 821(b)), to issue silver certificates against any silver bullion, silver, or standard silver dollars in the Treasury not then held for redemption of an outstanding silver certificates, to prescribe the denominations of such silver certificates, and to coin standard silver dollars and subsidiary silver currency for their redemption, and (b) By revoking subparagraphs (b) and (c) of paragraph 2 thereof.

There has been considerable confusion and misunderstanding over EO 11110. From the available evidence—and there appears to be missing and even altered data—with this order JFK was making a surreptitious effort to return money-creation power from the privately owned Federal Reserve to the Treasury Department.

On the surface, EO 11110 appeared to be a simple change to president Harry

Truman's Executive Order 10289 of 1951, which gave such power to the treasury through the issuance of treasury silver certificates. This silver, more than $100 million worth accumulated largely through reparations from World War I, was to be put in storage under the Agricultural Adjustment Act of 1933 and amended by the Gold Reserve Act of 1934. These acts also fully created the Commodity Credit Corporation and the Exchange Stabilization Fund, both of which held huge sums of money, some of which was being used for purposes such as funding covert intelligence activities.

In other words, EO 11110 allowed the treasury full access to silver certificates from the bowels of Fort Knox and would have drastically lowered the US government loan rate—and by inference interest payments—to the Federal Reserve. JFK was seeking to ease the inflation rate and this one order (EO 11110) would have accomplished just that. This would have placed more silver into the general population and paid off debt to the Federal Reserve.

JFK's EO 11110 expanded the Treasury Department's power to issue non-interest-bearing money from governmental reserves and edged out the US need to approach the Federal Reserve to print more interest-bearing Federal Reserve notes.

EO 11110 therefore allowed for the issuance of $4,292,893,815 in silver-backed treasury bills, called United States notes. That same day, Kennedy also signed a bill changing the backing of $1 and $2 bills from silver to gold, adding strength to the weakening US currency. Kennedy's successor, President Johnson, did nothing to change this situation. It was President Ronald Reagan who in September 1987 issued EO 12608 as part of a general clean-up of executive orders. EO 12608 revoked the section added by EO 11110. This effectively revoked the entire order. Today we continue to use interest-bearing Federal Reserve notes, and the deficit is more than $16 trillion, an all-time high.

The upshot of all this seemed to be Kennedy's attempt to increase the monetary and credit supply by infusing the economy with United States notes issued through the treasury rather than the private interest-charging Federal Reserve System.

And the fact remains that such interest-free United States notes were indeed issued and Kennedy showed signs of attempting to undercut the power of the heretofore unassailable Federal Reserve System.

Kennedy's comptroller of the currency, James J. Saxon, had been at odds with the powerful Federal Reserve Board for some time, encouraging broader investment and lending powers for banks that were not part of the Federal Reserve System. Saxon also had decided that non-Reserve banks could underwrite state and local general obligation bonds, again weakening the dominant Federal Reserve banks.

Considering that the battle over US monetary control by a monolithic central bank dates back to the founding of the Republic, some assassination researchers believe Kennedy's little-noted efforts to reform the money supply and curtail the Federal Reserve System may have cost him much more than just the enmity of the all-powerful international bankers. Many assassination researchers feel it was not a mere coincidence that Lincoln and Kennedy, the only two US presidents who attempted to issue interest-free money, were both shot in the head in public.

President Kennedy inched farther out on a limb with big business on January 17, 1963, when he presented both his administration's budget and proposals for tax reform that included a tax cut.

Kennedy's tax proposals included relieving the tax burden of low-income and elderly persons, revising tax treatment of capital gains for a better flow of capital funds, and broadening the base of individual and corporate income taxes to remove special privileges and loopholes and even to do away with the oil depletion allowance.

This last possibility brought the beleaguered president into direct confrontation with one of the most powerful and single-minded groups in America—wealthy oilmen.

Kennedy and Oilmen

The history of oil is replete with stories of unbounded greed, business chicanery, and even violence.

In 1923, the first major oil scandal occurred when it was discovered that president Warren G. Harding's secretary of the interior, Albert B. Fall, had accepted money from oilmen in exchange for secretly leasing drilling rights on government land in Wyoming known as the Teapot Dome.

By 1933, there were calls to make the vital oil industry a public utility with governmental controls. One of the men supporting this move was president Franklin Roosevelt's secretary of the interior, Harold Ickes. However, FDR was finally turned against the plan by Texas congressman Sam Rayburn, Lyndon Johnson's mentor, who faithfully represented Texas oil interests in Washington.

After World War II, the Marshall Plan began turning recovering European nations away from coal to oil. Refining capacity in Europe tripled in just a few years.

In 1950, a secret agreement was reached between the State Department and major oil companies that allowed all royalties paid to Arab nations to be applied as tax credits.

Dwight Eisenhower was elected with strong support from the oil industry and, early in 1953, in one of his first actions, he stopped a grand jury investigation into the "international Petroleum Cartel," citing reasons of "national security."

The same year, a CIA-backed coup reinstated the Shah of Iran and new oil arrangements were made with Iran. Ironically, the Iranian coup was masterminded by Kermit Roosevelt, Teddy's grandson, who went on to become a vice president of Gulf Oil. The Suez Crisis in 1956 signaled the end of British and French colonialism in the Middle East, and the major oil companies moved to consolidate their power.

When John F. Kennedy became president in 1961, the oil industry felt secure.

But then President Kennedy began to assault the power of the oil giants directly, first with a law known as the Kennedy Act, and later by attacking the oil depletion allowance. The Kennedy Act, passed on October 16, 1962, removed the distinction between repatriated profits and profits reinvested abroad. Both were now subject to US taxation. The measure also was aimed at preventing taxable income from being hidden away in foreign subsidiaries and other tax havens. While this law applied to industry as a whole, it particularly affected the oil companies, which were greatly diversified with large overseas operations.

By the end of 1962, oilmen estimated their earnings on foreign investment capital would fall to 15 percent, compared with 30 percent in 1955.

One of the most sacred of provisions in the eyes of oilmen was the oil depletion allowance, which permitted oil producers to treat up to 27.5 percent of their income as tax exempt. In theory this was to compensate for the depletion of fixed oil reserves but, in effect, it gave the oil industry a lower tax rate. Under this allowance, an oilman with a good deal of venture capital could become rich with virtually no risk. For example, a speculator could drill ten wells. If nine were dry holes and only the tenth struck oil, he would still make money because of tax breaks and the depletion allowance.

It was estimated at the time that oilmen might lose nearly $300 million a year if the depletion allowance was diminished. Attempts to eliminate or reduce the depletion allowance were rebuffed year after year by congressmen, many of whom were the happy recipients of oil-industry contributions.

Speaking of his tax reform act of 1963, President Kennedy pointed the finger at the oil companies, saying, "No one industry should be permitted to obtain an undue tax advantage over all others."

Included in Kennedy's tax package were provisions for closing a number of corporate tax loopholes, including the depletion allowance. Needless to say, oilmen both in Texas and elsewhere felt threatened by Kennedy and his policies. Kennedy's use of his personal power against the steel manufacturers had shown them that the young president meant to enforce his will in these matters.

John W. Curington, who for twelve years was special assistant to Dallas oil billionaire H. L. Hunt, reported in 1977, "Hunt was often heard by top aides and followers to say that America would be much better off without Kennedy." Curington, whose statements were assessed as truthful by Psychological Stress Evaluator analysis, also said the oilman sent him to check on Oswald's police security while in custody and was "elated" to find it was lax. Curington also is convinced that he saw Marina Oswald coming from Hunt's private offices several weeks after the assassination.

Hunt's former assistant said he believes that the wealthy oilman unwittingly influenced right-wing followers to participate in a conspiracy to kill Kennedy. He added that in later years, Hunt admitted that he knew an assassination conspiracy existed.

Angry talk in the corporate boardrooms may have grown into deadly plots on golf courses and at private parties. But despite their unparalleled wealth and power, oilmen could not have moved against Kennedy on their own. They needed allies within government and within the intelligence community and the military. Such allies were there—among the anti-Castro Cubans, in the CIA, in organized crime, in the Pentagon and even within the federal government—and all were most receptive to the idea of a change of leadership. Lyndon Johnson was especially sympathetic to oilmen, many of whom were fellow Texans and financial contributors.

One man with connections to government, intelligence, and the oil industry was Dallas oil geologist George DeMohrenschildt, identified by the Warren Commission as the last-known close friend to Lee Harvey Oswald.

Oswald's Friends

DeMohrenschildt—a man who was friends with both Jackie Kennedy's family and her husband's alleged assassin, Lee Harvey Oswald—is perhaps the most intriguing person in the entire cast of characters connected with the Kennedy assassination.

Despite this fascinating link, little was said about DeMohrenschildt at the time of the assassination as both he and his wife, Jeanne, were in Haiti during the events in Dallas.

A close study of DeMohrenschildt's life shows a string of intelligence connections, raising the possibility that DeMohrenschildt may have played a role—perhaps unwittingly—in furthering plans for the assassination. This possibility may have come to haunt DeMohrenschildt in the days just prior to his suspicious death in 1977.

DeMohrenschildt—his family, originally named Mohrenskuld, was of Swedish extraction—was born April 17, 1911, in Mozyr, a small Baltic town in czarist Russia near the Polish border.

An educated, sophisticated young man, DeMohrenschildt was introduced to many wealthy and influential Americans. He later told the Warren Commission:

> [I met] lots of people, but especially Mrs. [Janet] Bouvier. . . . Mrs. Bouvier is Jacqueline Kennedy's mother, also [I met] her father and her whole family. [Mrs. Bouvier] was in the process of getting a divorce from her husband [Jackie's father, John V. "Jack" Bouvier], I met him, also. We were very close friends. We saw each other every day. I met Jackie then, when she was a little girl. [And] her sister, who was still in the cradle practically.

After failing in attempts to sell insurance and perfume, DeMohrenschildt traveled by bus to Texas, where, thanks to family connections, he got a job with Humble Oil Company in Houston. Despite being friends with the chairman of the board of Humble, young DeMohrenschildt was confined to working as a "roughneck" in the Louisiana oil fields. He quit after being injured and contracting amoebic dysentery.

For years he claimed to have worked for French intelligence during the early years of World War II—he said he was never an official agent but had helped a good friend, Pierre Freyss, the head of French counterintelligence. In 1941, he was arrested by the FBI and charged with being a Nazi spy for sketching and photographing military installations near Aransas Pass, Texas. In later years he confessed to his wife that he had briefly worked for the Germans.

DeMohrenschildt also became closely connected with many exiled Russians who joined with the General Vlassov movement, anticommunist Russians who fought with the Nazis in hope of recovering their homeland. Springing up in cities with large Russian exile communities, these people referred to themselves as "solidarists," indicating the solidarity of their purpose. One of these groups existed in Dallas during the early 1960s, although DeMohrenschildt disclaimed being a member.

The Vlassov organization was eventually absorbed by the Nazi spy system under General Reinhard Gehlen; at the end of the war the system became a part of US intelligence. Many members of this apparatus ended up working for the CIA.

DeMohrenschildt's oil-related travels took him to France, Nigeria, Ghana, and Togoland.

In 1957, despite an unflattering background check by the CIA, he journeyed to Yugoslavia for the International Cooperation Administration, a branch of the US government's Agency for International Development. By this time, DeMohrenschildt apparently had some association with the agency, according to documents that became public in the late 1970s.

Researcher Michael Levy obtained one CIA memo from former agency deputy director Richard Helms that states that DeMohrenschildt's trip to Yugoslavia provided "foreign intelligence which was promptly disseminated to other federal agencies in 10 separate reports." Another CIA memo indicated that DeMohrenschildt also furnished lengthy reports on his later travels through Mexico and Central America.

Shortly before leaving for Yugoslavia, DeMohrenschildt met another Russian exile who lived in the same Dallas hotel with him. Jeanne Fromenke LeGon had already established a career as a dancer and clothing designer. Her family, too, had strong political and defense-related connections. Her Russian father had built the first railroads in China and was connected with Nationalist politics there while her brother, Sergio, had worked on the super-secret Manhattan atomic bomb project. Her former husband, Robert LeGon, was connected to security work for Douglas Aircraft and their daughter, Christiana, was married to a vice president of Lockheed Aircraft Corporation.

Jeanne and the outgoing DeMohrenschildt hit it off right away and she joined him in Yugoslavia. In a curious incident there, the couple was boating when they were shot at by communist guards who became anxious when they came too close to Marshal Tito's summer home. DeMohrenschildt claimed to have been simply sketching the shoreline.

Returning to the United States, George and Jeanne were soon married and shortly set off on an incredible odyssey through Central America.

Back in Dallas in late 1961, the DeMohrenschildts were at the center of prominent Dallasites. His business and social contacts read like a who's who of the Texas oil community. DeMohrenschildt knew Dallas oil millionaires H. L. Hunt and Clint

Murchinson, John Mecom of Houston, Robert Kerr of Kerr-McGee, and Jean De Menil, head of the worldwide oil firm Schlumberger Corporation. According to former New Orleans district attorney Jim Garrison, arms and explosives the CIA supplied to the anti-Castro Cuban exiles were hidden away in a Schlumberger facility near New Orleans in the summer of 1963.

But most intriguing was DeMohrenschildt's friendship with J. Walton Moore, a member of the CIA's Domestic Contact Service.

Moore, whom DeMohrenschildt described to the Warren Commission as "a government man—either FBI or Central Intelligence," debriefed the geologist upon his return from Yugoslavia and thereafter met with the DeMohrenschildts socially on many occasions. The Warren Commission, perhaps in an effort to deflect any attention from the CIA, listed Moore as "G. Walter Moore."

After DeMohrenschildt first met Lee Harvey Oswald, he checked on the ex-Marine with Moore. Less than two months after the assassination, DeMohrenschildt wrote to friends expressing shock and disbelief over Kennedy's death: "Before we began to help Marina and the child, we asked the FBI [he meant Moore but used the term FBI at that time, as the CIA was supposed to be secret] man in Dallas . . . about Lee and he told us that he was 'completely harmless.'"

These letters are part of DeMohrenschildt's FBI file, indicating the bureau was monitoring him during this time. Following the assassination, his statements that he had checked on Oswald with the bureau apparently caused great consternation. Dallas FBI chief J. Gordon Shanklin even ordered agent James Woods to go to Haiti and obtained a lengthy statement from DeMohrenschildt denying that he had ever spoken about Oswald to the bureau.

DeMohrenschildt himself may have been the object of a secret investigation in the months preceding Kennedy's death. Once DeMohrenschildt noticed small pencil marks on some of his papers and, convinced his home had been secretly entered, questioned Moore about it. Moore denied that government people had broken into DeMohrenschildt's home.

Another close friend of DeMohrenschildt's was Fort Worth attorney Max Clark, who at that time was connected with security at General Dynamics.

In later years, neither George nor Jeanne DeMohrenschildt could recall exactly who first mentioned the Oswalds to them. But in the summer of 1962, DeMohrenschildt made a business trip to nearby Fort Worth and decided to visit the Oswalds. He had learned through the Russian community in Dallas that the Oswalds had recently arrived in this country from Minsk and he was eager for news about the city of his youth.

DeMohrenschildt was appalled at the poorly furnished "shack" in which the Oswalds lived, but was impressed by Oswald's command of Russian. He told the Warren Commission, "He spoke fluent Russian, but with a foreign accent, and made mistakes, grammatical mistakes but had remarkable fluency in Russian. . . . Remarkable—for a fellow of his background and education . . . he preferred to speak Russian than English any time. He always would switch from English to Russian."

He said both his first impression of Oswald and his last were the same:

> I could never get mad at this fellow. . . . Sometimes he was obnoxious. I
> don't know. I had a liking for him. I always had a liking for him. There
> was something charming about him, there was some—I don't know. I just
> liked the guy—that is all. . . . With me he was very humble. If somebody
> expressed an interest in him, he blossomed, absolutely blossomed. If you
> asked him some questions about him, he was just out of this world. That
> was more or less the reason that I think he liked me very much.

In 1976, his opinion of Oswald had not wavered. He told one researcher:

> No matter what they say, Lee Harvey Oswald was a delightful guy. They
> make a moron out of him, but he was smart as hell. Ahead of his time really,
> a kind of hippie of those days. In fact, he was the most honest man I knew.
> And I will tell you this—I am sure he did not shoot the president.

In 1963, the DeMohrenschildts embraced the Oswalds and visited them with an idea of helping the struggling couple.

It is interesting to note how the Dallas Russian community split in reacting to the Oswalds. Most of them—being staunch anticommunists—wanted nothing to do with a man who had tried to defect to Russia. But some of the émigré members—especially those with intelligence connections, such as DeMohrenschildt—seemed quite at ease with the young would-be defector. Perhaps they, too, had been assured that Oswald was "harmless."

In October 1962, DeMohrenschildt managed to move Oswald to Dallas, where he dropped out of sight for nearly a month. Marina was left with DeMohrenschildt's daughter and son-in-law, the Gary Taylors. Oddly, Oswald did not even inform his mother of the move and he told friends he had been fired from his job at Leslie Welding in Fort Worth when actually he had quit.

Furthermore, during this time DeMohrenschildt was making regular trips to Houston, according to his friends Igor Voshinin and Paul Raigorodsky. Raigorodsky, a wealthy oilman and a director of the Tolstoy Foundation—an anticommunist organization of Russian exiles that was funded by the US government—told the Warren Commission he asked DeMohrenschildt about his frequent Houston trips. Raigorodsky stated, "He told me he was going to see Herman and George Brown. They are brothers." The Brown brothers were owners of Brown and Root Construction and close friends and financial contributors to Lyndon Johnson. Jeanne DeMohrenschildt said the only reason they didn't relocate to Houston during this time was her successful clothing business in Dallas.

At the time of the Cuban Missile Crisis, Oswald went to work for Jaggars-Chiles-Stovall, a Dallas printing and photographic firm that had contracts with the US Army Map Service. Although clearances were required to work in some areas of the plant, testimony before the Warren Commission showed security was sloppy and apparently Oswald had access to sensitive material. It was here, it was believed, that Oswald manufactured false identification papers both for himself and in the name A. J. Hidell, using company photographic equipment.

He once asked fellow employee Dennis Ofstein if he knew what the term "microdot" meant. The word "microdot" was found written in Oswald's address book next to the entry for Jaggars-Chiles-Stovall. When Ofstein replied no, Oswald proceeded to explain that it was a special photographic process whereby a great mass of documents could be reduced to the size of a dot. He said this technique was used frequently in espionage work. Ofstein wondered why Oswald would discuss such a subject.

Through the Christmas holidays of 1962–1963, DeMohrenschildt continued to try with only marginal success to get the Dallas Russian émigré community involved with the Oswalds.

He apparently tried to separate the Oswalds and, on at least two occasions, tried to find living quarters for Marina and her children. But Marina decided to reunite with Oswald, much to the disgust of her friends in the Russian community. On February 22, 1963, the DeMohrenschildts brought the Oswalds to the home of Everett Glover, where Marina was introduced to Ruth Paine. Mrs. Paine was separated from her husband, Michael, an employee of Bell Helicopter, and expressed an interest in seeing Marina again to learn the Russian language. Marina agreed and several visits between the women followed.

According to the Warren Commission, Oswald ordered the Carcano rifle from a mail-order firm under the name "A. Hidell" on March 12, 1963, and it arrived in Dallas on March 25. Just sixteen days later, Oswald reportedly fired a shot at General Walker.

The Walker incident occurred on a Wednesday night. Oswald arrived back home that evening and, according to Marina's Warren Commission testimony, told her he fired at Walker and had then buried his rifle. The rifle discovered in the Texas School Book Depository showed no sign of being buried. It was clean and well-oiled, yet no gun-cleaning material was ever found among Oswald's possessions.

And the following weekend, the rifle was observed in his home by Jeanne DeMohrenschildt during a visit. She and her husband brought a pink bunny toy to Oswald's young daughter and Marina was showing her around their new apartment when she saw a rifle in a closet. As Jeanne later recalled the incident, she asked Marina, "What on earth is that?" Marina replied, "A rifle. Lee bought it. I don't know why when we need money for food and things." Asked what Oswald did with the weapon, Jeanne said Marina answered, "He goes to the public park with little June [Oswald's daughter] and shoots leaves with it."

Jeanne DeMohrenschildt later told this author:

> Today that sounds very strange, but at the time, I was thinking of the times
> I had fired guns at small targets in amusement parks and I really didn't

think too much of her answer. When I told George about the rifle I had seen in the closet, he immediately boomed out, "Did you take that pot shot at General Walker, Lee?" George then laughed loudly. Looking back on this incident today, Lee and Marina did not appear to be shocked or upset. They merely stood there in silence while George laughed.

DeMohrenschildt told the Warren Commission his question about shooting at Walker was "frankly a stupid joke on my part." Marina told the Warren Commission that on another occasion, DeMohrenschildt asked Oswald, "Lee, how is it possible that you missed?" However, both DeMohrenschildts denied such a question was ever asked. It seems this may have been yet another example of Marina's being coached or misquoted by federal authorities.

This visit was to be the last meeting between the DeMohrenschildts and the Oswalds. On April 23, Marina moved in with the attentive Ruth Paine, and the next day Oswald left Dallas by bus for New Orleans.

About a week later, the DeMohrenschildts left for a new business venture in Haiti. As the DeMohrenschildts were preparing to leave for Haiti in May 1963, they stopped in Washington, where, according to CIA records, DeMohrenschildt met with a CIA representative and the assistant director of Army intelligence. What specifically was discussed at this meeting is not known, but at this same time, another CIA document shows that an agency officer "requested an expedite check on George DeMohren-schildt." At this meeting was DeMohrenschildt's Haitian business associate, Clemard Charles. Researchers have noted that Charles later was implicated in the sale of arms and military equipment involving a gunrunner named Edward Browder.

According to the House Select Committee on Assassinations, Browder leased a B-25 bomber under the name of a fictitious company and flew it to Haiti a year after the Kennedy assassination and later cashed a $24,000 check signed by Charles. Browder, a former Lockheed test pilot who served a twenty-five-year prison sentence for "security violations," told the committee he had been working for the CIA. According to information gathered by author David E. Scheim, Browder also was an associate of Jack Ruby in the 1950s when both men were arranging the sale of arms to Fidel Castro.

Herb Atkin, a former CIA operative, has stated that DeMohrenschildt was involved in a failed CIA plot to overthrow Haitian president Francois "Papa Doc" Duvalier in June 1963.

Following DeMohrenschildt's death in March 1977, Atkin told author Dick Russell, "I knew de Mohrenschildt as Philip Harbin. A lot of people in Washington have claimed that Harbin did not exist. But he's the one that ran me from the late fifties onward. I'm certain that DeMohrenschildt was my case officer's real name."

Recall that De Mohrenschildt's fourth wife, Jeanne, was born in Harbin, China.

The DeMohrenschildts were in Haiti when they learned of Kennedy's death. Reportedly DeMohrenschildt told friends there the FBI was behind the assassination. Whether or not he actually made such a comment, he did start to experience difficulties after Haitian president Duvalier reportedly received a letter from the FBI telling of DeMohrenschildt's friendship with Oswald and labeling him as a "Polish communist and a member of an international band."

The DeMohrenschildts were called to Washington to testify to the Warren Commission in April 1964. Oddly enough, when DeMohrenschildt tried to raise the issue of the damaging FBI letter, Warren Commission attorney Albert Jenner quickly told him, "I would say you have been misinformed on that." DeMohrenschildt replied, "Well, he did receive some kind of letter." Jenner then said, "But nothing that would contain any such statements. . . . It may have been a crank letter, but nothing official." DeMohrenschildt, catching the drift of Jenner's remarks depreciating the whole subject, suddenly agreed: "Yes, I am sure it is nothing official. I am sure it could not have been anything official."

Researchers are left with the question of how a Warren Commission attorney, supposedly searching for the truth of the Kennedy assassination, could have been so confident that the FBI letter was a "crank" and why he had closed the subject rather than trying to learn more about it.

Jeanne DeMohrenschildt claimed the Warren Commission did not appear eager to hear from her and her husband and that they had to ask to testify. She told this author:

> Much of our problems with government authorities came from our refusal to slander Lee's name. The Warren Commission, along with the mass media, depicted Oswald as a complete loner, a total failure, both as a man and a father. This is not the impression George and I had of this man. Lee was a sincere person. Although from a modest educational background, he was quick and bright. . . . Lee obviously loved his daughter June. We could not possibly consider him as dangerous.

During their stay in Washington, the DeMohrenschildts visited in the home of Jackie Kennedy's mother, Mrs. Hugh D. Auchincloss, who, according to an unpublished book by DeMohrenschildt, said, "Incidentally, my daughter Jacqueline never wants to see you again because you were close to her husband's assassin."

Returning to Haiti, the DeMohrenschildt's problems there increased to the point that in 1967 they were forced to sneak away from the island aboard a German freighter, which brought them to Port Arthur, Texas. Here, according to Jeanne, the DeMohrenschildts were met by an associate of former Oklahoma senator and oilman Bob Kerr. The returning couple were extended the hospitality of Kerr's home.

By the 1970s, the DeMohrenschildts were living quietly in Dallas, although once they were questioned by two men who claimed to be from *Life* magazine. A check showed the men were phonies.

DeMohrenschildt seemed content to teach French at Bishop College, a predominantly black school in south Dallas. Then in the spring of 1976, George, who suffered from chronic bronchitis, had a particularly bad attack. Distrustful of hospitals, he was persuaded by someone—Jeanne later could not recall who—to see a newly arrived doctor in Dallas named Dr. Charles Mendoza. After several trips to Mendoza in the late spring and summer, DeMohrenschildt's bronchial condition improved, but he began to experience the symptoms of a severe nervous breakdown. He became paranoid, claiming that "the Jewish Mafia and the FBI" were after him.

Alarmed, Jeanne accompanied her husband to Dr. Mendoza and discovered he was giving DeMohrenschildt injections and costly drug prescriptions. Jeanne said her husband's mental condition continued to deteriorate during this time. She now claims, "I have become convinced that this doctor, in some way, lies behind the nervous breakdown George suffered in his final months."

The doctor is indeed mysterious. A check with the Dallas County Medical Society showed that Dr. Mendoza first registered in April 1976, less than two months before he began treating DeMohrenschildt and at the same time the House Select Committee on Assassinations was beginning to be funded.

Mendoza left Dallas in December, just a few months after DeMohrenschildt refused to continue treatments, at his wife's insistence. Mendoza left the society a forwarding address that proved to be nonexistent. He also left behind a confused and unbalanced George DeMohrenschildt.

During the fall of 1976 while in this unbalanced mental state, DeMohrenschildt completed his unpublished manuscript, *I Am a Patsy! I Am a Patsy!* after Oswald's famous remark to news reporters in the Dallas police station. In the manuscript, DeMohrenschildt depicts Oswald as a cursing, uncouth man with assassination on his mind, a totally opposite picture from his descriptions of Oswald through the years.

The night he finished the manuscript, DeMohrenschildt attempted suicide by taking an overdose of tranquilizers. Paramedics were called, but they declined to take him to a hospital. They found DeMohrenschildt also had taken his dog's digitalis, which counteracted the tranquilizers.

Shortly after his attempted suicide, Jeanne committed her husband to Parkland Hospital in Dallas, where he was subjected to electroshock therapy. To gauge his mental condition at this time, consider what he told Parkland roommate Clifford Wilson: "I know damn well Oswald didn't kill Kennedy—because Oswald and I were together at the time." DeMohrenschildt told Wilson that he and Oswald were in downtown Dallas watching the Kennedy motorcade pass when shots were fired. He said that at the sound of shots Oswald ran away and DeMohrenschildt never saw him again.

This story, which was reported in the April 26, 1977, edition of the *National Enquirer* as "Exclusive New Evidence," is simply untrue since both George and Jeanne were at a reception in the Bulgarian embassy in Haiti the day Kennedy was killed. But the incident serves to illustrate George DeMohrenschildt's mental condition at the time.

In early 1977, convinced that evil forces were still after him, DeMohrenschildt fled to Europe with Dutch journalist Willems Oltmans, who later created a furor by telling the House Select Committee on Assassinations that DeMohrenschildt claimed he knew of Oswald's assassination plan in advance.

However, DeMohrenschildt grew even more fearful in Europe. In a letter found after his death, he wrote, "As I can see it now, the whole purpose of my meeting in Holland was to ruin me financially and completely."

In mid-March DeMohrenschildt fled to a relative's Florida home leaving behind clothing and other personal belongings. It was in the fashionable Manalapan, Florida, home of his sister-in-law that DeMohrenschildt died of a shotgun blast to the head on March 29, 1977, just three hours after a representative of the House Select Committee on Assassinations tried to contact him there.

Earlier that day, he had met author Edward J. Epstein for an interview. In a 1983 *Wall Street Journal* article, Epstein wrote that DeMohrenschildt told him that day that the CIA had asked him "to keep tabs on Oswald." However, the thing that may have triggered DeMohrenschildt's fear was that Epstein showed him a document that indicated DeMohrenschildt might be sent back to Parkland for further shock treatments, according to a statement by attorney David Bludworth, who represented the state during the investigation into DeMohrenschildt's death.

Although several aspects of DeMohrenschildt's death caused chief investigator Captain Richard Sheets of the Palm County Sheriff's Office to term the shooting "very strange," a coroner's jury quickly ruled suicide.

One other matter that involved the DeMohrenschildts with the assassination has proven as unfathomable as so many others. According to Jeanne, when the DeMohrenschildts arrived back in the United States in early 1967, they discovered a photograph of Oswald in some Russian-English language records they had loaned to Marina Oswald prior to leaving for Haiti. The picture is one of the famous backyard scenes depicting Oswald with his rifle and pistol while holding a communist publication. It is one pose of at least three separate photos believed by most researchers to be faked. On the back of the photo is one inscription in English reading "To my friend George from Lee Oswald." Beneath this is an inscription in Russian Cyrillic script that translates "Hunter of fascists Ha-ha-ha!!!"

The photo also bears the date "5/IV/63," apparently meaning April 5, 1963. The date is curious, mixing in Roman numerals as it does and written in the European style. The New Orleans–born Oswald more likely would have written "4/5/63" and, in fact, a check of dozens of other examples of dates in Oswald's mass of written material shows not one written in the manner on the photo.

Handwriting experts for the House Select Committee on Assassinations could not identify Oswald, Marina, or the DeMohrenschildts as authors of the inscription.

And Marina gave mixed accounts of the photo, which surfaced just at a time when many assassination researchers were first beginning to question the authenticity of the backyard photographs.

While testifying to the committee in 1978, Marina suddenly blurted out, "I remember being surprised at [Oswald] showing pictures like that to George [DeMohrenschildt], so apparently I saw them at the apartment. . . . Something strikes my memory that—how dare he show pictures like that to a friend?"

If her statement is true, and that's a big "if" since later in her testimony Marina suddenly could not remember much else about the episode, it would mean that George DeMohrenschildt—the man with numerous intelligence connections—was aware of Oswald's possession of weapons months before the assassination.

The DeMohrenschildts denied any knowledge of the photo with the incriminating inscription, and Jeanne swore to this author neither she nor her husband ever saw the photograph until discovering it upon their return in 1967. She was convinced that the picture had been planted among their possessions.

Looking over the fascinating life of George and Jeanne DeMohrenschildt, one is struck by the idea that this sophisticated couple may be one of the biggest "red herrings" of the assassination, as DeMohrenschildt had numerous and long-standing connections with intelligence—most notably the CIA and perhaps private intelligence groups connected with the oil industry and defense work. Through DeMohrenschildt, certain elements within oil, business, and intelligence circles could have become aware of Oswald, who with his procommunist background must have appeared to be a prime candidate for an assassination patsy.

After the assassination, DeMohrenschildt—with his connections to German, French, Polish, and US intelligence, wealthy right-wing Texas oilmen, and Caribbean business interests—provided a wonderful opportunity to draw investigators into a labyrinth of false leads. The mental deterioration near the end of his life caused DeMohrenschildt to make untrue statements that further clouded the issue.

If George DeMohrenschildt had a genuine liking for President Kennedy, as he stated on several occasions, this fondness was not shared by his conservative oil and business associates. They felt threatened by the young president, who was making decisions on finances, taxation, and foreign policy outside their control. This concern was shared by the military and intelligence communities.

President Kennedy's shift from Cold Warrior to seeker of world peace is well documented in James W. Douglass's 2008 book, *JFK and the Unspeakable*. Douglass drew the term "unspeakable" from author and social activist Thomas Merton, an ordained Catholic priest turned Trappist monk. The term refers to a hidden but insidious ideology of fascism that has so permeated American society that it must remain unmentioned in public. Douglass wrote, "The Vietnam War, the race to a global war, and the interlocking murders of John Kennedy, Malcolm X, Martin Luther King, and Robert Kennedy were all signs of the Unspeakable. It remains deeply present in our world."

Corporate heads initially may have been mollified to think that Kennedy was being guided by the hand of his father, Joseph P. Kennedy, a pro-Nazi former bootlegger and political boss. But in December 1961, Joseph Kennedy had a stroke that left him totally incapacitated. His son Jack was now in the highest office of the land with no direct control over him.

And the younger Kennedy was moving to restrict the predations of Wall Street and the corporations it funded. In his 1994 book, *Battling Wall Street: The Kennedy Presidency*, University of Pittsburgh professor Donald Gibson, who spent nearly forty years researching economic and political power in the United States, made a cogent argument that the primary motive behind the JFK assassination was that he was at loggerheads with the Wall Street Establishment, those same globalist financiers who first promoted communism in 1917 Russia and then national socialism, the Nazis, in Germany.

After detailing attacks on Kennedy's economic policies, beginning with his success in forcing the major steel manufacturers to reverse a price increase in 1962, Gibson stated, "The Establishment rejection of Kennedy became increasingly intense during his time in office." Gibson wrote that two prominent business publications—*Fortune* and the *Wall Street Journal*—were the most hostile critics of Kennedy and his economic policies and both "were related in numerous ways to the two most influential financial groups in the United States—Morgan and Rockefeller." He also noted, "By the early 1960s, the Council on Foreign Relations, Morgan and Rockefeller interests, and the intelligence community were so extensively inbred as to be virtually a single entity."

Other researchers also have revealed the closeness between the Wall Street Establishment and US intelligence, particularly the CIA. They are virtually two sides of the same coin.

As evidenced by the affair of Soviet defector Yuri Nosenko and the on-again, off-again anti-Castro Mongoose program, there appear to have been serious divisions within the CIA in the early 1960s. While some factions undoubtedly supported President Kennedy and his programs, others did not disguise their hatred of him.

The CIA had become highly compartmentalized. Often CIA employees working on one project would have no idea that people they came into contact with also were working for the agency. And for expediency, the agency employed and used some very unsavory characters—such as David Ferrie.

There can be little doubt that Oswald and many persons in contact with him were connected to the CIA. These contacts, plus the abundant evidence that Oswald was involved in intelligence work, point to who was maneuvering Oswald in the fall of 1963. Some individuals within the CIA may have played roles in an assassination conspiracy that later compelled their superiors to cover up their activities for fear that their connection to the agency might become public.

However, it seems highly unlikely that as an organization, the CIA initiated the Kennedy assassination. But senior corporate and intelligence officials were not overly concerned if something were to happen to the young president. Such officials traditionally have sought out politicians who would look out for their interests in Washington. So in the days of Kennedy's Camelot, intelligence chiefs along with oil and business titans may have looked to a man they knew they could deal with, if not completely trust—vice president Lyndon B. Johnson.

All the Way with LBJ

In Dallas on the day Kennedy died some people were iconoclastic enough to suggest that Vice President Johnson was behind the assassination. These were mostly long-time Texas residents who had heard vicious stories about Johnson for years and who knew the Texas politician had more to gain from Kennedy's death than just about anyone. Even today, many serious students of the assassination cannot discount the idea that Johnson in some way played a role in the Dallas tragedy. In fact, in recent years, a spate of books led by Barr McClellan's 2002 *Blood, Money & Power* have actually accused Johnson of masterminding the assassination. However, none have offered irrefutable evidence to support that charge. McClellan, whose son Scott was among George W. Bush's White House press secretaries, had worked for the Austin law offices of Clark, Thomas, Harris, Denius and Winters, a firm closely associated with Lyndon Johnson.

Johnson's actions following the assassination do little to stop such speculation. And a close study of the corruption and murder that dogged Johnson's political career only adds to the suspicion.

Lyndon Baines Johnson was born August 27, 1908, near Johnson City, Texas, which had been named for his grandfather, one of the area's original settlers. His father, Sam Ealy Johnson, who served in the Texas Legislature for twelve years, told neighbors, "A US senator is born today."

Young Johnson graduated from Johnson City High School as president of his senior class of six. After running away to California, he hitchhiked back home and enrolled in Southwest Texas State Teachers College at San Marcos.

After graduating at age twenty-two, Johnson got a teaching job in Houston, but it failed to hold the interest of this ambitious young man. So in 1931, Johnson was drawn into Texas politics, campaigning strenuously for conservative congressman Richard M. Kleberg. After Kleberg's victory, Johnson accompanied him to Washington as his secretary.

In 1934 Johnson was visiting in Austin when he met an attractive twenty-one-year-old journalism student named Claudia Alta Taylor, the daughter of an affluent merchant and landowner in Karnack, Texas. As the story goes, a black "mammy" took one look at the infant Claudia and declared, "Lawd, she's as pretty as a lady bird," and from then on, she was known as "Lady Bird." After a whirlwind courtship of two months, consisting mainly of daily telephone calls from Washington, Johnson returned to Texas and asked "Bird" to marry him. She agreed and the couple drove to San Antonio for a rushed wedding in St. Mark's Episcopal Church. After a brief honeymoon in Mexico, the Johnsons moved to Washington, where they rented a one-bedroom apartment and Johnson resumed his political work for Kleberg.

Watching the energetic Johnson was a close friend of the Johnson family, congressman Sam Rayburn, already a power on Capitol Hill. In August 1935, thanks to some help from Rayburn, president Franklin Roosevelt named Johnson as Texas director of the National Youth Administration, a New Deal program for employing youngsters.

Capitalizing on his authority to award loans and jobs, Johnson created a formidable political base in south Texas. He also used his new position to ingratiate himself with President Roosevelt, whom Johnson referred to as "my political daddy." By now his career designs were set firmly in politics.

In early 1937, with the sudden death of Austin congressman James P. Buchanan, Johnson saw an opportunity to advance. At the same time Johnson was looking for financial and political support to make a bid for Buchanan's seat, Austin attorney Alvin Wirtz and his client Herman Brown were looking for help in Washington.

Brown's construction company, Brown & Root, had already spent millions building the Marshall Ford Dam in south Texas. But the project had not been officially authorized by Congress; rather it had begun as a government grant obtained by Buchanan. With his death, the entire $10 million project was in limbo.

Backed by Wirtz, Brown, and their well-heeled business associates, the indefatigable Johnson raced through nearly 8,000 square miles of Texas hill country pledging total support of Roosevelt and his New Deal, a theme that sat well with impoverished farmers and laborers.

The senatorial election, climaxing with a raging blizzard and sudden surgery for LBJ to repair a ruptured appendix, was a victory, with Johnson outpolling five opponents by 3,000 votes.

Back in Washington, the twenty-nine-year-old Johnson managed to get authorization for the dam project as well as a contract for Brown & Root to build a huge Navy base at Corpus Christi.

Herman Brown and his friends were so pleased with Johnson's performance that in 1940 the young congressman was offered a share in very lucrative oil properties with no money down. Johnson was told he could pay for his share out of yearly profits. It was tantamount to a gift. Brown was shocked when Johnson, who had been complaining of lack of money, turned him down, saying the offer "would kill me politically." Since both a House and a Senate seat would come from Texas's reliable oil and gas constituency, Brown realized even at that time that Johnson's true political goal was the presidency.

As a congressman, Johnson continued to perform for his oil and business mentors back in Texas. In 1941, Brown & Root obtained a lucrative Navy contract to build four sub chasers, although as George Brown later recalled, "We didn't know the stern from the aft—I mean the bow—of the boat."

Just two days after Pearl Harbor, Johnson—who had been commissioned as a lieutenant commander in the Navy Reserve some months previously—was called to active duty, becoming the first congressman to leave for military service. After serving less than a year, Johnson arrived back in Washington after Roosevelt called on all congressmen serving in the armed forces to return home.

His wartime service had won Johnson at least one solid ally. After a period of cool relations due to Johnson's blatant ambitiousness, he again was accepted by powerful House Speaker Sam Rayburn. Rayburn taught Johnson his political philosophy, which he repeated often: "To get along, you have to go along."

J. Evetts Haley, a biographer critical of Johnson, wrote, "Lyndon became Rayburn's protégé; their relationship a fusion of experience and political sagacity with youthful ardor and enthusiasm, with no appreciable enhancement of the ideals and ethics of either."

Johnson entered a race for the Senate in 1948. It was a close race between Johnson, still identified with Roosevelt and the New Deal, and conservative Texas governor Coke Stevenson, who managed to defeat Johnson in the Democratic primary. However, Stevenson didn't have a clear majority, so a run-off election was called for August 28.

Due to slow communications and manual voting procedures, the election outcome was in doubt for several days. Finally on September 2, Johnson went on the radio with a "victory speech," which shocked the confident Stevenson forces. Veteran Texas newsman Clyde Wantland wrote:

> Their fears were validated the following day . . . when a source friendly to Stevenson reported from Jim Wells County that Precinct 13 had been recanvassed and a "correction" made favoring Johnson with 202 more votes. Johnson's radio broadcast on Thursday thus became a reality on Saturday.

This revision earned Johnson the sobriquet of "Landslide Lyndon" and began one of the longest legal feuds in Texas history.

Johnson's opponents claimed the eighty-seven-vote "correction." This eighty-seven-vote edge in the 1948 election came only after frantic phone calls between Johnson and George Parr, a powerful south Texas political boss known as the "Duke of Duval County."

The controversy continued into 1977, when Luis Salas, the local election judge, admitted to the *Dallas Morning News* that he had certified fictitious ballots for Johnson on orders from Parr, who committed suicide in 1975. Salas told news reporters, "Johnson did not win that election; it was stolen for him." But more troubling than this case of common political fraud was the series of deaths and federal government interference with investigations into Johnson's activities.

One of these deaths was Bill Mason, a south Texas newsman investigating the Duval incident, who was murdered by Sam Smithwick, a Parr associate who in turn was found hanged in his prison cell after saying he was willing to talk.

As far back as 1941, the IRS had initiated investigations of Johnson's finances, but had been blocked by orders from Johnson's mentor, President Roosevelt. In 1954, the Austin district IRS collector, Frank L. Scofield, was removed from office accused of forcing political contributions from his employees. Scofield was acquitted of these charges, but in his absence, all of the IRS files relating to Johnson and Brown & Root were placed in a Quonset hut in south Austin that mysteriously caught fire, destroying the evidence.

In the late 1940s and early 1950s, both Johnson and his protégé John Connally had offices in Fort Worth. Johnson operated out of the Hotel Texas, the site of Kennedy's breakfast speech the morning of November 22, 1963. Connally's offices were in the historic Flatiron Building, which later became the Press Club of Fort Worth.

It was in Fort Worth that both Johnson and Connally came into contact with gamblers, who in turn were later connected to Jack Ruby as well as anti-Kennedy Texas oilmen.

W. C. Kirkwood was known as a "gentleman gambler" because he never allowed anyone in his high-stakes poker games who was on a salary. He did not want to be the cause of someone's children going hungry. Kirkwood conducted his big-time gambling at a luxurious, sprawling Spanish-style complex known as the Four Deuces—the street address was 2222 on Fort Worth's Jacksboro Highway, once notorious for its taverns and prostitution. It was here, under the protective eye of off-duty policemen, that such men as H. L. Hunt and Clint Murchinson joined Sam Rayburn and his protégé Johnson for hours of Kirkwood-provided hospitality.

Retired Fort Worth policeman Paul Bewley recalled for this author that while providing security for Johnson's Hotel Texas office suite, the one man who had unquestioned access to Johnson was W. C. Kirkwood.

Assassination researchers noted that Kirkwood's son, Pat Kirkwood, hosted Kennedy's Secret Service guards in his Cellar club the night before his trip to Dallas—and that both the Kirkwoods and Dallas nightclub owner Jack Ruby shared a common close friend in gambler Lewis J. McWillie. McWillie—who at one time operated his own gambling establishment in Dallas, the Top of the Hill Club—had tried to open a casino in Cuba in 1959 and had participated in gunrunning schemes.

There may have even been some connection between Ruby and Texas governor John Connally only days before the assassination. Diane Bishop was nineteen years old and working at the message and reservation desk in the Sheraton Hotel in Houston on Wednesday night, November 20, 1963. Connally had taken a room there in preparation for meeting Kennedy the next day but the staff was under orders not to make his presence public. That night, Bishop, who said she wasn't even aware that Connally was governor, received a call from a man who had to speak up due to background noise "like an airport or public place." The man sounded like the message was urgent and asked to speak with Connally. As per orders, Bishop said no one with that name was registered there but the man asked to leave a message. The caller told her, "Tell Connally, if I don't see you tonight in Houston, I'll see you in Dallas. This is Jack Ruby."

Bishop thought no more of the call but filed the message away. She was shocked on November 24 to hear that Oswald had been shot by a Jack Ruby. On Monday, November 25, she went to work intending to retrieve the phone message but found the hotel "swarming" with federal agents. Although Bishop was questioned regarding the phone call, her written note, the only proof of the incident, was missing.

Yet, despite links between Jack Ruby's friend McWillie, the Kirkwoods, Texas oilmen, Lyndon Johnson, and John Connally, apparently neither the Warren Commission nor the House Select Committee on Assassinations felt the need to fully investigate these associations.

In 1951, Johnson was elected Democratic whip in the Senate. Two years later, at only forty-four years of age, Johnson became the Senate's majority leader.

Johnson used his powerful position to best advantage, according to biographer Robert Caro, who told the *Atlantic Monthly*:

> For years, men came into Lyndon Johnson's office and handed him envelopes stuffed with cash. They didn't stop coming even when the office in which he sat was the office of the vice president of the United States. Fifty thousand dollars in hundred-dollar bills in sealed envelopes was what one lobbyist for one oil company testified he brought to Johnson's office during his term as vice president.

There is evidence that Johnson also profited from cash contributions from the mob. Jack Halfen—a former associate of Bonnie and Clyde, Frank Costello, Vito Genovese, and Carlos Marcello—was the mob's gambling coordinator in Houston. On trial for income tax evasion in 1954, Halfen revealed how Houston gambling netted almost $15 million a year with 40 percent going to Marcello, 35 percent to Halfen, and 25 percent to Texas police officials and politicians.

In talks with federal officials while serving a prison term, Halfen told how Johnson had received more than $500,000 in contributions over a ten-year period while in the Senate. He said Johnson in turn had helped the crime syndicate by killing anti-racketeering legislation, watering down bills that could not be defeated, and slowing congressional probes into organized crime.

Halfen substantiated his close ties to Johnson with photographs of himself and Johnson on a private hunting trip and a letter from Johnson to the Texas Board of Paroles written on Halfen's behalf.

According to published reports, Johnson also received large-scale payoffs from Teamster president Jimmy Hoffa. A former senatorial aide, Jack Sullivan, testified that he witnessed the transfer of a suitcase full of money from a Teamster lobbyist through a Maryland senator to Johnson's chief aide, Cliff Carter.

Also recall that one of Johnson's "trusted friends," Bobby Baker, had long and documented mob connections. Baker once wrote, "A New Orleans businessman rumored to be well connected with the Mafia had once sought me out to inquire whether President Lyndon Johnson might be willing to pardon Hoffa in exchange for one million dollars."

The Johnson administration's anticrime record is dismal. Racket-busting came to a virtual halt. During the first four years following the assassination, Justice Department organized-crime section field time had dropped by 48 percent, time before grand juries by 72 percent, and the number of district court briefs filed by that section by 83 percent.

There also was a discernible lack of prosecution follow-up to corruption charges against Lyndon B. Johnson, such as the controversial awarding of a $7 billion contract for the TFX prototype fighter-bomber plane to Texas-based General Dynamics.

LBJ's close friend Fred Korth became secretary of the Navy when John Connally resigned to become Texas governor and was negotiating this TFX contract.

On October 7, 1963, Baker was forced to leave his post as LBJ's man in the Senate. This was soon followed by the resignation of Korth.

Yet another example of Johnson's willingness to circumvent the law for his career's sake came in 1960, when he decided to run for president despite continually denying this decision. At Johnson's urging, Democratic Party legislators in Texas rushed through a law that superseded an old statute forbidding a candidate from seeking two offices at the same time.

Thus, Texas voters witnessed the bizarre spectacle of Johnson running for vice president on Kennedy's liberal national ticket while also running for Texas senator on the state's conservative Democratic ticket.

One can easily imagine Johnson's anger and hurt when the Democratic Party in 1960 handed its presidential nomination not to this longtime standard bearer, but instead to John F. Kennedy, a relative newcomer. Johnson complained to friends, "Jack was out kissing babies while I was passing bills."

Knowing how Kennedy's top supporters detested him, Johnson must have seen Kennedy's nomination as a major roadblock in his drive for the presidency. He was therefore pleasantly surprised when Kennedy offered him the vice president's position on the ballot. This offer, coming as it did after an often-bitter contest between the two men, has been the subject of much debate. It now seems clear that Kennedy never really believed that Johnson would swap his Senate power for the empty honor of being vice president. He made the offer due to pressure from J. Edgar Hoover and as a conciliatory move, fully expecting Johnson to turn it down. But Johnson saw it as an opportunity to get one step closer to the presidency and promptly accepted. Reminded by friends that the office of vice president carried little importance, Johnson said, "Power is where power goes."

The Kennedy forces were shocked. How could Kennedy pick Johnson, who stood for almost everything they hated? It has been speculated that Kennedy accepted Johnson because it seemed necessary to have Johnson's help in swinging the 1960 election in southern and western states.

This proved prophetic. It was only through Johnson's tireless efforts that six crucial southern states—including Texas—were kept in the Democratic column.

In Texas this was accomplished very simply. According to biographer Haley, both Johnson and Rayburn warned the state's oilmen that if they voted for Nixon and the Democrats won, the oilmen could kiss the oil depletion allowance goodbye. So oil money helped swing the state for Kennedy-Johnson, despite a national Democratic Party platform that called for repealing the allowance—mute testimony to their belief in Johnson's power and hypocrisy. As vice president, Johnson was a changed man. Gone were his power and enthusiasm. There was almost constant friction between this old-style political powerbroker and the new breed of Kennedy men. Johnson's brother, Sam Houston Johnson, wrote about the treatment of his brother as vice president:

They made his stay in the vice presidency the most miserable three years of his life. He wasn't the number two man in the administration; he was the lowest man on the totem pole. . . . I know him well enough to know he felt humiliated time and time again, that he was openly snubbed by second-echelon White House staffers who snickered at him behind his back and called him "Uncle Corn Pone."

By the fall of 1963, rumors were rife that Johnson would be dumped from the 1964 Democratic national ticket. In fact, the day of Kennedy's assassination, the *Dallas Morning News* carried the headline: NIXON PREDICTS JFK MAY DROP JOHNSON. Consequently, Johnson made several trips abroad, most probably to escape the daily humiliations in the White House.

James Wagenvoord, editorial business manager and assistant to the executive editor of *Life* magazine, has revealed that his magazine was compiling information on Johnson's corrupt practices. "Beginning in later summer 1963 the magazine, based upon information fed from Bobby Kennedy and the Justice Department, had been developing a major news break piece concerning Johnson and Bobby Baker," said Wagenvoord. "On publication Johnson would have been finished and off the 1964 ticket (the reason the material was fed to us) and would probably have been facing prison time. At the time *Life* magazine was arguably the most important general news source in the US. The top management of Time Inc. was closely allied with the USA's various intelligence agencies and we were used by the Kennedy Justice Department as a conduit to the public." Immediately following the assassination, the exposé on Johnson was shredded and never saw publication.

Soon, yet another investigation into Johnson's dealings got under way. This time it involved a big-time Texas wheeler-dealer named Billic Sol Estes. Henry Marshall, a Department of Agriculture official, was looking into Estes's habit of acquiring millions in federal cotton allotment payments on land that was under water or actually owned by the government. Marshall was particularly interested in Estes's connections with his longtime friend Lyndon Johnson. However, before any official action could be taken, Marshall was found dead in a remote section of his farm near Franklin, Texas. He had been shot five times in the abdomen. Nearby lay a bolt-action single-shot .22-caliber rifle.

Five days later, without the benefit of an autopsy, a local peace justice ruled Marshall's death a suicide. Others knew better. Veteran Texas Ranger Clint Peoples once told this author, "If Henry Marshall committed suicide, I can ride a jackass to the moon."

In 1985 Estes, after being granted immunity from prosecution, told Texas media that Johnson had ordered Marshall's death to prevent his connections with Estes from being exposed. Later that year, a Texas district judge changed the official verdict of Marshall's death from suicide to homicide. At least three other men connected with the Estes case died in unusual circumstances.

By the time of the Kennedy assassination, dead witnesses, missing evidence, and interference with official investigations were nothing new to Lyndon Johnson.

It may also be highly significant that during Johnson's rise to power in Washington, one of his closest friends—in fact, a neighbor who frequently was his dinner guest—was none other than FBI director J. Edgar Hoover, also no stranger to the manipulation of politically sensitive investigations.

After becoming president, Johnson was encouraged to retire the crusty Hoover. But Johnson—possibly aware of the damaging evidence Hoover could provide against him—declined, saying, "I'd rather have him inside the tent pissing out, than outside pissing in."

Although it was against established security practice for the president and the vice president to be together in public, Johnson was riding only two cars behind Kennedy in the fateful Dallas motorcade.

At Parkland Hospital, Johnson was informed of Kennedy's death and then urged by Kennedy's assistant press secretary Malcolm Kilduff to make a public statement. As reported by author Jack Bell, Johnson told Kilduff:

> No, Mac. . . . I think I had better get out of here and get back to the plane before you announce [Kennedy's death]. We don't know whether there is a worldwide conspiracy, whether they are after me as well as they were after President Kennedy, or whether they are after Speaker McCormack or Senator Hayden. We just don't know.

It is significant to note that although Johnson mentioned fears of a "worldwide conspiracy" loudly in the hours immediately after Kennedy's death, there appears to have been no significant action to counter such a threat. While the Texas border was closed for a couple of hours, there was no widespread closing of US borders and major airplane and ship terminals were not shut down. Furthermore, while some units were placed on stepped-up status, there was no full-scale military alert, despite the commander in chief's stated concern.

Most significantly, at the same time Johnson was loudly decrying "a worldwide conspiracy," Warrant Officer Ira D. Gearhart, codenamed "Bagman" or "Football," who carried the launch codes for nuclear missiles in the event of sudden attack, was left behind not once but twice. He and Johnson became separated in the mad dash to Parkland and even then the Secret Service would not allow him in the room with Johnson at the hospital. In the rush to return to Love Field, Gearhart was left behind at Parkland and had to force his way onto a policeman's lap in an attempt to keep up with Johnson. Apparently Johnson had no real concern over hostilities with foreign powers.

It has seemed strange to researchers that while Kennedy's men wanted to leave Dallas as quickly as possible, it was Johnson who demanded that the entourage remain at Love Field until he could be sworn in as president by federal judge Sarah T. Hughes.

Hubert Humphrey, who later became Johnson's vice president, once correctly stated, "A vice president becomes president when there is no president. Later, when he takes the oath, he puts on the cloak of office. But that act is purely symbolic."

After arriving back in Washington, Jackie Kennedy explained to Robert Kennedy that the delay in returning was due to Johnson, who told her the attorney general had told him to take the oath of office in Dallas. Robert Kennedy was surprised and replied that he had made no such suggestion. Johnson compounded this lie months later in his deposition to the Warren Commission, when he again stated that it was Attorney General Kennedy who had urged him to take the oath immediately.

The new president was waiting on board presidential jet Air Force One when Kennedy's body reached Love Field. In his Warren Commission affidavit, Johnson said Kennedy's aide Kenneth O'Donnell specifically told him to take the presidential plane because it had better communication equipment. However, O'Donnell denied this, telling author William Manchester, "The President and I had no conversation regarding Air Force One. If we had known that he was going on Air Force One, we would have taken Air Force Two. One plane was just like the other."

O'Donnell later wrote that a Warren Commission attorney asked him to "change his testimony so that it would agree with the President's"—an offer O'Donnell declined.

While others were shocked into immobility by Kennedy's death, Johnson exhibited a strange—and perhaps suspicious—ability to press forward with his work. Johnson aide George Reedy commented that while "everything was chaotic, only the President knew what he was doing." While Kennedy's body still lay in state in the White House East Room, Johnson spoke with John Kenneth Galbraith, a liberal Harvard economist and confidant of Kennedy. Johnson laid out his 1964 election strategy to the flabbergasted Galbraith, saying, "I want to come down very hard on civil rights, not because Kennedy was for it, but because I am for it."

Author Jack Bell noted, "Almost from the moment he took the Presidential oath, Johnson had been unfolding a master plan designed to win the Presidency in his own right and . . . to carve for himself a favorable place in history."

During the course of the assassination investigation, a number of incidents occurred involving Johnson that suspicious researchers have viewed as destruction of critical evidence.

Within seventy-two hours of Kennedy's death—at Johnson's order—the presidential limousine SX-100, which carried Kennedy through Dallas, was shipped to Detroit, where the body was replaced and the interior completely refurbished. In any other case, this would have been destruction of evidence, since bullet marks on the windshield and blood traces could have provided essential clues as to the number and direction of shots.

After the assassination, Governor Connally's clothing—also vital evidence—was taken from the office of congressman Henry Gonzalez by Secret Service agents sent by Johnson aide Cliff Carter. Connally's clothing had been cleaned and pressed by the time it was handed over to the Warren Commission and, hence, useless as evidence.

One of Johnson's actions that caused researchers of the assassination no end of problems was Executive Order 11652, which locked an immense amount of assassination evidence and documents in the National Archives away from the American public until the year 2039. It was this act, more than any other, that has caused so much speculation about Johnson's possible role in the assassination. However, by the twenty-first century, thanks primarily to the creation of the Assassinations Records Review Board, much of this material had become public, though in 2013 there continued to be conflicts with the National Archives over the release of JFK assassination documents.

It is now publicly known that Johnson's mental state deteriorated significantly in the years following his predecessor's assassination. Former aide and speechwriter Richard Goodwin, who had helped fashion LBJ's "Great Society," has written that Johnson became obsessed with the idea that America was being taken over by his enemies—communists and "those Kennedys." Goodwin said he and aide Bill Moyers even consulted psychiatrists about his boss's behavior.

Another episode that may have had underlying psychological significance was related by Johnson's younger brother. Sam Houston Johnson said a few days after the assassination he got a long-distance call from the new president, who told him, "I've been waiting for the chance to talk to you and let you know how much I appreciated all you've done for me, Sam Houston." Sam, who said he had had a few drinks, jokingly replied, "I had nothing to do with Oswald." Lyndon flew off the handle, shouting into the phone, "Goddamit, Sam, what kind of remark is that?" Lyndon, widely known for his coarse humor, astonished his brother by launching into a thirty-minute tirade, getting angrier and angrier by the moment.

Madeleine Duncan Brown, whose claim to have been Johnson's mistress for twenty years has never been successfully refuted, publicly stated that Johnson had foreknowledge of the assassination. In her 1997 book, *Texas in the Morning*, Brown told of meeting with Johnson in Austin's Driskill Hotel at the end of December 1963. When she told him some people were accusing Johnson of playing some role in the assassination, he told her, "It was Texas oil and those fucking renegade intelligence bastards in Washington."

But did Johnson really have enough power to initiate the assassination and to force literally dozens of government officials and agents to lie and cover up that fact? Probably not.

However, if Johnson played some role in an assassination plot, he would have taken great pains to distance himself from such a conspiracy. Evidence of such a role would certainly not be readily available. Therefore, today it is possible only to point out that Johnson—above everyone else—benefited most from Kennedy's death. Plus, it only stands to reason that no one would kill the chief executive without some assurance that his successor would not move heaven and earth to pursue and punish the perpetrators.

With the assassination, Johnson achieved his lifelong goal of gaining the presidency, his business and oil backers were rid of Kennedy's interference, and his supporters who wanted an Asian war—notably Brown & Root and ranking officers at the Pentagon—were free to pursue a widening conflict.

A final point is that Johnson—always conscious of his role in history—must have feared appearing to be a dunce by continuing to support the Warren Commission's lone-assassin myth. In an interview with Walter Cronkite in the early 1970s, Johnson expressed the belief that the assassination involved more than one person, then asked network executives to delete his remarks from the broadcast—which they did.

In 1973, Johnson was quoted in *Atlantic Monthly* acknowledging, "I never believed that Oswald acted alone although I can accept that he pulled the trigger."

Johnson even voiced the suspicion that the CIA had a hand in the assassination, according to an FBI document released in 1977. The document quotes Johnson's postmaster general and close friend Marvin Watson as relaying to the bureau that "[Johnson] was now convinced there was a plot in connection with the assassination. Watson stated the President felt the CIA had something to do with this plot."

Yet this, too, was kept hidden from the public for years and is still not widely known.

Was Johnson well aware of such a plot and mentioned it in later years only so that future historians would not classify him as dense and naïve?

While this ambitiously driven man from Texas most probably did not initiate a death plot against Kennedy, everything known about the man—from the deaths and cover-ups of Texas scandals to his continued prosecution of the unpopular Vietnam War—indicates that Johnson may have had the willingness to join in a conspiracy that would place him in the White House.

As commander in chief of the armed forces and close confidant to the powerful J. Edgar Hoover, Johnson certainly had the ability to subvert a meaningful investigation into Kennedy's death—and a wealth of evidence suggests just such subversion. Did Johnson and Hoover contract with the mob to kill Kennedy? Or did the mob approach them? Or did they simply turn a blind eye to an existing plot? The truth of their involvement may not be proven for years, if ever. However, a conspiracy involving Lyndon Johnson and his buddy Hoover as an alternative to the Warren Commission's discredited lone-assassin theory goes farther in tying together the disparate bits of assassination evidence than any theory offered to date, and cannot be summarily dismissed.

Due to the demonstrable actions of both Johnson and Hoover in suppressing, altering, and fabricating evidence in this case, both men are clearly accessories after the fact. Under our legal system, accessories in murder cases are considered just as guilty as the person who pulled the trigger.

History will surely hold president and commander in chief Lyndon Johnson, along with his friend FBI director J. Edgar Hoover, guilty in the assassination—if not for orchestrating the assassination itself, at least for taking actions during their time in office to block any meaningful investigation into the plot.

Soldiers

During the past two hundred years the military forces of the United States have accumulated a distinguished history. From the Revolution-era citizen who could become a fighting man ready to protect his community in a minute to the professional Marines who grimly stand guard in the face of terrorism at US embassies around the world, the American soldier has proven his worth time and again. Amid the bitter dissension produced by US policy in Southeast Asia and currently the Middle East, few people seriously question the ability or bravery of the individual GI.

However, throughout world history, it has proven extremely difficult to return to civilian control of government in peacetime once power has been invested in the military. From the takeover of the Roman Empire by the Praetorian Guard up until today, military leaders have sought to maintain power and control.

This situation was aggravated in the United States during World War II by a combining of military and industrial power.

The Military-Industrial Complex

On January 17, 1961, three days before John F. Kennedy took office as president, president Dwight Eisenhower gave his farewell address to Congress. In this talk he coined the phrase "military-industrial complex" and warned against potential abuses by such an entity. He said:

> This conjunction of an immense military establishment and a large arms industry is new in the American experience. The total influence—economical, political, even spiritual—is felt in every city, every state house, every office of the federal government. . . . In the councils of government, we must guard against the acquisition of unwarranted influence, whether sought or unsought, by the military-industrial complex. The potential for the disastrous rise of misplaced power exists and will persist. We must never let the weight of this combination endanger our liberties or democratic processes.

Eisenhower's warning was especially timely, as the role of the military-industrial complex in American life has continued to grow under successive presidencies. By 2013, many police officers were wearing black bulletproof vests and Nazi-style helmets while remote-controlled drone aircraft prowled American skies.

The rise of the military-industrial complex can be charted by annual military budget expenditures. In 1950 the military budget was $13 billion; by 1961 this had risen to $47 billion; and by the end of the Vietnam War in 1975, it was $100 billion. By 1986 annual expenses by the Department of Defense had risen to nearly $170 billion. In 2012 this figure was up to $707.5 billion. By adding in the budgets of Homeland Security, the Department of Energy, and FBI counterterrorism, total expenditures for national security came to an astounding $1.4 trillion.

A large part of the argument for maintaining an ongoing war economy came from men and women who lived through the shock of Pearl Harbor. Vowing never again to allow the United States to be caught unaware by an enemy—although substantial evidence now shows that the Japanese attack was not wholly unexpected in certain Washington circles—such persons have argued that assembly and production lines must be kept operating so that America can convert to war production quickly, if needed. This argument—plus the fact that millions of American jobs depend on defense contracts—has been instrumental in maintaining the war economy.

Critics, on the other hand, claim the permanent war economy has actually been a drain on America's economic life—with its production of non-usable goods and its penchant for inefficiency and corruption.

A product of his time, senator John F. Kennedy parroted the Pentagon line during the 1960 campaign, promising increases in military spending.

Once in the Oval Office—with access to other sources of information—Kennedy changed his attitudes toward the military. Earlier he had echoed Pentagon figures showing that the Soviet Union possessed between five hundred and one thousand intercontinental ballistic missiles. According to later reports, the number was more like fifty. Kennedy complained that he had been ill-informed as to the actual number of missiles and suggested that this exaggeration was part of Pentagon strategy.

This complaint has been repeated over and over through the years, even by former CIA director William Colby in comments on the cover of the book *The Myth of Soviet Military Supremacy*, which he called "the greatest intelligence gap of all: the exaggeration of Soviet power in comparison with America's, which fuels the wasteful and dangerous nuclear arms race."

In addition to worries over the military, Kennedy also became concerned with the $3 billion federal deficit of his time—a paltry sum compared to today's nearly $16 trillion—and feared it would present a threat to the US dollar. Accordingly, Kennedy named a Ford Motor Company executive, Robert McNamara, as his secretary of defense and changes began to take place. On March 28, 1961, Kennedy told Congress, "In January, while ordering certain immediately needed changes, I instructed the Secretary of Defense to reappraise our entire defense strategy, capacity, commitments, and needs in light of present and future dangers."

Kennedy began to significantly modify the way defense and intelligence operated. Presidents Truman and Eisenhower had depended greatly on the National Security Council (NSC), a creation of the National Security Act of 1947. In 1963 the NSC consisted of the president, vice president, secretary of state, secretary of defense, and director of the Office of Emergency Planning.

Theoretically, the CIA was to be controlled by the NSC. But Kennedy had another way of getting things done. Accustomed to the quick-acting, hard-hitting world of political campaigning, Kennedy neglected the NSC method. Instead, he would call upon his friends and family to get things done. While this may have been effective at the time, it left both the Pentagon and the CIA largely to their own devices—a circumstance Kennedy came to regret.

During this same period, US foreign policy was being greatly influenced by a new vision of the role of the military in the world. This vision was codified in a May 15, 1959, document written by General Richard Stilwell as a member of a special presidential committee. Innocuously titled "Training Under the Mutual Training Program," this document offered nothing less than a plan to protect the noncommunist world by having nations ruled by a military elite with training and ideology supplied by Americans.

Initially Kennedy was fascinated by this concept, since by nature he was a strong believer in negotiation and limited response rather than simply using military options. Words such as "counterinsurgency," "pacification," and "special forces" began to creep into our political language.

Following the disastrous Bay of Pigs Invasion, a special board of inquiry was convened to dissect what went wrong. It was here that both John and Robert Kennedy began to learn what the new military doctrines of counterinsurgency, flexible response, civic action, and nation building really meant. They saw how the obsession with secrecy had completely changed the way the military and intelligence operated. Everything was on a "need-to-know" basis, with fewer and fewer responsible leaders included on the "need-to-know" lists. After the Bay of Pigs inquiry Kennedy became convinced that the CIA and the Pentagon had misled him terribly, and from that point on he was highly skeptical of information from those sources. Moreover, the inquiry showed the Kennedy brothers how powerful the military-industrial complex and its intelligence-security force had become.

Kennedy did learn something from this coalition—how to concoct a "cover story," which may account for his public support of the CIA while his private comments and actions showed otherwise.

Kennedy began to balk at his military advisers, who had assured him of victory in Cuba, and who now were urging military intervention, to include the use of nuclear weapons, in Laos, where communist insurgents were gaining ground. Military hawks became incensed when Kennedy negotiated with Soviet Premier Nikita Khrushchev a coalition government in Laos, forestalling armed conflict. They were further angered when Kennedy told them he would not send combat troops to South Vietnam.

The blending of the military and the political was seen most clearly in Vietnam, where it was the US ambassador who was in charge, not the senior military commanders.

War should be politicians' last resort. But once war is inevitable, it should be fought by professional soldiers with clearly defined goals and objectives.

After the CIA-sponsored Bay of Pigs fiasco Kennedy began to see that this nation's paramilitary and undercover operations were getting out of hand. He attempted to stem this trend by issuing two National Security Action Memoranda (NSAM) in June 1961. NSAM 55, signed personally by Kennedy, basically stated that he would hold the chairman of the Joint Chiefs of Staff personally responsible for all activity of a military nature during peacetime, the same as during wartime. In other words, Kennedy wanted all cloak-and-dagger operations as well as military expeditions under the control, or at least under the scrutiny, of the chairman—and hence under his control.

NSAM 57 attempted to divide paramilitary activity between the military and the CIA. Basically, this document stipulated that the CIA would be allowed only small covert operations, while any large operations must be studied and approved by the military. It seemed a reasonable division of responsibility. However, there were men in both the CIA and the Pentagon who did not appreciate this attempt to curb their power and prerogatives.

Not only did Kennedy attempt to curtail the power of both the military and intelligence, but he also presented a very different worldview from the past. On November 16, 1961, Kennedy told a Seattle audience, "We must face the fact that the United States is neither omnipotent nor omniscient—that we cannot impose our will upon the other 94 percent of mankind—that we cannot right every wrong or reverse every adversity—and that therefore there cannot be an American solution to every world problem."

With his words and actions, Kennedy became the first US president since World War II to address the myth of America's infallibility. This did not sit well with the military-industrial complex, which had so much to gain—including profits—by controlling the raw resources of other nations.

In the midst of Kennedy's reappraisal of US military and intelligence operations came the Cuban Missile Crisis.

In October 1962, information from satellites and U-2 flights revealed that the Soviets were preparing offensive missile bases in Cuba, only ninety miles from the United States. The military and the CIA were aghast. They prescribed nothing less than immediate bombing of the missile sites and another invasion of the island.

Kennedy chose a different approach. He personally struck a deal with Premier Khrushchev—the Russians would remove their missiles from Cuba and in return the United States would remove its offensive missiles from Turkey and Kennedy would pledge not to support a new invasion of Cuba. The Soviets appeared to back down and Kennedy's popularity rose significantly, except in offices at the Pentagon and at Langley, Virginia.

Meanwhile, the Kennedy administration continued its efforts to reduce military spending. On March 30, 1963, McNamara announced a reorganization program that would have closed fifty-two military installations in twenty-five states, as well as twenty-one overseas bases, over a three-year period.

Then on August 5, 1963, following lengthy negotiations, the United States, Great Britain, and the Soviet Union signed a limited nuclear test–ban treaty forbidding the atmospheric testing of nuclear weapons.

As part of this "first step" toward what later would be termed "détente," Kennedy and Khrushchev agreed to install a "hot line" telephone system between Washington and Moscow.

It was a serious deviation from the hard Cold War policies of the past, and military leaders—both retired and active—did not hesitate to voice their disapproval.

But for all his activities to reduce the risk of war and curtail the military and intelligence establishments, Kennedy's most momentous—and perhaps fatal—decisions came when he began to reevaluate US policy in Southeast Asia.

Kennedy and Vietnam

From the moment Lyndon B. Johnson took over the presidency, the idea was encouraged that he would simply carry on Kennedy administration policies. In some ways he did. It has been acknowledged that Johnson was able to push Kennedy's civil rights legislation through Congress where his predecessor may have failed. But one emerging Kennedy policy was not continued—that involved South Vietnam.

Early in his presidency, Kennedy simply went along with Eisenhower's policy to continue sending military "advisers" and materiel to South Vietnam. In fact, during 1961 and 1962, Kennedy actually increased the US military presence in that war-torn nation. This may have been due to his desire to avoid at all costs another foreign-policy disaster such as the Bay of Pigs.

But by summer 1963, Kennedy had begun to reevaluate US involvement.

By the time Kennedy was elected president in 1960, large-scale guerrilla warfare was being conducted against the South Vietnam regime. But because of Castro and Cuba as well as Soviet incursions in Berlin and the Congo, Vietnam was not an issue during the 1960 campaign. Three days after his election, Kennedy barely noticed that South Vietnam's President Diem was the object of an unsuccessful military coup d'état. In December 1960, the communists announced the formation of the Vietnamese National Liberation Front (the Viet Cong), and the internal guerrilla war got under way in earnest.

During 1961 Kennedy, though distracted by the Bay of Pigs Invasion, continued to support further US military assistance to Asia, particularly after communist forces seized the city of Phuoc Vinh, only sixty miles from Saigon. On December 11, two helicopter companies arrived in South Vietnam, beginning an expanded role for US advisers. By January 1962, total US military personnel in Vietnam numbered 2,646. And on January 13, a memorandum from the Joint Chiefs of Staff, titled "The Strategic Importance of the SEA [Southeast Asian] Mainland," stated that if the Viet Cong were not soon brought under control, the chiefs saw no alternative but to introduce US ground combat units.

Kennedy continued to hesitate about sending combat units to Vietnam. At a news conference on May 9, 1962, he said, "Introducing American forces . . . also is a hazardous course, and we want to attempt to see if we can work out a peaceful solution."

According to assistant secretary of state Roger Hilsman, one of Kennedy's key foreign policy planners, Kennedy told confidants, "The Bay of Pigs has taught me a number of things. One is not to trust generals or the CIA, and the second is that if the American people do not want to use American troops to remove a communist regime 90 miles away from our coast, how can I ask them to use troops to remove a communist regime 9,000 miles away?"

By mid-1963, after receiving conflicting advice and intelligence from his advisers regarding Vietnam, Kennedy began to further reassess US commitment there. He was especially concerned about the treatment of Buddhists under the Diem government. Thousands of Buddhists were demonstrating for freedom, and on June 11, the first Buddhist suicide by self-immolation occurred.

Reflecting Kennedy's concern, the State Department notified Saigon, "If Diem does not take prompt and effective steps to re-establish Buddhist confidence in him, we will have to re-examine our entire relationship with his regime."

Diem grew even more unmanageable as 1963 drew on, staffing his government with relatives and refusing to listen to the pleas of the Buddhists. Talk began about replacing Diem with leaders more agreeable to American policy.

The American government, including Kennedy, left no doubt of its displeasure with Diem, thus paving the way for yet another Vietnamese coup, which occurred on November 1, 1963, just twenty-one days before Kennedy arrived in Dallas.

Accompanied by CIA agent Lucien Conein, South Vietnam generals seized key installations and attacked the presidential palace. After hours of fighting, Diem and his brother, Ngo Dinh Nhu, surrendered. While being taken to the generals' headquarters, both were murdered.

Kennedy, who had approved the coup, then rejected it, then okayed it again, was genuinely shocked at the murders. Washington was forced to recognize the new military government in Saigon, but for the next twenty months, there were no fewer than ten changes of government as one general overthrew another.

It was time for a decision in Vietnam—to support a major American military expedition as the Pentagon desired or to simply withdraw and take the criticism of the anticommunists.

The assassination of the Diem brothers may have strengthened Kennedy's decision to disengage from Vietnam, and there is evidence that he would have curtailed the Vietnam War.

Kennedy, forever the astute politician, also was very much aware of the approaching 1964 election.

Senator Mike Mansfield of Montana told news reporters that once, following a White House leadership meeting, Kennedy had confided to him that he agreed "on a need for a complete withdrawal from Vietnam," but he couldn't do it until after being reelected.

The president also may have given a hint as to his plans in a broadcast on September 2, 1963. Speaking of Vietnam, he said, "In the final analysis, it is their war. They have to win or lose it."

People within the Pentagon and the CIA—who had so much to gain by widening the Vietnam War—continued to put out conflicting and often erroneous information.

Shortly before the Diem coup, McNamara and General Maxwell Taylor had returned from Saigon and told Kennedy that things were looking better in Vietnam and that the United States could withdraw all military personnel by the end of 1965. On hearing this optimistic assessment, on October 5, 1963, Kennedy approved an Accelerated Withdrawal Program, designed to carry out the promise to end the American military presence by the close of 1965.

National Security Action Memorandum (NSAM) 263 stated that at a meeting on October 11, 1963, the president considered the recommendations contained in the report of Secretary McNamara and General Taylor on their mission to South Vietnam. It read:

> The President approved the military recommendations [withdrawal by the end of 1965] . . . but directed that no formal announcement be made of the implementation of plans to withdraw 1,000 military personnel by the end of 1963.

Such unpublicized moves to disengage from Vietnam allowed anti-Kennedy forces to argue that no change of policy took place.

Less than one month after Kennedy's assassination, McNamara and Taylor changed their tune. They reported to President Johnson that conditions in Vietnam were grave and that a major effort—including American combat troops and a massive clandestine program—was needed to prevent a communist victory.

Kennedy's covert withdrawal plan ended a mere two days after Kennedy's assassination when President Johnson signed NSAM 273, which canceled the troop withdrawal. This document also subtly changed the US objective from simply assisting the South Vietnamese to assisting them "to win" against the communists, and authorized plans for expanding the war into North Vietnam and Laos. The memorandum also ordered senior government officials not to contest or criticize the changes.

It should be noted that a rough draft of NSAM 273, which essentially rescinded Kennedy's withdrawal policy, was found in the Johnson Presidential Library in Austin. It was dated November 21, 1963, the day before the assassination! Someone knew that JFK's troop reduction order would not be fulfilled.

Kennedy aide Kenneth O'Donnell confirmed this in his 1972 book, *Johnny, We Hardly Knew Ye*. He wrote, "The President's orders to reduce American military personnel in Vietnam by one thousand before the end of 1963 was still in effect on the day he went to Texas. A few days after his death, during the morning, the order was quietly rescinded."

Nine months after the assassination, the Vietnam War got into full swing when Congress passed the Gulf of Tonkin Resolution, which granted President Johnson the power to wage full-scale war in Southeast Asia. The US military had been secretly raiding the North Vietnamese coast, and in the adjacent Gulf of Tonkin jittery US sailors egged on by a CIA radio monitoring station had reported gunfire in the dark and were told they were under attack. By 2012, it was well documented and even presented in the mainstream media that the incident in the Gulf of Tonkin was phony. There was no attack by North Vietnam and no US sailor was killed. But within a month of this false-flag incident, Johnson had ordered ground combat troops into Vietnam.

Obviously, at this late date, no one wants to claim responsibility for a ten-year undeclared war that killed 58,000 Americans, caused domestic riots and demonstrations, engendered lasting hatred between classes and age groups, and according to many, nearly wrecked the American economy.

Was Kennedy's embryonic move to disengage in Vietnam a catalyst for his assassination? Was this the straw that broke the back of the military-industrial camel?

As terrible as it is to contemplate the involvement of the US military in the Kennedy assassination, there are many connections between the two. Several factors have raised suspicions concerning the military's role in the assassination.

It has been reported that the 112th Military Intelligence Group at 4th Army Headquarters at Fort Sam Houston in San Antonio was told to "stand down" that day rather than report for duty in Dallas, over the "violent" protests of the unit commander, Colonel Maximillian Reich. As noted by CIA-Pentagon liaison Colonel Fletcher Prouty, "Who has the power to make this kind of call? Not Lee Oswald, or Castro, or the Mafia . . . only someone with [military code] knowledge can make the call and use such code words that are needed to 'stand down' an entire Army unit."

Though apparently some elements of the military intelligence unit did arrive in Dallas, their activities there remain obscure. One member may have been with FBI agent James Hosty the morning Kennedy was killed. In Warren Commission testimony, Hosty said that forty-five minutes before the assassination he was in the company of a naval intelligence officer, but he added the meeting had no connection with Kennedy's visit.

Recall that Agent Hosty's name, address, phone number, and license number were found in Lee Harvey Oswald's personal notebook, which was originally deleted from the material turned over to the Warren Commission, and it was Hosty who destroyed a message from Oswald days after the assassination apparently on orders from superiors.

An Army intelligence officer involved in the assassination was special agent James Powell. Carrying a 35 mm Minolta camera, Powell had taken several photos in Dealey Plaza at the time of the assassination. He entered the Texas School Book Depository and his presence became public knowledge when he was forced to show his identification after Dallas police sealed the building. Powell told researcher Penn Jones he "worked with the sheriff's deputies at the rear of the Texas School Book Depository for about six or eight minutes" and that Powell had ordered a news reporter to hang up a telephone on the building's first floor so that he could use it.

The government has not pursued any meaningful investigation to determine what intelligence Agent Powell was conducting in Dealey Plaza at the time of the assassination or why he was photographing the exterior of the Depository prior to the shooting.

And the military connection becomes even more curious in light of other strange incidents that occurred in Dallas that day.

Dallas police lieutenant Jack Revill told the Warren Commission that a military intelligence officer rode with him from Dealey Plaza to the Dallas police station. It was Revill, as head of the police criminal intelligence division, who submitted a list of Texas School Book Depository employees. Heading Revill's list was the name "Harvey Lee Oswald," with the address given as 605 Elsbeth in Dallas.

During the House Select Committee on Assassinations investigation it was re-vealed that the 112th Military Intelligence Group, which maintained an office in Dallas, had possessed a file on a man named "Harvey Lee Oswald," identifying him as a procommunist who had been in Russia and had been involved in pro-Castro activities in New Orleans. This military file erroneously gave Oswald's address as 605 Elsbeth, the same mistake found on Revill's list.

Oswald had lived at 602 Elsbeth in late 1962 and early 1963 but had since moved, and the Elsbeth address had never been given to his employers at the Depository. And, of course, his name was Lee Harvey Oswald. It seems evident, based on this information, that military intelligence tipped off the Dallas police as to the identity of their suspect.

The erroneous information came from military intelligence files. In testimony to the House Select Committee on Assassinations, the 112th Military Intelligence Group's operations officer, Lieutenant Colonel Robert E. Jones, who was stationed at Fort Sam Houston, said the afternoon of the assassination he received a call from his agents in Dallas advising that a man named A. J. Hidell had been arrested.

Jones said he searched his intelligence indexes and located a file on A. J. Hidell that cross-referenced into one for Harvey Lee Oswald of 605 Elsbeth. He said he then contacted the FBI in both San Antonio and Dallas with his information.

However, in the vast documentation of Oswald's life he used the A. J. Hidell alias only twice—when he mail-ordered the Carcano rifle and the pistol and when he used the name Hidell on Fair Play for Cuba literature.

This indicates that it was US military intelligence that tipped off the Dallas po-lice as to the identity of their suspect and raises two possibilities. Either military intelligence had some independent knowledge of Oswald's purchase of the weapons, which took place long before he arrived in New Orleans, or they were monitoring his Dallas post office box. Or did someone, perhaps even Oswald himself, inform the military of his purchases?

The files on Hidell and Oswald gave detailed information about Oswald's trip to Russia as well as pro-Castro activities in New Orleans. Jones said he had become aware of Oswald in the summer of 1963 when information had been passed along by the New Orleans Police Department regarding his arrest there. He said the 112th Military Intelligence Group took an interest in Oswald as a possible counterintel-ligence threat.

The House committee, remarking on how quickly the military found files on Oswald, stated, "This information suggested the existence of a military intelligence file on Oswald and raised the possibility that he had intelligence associations of some kind."

The Warren Commission specifically asked to see any military files regarding Oswald but never saw the files mentioned by Jones or others.

In 1978, when the House Select Committee on Assassinations learned of these files and requested them from the military, they were told the files had been "destroyed routinely" in 1973. The committee concluded:

> The committee found this "routine" destruction of the Oswald file extremely troublesome, especially when viewed in light of the Department of Defense's failure to make the file available to the Warren Commission. Despite the credibility of Jones' testimony, without access to this file, the question of Oswald's possible affiliation with military intelligence could not be fully resolved.

It appears that the US military knew more about Oswald and his weapons than has been made public yet destroyed all the files when talk of a reinvestigation began in the early 1970s. But does that mean the military orchestrated the assassination?

It is ironic that of all our modern presidents, it was John F. Kennedy who received the only full military funeral in recent history. Why Kennedy? Why not Eisenhower? Was this the military's way of making atonement?

In early 2013, the Elsbeth apartment building was bulldozed on orders of Dallas officials despite protests by the owner, who said she tried to renovate it and preserve it.

The Man Who Was to Kill Oswald

[Since the first edition of *Crossfire*, readers have pondered the meaning of the heading above but that was followed by no copy. Apparently it was decided to delete the entire section in an effort to save costs but someone forgot to delete the heading. Here is the long-missing section. For an excellent and more detailed account of this story, see Dick Russell's 1992 book *The Man Who Knew Too Much*.]

According to one soldier's account, there was even an attempt to prevent the assassination by killing a key player—Lee Harvey Oswald.

The man's name was Richard Case Nagell and he told one of the strangest and most sinister stories to come out of the Kennedy assassination. As pieced together from interviews and court documents and a national magazine article in 1981 by writer and researcher Dick Russell, Nagell's story delved into the complex and murky world of military intelligence, the CIA, and the FBI.

Raised in an orphanage and foster homes, Nagell entered the Army in 1948 at age eighteen. During the Korean War, he was the youngest American to receive a battlefield commission. He was awarded three Purple Hearts and a Bronze Star while serving in Korea and honorably discharged in 1959 with the rank of captain.

Military papers disclosed that Nagell graduated from Army Military Intelligence School and a special leader's course, and served in the Counterintelligence Corps. According to his records, he was given a top-secret security clearance in 1950. One of his commendation certificates described Nagell as a "perennial calm and level-headed officer of superior intelligence."

According to courtroom testimony, in 1958 military intelligence "loaned" Nagell to "another intelligence agency" for assignments in Asia as part of a spy group called Field Operations Intelligence.

As a senior intelligence adviser in South Korea, Nagell admitted participating in political assassinations, kidnapping, blackmail, and counterfeiting operations. By 1957, he had told superiors he was "fed up" with committing crimes in the name of national security and was reassigned to counterintelligence duties in Japan. It was here, he said, he first met a young Marine stationed at Atsugi named Lee Harvey Oswald.

"We had a casual, but purposeful acquaintance in Japan," Nagell told Russell. "My relationship with Oswald there, and later in the United States, was strictly with an objective."

About this time, Nagell married a Japanese woman and, at her urging, resigned his commission, returned to the United States, and went to work for the State of California. In 1962, amid marital problems, he left his wife and two children and journeyed to Mexico City.

In Mexico, Nagell said, he contacted a CIA man he had previously known and signed a contract with the agency, becoming a double agent. He was to work for the Soviet KGB while actually serving the CIA.

The Soviets informed him of a plot to kill Kennedy involving the violent anti-Castro Cuban group known as Alpha 66 and ordered Nagell to return to the United States to learn more. The KGB even provided Nagell with a photograph of one of the plotters. Nagell was shocked to find it was his old acquaintance Lee Harvey Oswald.

Nagell echoed the story from Soviet defector Yuri Nosenko when he told Russell, "When he [Oswald] was in the Soviet Union, they suspected him as a spy and considered him emotionally unstable, prone to commit some act that could bring embarrassment to them."

Nagell would not give details about what he discovered concerning Oswald in the fall of 1962, but he did say, "He was just being used—by a lot of people, for their own reasons." Nagell said he became aware of at least two Kennedy assassination plots during this time, both involving Cubans, whose "war names" were "Angel" and "Leopaldo," the same names given to Silvia Odio.

According to Nagell, the CIA-backed Alpha 66 Cubans convinced Oswald they were members of Castro's intelligence service and solicited his help in assassinating Kennedy to avenge CIA assassination plots against Castro. Since the evidence suggests Oswald was actually playing as an undercover agent of the United States, he would, of course, have gone along with these schemes to learn all he could about the plots. Nagell said he actually got close enough to the plotting to tape a New Orleans meeting in late August 1963.

Nagell was then ordered by KGB officials fearful of being implicated in an assassination to disrupt the Kennedy plot. "[I was to] try to persuade Oswald that the deal was phony and if this didn't work, and if it looked like things were going to progress beyond the talking stage, to get rid of him," said Nagell, explaining that considering Oswald's background in Russia, the Soviets "were the last people that wanted Kennedy dead" in a plot involving Oswald.

Nagell said he met with Oswald in early September in New Orleans's Jackson Square. Unwilling to break his cover as a KGB operative, Nagell nevertheless tried to warn Oswald that "Angel" and "Leopoldo" were not Castro agents, but "counter-revolutionaries known to be connected with a violence-prone faction of a CIA-financed groupo." Later, Nagell related:

> He was informed that he was being "used" by fascist elements in an attempt to disrupt the Cuban revolution, and probably to incite the US Government to severe retaliatory measures against Cuba, etc. He denied that there had been any serious discussion to kill Kennedy. He seemed genuinely upset and visibly shaken. . . . He stated he was a friend of the Cuban revolution.

Frustrated that Oswald still maintained his own "cover," Nagell then sent a registered letter to FBI director J. Edgar Hoover, warning of the assassination plot and naming both Oswald and the Cubans but stating that the plot might occur in late September in Washington, DC.

After sending this letter, Nagell said, he again met with Oswald and told him a Soviet agent code-named "Oaxaca" wanted to meet Oswald in Mexico City. According to Nagell:

> He (Oswald) was instructed not to go near the Cuban or U.S.S.R. embassies. Oswald agreed to do so when he was advised that he would be provided with more than sufficient funds to make the trip to and from Mexico City by plane. He was told where and how he was to pick up the money order on 9/24/63, his expected date of departure from New Orleans.

On September 17, the day Oswald picked up his Mexican tourist card in New Orleans, Nagell was already on his way to Mexico City, carrying a .45-caliber Colt pistol to use on Oswald.

But Nagell began to have second thoughts about his role as a double agent and as an assassin. On September 20, he instead drove to El Paso and entered the State National Bank. According to Russell, "He had decided he could not go through with the KGB's assignment. Doubtful about which master he was really serving, unable to kill a man and then face life abroad without his children, he chose instead to get himself placed in federal custody."

After all, he had alerted the FBI, although the bureau predictably denied ever having received his letter. The matter was out of his hands. While in jail awaiting trial for bank robbery, Nagell was visited often by both FBI and Secret Service agents, according to jailer Juan Medina. Two FBI agents visited Nagell on November 19, only three days before the assassination. Early in 1964, Nagell was brought before US district judge Homer Thornberry in El Paso. The *El Paso Times* reported, "Instead of asking for a plea, Fred Morton, assistant US District Attorney made a motion to put Nagell in a federal institution in Springfield, Mo., for psychiatric observation. The motion was granted over Nagell's vigorous objections."

The newspaper also reported that FBI and Secret Service agents had questioned Nagell about Oswald and "subversive activities." On March 20, 1964, Nagell tried to communicate with the Warren Commission, writing, "Has the Commission been advised that I informed the Federal Bureau of Investigation in September 1963 that an attempt might be made to assassinate President Kennedy?"

Despite this letter and the attention paid to Nagell by the FBI and Secret Service, there is no mention of him in the Warren Report or its attendant twenty-six volumes. Nagell again wrote to Hoover:

> My responsibility concerning the then prospective action of Lee H. Oswald (alias) Albert Hidell, terminated with the dispatch of the registered letter from Richard Nagell to the FBI in September 1963. Since the information disclosed in that letter was judged to be mendacious by the FBI, as is quite evident, then with whom the responsibility lies for what subsequently happened in Dallas is rather obvious.

In March 1964, Nagell was declared competent to stand trial and, although he had no previous criminal record and the holdup was obviously faked, he was convicted of two counts of entering a bank with intent to rob and given the maximum sentence of ten years in the US Penitentiary in Leavenworth, Kansas.

His conviction was overturned in 1966 and a new trial ordered. Again he was found guilty and again drew a ten-year prison term. However, this was reversed in 1968 by the US Court of Appeals "in view of strong evidence that defendant was insane at time of offense." Nagell finally was set free.

But he was not truly free. He claimed he was followed and hounded and that attempts were made on his life. Nagell died of heart disease in 1995 at the age of sixty-five. It should be noted that the government has often used criminal and medical history documents, whether real or otherwise, to discredit testimony from people who might challenge the official version of an event.

But other military men apparently did not have such benign intentions toward President Kennedy and assassination.

Lone Gunmen on the Grassy Knoll

By 2013, numerous people had been identified as a possible Grassy Knoll gunman. But to this author's knowledge only four identified persons have actually confessed and all started out as American GIs. Of these four, only two offered any real evidence and even this was contradictory and far from conclusive.

The story of one of these men, Loy Factor, became public when researchers Mark Collom and Glen Sample self-published the 1995 book *The Men on the Sixth Floor*. Collom had met Lawrence Lloyd Factor when both were hospitalized in 1971. Factor's story seemed so farfetched that both the publishing world and most researchers ignored it.

Loy Factor was a Native American who claimed to have suffered brain damage while serving in the military during World War II. His story, as recounted by author Robin Ramsey in the 2007 book *Who Shot JFK?*, was this:

> Factor met a man he knew only as Wallace in 1962 at the funeral of a Texas politician. Factor said he went along just to see some famous people. In the course of their conversation, Factor boasted to Wallace of his shooting and hunting skills. Wallace was interested and asked for Factor's address. A year later he turned up and asked for a demonstration of Factor's shooting ability. Having seen it, the man told Factor that he might have a job for him in the future using his rifle, a job worth $10,000—$2,000 immediately and the rest when the job was done. Factor accepted the $2,000. . . . Later the man sent for Factor to do the job. Factor was taken to a house in Dallas where he met Jack Ruby, the man called Wallace, Lee Harvey Oswald and a young Hispanic woman, Ruth Ann. They ended up on the sixth floor of the book depository. [After firing coordinated shots at Kennedy, the group] fled quickly down the stairs—Ruth Ann and Factor to their parked car, Oswald and Wallace in different directions. Loy was driven to the bus depot, a few blocks away where he was to catch a bus back home. But in a short while Ruth Ann and Wallace both returned to the depot to pick up Factor and drive him out of town.

It would be easy enough to dismiss Factor's story, especially since he claimed to have collected $10,000 for his role yet never fired a rifle, except for the fact that years after publishing their book, Collom and Sample learned Wallace's first name was Malcolm or Mac and in 1998 heard that a group of Texas researchers had identified fingerprints found on the sixth floor of the Texas School Book Depository the day of the assassination could be traced to Malcolm "Mac" Wallace, a convicted killer for hire, a longtime associate of Lyndon B. Johnson's, and the man at the center of Factor's story. Factor also correctly recalled that the rear of the Depository faced north and there was a wooden loading dock there that was taken down not long after the assassination.

Wallace, who died in a car accident in 1971, was elected president of the Student

Union at the University of Texas at Austin after returning home from the Marines during World War II. In 1950, he was introduced to Lyndon Johnson by Johnson's attorney Ed Clark and soon was working for the US Department of Agriculture in Texas. In October 1951, Wallace was arrested and convicted in the murder-for-hire death of Austin miniature golf course owner John Kinser, who reportedly was in ill favor with Johnson due to his dating Johnson's sister, Josefa. Represented by Johnson's attorneys, Wallace nevertheless was convicted, with eleven of the jurors calling for the death penalty. However, the trial judge overruled the jury and announced a sentence of five years' imprisonment, which he immediately suspended.

This was not the only murder attributed to Wallace. Several deaths occurred during government investigations into Johnson's business dealings but the one that gained the most attention was the shooting death of Henry Marshall, the Agriculture Department official looking into illegalities by Texas cotton allotment kingpin Billie Sol Estes. Estes died in 2013 at age eighty-eight.

The Marshall case came to a climax in August 1984 when, after hearing Billie Sol Estes relate that he was present when Johnson, Wallace, and Johnson aide Cliff Carter plotted to "get rid" of Marshall, a Robertson County grand jury changed the Marshall suicide ruling to one of homicide.

On the day of the assassination, some twenty-odd fingerprints recovered from the sixth floor of the Depository could not be connected to either Oswald, other Depository employees, or investigators. These prints were placed in the National Archives and generally forgotten except by John F. "Jay" Harrison, a Dallas police reservist and JFK assassination researcher. Harrison arrived on the scene of the assassination within minutes and maintained his research until his death in May 2005.

In the late 1990s, Harrison enlisted the aid of Nathan Darby, the retired head of the Austin, Texas, Police Department's Identification and Criminal Records Section, in matching the Depository prints with a jail card belonging to Mac Wallace. According to Darby, there was a fourteen-point match between the prints. US courts generally accept a ten-to twelve-point comparison as proof of a match. These results were made public at a news conference in May 1998, where it was announced there was no doubt that Wallace was one of the shooters.

Naturally, opposition to any idea other than that of a lone assassin swung into gear, and controversy still reigns over the Wallace-fingerprint issue, especially since both Harrison and Darby are now deceased and cannot counter any accusations. Darby's analysis was submitted to the FBI for comment. Predictably, after dragging their feet for more than a year, bureau officials stated the print match was in error but failed to produce any supporting data or their own analysis.

It does stretch the imagination to the breaking point to believe that Lyndon Johnson would have been stupid enough to allow a convicted hit man who could be connected to him within fifty miles of Dallas on November 22, 1963. Some researchers theorize that Wallace's prints may have been planted on the sixth floor by someone else in an effort to ensure Johnson's ongoing cooperation.

James E. Files, born James Sutton, on the other hand, also was a soldier and has claimed to be the Grassy Knoll gunman. He definitely can be connected to both the government (both CIA and military) and the Chicago mob.

Entering the US Army in 1959, Files said he was eventually sent to Laos to operate with secret counterinsurgency US forces called "White Star" teams. Colonel Fletcher L. Prouty confirmed to this author that he was involved with such teams but had never heard of Files. While in the military, Files said, he was recruited into CIA operations by David Atlee Phillips, the same person Judyth Vary Baker named as Oswald's handler.

After leaving the military, Files said, he became a race car driver and was recruited as a driver by Charles "Chuckie" Nicoletti, described as a premier hit man for the Chicago Mafia. Files said it was Nicoletti who sent him to Dallas with a Chevrolet Impala loaded with guns after an assassination attempt on Kennedy in Chicago failed in early November 1963.

Once in Dallas, Files said, he called David Phillips to inform him he had arrived and soon he was visited at his motel by Lee Harvey Oswald, who arrived driving a green pickup truck similar to one owned by Jack Ruby. Although Oswald reportedly had no driver's license, such a technicality has never stopped others from driving. As will be seen, this was not the only incident of Oswald driving a vehicle. Files said Oswald drove him around showing road exits out of Dallas. Files said he then knew the operation was being orchestrated by Phillips, since no one in the Chicago mob knew Oswald.

By the morning of November 22, 1963, his boss Nicoletti had arrived in Dallas along with mobster Johnny Roselli, who claimed to have flown in on a "military flight." Files said on orders from Nicoletti, he drove Roselli to nearby Fort Worth, where he watched as Roselli received a package from a man at a pancake restaurant. On the drive back to Dallas, Roselli told Files the man was a mob-connected nightclub owner named Jack Ruby and that the package contained phony Secret Service identification as well as security plans for Kennedy's motorcade. As outlandish as this may sound, it is supported by Ruby's sister Eva Grant, who later told authorities that Ruby had the motorcade security plans in advance. A letter marked "personal and confidential" to Dallas police chief Jesse Curry from Dallas FBI chief J. Gordon Shanklin dated April 13, 1964, reported that Grant told the bureau that "we" had been given a copy of the security plans for Kennedy's visit prior to his arrival.

Later that morning, despite the overcast weather with some drizzle, Files said, he and Nicoletti strolled along the Grassy Knoll in Dealey Plaza, laying their plans. Nicoletti said Roselli mentioned an "abort team" to stop the assassination and that he was getting cold feet about involving CIA personnel. Files was told Roselli wanted out and that Nicoletti recruited him as backup. It was understood that Files was not to fire from the knoll unless it appeared that Kennedy might leave the plaza alive, and that Mrs. Kennedy was not to be harmed.

Files said the weapon he chose was an experimental model Remington XP-100 .222-caliber pistol with a foregrip called the "Fireball." A gunsmith for the mob had loaded the bullet tips with mercury, which created an explosive effect. According to Files, the mercury created "all the killing power of a 30.06" in the smaller weapon.

As the motorcade came into alignment with his position, Files said, he decided he must make his shot. He fired one round that struck Kennedy in his right temple (from Files's position, this was initially described as the left temple causing considerable confusion and criticism until he clarified it). After biting on the shell casing and leaving it behind on the knoll's wooden picket fence as a "calling card," Files then loaded the Fireball into a briefcase and casually walked away to join Nicoletti and Roselli at a car parked near the Dal-Tex Building, from where Files later learned Nicoletti had fired a rifle. The trio drove away unchallenged.

This whole convoluted story began in 1987 when a Dallas-area man named John Rademacher told Texas assassination researchers he had recently found two .222-caliber shell cases with the aid of a metal detector on the Grassy Knoll. One was located about ten feet east of the picket fence close to the pergola where Zapruder stood, while the other was some sixty feet farther to the northeast. One of the casings had an odd-shaped ring around the neck.

Among those who heard Rademacher's account was Texas private investigator Joseph H. West, who had already developed an intense interest in the JFK assassination case. West previously had gathered information that Nicoletti and Roselli may have been involved. Nationally syndicated columnist Jack Anderson wrote that Roselli on more than one occasion had indicated to him that he may have participated in the assassination. A 1999 book by Salvatore "Bill" Bonanno, the son of crime boss Joseph Bonanno, also claimed Roselli played a role in the assassination. Offering no evidence, Bonanno said Roselli fired from a drainpipe along Elm Street and was aided by French mobsters.

It must be emphasized that Files himself never sought publicity by going public with his story. This was the result of a tip from retired FBI agent Zechariah "Zack" Shelton, who had worked organized-crime cases during his time with the bureau. Shelton told West in the early 1990s that if anyone left alive knew about the assassination, it was most probably James Files, who by then was serving time in the Statesville Correctional Center in Joliet, Illinois, in a separate case involving the shooting of a police officer. West subsequently tracked down Files and approached him for his story. Files initially refused to talk but eventually warmed up to the personable West and finally agreed to talk, with the understanding that he would not betray anyone in the mob who was still alive.

West prepared for a formal taped interview with Files. About this same time, he filed a forty-five-page motion in federal district court to have the body of President Kennedy exhumed and examined by forensic pathologists, including Dr. Charles Wetli, the deputy chief medical examiner of Dade County, Florida. In an affidavit, Dr. Wetli said a postmortem examination could show whether Kennedy's body had been tampered with in an attempt to skew the autopsy results. "If we're given an opportunity to exhume, it will settle all these arguments," said West. His motion was rejected by federal judge Norman Black but West said he planned to appeal to the 5th US Circuit Court of Appeals.

Before either his appeal or the Files interview could take place, West entered a hospital for heart surgery in early 1993. He did not recover and those close to his situation, including his wife, did not believe his death was a natural one. His exhumation suit was dismissed for lack of prosecution and the Files interview was turned over to Houston photographer/researcher Robert G. Vernon, who proceeded with the Files interview.

After initial taping had been completed, Vernon learned from Files about his biting on a shell casing following the assassination and recalled the Rademacher story from West's notes. Vernon obtained the shell casing from Rademacher and sent it to Dr. Paul G. Stimson of Houston, a member of the American Board of Oral Pathology and the American Board of Forensic Pathology. No mention was made of the Kennedy assassination; Stimson was simply asked to analyze the .222 Remington spent casing. In a letter dated October 4, 1993, Dr. Stimson, after describing in detail the marks on the casing, concluded, "The indentations are oriented on the shell casing in a pattern that would be consistent with the maxillary right central incisor making the larger mark and the two smaller marks would be consistent with the lower right central and lateral incisors. It is my opinion that the marks are consistent with having been made by human dentition."

Human teeth marks on the casing appeared to be tangible evidence that connected Files with the Grassy Knoll. However, like so much else in the assassination case, giant holes began to appear in this story.

Once informed of the JFK assassination connection, Dr. Stimson backtracked on his analysis of the casing marks as from human teeth. In addition, there has never been any explanation for the second .222-caliber shell casing found on the Grassy Knoll. Files said he fired only one. Other details of Files's story also failed to check out. Some researchers suspected that West may have unconsciously passed along assassination information in the form of questions to Files that he used to bolster his claims.

A final blow to Files's account may have come in 2006, when researcher Allan Eaglesham, following a painstaking investigation into the little-known world of ballistics and headstamps on ammunition, published a paper titled "The Tell-Tale Dash: James Files and the Dented Cartridge Case," in which he demonstrated that the .222 shell casings Radenmacher found could not have been manufactured before 1971. If proven correct, this dismisses them, and hence Files's account, as true assassination evidence.

Then there is the strange case of John Christian, who in a 2010 deathbed confession claimed he was the Grassy Knoll gunman.

Calling himself a "wild child," Christian grew up hunting in rural Texas. He claimed he could "hit a frog's eye with a non-military rifle." His mother abused him, sometimes beating him with a two-by-four board. Christian said he ran away from home before he was ten years old and "took care of himself." Often in trouble with the law, he was given the choice between jail or the military. Finishing training at Fort Polk, Louisiana, in early 1963, Christian said, he was sent by train to Alaska, where he distinguished himself with his shooting prowess.

In late November 1963, Christian said he was pulled out of field maneuvers and told he was to eliminate a threat to national security. He learned his target was to be President Kennedy, who he was told was "doing a lot of drugs" and would likely start World War III. "I felt I was just a patriotic man doing my job," said Christian later.

On November 21, Christian said, he was flown by helicopter to Eielson Air Force Base near Fairbanks, Alaska, and from there via military plane to Carswell Air Force Base in Fort Worth, Texas. He was then taken to the Cellar club in downtown Fort Worth, where he slept on the floor of the kitchen while Secret Service agents were "debriefed" in the main club area. The next morning, he was driven to Dallas and given a choice of weapons in the vehicle's truck. "I chose one with an open sight—no scope," he said.

Lying prone on a mat along the north–south axis of the wooden picket fence atop the Grassy Knoll, Christian said, he fired a rifle through a small gap in the fence. He said there were men in suits to shield him from any interference. After he struck Kennedy in the head, he said he simply walked away while another man left with the rifle wrapped in a coat and yet another picked up the mat.

Christian's most astounding claim was that he was returned to his base in Alaska by a high-flying jet and arrived there in time to stand with an honor guard that evening for the fallen president.

He said he left the Army within two years on a hardship discharge and returned to north Texas. After a stint as a mercenary, he eventually became a rural county judge with a respectable reputation. In 2006 he was diagnosed with inoperable cancer and decided to tell his story to attorney Sheila Grace Neal of Azle, Texas. Neal confirmed one of Christian's claims—that he had paid no taxes since 1965. This apparently was partial payment for his role in the assassination. "I've seen his tax records," reported Neal. "He owed taxes but he was never required to pay them."

Christian died from cancer in June 2010, just days after giving his account to this author. Like other assassination stories, at this late date and because he claimed his military records were all stolen from him by "men in suits" in the late 1960s, there appeared no way to independently corroborate his confession.

A recent addition to the confessed gunmen is a man who only called himself "Anonymous." In the book *The Man on the Grassy Knoll*, reportedly published posthumously in 2011, he tells a compelling but dubious tale of being recruited out of college by a CIA operative named "Mr. Smith." This tale concerns a conspiracy of only three—the anonymous narrator, Smith, and Lee Harvey Oswald, whom he knew only as Ozzie Hidell. His story could have been acquired from assassination literature and there are some questionable statements: Jack Ruby acted entirely on his own, Oswald's employment at the Depository was a sheer accident, and the conspirators shared drinks in a downtown Dallas hotel at a time when no one could buy mixed drinks in the city.

The same problem of buying alcoholic drinks in dry 1963 Dallas appeared in the confession of an assassin called only "Saul" in a 1975 book, *Appointment in Dallas: The Final Solution to the Assassination of JFK*, by former Los Angeles County sheriff's detective Hugh C. McDonald. Saul confessed to McDonald during a one-time meeting in England that he fired on Kennedy from the Dallas County Records Building.

Serious researchers believe that as a means of cover-up, several credible persons were spoon-fed such false "confessions" to confuse future investigators, a common disinformation practice in the intelligence field.

While there is a lack of evidence to support such stories, they do serve as a good example of how a truly experienced sniper could have been insinuated into any number of assassination plots. The shooter could do his job and walk away without any contact or knowledge of any other participants. This type of redundant backup contingency also is typical of military/intelligence planning. Such a tactic ensures that a morass of false leads and red herrings are left behind to confuse investigators.

So it would appear that the best guess for the Grassy Knoll gunman is that of Roscoe White, whose story also has been dismissed by most due to the lack of verification even after nationwide publicity.

Roscoe Anthony White, nicknamed Rock, reportedly left behind a diary detailing his role in the assassination. This became known through his son, Ricky Don White, a high school football hero from Paris, Texas. Ricky White said involvement in the assassination case may have begun in early childhood, when he recalled a hunting trip with his father to west Texas in the fall of 1963. He saw his father practice shooting rifles with two other men from high positions into an open car.

He also recalled that on the Sunday Ruby killed Oswald, the elder White arrived home, appeared very agitated, and suddenly left Dallas with his family.

Earlier, on October 7, 1963, White had joined the Dallas Police Department. While in training he was assigned to the Crime Scene Search Section, which included work in the police photographic lab. He resigned from the police in October 1965 and in 1971 was killed in a freak explosion at a Dallas business where he worked as a shop foreman. He received a Masonic funeral on September 27, 1971.

Ricky White recalled that in 1975 investigators from the House Select Committee on Assassinations questioned his mother, Geneva, about her employment with Jack Ruby and a backyard photograph of Lee Oswald never before known to exist. The existence of this unpublicized third backyard Oswald photo—and especially the fact that the exact pose in this photo was re-created by authorities in a photo published by the Warren Commission—proved that evidence against Oswald was suppressed while in the hands of the government.

It was during the time of the committee that a neighbor warned Ricky that the HSCA might make public his father's name in connection with the assassination. He was told that Roscoe had belonged to something called "JTAG" ("Don't ask me what that means," said the neighbor who claimed to have worked for US intelligence), a team of specially trained soldiers sent into different countries to create wars and conflicts, including assassination plots.

When White's name was never mentioned by the HSCA, Ricky White tried to forget the whole thing. By 1982, he and his family were living in west Texas, when he received word that his grandfather W. S. Toland had died. The Toland family had acted as surrogate parents to Ricky.

Following the funeral, family members gathered at Toland's Paris home and were going through his effects. It was in a storage shed in the backyard that Ricky found an old Marine footlocker belonging to Roscoe. Inside were a Bell and Howell camera, several press clippings regarding the JFK assassination, a bank deposit box key, and a small book filled with handwritten notes. The book was a diary that mentioned $500,000 in bearer bonds in a bank deposit box.

Ricky found the diary entry for November 22, 1963, chilling. He read it over and over, committing it to memory. He recalled that it stated:

Lebanon [a code name for one of the assassins] (Sixth Floor), Saul [another code name] (Records Building), Mandarin [Roscoe White's code name] (Stockade Fence). Shots fired from upper buildings for diversion. Shots fired, looks as if target was hit. Shot from fence, definite hit. Man on other side fence in way. Shots again from upper buildings, no hit. Target open, fired, definite hit. Gun retrieved by man to the side, took to railroad area. Whirled over fence, took man down to protect myself. Ran around back of fence, down embankment to car. Drove to Oak Cliff, met officer. Told officer not to drive by house. Something was at this point wrong. Forced to take out officer at 10th and Patton. Not going as planned. Back tracked to car, drove back to the area of take out to locate other passenger. Failed to transport subject to Redbird. Realized what a mistake I had made, hope it is all over. Back to DPD awaiting information.

Ricky immediately took this information to his mother, who had briefly worked for Jack Ruby in the fall of 1963. She told him she knew nothing of the diary but that she had suspected Roscoe may have had something to do with the assassination.

Not certain how to proceed, in 1988 Ricky contacted Midland, Texas, district attorney Al Schorre for help in opening the bank deposit box. He also told Schorre about the diary. Schorre and his assistant initially were excited over the find, as were some local oilmen who financed Ricky's efforts to investigate the matter. The FBI was notified. Agents made a duplicate of the bank deposit box key but Ricky was never able to access the box. "I think the FBI made $500,000," he speculated later. With the federal government involvement, local interest waned.

Ricky was taken to FBI offices in Midland and questioned for five hours by agents Ron Butler and Tom Farris. They alternately coaxed Ricky for information and threatened him with charges of withholding evidence. After reading the diary, Agent Butler told Ricky, "Your father has a fanciful imagination."

Exhausted, Ricky was finally allowed to return home with his materials. As he rested, Agent Farris arrived and asked to retrieve a notepad he said he had inadvertently left in Ricky's belongings. The agent quickly returned from where Ricky had laid out his materials, said, "I got what I came for. Sorry for the interruption," and left. The diary has not been seen since.

However, in June 1990, further support for Roscoe's involvement came with the discovery of a steel canister at his grandfather's house. Inside were three coded messages that today are in the hands of an assassination researcher. All three messages carried the same heading, which read:

> Navy Int.
> Code A M R C
> Remark data
> 1666106
> NRC VRC NAC

The first message was dated on "? . . . 63." It stated:

> Foreign affairs assignments have been cancelled. The next assignment is to eliminate a national security threat to worldwide peace. Destination will be Houston, Austin or Dallas. Contacts are being arranged now. Orders are subject to change at any time. Reply back if not understood.

All are signed, "C. BowerS, OSHA, Re-rifle Code A A A destroy / on/"
A message dated September 1963 read:

> Dallas destination chosen. Your place hidden within the department. Contacts are within this letter. Continue on as planned.

The final message dated December 1963 stated:

> Stay within department. Witnesses have eyes, ears and mouth. You [unclear] do of the mix up. The men will be in to cover all misleading evidence soon. Stay as planned. Wait for further notice.

By 1990, the story of the diary had become known and Ricky was thrown into a world of publicity and entrepreneurs, culminating in an August 1990 press conference in the now-defunct JFK Assassination Information Center in Dallas. Here the entire story was made public along with the results of a lie detector test Ricky took a month earlier. It indicated truthfulness in all questions. Researchers rushed to examine the Roscoe White story.

It was learned that Roscoe White was stationed at the Marine base at El Toro, California, at the same time as Lee Harvey Oswald. Further, White shipped out from California to duty in Japan aboard the USS *Bexar*, the same ship carrying Oswald. Both White and Oswald served in the 1st Marine Aircraft Wing. Both Rock and Oswald were released from the Marines with a hardship discharge, like John Christian.

Based on White's broad, flat chin and a knot on his right wrist, it has been claimed that it was Roscoe White's body onto which Oswald's face was superimposed in the famous backyard photographs. In 1992, Beverly Oliver, the "babushka lady," told researcher Mark Oates that just after the shooting she saw a Dallas policeman coming down from the Grassy Knoll. She said she did not know him but recognized him as the husband of Geneva White, who she knew worked for Jack Ruby. Even Texas attorney general Dan Morales opened an investigation file on the Roscoe White issue.

Then it all fell apart.

Since the diary was missing and the coded messages did not specifically connect to the assassination, stronger proof was needed. Suddenly a second diary was made public but was almost immediately found to be a forgery. Someone—Geneva White was accused—had fabricated it. With this evidence of falsification, the attorney general, the media, and the public quickly lost interest in the Roscoe White case.

Today this issue is largely forgotten, although no one has explained the coded messages or even the original diary, which was seen by several people before disappearing into the hands of the FBI, yet another example of conspiracy evidence being suppressed by the government.

DEALEY PLAZA, DALLAS, TEXAS, 1963

1. Texas School Book Depository
   (today the Dallas County Annex)
2. The DalTex Building (today 801 Elm
   Building)
3. The Dallas County Records Building
4. The Dallas County Criminal Courts
   Building (then housing the sheriff's
   office and county jail)
5. Union Terminal Railroad Tower
6. The Grassy Knoll
7. Wooden picket fence
8. Concrete pergola
9. Parking lot
10. Old County Courthouse
11. Union Terminal Building

LOCATIONS OF SELECTED WITNESSES

A. Policeman J. W. Foster, Sam Holland,
   and other railroad workers
B. James Tague
C. Jean Hill and Mary Moorman
D. Beverly Oliver (the "babushka lady")
E. Charles Brehm and son
F. Emmett Hudson
G. Abraham Zapruder and Marilyn
   Sitzman
H. Railroad supervisor Lee Bowers
I. The Bill Newman family
J. AP photographer James Altgens
K. The John Chism family and
   A. J. Millican
L. Phillip Willis and family
M. Roy Truly, Billy Lovelady, and other
   Depository employees
N. Howard Brennan
O. Charles Bronson
P. Roger Craig and other deputy
   sheriffs
Q. The "umbrella man" and the
   "dark-complected man"

(*Above*) EVIDENCE IN FILM—The famous Zapruder film has provided evidence of misunderstanding and manipulation in the JFK assassination case. Alteration of Zapruder film frames (top) is demonstrated by comparing a painted black patch on the rear of JFK's head (frame 317) with normal shadow (frame 257). Hollywood film experts have agreed that the signs of retouching are both obvious and crude. Many people still believe the erroneous conspiracy theory that the driver, Secret Service agent William Greer, turned and shot Kennedy with a pistol. A clear blowup of Zapruder film frame 314 (bottom) clearly shows no pistol and that Greer's hands remained on the steering wheel. However, Greer's testimony contradicted his actions as seen in the film, prompting some suspicion of Secret Service complicity. What some people believed to have been a gun is merely sunlight reflecting off of Secret Service agent Roy Kellerman's greased hair.

(*Opposite Page*) SURVEYORS' MAP ALTERED—Dallas County surveyor Robert West and his associate, Chester Breneman, were both hired to survey Dealey Plaza, first by Time-Life, Inc., and later in 1964 by the Warren Commission. In both studies they said it was apparent that the assassination involved more than one gunman. Here is a copy of their original plat map provided by Breneman. They mention among other things a tree that obstructed any early shot from the Depository's sixth floor as well as an extraneous bullet strike on the south curb of Elm Street. These notations contradicted the government's conclusion of a lone assassin. Along with certain Zapruder film-frame numbers used to time the assassination, the West-Breneman information was altered by the Warren Commission before being made public. Without absolute accuracy in time, distances, and elevations, no computer analysis of the assassination can be considered valid.

"This area hid behind tree for any shot from depository as of this date—May '64"

First Shot

"Area of bullet shot on curb"

"Yellow mark on curb"

SMOKE ON THE GRASSY KNOLL—The long-standing controversy over whether or not smoke from a rifle was seen drifting down from the Grassy Knoll ended in the 1980s when this frame of a film by NBC cameraman Dave Weigman was made public. A modern rifle can produce a white puff of smoke, especially if recently oiled. This photo confirmed the presence of the puff of gun smoke (circled upper right) both seen and smelled by several witnesses as the Kennedy limousine entered the Triple Underpass (circled center). Bystanders quickly rushed up the Grassy Knoll where most of those in the west end of Dealey Plaza believed shots originated.

GUNMAN ON THE GRASSY KNOLL—
A blowup of a section of the Polaroid picture taken by Mary Moorman at the time of the fatal head shot reveals a man in the classic rifle-firing position behind the wooden picket fence atop the infamous Grassy Knoll. The smudge on the right of the photo is a fingerprint due to the failure to apply a fixative to the photo at the time. In the blowup, one can discern the figure's hairline, eyebrows, and left ear over a bright spot that could be either a muzzle flash or smoke from a weapon. The man is wearing a dark shirt with a bright spot on his left chest, which computer analysis showed to be metal, along with a semicircular patch on his left shoulder. These accoutrements have been compared to the black Dallas police uniforms with their badges and their semicircular patches on their left arms, leading the figure to be called the "badgeman."

Photoanalysis by Jack White and Gary Mack

THE SNIPER'S NEST—This view from the "sniper's nest" on the sixth floor of the Texas School Book Depository reveals several problems with the lone-assassin theory of the JFK assassination. The dark triangle at bottom right is the floor, only about a foot below the window, which was only half open on November 22, 1963, as shown here. Two pipes to the immediate left of the window provide serious obstacles to anyone attempting to aim a rifle down Elm Street. Additionally, the live oak tree on the street below obscures the line of sight from the window to the center of Elm where today an overhead highway sign marks the location of the first shot to strike Kennedy. This photo was taken in 1977, soon after the tree was trimmed back to its 1963 configuration for a television documentary. Today, no one can see this view because the window area has been closed off to the public with Plexiglass by the Sixth Floor Museum.

Photo by Jim Marrs

DISAPPEARING EVIDENCE—Here is one of a series of photos published by Dallas police chief Jesse Curry in 1967. Deputy sheriff Eddy Walters and uniformed policeman J. W. Foster watch as a sandy-haired man identified by Curry as an FBI agent picks something from the grass on the south side of Elm Street immediately following the assassination. It was at this location that witnesses, including Foster, claimed a bullet struck the ground near a manhole cover. This extraneous bullet was depicted in a news photograph published the next day. However, once taken away, there was no acknowledgement or even mention of this vital evidence.

TWO SUSPICIOUS CHARACTERS—Two of the most suspicious men in Dealey Plaza at the time of the assassination were a man brandishing an open umbrella despite the warm, balmy day and a dark-complected man with a bulge in his jacket. Although these men arrived and left separately, in the moments after the shooting they sat together on the Elm Street curb. While the umbrella lies at the man's feet, in other photos the dark-complected man appears to be speaking into a walkie-talkie. For nearly twenty years the federal government failed to identify these men and made no mention of them in official reports. Belatedly, the "umbrella man" was identified as a Louie Steven Witt by the House Select Committee on Assassinations. However, Witt's account did not correspond with the actions of the man depicted in assassination photos and many researchers have rejected him as a legitimate witness.

(*Top*) EVIDENCE ODDITIES—Oswald carried a draft card with his picture but in the name of Alek James Hidell. No Selective Service card in 1963 carried a photograph, which led researchers to suspect that this card was fabricated by Oswald himself. When the police demanded to know if he was Oswald or Hidell, Oswald was uncooperative. Yet at this same time—only two hours after the assassination—FBI director J. Edgar Hoover was already presenting a full background on Oswald's Marine service and attempted defection to Russia, declaring him a "mean-minded individual…in the category of a nut." How could Hoover have known more than the Dallas authorities, who were uncertain of their suspect's identity?

(*Bottom*) THREE TRAMPS?—These three men were arrested in a railroad car a short time after the shooting and were marched through Dealey Plaza under armed guard. For nearly thirty years their identities were unknown and no arrest records were found. But in 1992, when Dallas police opened their assassination files, three arrest reports listing three men were found, all written in the same hand and on the same date. Two of the men were located and they acknowledged being arrested on November 22, 1963. But the sudden appearance of the reports along with timing problems led many researchers to question whether the men in the photos were the same as the three tramps depicted in the arrest reports.

MOVING SANDBAGS—In 1979, the House Select Committee on Assassinations recreated the JFK assassination gunshots in Dealey Plaza as part of acoustical studies that ultimately led to its official conclusion that more than one gunman fired on the president. Notice that just below the light-colored van a pile of sandbags had been placed near the south curb of Elm Street. A sharpshooter on the Depository's sixth floor, using live ammunition, had ordered the bags moved from the center lane of the street, the actual location of the first shots into Kennedy's limousine. The police shooting expert said he ordered the move because he could not gain an unobstructed line of sight into the center of Elm because of an intervening live oak tree. The same problem existed in 1963. Two years before this test, the tree had been trimmed back to its 1963 configuration for the filming of a television documentary on the assassination. Neither the sharpshooter nor Oswald could have sighted a target in the center lane through the tree.

Photo copyright 1979 by Tom Blackwell

THE REMARKABLE PATH OF
THE PRISTINE BULLET,
ACCORDING TO WARREN COMMISSION

PATH OF THE MAGIC BULLET—The federal government's official "lone-assassin" theory rests on the idea that a single bullet, acting in the manner as seen in this diagram, caused seven wounds to two men, emerged in a "pristine" condition, and was fortuitously found on a stretcher in Parkland Hospital. In detail, this theory states that a rifle slug fired from sixty feet above ground level struck Kennedy in the back, at the level of the third thoracic vertebra, at a downward angle. Without hitting any bone, it coursed upwards to exit from his Adam's apple, then turned downward again to strike Connally near his right armpit, shattering his fifth rib. It then exited near Connally's right nipple and somehow struck and shattered his right wrist before turning left and lodging in his left thigh.

BULLET HOLES IN JACKET AND SHIRT—Adding confirmation to the fact that Kennedy was never shot through the neck but in the back is the bullet hole in his bloody jacket, which is still available for viewing in the National Archives. It has been argued that Kennedy's jacket bunched as he raised his arm to wave at the crowd, causing the bullet hole in the jacket to be much lower than the actual wound in his body. However, the bullet hole in his shirt also indicates that the shot from the rear was in the back rather than the neck. One's shirt does not bunch up when waving.

(*Top*) A COMPOSITE PHOTOGRAPH—When shown the famous photos depicting Oswald in his backyard with weapons and a communist publication, Oswald stated they were composite pictures with his face pasted on another's body. Proof of his statement came when graphics expert Jack White made the two known photos (Commission Exhibits 133 A and B) into transparencies and overlaid them. Nothing in the two separate pictures matched exactly, except Oswald's face. To create such a match with a handheld camera is impossible. Only a slight discrepancy was found on his mouth, apparently the result of later retouching. A third backyard photo turned up fifteen years after the assassination in the hands of Dallas policeman Roscoe White's widow. There was no chain of evidence or explanation for this photo. Yet when investigators recreated the backyard pose for the Warren Commission, they chose the pose of the third photo, proving suppression of evidence. Again, Oswald's face matched perfectly.

(*Bottom*) A CHIN TRANSPLANT—It is clear that the figure in the incriminating Oswald backyard photo has a broad flat chin. However, as seen in Oswald's Dallas police photo, he had a pointed, cleft chin. In the backyard photos, a perceptible line breaking the emulsion of the picture can be seen stretching from one side of the neck to the other. If Oswald was correct in stating that his face was pasted onto another's body, it would have been above the line across the chin.

Photoanalysis by Jack White

FRAGMENTS IN CONNALLY'S WRIST—The X-ray of Texas governor John Connally's right wrist shows bright spots, which are metal fragments from the bullet that shattered his radius, the largest and thickest of the wrist bones. Many other fragments were removed from his chest, wrist, and thigh. Still, there remained more bits of metal in his wrist and leg than were missing from Commission Exhibit 399 (left), the bullet the government claimed caused the wound. The small indention at the top of the slug is where FBI lab technicians chipped off a piece for spectrographic studies, the analysis of which remains in controversy.

(*Opposite Page*) CRITICAL EVIDENCE ALTERED—On the right is the Dallas Police Evidence Sheet as presented to the public as Warren Commission Exhibit 2003. In accordance with its "lone-assassin" theory, this inventory of assassination evidence shows that three spent 6.5 mm shell casings were recovered from the sixth floor of the Texas School Book Depository. The bottom of the sheet is clear. However, as can be seen on the evidence sheet from the Dallas police files, only two spent shell casings were found and logged. A Dallas police official belatedly turned over a third shell casing. He said he forgot he carried it around in his pocket for several days. At the bottom of the actual evidence sheet it states that the paraffin test on Oswald showed "positive on both hands and negative on face." However, though the paraffin report itself showed traces of nitrates on Oswald's hands, it showed no gunpowder on his hand or face—evidence that he did not fire a rifle that day. The Warren Commission concluded the paraffin test was unreliable but instead of explaining this, they chose to delete reference to the test on the evidence sheet, an explicit example of alteration and suppression of evidence.

EVIDENCE

1 Italian make 6.5 rifle, serial # C 2766, blue steel, wood stock, brown leather sling with 4 x 18 Coated Ordnance Optics Inc. Hollywood California. O 10 Japan telescopic sight.

   Found by Dept. Sheriff Weitzman on 6th floor, 411 Elm, 5' from west wall and 8' from stairway.

1 Green and brown blanket

   Found by Detr. Rose, Stovall, Adamcik 2515 W. 5th, Irving, Tex. taken from garage

1 .38 slug
1 button

   Taken from body of J. D. Tippit at Methodist Hospital by Dr. Paul Moellenhoff at 1:30 pm. He gave them to R. A. Davenport

X homemade paper bag resembling gun case

   Found by Johnson and Montgomery at 411 Elm and brought to Crime Lab.

1 .38 cal pistol, 2" barrel

   W. W. McDonald, FWD, took it fro Oswald at 231 W. Jefferson, gave it to Sgt. Jerry Hill who gave it to Det. Faker.

Pulled fragments taken from body of Governor Connally

Live round 6.5
6.5 spent rounds (3)

   Mrs. Audrey Bell, Operating room nurse, to Bob Nolan, D.P.S., to Capt. Fritz, to Crime Lab, to FBI.
   Recovered by Lept. Sheriff Luke Mooney at 411 Elm, 6th floor, southeast window.

1 Man's brown short shirt "Taken from Lee Harvey Oswald

*1 Piece cardboard containing palm print of suspect
*3 Empty cardboard boxes marked A, B, & C
*1 cardboard box, empty, size: 11 3/4" x 13 x 17½" "from which thumb print of suspect was found"
*1 Partial palm print "off underside gun barrel near end of foregrip" on rifle C 2766
*3 Negatives of partial prints "found on trigger housing of rifle nor. # C 2766.
* Taken from 6th floor, 411 Elm, by Lt. Day and Detective Studebaker and taken to Crime Lab, City Hall.

Paraffin test made on Oswald, was positive on both hands and negative on face.

Exh 443A

EVIDENCE

1 Italian make 6.5 rifle, serial # C 2766, blue steel, wood stock, brown leather sling with 4 x 18 Coated Ordnance Optics Inc. Hollywood California. O 10 Japan telescopic sight.

Carcano carbine

   Found by Dept. Sheriff Weitzman on 6th floor, 411 Elm, 5' from west wall and 8' from stairway.

1 Green and brown blanket

   Found by Detr. Rose, Stovall, Adamcik 2515 W. 5th, Irving, Tex. taken from garage

1 .38 slug
1 button

   Taken from body of J. D. Tippit at Methodist Hospital by Dr. Paul Moellenhoff at 1:30 pm. He gave them to R. A. Davenport

X homemade paper bag resembling gun case

   Found by Johnson and Montgomery at 411 Elm and brought to Crime Lab.

1 .38 cal pistol, 2" barrel, S&W, Rev. sandblast finish, brown wooden handles ser.# 510210. Rel. to FBI Agent 11-22-63 and again 11-26-63

   W. W. McDonald, FWD, took it fro Oswald at 231 W. Jefferson, gave it to Sgt. Jerry Hill who gave it to Det. Faker.

Bullet fragments taken from body of Governor Connally

Live round 6.5
6.5 spent rounds (3)

   Mrs. Audrey Bell, Operating room nurse, to Bob Nolan, D.P.S., to Capt. Fritz, to Crime Lab, to FBI.
   Recovered by Lept. Sheriff Luke Mooney at 411 Elm, 6th floor, southeast window.

1 Man's brown short shirt "Taken from Lee Harvey Oswald

   Found by Dep. Sheriff Mooney. Picked up by Det. R. M. Sims. See pages I-130 and P-252.

*1 Piece cardboard containing palm print of suspect
*3 Empty cardboard boxes marked A, B, & C
*1 cardboard box, empty, size: 11 3/4" x 13 x 17½" "from which thumb print of suspect was found"
*1 Partial palm print "off underside gun barrel near end of foregrip" on rifle C 2766
*3 Negatives of partial prints "found on trigger housing of rifle nor. # C 2766.
* Taken from 6th floor, 411 Elm, by Lt. Day and Detective Studebaker and taken to Crime Lab, City Hall.

DEAR MR. HUNT—This handwritten note, dated November 8, 1963, and signed "Lee Harvey Oswald," is addressed to a "Mr. Hunt," requesting "information concerding [sic] my position." The handwriting has been authenticated as that of Oswald. Some researchers believe the note was meant for Dallas oilman H. L. Hunt, who was open about his hatred of Kennedy. However, the fact that the note originated in Mexico City has lead other researchers to suspect the addressee may have been Watergate scandal figure E. Howard Hunt, a CIA officer working with anti-Castro Cubans in 1963. By some accounts, Hunt was in Mexico City at the time the note was written and some, including his son, St. John Hunt, have placed him in photographs taken in Dealey Plaza at the time of the assassination. In a dying declaration, the elder Hunt named the chief assassination conspirators as Lyndon Johnson, Cord Meyer and William Harvey of the CIA, operative David Morales, and a French assassin.

(*Opposite Page, Top*) A COMPOSITE OSWALD—The Warren Commission published this picture of Lee Harvey Oswald (Commission Exhibit 2963), reportedly taken about the time of his attempted defection to Russia. According to some researchers, this is a composite picture of two separate individuals—Lee Oswald on the left and Harvey Oswald on the right. Retouching can be seen on the lips and eyebrow. Also, although there is a light source from the person's right, his shadow on the rear wall falls to the left. An obvious line separating the two faces can be drawn from a break in the hairline at the top of his head through his mouth and chin and on through his necktie. Such composite photos have been used by intelligence agencies to allow an operative to pass cursory official examination when impersonating a similar-looking person. Adding to the evidence that Oswald was impersonated at various times are a memo from FBI director J. Edgar Hoover three years before the assassination, warning that an imposter was using the birth certificate of Lee Harvey Oswald, and a letter to the Russian embassy dated November 9, 1963, and signed by Lee Harvey Oswald, stating that he could not obtain a new Mexico visa "without using my real name." There are a number of accounts of Oswald's being seen in widely separated locations at the same time. (*Bottom*) When brought to same size, the Marine Oswald (left) appears to be taller than the Russian Oswald (right).

Photoanalysis by Jack White

HEALTH RECORD	CHRONOLOGICAL RECORD OF MEDICAL CARE
DATE	SYMPTOMS, DIAGNOSIS, TREATMENT, TREATING ORGANIZATION (Sign each entry)

USNAS, Navy #3835, c/o FPO, San Francisco, California

A 9/16/58

Diagnosis: Urethritis, Acute, due to gonococcus #0303
Origin: In line of duty, not due to own misconduct.
CC: Urethral discharge

PI: Patient complains of a slight discharge and a stinging sensation on urination.

PH: Previous V.D.:

PE: Essentially negative except for a thick mucopurulent discharge from the urethra.

LAB: Smear reveals gram negative intra-and extracellular diplococci having the morphology of N. Gonorrhea.

RX: Procain Penicillin 900,000 Units I.M. X 3 days

D 9/16/58

To duty under treatment and observation:

PES-1421(VD) submitted: No B 754

SUBMITTED P DERANIAN
CAPT. MC USN

APPROVED:

P. DERANIAN
CAPT MC USN
SENIOR MEDICAL OFFICER

SEX M	RACE C	GRADE, RATING, OR POSITION PVT	ORGANIZATION UNIT MACS 1 MAG 11 USMC	COMPONENT OR BRANCH	SERVICE, DEPT. OR AGENCY
PATIENT'S LAST NAME—FIRST NAME—MIDDLE NAME OSWALD, Lee Harvey				DATE OF BIRTH (DAY-MONTH-YEAR) 10/18/39	IDENTIFICATION NO. 1653230

CHRONOLOGICAL RECORD OF MEDICAL CARE
Standard Form 600

DONABEDIAN EXHIBIT No. 1—Continued

UNDERCOVER WORK—Tantalizing evidence that Lee Harvey Oswald participated in intelligence work is reflected in this Marine medical record dated September 16, 1958. Every branch of the US military cautions troops against contracting venereal disease. Some units, such as the Marine Corps, punish members who are treated for such disease. Yet, Oswald's military record indicates that his case of gonorrhea was contracted "In line of duty, Not due to own misconduct." This astonishing statement indicates that Marine Oswald may have been recruited into intelligence work while serving in Japan and ordered to consort with prostitutes suspected as foreign agents.

PART III

AFTERMATH

Dallas

The gunfire had barely died away in Dealey Plaza when an aftermath of odd and often unexplained events began in Dallas—and has continued for decades, a circumstance well beyond the means of any lone assassin.

Dallas police blocking the nearby intersections with no orders to the contrary—recall the eight-minute disruption of the Dallas police radio motorcade channel during the time of the shooting—released traffic, which began pouring through the crime scene.

Spectators from blocks away, having heard the shots and sirens, ran to the scene. Some bystanders were in shock. Others were shouting, "They shot the president!" while others sobbed out the news. Pandemonium was the order of the day.

There was no shortage of lawmen as nearly twenty sheriff's deputies, following sheriff Bill Decker's orders, ran to the railroad yards behind the Grassy Knoll. Dozens of Dallas police officers also were flooding the area. But all were receiving conflicting information—witnesses on the west end of Dealey Plaza pinpointed the picket fence on the Grassy Knoll as the source of the shots, while many people on the east end said shots came from the vicinity of the Texas School Book Depository.

It is significant to recall that James Tague, who was slightly wounded when a bullet or bullet fragment struck the Main Street curb near the Triple Underpass, last spoke with deputy sheriff Buddy Walthers before having to move his car once traffic got moving. Tague said this occurred about 12:40 p.m.

Yet Walthers was among the first officers to seal off the Depository, indicating that the building was still open for at least ten minutes after the shooting.

Actually the time may have been much longer. Captain Will Fritz, who headed the

Dallas police investigation, told the Warren Commission he began making detailed notes after hearing of the assassination at the Trade Mart. Fritz said he arrived at the Texas School Book Depository at exactly 12:58 p.m. Asked if the Depository exits were guarded at that time, Fritz replied, "I am not sure, but I don't—there had been some question about that, but the reason I don't think that—this may differ with someone else, but I am going to tell you what I know. . . . After I arrived, one of the officers asked me if I would like to have the building sealed and I told him I would."

Recall that witness Ed Hoffman was able to drive from Stemmons Freeway to the railroad yards behind the Depository, circle the area, and leave unchallenged.

The point is that there was no effective containment of the crime scene or of the Depository for at least ten minutes—and perhaps as much as twenty-eight minutes—after the shooting.

Officially it has been claimed that within an hour of the assassination, there was a roll call at the Texas School Book Depository. Employee Lee Harvey Oswald was the only person missing and authorities immediately began a search for him. Like so much other information in this case, this story is simply untrue.

To begin with, most Depository employees were outside viewing the motorcade at the time of the shooting and were prevented from returning to work by police. During the first roll call, dozens of Depository employees were missing. By the time it was determined that Oswald was gone—about 2:30 p.m.—he was already in police custody.

This was confirmed in 1981 by *Dallas Morning News* reporter Kent Biffle, who recalled that day in a lengthy article based on his notes of that day:

> Only two of us [reporters] had arrived at the ambush building [the Depository] by this point. . . . Getting in was no problem. I just hid my press badge . . . and went in with the first wave of cops. . . . Hours dragged by. The building superintendent showed up with some papers in his hand. I listened as he told detectives about Lee Oswald failing to show up at a roll call. My impression is that there was an earlier roll call that had been inconclusive because several employees were missing. This time, however, all were accounted for except Oswald. I jotted down the Oswald information. . . . Neither the police in the building nor the superintendent knew that Oswald already was under arrest.

In the confusion following the assassination, there was ample opportunity for conspirators to escape and for vital evidence to be eliminated.

One such incident occurred minutes after the shooting on the south side of Elm Street. Dallas policeman J. W. Foster, from his vantage point on top of the Triple Underpass, saw a bullet strike the grass on the south side of Elm near a manhole cover. He reported this to a superior officer and was told to guard the area. Photographs taken that day show both Foster and Deputy Sheriff Walthers standing over the manhole cover.

News reporters and spectators were kept at a distance and told that evidence—a bullet—was embedded in the grass inches from the manhole cover. News camera-man Harry Cabluck photographed the scene and recalled seeing more than one gouge in the ground. He, too, was told that a bullet had struck there. One photo-graph of the slug even appeared in the November 23, 1963, edition of the *Fort Worth Star-Telegram*, with the caption:

> ASSASSIN'S BULLET: One of the rifle bullets fired by the murderer of Pres-ident Kennedy lies in the grass across Elm Street from the building in which the killer was hiding and from where he launched his assault.

Inches from the bullet, which is circled in the newspaper photo, is the edge of the cement manhole.

Other witnesses to the bullet marks on the south side of Elm Street were Wayne and Edna Hartman, who were in Dallas for jury duty. After hearing shots in Dealey Plaza, the couple "ran like the devil" down to the grassy middle area of the plaza. Mrs. Hartman told this author:

> There were not many people in this area at the time, but a policeman was there. He pointed to some bushes near the railroad tracks on the north side of the street and said that's where the shots came from. . . . Then I noticed these two parallel marks on the ground that looked like mounds made by a mole. I asked "What are these, mole hills?" and the policeman said, "Oh no, ma'am, that's where the bullets struck the ground."

On Sunday, the Hartmans again visited Dealey Plaza but found that the crush of people bringing memorials had obliterated the marks.

In the summer of 1964, the Hartmans contacted the FBI after learning that the bureau was still seeking assassination information. Mrs. Hartman said FBI agents didn't seem too interested in what they had to say. One agent told them the marks had been made by bone fragments from Kennedy's head, an explanation that sounded "strange" to the Hartmans.

Both Hartmans told the FBI that the bullet marks did not line up with the Texas School Book Depository but rather with the picket fence on the Grassy Knoll. Years later, Mrs. Hartman recalled:

> I don't see how what we saw down there could have come from those win-dows up there because they were not the right angle. So we have always felt that it came from across the street . . . that was the angle . . . across the street from where we stood . . . the Grassy Knoll, we've always felt it came from there. . . . And at that time people were telling us the bullets came from over there. There was somebody over there shooting also. And they pointed across the street, which was south of the Depository.

Yet in an FBI report dated July 10, 1964, agents stated, "[The Hartmans] said this gouged out hole was in line with the general area of the Texas School Book Depository Building. [They] said some bystander had mentioned that he believed the shots had come from the Texas School Book Depository Building."

If one or more bullet slugs were in the grass, what happened to them? What role did an extra slug play in the assassination? Was the erroneous FBI report a mistake or was it meant to pinpoint the Depository as the assassin's lair? Was the slug in the grass proof that at least four shots were fired? The answers to these questions may never be known because, officially, this bullet never existed.

Within minutes of the shooting, a sandy-haired man in a suit appeared—identified in Dallas police chief Jesse Curry's book as an FBI agent. This man apparently had some authority, for in full view of both Walthers and Foster, he walked up, reached down, cupped some object in his hand, and stuck it into his left pants pocket.

The bullet was gone.

Later in 1964, when reports of this bullet reached the Warren Commission, the FBI was instructed to investigate the matter. Agents reported back that they had examined the manhole cover and there was no sign of a bullet striking it. There was no mention of the fact that the bullet in question landed inches away from the manhole cover. Apparently satisfied, the Commission dropped the matter of the bullet in the grass.

Later on the day of the assassination, the Stemmons Freeway sign, which according to some bystanders was struck by a bullet, disappeared. It is missing in photographs made in Dealey Plaza the next day. No official explanation of this disappearance has been offered, although some Dallasites recalled a brief local news segment at the time explaining that the sign was taken down by the city because a bullet hole in it would remind the public of the assassination.

In 2004 the Asahi Television Network of Japan procured two separate copies of the Zapruder film, both of which contained approximately six frames missing from the copies shown around the world to the public. *Life* magazine officials explained the missing frames were due to processing damage. In the missing frames it is apparent that a small hole appears in the Stemmons sign at the time of the shooting. Computer experts in England and Poland confirmed this as a bullet hole.

In 1974, Richard Lester, using a metal detector, discovered a bullet fragment on the far south side of Dealey Plaza just east of the Triple Underpass. Two years later, Lester turned the fragment over to the FBI. It was later studied by firearms experts of the House Select Committee on Assassinations who determined through ballistics that while the fragment was from 6.5-millimeter ammunition, it had not been fired through the Oswald rifle. Rather than view this as evidence that perhaps multiple rifles were used in the assassination, both the FBI and the committee left the impression that this discovery had no connection with Kennedy's death.

An intact .45-caliber bullet was discovered in May 1976 by Hal Luster buried in dirt by the four-foot-high cement retaining wall near where Abraham Zapruder had stood filming.

Yet another story of a found shell casing may shed much light on how some bullet fragments were traced to the Oswald rifle.

Dean Morgan of Lewisville, a suburb of Dallas, related that in 1975 his father was working on air-conditioning equipment on the roof of the Dallas County Records Building, located just catercornered from the Texas School Book Depository. The Records Building's west side faces onto Dealey Plaza and there is a waist-high parapet along the edge of its roof.

According to Morgan, his father, while searching for water leaks, discovered a 30.06-caliber shell casing lying under a lip of roofing tar at the base of the roof's parapet on the side facing Dealey Plaza.

The shell casing is dated 1953 and marks indicate it was manufactured at the Twin Cities Arsenal. One side was pitted by exposure to the weather, indicating it had lain on the roof for a long time. The casing, which remains in Morgan's possession, has an odd crimp around its neck.

Rifle experts have explained to Morgan that this is evidence that a sabot may have been used to fire ammunition from a 30.06 rifle. A sabot, also called a husk, is a plastic sleeve that allows a larger-caliber weapon to fire a smaller-caliber slug. The results of using a lighter-weight slug include increased velocity, producing more accuracy and greater striking power. And the smaller slug exhibits the ballistics of the weapon it was originally fired from, rather than, in this case, the 30.06, as the sabot engages the 30.06's rifling.

In other words, assassination conspirators could have fired 6.5-millimeter bullets from the Oswald rifle into water, recovered them, then reloaded them into the more accurate and powerful 30.06 with the use of a sabot—which is held in place by crimping the cartridge.

By this method, bullet fragments found in the presidential limousine would have the ballistics of Oswald's rifle rather than the 30.06 from which they were actually fired.

Warren Commission Exhibit 399—the nearly intact slug found at Parkland Hospital the afternoon of the assassination—displays all the characteristics of a slug fired into nothing more solid than water. It is just such a slug that can be reloaded and refired using a sabot, which comes apart on firing.

That such technology was available in 1963 is proven by a February 1962 ad in *Guns* magazine offering "Husk Bullets," and depicting a .22-caliber slug seated in a .308-caliber shell casing.

One such plastic sabot reportedly was found in Dealey Plaza the afternoon of the assassination by a member of the anticommunist Minutemen organization, led by Missouri biochemist Robert DePugh, who related the story to talk-show host Stan Major in the early 1990s. He claimed that a few months after he received the sabot, the FBI raided his home and took all his possessions. Eventually it was all returned, except for the plastic sleeve. DePugh died in 2009.

Bullets and a plastic sleeve were not the only evidence found in Dealey Plaza.

The day after the assassination, a college student named Billy Harper was taking pictures in the plaza when he found a piece of skull about twenty-five feet behind and to the left of the president's limo at the time of the head shot. Personnel at Methodist Hospital identified it as a piece from the occipital region at the right rear of the head. It, too, was never acknowledged by the Warren Commission.

And while evidence was disappearing from Elm Street, men were seen fleeing the rear of the Texas School Book Depository.

Richard Carr, a steelworker who saw a heavyset man on the sixth floor of the Depository minutes before the shooting, saw two men run either from inside or from behind the Texas School Book Depository minutes after the assassination.

Carr claimed the men got into a Nash Rambler station wagon on Houston Street by the east side of the Depository. He said the wagon left in such a hurry one of its doors was still open. He last saw the station wagon speeding north on Houston. Did it return moments later to pick up the Oswald figure as reported by Deputy Sheriff Craig?

After reaching ground level from his seventh-story vantage point on the courthouse under construction, Carr said he saw the same man he had seen earlier in the Depository window. Carr said the man was "in an extreme hurry and kept looking over his shoulder" as he walked hurriedly eastward on Commerce Street.

Carr's story was corroborated by that of James R. Worrell Jr., then a twenty-year-old high school senior who told the Warren Commission that seconds after the shooting, he saw a man wearing a sports coat come out of the rear of the Depository and walk briskly south on Houston (the direction of Carr's location). Worrell can't be questioned further about what he saw, as he was killed in a motorcycle accident on November 9, 1966, at age twenty-three. Carr, however, told researchers about his treatment at the hands of the authorities. In a taped interview, Carr said:

> The FBI came to my house—there were two of them—and they said they heard I witnessed the assassination and I said I did. They told me, "If you didn't see Lee Harvey Oswald up in the School Book Depository with a rifle, you didn't witness it." I said, "Well, the man I saw on television that they tell me is Lee Harvey Oswald was not in the window of the School Book Depository. That's not the man." And [one of the agents] said I better keep my mouth shut. He did not ask me what I saw, he told me what I saw.

Not long after this encounter with the FBI, Carr's home was raided by more than a dozen Dallas policemen and detectives armed with a search warrant. Claiming they were looking for "stolen articles," they ransacked Carr's home while holding him and his wife at gunpoint. Carr and his wife were taken to jail but later released. The day after the police raid, Carr received an anonymous phone call advising him to "get out of Texas."

Carr finally moved to Montana to avoid harassment, but there he found dynamite in his car on one occasion and was shot at on another.

After testifying in the Clay Shaw trial in New Orleans, Carr was attacked by two men in Atlanta. Although stabbed in the back and left arm, Carr managed to fatally shoot one of his assailants. After turning himself in, Carr was not indicted by an Atlanta grand jury.

Carr was not the only assassination witness to later claim they were victims of a pattern of intimidation. Acquilla Clemons, who saw two men at the scene of the Tippit slaying, said a man with a gun came to her home and told her to keep quiet. Ed Hoffman, who saw two men with a rifle behind the picket fence on the Grassy Knoll at the time of the assassination, was warned by an FBI agent not to tell what he saw "or you might get killed."

A relative of Depository superintendent Roy Truly recently told researchers that due to intimidation by federal authorities, Truly was fearful until his death. Truly's wife, Mildred, refused to discuss the assassination—even with family members.

Sandy Speaker, the supervisor of Warren Commission star witness Howard Brennan, would not discuss the assassination until recently, after getting a phone call from his friend and coworker A. J. Millican. Speaker said he got a call from Millican early in 1964. Millican was almost in tears and told him never to talk about the assassination. Millican said he had just received an anonymous call threatening not only his life, but the lives of his wife and her sister. He said the caller told him to warn Speaker to keep his mouth shut.

Speaker told this author:

> That call really shook me up because Millican was a former boxing champ of the Pacific fleet. He was a scrapper, a fighter. But he was obviously scared to death. I also got a call. And I still don't understand how they got my name because I was never interviewed by the FBI, the Secret Service, the police or anyone. They must be pretty powerful to have found out about me.

Whispered rumors, anonymous phone calls, and freakish "accidents" combined to create a tangible aura of fear in Dallas in the weeks following the assassination. Some of that fear lingered for decades.

Mysterious Secret Service Men

One of the most puzzling aspects of the post-assassination confusion involved encounters between Dealey Plaza witnesses and "Secret Service" agents.

The most notable incident was recounted by Dallas policeman Joe M. Smith. Smith had run into the parking lot atop the Grassy Knoll after a woman had told him, "They're shooting the president from the bushes!" While searching through the parked cars, he encountered a man who displayed Secret Service identification. Smith told author Anthony Summers:

> The man, this character, produces credentials from his hip pocket which showed him to be Secret Service. I have seen those credentials before, and

they satisfied me. . . . So, I immediately accepted that and let him go and continued our search around the cars.

Malcolm Summers was one of the bystanders who followed police up the Grassy Knoll immediately after the shooting. He said:

I ran across Elm Street to run up there toward that knoll. And we were stopped by a man in a suit and he had an overcoat over his arm. I saw a gun under that overcoat. And his comment was, "Don't y'all come up here any further, you could get shot . . . or killed."

The Secret Service subsequently asserted that none of their agents on duty that day were anywhere near Dealey Plaza either before or just after the assassination. All were either riding in the motorcade or at the Trade Mart.

In retrospect, Smith doubted the legitimacy of the man he encountered. In 1963, Secret Service agents, like their FBI counterparts, wore crew cuts, dark suits, and narrow ties.

Smith described the man thusly:

He looked like an auto mechanic. He had on a sports shirt and sports pants. But he had dirty fingernails, it looked like, and hands that looked like auto mechanic's hands. And, afterwards, it didn't ring true for the Secret Service. . . . At the time we were so pressed for time and we were searching. And he had produced correct identification and we just overlooked the thing. I should have checked the man closer, but at the time, I didn't snap on it.

In addition to Smith and Summers, GI Gordon Arnold also encountered a man who claimed to be with the Secret Service just moments before the assassination. Arnold said he was walking behind the wooden picket fence on top of the Grassy Knoll when he was approached by a man who told him he was with the Secret Service and that Arnold could not stay behind the fence. Moments later, Arnold said shots came from behind the fence.

Sam Holland, who was standing with two Dallas policemen and other railroad workers on the Triple Underpass, told the Warren Commission that "a plainclothes detective or FBI agent or something like that" was helping the police guard the railroad bridge. Holland told a Commission attorney, "There were two city policemen and one man in plainclothes. I didn't talk to him. I talked to the city policemen."

Holland said after hearing shots and seeing a white puff of smoke come from behind the wooden picket fence, he and others ran to the Grassy Knoll. He later said that while they found no one behind the picket fence, "somebody had been standing there for a long period. I guess if you could count them, about a hundred foot tracks [were] in that little spot, and also mud on the bumper of [a] station wagon."

Constable Seymour Weitzman, who had rushed behind the picket fence, met men he believed were Secret Service. Warren Commission lawyer Joseph Ball asked Weitzman if there were others with him behind the fence. Weitzman replied:

> Yes sir; other officers, Secret Service as well, and somebody started, there was something red in the street and I went back over the wall and somebody brought me a piece of what he thought to be a firecracker and it turned out to be, I believe, I wouldn't quote this, but I turned it over to one of the Secret Service men and I told them it should go to the lab because it looked to me like human bone. I later found out it was supposedly a portion of the President's skull.

It is not certain whether the proper authorities ever investigated this particular piece of bone. There is no mention of it in official reports, although Commission Document 1269 is titled "Location of Photos of a Bone Specimen." This document, however, is still classified.

Dallas police sergeant D. V. Harkness also encountered Secret Service men where none officially were supposed to be. Harkness told the Warren Commission that he ran to the rear of the Texas School Book Depository moments after the shooting and "there were some Secret Service agents there." Harkness told a commission lawyer, "Didn't get them identified. They told me they are Secret Service."

In later years Harkness told the *Dallas Morning News* that the men were dressed in suits and "were all armed." He told the newspaper, "[I] assumed they were with the Presidential party."

Dallas Secret Service agent in charge Forrest V. Sorrels was the only Secret Service agent to return to the scene of the assassination within an hour or so. Sorrels said he walked through a rear door of the Texas School Book Depository without showing any identification. His arrival was too late to have been that of one of the men Harkness encountered.

In 1978 Sorrels, then retired, was asked by a Dallas newsman to comment on the stories of bogus Secret Service agents in Dealey Plaza. Sorrels said, "[I'm] not answering any questions about this thing. I gave all my testimony in Washington and I don't put out anything else. As far as I'm concerned, that's a closed incident."

Another odd incident involving Secret Service agents who may have been bogus occurred within an hour of the assassination in the small town of Ferris, located just south of Dallas. Two high school students, Billy V. James and Ronnie Witherspoon, witnessed a speeding car being stopped by local police on Interstate 45. The students stopped to watch because they thought "we may have been witnessing the arrest of the assassins." However, according to the students, the men in the stopped car told police they were Secret Service agents "in a hurry to get to New Orleans to investigate something in connection with the assassination." James said the police believed the men and allowed them to go on without being ticketed. No Secret Service agent reported leaving Dallas for New Orleans that day and the identity of the men in the car remains a mystery.

Incredibly, even the accused assassin apparently had an encounter with one of these bogus agents.

Secret Service inspector Thomas J. Kelley was one of several officials who interrogated Lee Harvey Oswald on the Sunday morning he was shot by Ruby. In his report of that interview, Kelley wrote:

> [Oswald] asked me whether I was an FBI agent and I said that I was not, that I was a member of the Secret Service. He said when he was standing in front of the Textbook Building [Texas School Book Depository] and about to leave it, a young, crew-cut man rushed up to him and said he was from the Secret Service, showed a book of identification, and asked him where the phone was. Oswald said he pointed toward the pay phone in the building and that he saw the man actually go to the phone before he left.

It is significant that Oswald mentioned a "book of identification," as this accurately described the folding leather badge holder used by government agents. In later years, the theory was advanced that Oswald had merely mistaken a news reporter for an agent. Kelley's report dispels this notion, as news reporters merely carried press cards.

In fact, when the sixth-floor museum of the assassination opened in 1989, a taped tour of the exhibit was narrated by newsman Pierce Allman, who claimed to have been the reporter Oswald encountered. Amazingly, two other newsmen, Robert McNeil and Bill Moyers, also said they were told after the assassination that while looking for a telephone they had encountered Lee Oswald. Apparently none of these newsmen had any direct memory of this incident but said government agents planted the story in their mind by telling them months after the assassination they had encountered the accused assassin.

It seems incredible that the suspected killer of the president not only took the time to help someone he believed to be a Secret Service agent, but then stood around to watch him get to the telephone. It is claimed that less than an hour later, Oswald shot down a Dallas policeman who merely stopped him far from downtown in South Oak Cliff.

Considering the number of people claiming to have encountered agents in Dealey Plaza, it appears that Oswald may well have been correct in his identification of a Secret Service agent or someone posing as one.

But perhaps the strangest—and most ominous—incident involving the Secret Service happened to witness Jean Hill, who was standing beside her friend Mary Moorman on the south side of Elm Street at the moment Kennedy was killed. Moorman fell to the ground at the sound of the shooting, but Hill remained standing and watchful.

After seeing both a man fire from behind the wooden picket fence and a suspicious man rapidly walking west in front of the Depository, Hill ran across Elm Street and began to run up the Grassy Knoll. Hill told this author, "I don't know what I would have done if I had caught them, but I knew something terrible had happened and somebody had to do something."

As she ran up the Grassy Knoll, her attention was drawn to a "trail of blood in the grass just to the right of the steps." Thinking that "our guys had shot back and we got one of them," she followed the red droplets until she discovered they belonged to a snow cone—flavored ice packed in a cup. Someone had dropped a red-colored one that day on the Grassy Knoll.

After the distraction of the snow cone, Hill continued her run up the Grassy Knoll, but had wasted valuable seconds. She looked in vain for either the suspicious man behind the fence or the man she saw by the Depository. She recalled, "All I saw in that parking area were railroad workers and police."

Walking to the west of the Texas School Book Depository, Hill said, she encountered two men who identified themselves as Secret Service agents. She told interviewers in Texas:

> I was looking around but I couldn't see anything, when these two guys came up behind me. One of them said, "You're coming with us," and I replied, "Oh, no I'm not. I don't know you." "I said you're coming with us," one of them said and then put this horrible grip on my shoulder. I can still feel the pain when I think about it. I tried to tell them, "I have to go back and find my friend Mary." But then the other guy put a grip on my other shoulder and they began hustling me past the front of the Depository. "Keep smiling and keep walking," one of them kept telling me. They marched me across the plaza and into a building. We entered from the south side and I think it was the sheriff's office. They took me to a little office upstairs and they wouldn't let me out of this room. It was all such a shock. There was a lot of tension and it was like a lot of it was focused on this one area. The two men that grabbed me never showed me any identification but, after we got to this little room, some men came in who were Secret Service. They began to ask me a lot of questions. One man told me they had been watching Mary and I out of the window. He asked me, "Did you see a bullet hit at your feet?" I told him I didn't realize that one had struck near my feet. "Then, why did you jump back up on the curb?" he asked me and I told him how I had started to run at the President's car but thought better of it. Then I heard some booming sounds and it startled me and I jumped back on the curb by Mary. I guess they were up there the whole time and watched the whole thing. Then they sent those two guys to come and get me. I mean, I wasn't too hard to find that day—wearing that red raincoat.

Hill said she was kept in the room for some time before rejoining Mary Moorman in a downstairs office. There were other assassination witnesses in the office, such as Charles Brehm and others who signed sheriff's depositions that day.

A Dallas newspaperman Moorman and Hill initially believed to be a federal agent took all of the photographs Moorman had taken of the motorcade. Later that day three of the six snapshots were returned, and federal authorities returned the rest, but only after several weeks. The backgrounds on two of the returned photographs were mutilated.

Dallas police chief Jesse Curry summed up the import of a man with Secret Service identification when he told author Anthony Summers:

> Certainly the suspicion would point to the man as being involved, some way or other, in the shooting, since he was in the area immediately adjacent to where the shots were—and the fact that he had a badge that purported him to be Secret Service would make it seem all the more suspicious.

The House Select Committee on Assassinations briefly looked into the matter of men with Secret Service identification but came up with no real solution.

After establishing that "Except for Dallas Agent-in-Charge Sorrels, who helped police search the Texas School Book Depository, no [Secret Service] agent was in the vicinity of the stockade fence or inside the book depository on the day of the assassination," the committee wrote off most of the sightings as people mistaking plainclothes police for agents.

However, the committee could not dismiss Officer Smith's story so lightly. FBI agent James Hosty, who was named in Oswald's notebook and who destroyed Oswald's warning note, told the committee that Smith may have encountered a treasury agent named Frank Ellsworth. When deposed by the committee, Ellsworth denied the allegation.

Despite its inability to determine who was carrying Secret Service identification on the Grassy Knoll on November 22, 1963, the committee nevertheless concluded, "[We] found no evidence of Secret Service complicity in the assassination."

However, if Jean Hill's account is true, either men posing as federal agents were using offices in the Dallas County sheriff's building minutes after the assassination or genuine federal agents were monitoring the tragedy from an upper-story window.

One portion of Jean Hill's account that seemed unbelievable was her identification of the man she saw in front of the Depository as Jack Ruby. However, this story appears to have some corroboration.

First, recall the story of Julia Ann Mercer, who identified a man sitting in a truck just west of the Triple Underpass about an hour before the assassination as Jack Ruby. Also recall that both Mercer and Oswald's mother, Marguerite, said authorities showed them photographs of Jack Ruby before Ruby killed Oswald.

Then there is the Warren Commission testimony of Depository employee Victoria Adams, who said she and a coworker saw a man at the intersection of Elm and Houston minutes after the assassination "questioning people as if he were a police officer." She told the Commission that the man "looked very similar" to the photos of Jack Ruby broadcast after the Oswald slaying. Her companion, Avery Davis, was never asked for her opinion.

Malcolm O. Couch, a television cameraman for WFAA-TV in Dallas, also supported the idea that Ruby was in Dealey Plaza when he told the Warren Commission that another newsman, Wes Wise (who later became mayor of Dallas), had seen Ruby walking around the side of the Texas School Book Depository moments after the shooting. However, Couch was forced to admit his story was just "hearsay" by Commission lawyers who then declined to call Wes Wise to clarify the issue.

An FBI report from December 1963 gave the account of Lucy Lopez, who had been in Dallas visiting her daughter. They had joined others watching the motorcade from a window in the Dal-Tex Building when they recognized Jack Ruby walking back and forth outside the book depository. The women were acquainted with Ruby and also knew Oswald, who they recalled had once eaten with them at a nearby restaurant. Lopez told the FBI the women saw Ruby hand Oswald a pistol before walking off but were afraid to talk to the authorities.

Another story regarding Jack Ruby's possible presence in Dealey Plaza comes from Phil Willis, an amateur photographer and assassination witness. Willis, who knew Jack Ruby by sight at the time of the assassination, still claims to have seen and photographed Ruby minutes after the shooting, standing near the front of the Texas School Book Depository.

In publishing Willis's series of assassination photos, the Warren Commission cropped the face of the Ruby figure out of the picture.

Was Jack Ruby at the scene of the assassination?

The Warren Commission established that Ruby was in the offices of the *Dallas Morning News* at the time of the shooting. The Commission stated that Ruby arrived at the newspaper between 11 and 11:30 a.m., some thirty minutes after the incident at the Triple Underpass involving Julia Ann Mercer.

The Commission also determined that Ruby was with newspaper advertising employee Don Campbell until Campbell left for lunch about 12:25 p.m. About 12:45 p.m. another advertising employee, John Newnam, reportedly saw Ruby in the same spot Campbell had left him. However, Newnam and other newspaper employees said once word came that Kennedy had been shot (probably no sooner than 12:40 p.m., from employees who had been in Dealey Plaza returning to work), "confusion reigned" in the newspaper offices.

Years later employee Wanda Walker still recalled vividly how Ruby sat quietly in the near-empty newspaper office that noontime. Walker told researchers in 1986:

> The other secretary had gone to lunch and the ad salesmen were all gone and it was just me and Ruby up there. He was waiting for his regular ad man. He did an odd thing. I knew who he was, but we had never talked. But he got up and came over and sat by the desk where I was. It was like he didn't want to be alone. He said some things but I can't tell you what they were. Then some people started coming back in and they said the

President had been shot. Jack Ruby got white as a sheet. I mean he was really shaken up.

Despite Walker's certainty that Ruby remained at the newspaper office during the time of the assassination, it is possible that Ruby could have slipped away for a few minutes.

No one was keeping exact times, and the *Dallas Morning News* offices are only two short blocks from Dealey Plaza. It is conceivable that Ruby could have left the newspaper offices, been in Dealey Plaza, and returned unnoticed within the space of ten or fifteen minutes.

Ruby certainly was at Parkland Hospital after the assassination. In his 1978 book, *Who Was Jack Ruby?*, newsman Seth Kantor reported meeting and talking with Ruby at Parkland Hospital about 1:30 p.m. on November 22, 1963. This was supported by radio newsman Roy Stamps, also an acquaintance of Ruby's, who told this author he saw Ruby enter Parkland about 1:30 p.m. carrying some equipment for a television crew.

According to the Warren Commission, Ruby "firmly denied going to Parkland" and "video tapes of the scene at Parkland do not show Ruby there," and so the Commission concluded "Kantor probably did not see Ruby at Parkland Hospital." They failed to mention a photograph published by Penn Jones that appears to depict Ruby strolling through the crowd at Parkland Hospital.

The House Select Committee on Assassinations reversed this conclusion, stating that after reviewing the evidence concerning Ruby at Parkland Hospital an hour or so after the assassination, the panel decided, "While the Warren Commission concluded Kantor was mistaken, the Committee determined he probably was not."

If Ruby lied and the Warren Commission erred by denying Ruby's presence at Parkland, it could explain the sudden and unexplained appearance of Commission Exhibit 399—the intact bullet slug found at Parkland—that led to the single-bullet theory. It is entirely possible that Ruby planted the bullet. And it is possible that Ruby may have made his way—no matter how briefly—to the scene of the assassination.

Jean Hill said she recognized the man who shot Oswald as being the same man she saw "walking briskly" in front of the Texas School Book Depository seconds after the assassination. The man she saw was almost running west toward the Triple Underpass. She lost sight of the man after reaching the top of the Grassy Knoll.

This story may play a part in the account of one Dallas policeman who chased a man leaving the area of the Triple Underpass.

The Black Car Chase

On November 22, 1963, Dallas policeman Tom G. Tilson Jr. had taken the day off. A friend and fellow policeman, J. D. Tippit, was covering Tilson's regular beat that day. Three days later Tilson was a pallbearer at Tippit's funeral.

Tilson told Dallas news reporters of chasing a black car from the scene of the assassination that day and claims the man in the car bore a striking resemblance to Jack Ruby.

Tilson and his daughter Judy were going downtown to pick up another daughter who had been watching the presidential motorcade. As Tilson was turning east on Commerce from Industrial just west of the Triple Underpass, he said he learned from a police radio monitor he had in his car that Kennedy had been shot.

Tilson stated:

> I saw all these people running to the scene of the shooting. By that time I had come across under Stemmons. Everybody was jumping out of their cars and pulling up on the median strip. My daughter Judy noticed the [presidential] limousine come under the Underpass. They took a right turn onto Stemmons toward Parkland Hospital. Well, the limousine just sped past [this] car parked on the grass on the north side of Elm Street near the west side of the underpass. Here's one guy coming from the railroad tracks. He came down that grassy slope on the west side of the Triple Underpass, on the Elm Street side. He had [this] car parked there, a black car. And, he threw something in the back seat and went around the front hurriedly and got in the car and took off. I was on Commerce Street right there across from [the car], fixing to go under the Triple Underpass going into town. I saw all this and I said, "That doesn't make sense, everybody running to the scene and one person running from it. That's suspicious as hell." So, I speeded up and went through the Triple Underpass up to Houston . . . made a left . . . [came] back on Main . . . and caught up with him because he got caught on a light. He made a left turn and I made a left turn, going south on Industrial. I told my daughter to get a pencil and some paper and write down what I tell you. By this time, we had gotten to the toll road [formerly the Dallas–Fort Worth Turnpike, now Interstate 30] going toward Fort Worth. I got the license number and description of the car and I saw what the man looked like. He was stocky, about five-foot-nine, weighing 185 to 195 pounds and wearing a dark suit. He looked a hell of a lot more than just a pattern of Jack Ruby. If that wasn't Jack Ruby, it was someone who was his twin brother. Or pretty close. You know how Jack wore an old dark suit all the time? He always wore that old suit. He had that same old suit on. Anyway, I got the license number and all and exited off the turnpike and came back and picked up my other daughter down there at Commerce and Houston. Then I went to a phone and called in the information on the license number and what I had seen.

Tilson's story is corroborated by his daughter Judy Ladner, although photos taken west of the Triple Underpass at the time do not show the black car. Also, Dallas police radio logs for the day do not indicate any alert for the car Tilson described.

Tilson maintained that he gave the license number and man's description to the police homicide bureau, "but they never contacted me or did anything about it." Believing he had done his duty, Tilson threw away the scrap of paper with the license number on it. It was only much later that he discovered that his information had been ignored.

It would appear that someone in Washington also simply wanted to clear the case, as Tilson was never contacted by either the Warren Commission or the House Select Committee on Assassinations.

Back in Dealey Plaza, while Sam Holland and other railroad workers were finding evidence of someone waiting behind the picket fence and Jean Hill was being taken by men in suits to the sheriff's office, deputy sheriff Roger Craig thought he saw a suspect flee the scene in a station wagon.

The Account of Roger Craig

In 1963, Roger Dean Craig was an ambitious young deputy sheriff who was going places.

Having run away from his Wisconsin home at age twelve, Craig had received a high school diploma on his own and had served honorably in the US Army. By 1959 he had married and taken a job as a sheriff's deputy in Dallas. Craig already had received four promotions within the Dallas County Sheriff's Department and in 1960 had been named Officer of the Year by the Dallas Traffic Commission.

But then came November 22, 1963.

Craig's account of his experiences that day caused considerable problems for the official version of the assassination's aftermath.

He recalled that about 10:30 that morning, sheriff Bill Decker called plainclothes men, detectives, and warrant men into his office and told them that President Kennedy was coming to Dallas and that the motorcade would come down Main Street. According to Craig, Washington had advised Decker to stand down and he told his employees to stand out in front of the building but to take no part whatsoever in the motorcade security.

Craig later said the crowd of deputies was hostile. "The men about me felt they were being forced to acknowledge Kennedy's presence," he said, adding the deputies voiced "bitter verbal attacks on President Kennedy," Craig said. "They spoke very strongly against his policies concerning the Bay of Pigs incident and the Cuban Missile Crisis and they seemed to resent very much the fact that Kennedy was a Catholic."

Craig said just after the motorcade turned on Elm Street, he heard a shot and began running toward Dealey Plaza. He ran down the grassy incline between Main and Elm Street and saw a Dallas police officer run up the Grassy Knoll and go behind the picket fence near the railroad yards. Craig followed, noting "complete confusion and hysteria" behind the fence. He began to question people when he noticed a woman in her early thirties attempting to drive out of the parking lot. Craig recalled:

> I stopped her, identified myself, and placed her under arrest. . . . This parking lot was leased by Dallas deputy sheriff B. D. Gossett. He, in turn, rented parking space by the month to the deputies who worked in the courthouse, except for official vehicles. I rented one of these spaces. . . . I paid Gossett three dollars a month and was given a key to the lot. An interesting point is that . . . the only people having access to it were deputies with keys. . . . How did this woman gain access and, what is more important, who was she and why did she have to leave? I turned her over to deputy sheriff C. L. "Lummie" Lewis and . . . [he] told me that he would take her to Sheriff Decker and take care of her car. . . . I had no way of knowing that an officer with whom I had worked for four years was capable of losing a thirty-year-old woman and a three-thousand-pound automobile. To this day, Officer Lewis does not know who she was, where she came from, or what happened to her. Strange!

Meanwhile, Craig questioned people who were standing at the top of the Grassy Knoll, including Mr. and Mrs. Arnold Rowland. Craig said by approximately 12:40 p.m. he had turned the Rowlands over to Lummie Lewis and met E. R. Walthers back on the south side of Elm Street where "several officers and bystanders were looking at the curb on Elm Street where a nick caused by a bullet was reported to have hit."

He said his attention was attracted by a shrill whistle. In his report of November 23, 1963, Craig wrote:

> I turned around and saw a white male running down the hill from the direction of the Texas School Book Depository Building and I saw what I think was a light-colored Rambler station wagon with luggage rack on top pull over to the curb and this subject who had come running down the hill get into this car. The man driving this station wagon was a dark-complected white male. I tried to get across Elm Street to stop the car and talk with subjects, but the traffic was so heavy I could not make it. I reported this incident at once to a Secret Service officer, whose name I do not know, then I left this area and went at once to the [Depository] building and assisted in the search of the building. Later that afternoon, I heard that the city had a suspect in custody and I called and reported the information about the suspect running down the hill and getting into a car to Captain [Will] Fritz and was required to come at once to City Hall. I went to City Hall and identified the subject they had in custody as being the same person I saw running down this hill and get into the station wagon and leave the scene.

Craig later described the driver of the station wagon as a "very dark-complected" man with short, dark hair wearing a white windbreaker-type short jacket. Recall the witnesses who told of a dark man or a black man on the sixth floor of the Depository just before Kennedy's arrival.

Craig said since the two men were the only ones he saw trying to flee the scene, he believed the incident "important enough to bring to the attention of the authorities at a command post which had been set up in front of the Texas School Book Depository."

Here Craig may have had a brush with one of the bogus Secret Service men. Craig later said as he approached the Depository and asked for someone involved in the investigation, a man in a gray suit told him, "I'm with the Secret Service," and listened to Craig's report on assassination witnesses. Craig later recalled, "He showed little interest in the persons leaving [the scene]. However, he seemed extremely interested in the description of the Rambler [station wagon]. This was the only part of my statement which he wrote down in his little pad he was holding."

On April 1, 1964, Craig described to the Warren Commission his confrontation with Lee Harvey Oswald at Dallas police headquarters:

> I drove up to Fritz's office about, oh, after five—about 5:30 or something like that—and—uh—talked to Captain Fritz and told him what I had saw. And he took me in his office—I believe it was his office—it was a little office, and had the suspect sitting in a chair behind a desk—beside the desk. . . . And Captain Fritz asked me was this the man I saw—and I said, "Yes" it was. . . . Captain Fritz then asked him about the—uh—he said, "What about this station wagon?" And the suspect [Oswald] interrupted him and said, "That station wagon belongs to Mrs. Paine. . . . Don't try to tie her into this. She had nothing to do with it." . . . Captain Fritz then told him . . . "All we're trying to do is find out what happened and this man saw you leave from the scene."

Craig said Oswald then interrupted the interview by stating, "Everybody will know who I am now." In later years Craig explained Oswald was not boastful but made the statement in a dejected and dispirited tone, almost as if "his cover had been blown." This was all explosive testimony since Oswald officially acted alone and made his way home that day by bus and by taxi. Therefore, the Warren Commission stated it "could not accept important elements of Craig's testimony." It went even further, suggesting that the meeting between Craig and Oswald never occurred. According to the Warren Commission Report:

> Captain Fritz stated that a deputy sheriff whom he could not identify did ask to see him that afternoon and told him a similar story to Craig's. Fritz did not bring him into his office to identify Oswald but turned him over to

Lieutenant Baker for questioning. If Craig saw Oswald that afternoon, he saw him through the glass windows of the office.

The truth of Craig's claim to have been in Fritz's office came in 1969 with the publication of Dallas police chief Jesse Curry's assassination file. On page 72 is a photograph captioned "The Homicide Bureau Office under guard while Oswald was being interrogated." In the photograph, well inside the homicide office, stands deputy sheriff Roger Craig.

Craig also pointed out to Warren Commission attorneys that he had learned that Ruth Paine, with whom Oswald's wife, Marina, was living, indeed owned a light green station wagon. Support for Craig came in 1992 with the public release of Dallas Police files on the case. A December 23, 1963, "Criminal Intelligence" report made by Dallas detective T. T. Wardlaw regarding an attempted visit by Ruth Paine to Marina Oswald stated, "Mrs. Payne [sic] left at 12:20 p.m. She drove a 1955 Chevrolet station wagon, color two-tone green, bearing 1963 Texas license number NK 4041 which is registered to her at 2515 West Fifth Street, Irving, Texas."

His insistence on sticking with his story despite repeated attempts by authorities to have both Craig and Arnold Rowland change their testimony began to cause problems for Craig within the Sheriff's Department. Initially, Sheriff Decker had backed Craig, calling him "completely honest." But later, Craig's credibility began to slip within the department and on July 4, 1967, he was fired by Decker. Some say the cause was laxity and improprieties in his work, while others say it was due to his unyielding position on the assassination.

In recent years there seems to be growing corroboration for Craig's story. First, a photograph taken in Dealey Plaza minutes after the assassination shows Craig in the exact locations he described. There are even two photos of a station wagon moving west on Elm.

In later years, researchers discovered Warren Commission Document 5, independent corroboration of Craig's story that was not published in the Commission's twenty-six volumes. In this document, an FBI report dated the day after the assassination, motorist Marvin C. Robinson reported he had just passed Houston Street driving west on Elm Street in heavy traffic when he saw a station wagon, either gray or green, stop in front of the Texas School Book Depository and a white man walk down the grassy incline and get into the vehicle, which drove west on Elm.

In later years, Roger Craig—though vindicated in the controversy over his assassination testimony—continued to live with hard luck. His wife left him—some say due to pressure over his involvement in the assassination—and his back was injured in a car accident. His original account of his experiences began to grow in detail and complexity as he sought acceptance for his story. He even claimed to have been the object of murder attempts.

On May 15, 1975, Roger Craig, then only thirty-nine years old, was killed by a rifle bullet. His death was ruled a suicide.

The Three Tramps

Within an hour of the assassination, Dallas police sergeant D. V. Harkness had an encounter with three strange fellows, whom many researchers believe may have been involved in the shooting. It is one of the more convoluted of the assassination issues.

Union Pacific Railroad dispatcher Lee Bowers saw three men sneak into an empty railroad car in the train yards just behind the Texas School Book Depository moments after the assassination. Bowers ordered the train stopped by radio and then summoned Dallas police. Several officers, including Harkness, rousted the trio from the railcar at gunpoint and marched them to the Dallas County Sheriff's Office. Their route took them past the Depository and across the eastern portion of Dealey Plaza. At least three news photographers took pictures of the three men as they were marched through the plaza under guard. These photographs are the only proof that this incident occurred.

In later years Colonel L. Fletcher Prouty, who as chief of special operations for the Joint Chiefs of Staff under President Kennedy acted as liaison with the CIA, stated his immediate superior, General Edward Lansdale, was photographed walking by the three tramps in Dealey Plaza and perhaps even passing them some sort of signal. As Kennedy's assistant secretary of defense for special operations, Lansdale was the ranking member of Operation Mongoose, the secret war against Castro to include assassinations. Prouty's identification of Lansdale was corroborated in a 1985 letter to Prouty from Marine Lieutenant General Victor H. Kurlak, the highly decorated special assistant for counterinsurgency activities of the Joint Chiefs of Staff. Both Prouty and Kurlak had worked with Lansdale for a number of years.

Once in the sheriff's custody, the three tramps officially disappeared. Although reportedly transferred later to the Dallas police station, they reportedly were never booked and any names, information, or fingerprints taken were not seen before 1992. The House Subcommittee on Government Information and Individual Rights discovered in 1975 that Dallas police arrest records for November 22, 1963, compiled for the Warren Commission, were missing.

Were "tramps" actually near the assassination site at the time of the shooting? In 1981, Kent Biffle, a reporter for the *Dallas Morning News*, wrote an article detailing his experience that day that pinpointed the tramp arrests as shortly after the assassination:

> Everyone was pointing toward a fence that connected with the Underpass. . . . I ran that way. Some teenagers followed. One of them darted ahead and hit the fence before I did. . . . Puffing, I followed him. The other side of the fence revealed no gunman. There was just a maze of railroad tracks and three dazed winos. "What happened?" I asked one. "What happened?" he asked me. People were still climbing over the fence. I ran east toward the Texas School Book Depository.

Much like those of the "umbrella man" and the dark-complected man of Dealey Plaza, the identities of the three tramps were the object of speculation among assassination researchers. Although they were labeled "tramps," photos show the men had recent haircuts, shined shoes, and old but unsoiled clothing. In the photographs they hardly appear to be genuine tramps or winos.

In 1976 the three tramps drew national attention when comedian/social activist Dick Gregory and others claimed that two of the men were none other than CIA operatives and Watergate conspirators E. Howard Hunt and Frank Sturgis. This allegation was repeated in the book *Coup d'État in America*. It was quickly, though not conclusively, dismissed. In the summer of 1985, E. Howard Hunt lost a libel court case based on a national article that claimed CIA documents indicated he was in Dallas the day of the assassination. After the 1980 arrest of convicted assassin Charles V. Harrelson, researchers took a fresh look at the tramps, particularly the youngest of the trio. Many researchers now believe Harrelson was the tall tramp. Other men with CIA connections also were named, such as Thomas Vallee, Fred Lee Chrisman, and Daniel Carswell.

With the lack of records, other names were thrown into the mix. In 1991 Lois Gibson, a forensic facial recognition expert with the Houston Police Department, stated publicly that an investigation convinced her the three tramps were Harrelson; Charles Frederick Rogers, also known as Richard Montoya, who was wanted for the 1965 murder of his parents in Houston; and a man named Chauncey Holt.

Holt, located in California, gave a convincing, if not provable, account of his role in the assassination. He claimed to have once been an accountant for mobster Meyer Lansky but had also forged documents for the CIA. Holt said he delivered phony Secret Service identification to Dallas before the assassination in the company of Harrelson. Like so many other instances in the assassination case, those named by Holt who might have vouched for his story were either dead or missing. Holt died of cancer in 1997.

But just as the tramps story began to come together like the plot of a *Mission: Impossible* episode, it fell apart. As the public spotlight was once again focusing on the tramp issue, the Dallas City Council in 1992 decided to open their old police files, in which suddenly were found three arrest records naming the three tramps as a Harold Doyle, John Forester Gedney, and Gus W. Abrams. Abrams was dead but Doyle and Gedney were located in Oregon and Florida and both said they indeed were arrested in Dallas on November 22, 1963.

The FBI looked into the matter and a report later in 1992 described how the three men had arrived by rail in Dallas early on the morning of the assassination. After showering and receiving fresh clothes and a meal from an Irving Street mission, the trio again boarded a gondola car where they were arrested by Dallas police. According to this report, the three were convicted of vagrancy and sentenced to six days in jail only to be released four days later due to overcrowding. But problems remained.

Although by all accounts the trio were pulled out of the train cars only moments after the assassination, afternoon shadows and the lack of a crowd in the news photographs indicated the pictures were made later in the afternoon, long after the 12:30 p.m. shooting. The three arrest reports, all written and signed by the same Officer Chambers, gave an arrest time of 4 p.m. Other than the three reports, there were no jail records or court hearings concerning the trio.

Plus, the story of the three railroad tramps left no room for Charles Voyde Harrelson, a convicted hit man with some independent evidence to support the idea that he was involved.

Aside from being twice convicted of murder for hire, Harrelson—the father of actor Woody Harrelson—had a long history of involvement with Dallas underworld characters linked directly to Jack Ruby. This connection first came to the attention of JFK researchers when Harrelson was arrested near Van Horn, Texas, September 1, 1980. He had been identified as a suspect in the death of federal judge John Wood of San Antonio, who was shot in an ambush by a high-powered rifle.

High on cocaine, which is well-known for loosening the inhibitions, and pointing a pistol to his own head, Harrelson held lawmen at bay for six hours. During this time, according to the arresting officers, he not only confessed to the Judge Wood killing, but also claimed he had participated in the Kennedy assassination. This statement, repeated in some Texas newspapers, sent assassination researchers to their files looking for confirmation.

The late Fort Worth graphics expert Jack White, who testified before the House Select Committee on Assassinations, already had noticed the resemblance of Harrelson to the youngest tramp. Harrelson was forty-seven years old in 1985, making him twenty-five at the time of the assassination. This corresponds with the age of the youngest tramp, who was thought to have been between twenty-five and thirty years old.

In June 1981, Harrelson was interviewed by Chuck Cook, then a reporter for the *Dallas Morning News*. In a telephone interview with this author, Cook recalled, "I asked about the Kennedy assassination and he got this sly grin on his face. Harrelson is very intelligent and has a way of not answering when it suits him."

Cook said at a later interview he again brought the subject up and that Harrelson became very serious. Cook quoted Harrelson as saying, "Listen, if and when I get out of here and feel free to talk, I will have something that will be the biggest story you ever had." When Cook asked what that story might be, Harrelson would only reply, "November 22, 1963. You remember that!"

Intrigued with the possibilities, Cook said he later showed photographs of the three tramps to Harrelson's wife, Jo Ann Harrelson, who "was amazed at the similarities." Cook added, "Then I gave the photos to one of Harrelson's attorneys and he was supposed to show them to Harrelson. But that's the last I heard of it. He didn't want to talk about it because he felt his jail cell was bugged, and rightly so."

It was later revealed that Harrelson's jail conversations were indeed being monitored.

In an interview with Dallas TV newsman Quin Mathews, Harrelson offered further comments on the Kennedy assassination. "You said you'd killed President Kennedy?" commented Mathews. Harrelson replied:

> At the same time I said I killed the judge, I said I had killed Kennedy, which might give you an idea as to the state of my mind at the time. . . . It was an effort to elongate my life. . . . Well, do you believe Lee Harvey Oswald killed President Kennedy alone, without any aid from a rogue agency of the US Government or at least a portion of that agency? I believe you are very naïve if you do.

White became convinced that Harrelson was the youngest of the three tramps. White told this author, "I have done various photographic comparison tests and everything matches . . . the hair, the nose, the ear, the profile. It's Harrelson."

But over and above the comparisons of Harrelson's photograph with that of the youngest tramp, further evidence indicates Harrelson very well may have played a role in the assassination. When arrested, Harrelson was carrying the business card of R. D. Matthews. In subsequent interviews, Harrelson admitted to being a close friend of Matthews. In fact, Harrelson said he looked up to Matthews as a father.

Russell Douglas Matthews, a former Dallas underworld character, is mentioned in the Warren Report as a "passing acquaintance" of Jack Ruby's and is obliquely connected with a Ruby-backed jeep sale to Cuba in 1959.

The House Select Committee on Assassinations indicated Matthews's relationship with Ruby was more than "passing" and described Matthews as a man "actively engaged in criminal activity since the 1940s." The committee also documented Matthews's connections to Dallas gamblers Lewis McWillie, that close friend to the Kirkwoods of Fort Worth, and local gambler Benny Binion—both closely acquainted with Ruby. The committee further developed evidence that Matthews was in contact with associates of Florida crime chieftain Santos Trafficante Jr. and was linked to Texas underworld characters, such as Hollis de Lois Green, Jettie Bass, Nick Cascio, and James Todd—all acquaintances of Harrelson's.

In a strange sidelight, Matthews was best man at the wedding of a Dallas underworld figure named George McGann to Beverly Oliver. A friend to Ruby as well as several of his employees, Oliver became known to researchers as the "babushka lady."

The former chief counsel of the House committee, G. Robert Blakey, in his book *The Plot to Kill the President*, reiterated the committee's findings that Kennedy was assassinated as the result of a conspiracy involving organized crime and that more than one gunman was involved.

If organized crime in Dallas was involved—and Ruby's role would seem to justify that conclusion—then the entire spectrum of the Dallas underworld becomes suspect. And we come back to young Charles Harrelson.

But there is evidence that Harrelson's contacts went far beyond Dallas police characters. Indicted along with Harrelson in the plot to kill Judge Wood was the brother of reputed New Orleans crime boss Carlos Marcello, another of the organized-crime figures the House Select Committee on Assassinations named as possibly involved in the Kennedy assassination conspiracy. There was also Harrelson's involvement with criminals connected to intelligence agencies and even the military.

In April 1982, Florida law-enforcement officials identified Harrelson as being a member of a shadowy group of hired gunmen, mercenaries, and drug smugglers known as "The Company."

The Company, which according to lawmen took its nickname from the CIA, involved more than three hundred persons, many ex-police or ex-military men. Federal drug agents said the group imported billions of dollars' worth of narcotics from Central and South America as well as conducting gunrunning and mercenary operations. During one criminal trial involving members of the group, federal prosecutors claimed The Company owned more than $30 million in assets such as planes, ships, and real estate.

Florida lawmen investigating this group claimed Harrelson was a member and that Jimmy Chagra, the man who allegedly hired Harrelson to kill the judge, also once hired The Company for protection.

Oddly enough, the very day that Harrelson was formally charged with the Judge Wood assassination—April 16, 1982—a Dallas news reporter and a JFK assassination researcher were scheduled to meet with Harrelson to discuss his role in the Kennedy murder. Although Harrelson had been jailed for more than a year and a half, when the formal charges were filed, all visits to him were canceled. JFK researcher and author J. Gary Shaw claimed, "I feel this was done at that particular time to prevent Harrelson from revealing what he knows."

During Harrelson's trial, Joe Chagra, brother of Jimmy, testified that Harrelson got the Wood contract after telling his brother that he had participated in the JFK assassination. Researchers find it remarkable that a man reputed to be a high-ranking mobster by government agents should hire Harrelson on this claim rather than boot him out of his office—since everyone had been told the assassination was caused by only a lone nut.

Harrelson, who died in prison in 2007 while serving a life sentence in the Wood assassination, was never interviewed thoroughly about his role in Dallas, though his son's acting career prospered. Researchers are left only with his cryptic reminder: "November 22, 1963. You remember that!"

Today, Warren Commission apologists are content to lay the three-tramps controversy aside as a dead issue. But many researchers believe that some sort of shenanigan was pulled to distract from the truth. One offered explanation was that Doyle, Abrams, and Gedney were indeed railroad bums arrested in Dallas that day but in a separate incident and were not the same men photographed being marched through Dealey Plaza. If nothing else, the tramp issue illustrates the gaps, omissions, and general lack of meaningful investigation in the Kennedy assassination.

The "three tramps" were not the only persons arrested on the day of the assassination. More than a dozen people were taken into custody, and it will forever remain puzzling that few records were kept on any of them. It seems that once Oswald was captured, the authorities lost interest in anyone else.

A Catholic priest told this author of observing the arrest of a young man wearing a three-piece suit and gloves who was then escorted from the Texas School Book Depository to the Dallas County Sheriff's Office. He said he overheard the arresting officers say, "Well, we got one of them." There is no record of such an arrest.

Assassination witness Phil Willis told researchers that shortly after the shooting, police escorted a man in a black leather jacket and black gloves from the Dal-Tex Building—which lies directly east of the Depository and the building from which several researchers believe shots may have come. Again there is no record of such an arrest, though this man may have been Larry Florer, who was arrested in the Dal-Tex Building. In a statement to authorities, Florer said he tried to use a telephone in the Dal-Tex Building but found they were all busy. He was taken into custody as he tried to leave the building.

Another man arrested in the Dal-Tex Building was a Mafia-connected police character with a record of more than thirty arrests and oblique connections to Jack Ruby.

The Mafia Man in Dealey Plaza

Moments after the assassination, an elevator operator in the Dal-Tex Building noticed a man he did not recognize. The operator summoned deputy sheriff C. L. "Lummie" Lewis, who arrested the man. He identified himself as Jim Braden.

Taken to the sheriff's office for questioning, Braden said he was visiting Dallas on oil business and was staying at the Cabana Motel, a motor inn on Stemmons Freeway built with Teamster money. He said he had entered the Dal-Tex Building to use the telephone when he was taken into custody.

With no information to the contrary, authorities released Braden three hours later. It was an unfortunate decision. What is now known is that Braden had recently legally changed his name from Eugene Hale Brading. If the authorities had obtained that name on November 22, 1963, there perhaps would have been more interest in the man. Braden/Brading was a man with a police record stretching back to 1934 for such crimes as burglary, embezzlement, mail fraud, and conspiracy, including several arrests in Dallas.

Braden's story, which has been pieced together over the years by a variety of researchers and news reporters, indicated this man may have been more deeply involved in the assassination than was first suspected. On parole in California for mail fraud and interstate transportation of stolen property, Braden had informed his parole officer that he would be in Dallas from November 21 to 25, 1963. He said on November 21, 1963, he visited the offices of Texas oilman H. L. Hunt to meet with Hunt's son, Lamar. Interestingly, Jack Ruby also was at the Hunt offices about that same time, ostensibly to help a young woman get a job. Both Braden and Ruby denied these visits, though they have been verified by more than one office worker.

And Braden, along with ex-convict Morgan Brown, was staying at the Cabana Motel, the same motel Ruby visited the night of November 21.

Furthermore, in the book *Legacy of Doubt*, CBS newsman Peter Noyes documented Braden's connections to a number of underworld figures, including Meyer Lansky. Apparently Braden was known as a Mafia courier.

Most sinister of all, Braden may have been in contact with the New Orleans Mafia-CIA man, David Ferrie, Lee Harvey Oswald's former Civil Air Patrol leader.

Noyes found that in the weeks immediately preceding the assassination, Braden was in and out of Room 1701 of the Pere Marquette Building in New Orleans, just down the hall from Room 1707, where Ferrie was working for an attorney of Mafia boss Carlos Marcello.

Another fascinating connection between Braden and the assassination concerns two New York businessmen, Lawrence and Edward Meyers. Lawrence Meyers was a personal friend of Jack Ruby's. On November 20 and 21, 1963, Meyers also was staying at the Cabana Motel in Dallas. While in Dallas, Meyers told the FBI he was with Jean West, a "rather dumb, but accommodating broad." Edward Meyers was in Dallas to attend the bottlers convention—the same convention Richard Nixon attended. Both brothers were visited by Jack Ruby briefly at the Cabana Motel on the night of November 21—the night Braden was at the same motel.

While no direct connections between this group and Ferrie in New Orleans have been documented, it is fascinating to note that when New Orleans district attorney Jim Garrison began looking at long-distance telephone calls for David Ferrie he discovered something—the same day Oswald left New Orleans for his reported trip to Mexico City, Ferrie called a number in Chicago that belonged to Meyer's friend Jean West.

In Warren Commission Exhibit 2350—a listing of telephone calls made by Lawrence Meyers in November 1963—it was found that that same day he, too, called the Chicago number of Jean West, the woman who accompanied him to Dallas. While not conclusive, these documents suggest possible connections between Jack Ruby and David Ferrie via Meyers/West and Braden.

Meyers also told the Warren Commission that his friend Ruby had called him the night before shooting Oswald. The next day, upon hearing the news that Ruby had shot Oswald, Meyers decided not to contact Dallas police because "in light of the apparent hectic activities then ensuing at the police station, it would be better if he did not do so."

All of this occurred in the context of Braden's visit to Dallas. The House Select Committee on Assassinations tried to sort out the truth of Braden's visit as well as his contacts, to little avail.

First Braden said he made the trip to Dallas from California and met with a Dallas parole officer at the moment of the assassination. However, the parole officer could not recall such a meeting. If Braden had not notified his parole office that he was leaving California, he would have been in violation of parole and subject to arrest. Braden told the committee he walked as far as the Dal-Tex Building in an effort to find a telephone so he could call his mother and tell her about the assassination. He denied he ever was in Dealey Plaza.

However, due to statements made while in custody and the fact that Braden has definitely been identified in Dealey Plaza photographs, it is now widely accepted that Braden lied and was among the spectators gathered in Dealey Plaza minutes after the shooting.

This fact alone—that a known felon with many ties to Mafia figures, New Orleans, and Jack Ruby would be hanging around Dealey Plaza just after Kennedy's death—creates deep suspicion about the immediate Dallas investigation and, even more particularly, the subsequent federal investigation. This suspicion is heightened in light of the fact that in 1976, the National Archives revealed that at least two documents relating to the Braden arrest were missing.

One of the oddest arrests that day was reported only in a Dallas newspaper.

The November 22, 1963, edition of the *Dallas Times Herald* reported that a policeman arrested a man wearing horn-rimmed glasses, a plaid coat, and a raincoat after Depository employees pointed to him from a third-floor window. The news account said the man was taken under protest to the Sheriff's Department, while members of the crowd shouted, "I hope you die!" and "I hope you burn!"

Three weeks later, the same newspaper reported that "an early suspect in the assassination of President Kennedy was still in jail—but no longer a suspect in the killing." This account said the man was arrested minutes after the assassination after police swarmed into the railroad yards where "a man was reported seen in that area carrying a rifle." The story said the still-unidentified man was being held on "city charges."

Who was this man and what, if anything, did he know about the assassination?

Another odd arrest—that of Jack Lawrence—also deserves more serious study. Lawrence was arrested late on the afternoon on November 22, 1963, after his actions caused suspicions among his coworkers at Downtown Lincoln-Mercury, located two blocks west of Dealey Plaza.

Lawrence had obtained a job as a car salesman at the dealership just one month before the assassination with job references from New Orleans that later were found to be phony. Lawrence never sold a car and on the day before the assassination, he had borrowed one of the firm's cars, after telling his boss he had a "heavy date."

On Friday, November 22, Lawrence failed to show up for work. However, about thirty minutes after the assassination, he came hustling through the company's showroom, pale and sweating. He told coworkers he had been ill that morning and that he had tried to drive the car back to the dealership but had to park it due to the heavy traffic. Later, employees found the car parked behind the wooden picket fence on top of the Grassy Knoll overlooking Dealey Plaza.

Lawrence's activities were so suspicious that employees called police, who picked up Lawrence that evening. Lawrence, who reportedly was an expert marksman in the Air Force, left Dallas after being released the next day.

In 1991, after researcher Sheldon Inkol detailed Lawrence's story in *The Third Decade,* a JFK assassination newsletter, Inkol received a call from Lawrence, whom he described as "intelligent, articulate and good-humored" but irate. He denied any role in the assassination and said he parked his "loaner" car at the intersection of Ervay and Main Streets due to traffic and hurried to the car dealership so as not to be late for work.

A suspicious car salesman, a man held on nebulous charges for days, a Mafia man in Dealey Plaza, the three tramps—what could all this mean? Chauncey Holt, himself a suspect, may have provided the answer when he told *Newsweek* in 1991:

> Dallas that day was flooded with all kinds of people who ended up there for some reason. It's always been my theory that whoever was the architect of this thing—and no one will ever know who was behind it, manipulating all these people—I believe that they flooded this area with so many characters with nefarious reputations because they thought, "Well, if all these people get scooped up it'll muddy the waters so much that they'll never straighten it out."

Of course, the most prominent arrest of that day was when Dallas police nabbed Lee Harvey Oswald less than an hour and a half after the assassination. But such rapid police action was precipitated by yet another tragic shooting—the slaying of Dallas policeman J. D. Tippit.

The Shooting of J. D. Tippit

Of all the aspects of the Kennedy assassination, the shooting of Dallas policeman Jefferson Davis Tippit has received less attention than most others. Allegedly Tippit was shot down while attempting to arrest Lee Harvey Oswald forty-five minutes after the assassination in Oak Cliff, south of downtown Dallas. It was the slaying of this policeman that led to Oswald's arrest and in many ways became a cornerstone of the case for Oswald's guilt. Warren Commission attorney David Belin called the shooting the "Rosetta Stone to the JFK assassination." "After all," stated the conventional wisdom of 1963–1964, "Oswald killed that policeman. Why would he do that if he hadn't killed the president?"

Yet today a growing body of evidence suggests that Oswald did not kill Tippit— which, if true, reverses the above argument—if it can be shown that Oswald did not shoot the policeman, then perhaps he didn't shoot the president.

Little is known about Tippit or his life and personal contacts. This absence of information prompted researcher Sylvia Meagher to write:

Tippit, the policeman and the man, is a one-dimensional and insubstantial figure—unknown and unknowable. The [Warren] Commission was not interested in Tippit's life, and apparently interested in his death only to the extent that it could be ascribed to Oswald, despite massive defects in the evidence against him.

The commission failed to mention that Tippit's death occurred only two blocks from Ruby's home on Marsalis Street. Yet with no real knowledge of Tippit's background or associations and with a number of problems with the evidence, the Warren Commission nevertheless concluded that Oswald was his killer. This was based on four primary pieces of evidence.

1

Two witnesses who saw the shooting and seven who saw a man fleeing "positively identified Lee Harvey Oswald as the man they saw fire the shots or flee from the scene."

The chief witness for the Warren Commission was Helen Markham, whose credibility, even at the time of the Commission, was strained to the breaking point. Markham claimed to have talked for some time with the dying Tippit, yet medical authorities said he was killed instantly. She said she saw Tippit's killer talk with the policeman through his patrol car's right-hand window, although pictures taken at the scene show that window was shut.

She was in hysterics at the time and even left her shoes on top of Tippit's car. Later, in her testimony before the Warren Commission, Markham stated six times she did not recognize anyone in the police lineup that evening, before Commission attorney Joseph Ball prompted, "Was there a number-two man in there?" Markham responded, "Number two is the one I picked. . . . When I saw this man I wasn't sure, but I had cold chills just run all over me."

Furthermore, other witnesses at the scene—William Scoggins, Ted Calloway, and Emory Austin—even today claim they never saw Markham in the minutes immediately following the shooting.

Cabdriver Scoggins also identified Oswald that day, although Scoggins admitted he did not actually witness the shooting and his view of the fleeing killer was obscured because he ducked down behind his cab as the man came by. Scoggins and cabdriver William Whaley, who allegedly drove Oswald home that day, both viewed a Dallas police lineup composed of five "young teenagers" and Oswald. Whaley told the Warren Commission:

> You could have picked [Oswald] out without identifying him by just listening to him because he was bawling out the policemen, telling them it wasn't right to put him in line with these teenagers. . . . He showed no respect for the policemen, he told them what he thought about them. . . . They were

trying to railroad him and he wanted his lawyer. . . . Anybody who wasn't
sure could have picked out the right one just for that.

If his protestations weren't enough to guide the witnesses in identifying Oswald,
the suspect had conspicuous bruises and a black eye. Furthermore, Oswald stated
during the lineup he was asked his name and place of employment. By Friday evening, everyone in Dallas who attended the police lineups had heard that shots were
fired from the Texas School Book Depository.

On Saturday, Scoggins again identified Oswald, although in his Warren Commission testimony he admitted seeing Oswald's photograph in a morning paper
before viewing the police lineup. His identification of Oswald fell further into dis-
repute when he told the Commission that after the lineup, an FBI or Secret Service
agent showed him several pictures of men, which Scoggins narrowed down to two.
Scoggins recalled, "I told them one of these two pictures is him [Oswald] . . . and
then he told me the other one was Oswald."

These were the star government witnesses. Other witnesses, including Domingo
Benavides—the person closest to the killing—were never asked to view a lineup nor
were they able to identify Oswald as the killer.

Several other witnesses, including Acquilla Clemons, a black woman who claimed
two men were involved in the Tippit shooting but was ignored by the federal authorities. Clemons claimed she was threatened into silence by a man with a gun
and was never questioned. The Warren Commission denied knowledge of Clemons,
stating, "The only woman among the witnesses to the slaying of Tippit known to the
Commission is Helen Markham."

Markham's testimony was inconsistent. She initially stated Tippit's killer was
short and stocky with bushy hair. This is the same description given by Clemons,
who in a filmed interview said the killer was "kind of a short guy . . . kind of heavy."
Markham later denied giving this description.

Frank Wright lived near the scene of the Tippit shooting. He heard shots and ran
outside. His wife called the police, who contacted the Dudley M. Hughes ambulance service. The call slip carried the Wright's address and arrived, according to the
ambulance records, at 1:18 p.m. In an interview with private researchers less than a
year later, Wright said:

I saw a man standing in front of the car. He was looking toward the man
on the ground. . . . He had on a long coat. It ended just above his hands. I
didn't see any gun. He ran around on the passenger side of the police car.
He ran as fast as he could go, and he got into his car. His car was a little gray
old coupe. It was about a 1950–51, maybe a Plymouth. It was a gray car,
parked on the same side of the street as the police car, but beyond it from
me. It was heading away from me. He got in that car and he drove away as
fast as you could see. . . . After that a whole lot of police came up. I tried to
tell two or three people what I saw. They didn't pay any attention. I've seen

what came out on television and in the newspaper, but I know that's not what happened.

Another witness was Warren Reynolds, who chased Tippit's killer. He, too, failed to identify Oswald as Tippit's killer until after he himself was shot in the head two months later. After recovering, Reynolds identified Oswald to the Warren Commission. A suspect was arrested in the Reynolds shooting, but released when a former Jack Ruby stripper named Betty Mooney MacDonald provided an alibi. One week after her word released the suspect, MacDonald was arrested by Dallas police and a few hours later was found hanged in her jail cell. Neither the FBI nor the Warren Commission investigated this strange incident.

2

The cartridge cases found near the Tippit slaying "were fired from the revolver in the possession of Oswald at the time of his arrest, to the exclusion of all other weapons," claimed the Warren Commission.

There are many problems with this evidence. First, at the time of the Tippit shooting, Dallas police sergeant Gerald Hill radioed the police dispatcher, saying, "The shells at the scene indicate that the suspect is armed with an automatic .38 rather than a pistol." Oswald reportedly was captured with a .38 Special revolver. There is a significant difference between an automatic, which ejects spent shells onto the ground, and a revolver, which requires deliberate emptying of the weapon. These weapons also use different types of ammunition.

Other officers at the scene believed that an automatic weapon was used, based on the distance from Tippit's body to where the shells were found and what some perceived to be scratches from an automatic's ejector on the shells. If an automatic was used, then Oswald's revolver cannot be blamed for Tippit's death.

Then there's the problem of identification of the empty shells. Policeman J. M. Poe received two cartridge cases from witness Domingo Benavides at the scene. In an FBI report, Poe firmly stated that he marked the cases with his initials, "J.M.P." before turning them over to Dallas crime lab personnel.

However, on June 12, 1964, the FBI showed Poe the four .38-caliber Special cases used as evidence of Oswald's guilt by the Warren Commission. The bureau reported:

> [Poe] recalled marking these cases before giving them to [lab personnel], but he stated after a thorough examination of the four cartridges shown to him . . . he cannot locate his marks; therefore, he cannot positively identify any of these cartridges as being the same ones he received from Benavides.

Testifying to the Warren Commission, Poe vacillated, saying he couldn't swear to marking the cases. However, asked to identify the cartridges, Poe also stated, "I want to say these two are mine, but I couldn't swear to it." Poe's failure to find his initials on the cases, coupled with the fact that the cases were not turned over to the FBI until six days after other inventoried evidence, leaves many researchers with the suspicion that shell cases from Oswald's revolver were substituted for the ones Poe marked.

To further confuse the issue, the Warren Commission discovered that the shell cases allegedly recovered at the scene of the shooting do not match up with the slugs recovered from Tippit's body. Of the four cases, two are of Winchester-Western manufacture and two of Remington-Peters, while of the bullets removed from Tippit, only one is Remington-Peters and three are from Winchester-Western.

Weakly, the Warren Commission attempted to explain this anomaly by surmising that perhaps a fifth shot had been fired but not recovered, although most of the witnesses recalled no more than four shots, or that perhaps Oswald already had an expended Remington-Peters case in his pistol before shooting Tippit. The Commission even suggested that perhaps "to save money . . . he might have loaded one make of bullet into another make of cartridge case."

This, of course, would require Oswald to own or have access to reloading equipment. It should be pointed out that when arrested, Oswald reportedly was carrying five live Winchester-Western pistol bullets in his pocket in addition to the fully loaded revolver, which apparently was never tested to determine if it had been fired recently. With this exception, authorities found no other ammunition or gun-related materials in any of Oswald's possessions.

3

The Warren Commission determined that the revolver in Oswald's possession at the time of his arrest was purchased by and belonged to him. While this segment of the evidence against Oswald may be true—some researchers are not convinced that the weapons order signed by A. J. Hidell can conclusively be traced to Oswald—it does not prove that the gun was used to kill Tippit.

For instance, even the FBI's resources failed to prove that the slugs recovered from Tippit's body had been fired from Oswald's pistol. FBI officials claimed that since the Oswald revolver had been rechambered to accept .38 Special ammunition, the barrel was oversize for the bullet, causing inconsistent ballistic markings. Thus, "consecutive bullets fired in the revolver by the FBI could not even be identified with each other under the microscope," stated the Commission in an appendix to its report. This statement is most odd, for several firearms experts have told this author that similar .38 Special bullets do fit the rifling grooves and can be checked ballistically.

If the slugs from Tippit's body cannot be matched to Oswald's revolver, perhaps it is because they did not come from that gun. Adding fuel to this speculation is the statement of Eddie Kinsley, the ambulance attendant who drove the mortally wounded Tippit to a hospital. In recent years, Kinsley told newsman Earl Golz of an extraneous bullet. According to Kinsley, as he unloaded Tippit from his ambulance, "I kicked one of the bullets out of my ambulance that went into his button . . . onto the parking lot of Methodist Hospital. It didn't go in the body. . . . It fell off the ambulance still in this button."

Since Tippit reportedly was struck by all four bullets fired at him and these slugs were placed in evidence with the Warren Commission, what is the explanation for Kinsley's fifth slug? Kinsley told Golz he had never been questioned by the Warren Commission.

Recent work by Texas researchers indicates that the cases now residing in the National Archives and exhibited by the Warren Commission as the shells used in the Tippit slaying could not have been fired by Oswald's pistol. Oswald's pistol was originally a Military and Police Smith & Wesson 1905 Model .38-caliber revolver, the largest-selling quality revolver ever produced.

The pistol in question, serial number V510210, was converted to a .38 Special Model. This involved cutting off the barrel from its original five inches to two and a quarter inches. The Warren Commission said the pistol also was rechambered to accept .38 Special ammunition—slightly smaller in diameter but longer than. 38 Standard ammunition.

In the 1980s, Texas researcher and veteran hunter Larry Howard discovered after buying an exact duplicate of Oswald's .38 revolver that the .38 Special cartridges, when fired in a rechambered weapon, bulge noticeably in the center. Howard told this author:

> I have checked this with several expert gunsmiths. Since the rechambering cannot change the diameter of the cylinder, but only makes it longer to accept .38 Special ammo, the bullet bulges in the middle when fired. I've done it time after time. My wife can notice the bulge. The case looks like it's pregnant. Studying the shells depicted in the Warren Commission volumes and also in a close-up clear photograph in the November 1983 commemorative issue of *Life* magazine, it appears to everyone that the shell cases in the National Archives [supposedly the casings found at the scene of Tippit's death] do not show any bulging at all. This indicates to me and other experts that those cases could not have been fired from the .38 Special that was supposed to belong to Oswald.

Until further testing can be done on the cartridge cases in question, this is hardly solid proof of Oswald's innocence in the Tippit shooting. But it is a further example of the wide gaps still open in the case against Oswald.

4

According to the Warren Commission, Oswald's jacket was found along the path of flight taken by Tippit's killer.

The Warren Commission wrote:

> Oswald was seen leaving his rooming-house at about 1 p.m. wearing a zipper jacket. . . . The man who killed Tippit was wearing a light-colored jacket, that he was seen running along Jefferson Boulevard, that a jacket

was found under a car in a lot adjoining Jefferson Boulevard. . . . When he was arrested at approximately 1:50 p.m., he was in shirtsleeves. These facts warrant the finding that Lee Harvey Oswald disposed of his jacket as he fled from the scene of the Tippit killing.

But did the facts warrant such a conclusion? Not really, since almost every aspect of the jacket story has since come under question. Oswald, it is known, had only two jackets—one blue and one a lightweight gray zipper jacket. The blue one was later found in the basement lunchroom of the Depository building. At least two witnesses at the scene of Tippit's slaying reported his killer wore a white jacket.

One of these witnesses, Helen Markham, was shown Oswald's gray jacket by a Warren Commission attorney who asked, "Did you ever see this before?" Despite having been shown the jacket by the FBI prior to her testimony, Markham replied, "No, I did not . . . that jacket is a darker jacket than that, I know it was."

Witness Domingo Benavides was shown a jacket by Commission attorney David Belin, who said, "I am handing you a jacket which had been marked as 'Commission's Exhibit 163,' and ask you to state whether this bears any similarity to the jacket you saw this man with the gun wearing?" The accommodating Benavides responded, "I would say this looks just like it."

The problem here is that Commission Exhibit 163 is Oswald's dark blue jacket. The gray jacket is Commission Exhibit 162. Here is yet another example of a witness obligingly providing the answers he felt were desired.

Another example is cabdriver William Whaley, who reportedly drove Oswald home from downtown Dallas. Whaley identified the gray jacket as the one Oswald was wearing in his cab. Yet the Warren Commission, based on testimony from Earlene Roberts, Oswald's landlady, stated that Oswald put on the jacket *after* arriving at his lodgings.

Testifying to the Warren Commission, Roberts said:

[Oswald] went to his room and he was in his shirtsleeves . . . and he got a jacket and put it on—it was kind of a zipper jacket. [She then was shown Commission Exhibit 162, Oswald's gray jacket, and asked if she had seen it before] . . . Well, maybe I have, but I don't remember it. It seems like the one he put on was darker than that.

Barbara Davis, another witness at the Tippit slaying, stated the killer wore "a dark coat . . . it looked like it was maybe a wool fabric . . . more of a sporting jacket" and cabdriver William Scoggins also failed to identify Oswald's jacket, saying, "I thought it was a little darker."

Despite these problems of identification, the Commission went right on asserting that the jacket belonged to Oswald.

The Commission dissembled about the discovery of the jacket. The Warren Report stated, "Police Capt. W. R. Westbrook . . . walked through the parking lot behind the service station and found a light-colored jacket lying under the rear of one of the cars." However, in his testimony, Westbrook was asked if he found some clothing. He replied, "Actually, I didn't find it—it was pointed out to me by . . . some officer." According to the Dallas police radio log, a "white jacket" was found by "279 (Unknown)" a full fifteen minutes before Westbrook arrived on the scene. The Commission made no effort to determine who really found the jacket, if a jacket was actually found, or if it was a white jacket that only later was transformed into Oswald's gray jacket.

The owner of the Texaco station where the jacket reportedly was found told Texas researchers that no one—not the FBI, the Dallas police, or the Warren Commission—ever questioned him or his employees about this important piece of evidence.

In addition, the jacket identified by federal authorities as belonging to Oswald carried inside a laundry mark "30 030" and a dry-cleaning tag "B 9738." A full-scale search by the FBI in both Dallas and New Orleans failed to identify any laundry or dry cleaner using those marks.

Oswald's wife, Marina, testified she could not recall her husband ever sending his jackets to a cleaning establishment, but that she did recall washing them herself. Further investigation by the FBI turned up no laundry or dry-cleaning tags on any of Oswald's other clothing.

With all this, plus a broken chain of evidence, the jacket cannot be considered evidence of Oswald's guilt in the killing of Officer Tippit.

Then there is a matter of time and a strange incident at Oswald's lodging. Earlene Roberts, Oswald's landlady, told the Warren Commission she was watching television coverage of the assassination about 1 p.m. when Oswald—who had been registered at the rooming house as O. H. Lee—hurried in and went to his room.

She said soon after this, a Dallas police car pulled up in front of her house and honked. She explained, "I had worked for some policemen and sometimes they come by. . . . I just glanced out, saw the number [on the car]. . . . It wasn't the police car I knew . . . and I ignored it." She said the police car was directly in front of her home when the driver sounded the horn, like "tit-tit." She said the car then "just eased on . . . and they just went around the corner that way [indicating Zang Boulevard]."

According to Roberts, there were two uniformed policemen in the car, most unusual since daytime patrols in that area of the city were limited to one officer—such as Tippit. She could not recall the number of the car precisely, but said she did recall that the first two numbers of a possible three-digit combination were a 1 and a 0. Tippit was driving car number 10 that day and failed to respond to a dispatcher call at the approximate time of the police-car incident.

Immediately following the departure of the police car, Roberts said Oswald came out of his room and left hurriedly, zipping up a jacket. She said he left her house three or four minutes after 1 p.m.

Roberts said she looked out the window and last saw Oswald standing at a nearby bus stop at Zang Boulevard.

According to the Warren Commission, a man used Tippit's police radio microphone at 1:16 p.m., saying, "Hello police operator . . . We've had a shooting here . . . it's a police officer, somebody shot him." This, of course, referred to Tippit, who lay dead next to his patrol car about a mile from Oswald's North Beckley residence.

The Commission tried to establish that the Tippit shooting occurred moments after 1:15 p.m., hardly enough time to allow Oswald to run from his rooming house to the scene of the Tippit slaying at 10th and Patton. The Commission could not locate even one witness who saw Oswald walking or running between his rooming house and the scene of the Tippit slaying. None have been found to this day.

This time frame becomes stretched to the breaking point when one considers the Tippit witnesses' testimony. Even Helen Markham, who was so confused about other matters, was certain of the time because she was on her way to catch her usual 1:12 p.m. bus for work. Asked by a Warren Commission attorney about the time she saw the Tippit shooting, Markham responded, "I wouldn't be afraid to bet it wasn't six or seven minutes after one."

In this instance, Markham's recollection must be correct since another Tippit shooting witness, Jack Ray Tatum, told researchers that Markham did not want to remain at the scene because she feared missing her bus for work.

T. F. Bowley, the man who called the police dispatcher, was never called to testify to the Warren Commission. The reason may be that Bowley heard shots, saw Tippit's body lying next to his squad car, and looked at his watch. It was 1:10 p.m.

Other witnesses hid at the sound of the shots, afraid the gunman would turn on them. Only after the killer fled did they venture out. One of the first to reach Tippit was Domingo Benavides, who told the Warren Commission he was in a truck across the street from the shooting. After hearing only three shots, Benavides said:

> I sat there for just a few minutes. . . . I thought maybe [the killer] had lived in there [the house where he last saw the gunman] and I didn't want to get out and rush right up. He might start shooting again. . . . That is when I got out of the truck and walked over to the policeman. . . . The policeman, I believe, was dead when he hit the ground.

After checking on Tippit, Benavides said, he tried to call on the patrol car's radio but got no answer. Another bystander, Bowley, then got in the car and was successful in raising the police dispatcher and reported the shooting.

Obviously several minutes went by between the time of the shooting and 1:16 p.m., when the police radio log recorded the citizen's alert. This places the actual shooting closer to Bowley's time of 1:10 p.m.—a time frame that rules out the possibility that Oswald could have traveled on foot from his rooming house to the scene of the shooting.

The conversations of police regarding time sequences, orders, discovery of evidence, and so on were recorded on Dallas police radio recording equipment. These recordings should have provided accurate times and movement orders—in fact, the Warren Commission and subsequent investigations relied on them greatly.

Today, there is evidence that there may have been tampering with the Dallas police radio recordings. Soon after the assassination, the tapes may have been taken by federal authorities, who certainly have access to the most sophisticated audio equipment. Any police broadcasts not consistent with the lone-assassin theory could have been simply edited out and an altered copy returned to Dallas police for conveyance to the Warren Commission.

Is there any evidence that this occurred? Yes. Dr. James Barger, chief acoustic scientist for the House Select Committee on Assassinations, studied the "original" police tapes and discovered a break in the sixty-cycle hum background tone. He found two separate tones on the tape, which could result only from copying.

Although ignored publicly, the Ramsey panel, appointed by the National Academy of Sciences to review the acoustical studies of the House committee, did suggest in an appendix of its report that "the original Dictabelt could be studied more extensively for possible evidence . . . of being a copy."

Gary Mack reported that in recent years, former Dallas police sergeant J. C. Bowles, the radio-room supervisor who prepared transcripts for the Warren Commission, stated that a few days after the assassination, federal agents "borrowed" the original police Dictabelt and at the time he was under the impression that they took the tapes to a recording studio in Oklahoma.

Like the Zapruder film and so much of the Warren Commission's prime evidence, the Dallas police radio recordings are now open to question.

The House Select Committee on Assassinations supported the Warren Commission's conclusion that Oswald killed Tippit; however, it obliquely indicated that all is not known about the killing.

Committee investigators studied information developed by researcher Larry Harris that Tippit may have been killed as the result of personal problems. They also talked with yet another witness who had not been interviewed by the Warren Commission. Jack Ray Tatum told committee investigators that Tippit's killer, after shooting the officer from the sidewalk, walked toward the patrol car and shot Tippit once in the head at point-blank range. Correctly, the committee noted, "This action, which is often encountered in gangland murders and is commonly described as a coup de grace, is more indicative of an execution than an act of defense intended to allow escape or prevent apprehension."

There is a problem with Tatum's story, however. Most of the witnesses stated that four shots were fired in succession—with no interval between the shots.

Some serious students of the Tippit incident now believe that his death may have had no connection with the Kennedy assassination. And of the researchers who still believe such a connection exists, few cling to the belief that Oswald was the killer.

But the key objection to the idea that Oswald killed Tippit is that he was encountered inside the Texas Theater both before and during the Tippit slaying.

Regardless of who actually killed Officer Tippit, that event was the catalyst that set off a flurry of police activity in Oak Cliff resulting in the arrest of Lee Harvey Oswald.

Prior to his arrest, there were at least two incidents in which police were obviously seeking a suspect. Sometime after 1 p.m., a number of policemen stormed the Oak Cliff branch of the Dallas Public Library. One was heard to say, "He's not here!" Unable to locate who they were looking for, they quickly left. Oswald was a frequent visitor to that library. Then, shortly before being called to the Texas Theater, the scene of Oswald's arrest, police surrounded a church near the scene of the Tippit slaying in the belief that Tippit's killer had hidden there. However, before they could conduct a search of the building, they were called to the Texas Theater.

The Arrest of Oswald

The arrest of Lee Harvey Oswald appears straightforward enough in the official reports, but there are some strange aspects when viewed objectively.

By 1:45 p.m. on November 22, 1963, the president of the United States had been murdered just seventy-five minutes earlier, and only about thirty minutes before, Officer Tippit had been shot down on an Oak Cliff street. Dallas police were swarming like angry bees.

A report came in to police dispatchers. It seemed a man had slipped into the Texas Theater without paying. Immediately carloads of officers, including one federal agent and an assistant district attorney, converged on the theater.

The report had been instigated by a shoe store manager named Johnny Brewer. Brewer was listening to the radio when he learned of the Tippit murder. Hearing police sirens, he looked out the window of his store and saw a man duck into his doorway as a police car went by. Believing this to be suspicious activity, Brewer watched the man continue up the street to the Texas Theater, where he lost sight of him. Moments later, when Brewer asked the theater's ticket seller if she had sold a ticket to anyone, she replied she had not. Entering the theater, Brewer learned that the concession stand operator, W. H. "Butch" Burroughs, had heard the front doors open but had seen no one enter the theater lobby.

Between the theater's front doors and a second set of doors were stairs leading to the balcony. Burroughs was convinced that whoever entered had gone up to the balcony since no one had passed his concession stand. Brewer asked the ticket seller to call police while he and Burroughs unsuccessfully looked for the suspicious man.

The authorities arrived quickly. Several policemen went to the theater's rear exit and waited with drawn guns. Inside, police, including sergeant Gerald Hill, who had commanded the search of the sixth floor of the Texas School Book Depository, turned up the house lights and moved to the front of the theater.

Officer M. N. McDonald had come in the rear door and was standing at the side of the movie screen. In an article written the day after the assassination for the Associated Press, McDonald recalled:

I noticed about 10 to 15 people sitting in the theater [which seated 900] and they were spread out good. A man sitting near the front, and I still don't know who it was, tipped me the man I wanted was sitting in the third row from the rear of the ground floor and not in the balcony [as reported to the police dispatcher]. I went up the aisle and talked to two people sitting about in the middle. I was crouching low and holding my gun in case any trouble came. I wanted to be ready for it. I walked up the aisle and turned in Oswald's row. We were no more than a foot from each other when he suddenly stood up and raised both hands. "It's all over now," he told me. Then he hit me a pretty good one in the face with his fist. I saw him going for his gun and I grabbed him around the waist. We struggled and fell around the seats for a few seconds and I got my hand on the butt of his pistol. But he had his hand on the trigger. I was pulling the gun toward me and I heard the hammer click. The primer [which detonates the bullet] was dented and it didn't fire. . . . I'm sure glad that shell didn't fire.

McDonald's account of Oswald's gun misfiring was confirmed to the Warren Commission by theater patron John Gibson.

But in his testimony to the Warren Commission, Brewer never mentions speaking to McDonald. In fact, he said he was standing by a rear exit when he was grabbed by a couple of policemen and asked what he was doing there. Brewer told them he was suspicious of a man in the theater. Brewer continued:

And I and two or three other officers walked out on the stage and I pointed him out, and there were officers coming in from the front of the show . . . and officers going from the back. . . . I saw this policeman approach Oswald and Oswald stood up and I heard some hollering, I don't know exactly what he said, and this man hit Patrolman McDonald. . . . I didn't know his name [McDonald], but I had seen him quite a few times around Oak Cliff.

Was the sitting man who tipped off McDonald to Oswald's location Johnny Brewer? Apparently not, since Brewer stated he was standing and then on stage with several policemen. Brewer also never mentioned talking to McDonald, whom he said he recognized from around Oak Cliff. Who then was the man who tipped off McDonald to Oswald's location?

Brewer also told the Commission that as Oswald struggled with police, he heard one of the officers cry, "Kill the president, will you?"

If members of the police department somehow knew that Oswald was an assassination suspect at this time, it is strong evidence that something was going on behind the scenes. The Warren Commission, while not contradicting Brewer's account, nevertheless felt compelled to add, "It is unlikely that any of the police officers referred to Oswald as a suspect in the assassination."

George J. Applin, one of only two theater patrons questioned by the Warren

Commission, told the Commission he was watching the movie when the lights came on and a policeman with a rifle or shotgun began moving down his aisle. Applin said he was sitting in the downstairs middle aisle about six rows from the back when the commotion began. He moved down the aisle to ask what was going on, when a policeman (apparently McDonald) passed him moving toward the rear. Applin then witnessed Oswald's arrest.

At the close of his Warren Commission testimony, Applin said:

> But, there is one thing puzzling me . . . and I don't even know if it has any bearing on the case, but there was one guy sitting in the back row right where I was standing at, and I said to him, I said, "Buddy, you'd better move. There is a gun." And he says—just sat there. He was back like this. Just like this. Just watching. . . . I don't think he could have seen the show. Just sitting there like this, just looking at me.

Applin told Commission attorney Joseph Ball twice he didn't know the man, but in 1979, he told a news reporter that two days later, following the Oswald slaying, he recognized the man as Jack Ruby. Applin told the *Dallas Morning News*:

> At the time the Warren Commission had me down there at the Post Office in Dallas to get my statement, I was afraid to give it. I gave everything up to the point of what I gave the police there in town. . . . I'm a pretty nervous guy anyway because I'll tell you what: After I saw that magazine where all those people they said were connected with some of this had come up dead, it just kind of made me keep a low profile. . . . [Jack] Ruby was sitting down, just watching them. And, when Oswald pulled the gun and snapped it at [McDonald's] head and missed and the darn thing wouldn't fire, that's when I tapped him on the shoulder and told him he had better move be-cause those guns were waving around. He just turned around and looked at me. Then he turned around and started watching them.

Yet more questions have been raised by recent statements of concession stand operator Burroughs. In a 1987 interview with this author, Burroughs, who then had become assistant manager at the Texas Theater, reiterated his story of someone slipping in the theater about 1:35 p.m. that day. However, Burroughs claimed that it could not have been Oswald because Oswald entered the theater shortly after 1 p.m. Burroughs said Oswald entered only minutes after the feature started, which was exactly at 1 p.m.

He said several minutes later, about 1:15 p.m., the man later arrested by police and identified as Oswald came to his concession stand and bought some popcorn.

Burroughs said he watched the man enter the ground floor of the theater and sit down next to a pregnant woman. About twenty minutes after this, the outside doors opened and Johnny Brewer arrived.

Several minutes after the man—identified by Burroughs as Oswald—took his seat, the pregnant woman got up and went upstairs, where the ladies' restroom was located, said Burroughs. He said he heard the restroom door close shortly before Dallas police began rushing into the theater.

Burroughs said, "I don't know what happened to that woman. I don't know how she got out of the theater. I never saw her again."

The story of Oswald being in the Texas Theater at the time of the Tippit shooting is further supported by Jack Davis, who went on to host *Gospel Music Spotlight* on a Dallas Christian radio station.

Davis told this author that on the day of the assassination, he went to the Texas Theater to see the war movies. The eighteen-year-old Davis found a seat in the right rear section of the theater and recalled seeing the opening credits of the first film, which occurred a few minutes past the 1 p.m. starting time for the feature movie.

He said he was somewhat startled by a man who squeezed past him and sat down in the seat next to him. He found it odd that this man would choose the seat adjacent to him in a nine-hundred-seat theater with fewer than twenty patrons in it. Davis said the man didn't say a word but quickly got up and moved across the aisle and took a seat next to another person. Then shortly, the man got up and walked into the theater's lobby. A few minutes later, Davis, whose attention had returned to the movie, vaguely remembered seeing the same man enter the center section of the theater from the far side.

Twenty minutes or so after this incident, according to Davis, the house lights came on and when he walked to the lobby to ask why, he saw policemen running in the front door. He recalled:

> I was looking for the manager, but I never got to say anything because the policemen all came rushing past me. I did not see what went on in the theater, but I heard some scuffling going on. A few minutes later the police brought out this same man who had sat down next to me. He was shouting, "I protest this police brutality!" Later, of course, I learned that this was Lee Harvey Oswald.

If Oswald was already in the theater at the time of the Tippit slaying as claimed by Burroughs and Davis, then who slipped in about 1:35 p.m.?

Since it can be established that someone was impersonating Oswald in Dallas before the assassination, it is reasonable to suggest that someone besides Oswald lured police to the Texas Theater. But if this were the case, what happened to the man who slipped in without buying a ticket? Initial police reports stated the suspect was in the theater's balcony, this information perhaps coming from Burroughs's belief that the man who sneaked in went upstairs.

The Dallas police homicide report on J. D. Tippit of that day stated, "Suspect was later arrested in the balcony of the Texas Theater at 231 W. Jefferson." A separate arrest report also stated Oswald's arrest took place in the balcony.

Was someone else arrested in the Texas Theater? Not according to the official record. However, there is now evidence that perhaps another man was taken from the rear of the theater.

Bernard J. Haire owned Bernie's Hobby House, located two doors east of the Texas Theater on West Jefferson.

On November 22, 1963, Haire, who was unaware of the assassination, saw the street in front of his business fill up with police cars. He went outside and saw a crowd gathered at the Texas Theater but could not see what was happening. Haire was captured at the rear of the crowd in at least one photograph taken when Oswald was brought from the theater by police.

Haire walked through his store and went into the alley, which he said was also filled with police cars. Walking toward the theater, Haire was opposite the rear door when police brought a young white man out. He said the man was dressed in a pull-over shirt and slacks and appeared to be flushed as if having been in a struggle. Although Haire was unable to see whether the man was handcuffed, he was certainly under the impression that the man was under arrest. Haire watched police put the man in a patrol car and drive off.

For nearly twenty-five years Haire believed he had witnessed the arrest of Lee Harvey Oswald. He was shocked to discover that Oswald had been handcuffed and brought out the front door of the theater. He commented, "I don't know who I saw arrested."

Neither does anyone else, but it is eloquent testimony that apparently someone other than Oswald led police to the Texas Theater and someone other than Oswald shot Tippit.

The arrested Oswald was taken from the Texas Theater shortly before 2 p.m. and driven downtown to police headquarters. He was quickly taken to the third-floor office of captain Will Fritz, the crusty chief of the Homicide Bureau, and placed in a seat in the hallway.

Detective Guy Rose was already busy interviewing assassination witnesses. He soon took charge of Oswald. Rose recalled:

> I took the man to an interrogation office. I removed his handcuffs. I asked him to identify himself. He refused. In his pockets I found two pieces of identification. One card was for Lee Harvey Oswald, the other was for Alek Hidell. "Which are you?" He said, "You're the cop. You figure it out." He told me a lot of lies. Captain Fritz called me out at some time near 2:20 p.m. He said that the employees of the Texas School Book Depository were accounted for—except one. He told me to get some men together and get out to this address in Irving. I asked what the man's name was. He said, "Lee Harvey Oswald." I was stunned. "Captain," I said, "I think this is Oswald, right in there."

With a suspect in custody, the entire complexion of the assassination investigation changed.

Despite what was heralded as overwhelming proof of Oswald's guilt in both killings, it was not until late Friday, November 22, 1963, that he was charged with the murder of Officer Tippit. And it was well after midnight before he was reportedly charged with the murder of President Kennedy.

Dallas police and federal authorities quickly lost interest in any information, evidence, or detained suspects that did not fit in with the presumed activities of Lee Harvey Oswald.

Yet many puzzling aspects continued to crop up in the aftermath of the assassination. There were reports of a man seen with a rifle near Cobb Stadium, located on the Stemmons Freeway route from downtown to the Trade Mart. Nothing came of this report.

At Redbird Airport, a private field located just south of Dallas, it was reported that federal officials seized a plane with its engine running the afternoon of the assassination and placed it in a closed hangar under tight security. Two days before the assassination, the airport's manager, Wayne January, said three men talked to him about renting an airplane on November 22 to fly to Mexico. He said one of the men remained sitting in a car and closely resembled Lee Harvey Oswald. None of these stories regarding possible escape plans were properly investigated.

It is clear that someone was impersonating Oswald and if this "Oswald" did not leave Redbird, how did that person get out of Dallas?

The answer perhaps may be found in the 2008 book by James W. Douglass, *JFK and the Unspeakable*. Here Douglass recounts the story of Air Force Sergeant Robert G. Vinson, a staff member of the North American Air Defense Command (NORAD) who by happenstance hitched a ride on an unmarked military transport plane from Washington to his home in Colorado. Vinson soon found himself flying over mid-America all alone in the C-54 transport. At one point an unemotional voice came over the plane's radio stating, "The president was shot at 12:29." The craft suddenly banked left and headed south, arriving some time later in Dallas, a city with which Vinson was familiar. Vinson was surprised when the plane made a sudden landing on a dirt strip near the Trinity River and picked up two men, who sat near him without saying a word. The taller of the pair, both wearing beige coveralls, appeared to be Latino, a Cuban perhaps, while the second man was a nondescript young white male. The transport, which had never turned off its engines, immediately took off in a westerly direction.

Just after dusk, Vinson said, they landed at Walker Air Force Base at Roswell, New Mexico, which Vinson was told was closed and under alert. A few hours later, Vinson was able to continue his trip home. Watching the constant news coverage of the assassination, he was shocked to realize the man he saw get on the transport in Dallas was Lee Harvey Oswald. "He's in jail," Vinson's wife argued, adding, "Keep quiet about it." Vinson did keep quiet even after being assigned to CIA projects, apparently in an effort to keep him under surveillance and control. Finally, his conscience prompted Vinson to tell his story to a TV news reporter in 1993 and eventually write down his account in a book published in 2003. Needless to say, Vinson's story never garnered national media attention.

But if doubts remained in Dallas as to Oswald's guilt, there were none in Washington. Less than two hours after the assassination—at a time when Dallas police were not even certain of the identity of the man they had in custody, FBI Director Hoover called Robert Kennedy. In a bureau document released to the public in 1977, Hoover wrote, "I called the attorney general at his home and told him I thought we had the man who killed the President down in Dallas."

Hoover went on to describe Oswald as an ex-Marine who had defected to Russia, a procommunist and a "mean-minded individual . . . in the category of a nut." This incident raises the troubling question of how Hoover could have had all this information on Oswald at a time when the Dallas authorities were not even certain of their prisoner's identity.

On November 24, less than two hours after Oswald was killed in Dallas, Hoover telephoned the Johnson White House, saying, "The thing I am most concerned about . . . is having something issued so we can convince the public that Oswald is the real assassin."

In 1976 a Senate Select Committee report stated, "Almost immediately after the assassination, Director Hoover, the Justice Department and the White House 'exerted pressure' on senior Bureau officials to complete their investigation and issue a factual report supporting the conclusion that Oswald was the lone assassin."

Over the assassination weekend, information on—and evidence against—Oswald continued to pile up. The news media was on around-the-clock alert. No bit of information was too insignificant to broadcast or publish.

The *Dallas Morning News* of November 23, 1963, carried a story stating:

> [District Attorney Henry] Wade said preliminary reports indicated more than one person was involved in the shooting which brought death to the President and left Gov. John Connally wounded. . . . "This is the most dastardly act I've ever heard about," Wade said. "Everyone who participated in this crime—anyone who helped plan it or furnished a weapon, knowing the purposes for which it was intended—is guilty of murder under Texas law. They should all go to the electric chair."

But Wade's initial claim of evidence of a conspiracy was quickly dropped as official statements began to center more and more on Oswald. Years later, Wade recalled why:

> Cliff Carter, President Johnson's aide, called me three times from the White House that Friday night. He said that President Johnson felt any word of a conspiracy—some plot by foreign nations—to kill President Kennedy would shake our nation to its foundation. President Johnson was worried

about some conspiracy on the part of the Russians. Oswald had all sorts of connections and affections toward Castro's Cuba. It might be possible to prove a conspiracy with Cuba. But it would be very hard to prove a conspiracy with Russia. Washington's word to me was that it would hurt foreign relations if I alleged a conspiracy—whether I could prove it or not. I would just charge Oswald with plain murder and go for the death penalty. So, I went down to the Police Department at City Hall to see Captain Fritz—to make sure the Dallas police didn't involve any foreign country in the assassination.

With an ever-growing pile of evidence of conspiracy in the assassination, the federal government began to assert itself as early as the afternoon of the assassination.

The FBI Takes Control

What criminal wouldn't like to gain complete, secret, and unsupervised control over all the evidence in his case for two full days? Wouldn't the verdict in his criminal trial be a swift "not guilty" if he had the opportunity to "doctor" the evidence?

This is exactly the situation that occurred in the murder of President John F. Kennedy beginning the very day of the assassination. Although the proof of the disappearance and reappearance of the JFK evidence has been lying right in front of researchers since the fateful weekend, no one seems to have perceived the significance of the matter. However, at least one person with access to official federal government documents apparently recognized this significance and took steps to conceal it from the public.

This issue began the evening of November 22, 1963, when Dallas police chief Jesse Curry began receiving calls from Washington. Curry told the Warren Commission:

> The FBI actually had no jurisdiction over [the murder of Kennedy], the Secret Service actually had no jurisdiction over it. But, in an effort to cooperate with these agencies we went all out to do whatever they wanted us to do. . . . We kept getting calls from the FBI. They wanted this evidence up in Washington . . . there was some discussion, [Captain] Fritz told me, he says, "Well, I need the evidence here, I need to get some people to try to identify the gun, to try to identify this pistol and these things, and if it's in Washington, how can I do it?" But, we finally . . . about midnight of Friday night, we agreed to let the FBI have all the evidence.

As he related to Warren Commission member Allen Dulles, "We kept getting calls from the FBI. They wanted this evidence up in Washington, in the [FBI] laboratory, and there was some discussion." Curry made it clear that "we felt this was a murder that had been committed in the county, city and county of Dallas, and that we had prior, I mean we had jurisdiction over this.

But someone in Washington was most persistent. "We got several calls insisting we send this [evidence], and nobody would tell me exactly who it was that was insisting, 'Just say I got a call from Washington, and they wanted this evidence up there,' insinuated it was someone in high authority that was requesting this, and we finally agreed as a matter of trying to cooperate with them, actually," explained Curry. Rumors in Dallas have long been that the calls were made by President Lyndon B. Johnson's assistant Cliff Carter.

On the basis of this pressure from Washington and against their better judgment, the Dallas police reluctantly released all of the assassination evidence to the FBI. "We finally, the night, about midnight of Friday night, we agreed to let the FBI have *all* [emphasis added] the evidence and they said they would bring it to their laboratory and they would have an agent stand by and when they were finished with it to return it to us," stated Curry.

However, much of the evidence was never returned to Dallas. Curry told the Warren Commission on April 22, 1964, "Subsequently they photographed these things in Washington and sent us copies, some 400, I think 400 copies of different items. So far as I know, we have never received any of that evidence back. It is still in Washington, I guess. Perhaps the Commission has it."

"Yes; the Commission is still working with it," responded Commission general counsel J. Lee Rankin. According to Fritz, what the Dallas authorities eventually received was "very poor reproductions of some of these items on microfilm."

Yet the journey of this vital evidence was unofficial and was never made clear to the public. The first official word on the transfer of assassination evidence came on Tuesday, November 26, when both Dallas newspapers carried stories announcing that the evidence was to be turned over to federal authorities.

"The Dallas Police Department Tuesday prepared to turn over all evidence in the assassination case against Lee Harvey Oswald to the Federal Bureau of Investigation," stated the *Dallas Times Herald*. "FBI agents Tuesday took control of all evidence gathered by Dallas police against accused assassin Lee Harvey Oswald on an agreement between Police Chief Jesse E. Curry and Dist. Atty. Henry Wade," announced the *Dallas Morning News*.

The *News* went on to explain, "Curry went before reporters at noon Tuesday to make the announcement. The disclosure came after Curry held several morning conferences with top aides. The transfer of evidence from city police to federal control was completed four hours later."

So now the FBI was officially on the case and officially in charge of the evidence. But what could have happened during the two days while the evidence was unofficially in their hands? Fabrication, substitution, elimination, alteration—anything could have been done to the evidence, with no effective chain of custody. Unlike in 1963, today the FBI has come under suspicion of poor management of evidence at best and downright falsification of evidence at worst. In the late 1990s, Frederic Whitehurst, who served as supervisory special agent in the FBI's laboratory from 1986 to 1998, went public with charges that the lab was involved in ongoing deficiencies ranging from mishandling of evidence to falsifying documents. His charges echoed those of researchers who have claimed similar activities with JFK assassination evidence.

Under Hoover's iron control, it would have been an easy matter for certain ranking bureau officials to do with the evidence whatever they pleased.

The fact that federal authorities had all the assassination evidence under covert control for two days could go far in explaining the contradictions and questionable conclusions of the official investigation. Apparently at least one person understood the gravity of this issue as there was an attempt to obscure it in the Warren Commission materials.

In 1992, the National Archives made public the "confidential" deposition of FBI fingerprint expert James C. Cadigan. In his April 30, 1964, testimony to Warren Commission attorney Melvin A. Eisenberg, the following exchange took place during routine questioning regarding fingerprint matters:

MR. EISENBERG: Do you know why [Exhibit] 820 was not reprocessed or desilvered?
MR. CADIGAN: I could only speculate.
MR. EISENBERG: Yes?
MR. CADIGAN: It may be that there was a very large volume of evidence being examined at the time. Time was of the essence, and this material, I believe, was returned to the Dallas Police within two or three days, and it was merely in my opinion a question of time. We have (*sic*) a very large volume of evidence. There was insufficient time to desilver it. And I think in many instances where latent fingerprints are developed they do not desilver it.
MR. EISENBERG: Can you explain why the signature, "Lee H. Oswald" or "L.H. Oswald is apparent while the signature "A.J. Hidell" is not?
MR. CADIGAN: Different inks.

During this otherwise unremarkable questioning, Cadigan had inadvertently let the cat out of the bag. He had declared to one and all that the FBI had a "large volume" of assassination evidence only some of which was returned to the Dallas police. Later in his deposition, Cadigan made it absolutely clear when this evidence was being handled:

MR. CADIGAN: Initially the first big batch of evidence was brought into the laboratory on November 23rd of 1963 and this consisted of many, many items.
MR. EISENBERG: `63?
MR. CADIGAN: November 23, 1963. It was a very large quantity of evidence that was brought in. There were several agent examiners available to evaluate this material. There were supervisory officials, there were representatives from our Internal Security Division, all of whom had an interest in this matter, and it was decided they wanted certain items treated for latent fingerprints.

So a virtual posse of ranking FBI officials swarmed over the assassination evidence all day Saturday and Sunday. Obviously this unpublicized and unmonitored access to all the evidence might cause a suspicious mind to question the validity of the evidence later used to establish Oswald's guilt.

It is doubly suspicious that in Cadigan's original deposition some unknown person scratched out his statement about being rushed to return the evidence to Dallas and scribbled "delete" in the margin. This same person marked out Cadigan's statement that "I could only speculate" and wrote in "No, this is a latent fingerprint matter."

Sure enough, in the version published by the Warren Commission, we read:

MR. EISENBERG: Do you know why Exhibit 820 was not reprocessed or desilvered?
MR. CADIGAN: No, this is a latent fingerprint matter.
MR. EISENBERG: Can you explain why the signature, "Lee H. Oswald" or rather "L.H. Oswald" is apparent, while the signature "A.J. Hidell" is not?
MR. CADIGAN: Different inks.

Why did someone commit a crime by illegally altering an official government deposition and why did the Warren Commission print an altered version of Cadigan's statement. Were they unaware of the alteration? Or did someone recognize the significance of the assassination evidence being in the hands of the FBI with no publicity or accountability for two days?

Perhaps a study of the stenographic notes and tapes might reveal other alterations to the testimony of Cadigan and others. But don't count on it. According to a notice on the cover sheet of Cadigan's deposition, "Stenotype Tape, Master Sheets, Carbon and Waste turned over to Commission for destruction."

The assassination had become a federal government matter, and although the assassination evidence is often ambiguous and contradictory and will certainly be in controversy for years to come, the handling of the evidence clearly points to manipulation and obfuscation at the highest levels of federal authority, clear proof of who was responsible for at least the demonstrable cover-up, if not the assassination itself.

The next major shock came about 11:20 a.m. Sunday, November 24, 1963, when the prime suspect was fatally shot while handcuffed in the basement of Dallas police headquarters.

Five days later, Lyndon Johnson moved to block any further investigation of the curious events in Dallas by appointing a "blue ribbon" commission to probe the entire affair. It was the beginning of total federal control over the evidence and witnesses in the assassination case. The key to the JFK assassination may be in the aftermath of the crime—the unfollowed leads, the presence of Secret Service agents—real or bogus—in Dealey Plaza where none should have been, the intimidation of witnesses, the destruction and suppression of vital evidence.

As with any good investigation dealing with criminal violence, much of the work in the first hours after the assassination centered on the medical evidence, which should have clearly shown how many bullets struck Kennedy and from which direction they came.

Therefore, on the day of the assassination, attention was centered on two hospitals—Parkland Memorial Hospital in Dallas and Bethesda Naval Hospital near Washington, DC.

Two Hospitals

As the echo of shots died away in Dealey Plaza, Dallas police chief Jesse Curry, riding in the lead car of Kennedy's motorcade, radioed his police dispatcher, "Looks like the president has been hit. Have Parkland stand by."

The motorcade sped up, reaching speeds of nearly eighty miles per hour during the four-mile race along Stemmons Freeway to the hospital.

Parkland Memorial Hospital remains the major public hospital in Dallas County today. Almost every victim of violence—from wrecks to gunshot wounds—is brought to Parkland. Its emergency room is constantly staffed with doctors and interns well experienced in trauma situations. President Kennedy could not have asked for more experienced and competent medical attention.

Yet following his autopsy that evening at the National Naval Medical Center at Bethesda, Maryland, serious and continuing discrepancies in the medical evidence arose. These discrepancies have provided a source of controversy that continues even today.

If one assumes there was some sort of conspiracy involved in the assassination, the questions over the medical evidence provide a good starting point for determining its scope.

But before examining the tangled morass of medical evidence, there is a small question of the presidential limousine's arrival at Parkland. Secret Service driver William Greer testified to the Warren Commission that he did not know the way to Parkland and so followed sheriff Bill Decker and Chief Curry in the lead car. Greer's story is buttressed by the testimony of two other Secret Service officials, Forrest Sorrels and Winston Lawson. However, in his testimony, Chief Curry is strangely vague, saying only that the limousine went to the hospital under "siren escort."

What's the problem? During the time of the House Select Committee on Assassinations, a film taken by Dallasite Jack Daniel was seen widely for the first time. Taken just as the motorcade exited from the west end of the Triple Underpass and entered Stemmons Freeway, this film clearly shows that both the presidential limousine and the Secret Service backup car had passed Curry's lead car and were leading the race to the hospital.

How could Washington-based Agent Greer know how to find Parkland and, more important, why did he state in his Commission testimony, "I never passed [Curry's car]. . . . I was led to the hospital by the police car who was preceding me"?

Either these highly trained agents panicked and forgot what actually happened or they lied about it. Since the Daniel film can't lie, the question remains—how did Greer know how to locate Parkland?

Upon arrival at Parkland at 12:35 p.m., Governor Connally regained consciousness long enough to attempt to rise, but fell back into the car in great pain. Connally was lifted onto a stretcher and wheeled into the hospital. Secret Service agent Clint Hill removed his suit coat and placed it over the president's gory head wound to prevent photographs.

However, several persons saw Kennedy's body, including Fort Worth newsman Roy Stamps, who told researchers, "I rushed up and saw Kennedy lying in the car on his side. His foot was hanging over the side of the car. The back of his head was gone."

As other vehicles in the presidential motorcade began arriving at the Parkland emergency entrance and Connally was placed in Trauma Room 2, Secret Service agents Greer, Roy Kellerman, and Winston Lawson pulled the fatally wounded president away from Mrs. Kennedy, placed him on a stretcher, and pushed it into Trauma Room 1. There Kennedy was attended to by no fewer than twelve of Parkland's doctors—including four surgeons, the chief neurologist, an oral surgeon, and a heart specialist.

Dr. Charles J. Carrico, a resident surgeon, was the first doctor to examine Kennedy. He noted the president was ashen in color, his breathing lacked coordination, there were no voluntary movements, and his eyes were open with pupils dilated, showing no reaction to light. However, a few chest sounds thought to be heartbeats were heard and immediately resuscitation efforts were begun. Carrico inserted a cuffed endotracheal tube in a small puncture wound just below Kennedy's Adam's apple. The tube was connected to a respirator.

Other doctors began arriving and treating the president; fluids and stimulants were injected and oxygen administered. Cardiac massage was begun—to no avail.

President Kennedy was pronounced dead at 1 p.m. (CST) by Dr. Kemp Clark, Parkland's director of neurological surgery.

Dr. Charles A. Crenshaw, who retired as chairman emeritus of the Department of Surgery at Fort Worth's Peter Smith Hospital and a director of the Tarrant County Hospital District, was among the team that worked to save the president. In 1992, he was vilified by the *Journal of the American Medical Association* (*JAMA*) after publicly stating that Kennedy was shot from the front and that the Dallas doctors had engaged in a "conspiracy of silence" concerning his wounds. The publication even suggested that Crenshaw was never in Parkland's emergency room. He noted:

> My observations contradicted the "official" version of the assassination, as reported in the Warren Report. I stated that President Kennedy was shot at least once, and I believe twice, from the front, and Oswald could not have been a "lone gunman." I had anticipated criticism from some, but I never expected the vicious attack from my medical colleagues.

A retraction and financial settlement were later given by *JAMA* when it was pointed out that five doctors and nurses had mentioned Crenshaw's presence in their Warren Commission testimony.

Crenshaw also raised official ire when he related how he received a call from Lyndon Johnson while trying to save the life of Lee Harvey Oswald. Phyllis Bartlett, chief telephone operator for Parkland Hospital, recalled, "The call came in and said 'hold the line for the President,' and for a second I was still thinking Kennedy, and I . . . was kind of taken aback for a minute and a few seconds. It was just a matter of a second, that's when he came on in a loud voice and said, 'This is Lyndon Johnson. Connect me to the accused assassin's doctor.' It sounded the same as it had been on newscasts when I would hear him speak."

Crenshaw said Johnson told him, "Dr. Crenshaw, I want a death-bed confession from the accused assassin. There's a man in the operating room who will take the statement. I expect full cooperation in this matter."

Crenshaw said the incident confounded logic and bothered him for the rest of his life. "Why the President of the United States would get personally involved in the investigation of the assassination, or why he would take the inquest out of the hands of the Texas authorities was perplexing," he mused.

While one set of Parkland doctors worked on Kennedy, another worked feverishly to save Connally. A large sucking chest wound caused the greatest concern for the governor. A bullet had shattered the fifth rib on his right side, sending bits of bone and metal tearing through his chest, collapsing one lung. And his right wrist had been broken, the bullet entering from the top and exiting from the bottom of his wrist. Doctors also discovered a wound in Connally's left thigh. This wound was cleaned and sutured shut, although according to the Warren Report, "a small metal fragment remained in the Governor's leg."

Vice president Lyndon Johnson also had entered Parkland, but was kept secluded in a room near where efforts were being made to revive the president. About 1:20 p.m., presidential aide Kenneth O'Donnell informed Johnson that Kennedy was dead. According to the Warren Report, O'Donnell advised Johnson to return to Washington as soon as possible. However, Mrs. Kennedy refused to leave without her husband's body and Johnson refused to leave without Mrs. Kennedy.

It was finally decided to leave immediately and to return on Air Force One because the presidential plane had better communication equipment. The decision created one of the assassination's most enduring problems—with the president's autopsy performed at Bethesda, two sets of doctors viewed the body at different times and their descriptions of wounds differed so widely that controversy remains to this day.

The president's death was legally a Texas homicide and by law, the body could not be removed until after an autopsy or a coroner's ruling, which would have involved further medical investigation. Dallas County medical examiner Dr. Earl Rose, who died in 2012 at age eighty-five, tried to block the efforts of Secret Service agents trying to remove Kennedy's body from Parkland. But after some shouting, including profanities and, by some accounts, even drawn weapons, Rose was forced to step aside. In 2003, Rose told the Associated Press he and his staff should have conducted an examination as required by law. "We had the routine in place to do it and it was important for the chain of evidence to remain intact. That didn't happen when the body was taken to Bethesda," he explained.

Totally against prevailing law and despite the protest of Texas officials, a coffin was ordered from O'Neal Funeral Home and Kennedy's body was whisked away from Parkland Hospital. Ambulance driver Aubrey Rike told this author that even though his ambulance was on standby at Parkland, his boss, Vernon O'Neal, arrived with an expensive bronze casket into which Kennedy's body was placed. Government agents then drove off in the newly arrived ambulance leaving both O'Neal and Rike standing at the hospital's loading dock. Both men then climbed into Rike's ambulance and trailed the first ambulance to Love Field. Rike said there were no stops.

After Kennedy's body left Parkland and while Dallas doctors worked on Connally in a second-floor operating room, another incident occurred in the hospital that was to have long-reaching effects on the official theory of the assassination—a hospital worker discovered a bullet in a hallway.

During the feverish activity in the emergency room, the hospital's senior engineer, Darrell C. Tomlinson, was asked to manually operate an elevator that connected the ground-floor emergency room to the second-floor operating theaters. It was Tomlinson who found an intact bullet, which became the key exhibit of the Warren Commission.

Despite efforts by Warren Commission attorney Arlen Specter to confuse the issue during testimony, Tomlinson was remarkably clear on what had happened that day. Tomlinson stated that one hospital stretcher containing two rolled-up bloody sheets, some surgical instruments, and some sterile packs was sitting against a wall near the elevator.

No effort apparently was made by the Commission to determine the true origin of this stretcher. Some researchers believe it may have held Kennedy's body while in the emergency room. But this is extremely doubtful since Kennedy's body remained on his stretcher until the Dallas casket arrived about 1:40 p.m. At this time, his body was placed in the casket and the stretcher was stripped of sheets and rolled across the hall to Trauma Room 2, according to nurse Diana Bowron. Since Tomlinson claimed to have discovered a bullet at this same time and two nurses reported placing Kennedy's empty stretcher in Trauma Room 2, it is virtually impossible to believe that the hallway stretcher carried the president.

Today, it is more likely that this stretcher was used in treating two-year-old Ronald Fuller, who entered the Parkland emergency room at 12:54 p.m. with a bad cut on the chin. The child's mother, Mrs. Ross Fuller, years later told the *Dallas Morning News* what happened:

> I was watching the President's parade on television when they announced he had been shot. I knocked over the bottle of soda pop I was drinking and it broke into pieces. My little boy Ronnie fell on it and started bleeding badly. My husband and I ran to the car and headed for Parkland with the baby.

Mrs. Fuller finally reached the Parkland emergency room and handed her son to medical personnel. Then she fainted. She recalled, "When I came to, they told me Ronnie was all right. They were sewing him up. Then they told me the President was dead. It happened in the cubicle right next to us. The doctor said I was living a part of history."

The Fuller child was briefly placed on a stretcher and his cut was treated with sutures and gauze packs, which could have been left behind on the cart.

Considering both the condition—bloody sheets, instruments, sterile packs—and the location of Fuller's stretcher—the child originally was placed on a stretcher in the same hallway leading to Trauma Rooms 1 and 2—it is most likely this stretcher on which the bullet was found.

Tomlinson said a second stretcher was on the elevator—perhaps the one that carried Connally to the second-floor operating room—and that he pulled it out and placed it near the first stretcher. Specter designated the stretcher pulled off the elevator as stretcher A and the stretcher already in the hall near the elevator (Fuller's?) as stretcher B.

After making a few trips in the elevator, Tomlinson said one of the stretchers was moved away from the wall so he could enter a men's restroom. Tomlinson told Specter as he pushed the stretcher back up against the wall to clear the hallway, "I bumped the wall and a spent cartridge or bullet rolled out that apparently had been lodged under the edge of the mat." "And that was from which stretcher?" asked Specter. "I believe that it was B," replied Tomlinson.

Later in his testimony, Specter tried to shake Tomlinson's recollections. Specter asked, "And at the time we started our discussion, it was your recollection at that point that the bullet came off of stretcher A, was it not?" "B," Tomlinson quickly responded.

Finally, after Specter continued to confuse the matter by telling Tomlinson that he had identified stretcher A during a Secret Service interview, the hospital worker said:

> I really don't remember. I'm not accustomed to being questioned by the Secret Service and the FBI and by you and they are writing down everything,

I mean . . . I'm going to tell you all I can, and I'm not going to tell you something I can't lay down and sleep at night with either.

From Tomlinson's testimony, it appears more than likely that the stretcher holding the bullet did not belong to Connally. But this would be evidence of planted evidence, which would mean an accomplice to the assassination—a conspiracy. Therefore, the Warren commissioners, while acknowledging Tomlinson's uncertainty, nevertheless concluded that the intact bullet came from Connally's stretcher. "That conclusion is buttressed by evidence which eliminated President Kennedy's stretcher as a source of the bullet," they explained, closing off any suspicion that the slug might have come from anywhere else.

It was this bullet—Commission Exhibit 399—that became the foundation of the single-bullet theory of the assassination. It has also been called the "magic bullet."

Tomlinson turned the bullet over to Parkland's chief of security, O. P. Wright, who gave it to Secret Service agent Richard Johnsen.

Interestingly, Wright was the father-in-law of Dallas police sergeant Patrick T. Dean, the officer blamed by the Warren Commission for allowing Jack Ruby into the police department basement just before Oswald's slaying. Dean's mother-in-law, Mrs. O. P. Wright, was director of nursing at Parkland and on duty when Kennedy was being treated.

Neither Wright nor Agent Johnsen were interviewed by the Warren Commission—perhaps because, in later interviews with researchers, neither man could positively identify Commission Exhibit 399 as the bullet found that day. Oddly, Tomlinson never was asked to identify Commission Exhibit 399.

In fact, during a 1966 interview with author Josiah Thompson, Wright, a professional security officer, picked a pointed-tip bullet shape as more nearly like the bullet discovered at Parkland. He rejected round-nose bullet shapes similar to Commission Exhibit 399. Likewise, Tomlinson selected a pointed shape as resembling the bullet he found.

The whole bullet matter becomes even more clouded when the possibility of substitution and planting is considered. The hallway in which both stretchers A and B were left unattended was a public corridor and neither stretcher belonged to either Kennedy or Connally. Although the Warren Commission apparently never considered that Commission Exhibit 399 may have been planted on one of the stretchers or later substituted for the found bullet, these possibilities find favor in the minds of assassination researchers.

Adding to this suspicion is the presence of Jack Ruby at Parkland Hospital while Kennedy's body was still there.

Jack Ruby at Parkland

Veteran newsman Seth Kantor told the Warren Commission that he encountered Jack Ruby at Parkland Hospital about the time Kennedy's death was publicly announced. Kantor said he and Ruby even shared a brief conversation. Kantor recognized Ruby, having worked in Dallas for some years. He said he spoke to Ruby at 1:30 p.m. and recalled that Ruby asked if he should close his club out of respect for the slain president.

When asked about his presence at Parkland, Ruby denied ever being there, and the Commission chose to believe him and concluded that Kantor must have been mistaken.

Ignored by the Commission were FBI interviews with a Dallas woman whose experiences on the day of the assassination fully supported Kantor's account of his Parkland meeting with Ruby. Wilma Tice was home when she heard the news of the Dealey Plaza shooting. Curious, she drove to Parkland Hospital, arriving about 1:30 p.m., and joined the throng of bystanders awaiting word on the president's condition.

Some months later, she told the FBI she stood beside a heavily built man in a dark suit who was hitting his hat against his leg. She was only three or four feet from the man when another man approached him and said, "How are you doing there, Jack?" She said the two men had a brief conversation during which the man named Jack offered to donate a kidney to John Connally.

Two days later Tice was astounded to see the man called Jack on television identified as Jack Ruby, the slayer of Oswald. However, she assumed that the authorities knew about his presence at Parkland and did not notify anyone until late in the spring of 1964.

Tice had telephoned Ruby's sister, Eva Grant, to express her condolences over Ruby's death sentence when she mentioned her encounter at Parkland and learned that Ruby had denied being there. It was at this point that Tice contacted the FBI and told her story.

On April 12, 1964, she received a call from a man claiming to be a newspaper reporter. He asked about her Parkland encounter and then advised her not to talk about the incident. On July 19, Tice received a letter asking her to testify for the Warren Commission. The next day she received an anonymous call from a man who warned her, "It would pay you to keep your mouth shut."

On July 22, Tice called police because someone tried to break into her home while her husband was away. This incident was followed by other phone calls, but she had a fourteen-year-old niece answer the phone and the caller would hang up.

The account of Ruby at Parkland has been further supported in recent years by former radio newsman Roy Stamps, who said he had met Ruby on about forty-five occasions before November 22, 1963. Stamps told Texas researchers that he was in the hall of Parkland holding open a telephone line to his radio station when he noticed Ruby enter the hospital. He said Ruby was carrying some television equipment and trailing behind a TV crew.

In 1979, the House Select Committee on Assassinations reversed the Warren Commission's decision that Kantor was mistaken about his Parkland meeting with Ruby, stating, "While the Warren Commission concluded that Kantor was mistaken, the Committee determined he probably was not."

With the presence of Ruby in Parkland plus the lack of firm identification, the possibility that Commission Exhibit 399 was planted appears more than likely.

Of course, virtually anyone could have planted the bullet, since the stretcher in question sat unattended in the public hallway for some time. But even if the bullet were not planted—and there is some evidence to suggest that a bullet slug may have worked its way out of Kennedy's back wound—there is also the possibility that Commission Exhibit 399 was substituted for the bullet found on the stretcher. There is even the possibility that Commission Exhibit 399 represented an entirely different bullet, a suggestion strengthened by John Connally, who wrote in 1993:

> But the most curious discovery of all took place when they rolled me off the stretcher and onto the examining table. A metal object fell to the floor, with a click no louder than a wedding band. The nurse picked it up and slipped it into her pocket. It was the bullet from my body, the one that passed through my back, chest, and wrist, and worked itself loose from my thigh. . . . I have always believed that three bullets found their mark. What happened in the hospital demonstrated how easily a bullet could have been swept aside and lost.

But this extraneous bullet was not lost. According to several reports, it was given by the nurse to Texas highway patrolman Bobby Nolan, who said he turned it over to Captain Will Fritz. From that point onward, it was in the hands of federal authorities. Of course, if bullets were switched, it could have been done only while in the hands of authorities—a most ominous suspicion.

After Kennedy's body was returned to Air Force One at Love Field, Lyndon B. Johnson was sworn in as thirty-sixth president of the United States by federal judge Sarah T. Hughes.

On the plane flight back to Washington, it seems the original destination for Kennedy's body was to have been Walter Reed Army Hospital—long the major military medical facility for Washington. Examining US Army Signal Corps transcripts of radio messages from Air Force One that day, researchers have found several references indicating that military officers were going to send the body to the Army hospital. General Chester Clifton, senior military aide, radioed:

> This is Gen. Clifton. We do not want a helicopter to go to Bethesda Medical Center. We do want an ambulance and a ground return from Andrews to Walter Reed, and we want the regular post-mortem that has to be done by law under guard performed at Walter Reed. Is that clear?

Even the official history of the 1001st Air Base Wing, which included Air Force

One, reported, "The body of the slain President was removed to Walter Reed General Hospital."

Why the sudden change to Bethesda?

Kennedy's personal physician, Dr. George G. Burkley, wrote in his report of that day:

> During the course of the flight [back to Washington], determination of the immediate action on arrival in Washington was made to assure complete compliance with Mrs. Kennedy's wishes. I spoke to her while kneeling on the floor so I would be at the level of her face rather than leaning forward, and expressed complete desire of all of us and especially of myself to comply with her wishes, stating that it was necessary that the President be taken to a hospital prior to going to the White House. She questioned why and I stated it must be determined, if possible, the type of bullet used and compare this with future material found. I stated frankly that I had no preference that it could be any hospital, but that I did feel that, if possible, it should be a military hospital for security measures. The question was answered by her stating that she wanted the President taken to Bethesda Naval Hospital.

Oddly, having just received Mrs. Kennedy's wishes, Dr. Burkley then added, "Arrangements were made on the ground for departure to Walter Reed Army Hospital or Bethesda Naval Hospital, as the case may be."

Why such confusion over military hospitals? Was Mrs. Kennedy's natural desire to take her husband, a former naval officer, to the naval hospital an unexpected hitch in a plan for an autopsy at Walter Reed?

It certainly appears that Bethesda was not prepared for this most important autopsy. The three military physicians who performed Kennedy's autopsy were clinical pathologists with little experience in gunshot wounds. Neither Navy Commander James J. Humes nor Navy Commander J. Thornton Boswell had practical, firsthand experience with bullet wounds. Army Lieutenant Colonel Pierre Finck did have some such experience, but he later said he was hampered in his autopsy procedures by officials in the room. The military autopsy doctors apparently were surrounded by both military and civilian superiors who directed much of the autopsy—some of this direction contrary to normal autopsy procedures.

During the Clay Shaw trial in New Orleans, Dr. Finck was asked under oath if Dr. Humes had been in charge of the president's autopsy. He replied:

> Well, I heard Dr. Humes stating that—he said, "Who's in charge here?" And I heard an Army general, I don't remember his name, stating, "I am." You must understand that in those circumstances, there were law-enforcement officers, military people with various ranks, and you have to coordinate the operation according to directions.

An unnamed Army general in charge? Directions to the doctors? Finck continued to describe the scene:

> The autopsy room was quite crowded. It is a small autopsy room, and when you are called in circumstances like that to look at the wound of the President of the United States who is dead, you don't look around too much to ask people for their names and take notes on who they are and how many there are. I did not do so. The room was crowded with military and civilian personnel and federal agents, Secret Service agents, FBI agents, for part of the autopsy, but I cannot give you a precise breakdown as regards the attendance of the people in that autopsy room at Bethesda Naval Hospital.

New Orleans executive assistant district attorney Alvin Oser then pressed Finck on why, as an autopsy pathologist, he had not tracked the bullet wound through Kennedy's body to determine its exact path.

After dodging the question for a time, Dr. Finck finally was ordered by the court to answer Oser's question. Dr. Finck stated, "As I recall I was told not to, but I don't remember by whom." "Could it have been one of the admirals or one of the generals in the room?" asked Oser. "I don't recall," said Dr. Finck.

Finck, the only member of the autopsy team who was a member of the American Academy of Forensic Sciences, asked to examine Kennedy's clothing—a normal and acknowledged autopsy procedure. His request was denied.

Further, the autopsy doctors were ordered not to talk about what they had seen in the autopsy room. Finck again:

> When you are a lieutenant colonel in the Army you just follow orders, and at the end of the autopsy, we were specifically told—as I recall it, it was by Admiral [Edward C.] Kenney, the surgeon general of the Navy . . . not to discuss the case.

In 1977 Dr. Humes appeared before a medical panel gathered by the House Select Committee on Assassination. Because of long-standing questions concerning the possibility that Kennedy suffered from Addison's disease (which can be detected by studying the adrenal glands), Humes was asked about the glands by committee medical panel member Dr. Charles Petty "because normally we examine adrenals in the general course [of an] autopsy, as we undertake it." Humes replied:

> Since I don't think it bore directly on the death of the President, I'd prefer not to discuss it with you, doctor. . . . I'd only comment for you that I have strong personal reasons and certain other obligations that suggest to me that it might not be preferable.

Certain other obligations? To whom?

But for all the puzzles and the directions of superiors, Humes had come to some definite conclusions by the end of the autopsy.

—One bullet entered the rear of Kennedy's head and exited from the top of his skull.

—Another bullet entered the president's back and apparently worked its way out during cardiac massage at Parkland.

The autopsy, which began at 8:15 p.m. the evening of the assassination, was concerned with only two of Kennedy's wounds. Humes studied the head wound and found about forty pieces of bullet metal, indicating a bullet had fragmented while passing through the skull area. He concluded that a high-velocity rifle bullet had entered the rear of the skull, fragmented, and then exited through the top of the skull. Death was attributed to the head wound.

Not so easily explained was a wound in the president's back. The Dallas doctors said they never saw this wound because they never examined Kennedy's back. However, the autopsy doctors studied this wound carefully and wrote clear records of it. On the autopsy face sheet diagram marked by Dr. Humes, a wound is depicted in Kennedy's back between the shoulder blades.

Kennedy's death certificate states, "A second wound occurred in the posterior back at about the level of the third thoracic vertebra." The third thoracic vertebra is located almost midway between the shoulder blades.

Two FBI agents, Francis X. O'Neill Jr. and James W. Sibert, were ordered to attend the autopsy and make a report. Their report, which the Warren Commission kept classified for several years, said, "During the latter stages of this autopsy, Dr. Humes located an opening which appeared to be a bullet hole which was below the shoulders and two inches to the right of the middle line of the spinal column."

This description on the wound's location was supported by the testimony of Secret Service agents and bullet holes in Kennedy's clothing. Yet it presented a real problem to the Warren Commission. If the president's wound was between the shoulder blades, this was lower than the position of the neck wound, making for an upward trajectory—totally inconsistent with shots fired from sixty feet above and behind the president.

The solution to this dilemma was simple—the Commission simply reported the back wound as located five and a half inches higher than determined by the evidence. They reported, "A bullet had entered the base of the back of [Kennedy's] neck slightly to the right of the spine. It traveled downward and exited from the front of the neck, crossing a nick in the left lower portion of the knot in the President's necktie."

Later, when questioned about the location of the wound as marked on the autopsy face sheet, Dr. Boswell stated the drawing was a "diagram error." And Humes was quoted as saying the back wound was higher than the throat wound, although he had marked it well below the neck wound.

The issue of the autopsy diagram was resolved in 1975 when researcher Harold Weisberg obtained the original autopsy face sheet through a Freedom of Information Act suit.

Researchers discovered that the original diagram—depicting a wound in the low back—had been marked "verified" by Kennedy's personal physician, Dr. George Burkley. This verification of the autopsy sheet had been eliminated in copies of the document presented by the Warren Commission to the public. Curiously, Dr. Burkley was never called to testify to the Commission, although he was the only medical authority who rode in the motorcade, viewed Kennedy's body at Parkland Hospital, and was present at the autopsy. In 1982, Burkley reportedly told author Henry Hurt that he believed Kennedy's death was the result of a conspiracy. However, Burkley declined to elaborate further.

This issue became more understandable in 1997 with the release of documents from the Assassination Records Review Board, which discovered Warren Commission documents showing that commission member—and America's only appointed president—Gerald R. Ford told the authors of the Warren Report to change their wording before issuing the report. The writers correctly had written, "A bullet entered his [Kennedy's] back at a point slightly below the shoulder to the right of the spine." Ford "suggested" they change this wording to "a bullet had entered the back of his neck slightly to the right of the spine." Ford's wording was adopted and the final report stated, "A bullet had entered the base of the back of his neck slightly to the right of his spine."

Ford explained to the Associated Press, "My changes had nothing to do with a conspiracy theory. My changes were only an attempt to be more precise." However, critics such as Robert Morningstar pointed out this allowed for the single-bullet theory and claimed, "This is the most significant lie in the whole Warren Commission Report."

The Sibert-O'Neill FBI report further stated:

> This opening [the back wound] was probed by Dr. Humes with the finger, at which time it was determined that the trajectory of the missile entering at this point had entered at a downward position of 45 to 60 degrees. Further probing determined that the distance traveled by this missile was a short distance inasmuch as the end of the opening could be felt with the finger. Inasmuch as no complete bullet of any size could be located in the brain area and likewise no bullet could be located in the back or any other area of the body as determined by total body X rays and inspection revealing there was no point of exit, the individuals performing the autopsy were at a loss to explain why they could find no bullets.

Commander J. Thornton Boswell, Humes's assistant, told author Josiah Thompson that all three doctors probed the back wound with their fingers but could not penetrate past an inch or so. According to Boswell, a thin metal probe also was used but no bullet track could be located.

After failing to find any bullet, agents Sibert and O'Neill called the FBI laboratory and were informed of the bullet that had been found on a stretcher at Parkland Hospital. This information was relayed to Humes and the autopsy doctors and led them to a conclusion expressed in Sibert and O'Neill's FBI report: "Since external cardiac massage had been performed at Parkland Hospital, it was entirely possible that through such movement the bullet had worked its way back out of the point of entry and fallen on the stretcher."

At the end of the autopsy, the military doctors concluded, as recorded in the Sibert-O'Neill report, "The one bullet had entered the President's back and had worked its way out of the body during external cardiac massage and that a second high-velocity bullet had entered the rear of the skull and had fragmentized prior to exit through the top of the skull."

But if the back wound caused problems, they were nothing compared to the problems that arose after Humes learned that the autopsy doctors had completely missed one of the president's wounds.

On the day after the autopsy—with the president's body already prepared for burial and lying in state at the White House—Humes contacted the medical officials in Dallas. He was shocked to learn that they had observed a bullet wound in Kennedy's throat. The autopsy doctors had noticed an opening in the throat but had assumed it had been made at Parkland to facilitate a tracheal tube.

Here is one of the most suspicious of the differences recorded in Kennedy's wounds: Dr. Perry at Parkland described the throat wound as a small hole about three to five millimeters—or about one-fifth of an inch—in diameter that had the appearance of an entrance wound. He reiterated this size in interviews in 1966, 1989, and 1998, although he backed off somewhat from his description of an entrance wound after being ordered to change his testimony by Dallas Secret Service agent Elmer Moore, who explained years later that he was acting "on orders from Washington and Mr. Kelly of the Secret Service Headquarters."

Perry said he made a surgical incision laterally across this hole to facilitate a tracheotomy, but did not obliterate the bullet wound. But by the time the autopsy doctors examined Kennedy's throat, this wound had elongated to almost three inches—such a gash that they didn't realize it obliterated a wound from the assassination. Furthermore, all of the Dallas doctors said Kennedy had a large blasted hole in the right rear portion of his head—not at all like the gaping wound in the right top portion of his skull as reported by the autopsies.

These differences in the descriptions of the throat and head wounds suggest only three explanations:

1. The Dallas medical personnel lied about what they saw.
2. The autopsy doctors lied about what they saw.
3. No one lied—thus indicating the wounds were altered between the time they were seen in Dallas and the autopsy.

The latter explanation is buttressed by the Sibert-O'Neill FBI report of the Bethesda autopsy, which states:

> The President's body was removed from the casket . . . and placed on the autopsy table, at which time the complete body was wrapped in a sheet and the head area contained an additional wrapping which was saturated with blood. . . . It was also apparent that a tracheotomy had been performed, as well as surgery of the head area, namely, in the top of the skull.

Surgery in the top of the skull? No such surgery was ever mentioned by the Parkland medical staff.

This oddity became one of the focal points of an investigation by researcher and author David Lifton, who reached some startling and well-publicized conclusions.

The Switching of Bodies

David Lifton, a former NASA computer engineer who researched the assassination for more than fifteen years, was the first person to interview both medical personnel in Dallas and at Bethesda Naval Medical Center. What he discovered shocked him.

In his best-selling 1980 book, *Best Evidence*, Lifton reported that there were discrepancies not only in the descriptions of Kennedy's wounds, but also in reports of how the body was transported.

It has been well documented how Kennedy's body was wrapped in a sheet in Dallas and placed in an expensive bronze ceremonial casket for shipment to Washington. Yet Lifton found Bethesda technicians who said they removed Kennedy's body from a black zippered body bag that was inside a cheap, gray military-style shipping casket, similar to those used to transport bodies back from Vietnam.

Paul K. O'Connor, who was studying to be a medical technician, was working in Bethesda's laboratory when Kennedy's body arrived. He said the body arrived in a "shipping casket . . . kind of slate-type gray and a kind of light pinkish color on the edges." Asked by Lifton the condition of the body when the casket was opened, O'Connor replied, "He was in a body bag." O'Connor's recollection was confirmed by others, including Captain John Stover, Bethesda's commanding officer.

Just as startling was an interview with Bethesda X-ray technician Jerrol F. Custer. He said he had already made X-ray photographs of Kennedy's body, had gone to an upper floor to process them, and was returning to the morgue area of the hospital when he encountered a bloodstained Jacqueline Kennedy, surrounded by news reporters and Secret Service agents, entering Bethesda. Outside in an ambulance was the bronze Dallas casket supposedly containing the president's body.

By 1992, not only Custer but also Floyd Riebe, who took autopsy photographs, were disclaiming that evidence in the National Archives. In a news conference called to rebut articles published by the American Medical Association (AMA), Custer stated that X-rays presented by the AMA showed a hole on the right side of Kennedy's face indicating that portion was destroyed. "There was no damage to his face and no part of his skull was missing on the forward part of his head." Custer concluded, "These are fake X-rays." He added that later a Navy admiral threatened him with prison if he spoke out regarding the autopsy.

After pointing to dozens of autopsy photographs, Riebe announced, "These films are doctored one way or another. . . . [They are] phony and not the photographs we took." As usual, this bombshell testimony from the technicians who actually took JFK's X-rays and photographs received scant attention from the national mass media.

Based on this and much more information gleaned from official reports and witnesses, Lifton concluded that the assassination was the result of a plot "involving the Executive Branch of the Government." His hypothesis was this:

> Since it was unbelievable that the doctors at both Parkland and Bethesda lied about their observations, the alternative belief was that Kennedy's body was altered. Lifton discovered a brief time period during the swearing-in ceremonies for Lyndon Johnson aboard Air Force One when everyone gathered forward, leaving Kennedy's body unattended. It was during this time that he believed JFK's body was taken from the bronze Dallas casket, placed in a military body bag, and stowed elsewhere in the plane. [Autopsy photos showed several scratches on Kennedy's back that could be explained by the hasty handling of his body.] At Andrews Air Force Base, Kennedy's body was taken off the right side of Air Force One and placed in a helicopter, which immediately took off while the news media and officials concentrated on Mrs. Kennedy and the Dallas casket, which were unloaded from the left side of the plane. Either at Walter Reed or Bethesda, someone altered the President's wounds to conform to the shots-from-behind thesis and then the body was wrapped in a sheet and placed on the Bethesda autopsy table ready for Dr. Humes and the others.

This theory—incredible as it may seem—is supported by the available evidence. Attempts to discredit either Lifton or his sources have proven unconvincing. Some researchers suspect that alternatively the body may have been flown separately to Washington in a military jet, arriving before the official party.

In 2009, the chief analyst for military records for the 1990s Assassination Records Review Board published a five-volume set of books based on the most recent interviews and studies of the JFK autopsy. The autopsy was conducted by the military at Bethesda Naval Hospital the night of the assassination and many issues connected to it remain in controversy.

Douglas P. Horne was meticulous and detailed in his accounts of obfuscation and downright dissembling of autopsy statements and documents. His work, which included the reinterviewing of autopsy observers, technicians, and photographers, provided strong support for Lifton's thesis.

There is no doubt that long-standing and serious questions have arisen over the medical evidence. The idea that Kennedy's body was altered while in the hands of federal officials, along with the knowledge that all assassination evidence was illegally in the hands of the FBI for two full days with no chain of evidence, goes a long way in explaining the puzzles and inconsistencies of the medical evidence.

———

Upon learning of the throat wound the day after the autopsy, Humes was forced to revise his autopsy report. The autopsy doctors determined that the back wound was four to seven millimeters in diameter and the Dallas doctors said the throat wound was three to five millimeters in diameter. Since the back wound was larger, this normally would suggest that the neck wound was one of entrance and the back wound one of exit—assuming both holes represented the path of a single bullet.

However, Humes saw it another way. Testifying to the House Select Committee on Assassinations, Humes said upon learning of the throat wound, "Lights went on, and we said, ah, we have some place for our missile to have gone."

After revising his autopsy report, Humes walked to his fireplace and burned autopsy material—alternatively described as original notes, a first draft, or other written notes. This highly questionable activity preceded his final autopsy report, which stated definitively, "One missile entered the back of the President and exited in the front of the neck."

Considering that the wound in Kennedy's throat was too small to have been caused by a rifle slug and that FBI experts could not find any traces of metal on Kennedy's shirt or tie and that the Dallas doctors noted bruises on Kennedy's neck, it has been theorized that the neck wound may have been caused by bone fragments blasted downward at the time of the fatal head shot.

Author Josiah Thompson wrote, "If we suppose that a bullet (or more likely a bone) fragment was driven downward on a slight left-to-right trajectory through the midbrain, we have a hypothesis that accords with all the known facts surrounding the throat wound."

But Humes was not bothered by such theories. He now had a revised idea of how Kennedy died:

—One bullet entered Kennedy's back and exited from his throat.
—Another bullet struck the back of his head and exited from the top of the skull.

Even Kennedy's personal physician, Dr. Burkley, had problems accepting these findings, which may explain his belief in a conspiracy as revealed to author Henry Hurt.

Adding to this confusion is the possibility of yet another bullet being recovered from Kennedy's body during the autopsy. In the *New York Times* of November 27,

1963, Dallas doctor Kemp Clark stated one bullet struck Kennedy at the necktie knot, "ranged downward in his chest, and did not exit." This statement was supported by Dr. Robert Shaw, who told *New York Herald-Tribune* reporter Martin Steadman on November 27 that a bullet entered the front of Kennedy's throat, "coursed downward into his lung [and] was removed in the Bethesda Naval Hospital where the autopsy was performed."

The idea of a bullet being removed during autopsy gains additional strength in light of two government documents now available. One is a letter of receipt signed by FBI agents Sibert and O'Neill, who monitored the autopsy. The two-line letter, dated November 22, 1963, states, "We hereby acknowledge receipt of a missile removed by Commander James J. Humes, MC, USN on this date." The other is another letter of receipt, but this time from the Protective Research Section of the Treasury Department, dated November 26, 1963. Among the items it listed as received from Kennedy's personal physician, Dr. Burkley, is "one receipt from FBI for a missile removed during examination of the body." FBI agents normally would know the difference between bullet fragments and an intact slug. It is curious that both documents refer to a "missile" rather than fragments or pieces of bullet.

All of this suggests yet another bullet was discovered but kept secret, since another bullet would have destroyed the lone-assassin theory, which already was being strained to the limit.

Further evidence that more than two bullets struck President Kennedy came in 1968 when then–attorney general Ramsey Clark gathered a panel of physicians headed by Dr. Russell Fisher, a Maryland medical examiner, to study the JFK autopsy photographs and X-rays.

In addition to noting that the rear head wound had changed both size and shape from its description by the autopsists, the Clark panel found at the base of Kennedy's skull "a large metallic [bullet] fragment which . . . is round and measures 6.5 mm in diameter."

This could be construed as strong evidence against Lee Harvey Oswald, since he reportedly used a 6.5 mm rifle. However, recall that the official version states that one bullet—the "Magic Bullet"—traversed the president's neck, penetrated Connally, and was found intact at Parkland Hospital.

Since officially no large fragments had been noted by the autopsy doctors and no such fragments could have come from the whole bullet found at Parkland, it seems probable that either more than two shots struck Kennedy in the head area or that the autopsy materials viewed by the Clark panel were fraudulent.

Furthermore, yet another bullet base, about 6.5 mm in diameter, was said to be found in the front seat of the presidential limousine. All this goes far to prove that more than two bullets struck Kennedy.

A Navy officer who might have been able to clarify some of the questions about the president's autopsy is unavailable. Bethesda television technician Lieutenant Commander William Pitzer, according to Chief of the Day Dennis David, may have surreptitiously taken both film and photos of the autopsy and participants. David later said these materials depicted an entry wound in Kennedy's right temple area with a corresponding exit wound in the lower right portion of the skull. In October 1966, Pitzer was found shot in the head under questionable circumstances. The death was ruled a suicide due to self-inflected pistol wound but no nitrates or gunpowder were found on his hand. Among other oddities in the death was a claim in recent years by Special Forces Colonel Daniel Marvin that at that time he was approached by a CIA operative who wanted Marvin to "terminate" Pitzer.

Over the years, as attempts have been made to clarify and substantiate the medical evidence, the wounds seem to take on a life of their own.

The head wound as seen by the Dallas doctors consisted of a large blasted-out area in the right rear of the skull. Both medical and nonmedical persons in Dallas gave consistent descriptions of this wound.

Secret Service agent Clint Hill told the Warren Commission, "The right rear portion of his head was missing."

Dr. Charles J. Carrico noted a large hole "in the posterior skull, the occipital region. There was an absence of the calvarium or skull in this area."

Dr. Malcolm Perry: "I noted a large avulsive wound of the right parietal occipital area [the occipital is the large bone on the back of a human skull], in which both scalp and portions of skull were absent."

Dr. William Kemp Clark: "I then examined the wound in the back of the President's head. This was a large, gaping wound in the right posterior part, with cerebral and cerebellar tissue being damaged and exposed." (The cerebellum controls muscle coordination and is located at the low rear portion of the head behind the occipital bone.)

Dr. Robert McClelland: "I noted that the right posterior portion of the skull had been extremely blasted."

Yet the autopsy doctors saw a head wound that stretched from the upper side of the rear to the right front of Kennedy's head.

The autopsy doctors said a small entrance wound was located in the back of the skull at about the hairline, while the House Select Committee on Assassinations' medical panel placed the entrance wound four inches higher, near the top of the head.

Neither the Warren Commission nor the House committee spoke of a hole blasted out of the right rear portion of the president's head. The House committee even produced a drawing reportedly made from an autopsy photograph that depicts the rear of Kennedy's head. It is entirely intact except for what appears to be a small hole—the entrance wound—near the top.

Humes had problems with this drawing, stating he had never seen the small hole before. He suggested it might be dried blood. His thought was confirmed later when the actual photographs were released to the public. The photo clearly showed the hole as a spot of transparent dried blood with hair growing through it. Humes was certain he had seen no entrance wound in that location.

Robert Groden, photographic consultant to the House Select Committee on Assassinations, had a simple explanation for the mystery surrounding the autopsy photographs. After careful study, he agreed with photographer Floyd Riebe that the autopsy photos now available to the public are forgeries. After discovering evidence of retouching, Groden wrote:

> The vital autopsy photos of the back of the President's head were altered immediately after the autopsy in order to cover up the fact that the President received two bullets in the head, one from the rear and one from the front, and this second shot blew out the back of his head, as Jackie Kennedy testified to the Warren Commission.

X-rays and other autopsy materials such as photographs, tissue samples, and blood smears—including Kennedy's brain, which was removed and preserved—could have provided definitive proof of the location of the wounds. However, much of this material is missing from the National Archives. The House Select Committee on Assassinations hinted that the brain may have been taken by Robert Kennedy to prevent future public display; however, this has not been proven and Kennedy is not alive to answer the charge.

It also should be noted that the Warren Commission—the group officially charged with finding the truth of Kennedy's assassination—apparently never was allowed to view for themselves the president's autopsy photographs and X-rays. Commission attorney Arlen Specter, in an October 10, 1968, interview in *US News & World Report*, stated:

> The complete set of pictures taken at the autopsy was not made available to me or to the Commission. I was shown one picture of the back of a body which was represented to be the back of the President, although it was not authenticated. It showed a hole in the position identified in the autopsy report. To the best of my knowledge, the Commission did not see any photographs or X-rays. . . . The photographs and X-rays would, in the thinking of the Commission, not have been crucial, because they would have served only to corroborate what the autopsy surgeons had testified to under oath as opposed to adding any new facts for the Commission.

But they are crucial—if not in truthfully understanding Kennedy's wounds, then in understanding the manipulations surrounding the medical evidence. Not studying the autopsy materials did not dissuade Specter from formulating the convoluted "single-bullet" theory.

Dr. Cyril H. Wecht, an experienced coroner and former president of the American Academy of Forensic Medicine, was blunt. He stated:

[Kennedy's autopsy was] extremely superficial and sloppy, inept, incomplete, incompetent in many respects, not only on the part of the pathologists who did this horribly inadequate medical-legal autopsy but on the part of many other people. This is the kind of examination that would not be tolerated in a routine murder case by a good crew of homicide detectives in most major cities of America.

As Groden later wrote:

The key to understanding who killed Kennedy lies with the autopsy photographs. These photographs may tell us more about the assassination than all of the official investigations. Perhaps the single most important question in the investigation was never asked: Why were the autopsy photographs and X-rays never officially shown to the numerous doctors and nurses in Dallas who treated President Kennedy? Had this question been pursued, the true nature of the conspiracy would then have been exposed, because the crucial pictures allegedly of the back of the President's head are forged! That forgery is one of the keys to the conspiracy. Who would have had that kind of access to the evidence in order to alter it? Who had the capability to alter it?

Jack Ruby

On the day before Kennedy's assassination there was a continuing parade of defendants, lawyers, and police officers in the Dallas County District Attorney's Office. One officer, Dallas police lieutenant W. F. Dyson, later told the Warren Commission that it was here that he and other officers encountered a short, stocky nightclub owner who was going out of his way to make their acquaintance. Dyson overheard this man—Jack Ruby—tell the officers, "You probably don't know me, but you will."

The following Sunday the entire world knew Jack Ruby—the man who killed Lee Harvey Oswald.

When on November 24, 1963, Ruby silenced the one man whom authorities blamed for Kennedy's death, a rumble of discontent and suspicion began that persists even today. Many people could accept the idea of a "lone-nut assassin," but balked at the idea of two such characters.

In the months following the assassination, the American public was told—first by news media accounts and then by the Warren Commission—that Ruby was a small-time Dallas nightclub operator with no significant ties to organized crime, to Dallas authorities, or to Oswald. It was said that his killing of Oswald was simply the spontaneous act of a man hoping to right the wrong of the president's death.

Today there is evidence that Ruby, a fixture on the Dallas scene in 1963, was more intimately connected with organized-crime figures than earlier believed and that he in fact stalked Oswald throughout the assassination weekend. Furthermore, the evidence of an association between Ruby and Oswald prior to the assassination is substantial.

It also is now known that Ruby tried to tell what he knew about the plot to kill Kennedy but was shrugged off by both government investigators and the news media. To a radio news reporter, Ruby said, "I know there is a terrible conspiracy going on in the world right now. . . . I'm speaking the truth. . . . The world has the right to hear the truth."

Shortly after Ruby was granted a new trial, he was filmed by a Texas television station stating, "Everything pertaining to what's happened has never come to the surface. The world will never know the true facts of what occurred—my motive, in other words. I am the only person in the background to know the truth pertaining to everything relating to my circumstances."

Asked by the interviewer if this truth would ever come out, Ruby replied, "No. Because unfortunately these people, who have so much to gain and have such an ulterior motive to put me in the position I'm in, will never let the true facts come aboveboard to the world."

"Are these people in high positions?" asked the interviewer. Ruby answered, "Yes." In letters smuggled out of the Dallas County Jail, Ruby even named Lyndon Johnson as the person behind the assassination and called him a Nazi.

Jack Ruby was born Jacob Rubenstein in 1911, the fifth of eight siblings. His exact birth date is not known. Various documents show different birth dates, although Ruby himself used March 25, 1911, most frequently. Despite several moves, the family always remained in what was described by one brother as a "ghetto," complete with noisy streets filled with pushcarts and peddlers.

When Ruby was ten years old, his parents separated and he, along with his three brothers and four sisters, was placed in various foster homes by the Jewish Home Finding Society. During this time, young Rubenstein was learning more on the streets of Chicago than in the schoolroom. Like young Oswald, Ruby was caught by truant officers after skipping school. Unlike Oswald, who found diversion in the local library and zoo, Ruby gravitated toward street gangs and amusement parks.

On the streets, young Ruby was nicknamed "Sparky." According to his sister Eva Grant, the name came from Ruby's swaggering walk, which reminded some people of the wobbling gait of Sunday comic strip character Barney Google's horse, "Sparkplug." Others believed "Sparky" was a tag reflecting Ruby's volatile temperament.

Young streetwise Sparky gained a reputation with his fists, although the accounts of his aggressiveness differed with those who knew him. Barney Rasofsky, who gained fame in the 1930s as World Welterweight Boxing Champion Barney Ross, in 1964 told the FBI that he and Ruby along with other young toughs were paid $1 per trip to deliver sealed envelopes for gangster Al Capone. If this information was passed along to the Warren Commission, it was never reported. Rasofsky also said Ruby was never a troublemaker, although he always was ready to defend himself against any attack.

Others, too, recalled Ruby as one to avoid a fight if possible. These recollections clash markedly with those of others who recalled Ruby as a street brawler, eager to take up any challenge, even to the extent of aiding someone else in trouble.

Ruby was also militantly proud of his Jewish ancestry. Although not particularly devout, he had nevertheless received some instruction in Orthodox Judaism. In addition to fights with other street gangs because of racial and ethnic differences, Ruby reportedly joined with Jewish toughs in fights with the pro-Nazi group the German American Bund during the late 1930s.

In 1933 Ruby, along with several Chicago friends, went to Los Angeles and then San Francisco seeking employment. In 1936, he was still in San Francisco living for a brief time with his sister Eva and her husband.

Despite some evidence to the contrary, Ruby later told authorities he returned to Chicago in 1937—the same year his mother was committed to Elgin State Hospital with mental disorders. For more than twenty years, Fannie Rubenstein had frequented doctors and clinics reporting that a fishbone was lodged in her throat despite continuing reassurances that nothing organic could be detected.

Having returned to Chicago about 1937, Ruby began working for the Scrap Iron and Junk Handlers Union, according to Social Security Administration records. Chicago attorney Leon R. Cooke, a close friend to Ruby, had founded the union and was financial secretary. When gangsters connected to the Chicago underworld began taking control of the union and its funds, Ruby went along. Union president John Martin, who earlier had been indicted along with a major Chicago mobster for withholding tax information, named young Rubenstein union secretary. However, according to a statement Ruby made to police at the time, he was little more than a bagman for union thugs.

On December 8, 1939, Martin fatally shot Cooke in the union's offices after an argument over missing funds. Martin fled and Ruby was arrested. The incident was splashed all over the Chicago newspapers at the time. Although Cooke was shot in the back, Martin claimed self-defense and never served time for the murder.

While Ruby claimed such close friendship for the slain man that he eventually took the name Leon as his own middle name, he nevertheless stayed on with the corrupt union after Cooke's brutal murder.

Following the bad publicity over Cooke's killing, the union was reorganized as the Waste Material Handlers Union, Local 20467, American Federation of Labor. Martin was replaced and the reorganized union was dominated by its secretary-treasurer, Paul J. Dorfman, a man with long-standing connections to Chicago racketeers.

Several months after Dorfman took over, Ruby suddenly left the union. In 1964, Ruby told the Warren Commission, "I was with the union back in Chicago and I left the union when I found out a notorious organization had moved in there. . . . I have never been a criminal. . . . I am not a gangster. . . . I had a very rough start in life, but anything I have done, I at least tried to do it in good taste."

By mid-1943, Ruby had found a permanent home—the US Army Air Corps. At the beginning of World War II, he had been granted a draft deferment for reasons not entirely clear. One version is that he feigned a hearing disability by wearing a hearing aid, while another is that he was granted an "economic hardship" deferment because he was the only Rubenstein child remaining at home. Whatever the reason, it was insufficient in 1943 when he was reclassified 1-A and, despite an appeal to his local board, inducted into the Army Air Corps on May 21.

Upon his discharge from the air force in February 1946, Ruby returned to Chicago, where he entered an unsuccessful sales business with his three brothers, Hyman, Sam, and Earl. As in their childhood, the four Rubenstein brothers constantly argued with one another—this time over how to run the business. One of the few things they agreed on was the need to obtain a more "American" name. After Hyman left the business, Sam, Earl, and Jack all shortened their name from Rubenstein to Ruby. Their stormy partnership lasted only one year, and by 1947 Jack Ruby had left Chicago for Texas.

Shortly after Jack arrived in Dallas his name change was made official by a decree from the 68th Judicial District Court of Dallas on December 30, 1947.

Although the official story of Ruby's move is that he went to help his sister operate a nightclub, several different sources—some within the mob—have claimed that Ruby was part of a plan to bring Dallas rackets under the control of the Chicago underworld. Shortly after the JFK assassination, Dallas businessman Giles Miller added support for this idea by telling the FBI that in 1959 Ruby had told him he wanted to go back to California in 1947 but "was directed" to go to Dallas.

But further evidence of Ruby's move as part of a mob offensive into Texas came from former Dallas County sheriff Steve Guthrie. During the late 1930s and 1940s, Dallas gambling operations were virtually wide open under the control of home-grown bosses like Benny "Cowboy" Binion and Herbert Noble. However, by the late 1940s a bloody feud between these two top gamblers had resulted in Noble's bombing death and Binion's departure for the quieter environs of Las Vegas. It was then that the Chicago mob made its bid for a takeover in Dallas.

In late 1946, an emissary from the Chicago syndicate named Paul Roland Jones contacted Dallas lawmen in an effort to open the city for the mob. Jones held meetings with Sheriff Guthrie and an obscure Dallas police lieutenant named George Butler. Jones said he was an advance agent of the Chicago crime syndicate and was prepared to offer the district attorney and the sheriff $1,000 a week each or a 12.5 percent cut on the profit if the syndicate were permitted to operate in Dallas under "complete protection." He also said local people would "front" for the Chicago mob. Sometime later Jones was indicted for attempted bribery when Guthrie and Butler blew the whistle.

At this time the two top Chicago mob leaders were Sam Giancana (the coordinator of Mafia-CIA assassination plots) and Anthony Accardo.

Was Ruby one of the "fronts" mentioned by his friend Jones? Sheriff Guthrie told the Warren Commission that Ruby was himself involved in the bribery plan of Jones and that both Jones and his Chicago associates "frequently mentioned that Ruby would operate a 'fabulous' restaurant as a front for gambling activities." The Commission went on to state, however, that since Ruby was not mentioned in Jones's bribery scheme, the Commission "found it difficult to accept [Guthrie's] report." The Commission also ignored a story by Chicago newsman Mort Newman, who reported that Butler told him that "Jack Ruby came to Dallas from . . . Chicago in the late 1940s and was involved in an attempt to bribe Sheriff Steve Guthrie."

The Warren Commission also ignored testimony that showed that Jones met Ruby through two mutual friends, Paul "Needle Nose" Labriola and Jim Weinberg—both well-known associates of Giancana.

In fact, to arrive at their conclusion that Ruby was not connected to the mob, they had to ignore an FBI interview with Jones in which he stated that when he first met Ruby, both Weinberg and Labriola told him Ruby was "all right" as far as the syndicate was concerned. Weinberg and Labriola in 1954 were found garroted and stuffed in a car trunk in a double gangland slaying.

When interviewed for the Warren Commission in 1964, Jones said he believed Butler was serious about accepting mob payoffs, changing his position only after learning that the Texas Rangers had become aware of the deal.

It was Butler—then assigned to the juvenile division—who was in charge of the fatal transfer of Lee Harvey Oswald on November 24, 1963. Butler apparently was also close to right-wing causes in Dallas. According to Penn Jones, former editor of the *Midlothian Mirror*, Butler approached him in 1961 about publishing right-wing literature. Jones told this author, "[Butler] offered me the job of printing a regional newspaper under the auspices of the Ku Klux Klan. He told me that half of the Dallas police were members of the KKK." Butler also was known to have provided personal police security for right-wing Dallas oil billionaire H. L. Hunt.

Butler's veracity comes into further question when one considers Commission Exhibit 2249, which includes the statements of two Dallas policemen who claimed that shortly after Ruby killed Oswald, Butler approached them with "important" information, namely that young Oswald was actually the illegitimate son of Jack Ruby. Some researchers have speculated that it was Butler who let Ruby into the police department basement to kill Oswald through a rear door leading to an alleyway by the Western Union office.

Whether or not Ruby participated in the 1947 bribe attempt, it is certain that his relationship with Paul Roland Jones continued. On October 24, 1947, Jones was arrested and charged with smuggling opium into the United States from Mexico. In Chicago, both Ruby and his brother Hyman were questioned by Bureau of Narcotics agents investigating the case.

And over the next two years, while Jones appealed his narcotics conviction, he frequented Dallas's Singapore Club, which by then was operated by Jack Ruby.

Despite Jack Ruby's ongoing gangster connections, the Warren Commission and subsequent assassination investigations attempted to portray him as simply a rambunctious, self-ingratiating nightclub owner striving for success in a rather shabby business—almost a Damon Runyan racetrack character.

It may also be significant that Ruby was much better connected socially in Dallas than federal investigations have publicly stated. As a man-about-town, Ruby was well-known not only to police and law-enforcement officials, but also to the city and county officials and businessmen who frequented his clubs and attended area gambling parties.

One significant contact may be found in an account by Madeleine Brown, a former mistress to Lyndon Johnson. She claimed to have first met Jack Ruby through Johnson attorney Jerome Ragsdale of Dallas. She told this author:

> One day in the early 1950s, I was coming out of Nieman-Marcus in downtown Dallas when I encountered Jerome Ragsdale and another man talking on the sidewalk. They seemed to be good friends and Jerome introduced me to the man, who was Jack Ruby. Ruby told me he owned a club downtown and invited me to visit. He also gave me a card. Of course, later I saw Ruby frequently. A bunch of us would see him around town. Lots of people in town knew him, especially people in the downtown area like H. L. Hunt, Henry Wade, Earl Cabell, they all knew him. But after the assassination weekend, everyone was scared to say they knew him.

According to Ester Ann Mash, a former employee who dated Ruby during the spring of 1963, Ruby was no stranger at the homes of prominent Dallasites. She told this author, "Several times he took me to big nice homes where there were important people in town, including District Attorney Henry Wade. I think he only took me so he didn't have to go alone. Once we got there, I never saw Jack. He would be off gambling."

But the record shows Ruby was a much more important criminal than previously believed.

Jack Ruby—Gangster

From the prewar union murder of Leon Cooke to the 1963 killing of Lee Harvey Oswald in Dallas, Jack Ruby's life was one of close association with gangsters and close calls with the law.

Consider these Ruby associates:

Barney Baker: Described by Robert Kennedy as Jimmy Hoffa's "roving organizer and ambassador of violence," Baker had moved from criminal activities involving mobsters Jake Lansky and Bugsy Siegel to Teamster organizer for the Central States Conference under Hoffa. According to the Warren Commission, Baker received at least two calls from Ruby in a three-week period preceding the assassination and Baker called Ruby on November 7, 1963. Three of Baker's phone numbers were found in Ruby's notebooks.

Joseph Campisi: An associate of Dallas Mafia member Joseph Civello, Campisi operated several businesses in Dallas, including a restaurant notorious as a gangster hangout, and has been linked closely to the New Orleans Marcello family. Both Ruby's sister Eva Grant and his business partner and roommate, George Senator, described Campisi as one of Ruby's closest friends. And though trying to distance himself from Ruby, Campisi himself told the FBI in December 1963 he had been in contact with Ruby the night before the assassination and had visited Ruby in jail on November 30, 1963.

Frank Caracci: Described by *Life* magazine as a "Marcello Mobster," Caracci was arrested by Houston police in 1969 with three members of the Marcello group who later attended the Dallas wedding of Joseph Campisi's son. One of these men was Frank "Tickie" Saia, a prominent Louisiana gambling and political figure who was close friends with Senator Russell Long. In the months preceding the Kennedy assassination, Ruby met with Caracci at least once and was in telephone contact on several occasions.

Frank Chavez: Another Teamster thug with arrests for obstruction of justice and attempted murder, Chavez told associates that in the fall of 1961 he had met with Ruby and other Teamster officials, including Richard Kavner, whom author Dan Moldea described as "another key member of the Hoffa circle." A Justice Department memorandum also linked Ruby and Chavez to mobster Tony Provenzano.

Joseph Civello: The Dallas Mafia chief who was one of those arrested at the 1957 Apalachin, New York, mob meeting, Civello admitted to the FBI after the assassination that he had known Ruby "for about 10 years." Like Campisi, Civello tried to downplay his close connections with Ruby, and someone within the Warren Commission aided this effort by deleting an entire page covering Civello from Commission Exhibit 1536 and by blanking out several paragraphs within the document.

Mickey Cohen: A news reporter claimed that Ruby was acquainted with famed mobster Cohen through his girlfriend Candy Barr, a close friend of Ruby's who had been jailed on a narcotics charge earlier in the 1960s.

Al Gruber: A former roommate of Ruby's from Chicago, Gruber told the FBI he had no mob connections. Yet in 1970, a two-page FBI report that had been suppressed for years showed Gruber had been arrested six times using two aliases in three states. Gruber, too, was associated with top Teamster officials as well as thugs working for Mickey Cohen. Gruber reportedly had not seen his old friend Ruby for ten years when he showed up in Dallas in mid-November 1963 for an extended visit. Ruby called Gruber in Los Angeles three hours after the assassination.

Russell D. Matthews: An underworld character with a lengthy arrest record, Matthews has been linked to Campisi and Florida mob chief Santos Trafficante. He also was described as a father figure by convicted hit man Charles V. Harrelson. Several people told the Warren Commission that Ruby and Matthews were friends and on October 3, 1963, a call was placed from Ruby's Carousel Club to Matthews's former wife in Louisiana.

Lenny Patrick: According to his sister, Ruby also placed calls to Patrick in late 1963. Identified in a 1965 US Senate report as a high-ranking associate of the Chicago Mafia, Patrick reportedly was close to Chicago mob chieftain Sam Giancana.

Nofio J. Pecora: Described by various crime investigations as an ex-convict with several arrests, Pecora has been identified as one of Carlos Marcello's most trusted aides. As late as October 30, 1963, a call was logged between the Dallas phone of Ruby and a New Orleans phone listed to Pecora.

Johnny Roselli: A former associate of Al Capone, Roselli was one of the Mafia chiefs involved in the CIA-Mafia assassination plots against Castro and the man CIA pilot Tosh Plumlee claimed to have flown into Dallas the morning of the assassination. His mutilated body was found in an oil drum in Florida's Biscayne Bay in 1976 just before Roselli was scheduled to testify before the House Select Committee on Assassinations. According to columnist Jack Anderson, Roselli knew Ruby and described him as "one of our boys." According to reports from federal sources in Florida, Roselli and Ruby twice met secretly in Miami motel rooms during the two months preceding the assassination. These meetings were monitored by the FBI, which was keeping Roselli under surveillance. However, no mention of these meetings was made to the Warren Commission.

Irwin S. Wiener: A close associate of Hoffa as well as other Teamster officials, Wiener has been connected to mob bosses Trafficante and Giancana. On October 26, 1963, Wiener received a twelve-minute person-to-person call from Ruby's Carousel Club. He later gave contradictory accounts of the content of this call.

Lewis McWillie: A notorious Dallas gambler, McWillie worked for several gambling houses there during the 1940s, including Benny Benion's Top of the Hill Club and W. C. Kirkwood's Four Deuces Club in nearby Fort Worth. McWillie then joined such famed gangsters as Santos Trafficante, Meyer and Jake Lansky, and Dino Cellini in gambling operations in Havana, Cuba, before being thrown out by Castro. One of Ruby's closest friends, McWillie received guns from Ruby while still in Cuba and, in fact, received a .38 Smith & Wesson from him as late as May 10, 1963. Ruby told the Warren Commission, "I called him frequently. . . . I idolized McWillie." The Kirkwoods, who conducted high-stakes poker games involving wealthy Texans such as H. L. Hunt, Clint Murchinson, and Amon Carter Sr., also played host to Texas politicians Sam Rayburn, Lyndon Johnson, and John Connally. Kirkwood's son, Pat, served alcoholic drinks to President Kennedy's Secret Service guards well into the morning hours of November 22, 1963. Kirkwood told the House Select Committee on Assassinations that "Chilly" McWillie was a close family friend. Warren Commission staffers saw several conspiratorial leads in McWillie and recommended that he be called to testify about Ruby's Cuban and mob connections, a recommendation that the Commission ignored.

Despite these revealing associations, the Warren Commission Report stated, "The Commission believes that the evidence does not establish a significant link between Ruby and organized crime."

But Jack Ruby's connection to crime was not limited to his friends and associates. The record shows his involvement in a number of criminal activities including gambling, narcotics, prostitution, and gunrunning.

In an interview with FBI agents on December 6, 1963, a small-time bookie named William Abadie described how he had worked briefly for Ruby writing gambling "tickets" as well as serving as a "slot machine and jukebox mechanic." According to this FBI report, only partially reported by the Warren Commission in Document 86—the first page containing the FBI's information about Ruby's gambling activities was inexplicably missing from the Commission document—Abadie stated, "It was obvious [to me] that to operate gambling in the manner that he [Ruby] did, that he must have racketeering connections with other individuals in the City of Dallas, as well as Fort Worth, Texas. . . . [This] applied also to police connections with the two cities."

In fact, Abadie told agents that he had observed policemen coming and going while acting as a bookie in a Ruby establishment.

There is simply no question of Ruby's connections to gambling and to gamblers, both local and national. Not so clear is Ruby's connection to drugs.

In one case, a drug offender named James Breen traveled to Dallas, where he made contact with "a large narcotics setup operating between Mexico, Texas, and the East," according to Eileen Curry, Breen's female companion. Curry told the FBI that Breen's contact with this drug ring was Jack Ruby. After Ruby killed Oswald, the FBI again contacted Curry. She repeated her earlier contention that Ruby and Breen had been mixed up in a narcotics smuggling ring.

There is also an abundance of evidence that Ruby was involved in other criminal activities, such as prostitution, pornography, and bribery.

The fact that Ruby was a pivotal contact man for criminal activity in Dallas seems affirmed by his lack of prosecution by Dallas authorities.

Ruby's Dallas rap sheet showed he was arrested nine times in sixteen years—on charges ranging from operating his club after legal hours to using a gun to slug an off-duty Dallas policeman in a fight outside the Carousel Club—yet the toughest conviction shown in his criminal record was a $35 fine for ignoring a traffic summons.

Jack Ruby's criminal activity reached a peak in 1959, when he became even more closely connected to the mob and the Feds through their common interest in Cuba.

Jack Ruby—Gunrunner and FBI Informant

The year 1959 was a busy time for Jack Ruby. He made at least two trips to Cuba, making contact with gunrunners who had been arming Castro but were beginning to turn against the bearded leader, and he began serving as an informant for the FBI.

Just prior to Castro's takeover, American mobsters had helped supply the revolutionary with arms for his fight with Batista. While the dictator Batista was friends with the mob, the gangsters were playing both sides of the fence, believing that if they helped Castro, they would be allowed to remain in Cuba should he succeed in his revolution.

The smuggling of arms to Castro was overseen by Norman "Rough-house" Rothman, a burly associate of Miami mob boss Santos Trafficante Jr., who managed Trafficante's Sans Souci casino in Havana. At the same time, Rothman reportedly was splitting Havana slot machine revenues with Batista's brother-in-law.

After the assassination, the sister of a Cuban gunrunner gave information indicating that Ruby was part of the Rothman operation. Mary Thompson said she and her daughter traveled to the Florida Keys during June 1958, where her brother introduced them to a man named "Jack." The women were told that Jack owned a nightclub in Dallas and was a member of "the syndicate" who was running some guns to Cuba.

This story later was corroborated by bureau informant Blaney Mack Johnson, who stated that in the early 1950s, Ruby had an interest in a notorious nightclub and gambling house in Hallandale, Florida, along with Meyer and Jake Lansky and other prominent mobsters. Johnson said Ruby was active in arranging illegal flights of weapons to Castro forces and named Edward Browder as one of the pilots operating for Ruby.

Browder, a flamboyant Miami arms dealer, was a central figure in Rothman's gunrunning operation, according to federal court documents. Another soldier of fortune operating with Browder during this time was Frank Sturgis, who would much later be caught burglarizing the Watergate building along with men connected to the Nixon White House.

Although the FBI file on Browder reportedly contains more than 1,000 pages, the bureau gave only three small, innocuous reports to the Warren Commission.

According to Wally Weston, the Carousel Club's emcee who visited his former employer in the Dallas County Jail, Ruby said, "Wally, you know what's going to happen now? They're going to find out about my trips to Cuba and my trips to New Orleans and the guns and everything."

In mid-1959, the Rothman gunrunning operation was rocked when its chief was arrested in connection with an $8.5 million Canadian bank burglary. Federal authorities linked the bank job with a large theft of arms from an Ohio National Guard armory through a $6,000 airplane rental agreement by Rothman. Authorities agreed it appeared to all be part of a massive gunrunning operation to Cuba.

And it was during this time that Ruby's travels to Cuba increased significantly, thanks to Ruby's mob idol, Lewis J. McWillie.

McWillie—potentially a key central character in this swirl of gunrunners, drug smugglers, mob hit men, CIA-Mafia assassination plots, and Texas gamblers—has received scant attention from the two major government assassination investigations.

In his Warren Commission testimony, Ruby made no secret of his closeness to McWillie, stating, "I called him frequently. . . . I idolized McWillie."

Despite Ruby's accolades, Commission members declined to follow through on a staff recommendation to call McWillie to testify about his relationship with Ruby and Mafia figures. The Warren Report made no mention of McWillie's mob ties or of McWillie's FBI record, No. 4404064, which gives a list of aliases and characterizes him as a gangland killer.

While the Warren Commission took Ruby's and McWillie's word that the 1959 trips to Cuba were "purely social," the House Select Committee on Assassinations did not. After listing a number of visits to Cuba based on visas, airline tickets, and even a postcard, chief counsel Blakey wrote:

> We established beyond reasonable doubt that Ruby lied repeatedly and willfully to the FBI and the Warren Commission about the number of trips he made to Cuba and their duration. . . . It was clear, for example, that the trips were not social jaunts; their purpose, we were persuaded, was to courier something, probably money, into or out of Cuba. . . . The evidence indicated strongly that an association (with Trafficante) existed and that Ruby's trip was related to Trafficante's detention and release. We came to believe that Ruby's trips to Cuba were, in fact, organized-crime activities.

Lewis J. McWillie was born May 4, 1908, in Kansas City, Missouri. From 1940 until 1958 he lived in Dallas, where he managed several gambling operations, including the Four Deuces Club in nearby Fort Worth owned by gentleman gambler W. C. Kirkwood. Recall it was his son, Pat Kirkwood, who hosted Kennedy's Secret Service agents the night before the assassination.

In the summer of 1958, McWillie relocated to Havana, Cuba, where he worked for Norman Rothman as a pit boss in Trafficante's Sans Souci casino. It was during this time that Ruby was encountered in the Florida Keys involved in gunrunning schemes run by Rothman.

By September 1958, McWillie was manager of the Tropicana Hotel's luxurious casino, then styled as "the largest nightclub in the world." It was here that McWillie became a close associate of some of the mob's most powerful leaders.

Yet over the years, McWillie maintained that he knew these men only "casually," but did admit an acquaintanceship with Dallas crime figures R. D. Matthews and Joseph Civello.

It is interesting to note that both McWillie and Matthews were connected to Dallas gambling operations during the 1950s; both went to work gambling in Havana, Cuba, in 1958–1959; and in later years, both were employed at Benny Binion's Horseshoe Club in Las Vegas.

When Castro closed the Tropicana, McWillie became pit boss at the Capri Hotel's casino, another Trafficante property. The Capri was then run by Charlie "The Blade" Tourine, whose mistress later confirmed that she was assisting Frank Sturgis in an attempt to poison Castro.

McWillie finally left Cuba in January 1961. According to Ruby and others, he was one of the last American mobsters to leave the island.

It should be pointed out that during the first half of 1961 McWillie was in Miami, the site of the CIA-Mafia assassination meetings involving Trafficante, Giancana, and Roselli. After that time, McWillie worked at a number of Nevada gambling casinos.

In early 1959, McWillie's boss Trafficante was arrested and jailed in the Trescornia Camp outside Havana. Within days of this incident, Jack Ruby contacted convicted Texas gunrunner Robert Ray McKeown, who in 1958 had received a two-year suspended sentence and five years on probation when convicted by US authorities of conspiring to smuggle arms to Castro. His gunrunning activities brought McKeown into close contact with two notable Cubans—one of whom was Fidel Castro. McKeown was photographed with the bearded leader during a visit to Houston in April 1959. He was also close to Carlos Prio Socarras, former president of Cuba, who quickly turned against Castro and became a leader of the anti-Castro Cubans in the United States.

It was due to this closeness to Cuban leaders that McKeown was contacted by telephone by a man who identified himself as "Jack Rubenstein of Dallas." The caller said he had obtained McKeown's phone number through a member of the Houston County Sheriff's Office and had thought his name was "Davis."

"Davis" was the same name that Ruby mentioned to his attorneys when asked if he knew of anyone who could damage their legal plea of momentary insanity for Ruby. Indeed, a gunrunner named Tommy E. Davis not only was active in Texas at that time but during Ruby's trial showed up in Dallas and told Ruby's attorneys that he and Ruby had met several times to discuss the possibility of running arms to Cuba. However, Davis denied that anything came of this planning. Tommy Davis was linked to both US intelligence and crime circles.

McKeown told the House Select Committee on Assassinations that Ruby told him he represented Las Vegas interests that were seeking the release of three prisoners in Cuba. Ruby offered $5,000 each for help in obtaining release of the prisoners. McKeown told the caller he would accept the offer if money were forthcoming. The caller said he would think about it.

About three weeks later, McKeown said he was visited by Ruby at his business near Houston. Ruby said he had access to a large number of jeeps in Shreveport, Louisiana, which he was going to sell in Cuba. He offered McKeown $25,000 for a letter of introduction to Castro. Again, McKeown asked for money up front. He later claimed that Ruby "never returned nor did he ever see him again."

Of equal interest is McKeown's claim in later years that just weeks before the assassination, he was contacted by yet another man who wanted to buy weapons, particularly high-powered rifles with scopes. McKeown said this man identified himself as "Lee Oswald."

In this story, which has been corroborated by a McKeown friend, Sam Neill, "Lee Oswald" and a man named Hernandez showed up at McKeown's home in late September or early October 1963, saying they were involved in planning a revolution in El Salvador. McKeown said he refused to sell arms to "Oswald."

Both McKeown and his friend Neill independently recognized Oswald on November 22, 1963, as the man who had visited a few weeks earlier. However, both men decided to keep quiet about the Oswald visit, saying later they were "scared" to tell the FBI in 1964 what they knew. Indeed, a January 28, 1964, FBI document pertaining to McKeown's interview states, "To his knowledge, he has never seen or met Lee Harvey Oswald."

Although the House committee pointed to inconsistencies in McKeown's various accounts of his contact with both Ruby and Oswald, on the whole—especially with the Neill corroboration—his story has gained credence with many researchers.

Yet another incident occurred in 1961 that indicates that Ruby's gunrunning activities may not have ceased in 1959. Nancy Perrin Rich worked for Ruby and became involved in Cuban gunrunning activities while married to Robert Perrin in Dallas. In interviews with both the FBI and Warren Commission, she related how her mob-connected husband met with a group of anti-Castro Cubans in a Dallas apartment, presided over by a US Army lieutenant colonel. During this meeting, her husband was offered $10,000 to bring a boatload of Cuban refugees to Miami. The couple demanded a cash retainer.

A few nights later, the Perrins met again with the Cubans, who promised money was on the way. Rich told the Warren Commission, "I had the shock of my life. . . . A knock comes on the door and who walks in but my little friend Jack Ruby . . . and everybody looks like . . . here comes the Savior." She detected a bulge in Ruby's jacket that disappeared quickly, leading her to conclude Ruby was the "bag man" bringing funds to the Cubans.

Less than a year after this Ruby-Cuban meeting, Robert Perrin was found dead of arsenic poisoning. His death was ruled a suicide.

On November 26, 1963, long before any in-depth investigation was done on Ruby's background, British journalist John Wilson informed the American embassy in London that he had been held in the Trescornia Camp outside Havana with Trafficante in the summer of 1959. Wilson said there he met an American gangster called Santos and that "Santos was visited several times by an American gangster type named Ruby." Wilson claimed the man named Ruby would come to the prison with people bringing food to Trafficante.

Although Wilson is now dead, there is considerable corroboration to his story.

Gerry Patrick Hemming, a CIA agent who in 1959 was serving with Castro's forces, saw Ruby in a meeting with Castro leader Captain William Morgan during this time and the talk centered around efforts to release Trafficante from prison. Sources within the Dallas underworld claimed Ruby was the middleman who, acting on McWillie's orders, bought Trafficante's freedom from Cuba with the sale of black-market jeeps to Castro.

While this has not yet been officially confirmed, it is certainly significant that there appears to have been much closer contact between Jack Ruby, Oswald's slayer, and Santos Trafficante, the mob boss who predicted that Kennedy would be "hit." The fact that Ruby idolized the stylish, gray-haired McWillie and would do "anything" for his mentor is especially intriguing in light of the close association between McWillie and Trafficante.

And during those active days in 1959, Ruby made another astonishing contact— the Federal Bureau of Investigation. The Warren Commission was quietly notified in early 1964 that the bureau had contacted Jack Ruby in 1959 as an informant but asked that the Commission keep this explosive fact a secret. The contents of this February 27, 1964, memo from Director Hoover to Warren Commission general counsel J. Lee Rankin was not made public until 1975. The memo, belatedly discovered through "a search of all files in the Dallas [FBI] office wherein references to Jack Ruby appeared," stated:

> For your information, Ruby was contacted by an Agent of the Dallas Office on March 11, 1959, in view of his position as a nightclub operator who might have knowledge of the criminal element in Dallas. He was advised of the Bureau's jurisdiction in criminal matters, and he expressed a willingness to furnish information along these lines. He was subsequently contacted on eight occasions between March 11, 1959, and October 2, 1959, but he furnished no information whatever and further contacts with him were discontinued. Ruby was never paid any money, and he was never at any time an informant of this Bureau.

The Commission not only failed to see the significance of the nine meetings between the FBI and Ruby during the very time he was trying to free mob boss Trafficante, but also did not bother to question the FBI agent who had met with Ruby.

But many law-enforcement officers, both state and federal, have privately stated that both the frequency and duration of these Ruby contacts suggests there was more to the relationship than Hoover would admit.

The House Select Committee on Assassinations did interview Charles W. Flynn, the FBI agent who met with Ruby. According to Flynn, Ruby initiated the contacts on March 11, 1959, rather than the bureau as stated in the Hoover memo. Flynn said Ruby told him he wanted to give information on a confidential basis and so Flynn opened a potential criminal informant (PCI) file on Ruby. Flynn said he closed the file on November 6, 1959, because Ruby had not been particularly helpful.

The House committee staff was intrigued by this connection between Ruby and the FBI at the time Ruby was making trips to Cuba. The committee's chief counsel later wrote:

> Ruby could, of course, have contacted the FBI with no ulterior motive, and it could have been wholly unrelated to his Cuban activities. . . . We [the committee staff] believed, however, that Ruby's behavior was consistent with the pattern of seasoned offenders, who often cultivate a relationship with a law enforcement agency during a period when they are engaging in a criminal activity in the hope that, if they are caught, they can use the relationship to secure immunity from prosecution.

On April 27, 1959, shortly after his first contact with Agent Flynn and the day before their next scheduled meeting, Ruby rented safety deposit box 448 at Merchants State Bank in Dallas, where he maintained a small business checking account.

Sometime before he rented the bank box, Ruby bought more than $500 worth of tape-recording equipment. The saleswoman, contacted by Secret Service agents shortly after the assassination, recalled that Ruby bought "a wristwatch which held a microphone for the equipment, and also an instrument to bug a telephone . . . [and a] tie clip and attaché case." An FBI agent also interviewed the saleswoman but filed a meager two-paragraph report, omitting the descriptions of the electronic bugging equipment.

From the time Ruby acquired the safety deposit box through the fall of 1959, researchers have discerned a pattern—both before and after making a trip to Cuba, Ruby would enter this deposit box and then contact the FBI.

Flynn denied to the House committee that he and Ruby had discussed the Cuban visits, but in later years Flynn reportedly admitted to news reporters that Ruby may have mentioned one trip to Cuba.

And apparently Ruby was making no secret of his Cuban sojourns at the time. He sent a postcard from Havana to a girlfriend in Dallas and he was overheard telling one of his employees not to say where he was going "unless it was to the police or some other official agency."

It also should be noted that three days after Ruby shot Oswald, authorities in New Orleans received a tip that Jack Ruby had bought some paintings while in that city in the summer of 1959. While this information seemed hardly germane to the assassination, its source points to the involvement of US intelligence, for this bit of art news came from William George Gaudet, the CIA operative who accompanied Oswald to Mexico.

So apparently the CIA was tracking Ruby's movements in 1959, and after the assassination, Ruby was fearful that his activities in New Orleans—which obviously involved Cuba—would be found out.

The House Select Committee on Assassinations determined that Ruby may have made as many as six trips to Cuba, but most significantly, this issue was clouded and passed off by both the FBI and the Warren Commission.

When Warren Commission attorneys Leon Hubert and Burt Griffin—both assigned to the Ruby aspect of the investigation—requested further probing of Ruby's Cuban connections, they were rebuffed by both the CIA and other Commission staff members. In later years, Warren Commission staffer Howard P. Willens, the liaison with the Department of Justice, explained the commission's reluctance to probe deeper by telling newsman Seth Kantor, "These Cuban pursuits represented some kind of bottomless pit and our overall investigation had to be wrapped up."

Considered all together, the activities of Jack Ruby involving Cuba, Trafficante, McWillie, and the FBI represent a whole new dimension of the assassination—one that has yet to be fully explored.

But these connections, especially in light of the theory on mob involvement in the assassination, certainly elevate Ruby far above the simple, emotional nightclub owner pictured by the Warren Commission.

As the day of Kennedy's assassination approached, Jack Ruby remained in contact with a variety of mob figures both by telephone and in person.

One of the most intriguing incidents involved Johnny Roselli, the gangster involved with Santos Trafficante and Sam Giancana in the CIA-Mafia assassination plots and the man said to have been flown into Dallas on the morning of November 22, 1963, by "black ops" pilot Tosh Plumlee.

It has become known that beginning in the summer of 1963 and continuing into November, the FBI had Roselli under surveillance.

Researchers were surprised in later years that the bureau had monitored two separate meetings between Roselli and Jack Ruby that occurred within two months of Kennedy's death. Roselli, who later began to speak openly to columnist Jack Anderson, admitted to knowing Ruby, calling him "one of our boys." What these meetings were about and why they were not reported to the Warren Commission is not known, but to most researchers this is yet another clear example of the FBI's suppression of evidence.

The Woman Who Foresaw the Assassination

One of the most intriguing stories to come out of the assassination case involved a woman who claimed to have worked for Ruby and who is on record with foreknowledge of Kennedy's death.

On November 20, 1963, two days before the assassination, Louisiana State Police lieutenant Francis Fruge journeyed to Eunice, Louisiana, to pick up a woman who had received minor abrasions when she was thrown from a moving car. This scene was depicted at the beginning of the Oliver Stone film but with no identification of the woman or any explanation of its meaning.

The woman appeared to be under the influence of some drug. She later was driven to the state hospital in Jackson, Louisiana. On the way she told Fruge that she had been traveling with two men "who were Italians or resembled Italians" from Florida to Dallas. When Fruge asked her what she planned to do in Dallas, the woman replied, "Number one, pick up some money, pick up [my] baby and . . . kill Kennedy."

Thus began the strange saga of Melba Christine Marcades, better known as Rose Cheramie.

While at the state hospital, Cheramie told doctors there that Kennedy was to be killed in Dallas. She appeared quite lucid and hospital records studied by the House Select Committee on Assassinations reflect the woman was diagnosed as "without psychosis. However, because of her previous record of drug addiction she may have a mild integrative and pleasure defect."

Dr. Victor Weiss told committee investigators that Cheramie said she had worked for Jack Ruby and that her knowledge of the assassination came from "word in the underworld."

The day of the assassination, Lieutenant Fruge immediately remembered the woman and her apparent foreknowledge. He returned to the state hospital and took Cheramie into custody. During questioning she said the two men were on their way from Florida to Dallas to kill Kennedy. She said she was to receive $8,000 for her part in this activity and was then to accompany the two men to Houston to complete a drug deal and pick up her young son. She even gave Fruge the name of both a seaman and a ship that were involved in the drug deal and Fruge verified this information through US Customs.

Fruge also confirmed the woman's story by talking to a Louisiana lounge owner. The owner related how two men and a woman had stopped at his lounge about November 20 and that the owner knew the men to be two pimps who regularly transported prostitutes from Florida. He said the woman became intoxicated and was taken outside after one of her companions "slapped her around."

Fruge said he soon contacted Dallas police captain Will Fritz, the man in charge of the assassination investigation, believing that he had uncovered valuable information. However, after Fritz told him he "wasn't interested," Fruge dropped his investigation.

Interestingly, the House committee found that although the FBI had no record of Cheramie's prediction of the assassination, it did have reports that a Melba Marcades (Cheramie) had tipped bureau agents that she was traveling to Dallas to deliver heroin to a man in Oak Cliff, then to Galveston to pick up a shipment of drugs. The bureau had looked into the matter but, unsurprisingly, decided that the woman's information was "erroneous in all respects."

On September 4, 1965, one month after yet another attempt to contact the FBI with similar information, Marcades/Cheramie was found dead by a highway near Big Sandy, Texas—a small town in east Texas about midway between Dallas and Louisiana. A man told authorities that Cheramie was lying in the roadway, apparently after being thrown from a car, and that he drove over her head while trying to avoid her. Police could find no relationship between the woman and the driver and the case was closed. However, Fruge later told researchers that when he attempted to contact the driver, he found the man's Tyler, Texas, address to be nonexistent.

While the entire Rose Cheramie episode was extensively covered in a staff report to the House Select Committee on Assassinations and essentially verified, oddly there was no mention of her in the committee's report.

Did Ruby and Oswald Know Each Other?

Both federal investigations of the assassination announced publicly that they could not establish any link between Jack Ruby and Lee Harvey Oswald.

The Warren Commission flatly stated, "There is no evidence that Oswald and Ruby knew each other or had any relationship through a third party or parties."

Yet according to the Commission's own internal memos, staffers were not all that certain. Arguing that further investigation was needed, Commission lawyers Burt Griffin and Leon Hubert wrote, "In short, we believe that the possibility exists, based on evidence already available, that Ruby was involved in illegal dealings with Cuban elements who might have had contact with Oswald."

In its report, the House Select Committee on Assassinations also seems to question the Warren Commission's conclusion by pointing out:

> The Commission also found no evidence that Ruby and Oswald had ever been acquainted, although the Commission acknowledged that they both lived in the Oak Cliff section of Dallas, [both] had post office boxes at the Terminal Annex, and had possible but tenuous third party links. These included Oswald's landlady, Earlene Roberts, whose sister, Bertha Cheek, had visited Ruby at his nightclub on November 18, and a fellow boarder at Oswald's rooming house, John Carter, who was friendly with a close friend and employee of Ruby, Wanda Killam.

While leaving the impression that no link existed between Ruby and Oswald, the House committee in fact left the possibility open by concluding, "The Committee's investigation of Oswald and Ruby showed a variety of relationships that may have matured into an assassination conspiracy. Neither Oswald nor Ruby turned out to be 'loners,' as they had been painted in the 1964 investigation."

And the body of evidence connecting Ruby and Oswald continues to grow.

As far back as 1964, General Edwin A. Walker—himself a figure in the assassination case—told this author, "The Warren Commission Report was ridiculous and a sham as well as an insult to the public's intelligence. Rubenstein knew Oswald; Oswald knew Rubenstein. The report would have to start all over on this basic fact."

Recall that Julia Ann Mercer identified both Ruby and Oswald as the men she saw near the Triple Underpass with a rifle shortly before the assassination and that Oswald's mother, Marguerite, claimed an FBI agent showed her a photograph of Jack Ruby the night before Oswald was shot.

Stories have circulated around Dallas since 1963 about Ruby and Oswald being seen together. On November 26, 1963, the *Dallas Morning News* quoted assistant district attorney Bill Alexander as saying, "[Investigators] have received at least a hundred tips [linking Oswald to Jack Ruby] and are checking out each one. As far as I know, none has panned out." This merely meant none were accepted.

As early as Monday, November 25, 1963, news reporters were receiving information of a Ruby-Oswald link. Some were not easy to dismiss, especially the number from Ruby's Carousel Club.

Madeleine Brown worked for one of Dallas's leading advertising firms in 1963. She handled some of the agency's biggest accounts. After work, she and coworkers would unwind at various watering holes, including the Carousel Club. Brown recalled that in the spring of 1963 as she and her friends sat in the Carousel Club the conversation turned to speculation over who might have taken a shot at General Edwin A. Walker. The group was surprised to hear Jack Ruby blurt out that the man who shot at Walker was Lee Oswald.

Brown took note of the name because she had never heard it before and because Ruby seemed so confident of the name of Walker's assailant. She was shocked the following November to see the names Ruby and Oswald tied to the assassination. She told this author, "I asked around and found out that many people knew that Oswald and Ruby knew each other. In fact, I just assumed that everyone knew this. I was surprised when, well into the 1980s, I learned that officially they were not supposed to be connected."

Another fascinating story was offered by former Dallas cabdriver Raymond Cummings. During the Garrison investigation, Cummings saw a news story with a photograph of David Ferrie, who claimed that he had never been in Dallas. Cummings contacted Garrison's office to say he had driven David Ferrie and Lee Harvey Oswald to Ruby's Carousel Club in the early part of 1963.

Even more convincing are the accounts of Ruby and Oswald seen together by employees of the Carousel Club. William D. Crowe Jr., a magician and entertainer who was using the stage name Bill DeMar and performing in Ruby's Carousel Club at the time of the assassination, called a news media friend right after Oswald's arrest. He said Oswald had participated in his act about a week prior to the assassination.

On November 25, Crowe told the Associated Press he was "positive" Oswald had patronized Ruby's club: "I have a memory act in which I have 20 customers call out various objects in rapid order. Then I tell them at random what they called out. I am positive Oswald was one of the men that called out an object about nine days ago."

Crowe later told the *Dallas Morning News* that after the Associated Press story appeared, he was contacted by FBI agents who told him to check out of his Dallas hotel and go into hiding.

The Warren Commission Report went to great lengths to downplay Crowe's story, including quoting Crowe as saying, "I never stated definitely, positively [that I saw Oswald], and they said I did, and all in all, what they had in the paper was hardly even close to what I told them." Crowe was not asked if he had been intimidated or why he told the same story of seeing Oswald to *Dallas Morning News* reporter Kent Biffle several days later.

The Warren Commission likewise brushed off the testimony of Dallas electronics salesman Robert K. Patterson, who said that Jack Ruby along with a man who looked like Oswald bought some equipment from him on November 1, 1963. Commissioners said Ruby's companion most likely was a Carousel Club employee named Larry Crafard who "bears a strong resemblance to Oswald."

The Commission noted that at least four other persons had told them of seeing Oswald in the Carousel Club, but these stories also were dismissed. No mention was made of Rose Cheramie or Beverly Oliver, the Dealey Plaza assassination witness who told researchers Ruby introduced her to "Lee Oswald of the CIA" a few weeks before the assassination.

Oliver, now a Christian evangelist using another name, told British television:

> I purposely waited this long [to publicly tell the story] because I felt threatened. . . . I didn't want to become another statistic. About two weeks prior to the assassination, between shows [she was a singer at the nearby Colony Club and would frequently visit Ruby's Carousel Club], I trotted over. There was this girl who danced there by the name of Jada. And she was sitting at a table with Jack Ruby and another man. I went and sat down with them to have a drink. As I sat down, Ruby introduced me to this man. He said, "Beverly, this is my friend Lee." And after Jack Ruby went into the police station and killed Lee Harvey Oswald, it was then I realized it was the man I had met in the club two weeks before the assassination. . . . Jack Ruby and Lee Harvey Oswald were linked together but I don't know how. . . . But I know in my heart that Lee Harvey Oswald, or the man shot in the police station, was the man I met in the club two weeks before the assassination.

She told this author of meeting David Ferrie in the Carousel Club. She said Ferrie was there so often that she initially took him to be assistant manager of the club. Her story was supported by other Carousel employees who also recalled seeing Ruby and Oswald together.

Karen Bennett Carlin, who danced in Ruby's club using the name "Little Lynn," was the woman to whom Ruby mailed a $25 money order minutes before shooting Oswald. Interviewed by the FBI on November 24, 1963, Carlin "seemed on the verge of hysteria." FBI agent Roger C. Warner reported:

> Mrs. Carlin was highly agitated and was reluctant to make any statement to me. She stated to me that she was under the impression that Lee Oswald, Jack Ruby, and other individuals unknown to her, were involved in a plot to assassinate President Kennedy and that she would be killed if she gave any information to the authorities.

Janet Adams Conforto, known as "Jada," told Dallas news reporters shortly after the assassination that she had seen Oswald in the Carousel Club. Likewise, Bill Willis, a musician at the club, reportedly recalled Oswald sitting "right in the corner of the [club's] stage and runway."

Ruby stripper Kathy Kay told the *Dallas Times Herald* in 1975 that she recalled seeing Oswald in the club and even danced with him on one occasion.

This account is supported by Bobbie Louise Meserole, who danced at the Carousel Club under the name Shari Angel. Meserole, who went on to become an ordained minister in Dallas, remembered Jack Ruby fondly. She told this author she recalled conversations with Kathy Kay and others in which they laughingly told how Ruby had ordered Kay to dance a bump and grind to embarrass Oswald.

Shari Angel's husband, Walter "Wally" Weston, who was the Carousel Club's master of ceremonies until five days before the assassination, told of striking Oswald. In a 1976 interview with the *New York Daily News*, Weston said he had seen Oswald with Ruby in the Carousel Club at least twice prior to the assassination. Weston recalled:

> I was working in the club one night approximately three weeks before the assassination. I was on stage, doing my bit, and this guy was standing near the back wall. The club was pretty crowded. The guy walked up in the middle of the club, right in front of the stage, and for no reason he said, "I think you're a communist." I said, "Sir, I'm an American. Why don't you sit down." He said, "Well, I still think you're a communist," so I jumped off the stage and hit him. Jack was right behind him when I hit him. He landed in Jack's arms and Jack grabbed him and said, "You [son of a bitch], I told you never to come in here." And he wrestled him to the door and threw him down the stairs.

After the assassination, Weston said he recognized Oswald as the man in the club but did not say anything when questioned briefly by the FBI and a Dallas detective because he was afraid after discussing the matter with other Carousel employees. He said, "[Carousel drummer] Billy Willis saw me hit [Oswald]. When I discussed it with him [and dancer Kathy Kay], he said, 'Wally, the best thing to do is to stay out of it. Just keep your mouth shut. Don't say anything. That's what I'm going to do. I don't want any part of this.'"

Willis later told a former FBI agent that he changed both his name and Social Security number after all the other members of the Carousel band were killed. Willis said he definitely recalled one incident shortly before the assassination in which he returned a satchel to Oswald in the club's parking lot after Oswald had left it in a circular booth.

Weston visited Ruby in jail several times. He recalled, "The one time I mentioned it to him, I said, 'Jack, wasn't that the guy I hit in the club?' He just looked at me and didn't say yes or no."

Another reason Weston decided to talk in 1976 was that he claimed to have "bumped into" a gangster in Fort Lauderdale, Florida, who had been at a meeting with Ruby in the Carousel Club five days before the assassination. In a published interview, Weston said, "[This guy] said to me, 'I know you, you were Jack Ruby's emcee.' I asked him when he had been at the Carousel Club and he told me he was at the table the night the gun went on the floor."

The shaken Weston vividly recalled that night:

> There was a meeting held at Jack Ruby's club the night I left there, which was five days before the assassination of President Kennedy. There were approximately six to eight guys from Chicago who came into the club—friends of Jack Ruby. I first really noticed them at about 1:30 in the morning, right before closing. Four of them were sitting at a front table, the rest hung around the bar. I was on stage telling jokes and while I was up there, the ones at the table were talking to each other. So I walked to the front of the stage where they were sitting and said, "Hey, you guys, cool it." One of them looked at the others and said, "Who is this son of a bitch?" and he pulled a gun out of his waistband. . . . It looked like a cannon pointed in my direction. At this precise time, two uniformed policemen came in the front door. They just happened to walk in—which was not unusual at Jack's club. I said to the four guys at the table, "The police are here." The gun went to the floor immediately and was kicked over to the side. Jack Ruby, in the meantime, was explaining to the policemen that everything was all right and that there was no problem. After the show, Jack introduced me to the men. . . . He didn't introduce them to me by name, he just said, "These are friends of mine from Chicago."

Weston might not have thought too much about this incident except that he returned to the club after closing to retrieve his jacket. One of the men from Chicago opened the door but refused to allow him inside. When he asked the man to go get Jack Ruby the man also refused, saying, "You can't come in now." Understanding that something very secret was going on in the club, Weston left.

In 1976, after encountering one of the Chicago toughs who had been at the meeting, Weston decided he should tell his story. Incredible as Weston's story seems, at least two people have corroborated it. A convicted murderer and mobster named Myron Thomas Billet, also known as Paul Buccilli, admitted in 1976 that he attended just such a meeting in Ruby's club. Billet stated:

> I was at the Whitemarsh Valley Country Club back in the late part of 1963 when I was contacted by the Mob for a meeting in Dallas at Jack Ruby's Carousel Club. As I remember it, there was myself, Jack Ruby, Lee Oswald, Sam Giancana, John Roselli, and an FBI man. The meeting was to set up

a "hit" on John F. Kennedy. I can't say what the arrangement was because Sam and I left. Sam told me he wanted nothing to do with it. Hell, he helped put Kennedy in office. But three weeks later, JFK was hit and we all knew it wasn't done by one man. Sam told me then that he figured this would get us all killed before it was over.

One man never questioned by the government was C. B. Caldera, a resident of Neely Street. In 1990, he told of seeing Oswald, whom he recognized as his neighbor, inside Ruby's Carousel Club.

Then there is the experience of Ester Ann Mash, who came forward only in recent years. Mash told this author she served drinks at a meeting in the Carousel Club that included "gangsters" from Chicago, Jack Ruby, and Lee Harvey Oswald.

She had been a waitress at a restaurant near Love Field when a Dallas detective introduced her to Ruby early in 1963. Shortly after their introduction, Ruby enticed her into working at the Carousel Club, but only as a waitress and champagne hostess. She explained, "He wanted me to strip, but I just couldn't bring myself to do that." In addition to her club duties, Mash became a lover to Ruby, who she said took her to gambling parties around Dallas.

In the late spring of 1963, she said, Ruby asked her to serve drinks at a gathering in a meeting area of the Carousel Club. Mash said the meeting was composed of Ruby, five "gangster types," and a young man who only sipped beer. She described the meeting:

> I had to follow Jack's orders to the letter for that meeting. He demanded absolute privacy and no interruptions. I was the only person allowed to enter the room and that was just to serve the drinks and then get out. Five men dressed in suits, looking very businesslike, came in about ten thirty that night. They were all dark, swarthy men who looked like gangsters out of some movie. There was another man, dressed real casual—he didn't look like he fit in with the rest of the group at all. There were seven all together [including Ruby]. They talked until about one o'clock in the morning. Then the men in suits left. Jack went to his apartment behind the club. And the other guy stayed until closing watching the strippers. He couldn't take his eyes off them. That man was Lee Harvey Oswald. I really remember him because he was so unusual from the rest. He kept ordering beer. Everyone else drank mixed drinks but this wimpy-looking little guy. I might not remember a name, but I always remember a face. It was a serious meeting and although I did not overhear what they were talking about at the time, I am convinced that they were discussing killing Kennedy. I knew it had something to do with the Mafia because everybody in town in those days knew Ruby had something to do with the mob. Also, Jack asked me to take care of these guys, so later I played up to them a little and discovered they were Mafia guys from Chicago.

About two months after this meeting, Mash had a falling-out with Ruby. She explained:

> He accused me of bringing the vice squad to the club but I didn't. But he wouldn't listen to me. He cussed me out. It upset me, so I left. Also, it was real strange, but I had a very bad feeling, a premonition, that I had better get away from Dallas. So I moved to Euless and got a job in a restaurant, then later moved to Phoenix. I was not even in Dallas the day of the assassination. I did not pay much attention to the news after the assassination. But then on Sunday morning, my children were watching TV when they were showing them moving Oswald. Ruby shot him and I screamed, "Oh, my god!" I couldn't believe my eyes. I thought, "That's the weird little man who was at that secret meeting with Jack and those Mafia types." I saw that grin on Oswald's face on TV the day Jack shot him. He was smiling because Jack was his friend. I didn't want to be involved, so I kept quiet. But now I have a blood clot on the right side of my brain as a result of a car accident. I've already lived longer than I am supposed to. That's the reason I'm telling you this now. Somebody needs to know this before I die.

But an even more damning story concerning Ruby and Oswald comes from Carroll Jarnagin, a credible, if eccentric, attorney. Jarnagin explained to this author that he visited Ruby's Carousel Club on October 4, 1963, to discuss a legal case with one of Ruby's strippers. While seated in a booth at the club, Jarnagin overheard Jack Ruby—whom he knew well—talking with another man. Jarnagin heard the man tell Ruby, "Don't use my real name. I'm going by the name of O. H. Lee." This, of course, was the name Lee Harvey Oswald used to rent a room on North Beckley in Oak Cliff.

Jarnagin described this meeting:

> These men were talking about plans to kill the governor of Texas. Ruby explained, "He [Governor Connally] won't work with us on paroles. With a few of the right boys out we could really open up this state, with a little cooperation from the governor." Then Ruby offered Lee a drug franchise. Ruby also said that the boys really wanted to kill Robert Kennedy. Lee offered to go to Washington to do the job. They then discussed using public lockers and pay telephones as part of hiding their plot. Ruby assured Lee that he could shoot Connally from a window in the Carousel Club and then escape out a back door. Lee was asking for money. He wanted half of the money in advance, but Ruby told him he would get one lump sum after the job was done.

One thing that sets Jarnagin's story apart from the others is that he contacted authorities with his information prior to the assassination. The day after hearing

Ruby's conversation, Jarnagin telephoned the Texas Department of Public Safety. Nothing came of this.

Jarnagin stated, "[After Ruby shot Oswald] I definitely realized that the picture in the November 23, 1963, *Dallas Times Herald* of Lee Harvey Oswald was a picture of the man using the name O. H. Lee, whose conversation with Jack Ruby I had overheard back on October 4, 1963."

After the assassination, Jarnagin again contacted the authorities, this time the Dallas police and the FBI. He was interviewed but his startling account of a Ruby-Oswald plot was buried deep in the volumes of the Warren Commission and never mentioned in its report.

In fact, the Warren Commission quickly dismissed rumors circulating throughout Dallas in 1963–1964 that Ruby and Oswald knew each other by stating, "All assertions that Oswald was seen in the company of Ruby or anyone else at the Carousel Club have been investigated. None of them merits any credence."

Jarnagin said when he tried to tell the FBI what he knew, agents accused him of having hallucinations. The attorney huffed, "It was clearly abuse of a witness."

His tale of an Oswald-Ruby plot finally garnered headlines, this time in 2008. It seems district attorney Henry Wade revamped Jarnagin's account, turning it into a script of Ruby and Oswald plotting, not against Governor Connally, but against President Kennedy. His script adaptation was found in an old safe in the district attorney's office.

The media as well as Gary Mack, by then Sixth Floor Museum curator, laughed off the find as simply an attempt at making a "bad B movie." No mention was made of the fact that the Ruby-Oswald plot was a genuine report to authorities Jarnagin made prior to the assassination.

The disparate meeting times given in these reports—Mash said late spring 1963, Weston indicated about mid-October, and Jarnagin pinpointed October 4, 1963—and the people involved indicate the possibility that more than one meeting involving Ruby and Oswald occurred.

And neither the FBI nor the Warren Commission ever talked to Rose Cheramie, Beverly Oliver, Ester Mash, Wally Weston, Shari Angel, Billy Willis, C. B. Caldera, or Madeleine Brown.

There is tantalizing evidence that authorities knew more than they were telling about a relationship between Oswald and Ruby. In 1976, four Dallas deputy constables told the *Dallas Morning News* that shortly after the assassination they had examined a boxful of handwritten notes and other papers in the Dallas County Courthouse that linked Ruby and Oswald together.

Deputy Billy Preston said he and constable Robie Love, now deceased, handed the box of documents over to Dallas County district attorney Henry Wade in late 1963 or early 1964. Wade told the paper he didn't recall receiving the papers.

Preston, along with deputy constables Mike Callahan and Ben Cash, said the box of papers came from the apartment of a Dallas woman. Preston explained, "She was really scared because she had all that stuff. She wanted me to pick it up for her. And I just wished I had made some more copies now."

Preston could not recall the woman's name other than "Mary," but then and now he believes she had some connection with Oswald because most of the box's contents appeared to have been written by him.

Cash, however, recalled that the box came from the woman's roommate, who had kept it for a Latin American boyfriend. Cash told reporter Earl Golz, "The impression I got [was that] the papers were from the Latin American because he mentioned Ruby and he mentioned Oswald in the writings. He didn't mention the third party but he kept referring to a third party. And the third party would have to be him."

Among the papers in the box, according to the deputies, were newspaper clippings from Mexico, a photocopy of a press card with the words "Daily Worker" issued to Ruby, a receipt from a motel near New Orleans dated several weeks before the assassination with both the names Ruby and Oswald on it and references to calls to Mexico City, papers pinpointing a landing strip somewhere in Mexico, and references to meetings with "agents" in the border towns of McAllen and Laredo, Texas. There was also a church brochure with markings indicating something about going to Cuba.

Preston said one handwritten note referred to a plan to assassinate President Kennedy during the dedication of a lake or dam in Wisconsin. Lawmen in Wisconsin had speculated in December 1963 about the existence of just such a plan after discovering what appeared to be Lee Harvey Oswald's signature on the registry of a restaurant in Hubertus, Wisconsin, dated September 16, 1963. Kennedy indeed had made a speech on September 24, 1963, in Ashland, Wisconsin, as part of a nationwide conservation tour. The FBI rejected the signature as Oswald's and this subject received little attention outside Wisconsin.

Deputy Cash explained why the men had not made this story public earlier:

At that time it was a pretty hot issue, you remember. So we kept quiet and went along with the game. We figured it would be handled on a higher level [than us]. And when it didn't come out, we thought at that time possibly they [the Warren Commission] thought that kind of information tying it into the Cubans or Russians couldn't be released at that time because it might put us in World War III.

Wade finally admitted the incident with the box of documents "might well have happened," but added, "but I know that whatever they had didn't amount to nothing." Whether it did or not may never be known because as far as any official investigation, the box simply never existed.

It would appear that despite the protestations of the two federal investigations, the evidence of an Oswald-Ruby connection is overwhelming.

Even former Dallas police chief Jesse Curry seems to indicate such a relationship existed in his 1969 book by noting, "Witnesses to the shooting [of Oswald] wondered if there wasn't a gleam of recognition in Oswald's eye when Ruby stepped out from the newsmen."

———————

Whether it may ever be conclusively proven that Ruby and Oswald were in contact, there is no doubt that Ruby was in touch with associates of mob and Teamster leaders—and that telephone calls with them markedly increased in the days leading up to the assassination.

In March 1963, Ruby made fewer than ten long-distance calls and from May to September this number averaged monthly between twenty-five and thirty-five. But Ruby's toll calls climbed to more than seventy in October and almost one hundred in November.

This surge in phone traffic also intrigued Warren Commission investigators Hubert and Griffin, who asked the FBI to thoroughly examine all calls by Ruby, his family, and his associates. They also requested that the bureau have phone companies in Texas, Nevada, Los Angeles, San Francisco, Chicago, Detroit, Boston, New York, Washington, Miami, and New Orleans freeze all records until Commission staff could study them.

Apparently this was never done. Griffin later told the House Select Committee on Assassinations that while the bureau did compile some telephone information, it was not the comprehensive check he had asked for and that "no request to freeze records was made to telephone companies." When the House committee got around to requesting these same records, most had been routinely destroyed.

Nevertheless, enough information on Ruby's calls has become available to paint a portrait of a man frantically touching bases across the nation as November 22, 1963, approached. While some of Ruby's calls could be dismissed as obviously personal or business communications, some—such as frequent calls to Harold Tannenbaum, who ran several New Orleans nightclubs that were owned at least in part by mob boss Carlos Marcello—may have served sinister purposes. Near the end of October, Ruby placed a call to Nofio Pecora, one of Marcello's closest associates. The House committee developed information that Pecora owned the Tropical Court Tourist Park, a New Orleans trailer court in which Tannenbaum lived.

Ruby made at least seven traceable calls to his "mentor," gambler Lewis McWillie, beginning in June 1963. He also was in touch with Irwin S. Weiner, a bondsman and insurance agent connected with Santos Trafficante, Sam Giancana, and several other crime-syndicate figures. He also placed a seventeen-minute call in early November to Robert "Barney" Baker, identified as "Hoffa's ambassador of violence" by attorney general Robert Kennedy.

When questioned by House investigators, all of these telephone contacts said the Ruby calls were innocuous and pertained only to some union problems Ruby was having with the American Guild of Variety Artists. The committee concluded,

"We were no more satisfied with [this] explanation than we were with McWillie's, Weiner's, or Baker's."

Union disagreements were not the only problem Ruby faced in the fall of 1963. His problems with the IRS alone were enough to motivate him to follow orders to kill Oswald.

According to the Warren Commission:

In 1960, the government filed tax liens for more than $20,000 [against Ruby]. In November 1962, the government rejected Ruby's offer to pay $8,000 to compromise the assessed taxes of more than $20,000 because he had not filed returns for other federal taxes and had not paid these taxes as they became due. These other taxes . . . amounted to an additional $20,000.

Testimony from Ruby's friends and acquaintances confirmed that he was complaining of his tax debts to anyone who would listen and the House committee determined that Ruby's tax liability may have been closer to $60,000 than the $40,000 the Warren Commission mentioned.

One June 6, 1963, Ruby's attorney, Graham R. E. Koch, informed the Internal Revenue Service that his client would settle his debts "as soon as arrangements can be made to borrow money." However, an FBI check of more than fifty banking institutions revealed no attempt by Ruby to borrow money legitimately.

Did Ruby turn to the mob for help? His flurry of phone calls would seem to indicate this as well as a quick trip to Las Vegas two weekends before the assassination.

Recall that Marguerite Oswald claimed she was fired from her job after her employer, Fort Worth publisher and high-stakes gambler Amon G. Carter Jr., traveled to Las Vegas at the same time Ruby was there. Some have speculated that Carter got word from Vegas sources that Marguerite should be dropped from the family's employment before her son was named as a presidential assassin. The Warren Commission rejected the idea that Ruby visited America's gambling capital, but the House committee found "credible evidence" that Ruby was there. Both a cashier and the credit manager of the Stardust Hotel recalled that a man named Ruby, who claimed to own a club in Dallas, attempted to cash a check one weekend in mid-November. The FBI confirmed this trip through "confidential information."

Ruby's lawyer later told newsman Seth Kantor that it was right after this alleged trip that Ruby told him "he had a connection who would supply him with money to settle his long-standing government tax problems."

Taking the long view, House committee chief counsel Robert Blakey noted, "Ruby's business was in deep financial difficulty, complicated by the dispute with AGVA [the American Guild of Variety Artists] over 'amateur' strippers and serious tax problems."

After pointing out Ruby's union and tax problems as well as his capacity for violence, his underworld missions to Cuba, and his familiarity with the Dallas police, Blakey concluded, "Whatever else may be inferred from Ruby's conduct in the summer and fall of 1963, it at least established that he was an available means to effect Oswald's elimination."

The Shooting of Lee Harvey Oswald

The Warren Commission—and hence the news media—reported in 1963–1964 that the shooting of Lee Harvey Oswald by Jack Ruby was the spontaneous act of a grief-stricken man who was concerned with the possibility of Mrs. Kennedy having to return to Dallas to testify against Oswald. Today that story, still repeated in the news media, has been shown to be a lie and a legal ploy.

Less than three hours after shooting Oswald, Ruby was visited by Dallas attorney Tom Howard. Months later during his trial, Ruby scribbled a note to attorney Joe H. Tonahill saying, "Joe, you should know this. Tom Howard told me to say that I shot Oswald so that Caroline and Mrs. Kennedy wouldn't have to come to Dallas to testify. Okay?"

Ruby also admitted this ploy to attorney Melvin Belli, as recorded in his book, *Dallas Justice.* Belli wrote that Ruby told him, "We know I did it for Jackie and the kids. . . . Maybe I ought to forget this silly story that I'm telling, and get on the stand and tell the truth."

These confessions coupled with Ruby's movements during the assassination weekend all portray a man who consciously stalked Oswald—propelled by motives that were not his own—before finally shooting him in the basement of the Dallas police station.

According to information developed by both the Warren Commission and the House Select Committee on Assassinations, Ruby awoke about 9:30 a.m. on the day of the assassination and drove to the offices of the *Dallas Morning News*, where he tried to visit entertainment columnist Tony Zoppi. Failing to find Zoppi, Ruby said, he went to the paper's advertising office and began to compose ad copy for his club.

Ruby claimed to have remained at the paper from nearly 11 a.m. until well after the assassination and several *News* employees, such as John Newnam and Wanda Walker, confirmed this. However, all the accounts of Ruby at the newspaper contain gaps when he was out of sight. One reporter told the FBI that Ruby was "missed for a period of about twenty to twenty-five minutes" before reappearing shortly after the assassination.

According to Ruby, he drove back to the Carousel Club after learning of the assassination at the newspaper. However, club employee Andrew Armstrong later stated that Ruby did not come to the club until nearly 2 p.m. and several witnesses placed Ruby at Parkland Hospital.

Ruby made several phone calls from the Carousel Club that afternoon and was visibly upset, according to employees' accounts.

He claimed he left the club late in the afternoon, but was seen in the crowded Dallas police headquarters between 4 and 4:30 p.m. Various persons, including a reporter and policemen, placed Ruby at the police station at different places and times between 4 and 7:30 p.m.

By 9 p.m., according to phone records, Ruby was back at his apartment, and at 10 p.m., he visited a Dallas synagogue.

Shortly after 11 p.m. Ruby was back at Dallas police headquarters armed with about a dozen sandwiches he had bought to give to officers.

One officer has even told Texas researchers he saw Ruby enter Captain Fritz's office while Oswald was undergoing interrogation.

Ruby was still there shortly after midnight when Oswald was taken to a basement assembly room for a news conference. Mingling with news reporters, Ruby ended up in the rear of the room, where he elbowed his way onto a table past news photographer Tony Record. Record later said he thought Ruby was a fellow newsman but could not understand his insistence on standing on the table when he didn't carry a camera.

It was during this news conference that a singular incident occurred that many researchers have pointed to as evidence of Ruby's intimate knowledge of Oswald and his activities. Dallas County district attorney Henry Wade, in briefing news reporters about Oswald's background, stated he belonged to the Free Cuba Committee, whereupon Ruby corrected Wade by shouting out, "Henry, that's the Fair Play for Cuba Committee."

While Ruby later claimed to have heard of Oswald's Fair Play for Cuba Committee affiliation over a local radio station that afternoon, it nevertheless struck researchers as most odd that this nightclub owner with no known politics would note the difference between the anti-Castro Free Cuba Committee and the pro-Castro Fair Play for Cuba Committee. Of course, this knowledge would not seem at all odd if the accounts of a Ruby-Oswald relationship are true.

The midnight news conference was tumultuous and if Ruby's plan was to silence Oswald there, there was never a clear shot.

The remainder of the night Ruby was a nervous bundle of activity. He reportedly helped arrange a radio interview for District Attorney Wade, brought sandwiches and drinks to news personnel at KLIF radio, and sometime after 2 a.m. drove around downtown encountering one of his strippers, Kay Coleman (known as Kathy Kay) with Dallas policeman Harry Olsen. During this supposedly chance meeting, Ruby was exhorted to move against Oswald, if his account can be believed. He told the Warren Commission:

> They talked and they carried on, and they thought I was the greatest guy in the world, and he stated they should cut this guy [Oswald] into ribbons, and so on. And she said, "Well, if he was in England, they would drag him through the streets and would have hung him." . . . They kept me from leaving. They were constantly talking and were in a pretty dramatic mood. They were crying and carrying on.

All in all, even considering that much of what is known of Ruby's movements during that weekend is confusing and contradictory, the man evidently was in a nervous, anxious condition and touching bases all over town—especially the Dallas police station, where Oswald was being held.

The House Select Committee on Assassinations concluded, "These sightings, along with the one on Friday night, could indicate that Ruby was pursuing Oswald's movements throughout the weekend."

Jack Ruby's Warnings

And it was in the early morning hours of November 24, 1963, that Ruby may have tried to avert his rapidly approaching confrontation with Oswald. Even the Warren Commission noted this strange incident by reporting, "Between 2:30 and 3 a.m., the local office of the FBI and the sheriff's office received telephone calls from an unidentified man who warned that a committee had decided 'to kill the man that killed the President.' . . . The police department and ultimately Chief Curry were informed of both threats."

What the public was not told was that the man who took one of the calls recognized the voice of Jack Ruby. Dallas police lieutenant Billy R. Grammer was a young officer working in the communications room early on November 24, 1963. A man called and asked to know who was on duty that morning. After hearing Grammer's name, the caller asked to speak with him. Refusing to give his name—the caller said cryptically, "I can't tell you that, but you know me"—the man described in detail to Grammer the plans to transfer Oswald, even to the use of a decoy vehicle, and added, "You're going to have to make some other plans or we're going to kill Oswald right there in the basement." Grammer and his superior took the warning seriously to the extent of writing up a report for Chief Curry.

Later in the morning Grammer was awakened by his wife, who told him that Jack Ruby had just shot Oswald in the basement of the police station. A stunned Grammer told his wife that he suddenly realized that the familiar voice on the phone was Ruby's. In 1988, Grammer told British television that he remained convinced that the caller was Ruby—especially in light of a chance meeting and conversation he had with Ruby in a restaurant near police headquarters only a week before the call.

Of course, if the caller was Ruby and if he did have inside knowledge of the Oswald transfer, then it is clear that Oswald's shooting was premeditated and involved others.

Despite these clear warnings and a few minor changes in the transfer plans as a result, the execution of Oswald went off according to plan.

Ruby told the FBI and the Warren Commission that he remained at his apartment until after 10 a.m. on that Sunday when he left to mail a money order to Lynn Carlin, but several witnesses and a call from a cleaning lady seem to belie that notion.

Ruby's roommate George Senator also tried to say that Ruby was home in the early morning but his story proved inconsistent and even the Warren Commission expressed suspicions about it.

As early as 8 a.m. Warren Richey, a cameraman for WBAP-TV in nearby Fort Worth, reported seeing a man that he was "positive, pretty sure in my own mind" was Jack Ruby in front of the Dallas police station. Richey's observation was corroborated by two other WBAP newsmen, Ira Walker and John Smith. Smith also saw the man about 8 a.m. and, with Walker, about 10 a.m. when the same man approached them and asked, "Has [Oswald] been brought down yet?"

The three newsmen were amazed a short time later when Ruby's mug shot was broadcast over the air. Walker told the Warren Commission, "Well, about four of us pointed at him at the same time in the [mobile broadcast] truck, I mean, we all recognized him at the same time." Characteristically, the Warren Commission downplayed the testimony and suggested the men were all mistaken, choosing rather to believe Ruby.

The Commission also failed to seriously consider the statements of Ray Rushing, a Plano, Texas, preacher who had tried to visit Oswald at the police station that morning. Shortly after Oswald's death, Rushing told Dallas police lieutenant Jack Revill that he had held a brief conversation with Ruby about 9:30 a.m. during a ride in a police station elevator. In his report, Revill evaluated Rushing as "truthful" but noted that District Attorney Wade "didn't need [Rushing's] testimony, because he had placed Ruby there the morning of the shooting."

Was Ruby at his apartment as he claimed or skulking about the police station? A call from a cleaning woman has been used to show that he was indeed home. However, consider the call, made by sixty-year-old Elnora Pitts, who cleaned Ruby's apartment every Sunday. Pitts called sometime just after 8 a.m. November 24. She told the Warren Commission she called each Sunday to verify whether she should work that day.

She said a man answered and she identified herself but the man didn't seem to recognize her name or the fact that she was to clean the apartment. Finally the man said, "Yes, you can come, but you call me." "That's what I'm doing now," replied the exasperated Pitts. By now the woman was frightened by this man, who didn't seem to know her. She also said the man "sounded terrible strange to me. . . . He never did sound like himself."

But regardless of where Jack Ruby was earlier on Sunday morning, he was definitely in the Western Union office just down the street from the police station at 11:17 a.m. That is the time stamped on Ruby's receipt for a $25 money order, which he was sending to Karen Carlin in Fort Worth. Carlin, who also had worked for Pat Kirkwood's Cellar in Fort Worth, told Dallas police she had talked to Ruby earlier that morning and that Ruby obviously was very upset.

The time Ruby sent the money order was only four minutes from the time he shot Oswald. For years, supporters of the official version of the assassination have argued that if Ruby intended to shoot Oswald, he could not have known that Oswald's jail transfer would be delayed almost an hour and he would not have sent the money order. Therefore, they say, Ruby's shooting of Oswald must have been a spontaneous act.

Most serious researchers now understand that the shooting of Oswald was not predicated on Ruby's knowing the exact time of his transfer, but rather conversely that Oswald was transferred only after Ruby was in a position to shoot him.

This idea of a conspiracy to silence Oswald is based on several known facts. One of the most tantalizing of these is the story told by respected reporter Seth Kantor, author of *Who Was Jack Ruby?* According to Kantor, George Senator, Ruby's roommate, was at the Eatwell Café near the police station the morning Ruby shot Oswald. Reportedly Senator went to a pay phone and called Dallas attorney Jim Martin, whom he asked to represent his friend Ruby for murdering the accused assassin, Lee Harvey Oswald.

Minutes later news came over the radio that Oswald had been shot. Ruby's roommate had arranged legal representation *before* the event.

Other facts pointing to a conspiracy to kill Oswald include that Ruby was in and out of the police station the entire weekend, stalking Oswald; Ruby (or someone) tried to warn the authorities of Oswald's death, even relating specific police precautions; and both the mob and the federal government had enough leverage on Ruby to force him to such an act.

Only a minute or so before the Oswald shooting, Ruby's initial lawyer, Tom Howard—the one who cooked up his concern over Mrs. Kennedy as a motive—entered the police station and peered through the basement jail office window just as Oswald was being taken off the elevator. Dallas detective H. L. McGee later that day reported, "At this time, Oswald was brought off the jail elevator and Tom Howard turned away from the window and went back toward the Harwood Street door. He waved at me as he went by and said, 'That's all I wanted to see.' Shortly after that I heard a shot."

Detective Jim Leavelle, one of the men handcuffed to Oswald, told this author he never understood the reason for the nearly one-hour delay in transferring Oswald, but that captain Will Fritz gave him the order to move just after conferring with FBI and Secret Service officials. Leavelle said he had been standing around still handcuffed to Oswald for nearly an hour past the announced movement time when Fritz turned from the federal officers and said, "Everything's all set. Take him down."

In 1963–1964, the federal government in the form of the Warren Commission offered a simple explanation for Oswald's death. It stated that Ruby strolled down the police department's Main Street ramp to the basement minutes after mailing the money order and, by sheer happenstance, arrived within shooting distance of Oswald.

The House Select Committee on Assassinations turned history around by concluding that

> Ruby probably did not come down the ramp, and that his most likely route
> was an alleyway located next to the Dallas Municipal Building and a stair-

way leading to the basement garage of police headquarters. . . . Ruby's shooting of Oswald was not a spontaneous act in that it involved at least some premeditation. Similarly, the committee believed it was less likely that Ruby entered the police basement without assistance, even though the assistance may have been provided with no knowledge of Ruby's intentions. . . . The Committee was troubled by the apparently unlocked doors along the stairway route and the removal of security guards from the area of the garage nearest the stairway shortly before the shooting. . . . There is also evidence that the Dallas Police Department withheld relevant information from the Warren Commission concerning Ruby's entry to the scene of the Oswald transfer.

Ruby himself appeared to support the idea of police aid in reaching Oswald when he told the Warren Commission, "Who else could have timed it so perfectly by seconds. If it were timed that way, then someone in the police department is guilty of giving the information as to when Lee Harvey Oswald was coming down."

Then there are the words of mob boss Johnny Roselli. According to columnist Jack Anderson, Roselli once told him, "When Oswald was picked up, the underworld conspirators feared he would crack and disclose information that might lead to them. This almost certainly would have brought a massive U.S. crackdown on the Mafia. So Jack Ruby was ordered to eliminate Oswald."

Studying the films of the Oswald shooting has given researchers valuable insight into what happened—particularly a film still held by WBAP-TV in Fort Worth. The station was the NBC affiliate in the Dallas–Fort Worth Metroplex and on November 24, 1963, had a remote truck and cameras at the Dallas police station.

One camera was set up across the Main Street ramp driveway and was running more than thirty minutes before Oswald's arrival in the basement. The transfer, originally set for about 10:30 a.m., was delayed by further questioning of Oswald in Fritz's office. Oswald finally arrived in the basement about 11:20 a.m. He was shot moments later. The camera continued filming long after the shooting.

This documentary of the incident is intriguing seen in its entirety:

About a quarter of an hour prior to Oswald's arrival, a car moves out of the basement garage area and up the Main Street ramp. Its horn is sounded loudly as a warning to people on the sidewalk above. Newsmen and police, both uniformed and plainclothes, mill about in expectation. Then more than a minute or so before Oswald arrives, another horn blows but the sound is more muted, indicating that the car may be farther back in the garage area. Moments later, the jail elevator doors open and Oswald is brought out. "Here he comes," shout the newsmen, crowding up toward the jail office door. Police push them back forming a corridor through the crowd. One reporter jams a microphone near Oswald's face and shouts, "Do you have anything to say in your defense?" Just at that moment, Jack Ruby moves in from behind the camera and shoves his .38-caliber snub-nosed revolver into Oswald's stomach. The bang is quite audible and Oswald cries out in pain.

Police immediately swarm over Ruby, knocking him to the floor. One of them calls out, "Jack, you son of a bitch!" Both Oswald and Ruby are hustled back into the jail office while stunned newsmen are reporting, "Oswald has been shot! Oswald has been shot!" Soon these reporters are interviewing the officers who, moments before, had been standing unnoticed beside them. Their questions tumble out, "What happened? Did you know that man? Where did he come from?" Their responses are intriguing. More than a couple indicated that they indeed recognized Jack Ruby but they declined to give his name or say more. More than one officer says he thought Oswald's assailant came from the vicinity of a green car parked back in the police garage.

Taken in total, this film of the shooting indicates that Ruby came through the parked cars in the basement and may have paused near a green car, perhaps the very car that sounded its horn moments before Oswald was brought down. Some researchers believe this horn honk may have been a signal to move Oswald because Ruby was in position.

The film also indicates that many of the officers in the police basement recognized Ruby right away.

Detective Leavelle told this author he both recognized Ruby and saw the gun in his hand as he stepped from the crowd of reporters, but that he was powerless to do anything in the split second it took to shoot Oswald. Leavelle recalled the shooting:

Out of the corner of my eye I saw Ruby step out from the crowd. He was crouched and he had a pistol. He took a couple of steps and pulled that trigger. Ruby was aiming dead center at Oswald. I had a grip on the top of Oswald's trousers. When I saw Ruby, I tried to jerk Oswald aside to get him out of the way. I succeeded in turning him. The bullet hit him in the side rather than straight into the stomach.

Oswald was pushed to the floor by Leavelle while detective L. C. Graves on the opposite side of Oswald grabbed Ruby. Graves told researcher Edward Oxford:

By the time Ruby got that shot off, why I had him down. His hand was still flexing. I was saying to him, "Turn it loose! Turn it loose!" I pried his finger off the trigger. He was still trying to work it. Empty the gun into Oswald, I expect, if he could. Officers were jumping on Ruby to get him to the floor. Oswald said, "Owww!" and fell back. That was the last thing he ever said.

Researchers over the years have been struck by an odd fact. Part of the plan for security in the transfer involved focusing attention on an armored car that news reporters were told would carry Oswald to the county jail. The armored car was a decoy. Oswald was to have been transported in an unmarked police car, which was only feet from where he was shot.

Yet rather than load Oswald into the police car standing by and rush him to a hospital, the mortally wounded prisoner was taken back into the jail office where police gave him artificial respiration while waiting for an ambulance to arrive.

Ruby's one shot had been remarkably efficient. It transversed Oswald's lower abdomen, rupturing two main arteries carrying blood to the heart, and tore through the spleen, pancreas, liver, and right kidney.

Obviously, pumping Oswald's chest was the worst possible reaction to the internal bleeding the abdominal wound had caused.

Chief Curry, who had been told to remain in his office for a call from Mayor Cabell, finally arrived in the basement. He noted when the ambulance arrived, "Oswald was already white as a sheet and looked dead as he was loaded on a stretcher."

Oswald was taken to Parkland Hospital, where he was pronounced dead at 1:07 p.m.

Meanwhile, Jack Ruby had been hustled out of the police basement and taken, ironically enough, to the jail cell that Oswald had just vacated. Ruby asked his captors, "What happened?" He displayed an odd inability to recall the Oswald shooting with any clarity.

One of the auto-theft detectives in charge of placing Ruby in jail was struck by his strange behavior immediately after the shooting. Don Ray Archer told British television in 1988:

> His behavior to begin with was very hyper. He was sweating profusely. I could see his heart beating. We had stripped him down for security purposes. He asked me for one of my cigarettes. I gave him a cigarette. Finally after about two hours had elapsed . . . the head of the Secret Service came up and I conferred with him and he told me that Oswald . . . had died. This should have shocked [Ruby] because it would mean the death penalty. I returned and said, "Jack, it looks like it's going to be the electric chair for you." Instead of being shocked, he became calm, he quit sweating, his heart slowed down. I asked him if he wanted a cigarette and he advised me he didn't smoke. I was just astonished at this complete difference of behavior from what I had expected. I would say his life had depended on him getting Oswald.

On November 27, 1963, a Dallas grand jury indicted Jack Ruby for Oswald's murder.

There was never any doubt he did it. After all, only a handful of Americans failed to see what undoubtedly was the most widely viewed homicide in history. The networks ran replays of the shooting over and over. Because of this publicity, a change-of-venue hearing was conducted on February 10, 1964, but changing the location of Ruby's trial was denied. Jury selection began on February 17 and ended on March 3. The trial began the next day.

Ten days later, on March 14, 1964, the jury—eight men and four women—returned a guilty verdict, with the judge handing down a death sentence. The verdict was appealed.

Many people considered Ruby a hero for eliminating Kennedy's presumed assassin. Cards and letters—even money—came from all over. Ruby's attorney Tom Howard echoed their sentiment when he stated, "I think Ruby deserves a congressional medal."

But despite the favorable pretrial publicity, Ruby never had much of a chance in the Dallas of those days. As right-wing assistant district attorney Bill Alexander explained to newsman Seth Kantor, "Jack Ruby was about as handicapped as you can get in Dallas. First he was a Yankee. Second, he was a Jew. Third, he was in the nightclub business."

To appeal to the mind-set of Dallas at that time, attorney Joe Tonahill was asked to join in his defense. Tonahill had the east Texas drawl and the rural mannerisms more acceptable to a Dallas jury.

But the heavyweight of Ruby's defense was flamboyant San Francisco super-attorney Melvin Belli, who quickly set himself at odds with the down-home provincialism of Dallas.

Belli's avenue of defense was to have Ruby declared a victim of "temporary insanity" due to "psychomotor epilepsy." To this end, Belli put a string of psychiatrists on the stand to testify. It also meant that he would not allow Ruby to take the stand on his own behalf.

This failure to allow Ruby to testify, coupled with the tight security in the Dallas County Jail, effectively kept Ruby isolated from the news media and the public. Ruby even cautioned his few visitors to the jail that his conversations were being recorded and monitored.

The only reporter to get a private interview with Ruby during his trial in March 1964 was nationally syndicated columnist Dorothy Kilgallen, who prevailed on lawyer Tonahill to arrange the meeting with presiding judge Joe B. Brown. She claimed to have a message for Ruby from a mutual friend who "may have been some kind of singer."

Judge Brown, impressed with the famous Broadway newspaperwoman, agreed and, according to Kilgallen biographer Lee Israel, the pair met in a small office behind the judge's bench without the four sheriff's deputies who were always at Ruby's side. Israel wrote, "They were together privately for about eight minutes in what may have been the only safe house Ruby had occupied since his arrest."

Although Kilgallen mentioned this unique private meeting with Ruby to close friends, she did not publicly write about it. The fact that she did not publicly disclose what she learned in this meeting prompted biographer Israel to write:

> That she withheld suggests strongly that she was either saving the information for her book, *Murder One*, a chapter of which she had decided to devote to the Ruby trial; that he furnished her with a lead which she was actively pursuing; that he exacted a promise of confidentiality from her; or that she was acting merely as a courier. Each possibility puts her in the thick of things.

Israel also records that toward the end of her life, Kilgallen may have obtained inside assassination information from yet another source. He wrote, "Dorothy began to draw drinking companions to her. Joan Crawford . . . was among them. She tooled around with Crawford. . . . They boozed abundantly together in the back of Crawford's touring car, which was well stocked with hundred-proof vodka."

Upon her husband's death, Crawford had become a principal owner of Pepsi-Cola, the firm that counted Richard Nixon as an attorney. Both Nixon and Crawford had been in Dallas the week of the assassination and may have been privy to inside information.

Whatever information Kilgallen learned and from whatever source, it fired her desire to solve the JFK assassination. She told attorney Mark Lane, "They've killed the President, [and] the government is not prepared to tell us the truth" and that she planned to "break the case." To other friends she said, "This has to be a conspiracy! [The Warren Commission is] laughable. . . . I'm going to break the real story and have the biggest scoop of the century." And in her last column item regarding the assassination, published on September 3, 1965, Kilgallen wrote, "This story isn't going to die as long as there's a real reporter alive—and there are a lot of them."

But on November 8, 1965, there was one less reporter. That day Dorothy Kilgallen was found dead in her home. It was initially reported that she died of a heart attack, but quickly this was changed to an overdose of alcohol and pills. Her death certificate, dated November 15, 1965, stated the cause of death was "acute ethanol and barbiturate intoxication—circumstances undetermined."

Israel later wrote, "After three years of investigating the events surrounding Dorothy's death, it is clear to me that she did not die accidentally and that a network of varied activities, impelled by disparate purposes, conspired effectively to obfuscate the truth."

No trace of her notes or writings about what she may have learned from Ruby or Crawford was ever found.

During Ruby's trial, Dallas County district attorney Henry Wade made a strong case for premeditation but carefully skirted the issue of conspiracy. He explained that he was given instructions from Johnson's aide Cliff Carter, who called from Washington at least three times on Friday afternoon: "Any word of a conspiracy . . .

to kill President Kennedy would shake our nation to its foundation. President Johnson was worried about some conspiracy on the part of the Russians [saying] it would hurt foreign relations if I alleged a conspiracy—whether I could prove it or not—I was to charge Oswald with plain murder."

But according to the *Fort Worth Star-Telegram* of March 18, 1964, Wade's "big decision" later was to not call witnesses "who insisted they had seen Ruby and Oswald together at various times."

A parade of police witnesses recalled various remarks Ruby reportedly made at the time of the shooting, such as:

> You rotten son of a bitch, you shot the President. . . . I intended to get off three shots. . . . I did it because you [the police] couldn't do it. . . . I did it to show the world that Jews have guts. . . . I first thought of killing him at the Friday night press conference.

It was such publicized statements as these, as well as Judge Brown's refusal of a change of venue, that prompted the Texas Court of Criminal Appeals to reverse Ruby's conviction on October 5, 1966. The appeals court ordered a new trial but Ruby did not live to see it.

Although Ruby was not allowed to testify at his trial, he was interviewed by the Warren Commission on June 7, 1964. Representing the Warren Commission were US Supreme Court chief justice Earl Warren and representative Gerald R. Ford along with general counsel J. Lee Rankin and staff attorneys Arlen Specter and Joseph Ball. Also present were attorneys Leon Jaworski and Robert G. Storey, who were acting as liaisons between the Commission and Texas authorities; Secret Service agent Elmer W. Moore; Dallas County assistant district attorney Jim Bowie; sheriff Bill Decker; Ruby attorney Joe Tonahill; and several Dallas police officers.

Oddly enough, due to an internal squabble over the handling of Dallas witnesses, the two Commission staffers who were in charge of the Ruby investigation—Leon Hubert and Burt Griffin—were not allowed to sit in on this important interview.

During this interview, Ruby vacillated. After about an hour of a rambling account of his activities prior to shooting Oswald and some rather innocuous questions, it appeared that Warren was ready to wrap up the interview. Apparently sensing this, Ruby said, "You can get more out of me. Let's not break up too soon."

Ford then began questioning Ruby about his trips to Cuba in 1959, but just as the answers appeared to be leading into fruitful territory, Warren cut Ford off and changed the subject.

Tonahill later told newsman Seth Kantor, "Ford never did finish his interrogation on Cuba. Warren blocked Ford out on it. That was very impressive, I thought. Ford gave him a hard look, too. I was sitting right there and saw it happen."

Ruby became desperate, pleading:

> Gentlemen, my life is in danger here. . . . Do I sound sober enough to you

as I say this? . . . Then follow this up. I may not live tomorrow to give any further testimony. . . . The only thing I want to get out to the public, and I can't say it here, is with authenticity, with sincerity of the truth of everything and why my act was committed, but it can't be said here. . . . Chairman Warren, if you felt that your life was in danger at the moment, how would you feel? Wouldn't you be reluctant to go on speaking, even though you request me to do so?

Having previously voiced the suspicion that his words and actions were being monitored in Dallas, Ruby then asked to be taken out of his present circumstances, saying, "Gentlemen, if you want to hear any further testimony, you will have to get me to Washington soon, because it has something to do with you, Chief Warren. . . . I want to tell the truth and I can't tell it here. Does that make sense to you?"

Ruby begged to be taken to Washington, away from Dallas, at least eight times. He complained that his "life was in danger. . . . [My] whole family is in jeopardy." He was shrugged off by Warren, who replied, "There are a good many things involved in that, Mr. Ruby."

Asked to explain, Warren replied, "Well, the public attention that it would attract, and the people who would be around. We have no place for you to be safe when we take you out, and we are not law enforcement officers, and it isn't our responsibility to go into anything of that kind. And certainly it couldn't be done on a moment's notice this way."

Ruby grew more blunt:

If you don't take me back to Washington tonight to give me a chance to prove to the President that I am not guilty, then you will see the most tragic thing that will ever happen. And if you don't have the power to take me back, I won't be around to be able to prove my innocence or guilt. . . . All I know is maybe something can be saved. Because right now, I want to tell you this. I am used as a scapegoat. . . . Now maybe something can be saved. It may not be too late, whatever happens, if our President, Lyndon Johnson, knew the truth from me. But if I am eliminated, there won't be any way of knowing.

Asked if he knew Officer Tippit, he replied that "there was three Tippits on the force" but he knew only one and didn't think he was the murdered policeman. Incredibly, no one followed up on this to find out which Tippit Ruby did know and how he knew it wasn't the murdered officer. To this author's knowledge, there were no other Tippits on the police force at that time.

Then Rankin asked him about a rumor that Ruby had been seen in the Carousel Club shortly before the assassination with a Mr. Weissman—the man who had paid for an anti-Kennedy newspaper ad—Officer Tippit, and a rich Dallas oilman.

Ruby said the story was untrue, then may have uttered an ironic truth. Looking around the room, he proclaimed, "I am as innocent regarding any conspiracy as any of you gentlemen in the room."

As early as December 1963, Ruby had asked to be given a lie detector test, perhaps reasoning that such a test would bring out the truth by revealing his account of events to be false. During his meeting with Warren he again begged to be given a polygraph test and the Commission dutifully agreed. A polygraph test was administered to Ruby on July 18, 1964, and his answers did not indicate he was lying. These test results have been used during the years to support the contention that Ruby was not part of any conspiracy and shot Oswald only out of personal motives.

Few people bothered to read the last page of the Warren Report, where in Appendix XVII, J. Edgar Hoover commented:

> It should be pointed out that the polygraph, often referred to as "lie detector" is not in fact such a device. . . . During the proceedings at Dallas, Texas, on July 18, 1964, Dr. William R. Beavers, a psychiatrist, testified that he would generally describe Jack Ruby as a "psychotic depressive." In view of the serious question raised as to Ruby's mental condition, no significance should be placed on the polygraph examination and it should be considered nonconclusive as the charts cannot be relied upon.

Apparently unwilling or unable to see that Ruby was desperately trying to tell them something outside the surveillance of Dallas authorities, the Warren Commission entourage prepared to leave Ruby's interview. Failure to fully question Jack Ruby was one of the Commission's greatest mistakes—if it was a mistake.

A resigned Ruby told them, "Well, you won't ever see me again. I tell you that. . . . A whole new form of government is going to take over the country, and I know I won't live to see you another time."

He didn't.

The Sudden Death of Jack Ruby

In the days following his trial and interview by the Warren Commission, Jack Ruby's moods went from confident highs to suicidal lows. A prisoner with few opportunities to communicate with the outside, Ruby nevertheless was given the run of sheriff Bill Decker's jail. He reportedly was able to roam freely, occasionally use the telephone, and even sleep in a corridor. But at all times he was under close guard, especially after several inept suicide attempts.

On one occasion he tried to hang himself but there was not enough time to rip his clothing and fashion a knot before a guard got to him. Another time, Ruby became so despondent he tried to split his skull by running headlong into a wall. This attempt merely left him with a large knot on his head.

His most pathetic attempt took place when a guard went off for a drink of water. Quickly Ruby unscrewed an overhead lightbulb, then threw water from his own glass onto his feet as a conduit. However, he couldn't reach the light socket with his finger while standing in the water. His guard, deputy sheriff Jess Stevenson, found him ineffectually jumping up and down trying to complete the circuit. The attempt was "something nearly comical," Stevenson told newsman Seth Kantor.

As time dragged on and his isolation began to take its toll, Ruby became more despondent. His mood worsened after he came to believe that Stevenson, who had chatted at length with the prisoner after preaching the Bible to him, actually was passing information gleaned through their conversations back to Dallas authorities.

Long after the Warren Commission had issued its report in the fall of 1964, while waiting for the outcome of his conviction appeal, Ruby apparently wrote a sixteen-page letter to a fellow prisoner who was leaving the jail. Ruby asked the prisoner to memorize names and facts in the letter, then destroy it. The prisoner, identified only as "John," decided instead to sell the letter, and it ended up in the hands of longtime researcher Penn Jones. Jones purchased the letter from New York autograph dealer Charles Hamilton, who had the document appraised as authentic.

The letter is disjointed, rambling, and full of references to Nazis, the death of Jews, and, most intriguing, derogatory references to Lyndon Johnson. Many researchers, as improbable as it seems, feel Ruby's letter, though written in a state of questionable mental equilibrium, laid bare some of his secret knowledge and fears. He wrote:

> First, you must realize that the people here want everyone to think I am crazy, so if what I know is actually [*sic*], and then no one will believe me, because of my supposed insanity. Now, I know that my time is running out . . . they plan on doing away with [me]. . . . As soon as you get out you must read Texan looks at Lyndon [*A Texan Looks at Lyndon: A Study in Illegitimate Power*, by J. Evetts Haley] and it might open your eyes to a lot of things. This man [Johnson] is a Nazi in the worst order. For over a year now they have been doing away with my people. . . . Don't believe the Warren report, that was only put out to make me look innocent in that it would throw the Americans and all the European country's [*sic*] off guard. . . . There are so many things that have been played with success that it would take all nite [*sic*] to write them out. . . . There wouldn't be any purpose of my writing you all of this unless you were convinced of how much I loved my country. . . . I am going to die a horrible death anyway, so what would I have to gain by writing all this. So you must believe me. . . . Johnson is going to try to have an all-out war with Russia and when that happens, Johnson and his cohorts will be on the side-lines where they won't get hurt, while the Americans may get wiped out. The only way this can be avoided is that if Russia would be informed as to [who] the real enemies are, and in that way they won't be tricked into starting a war with the U.S. . . . One more thing, isn't it strange that Oswald who hasn't worked a lick most of his life, should be fortunate enough to get a job at the Book Bldg. two wks. before the president himself didn't know as to when he was to visit Dallas, now where

would a jerk like Oswald get the information that the president was coming to Dallas. Only one person could have had that information, and that man was Johnson who knew weeks in advance as to what was going to happen because he is the one who was going to arrange the trip for the president, this had been planned long before the president himself knew about [it], so you figure that one out. The only one who gained by the shooting of the president was Johnson, and he was in a car in the rear and safe when the shooting took place. What would the Russians, Castro or anyone else have to gain by eliminating the president? If Johnson was so heartbroken over Kennedy, why didn't he do something for Robert Kennedy? All he did was snub him.

In a second letter smuggled out of the Dallas County Jail, Ruby was more blunt in his accusations. He wrote:

They found some very clever means and ways to trick me and which will be used later as evidence to show the American people that I was part of the conspiracy in the assassination of [the] president, and I was used to silence Oswald. . . . They alone planned the killing, by they, I mean Johnson and others. . . . Read the book Texas Looks At Lyndon [another reference to Haley's book] and you may learn quite a bit about Johnson and how he has fooled everyone. . . . In all the history of the U.S. never has a president been elected that has the background of Johnson. Believe me, compared to him I am a Saint.

Not long before his death, Ruby was interviewed by psychiatrist Werner Teuter. Perhaps realizing his end was near, Ruby told Teuter the assassination was "an act of overthrowing the government" and that he knew "who had President Kennedy killed." He added, "I am doomed. I do not want to die. But I am not insane. I was framed to kill Oswald."

These comments will always intrigue researchers. Was Ruby merely speculating or were his messages born of secret knowledge? Did he know that Johnson and the people behind him wanted war—only mistaking Russia for Asia? And were his warnings of Nazis taking over rooted somewhere in a knowledge of the mentality of the people he knew were behind the assassination? A Nazi connection to the assassination is both well documented and considerable. See *The Rise of the Fourth Reich* by this author.

Or were his missives only the delusions of a man unhinged by his captivity and the belief that forces were out to destroy him?

The answer may be found in a study of Ruby's mysterious death.

The Texas Court of Criminal Appeals overturned Ruby's conviction on October 5, 1966, and ordered a new trial. On December 7, 1966, his new trial was ordered moved from Dallas to Wichita Falls, a small Texas city near the Oklahoma border.

There was every likelihood that within another month or two, Ruby would walk free, as his time in jail would be counted against a probable short prison term for murder without malice. He certainly would have been allowed to post bond and become accessible to the public.

On December 9, 1966, two days after his new trial site had been announced, Ruby was moved from the Dallas County Jail to Parkland Hospital after complaining of persistent coughing and nausea.

Doctors initially diagnosed his problem as "pneumonia." The next day, however, the diagnosis was changed to cancer and within just a few more days, it was announced that Ruby's cancer was too far advanced to be treated by surgery or radiation.

On the evening of January 2, 1967, doctors suspected that blood clots were forming and they administered oxygen and Ruby seemed to recover. But about 9 a.m. the next day, he suffered a spasm and, despite emergency procedures, he was pronounced dead at 10:30 a.m. January 3, 1967.

One of his attorneys told newsmen, "His death was a merciful release."

Shortly before his death, Ruby's brother Earl smuggled a tape recorder into Parkland and later produced a short record that was sold to Capitol Records. The proceeds from this record, in which Ruby simply reiterated the official account of his actions—including his Cuban travels, which the House Select Committee on Assassinations proved false—was used to pay for his burial expenses. This record also once again put the public off the trail of evidence by repeating the same story reported in 1963–1964.

An autopsy by Dallas County medical examiner Dr. Earl Rose showed the heaviest concentration of cancer cells in Ruby's right lung. However, Dr. Rose determined the immediate cause of death was pulmonary embolism—a massive blood clot had formed in a leg, passed through the heart, and lodged in Ruby's lung. Ruby's doctors had said they believed his cancer had originated in the pancreas, but Dr. Rose found Ruby's pancreas perfectly normal.

With the announcement of his inoperable cancer, there was immediate and widespread suspicion that Ruby had been maneuvered into killing Oswald knowing he had only a short time to live. Dr. Rose was asked by the House committee if there was any chance that Ruby could have known about his cancer in November 1963. He said no.

Yet questions remain.

In the later summer of 1966, jail doctor Julian Mardock found Ruby was in good health. But several weeks later he was told that he was no longer needed, as a doctor "down from Washington" would take over Ruby's case.

Deputy sheriff Al Maddox also mentioned the new doctor who arrived to attend Ruby:

> We had a phony doctor come in to [the Dallas County Jail] from Chicago, just as phony and as queer as a three-dollar bill. And he worked his way in through—I don't know, whoever supplied the county at that time with

doctors. . . . You could tell he was Ruby's doctor. He spent half his time up there talking with Ruby. And one day I went in and Ruby told me, he said, "Well, they injected me for a cold." He said it was cancer cells. That's what he told me, Ruby did. I said you don't believe that shit. He said, "I damn sure do!" I never said anything to Decker or anybody. . . . [Then] one day when I started to leave, Ruby shook hands with me and I could feel a piece of paper in his palm. . . . [In this note] he said it was a conspiracy and he said . . . if you will keep your eyes open and your mouth shut, you're gonna learn a lot. And that was the last letter I ever got from him.

Maddox was not the only law-enforcement officer to suspect that Ruby's death was not entirely natural. Policeman Tom Tilson told researchers, "It was the opinion of a number of other Dallas police officers that Ruby had received injections of cancer while he was incarcerated in the Dallas County Jail following the shooting of Lee Harvey Oswald."

The new physician has been identified as none other than Dr. Louis Joyon "Jolly" West, professor and director of the Neuropsychiatric Institute at the University of California–Los Angeles. He also was a government expert on torture and brainwashing who also turned up in the cases of Sirhan Sirhan and Patty Hearst. West's name has cropped up in many reports and documents pertaining to the government's MK-ULTRA mind-control experiments and may also have been connected to covert cancer research.

According to a January 7, 1999, Reuters report, "After examining Ruby, the killer of President John F. Kennedy's assassin, Lee Harvey Oswald, West concluded Ruby was suffering from 'major mental illness precipitated by the stress of [his] trial.'"

Many researchers believe that Ruby's cancer was induced, either by ingestion or injection. At least one former Dallas law-enforcement officer offered a more mundane explanation for Ruby's sudden and rampant cancer. He told this author, "Hell, it wasn't any big deal. They just took Ruby in for X-rays and had him wait in the X-ray room. While he sat there for fifteen or twenty minutes or more, they just left the X-ray machine on him."

Bruce McCarty operated an electron microscope at Southwest Medical School near Parkland. He told this author that he was called back to work during the holidays in 1966 to study Ruby's cancer cells. McCarty explained that there are two types of cancer cells—cilia, which indicate an origin in the respiratory system, and microvilli, indicating an origin in the digestive system. These cells are difficult to differentiate with a regular microscope, hence the need for his electron microscope.

McCarty confirmed that Ruby's cells were microvilli, indicating his cancer originated in the digestive system. He was shocked when it was announced that Ruby died from lung cancer.

Could Ruby have been injected with live cancer cells, which could account for the presence of the microvilli? Traditional medical science has claimed this is impossible but recall the account of just such a process as described by Judyth Vary Baker, who claimed to have met Ruby in New Orleans while working in David Ferrie's covert cancer lab.

While none of this information establishes beyond doubt that Jack Ruby was somehow eliminated through cancer, it certainly shows there is cause enough for researchers to be highly suspicious of his sudden and convenient death.

With the death of the two men who might have shed light on the lines of communication within a plot to kill the president—Oswald and Ruby—researchers were left only with a vast amount of evidence, much of which seems substantial until studied closely.

The Evidence

There has never been a lack of evidence in the assassination of President Kennedy. In addition to the several hundred witnesses in Dealey Plaza, there was an abundance of film and still pictures as well as documentation and a great deal of physical evidence.

In the hours following the assassination, this evidence grew to include a rifle, empty shell cases, a "sniper's nest" and even a convincing—if belated—palm print on the suspected murder weapon.

The rapid accumulation of evidence prompted Dallas County district attorney Henry Wade to proclaim to the media he had an open-and-shut case against Lee Harvey Oswald the day after the shooting.

However, a long and thoughtful look at most of the evidence reveals just as many questions and as much confusion as the medical evidence.

The Warren Commission questioned 126 of the 266 known witnesses either by testimony or affidavit. Regarding the source of the shots, thirty-eight gave no opinion—most were not asked—thirty-two indicated the Texas School Book Depository, and fifty-one placed the shots in the vicinity of the Grassy Knoll. Several believed shots were fired from locations other than those two.

Even veteran law-enforcement officers, who should have been expected to provide expert opinions as to the source of the shots, were divided in their beliefs. Of the twenty sheriff's deputies watching the motorcade from in front of the sheriff's office, sixteen placed the origin of the shots near the Triple Underpass, three gave no opinion, and only one implied the Depository. Of twelve Dallas policemen stationed in the plaza interviewed, four placed shots from the Grassy Knoll, four said shots came from the Depository, and four gave no opinion.

While it is understood that eyewitness testimony cannot be relied on for absolute truth, statements of otherwise ordinary citizens regarding second gunmen, muzzle flashes, and smoke on the Grassy Knoll must be considered in any impartial desire to learn the truth.

The best evidence would have been the medical reports. With a competent autopsy, it should have been well established how many bullets struck Kennedy and from which direction. However, as discussed earlier, the medical evidence in this case continues to be a source of controversy—filled with inconsistencies, errors, missing items, and phony photographs and X-rays. About all one can say for certain based on the medical evidence is that Kennedy was shot at least twice.

So it remains for other pieces of evidence—ballistic and physical evidence—to prove the official version of the assassination. Unfortunately, this area, too, is filled with doubts, questions, deceit, and ambiguity.

Some of the first physical evidence to be found was in the Texas School Book Depository. Many of the press accounts at the time mentioned fingerprints traced to Lee Harvey Oswald being found on boxes on the Depository's sixth floor, the shield of boxes around a "sniper's nest" in the southeast corner of that floor, and the remains of a chicken lunch discovered nearby.

The presence of Oswald's fingerprints on the sixth floor means nothing, since he was a Depository employee and by all accounts had worked on the sixth floor that day. Furthermore, it is clear that the Dallas police failed to follow even the most rudimentary methods of handling evidence. Of the nine fingerprints and four palm prints found on book boxes from the sixth floor, only one fingerprint and palm print could be traced to Oswald. All remaining prints belonged to Dallas policeman R. L. Studebaker, FBI clerk Forest L. Lucy, or others, with a few unidentified. In other words, the forensics evidence was a mess.

The stacking of book boxes both around the sixth-floor window and on the windowsill cannot be used as proof of Oswald's guilt since there is no proof he placed them and since it is now known that the entire "sniper's nest" scene was later staged for the official photographs.

At least three Warren Commission photographs of the scene—Commission Exhibits 509, 724, and 733—show three versions of the boxes stacked near the sixth-floor window. R. L. Studebaker, Dallas police photographer, told the Warren Commission that some of his photos were taken as late as the Monday following the assassination.

Jack Beers, a photographer for the *Dallas Morning News*, took pictures of the "sniper's nest" less than three hours after the assassination. His photos show yet a different configuration of boxes from that shown in the Commission photos.

Dallas police lieutenant J. C. Day of the Crime Scene Search Unit admitted to the Warren Commission that the boxes had been moved around. In Commission testimony, the following exchange took place between Day and Commission attorney David Belin:

BELIN: Were those boxes in the window the way you saw them, or had they been replaced in the window to reconstruct it?

DAY: They had simply been moved in the processing for prints. They weren't put back in any particular order.

BELIN: So [the "sniper's nest" photograph] does not represent, so far as the boxes are concerned, the crime scene when you first came to the sixth floor, is that correct?

DAY: That is correct.

So the evidence of the "sniper's nest" is virtually useless since even the Dallas police crime scene official stated the boxes had been moved about.

Unfortunately, it was the same story with the three cartridge hulls reportedly found on the sixth floor. Day said he took two photographs of the three hulls lying near the sixth-floor window. Two hulls can been seen lying near to each other on the floor beneath the windowsill while a third is some distance away. It has been assumed that this was the position of the hulls. However, today there is evidence that this evidence also was staged.

Gary Mack, based on a 1985 interview with WFAA-TV cameraman Tom Alyea, wrote:

[Alyea] managed to get inside the Texas School Book Depository before it was sealed by police. As he entered the building, Alyea heard someone shout, "Don't let anyone in or out!" Alyea reached the sixth floor and filmed Dallas police searching for evidence. He said the federal authorities there were "bent on getting me out of the place" and did not want him taking any film but his friendly local police contacts allowed him to stay. Alyea said he noticed shells lying on the floor but couldn't film them because of book boxes in the way. Noting Alyea's predicament, Captain Will Fritz scooped up the shells and held them in his hand for Alyea's camera—then threw the hulls down on the floor. All of this occurred before the crime scene search unit arrived. Alyea said film of the shells lying in their original positions on the floor was apparently thrown out with other unused news film on orders of his WFAA news director.

Two lawmen on the sixth floor at the time—deputy sheriffs Roger Craig and Luke Mooney—have told researchers they saw the three hulls lying side by side only inches apart under the window, all pointing in the same direction. Of course this position would be impossible if the shells had been normally ejected from a rifle to the right rear. So the evidence of the empty shell cases became suspect.

Just as a matter of speculation, it seems incredible that the assassin in the Depository would go to the trouble of trying to hide the rifle behind boxes on the opposite side of the sixth floor from the southeast window and then leave incriminating shells lying on the floor—unless, of course, the hulls were deliberately left behind to incriminate Oswald.

There is yet another problem with the empty rifle hulls. Although the Warren Commission published a copy of the Dallas police evidence sheet showing three shell cases were taken from the Depository, in later years a copy of that same evidence sheet was found in the Texas Department of Public Safety files that showed only two cases were found. This is supported by the FBI receipt for assassination evidence from the Dallas police that indicates only two shell cases arrived in Washington just after the assassination.

Reportedly Fritz held on to one of the cases for several days before forwarding it to the FBI. This breach of the chain of evidence causes suspicion to be raised about the legitimacy of the third shell. This suspicion is compounded by the fact that while the FBI crime lab determined that two of the hulls show a small dent, this anomaly was found only on shell cases loaded in the Oswald rifle. The third casing showed no such evidence.

In fact, the third hull—designated Commission Exhibit 543—had an indention on its lip that would have prevented the fitting of a slug. In its present condition, it could not have fired a bullet on that day.

The FBI determined that Commission Exhibit 543 had been loaded and extracted from a weapon "at least three times" but could not specify that the weapon belonged to Oswald. Some researchers speculate this shell may have been the one used to fire the slug from the Oswald rifle that later turned up at Parkland Hospital and has been designated as Commission Exhibit 399—the "magic bullet." However, FBI experts said Commission Exhibit 543 did show marks from the magazine follower of Oswald's rifle. What went unexplained was how these marks were made, since the magazine follower marks only the last cartridge in the clip. This position was occupied by a live round found that day, not by Commission Exhibit 543.

Again, too many questions arise to accept the shell cases as legitimate evidence.

The rifle reportedly belonging to Oswald also is surrounded by controversy and inconsistencies. The rifle found behind boxes on the sixth floor of the Depository was initially described as a 7.65 mm bolt-action German Mauser. It was described as such by deputy sheriff E. L. Boone, discoverer of the rifle, in his report of that day. Boone's report is supported by that of deputy constable Seymour Weitzman. Both lawmen reportedly had more than an average knowledge of weapons.

As late as the day after the assassination, Weitzman wrote in a report:

> I was working with Deputy Boone of the Sheriff's Department and helping in the search. We were in the northwest corner of the sixth floor when Deputy Boone and myself spotted the rifle about the same time. This rifle was a 7.65 Mauser bolt action equipped with a 4/18 scope, a thick leather brownish-black sling on it. The rifle was between some boxes near the stairway. The time the rifle was found was 1:22 p.m.

This account was confirmed by Deputy Craig, who told Texas researchers he actually saw the word "Mauser" stamped on the weapon's receiver. When asked about the make of rifle shortly after midnight the day of the assassination, Dallas County district attorney Henry Wade replied, "It's a Mauser, I believe."

However, by late Friday afternoon the rifle was being identified as a 6.5 mm Italian Carcano.

While a German Mauser and the Carcano do look somewhat similar, anyone vaguely familiar with these weapons—Weitzman, Boone, and Craig should certainly qualify—can distinguish between them. Why the discrepancies? The Warren Commission indicated that Weitzman was simply mistaken in his identification of the rifle and that the others, including Wade, probably repeated this mistaken identification. However, Wade never gave any indication as to the source of his idea that the rifle was a Mauser. And Boone told the Commission he thought it was Captain Fritz who termed it a Mauser.

Asked to identify the Carcano, Boone would only say, "It looks like the same rifle. I have no way of being positive." Weitzman, who managed a sporting-goods store and was considered an expert on rifles, had identified the gun as a Mauser. He testified to the Warren Commission only by affidavit and was not asked to identify the Carcano as the gun he held in the Depository.

Author Sylvia Meagher noted, "The failure to obtain such corroboration from Weitzman leaves open the possibility that a substitution of rifles took place, or that a second rifle may have been found at the Book Depository, but kept secret."

Also consider that Lieutenant Day and another Dallas policeman mentioned writing contemporary descriptions of the rifle, yet neither of these documents was included in the mass of Warren Commission materials.

Even the CIA had doubts as to the true identity of the assassination rifle. Five days after the assassination, in an internal report transmitted from Italy to Langley headquarters, CIA officials noted that two different kinds of Italian-made carbines were being identified as the single murder weapon. The CIA document stated, "The weapon which appears to have been employed in this criminal attack is a Model 91 rifle, 7.35 caliber, 1938 modification. . . . The description of a 'Mannlicher-Carcano' rifle in the Italian and foreign press is in error."

The possibility of a rifle substitution was even admitted by Dallas police chief Jesse Curry in 1976. In an interview with the *Detroit News*, Curry agreed "it's more than possible" the rifle originally found in the Depository could have been exchanged for the gun now in the National Archives. Curry said anyone wanting to substitute one suspected murder weapon for another "could have gotten away with it at the time" because no special precautions were taken to isolate the weapon as historic evidence.

But even accepting that the Carcano was the assassination rifle, it is hard to envision a worse weapon. In testimony to the Warren Commission—conveniently left out of its report—FBI reports quoted firearms experts as calling the rifle "a cheap old weapon," "a very cheap rifle [which] could have been purchased for $3 each in lots of 25," and a "real cheap, common, real flimsy-looking [gun] . . . very easily knocked out of adjustment."

The FBI also noted that the Carcano was part of a gun shipment that was the subject of "a legal proceeding by the Carlo Riva Machine Shop to collect payment for the shipment of rifles which Adam Consolidated Industries, Inc., claims were defective." A defective gun managed to strike two men with three shots at a range of more than two hundred feet within six seconds?

There are many other questions concerning the rifle and its purchase.

The Warren Commission published a "duplicate" of the ad from which Oswald reportedly ordered the rifle from Klein's Sporting Goods Co. of Chicago on March 13, 1963. According to Klein's records, a rifle bearing serial number C2766 was shipped to one A. Hidell, Post Office Box 2915, Dallas, Texas, on March 20, 1963.

Why publish a duplicate ad? Why not publish the original ad? The order form reportedly came from the February 1963 issue of *American Rifleman* magazine. Yet the ad from that issue advertises a "36-inch overall" rifle. Perhaps that is why the Commission chose to present a "duplicate" ad, which depicts a forty-inch-long rifle—the same length as the weapon identified as Oswald's.

Perhaps the discrepancy between rifle lengths had a logical explanation. But the manner in which the Commission tried to conceal this problem only further demonstrates manipulation of the evidence.

This problem is heightened by the fact that no record exists to show that either Oswald or A. Hidell actually took possession of the rifle. Despite postal regulations requiring that Form 1039, which lists those persons with access to a post office box, be kept a minimum of two years after a box is closed—the Commission was told Oswald's form had been thrown away. Likewise, there are no official records to show that Oswald signed for the .38 caliber pistol that reportedly was shipped to him by Railway Express.

In fact, according to Warren Commission documents, Oswald told Captain Will Fritz "he had bought [the pistol] several months before in Fort Worth, Texas."

It should also be noted that Kennedy's death certificate, the Warren Commission, the House Select Committee on Assassinations and the *Journal of the American Medical Association* article all claimed Kennedy was killed by bullets from a "high-powered" or "high-velocity" rifle. Yet, the Warren Commission stated the 6.5 mm Carcano only reached a velocity of less than 1,779 feet per second while a high-velocity rifle exceeds 2,000 feet per second. Based on this discrepancy, the Oswald rifle could not be the death weapon.

But the strongest evidence that the Carcano was not the assassination weapon came from Ronald Simmons, chief of the Infantry Weapons Evaluation Branch of the Ballistics Research Laboratory of the Department of the Army, who headed the team evaluating the rifle. During testimony to the Warren Commission, Simmons was asked if his team had experienced any difficulties sighting in the rifle. He replied, "Well, they could not sight the weapon in using the telescope, and no attempt was made to sight it in using the iron sight. We did adjust the telescopic sight by the addition of two shims, one which tended to adjust the azimuth and one which adjusted an elevation."

Moments later, the Warren Commission attorney stated, "For the record, Mr. Chairman, these shims were given to me by the FBI who told me that they removed them from the weapon after they had been placed there by Mr. Simmons's laboratory." There were, in fact, three metal shims, which the Warren Commission dutifully depicted in Commission Exhibits 567, 577, and 578.

What an astounding admission—the Oswald rifle needed three metal shims placed under the telescopic sight before the Army laboratory could test its accuracy. And this evidence was known to both the FBI and the Warren Commission, but never adequately relayed to the media or the public.

The experts also indicated that the telescopic sight was adjusted for a left-handed shooter, yet both Oswald's wife and his brother told the Commission Oswald was right-handed. Robert Oswald said, "I would say without qualification . . . he [Lee] was instinctively a right-handed person."

Added to the inferior quality and the inaccuracy of the rifle, recall Oswald's well-documented inability to achieve marksmanship standards while in the Marines.

The Warren Commission stated authoritatively, "The number C2766 is the serial number. This rifle is the only one of its type bearing that serial number." Yet an FBI report dated April 30, 1964, and signed by J. Edgar Hoover stated:

> The Mannlicher-Carcano rifle was manufactured in Italy from 1891 until 1941; however, in the 1930's Mussolini ordered all arms factories to manufacture the Mannlicher-Carcano rifle. Since many concerns were manufacturing the same weapon, the same serial number appears on weapons manufactured by more than one concern. Some bear a letter prefix and some do not.

Plainly, there could be more Carcanos around with the serial number C2766—a fact that further weakens the case against Oswald.

Without going into minute details, it should be noted that the sling on Oswald's rifle was not a standard rifle sling but instead seemed to come from a musical instrument or a camera carrying strap. No attempt was made to determine where this sling came from, although Commission experts, after explaining that the purpose of such a strap is to steady the aim, stated, "The sling on the rifle was too short to use in the normal way."

Despite two massive federal investigations, not one bit of evidence has been brought forward as to where or when Oswald might have purchased ammunition or the ammunition clip for the rifle. Bear in mind that no gun oil or other cleaning materials, including ammunition, were found in Oswald's belongings.

Another important piece of evidence involved a paraffin test made on Oswald the day of the assassination. The results of this test presented evidence that he may not have fired a rifle that day, yet these results were downplayed and even suppressed by the federal authorities.

In this test, layers of paraffin are applied to a suspect's skin and the sticky, warm wax opens the pores and then picks up any foreign material that may be present on the skin. When the wax cools, it forms a hard cast that is treated with chemicals that turn blue if nitrates are present. The idea is that the skin of someone who has recently fired a weapon will bear traces of nitrates. While the presence of nitrates is not conclusive evidence that a gun was fired—tobacco, urine, cosmetics, matches, soil, and certain drugs can cause a positive reaction—the absence of nitrates is compelling evidence that the person has not fired a weapon.

Oswald's hands both reacted positively to the paraffin test, indicating the presence of nitrates but no gunpowder. A cast of his right cheek showed no reaction for either. Any competent defense attorney would have pointed to this test as evidence that his client had not fired a rifle.

However, in its report the Warren Commission termed this routine police test "completely unreliable," adding that an FBI agent fired three rounds through the Oswald rifle in rapid succession and tested negative on both his hands and face afterward.

The odd part of this issue is that in publishing the Dallas police evidence sheet, the Commission deleted reference to the paraffin test at the bottom of the page. Why obscure this test result, which appeared to present evidence of Oswald's innocence, if the test can be demonstrated to be faulty or unreliable?

In all criminal cases, police always hope for that most important piece of evidence linking the crime to the suspect—a fingerprint.

An Incriminating Palm Print

The sole piece of hard evidence linking Oswald to the Carcano rifle was a palm print reportedly found on the underside of the gun's barrel when disassembled.

It seems strong evidence until inspected closely. To begin with, the palm print would never have been admitted as evidence in any courtroom trial because it lacked a chain of evidence—the unquestioned and documented path from discovery to presentation in court.

According to Dallas police lieutenant John Carl Day, he discovered the palm print shortly before turning the rifle over to the FBI about midnight on November 22, 1963. Yet, he mentioned it to no one and there is no record of his discovery. Day even admitted to the Warren Commission that "it was his customary practice to photograph fingerprints in most instances prior to lifting them." Yet this was not done.

About midnight, the rifle was given to FBI agent Vincent Drain, who flew with the gun to Washington in an Air Force plane.

Early on November 23, 1963, the rifle was turned over to the FBI laboratory and examined for fingerprints. A report made that day and signed by J. Edgar Hoover reported, "No latent prints of value were developed on Oswald's revolver, the cartridges cases, the unfired cartridge, the clip in the rifle or the inner parts of the rifle."

The FBI had no indication of any useful print. Before the Warren Commission, FBI expert Sebastian Latona stated, "We had no personal knowledge of any palm print having been developed on the rifle. . . . Evidently the lifting had been so complete that there was nothing left to show any marking on the gun itself as to the existence of such—even an attempt on the part of anyone to process the rifle."

On the morning of November 24, Oswald was killed in the basement of the Dallas police station and that afternoon the rifle was flown back to Dallas.

On Monday, following a competent autopsy, Oswald's body was lying in Miller Funeral Home in Fort Worth when, according to the *Fort Worth Press*, "An FBI team, with a camera and a crime lab kit, spent a long time in the morgue." Miller Funeral Home director Paul Groody told this author that the FBI fingerprinted

Oswald's corpse. Groody complained, "I had a heck of time getting the black finger-print ink off of [Oswald's] hands in time for burial."

In 1978, FBI agent Harrison confirmed to researcher Gary Mack that he, along with Agent Drain, had personally driven the "Oswald" rifle to the Miller Funeral Home. Harrison said at the time he understood Drain intended to place Oswald's palm print on the rifle "for comparison purposes."

Oswald had been fingerprinted three times while in Dallas police custody. There has been no explanation for this postmortem fingerprinting.

Later that Monday, while talking to reporters, District Attorney Wade casually mentioned, "Let's see . . . his fingerprints were found on the gun. Have I said that?" It was the first mention of any prints being found. By Monday evening, the news was all over the media. The *Dallas Times Herald* proclaimed: OSWALD'S PRINTS REVEALED ON RIFLE KILLING KENNEDY.

Asked about the strongest evidence of Oswald's guilt, Wade responded, "If I had to single out any one thing, it would be the fingerprints found on the rifle and the book cartons which [Oswald] used to prop the weapon on." On November 26, the rifle was again sent to Washington. But the incriminating palm print did not arrive at the FBI lab until November 29, three days after all other Dallas police evidence had been officially turned over to the bureau.

By this time, FBI officials were able to confirm that the palm print matched that of Lee Harvey Oswald.

Day continued to maintain he found the print and failed to mention it, photo-graph it, or send it to the FBI quickly because he believed that "sufficient traces of the print had been left on the rifle barrel." Day told author Henry Hurt that he spe-cifically pointed out the print to Agent Drain when he gave him the rifle. However, Drain denied this. According to Hurt, Drain told him, "I just don't believe there ever was a print. . . . All I can figure is that it was some sort of cushion, because they were getting a lot of heat by Sunday night. You could take the print off Oswald's [arrest] card and put it on the rifle. Something like that happened."

Considering the movements of the rifle, some researchers believe Oswald's dead hand was placed directly on the rifle barrel. Others believe Oswald's palm print was taken either from jail records or the Depository and superimposed over marks from the rifle barrel.

No serious researcher today believes that Oswald's palm print was legitimately lifted from the rifle barrel on November 22, 1963. Even the Warren Commission found this piece of evidence hard to swallow. An internal FBI memorandum made public only in 1978 disclosed that on August 28, 1964:

> [Warren Commission general counsel J. Lee] Rankin advised because of the circumstances that now exist there was a serious question in the minds of the commission as to whether or not the palm impression that has been obtained from the Dallas Police Department is a legitimate latent palm

impression removed from the rifle barrel or whether it was obtained from some other source and that for this reason this matter needs to be resolved.

Commission fingerprint experts admitted, "It was not possible to estimate the time which elapsed between the placing of the print on the rifle and the date of the lift." The FBI then attempted to have Lieutenant Day certify a statement concerning his lifting of the palm print, but Day declined to sign it. One FBI fingerprint expert declined to answer researchers who merely asked if he could determine whether a fingerprint came from living or dead flesh.

The Commission apparently made no effort to resolve the matter. It instead presented the belated palm print as strong evidence of Oswald's guilt. Like so much of the "hard" evidence in this case, the closer one looks, the softer it becomes.

After considering the rifle, the empty shells, and the palm print, one must again consider the "hero of the Warren Commission"—Commission Exhibit 399, the "magic bullet."

The discovery of Commission Exhibit 399 has been dealt with earlier. Now consider the highly technical studies of this bullet and other bullet fragments involved in the assassination.

The Commission attempted to duplicate the feat of Commission Exhibit 399—passing through seven layers of skin and muscle, striking bones in two male adults, and emerging in near-perfect condition—but with no success. Similar ammunition fired into goat carcasses, human bodies, and gelatin blocks all showed more deformity than Commission Exhibit 399.

In an attempt to explain away the unscathed condition of this bullet, members of the forensic pathology panel of the House Select Committee on Assassinations argued that other bullets had done similar damage and remained in pristine condition.

However, one member of the panel, Dr. Cyril Wecht, challenged the group to produce even one single bullet that had broken two human bones and remained unchanged. The forensics panel declined. Dr. Wecht concluded, "It is clear to me that their reluctance was based upon their knowledge that such studies would further destroy the single-bullet theory."

Since neither the Warren Commission nor the House Select Committee on Assassinations was able to convincingly prove the feat ascribed to Commission Exhibit 399, the emission spectrography tests assume more importance. These spectrographic tests are a scientific means of determining whether the various bits of bullet metal taken from both Kennedy and Connally came from the same bullet. These tests could have provided what is missing from all Kennedy assassination investigations—clear, irrefutable proof that metal found in the victims could be traced to Commission Exhibit 399. The tests failed to do this and the handling of this evidence raised a great deal of suspicion toward federal authorities.

Under such testing it is a simple matter to determine whether two bits of metal have the same percentage of basic elements, such as lead, copper, and antimony. It is much more difficult to prove that such bits are from the same source.

Concerning the tests, the Warren Commission chose not to ask one single question of the spectrographic expert who conducted the tests. They were content to simply report that several bullet fragments were "similar in metallic composition," which proved nothing.

In the years following the assassination, researcher Harold Weisberg sought unsuccessfully to obtain the spectrographic test results from the US government. Government attorneys argued that revealing the results was not in the "national interest," although they would not explain why.

Then in 1973, a batch of Warren Commission documents were released to the public that contained letters from FBI director J. Edgar Hoover. In these, Hoover reported that composition of the fragments was "similar" and "that no significant differences were found."

The fact that differences—no matter how "significant"—were found means they are not from the same source.

The real significance in this matter is that the results of these spectrographic tests have been kept from the public all these years. Obviously, if the tests proved conclusively that the fragments and Commission Exhibit 399 all came from the same ammunition, the case against Oswald would have been strengthened considerably. In fact, the opposite occurred. And by concealing the test results, the Commission raised further suspicion about government handling of the case.

Unreported in the Commission's report or volumes was an account of even further scientific testing, this time using neutron activation analysis, a sophisticated method of determining differences in composition by bombarding the test object with radiation.

In referring to this test in a letter made public in 1973, Hoover wrote, "While minor variations in composition were found by this method, these were not considered to be sufficient to permit positively differentiating among the larger bullet fragments and thus positively determining from which of the larger bullet fragments any given small fragment may have come."

This wording is suspiciously deceptive, since any difference in composition is evidence that the fragments are not from the same ammunition.

Faced with scientific evidence that Kennedy and Connally were not struck by the same bullet, the House Select Committee on Assassinations decided to conduct its own tests. But researchers' hopes for a final, clear determination on this matter dimmed with the committee's selection of Dr. Vincent P. Guinn to conduct the tests. Guinn admitted he had been an informal consultant to the FBI even prior to the Kennedy assassination. And predictably, Guinn concluded that it was "highly probable" that fragments taken from Connally's wrist came from Commission Exhibit 399.

This seemed to be the strong, clear evidence researchers had been looking for, even though it appeared to support the single-bullet theory. Guinn's conclusions were warmly embraced by the House committee. But it was later learned that the wrist fragments originally tested in 1964 were missing. And Guinn admitted publicly that the fragments he tested were not the originals from the National Archives.

Author Henry Hurt quoted Guinn as admitting that fragments from Commission Exhibit 399 could have been substituted for the missing fragments: "Possibly they would take a bullet, take out a few little pieces and put it in a container, and say, 'This is what came out of Connally's wrist.' And naturally if you compare it with CE 399, it will look alike. . . . I have no control over these things."

Guinn also reported that he had examples of the ammunition from the four production runs in 1954 made at Western Cartridge Company, manufacturers of the Mannlicher-Carcano bullets. "Reportedly those are the only lots they ever produced, and we have boxes from each of those lots," Guinn told the committee.

If this was indeed the only ammunition ever produced, the results of Guinn's tests gain credibility. However, a Warren Commission document dealing with an interview of a Western Cartridge representative revealed this comment:

> The Western Cartridge Company . . . manufactured a quantity of 6.5 . . . Mannlicher-Carcano ammunition for the Italian government during World War II. At the end of the war the Italian Carcano rifle, and no telling how much of this type of ammunition, was sold to United States gun brokers and dealers and subsequently was distributed by direct sales to wholesalers, retailers and individual purchasers.

If the ammunition supposedly used in the Oswald rifle came from this World War II batch, then Dr. Guinn tested the wrong bullets. This is another example of how seemingly indisputable evidence in the assassination diminishes upon closer examination.

Without arguing the technical aspects of Dr. Guinn's analysis, it should be pointed out that he failed to recall or report on his prior governmental connections with the JFK case. House Select Committee on Assassinations subcommittee member Floyd J. Fithian asked:

> Dr. Guinn, this is not meant to be an embarrassing question, but I think I must ask it. Mr. Chairman, a recent article in the *New York Times* magazine stated that you had worked for the Warren Commission and therefore, your conclusions for this committee would be implicitly biased. Did you ever work for the Warren Commission or work for the FBI in connection with the analysis of these evidence samples?

Dr. Guinn responded:

> Neither one. I think Mr. Wolf called my attention to the existence of this article, which I haven't seen, and I don't know where they got their mis-

information, but I never did anything for the Warren Commission, and although I know people in the FBI, I have never done any work for them.

In reality, it seems Dr. Guinn had a long record of working to prove Oswald's guilt. On August 28, 1964, the *New York Times* reported:

The use of radioactivity in criminology may determine whether Lee Harvey Oswald killed President Kennedy, a San Diego, Calif., chemist said today. Dr. Vincent P. Guinn, head of the activation analysis program of the General Atomic division of General Dynamics Corporation, has been working on the problem with the Federal Bureau of Investigation. Dr. Guinn said he was working even then with radioactive analysis but could not make public his findings until released by the Warren Commission.

Sherry Fiester, a retired certified senior crime scene analyst with more than twenty-five years' experience, studied Guinn's work and characterized it as "grossly flawed." She noted, "Scientific testing in 2006 and 2007 indicate the available evidence is consistent with between two and five bullets being fired in Dealey Plaza at the time of the assassination. This number of bullets would be consistent with more than one shooter and indicates the single-gunman theory can't be supported by science."

Another major piece of evidence against Oswald was a brown paper bag reportedly discovered in the Texas School Book Depository on the afternoon of the assassination—although it is not depicted in any of the crime scene photographs. The Warren Commission claimed Oswald used the bag to transport the Carcano rifle from a home in Irving, Texas, to the Depository on the morning of November 22, 1963.

If this bag indeed belonged to Oswald and if it could be traced to the Depository, it becomes strong evidence of Oswald's guilt. But again, upon closer inspection, this piece of evidence becomes highly questionable. First, while the Oswald rifle was found to be well oiled, there is absolutely no trace of gun oil on the paper bag. Second, federal authorities claimed to have found cloth fibers on the bag that matched those of a blanket used to wrap the rifle at the Irving home. However, a Dallas police photograph of assassination evidence shows the bag touching the blanket, which thus could have produced the incriminating fiber evidence. To add credence to this idea, the FBI found no traces of paper bag particles on the rifle.

When the Dallas evidence was shipped to the FBI laboratory early on November 23, there was no mention of the paper bag. Instead, Dallas FBI agent in charge J. Gordon Shanklin mentioned the blanket, which he suggested was used to carry the rifle into the Depository.

Both Wesley Frazier and his sister, Linnie Mae Randle, testified that Oswald took a paper bag to work with him on the morning of the assassination. However, both said they did not believe the bag they saw was like the one the Warren

Commission showed them. Frazier said Oswald told him the bag contained curtain rods for his room in Dallas. Frazier also said Oswald carried the package into the Depository tucked under his arm, with one end cupped in his hand and the other under his armpit.

Since the disassembled rifle measured thirty-five inches long, it would have been impossible for someone of Oswald's height to carry it in this position. Jack Dougherty, a Depository employee who saw Oswald arrive for work, said he had seen no bag.

Yet the paper bag was a necessary piece of evidence, for if Oswald did not carry the rifle into the Depository on November 22, then it must have gotten there in some other manner. This possibility opened too many areas of investigation. But if Oswald fashioned the bag from wrapping paper at the Depository—as the Warren Commission concluded—how did he get it to the Irving home, where he spent the night before the assassination?

Frazier, who drove Oswald to Irving, repeatedly said Oswald had no package with him at that time. The Commission decided Oswald must have hidden the paper bag in his jacket, although there was no reason to do so and despite the discomfort and rustling noise sure to have been made by a forty-two-inch-by-eighteen-inch folded paper bag.

This whole issue is further clouded by a duplicate FBI report that claims two opposite facts concerning the paper bag. In a November 29, 1963, report numbered Dallas 89-43 released with other FBI documents in 1968, agent Vincent Drain wrote, "This paper was examined by the FBI laboratory and found to have the same observable characteristics as the brown paper bag shaped like a gun case which was found near the scene of the shooting on the sixth floor of the Texas School Book Depository building."

In 1980, researcher Gary Shaw discovered what appeared to be this same FBI report in the National Archives. It bore the same dates and the same identification number—Dallas 89-43.

However, in this version of Drain's report, it stated, "This paper was examined by the FBI laboratory and found not to be identical with the paper gun case found at the scene of the shooting."

When pressed to explain the two opposite versions of the same report, William Baker, then the FBI's assistant director of the Office of Congressional and Public Affairs, told researcher Edgar F. Tatro the version that states Depository paper and the paper bag are not the same was "inaccurate." Baker said the inaccuracy in Drain's original report was caught at FBI headquarters and the Dallas office was instructed to "make corrections at that time." He added that the "inaccurate" report was mistakenly passed along to the Warren Commission. Baker concluded, "We hope the above explanation resolves the problem."

Far from resolving the problem of identical FBI reports that state opposite facts, this incident raises the question of how many other assassination documents stated one thing and were subsequently "revised." And if there do exist "revised" documents in federal files, how would anyone know unless the originals accidentally slip out, as appeared to have happened in this case?

Considering all of the above and considering that not one of the lawmen who searched the Depository mentioned finding the bag in their testimony, the evidence of the paper bag must be viewed skeptically. Recall the two days that all assassination evidence was in the hands of the FBI unbeknownst to the media and public.

Two other observations should be made concerning primary pieces of evidence— the presidential limousine and the rifle.

Even while the limousine was parked at the emergency-room door of Parkland Hospital, federal agents and even Dallas police apparently mopped up blood, picked up bullet fragments, and otherwise tampered with this important evidence, contrary to basic crime scene protection procedures in place even at that time. White House photographer Cecil Stroughton noticed agents at the limousine. The trunk was open and the plastic top was being placed on the car. He recalled a man washing the seat "with a cloth and he had a bucket."

Within forty-eight hours the limousine was shipped to the manufacturer Hess & Eisenhardt and completely dismantled, thus destroying any important bloodstains, bullet holes, or more bullet fragments that could have shed light on the assassination. Although government agents examined the car the day after the assassination, there is no evidence that members of the Warren Commission closely studied this important piece of evidence, including photographs of a controversial bullet or fragment strike on the windshield.

And although the Carcano was checked for fingerprints, apparently it was never given the simple test by Dallas police or federal authorities to determine whether it had been recently fired. This normal testing might have proved conclusively whether the rifle had been used in the assassination. Researchers view the failure to conduct such a test as strong evidence of fabrication in the case against Oswald.

Other vital evidence was destroyed. After receiving Governor Connally's blood-stained clothing at Parkland Hospital, congressman Henry Gonzalez kept this potential evidence in a closet in his Washington office. Several months later, while Gonzalez was home in Texas, Clifton Carter, an aide to Lyndon Johnson, notified a Gonzalez secretary that the Secret Service was coming to pick up Connally's clothing.

Sometime later, this clothing was presented as evidence to the Warren Commission. But by this time, it had been cleaned and pressed, thereby eliminating metal traces at the bullet holes that could have been studied to determine the type of ammunition and the direction of shots.

It is interesting that it was Gonzalez who formally called for a reopening of the assassination investigation in 1975, which led to the forming of the House Select Committee on Assassinations.

But the one piece of evidence that did more than all others to convict Oswald as the assassin in the minds of the American public was the famous backyard photographs depicting Oswald with a rifle and a communist publication.

Questionable Backyard Photos

Dallas police claimed to have discovered two prints and one negative of pictures showing Lee Harvey Oswald standing in his backyard wearing a holstered pistol and holding a rifle and some communist literature. According to police reports, these photos were found among Oswald's possessions in the garage of the Paine home in Irving, Texas, on Saturday, November 23, 1963, although a search the day before failed to turn up such photos.

One of these photos became the cover of the February 21, 1964, issue of *Life* magazine. This now-famous issue, published seven months before the Warren Commission issued its verdict, convicted the suspect by proclaiming, "Lee Oswald with the weapons he used to kill President Kennedy and Officer Tippit."

The Warren Commission heard from Oswald's accommodating wife, Marina, that she had taken the snapshots with a handheld Imperial Reflex camera at her husband's insistence. Based on Marina's testimony and the order form for Oswald's rifle, the Commission pinpointed the date as March 31, 1963. She said she took one shot, then handed the camera back to Oswald, who advanced the film and handed it back for her to take another picture.

The Commission asserted that the rifle in the picture is the same rifle found on the sixth floor of the Texas School Book Depository.

Yet when shown the photographs by Dallas police, captain Will Fritz said Oswald made the following comments:

> He said the picture was not his, that the face was his face, but that this picture had been made by someone superimposing his face, the other part of the picture was not him at all and that he had never seen the picture before. . . . He told me that he understood photography real well, and that in time, he would be able to show that it was not his picture, and that it had been made by someone else.

Of course, Oswald never got the opportunity to explain the backyard photos. But various researchers have spent years studying this incriminating evidence, and today most are convinced Oswald was truthful about the pictures' being fabricated.

To begin with, it appears there were actually four backyard pictures. One was described by Marguerite Oswald as depicting her son holding a rifle above his head with both hands. She was shown this photo by Marina at the Paines' Irving home the night of the assassination. On Marguerite's insistence, the incriminating photo was burned and flushed down a toilet.

In 1976 the Senate Intelligence Committee discovered yet a fourth backyard photo in the hands of the widow of a Dallas policeman. Mrs. Roscoe White said her husband, who worked in the Dallas photographic lab, once told her the picture would be very valuable someday. In this heretofore unknown version of the backyard photo, Oswald is depicted holding the rifle in his left hand and the communist material in his right. This is the same pose Dallas police used in reenacting the photo for the Warren Commission—strong evidence that authorities were aware of the suppressed picture long before it became known to the public.

Photo experts told the House Select Committee on Assassinations that the most famous backyard picture—the one used on the cover of *Life* magazine—was obviously made from the original negative while in the hands of Dallas authorities. Yet this negative was never accounted for by the Dallas police. The committee noted, "There is no official record explaining why the Dallas Police Department failed to give the Warren Commission the other original negative."

To further cloud this issue, two Dallas commercial photographic processors have told this author they saw copies of the backyard photo the night of the assassination—more than twelve hours before they were reported found in the Paine garage.

Robert Hester, who was called from home on November 22, 1963, to help process assassination-related photographs for the FBI and Dallas police at National Photo, said he saw an FBI agent with a color transparency of one of these pictures and that one of the backyard photos he processed showed no figure in the picture. Hester's claim was corroborated by his wife, Patricia, who also helped process film on the day of the assassination.

There is also considerable question regarding the camera reportedly used to make these photographs. Oswald's brother Robert claimed to have obtained the camera from the Paine home on December 8, 1963. He said he did not mention it to authorities because he didn't realize anyone would be interested.

Robert was only told the camera belonged to his brother by Ruth Paine and the FBI did not receive the camera until February 24, 1964. About that time, Marina was shown two cameras but failed to identify either as belonging to her husband.

When the government got the camera, it was inoperable. FBI photographic expert Lyndal L. Shaneyfelt told the Warren Commission, "In order to be able to make a photograph with the camera, I had to make slight repairs to the shutter lever, which had been bent. I straightened it and cleaned the lens in order to remove the dirt which had accumulated."

Finally, in June 1964, Marina identified the camera as the one she used to take the photographs. Marina, who originally claimed to have taken only one picture, revised this statement in her testimony to the commission in February 1964. She said, "I had even forgotten that I had taken two photographs. I thought there was only one. I thought there were two identical pictures, but they turned out to be two different poses."

She, of course, never mentioned the other two photographs. But then this incident was not the only time Marina's testimony reflected inconsistencies and rehearsal.

An objective viewing of the three available backyard photographs reveals internal problems aplenty. Although all three pictures were reportedly taken with a handheld camera, the background of all three is identical when brought to the same size. That is, though cropped differently in the three photos, the elements of the background—shadows, leaves, branches, stairs, etc.—are exactly identical. This sameness of background could possibly be produced with a stationary camera on a heavy tripod but is impossible with a handheld camera.

The V-shaped shadow under Oswald's nose remains the same in all three pictures, although his head is tilted in different directions.

And the photos all show a discernible line marking a break in the print's emulsion across Oswald's face just above a flat, broad chin. In Dallas police photos, it is clear that Oswald had a sharply pointed, cleft chin.

And when all three photos are brought to the same size and placed on top of each other as transparencies, nothing matches except the face of Lee Harvey Oswald

Oswald's assessment that the photos are superimposed fakes has been confirmed by two foreign authorities. In 1977, Major John Pickard, commander of the photographic department at the Canadian Defense Department, made these statements after studying the backyard pictures:

> The pictures have the earmarks of being faked. The shadows fall in conflicting directions. The shadow of Oswald's nose falls in one direction and that of his body in another. The photos were shot from a slightly different angle, a different distance, with the gun in a different hand. So, if one photo is laid on top of another, nothing could match exactly. Yet, impossibly, while one body is bigger, in the other the heads match perfectly, bearing out Oswald's charge that his head was pasted on an incriminating photograph.

Author and British Broadcasting Corporation investigative reporter Anthony Summers had the photos studied by retired detective superintendent Malcolm Thompson, a past president of the Institute of Incorporated Photographers in England. Thompson said he detected retouching in the photos around the area of Oswald's head and on the butt of the rifle. He also noted inconsistencies in the location of shadows and the different chin on Oswald. Thompson stated, "One can only conclude that Oswald's head has been stuck on to a chin which is not Oswald's chin. . . . My opinion is that those photographs are faked. . . . I consider the pictures to be the result of a montage."

However, neither Pickard nor Thompson studied the original photos. The Photographic Evidence Panel of the House Select Committee on Assassinations, which did study the originals, concluded in 1978 that it could find no evidence of fakery in the backyard photos.

This conclusion rested primarily on studies that showed markings on the edges of the negative of one of the original photographs were identical to markings on other photographs made by the Imperial Reflex camera. This ballistics-type evidence convinced the panel that the photos must be genuine.

However, Texas graphics expert Jack White pointed out that if a knowledgeable person wanted to fake the backyard pictures, it would have been a simple matter to produce a high-quality montage photograph using one backyard scene, a figure with rifle and papers, and a head shot of Oswald, which then could be photocopied using the Imperial Reflex camera. This procedure would produce a faked backyard photo that could be proven to have come from the camera traced to Oswald. Another method to achieve the same results, according to White, would be to make an exposure through the Imperial Reflex camera that would include the markings on the edge but nothing else. Then, when the composite photo is combined with this, the markings become part of the negative.

Asked to study the sameness of the different photos' backgrounds, the House committee's experts said they measured the distances between certain objects in the pictures—such as wooden fence posts—and determined some differences in distance, indicating that the photos were indeed separate shots.

White, who died in 2012, argued that these differences were simply the result of "keystoning" or tilting the easel on which the photograph was exposed in an enlarger. He said he, too, had been concerned with what appeared to be differences in the photos but discovered that by simply tilting the photographic print in an enlarger's easel, the backgrounds of the supposedly separate pictures overlapped and matched perfectly.

Furthermore, in recent years White discovered other problems with the backyard photos. In one picture, the tips of Oswald's fingers appear to be missing as does one end of the rifle's telescopic sight. White claimed this was due to sloppy airbrushing on the part of whoever faked the picture. In one photo, the figure can be seen to be wearing a large ring on his right hand, yet the ring is missing in the other photos.

Sameness of backgrounds and Oswald's face, conflicting shadows and distances, loss of portions of the photos—again, a vital piece of evidence remains in "controversy" despite the studied opinions of experts and inconsistencies that can be viewed by any layperson.

Yet the federal government continues to vouch for the authenticity of the incriminating photos. The reason for this steadfast support may have been voiced by House committee chief counsel Robert Blakey, who stated, "If [the backyard photographs] are invalid, how they were produced poses far-reaching questions in the area of conspiracy, for they evince a degree of technical sophistication that would almost necessarily raise the possibility that [someone] conspired not only to kill the President, but to make Oswald a patsy."

Reenactment Problems

In light of the controversies surrounding the physical evidence attempting to link Lee Harvey Oswald to the assassination, the Warren Commission tried to strengthen the case against the ex-Marine through the use of reenactments.

However, at least two of the participants have questioned the results of these reenactments.

Chester Breneman, a surveyor who participated in two separate reenactments of the Kennedy assassination, said the studies proved that more than one man was involved in the shooting. Breneman, who went on to become county surveyor of

Eastland County, Texas, told this author in 1978 that distance and time figures the Warren Commission published were "at odds" with figures obtained in the reenactment staged for the FBI and Secret Service in 1964.

Height and distance figures altered by the federal government mean that all subsequent computer analyses based on such figures are erroneous and baseless.

Breneman's story was confirmed by Dallas County surveyor Robert West, who also participated in both reenactments. Both men were in West's office on the Monday following the assassination when a man entered. Breneman recalled:

> [He] said he was a special investigator for *Life* magazine. He asked if we would make an investigation down there [in Dealey Plaza] and see if any other bullets were fired and from which direction they came. They were aware at that time that something was haywire. . . . So, we went down there and roped the area off. I stood on the parapet where [Abraham] Zapruder stood and took those pictures. *They had still pictures of all the frames of Zapruder's film.* [Author's emphasis—Reportedly *Life* did not take possession of the Zapruder film until that same day and evidence indicates the film was actually processed and manipulated by the CIA in New York state.]

Breneman and West took measurements of the plaza and distances from the Texas School Book Depository and matched everything against the Zapruder stills.

Later that day, Breneman accompanied *Life*'s investigators to the thirteenth floor of Dallas's Adolphus Hotel, where they were headquartered. He said at that time everybody involved agreed that no one man could have done all the shooting.

Breneman said the magazine investigators also had obtained a Carcano rifle and attempted to work the bolt in the time frame attributed to Oswald. Breneman, a former Marine medal winner for marksmanship, said he, too, worked the rifle's bolt for hours. He said, "We came to the conclusion that it couldn't be done in the time limit they were trying to get me down to."

He also recounted a strange incident that occurred during his time with the magazine people. "This [one] man told me, 'My life isn't worth a plug nickel on this investigation.' Then he pulled his shirt back and showed me this bulletproof vest. I thought that was a little odd."

Breneman again was visiting his friend West on May 31, 1964, when the FBI and Secret Service reenacted the assassination for the Warren Commission. Both surveyors participated in the tests. Breneman recalled:

> We again measured distances and elevations by matching the frames of the Zapruder film. We examined a bullet mark on the curb on the south side of [Elm] street. This part of the curb was replaced shortly after the assassination. Also, right after the assassination, they were mentioning a [highway] sign which had a stress mark from a bullet on it. It's my understanding that

this particular sign was quickly taken down and no one has been able to locate it.

During the May reenactment, Breneman said the FBI used a big Cadillac as a substitute for Kennedy's Lincoln Continental. "It was in no way like Kennedy's limousine," said Breneman.

West added, "That was one thing that was always funny to me. They brought this big old Cadillac down to use in the tests, but it was thirteen inches higher than Kennedy's car." Breneman agreed, "They were all crunched up in there, shoulder to shoulder. In that condition it could have been possible for one man to shoot two of them."

West said his study showed that one of the alleged shots from the Depository followed a path straight through a leafy tree. "If he shot through a hole in that tree, it was absolutely fantastic," commented West. Breneman concluded, "I wish to state that both investigations led us to believe beyond any doubt that there were two assassins. *Life* magazine's special investigators believed this to be true. The Secret Service would not say. But at the time, that seemed to be the reason we were there and we felt the Secret Service felt that way too."

After the Warren Commission published the figures from the government reenactment, Breneman and West were shocked to find that the figures did not match those they made at the time. Both Breneman and West retained copies of the Dealey Plaza reenactment figures.

Breneman said:

They [the figures] were at odds with our figures. After checking a few figures, I said, "That's enough for me," and I stopped reading. . . . For instance, on our map, we marked the spot corresponding to Zapruder film frame 171. The Warren Commission changed this to 166 before they used it in the report. The Warren Report shows a 210 where we show a 208. . . . It would seem to me that . . . these figures were changed just enough that the Warren Commission could come up with the idea that another shot came from the same direction as the first. But all I have been concerned with is, did another shot come from another direction? I know danged well it did.

Neither Breneman nor West—the actual surveyors used for the government's reenactment studies—was asked to testify to the Warren Commission. Further, the Commission declined to publish the map Breneman and West drew, claiming it was inaccurate.

This map indicates a bullet hit on the south curb of Elm Street. Breneman said, "We were told not to study those bullet marks by the FBI."

Again, any meaningful search for the truth of the assassination was ended by altered figures and orders not to note extraneous bullet marks—all from federal authorities.

The Warren Commission

The federal government, led by president Lyndon Johnson, began to assert itself immediately following Kennedy's death. Against normal procedure of that time, all evidence was removed from Dallas that night and sent to FBI headquarters in Washington.

The day after the assassination, despite tremendous confusion in Dallas and elsewhere, FBI director J. Edgar Hoover forwarded to Johnson a preliminary report supporting the idea of Lee Harvey Oswald's sole guilt. At this time, only selected FBI officials had seen all the evidence and the plausible suspicion of fabrication and substitution grew.

Following the death of the accused assassin on November 24, calls increased for an investigation independent from that of the Dallas police, who in many circles were being held responsible for Oswald's death.

That same day, Hoover talked with Johnson aide Walter Jenkins, stating, "The thing I am concerned about, and so is [deputy attorney general Nicholas D.] Katzenbach, is having something issued so we can convince the public that Oswald is the real assassin. Mr. Katzenbach thinks that the President might appoint a Presidential Commission of three outstanding citizens to make a determination."

On November 25, President Johnson ordered his friend Hoover to prepare a detailed report on the circumstances surrounding Kennedy's death. The news media were already reporting leaks from the bureau, including, "Rumors that will be spiked by the [FBI] report . . . is one that there was a conspiracy involved, and another one that shots fired at Kennedy came from different guns."

That same day, Katzenbach wrote a memo to Johnson aide Bill Moyers and outlined his thoughts on an assassination investigation:

> It is important that all of the facts surrounding President Kennedy's assassination be made public in a way which will satisfy people in the United States and abroad. That all the facts have been told and that a statement to this effect be made now.
>
> 1. The public must be satisfied that Oswald was the assassin; that he did not have confederates who are still at large; that the evidence was such that he would have been convicted at trial.
>
> 2. Speculation about Oswald's motivation ought to be cut off, and we should have some basis for rebutting the thought that this was a communist conspiracy or (as the Iron Curtain press is saying) a right-wing conspiracy to blame it on the communists. Unfortunately the facts on Oswald seem about too pat—too obvious (Marxist, Cuba, Russian wife, etc.). The Dallas Police have put out statements on the communist conspiracy theory, and it was they who were in charge when he was shot and thus silenced.
>
> 3. The matter has been handled thus far with neither dignity nor conviction; facts are mixed with rumor and speculation. We can scarcely let the

world see us totally in the image of the Dallas Police when our President is murdered.

I think this objective may be satisfied and made public as soon as possible with the completion of a thorough FBI report on Oswald and the assassination. This may run into the difficulty of pointing to inconsistency between this report and statements by Dallas Police officials; but the reputation of the Bureau is such that it may do the whole job.

The only other step would be the appointment of a Presidential Commission of unimpeachable personnel to review and examine the evidence and announce its conclusions. This has both advantages and disadvantages. I think it can await publication of the FBI report and public reaction to it here and abroad.

Also on November 25, Texas attorney general Waggoner Carr announced he planned to conduct a court of inquiry concerning the deaths of both Kennedy and Oswald. Carr named two prominent Texas attorneys—Leon Jaworski (who went on to become the special Watergate prosecutor) and Dean Storey—as special counsel for the probe.

The next day, Senator Everett Dirksen announced that a Senate investigation of the assassination would be conducted by a special committee headed by senator James O. Eastland, chairman of the powerful Judiciary Committee. One Republican senator told newsmen, "Too many people are disturbed about the strange circumstances of the whole tragic affair." Not to be outdone by the Senate, the House of Representatives announced an attempt to create yet another investigative committee the next day.

The grief-stricken attorney general, Robert Kennedy, was never consulted about any of these attempts. But the next-ranking officials of the Justice Department— Deputy Attorney General Katzenbach and solicitor general Archibald Cox (also of Watergate fame)—met with Johnson's close friend attorney Abe Fortas, who had blocked the 1948 election investigation of Johnson by obtaining a court order from Supreme Court Justice Hugo Black.

These men, aided by Yale law professor Eugene Rostow, secretary of state Dean Rusk, and columnist Joseph Alsop—all members of the elitist Council on Foreign Relations—convinced President Johnson that the public could misinterpret his plan for a Texas investigation as an attempt to cover up the crimes in Johnson's home state. They argued a national commission headed by men of supposedly unimpeachable integrity was needed.

In explaining the formation of what came to be known as the Warren Commission, the *Dallas Morning News* commented, "Creation of the Presidential commission appeared certain to head off several congressional inquiries into the slaying of President Kennedy in Dallas a week ago."

The newspaper was absolutely correct. With the creation of the Warren Commission, not only had Johnson blocked any congressional investigations but, by the next week, Texas attorney general Carr had announced postponement of his state board of inquiry.

Despite massive media coverage of Oswald's arrest, his slaying, and the amount of evidence offered to the public by both Dallas and federal authorities, a Gallup poll taken the first week of December 1963 showed a majority of respondents—52 percent—continued to believe that Oswald had not acted alone.

Rumors were widespread in Texas that Johnson in some way had a hand in the assassination. A man of distinction and credibility was needed to stop such rumors. That man was chief justice Earl Warren.

The Reluctant Chairman

Earl Warren had no middle name. He once said, "My parents were too poor to afford the luxury of a middle name." Born to Scandinavian immigrants on March 19, 1891, Warren grew up in Los Angeles and nearby Bakersfield. By delivering newspapers, working for the railroad where his father was employed, and performing other odd jobs, Warren managed to save enough money to enroll at the University of California at Berkeley.

After receiving a bachelor of letters degree he entered law school. Warren graduated from the University of California Law School near the bottom of his class on May 14, 1914.

His law practice was interrupted by World War I. After enlisting as an infantry private, Warren was accepted for officer training and became a lieutenant. However, the Armistice was signed before Lieutenant Warren could leave the United States. After the war, Warren became an assistant attorney for the City of Oakland and later a member of the district attorney's staff. By the late 1920s, he had married Nina Palmquist Meyers and was elected as one of the nation's youngest district attorneys.

Building a reputation for honesty, hard work, and court convictions, Warren easily won reelection in 1930. As his family grew, so did his political reputation.

In the late 1930s, Warren campaigned for and won the office of California attorney general.

Almost immediately, Republican Warren was in a heated contest with the California Democratic governor Culbert Olson. Adding to their political differences were Olson's support of unions and his outspoken isolationism on the eve of World War II. This conflict reached a breaking point when, after Pearl Harbor, Olson proclaimed a state of emergency in California. As attorney general, Warren challenged his authority to do so and shortly afterward declared himself a candidate for governor.

In a surprising upset—Roosevelt and the Democrats were still in firm control nationally—Warren was elected governor of California in late 1942 by more than 342,000 votes.

In 1946, Warren handily won reelection as governor and began to look toward Washington. During the 1948 Republican National Convention, Warren reluctantly agreed to run for vice president with Thomas Dewey, the former governor of New York. He may have actually been relieved when the team was defeated by Truman in the greatest upset victory in American politics.

Still hoping for a national office, Warren announced he would seek the GOP presidential nomination in 1952. He was chagrined to quickly find himself pitted against the war hero Dwight "Ike" Eisenhower. Richard Nixon, who had signed a pledge to support Warren, nevertheless began to campaign for Eisenhower, hoping for the vice presidential nomination that he indeed later received. Eisenhower got the nomination and then the presidency. Nixon, who had been in public office for only six years, was the nation's number-two man.

Warren had been a strong contender and Nixon feared his clout in the next election. According to Warren biographer Jack Harrison Pollack:

> Nixon . . . badgered Eisenhower to find a suitable appointment for Governor Warren which would effectively separate him from his electoral constituency. The ideal solution presented itself in September 1953, when a vacancy arose on the Supreme Court after Chief Justice Fred Vinson suddenly died. Warren, who already had decided not to seek a fourth term as governor, was offered the prized seat and, to Nixon's delight, accepted.

New on the job and with the naïve Eisenhower years as a backdrop, Warren made initial decisions as chief justice that tended to support the status quo. But as he grew more comfortable in his position, his decisions began to reflect the progressive policies he advocated as California governor. It was under Warren's leadership that the Supreme Court—after years of foot dragging—finally ruled on the touchy desegregation issues raised by *Brown v. Board of Education of Topeka, Kansas*. Using private discussions as well as judicial conferences, where the justices took no positions, Warren was able to guide the court to its unanimous decision in favor of Brown, which virtually eliminated the old "Jim Crow" separate-but-equal segregation laws and paved the way for racial equality in the United States.

Brown was a landmark decision and one that caused archconservatives to begin a campaign of bitter attacks against the chief justice. IMPEACH EARL WARREN signs were commonplace throughout the South. Later court opinions dealing with the rights of accused persons and the persecution of suspected communists added further fuel to the fires of Warren's opponents.

In the squeaky-close election of 1960, the Republican Warren found himself voting for young John F. Kennedy, apparently because he could not bring himself to vote for the ever-ambitious Nixon. Displaying considerable foresight, Warren told a California friend, "Nixon is a bad man."

Warren and Kennedy voiced mutual respect for each other and the new president supported the Warren Court's progressive activism, even in such controversial cases as the June 1963 decision that outlawed compulsory prayer in public schools.

Six months later, Warren was asked to head a federal panel to decide who had killed Kennedy.

On November 29, the same day President Johnson announced his plans for a special commission, Warren was visited by deputy attorney general Nicholas

D. Katzenbach and solicitor general Archibald Cox (years later fired by Nixon as special Watergate prosecutor). Warren was told he was being asked to serve as chairman of the presidential commission. He declined, saying, "Please tell the President that I am sorry but I cannot properly undertake this assignment." Warren then explained that he did not feel it proper for a member of one branch of government to be employed by another branch.

Two hours later, Warren received a telephone call from President Johnson. The new president wasn't going to take no for an answer. He summoned Warren to his office. Dutifully, the chief justice reported to his president and received the famous "Johnson treatment"—a combination of back-patting and arm-twisting. According to Warren biographer Pollack:

> The President spoke gravely of the desperate need to restore public confidence. He hinted darkly at the possibility of dangerous international repercussions. He invoked Warren's sense of duty and patriotism. . . . By the end of the interview, he had succeeded in making Warren feel that to refuse the President would be a betrayal of a public trust. As a man-to-man persuader, Lyndon Johnson had no equal. His trump card was: "Mr. Chief Justice, you were a soldier in World War I. There's nothing you then did that compares with what you can do now for your country. As your Commander-in-Chief, I am ordering you back into service."

There may have been matters of more personal concern that Johnson transmitted to Warren. In an internal memorandum written on February 17, 1964, Warren Commission attorney Melvin Eisenberg mentioned what Warren told fellow commissioners regarding how he had been "pressured" by Johnson. Eisenberg wrote:

> The President stated that rumors of the most exaggerated kind were circulating in this country and overseas. . . . Some rumors went so far as attributing the assassination to a faction within the government wishing the presidency assumed by President Johnson. Others, if not quenched, could conceivably lead the country into a war. . . . No one could refuse to do something which might help prevent such a possibility. . . . He placed emphasis on the quenching of rumors and precluding further speculation.

Warren left the emotional meeting with tears in his eyes, perhaps thinking of what had become of the country he loved. He had reluctantly agreed to chair the commission. It is obvious that Warren's sense of patriotism outweighed his sense of legality in his acceptance of the Commission chairmanship.

Later that same afternoon, Johnson signed Executive Order 11130, creating the seven-man Warren Commission.

Commission members saw their work as having a dual purpose—one, to find the facts of the Kennedy assassination, the other, to calm public fears and suspicions both at home and abroad. Allen Dulles told author Edward Jay Epstein that since an atmosphere of rumors and suspicion interferes with the functioning of the government, especially abroad, one of the Commission's main tasks was to dispel rumors.

Other Commission members also thought it their duty to protect the US image as reflected in these public statements:

JOHN McCLOY: [It was of paramount importance to] show the world that America is not a banana republic, where a government can be changed by conspiracy.

JOHN COOPER: [An important purpose was] to lift the cloud of doubts that had been cast over American institutions.

When evidence presented to the Commission supported this duality of purpose, there was no problem. But since so much evidence contradicted the official assassination theory and called into question certain government institutions, it must be asked which purpose became paramount to the commissioners.

Johnson's old friend, lawyer Abe Fortas, and Katzenbach had prepared a list of seven prominent persons to serve on the new presidential commission. President Johnson promptly approved this list without change.

Headed by Chief Justice Warren, the Commission members were:

Representative Hale Boggs (D-Louisiana): The most vocal critic among Commission members, Boggs became frustrated with the panel's total reliance on the FBI for information. Speaking of the "single-bullet theory," Boggs once commented, "I had strong doubts about it." On April 1, 1971, House Majority Leader Boggs delivered a blistering attack on J. Edgar Hoover, charging that under his directorship the FBI had adopted "the tactics of the Soviet Union and Hitler's Gestapo." Boggs, who undoubtedly would have become Speaker of the House and a powerful ally in any reopening of the JFK assassination investigation, vanished on October 16, 1972, while on a military junket flight in Alaska. Despite a massive search, no trace of the airplane or of Boggs has ever been found.

Senator John Sherman Cooper (R-Kentucky): A former member of the Kentucky General Assembly and county judge, Cooper served with the US 3rd Army in Europe during World War II and helped reorganize the judicial system in Bavaria. He also was a former ambassador to India and Nepal in the mid-1950s. Like Boggs, Cooper later voiced dissatisfaction with the Commission's "single-bullet theory," stating he was "unconvinced."

Allen W. Dulles: Dulles had been fired as director of the Central Intelligence Agency by Kennedy following the ill-fated Bay of Pigs Invasion. Today it seems more than ironic that Dulles would have been selected to sit in judgment on Kennedy's death.

Dulles also was tightly connected to the military, not only because of his years with the CIA, but because of his service in World War II, which included arranging the surrender of German troops in Italy. It is now acknowledged that Dulles withheld CIA information from the Warren Commission, particularly concerning assassination plots between the agency and organized crime.

Representative Gerald Ford (R-Michigan): Former President Ford is now recognized as the FBI's "spy" on the Warren Commission. This is confirmed by a memo from Cartha DeLoach, a close aide to Director Hoover, in which he noted:

> I had a long talk this morning [December 12, 1963] with congressman Gerald R. "Jerry" Ford. . . . He asked that I come up and see him. . . . Ford indicated he would keep me thoroughly advised as to the activities of the Commission. He stated this would have to be on a confidential basis, however, he thought it should be done. He also asked if he could call me from time to time and straighten out questions in his mind concerning our investigation. I told him by all means he should do this. He reiterated that our relationship would, of course, remain confidential.

According to former New Orleans district attorney Jim Garrison, "Ford [also] enjoyed the reputation of being the CIA's best friend in the House of Representatives."

Ford's name as a member of the Warren Commission was recommended to President Johnson by Richard Nixon. A World War II Navy veteran, Ford became the Commission's most industrious member, hearing seventy out of the ninety-four witnesses who actually met with commissioners. He also profited from his time on the Commission. Ford had his first campaign manager and former Nixon presidential campaign field director John R. Stiles hired as his special assistant. Ford and Stiles went on to write *Portrait of the Assassin*, a book that presented selective evidence of Oswald's guilt. When their publisher found the book dull reading, Ford and Stiles spiced it up with rewritten transcripts of the January 27, 1964, Commission meeting where Oswald's possible connection to the FBI was discussed. The minutes of this meeting were classified top secret and remained closed to the public. During confirmation hearings before the Senate Judiciary Committee in 1973, Ford was asked specifically about his use of classified Warren Commission material in his book. Ford replied, "We did not use in that book any material other than the material that was in the 26 volumes of testimony and other exhibits that were subsequently made public and sold to the public generally."

When it was discovered that the January 27, 1974, meeting transcripts were still classified, Ford belatedly said, "I cannot help but apologize if the circumstances are such that there was this violation, but there certainly was no attempt to do it."

Despite being caught in perjury, Ford was dutifully confirmed by his old friends in Congress and sworn in as this nation's first appointed president. Six months later, Ford ordered the Commission material in question declassified.

John J. McCloy: As coordinator for the Kennedy administration's disarmaments activities since 1961, McCloy had a background for supporting Nazis, both before and after the war, and was a ranking member of the Council on Foreign Relations. He had been assistant secretary of war throughout World War II, military governor and high commissioner for Germany from 1949 to 1952, and president of the World Bank from 1947 to 1949. He also help build the US intelligence Establishment after the war. Despite his continued defense of the Warren Commission, McCloy himself voiced a prophetic skepticism of its work on December 5, 1963, stating, "The Commission is going to be criticized . . . no matter what we do, but I think we would be more criticized if we simply posed before the world as something that is evaluating Government agencies' reports, who themselves may be culpable."

In Commission arguments over the "single-bullet theory," it was McCloy who finally proposed that the evidence supporting this theory be called "persuasive," a term all members finally agreed upon.

Senator Richard B. Russell (D-Georgia): As chairman of the powerful Senate Armed Services Committee, Russell carried much clout on Capitol Hill, usually employed to further the aims of the Pentagon. His work on behalf of defense projects brought sizable government contracts to Georgia. Governor there from 1931 to 1933, Russell was elected to the Senate in 1933. Russell also sat on the watchdog Subcommittee on CIA Oversight. Russell, widely regarded as one of the most intelligent senators, became the first Warren Commission member to publicly question its conclusions. In a 1970 *Washington Post* article, Russell said he had come to believe that a criminal conspiracy had resulted in Kennedy's death. The senator even worked with assassination researcher Harold Weisberg in an effort to obtain Commission transcripts. In a court affidavit, Weisberg stated, "Privately Senator Russell told me that he was convinced that there were two areas in which Warren Commission members had been deceived by Federal agencies responsible for investigating the assassination of President Kennedy. These two areas were: (1) Oswald's background; and (2) the ballistics evidence."

As can be seen, all of the Commission members had long-standing ties to both the military and intelligence establishments of the United States. They also were men accustomed to the delicacy of dealing with highly sensitive political issues.

Each had received a copy of White House Executive Order 11130, which after naming the seven members of the President's Commission, stated the Commission's purpose was to "uncover all the facts concerning the assassination of President Kennedy and to determine if it was in any way directed or encouraged by unknown persons at home or abroad," and that "necessary expenses" of the Commission would be paid from the "Emergency Fund for the President."

In an effort to obtain fairness for her son, Marguerite Oswald wrote to Warren Commission general counsel J. Lee Rankin and even President Johnson, stating, "I [am] . . . imploring both in the name of justice and our American way of life to let my son Lee Harvey Oswald be represented by council [*sic*] so that all witnesses including my son's widow will be cross-examined."

Her request was denied.

New York attorney Mark Lane, who in 1959 helped found the Reform Democratic Movement, volunteered to represent Oswald.

His request was denied.

In 1964, Lane was retained by Marguerite Oswald to represent her son's interest but the Commission refused to accept him. Lane explained his persistence by writing:

> In all likelihood there does not exist a single American community where reside 12 men or women, good and true, who presume that Lee Harvey Oswald did not assassinate President Kennedy. No more savage comment can be made in reference to the breakdown of the Anglo-Saxon system of jurisprudence. At the very foundation of our judicial operation lies a cornerstone which shelters the innocent and guilty alike against group hysteria, manufactured evidence, overzealous law enforcement officials, in short, against those factors which militate for an automated, prejudged, neatly packaged verdict of guilty. It is the sacred right of every citizen accused of committing a crime to the presumption of innocence.

In fact, every basic legal right guaranteed to even the lowliest street criminal—the right to legal representation, to face accusers, to cross-examine witnesses and evidence—was denied Lee Harvey Oswald. The Commission met behind closed doors, heard secret testimony, and emerged to announce its conclusions.

The Warren Commission's first official meeting took place on December 5, 1963. The primary purpose of this meeting was to get the investigation organized. During this process, Warren suggested that the Commission need not hire its own investigators or obtain subpoena powers from Congress. He was, however, overridden in this matter by other Commission members. McCloy stated:

> I have a feeling that we have another obligation than the mere evaluation of the reports of agencies, many of which as you suggested, or some of them at least, may be interested, may be involved. There is a potential culpability here on the part of the Secret Service and even the FBI, and these reports . . . may have some self-serving aspects in them. And I think that if we didn't have the right to subpoena documents, the right to subpoena witnesses if we needed them, that this Commission's general standing might be somewhat impaired.

Not wishing to appear as simply a conduit for information from federal agencies, Commission members appealed to Congress for the right to issue subpoenas. This was granted on December 13, 1963, by the passage of Senate Joint Resolution 137. This law also authorized the Commission to compel testimony by providing immunity from prosecution—an authority that the Commission never once used.

During this meeting, Senator Russell noted the ongoing leaks of assassination information by the FBI while Commission members were still awaiting the bureau's first full report. He asked pointedly, "How much of their findings does the FBI propose to release to the press before we present the findings of this Commission?"

This was the beginning of a quiet—yet intense—feud between the Commission and Hoover's bureau.

The Commission's second meeting was on December 6. There was considerable discussion about the proposed Texas court of inquiry. State Attorney General Carr had traveled from Texas to Washington but was put off from meeting with Warren for three days because the chief justice wanted a formal promise that there would be no Texas hearings until after his commission had completed its investigation. Warren read from a letter he had sent Carr stating, "It is the view of this Commission . . . that a public inquiry in Texas at this time might be more harmful than helpful in our search for the truth."

It was during this meeting that the name of J. Lee Rankin was advanced as a possible general counsel for the Commission. Warren originally wanted Warren Olney III, head of the FBI Criminal division from 1953 to 1957, as chief counsel. However, Olney, an outspoken critic of director J. Edgar Hoover and most knowledgeable about the internal workings of the bureau, was rejected after the powerful Hoover voiced fierce opposition to his appointment, an indication of the director's power over the investigation.

The Commission then recessed until December 16, when it reviewed the first formal report on the assassination issued by the FBI on December 9. Warren set the tone by commenting, "Well, gentlemen, to be very frank about it, I have read that FBI report two or three times and I have not seen anything in there yet that has not been in the press."

Boggs commented, "Reading that FBI report leaves a million questions."

Dulles said the CIA couldn't finalize a report until the agency received more documents from the FBI. He commented, "They've been working for a long while, I know. It started when I was there." This was the first admission that the CIA had been keeping an eye on Oswald since his trip to Russia in 1959.

On December 8, 1963, J. Lee Rankin, a fifty-six-year-old corporate attorney and US solicitor general under Eisenhower, had accepted the appointment as general counsel for the Commission and met for the first time with the commissioners. Rankin would take charge of the Commission's investigation, serve as the primary liaison between the Commission and both the FBI and CIA, and act as coordinator between Commission members and the staff. Years later, one Commission attorney commented, "It was, very simply, a Rankin operation." And Rankin appeared more concerned with wrapping up the Commission's investigation swiftly than with fully probing each assassination issue.

When Commission assistant counsel Wesley Liebeler submitted a twenty-six-page memorandum to Rankin carefully outlining the serious deficiencies of the evidence against Oswald as the lone assassin, Rankin reportedly replied, "No more memorandums. The report has to be published."

On another occasion when Liebeler tried to address the problems arising from the Silvia Odio affair, an angry Rankin said, "At this stage, we are supposed to be closing doors, not opening them."

Initially, even Rankin voiced the suspicion that the Commission might have to do more than simply evaluate FBI reports. During the December 16 meeting, he stated:

> The Chief Justice and I finally came to the conclusion . . . that we might have to . . . ask for some investigative help . . . because we might not get all we needed by just going back to the FBI and other agencies because the [FBI] report has so many loopholes in it. Anybody can look at it and see that it just doesn't seem like they're looking for things that this Commission has to look for in order to get the answers that it wants and is entitled to. . . . [This] might be a tender spot. I am sure the FBI is certainly tender about the knowledge they had [concerning Oswald's presence in Dallas] and the fact that the Secret Service did not have that knowledge in order to do anything about it.

On January 21, 1964, the Commission met for the fourth time. Warren optimistically predicted an early end to the investigation, although there continued to be debate over whether to hurry up the Commission's work prior to the election-year conventions or slow it down pending the outcome of the Texas trial of Jack Ruby, which was about to begin.

A lengthy discussion ensued regarding the Commission's responsibility to question Mrs. Kennedy and the new president, Lyndon Johnson. However, almost a dozen pages of this discussion were marked "classified" and kept from the public.

The Commission then discussed the possibility of moving Oswald's body, including another autopsy and even cremation. Although the transcripts make no mention that they suspected impersonation at this time, it is significant to note the Commission's interest in Oswald's body. McCloy said, "I don't think we ought to have on the record that we are moving in this thing [an Oswald exhumation]. We are not saying anything about it." In response to news articles that Marina Oswald was being held against her will, Warren suggested allowing someone with the American Civil Liberties Union to meet with her. Rankin added, "We do have a little problem because the Secret Service came to us and said, 'Shall we quit our surveillance over her?' . . . I said we can't do that because she would slip right across the border and be gone."

The Commission again grappled with the problem of interagency rivalries. And again the issue of FBI reliability was raised, this time in connection with the conflicting information commissioners were getting concerning the president's wounds. McCloy said, "Let's find out about these wounds, it is just as confusing now as could be. It left my mind muddy as to what really did happen. . . . Why did the FBI report come out with something which isn't consistent with the autopsy?"

Senator Russell even suggested double-checking the FBI studies, but no action was taken.

Oswald and the FBI

On January 22, 1964, the Warren Commission was hurriedly called into secret session because of the explosive news that Texas authorities had information that Oswald had been an undercover informant for the FBI. Reports of this meeting were not made public until 1975.

Rankin told members:

> Yes, it was being rumored that [Oswald] was an undercover agent. Now it is something that would be very difficult to prove out. There are events in connection with this that are curious, in that they might make it possible to check some of it out in time. I assume that the FBI records would never show it . . . or if their records do show anything, I would think their records would show some kind of number that could be assigned to a dozen different people according to how they wanted to describe them. . . . [Oswald] did use postal boxes practically every place he went, and that would be an ideal way to get money to anyone that you wanted as an undercover agent.

Rankin wondered aloud if Oswald had been operating for the FBI during his trip to Russia, but Warren pointed out "They haven't any people in Russia." Rankin was still wondering, "One of the strange things that happened . . . is the fact that this man who is a defector, and who was under observation at least by the FBI . . . could [obtain] a passport that permitted him to go to Russia."

Rankin then connected his musings to the Commission's problems with the bureau:

> The FBI is very explicit that Oswald is the assassin or was the assassin, and they are very explicit that there was no conspiracy, and [yet] they are also saying in the same place that they are continuing their investigation. Now in my experience of almost nine years, in the first place it is hard to get them to say when you think you have got a case tight enough to convict somebody. . . . In my experience with the FBI, they don't do that. They claim that they don't evaluate. . . . Secondly, they have not run out of all kinds of leads in Mexico or in Russia and so forth which they could probably. . . . But they are concluding that there can't be a conspiracy without those [leads] being run out. Now that is not [normal] from my experience with the FBI. . . . It raises questions.

The specter of Oswald's being identified as an FBI agent caused great difficulty for the Commission. There appeared no way to fully resolve the matter, and as Representative Boggs pointed out, "[The] implications of this are fantastic, don't you think so? . . . I don't even like to see this being taken down."

Dulles agreed, "Yes, I think this record ought to be destroyed." But it wasn't.

Five days after this secret meeting, the Commission met formally. The minutes of this meeting, on January 27, 1964, show that commissioners were still agonizing over Oswald's possible involvement with the FBI. More than two hours of its three-and-a-half-hour afternoon session were spent trying to decide how to broach the subject with director J. Edgar Hoover. The problem was compounded by rumors that added the CIA to Oswald's suspected intelligence connections.

The stories of Oswald's spy connections were traced back from Texas attorney general Waggoner Carr to Dallas County district attorney Henry Wade and more specifically assistant district attorney William Alexander. Alexander claimed he got the story from *Houston Post* reporter Alonzo Hudkins, who said he got it from Dallas County deputy sheriff Allan Sweatt. Sweatt revealed his source for the story was none other than Alexander—who was on the scene of the Tippit slaying and reportedly also present at Oswald's capture at the Texas Theater.

Apparently no attempt was made to determine just where Alexander got his information that Oswald was being paid $200 a month as FBI informant S-179.

Rankin dismissed the possibility of approaching attorney general Robert Kennedy with the problem, saying, "As the head of the [Justice] department, the FBI, of course, is under the attorney general, but I think we must frankly recognize amongst ourselves that there is a daily relationship there . . . and we wouldn't want to make that more difficult."

He then raised the possibility of going straight to FBI director J. Edgar Hoover. But since Hoover was already on record denying that Oswald had any connection with the bureau, Commission members were hesitant to anger the dour Hoover by initiating their own inquiries. Senator Russell noted, "There is no man in the employ of the federal government who stands higher in the opinion of the American people than J. Edgar Hoover."

Furthermore, Commission member Allen Dulles, former head of the CIA, while admitting that government agencies and even local police departments employed "terribly bad characters" as undercover agents, bluntly implied there was no way to prove such allegations during the following exchange:

Rep. Boggs: Let's say [someone] . . . was recruited by someone in the CIA. The man who recruited him would know, wouldn't he?

Dulles: Yes, but he wouldn't tell.

Chairman Warren: Wouldn't tell it under oath?

Dulles: I wouldn't think he would tell it under oath, no. . . . He ought not tell it under oath. Maybe not tell it to his own government but wouldn't tell it any other way.

McCloy: Wouldn't he tell it to his own chief?

Dulles: He might or might not. If he was a bad one then he wouldn't.

Dulles added that he would not reveal CIA business to anyone except the president and that questioning Hoover would not necessarily get to the truth. He explained:

If [Hoover] says no, I didn't have anything to do with it. You can't prove what the facts are. There are no external evidences. I would believe Mr. Hoover. Some people might not. I don't think there is any external evidence other than the person's word that he did or did not employ a particular man as a secret agent. No matter what.

McCloy voiced the Commission's exasperation with its total dependence on the FBI: "The time is almost overdue for us to have a better perspective of the FBI investigation than we now have. . . . We are so dependent upon them for our facts."

Commission members also were becoming suspicious that the bureau was not being totally open with them regarding certain aspects of the assassination. For example, Rankin recalled that Marina Oswald said her husband met with two FBI agents for nearly two hours shortly after their return from Russia, but added, "We don't have any report that would cover anything like a two-hour conversation."

Senator Russell summed up the Commission's dilemma: "It seems to me we have two alternatives. One is we can just accept the FBI's report and go on and write the report based on their findings and supported by the raw materials they gave us, or else we can go and try to run down some of these collateral rumors that have just not been dealt with directly in this raw material that we have."

The Commission decided to allow Rankin to approach Hoover in the manner he thought best. But after all was said and done, the Warren Commission elected to accept the FBI's information and conclusions without independent verification.

During the same meeting that commissioners agonized over Oswald's possible connection with the FBI, Rankin outlined at length the six major areas of the Commission's investigation.

Area one was "The Basic Facts of the Assassination," dealing with the number and source of the shots. In charge of this area were Commission assistant counsels Francis W. H. Adams, who had served as a special assistant to the US attorney as well as police commissioner and chief assistant US attorney in New York City, and Arlen Specter, a Yale Law School graduate and an assistant district attorney in Philadelphia. In March 1964, Adams announced he could not fulfill his responsibility in the investigation. Specter went on to singlehandedly manage this critical area.

Area two was to establish the "Identity of the Assassin." In charge were David Belin, an Iowa attorney with a distinguished academic record, and Joseph A. Ball, an Iowa-born attorney who was teaching criminal law and procedure at the University of Southern California. An investigation into the murder of policeman J. D. Tippit belatedly was added.

Area three was a study of "Oswald's Background," an aspect of the probe that clearly indicated the Commission's predisposition toward Oswald's guilt.

Area four was to determine "Possible Conspiratorial Relationships." It was headed by William T. Coleman Jr., a Pennsylvania attorney who had served as law clerk to US Court of Appeals judge Herbert F. Goodrich and Supreme Court Justice Felix Frankfurter as well as a consultant with the US Arms Control and Disarmament Agency, and W. David Slawson, a Denver, Colorado, attorney educated at Amherst College, Princeton, and Yale.

Area five was the study of "Oswald's Death." In charge were Burt Griffin and Leon Hubert, both former assistant US attorneys.

Area six was added later and dealt with "Presidential Protection," a study of the security precautions of the Secret Service and the FBI. Samuel Stern, a former law clerk to Chief Justice Warren, was assigned to the job, but Chief Counsel Rankin supervised this "politically sensitive area."

Rankin also outlined the questions already arising over the medical evidence. He said:

> We think that the wound in the neck has to be related to one of these others, but the problem is difficult to determine because we have a statement from the hospital that the bullet that was more whole than the other was found on the stretcher which they brought the President in to the hospital on and then we have testimony later that goes back over the same ground . . . [saying] that this bullet was found under the blanket on the stretcher Gov. Connally was on.

It was the beginning of years of controversy over the basic medical and ballistic evidence.

As with the later House Select Committee on Assassinations, the Warren Commission asked many experts with lengthy credentials to evaluate various assassination evidence, such as Oswald's fingerprints and ballistics. And as with the House committee, while these experts supported the government's conclusions, none of them could later state with any certainty that the materials they received from the government were originals. But the possibility that someone within the government would substitute or fabricate evidence never seemed to cross the minds of the experts or the commissioners.

There also was controversy over Oswald's description as a loner. Rankin told the commissioners, "We have no evidence that is clear that Oswald was connected with anybody but we also have very great problems." In regard to Oswald's life in Russia, Rankin commented, "That entire period is just full of possibilities for training, for working with the Soviets, and its agents."

On February 24, 1964, Warren, senator John Cooper, representative Gerald Ford, Allen Dulles, and Rankin met for about ten minutes. Rankin reported no significant progress in the problem area of Oswald's possible connection with the FBI. He said affidavits from Hoover, FBI agents, and even Dallas officials "show negative." However, he also reported one instance of the bureau's lack of candor with the Commission, explaining:

As you recall, we informed you before that the address in the telephone book of Lee Oswald had in it the name of [FBI agent James] Hosty and his telephone number and his automobile license, and that it wasn't in the transcript of that information which was furnished to us by the FBI. And we have written to the FBI to ask them, an official inquiry, how that could happen, and to furnish us all of the information concerning that occurrence. And we have not received a reply yet.

On March 16, 1964, three and a half months after its inception, the Warren Commission met again. This three-minute session was to approve a resolution governing the questioning of witnesses by Commission staff members. Only Warren, Cooper, Ford, McCloy, and Rankin attended.

Jack Ruby's trial had ended on March 14, and at this point the real Warren Commission investigation began. On March 18, Commission staff attorneys flew to Dallas and set up a field station in the offices of US Attorney Barefoot Sanders.

Also in March the "more important" witnesses were called to testify over a period of fourteen days. By April, the number of days spent hearing testimony had dropped to seven.

On April 30, 1964, the Commission met again. Commissioners Ford, Boggs, and Russell were absent. Senator Cooper left the two-hour meeting after only thirty minutes. Though nearly five months had passed, Commissioners were still concerned about the contradictions in the investigative material. The question of Oswald's involvement with the FBI and CIA remained unresolved.

Cooper expressed his concern over contradictions between the testimony of witnesses to Commission attorneys and news media reports of interviews with the same witnesses.

Conflicts in the Testimony

The questions Cooper raised remain valid today. Only a few assassination researchers have seen fit to study the problems between what some Commission witnesses actually said and what was reported.

If basic conflicts exist in the Warren Commission testimony, then all of it—used as primary evidence in all studies of the Kennedy assassination—must be reevaluated. In fact, a close scrutiny of this issue brings out deeply troubling instances of suppressing evidence and intimidating witnesses.

The first problem with Warren Commission testimony is omissions. Despite what was hailed at the time as one of the most thorough investigations of all time, a review of the Warren Commission's performance reveals glaring deficiencies.

In their report, commissioners devoted more than a page to a detailed discussion of Lee Harvey Oswald's pubic hair. In their volumes, several pages were used to reproduce Marguerite Oswald's tax and house payment receipts, some dating back into the 1930s, and the dental records of Jack Ruby's mother.

Many other pages were filled with meaningless and irrelevant testimony, such as that of Anne Boudreaux, who never met either Oswald or his mother but did know a woman who once babysat for the infant Oswald; that of Viola Peterman, a former neighbor of Marguerite Oswald's who had not seen her for twenty-seven years; and that of Professor Revilo Pendleton Oliver, who took up thirty-five pages of testimony to discuss an article he had written that had no bearing on the JFK assassination.

Yet many pertinent witnesses were never asked to tell what they knew. These included:

—James Chaney, the motorcycle policeman closest to Kennedy during the assassination who told newsmen he saw the president "struck in the face" by the final shot.

—Bill and Gayle Newman, two of the bystanders closest to Kennedy at the time of the fatal head shot, who stated that shots came from directly behind them on the Grassy Knoll.

—Charles Brehm, a former US Army Ranger combat veteran and one of the closest bystanders to Kennedy when he was shot.

—J. C. Price, who from his bird's-eye perch on top of the Terminal Annex building witnessed the entire assassination and then told of seeing a man with a rifle running behind the wooden picket fence on top of the Grassy Knoll.

—Milton Jones, who told the FBI that he was on a Dallas bus that was boarded and searched by Dallas police after Oswald had gotten off, although at that time no one knew that Oswald was a suspect.

—Mary Dowling, a waitress at Dallas's Dobbs House restaurant who told the FBI that Policeman Tippit had been in the restaurant on November 20, when Oswald was there making a fuss over his food.

—James Simmons, a Union Railroad employee who supported Sam Holland in his contention that shots came from behind the picket fence on the Grassy Knoll.

—Richard Dodd, another railroad employee who told of hearing shots and seeing smoke come from behind the picket fence.

—Alonzo Hudkins, the Houston newspaperman who reported that Dallas officials told him that Oswald was an informant for the FBI.

—Ray Rushing, an evangelist who claimed to have ridden in an elevator at Dallas police headquarters with Jack Ruby about two hours before Ruby murdered Oswald and at a time when Ruby reportedly was at his home.

—Lieutenant George Butler, the Dallas police official in charge of Oswald's transfer November 24 and who was reported to have been in an extremely agitated condition by newspaperman Thayer Waldo.

—Admiral George Burkley, Kennedy's personal physician who rode in the motorcade, was with Kennedy at Parkland Hospital, rode with Air

Force One on the trip back to Washington, was present at the Bethesda autopsy, and received all of the official medical evidence, much of which is now in controversy.

—John T. Stringer and Lieutenant William Pitzer, who photographed and X-rayed Kennedy's body at Bethesda Naval Hospital.

—James Sibert and Francis O'Neill, two FBI agents who attended Kennedy's autopsy and made a report that contradicts some of the official conclusions.

—Richard Randolph Carr, a steelworker who reported seeing two men run from behind the Texas School Book Depository and drive off in a Rambler station wagon.

—Marvin Robinson, a motorist in Dealey Plaza who corroborated deputy sheriff Roger Craig's claim that Oswald entered a westbound Rambler station wagon in front of the Depository minutes after the assassination.

The omission of these people's testimony appears to go far beyond inefficiency or oversight. It seems rather to support the charges by Warren Commission critics that the panel avoided information that conflicted with their preconceived determination that Oswald was the lone assassin.

Conclusions reached by the Warren Commission—particularly the single-bullet theory—were contradicted by medical evidence, the witnesses, and governor John Connally. Therefore, the Commission chose to simply ignore them.

Some witnesses the Commission questioned, either directly or by deposition, have told researchers and news reporters that their testimony was altered. Others simply shrugged off their superficial questioning. Railroad supervisor Lee Bowers later said, "I was there to tell them only what they asked and when they wanted to cut off the conversation, I figured that was the end of it."

Witnesses Butch Burroughs, Jean Hill, Phil Willis, Orville Nix, James Tague, and others have stated that their testimony as presented by the Commission did not accurately reflect what they said.

While every Commission witness had the opportunity to review his or her testimony for accuracy, as far as can be determined, few took advantage of the offer. As one person put it, "I trust you."

One Warren Commission witness voiced her complaints to the FBI. Nancy Powell, better known as Ruby stripper Tammi True, talked to agents in August 1964. In their report, the agents stated:

> Mrs. Powell complained that she did not feel that her testimony had been recorded accurately in the deposition. It was explained to Mrs. Powell that persons, while conversing, give meaning to their words through voice inflections, and that reading the words without inflections sometimes gives different meaning to the words which was not meant. . . . At that time she stated to me that the deposition as written was not acceptable to her, particularly in

the area where she was questioned relative to Jack Ruby and to any part that Ruby may have played in the assassination. . . . Mrs. Powell stated it would be impossible for her to make corrections in the deposition as written because to make her testimony "sound right I would have to change the questions of [Commission attorney Burt] Griffin."

Witness Sam Holland was one of the few to attempt to correct his Warren Commission testimony. Holland told author Josiah Thompson he and his attorney attempted to correct the transcript. "We red marked . . . red penciled that statement from beginning to end because there were a lot of errors in it," he recalled. Holland said apparently his corrections were lost somewhere along the line, because "the statement that I made, as well as I remember, isn't in context with the Warren Commission." He told Commission critic Mark Lane, "The Warren Commission, I think, had to report in their book what they wanted the world to believe. . . . It had to read like they wanted it to read. They had to prove that Oswald did it alone."

Ronald Fischer, one of the bystanders who saw a man in the sixth-floor window in the minutes preceding the assassination, later said he almost got into a fight with a Commission attorney who was trying to get him to change his story. In an interview with the *Dallas Morning News* in 1978, Fischer said assistant counsel David Belin tried to intimidate him: "[Belin] and I had a fight almost in the interview room over the color of the man's hair. He wanted me to tell him that the man was dark-headed and I wouldn't do it. [Oswald's hair] doesn't appear to me in the photographs as light as the man that I saw and that's what Belin was upset about. I see it now, but I didn't see it at the time."

Roger Craig, the Dallas deputy sheriff who claimed to see Oswald escape in a station wagon, years later wrote about his experience with the Warren Commission: "Combine the [harassment at his work] with the run-in I had with Dave Belin, junior counsel for the Warren Commission, who questioned me in April, 1964, and who changed my testimony fourteen times when he sent it to Washington, and you will have some ideas of the pressure brought to bear."

Julia Ann Mercer, the woman who claimed to have seen Jack Ruby behind the wheel of a truck in Dealey Plaza about an hour and a half before the assassination, subsequently told investigators for New Orleans district attorney Jim Garrison that the FBI altered several key portions of her statement and that even her signature was forged on a Dallas County sheriff's report that supported the altered FBI documents.

Phil Willis, who took a series of photographs of the assassination, was surprised when he was asked only to give a deposition rather than to testify. He told this author:

This guy came to Dallas and took my deposition. He took down only what he wanted to hear. I tried to tell him about the shots and the echoes but he wasn't interested. He just seemed to want to get it over with. The Warren Commission never subpoenaed any photographer. They weren't interested in talking to me or Zapruder. It seems strange to me. It's not much of a way to conduct an investigation.

Willis's daughter, Linda Pipes, also witnessed the assassination. She said, "I very much agree [with Willis] that shots came from somewhere else other than the Depository. And where we were standing [across Elm from the Depository], we had a good view. . . . [Representatives of the Warren Commission] talked to me later, but they didn't seem to be investigating very thoroughly."

Phil Willis summed up his experience in a 1988 British TV interview: "All they wanted to know was that three shots came from the Book Depository. That's all that got into the Warren Commission [Report]. . . . I'm certain that at least one shot came from the right front. I'll stand by that to my grave!"

Recall that Chester Breneman and Robert West, the two Dallas surveyors who in May 1964 produced the height and distance figures for the Commission's reenactment of the assassination, reported their figures "at odds" with the figures the Warren Commission published. The consequence of these altered numbers was to make the controversial single-bullet theory more plausible by simply moving back the time when both Kennedy and Connally were wounded.

The experience of former Texas senator Ralph Yarborough also sheds light on the manner in which the Commission allowed key witnesses to be handled. The fact that Yarborough was riding beside Lyndon Johnson in the motorcade may explain his treatment in the summer of 1964. He described it this way:

After I wrote them, you see, a couple of fellows came to see me. They walked in like they were a couple of deputy sheriffs and I was a bank robber. I didn't like their attitude. As a senator I felt insulted. They went off and wrote up something and brought it back for me to sign. But I refused. I threw it in a drawer and let it lay there for weeks. And they had on there the last sentence which stated "This is all I know about the assassination." They wanted me to sign this thing, then say this is all I know. Of course, I would never have signed it. Finally, after some weeks, they began to bug me. "You're holding this up, you're holding this up" they said, demanding that I sign the report. So I typed one up myself and put basically what I told you about how the cars all stopped. I put in there, "I don't want to hurt anyone's feelings but for the protection of future presidents, they should be trained to take off when a shot is fired." I sent that over. That's dated July 10, 1964, after the assassination. To my surprise, when the volumes were finally printed and came out, I was surprised at how many people down at the White House didn't file their affidavits until after the date, after mine the 10th of July, waiting to see what I was going to say before they filed theirs. I began to lose confidence then in their investigation and that's further eroded with time.

Yarborough also was shocked to find that all vital assassination information was sent to President Johnson before it ever went to the Warren Commission or even attorney general Robert Kennedy.

Perhaps one of the most shocking statements regarding treatment at the hands of the Warren Commission came from witness Jean Hill. Fearful to speak out for years, Hill came forward in the spring of 1986 and told her story to a group of assassination researchers at the University of Texas at Arlington.

After witnessing a rifleman firing from the Grassy Knoll and immediately being grabbed by two men who claimed to be Secret Service agents, she was advised by friends in the Dallas Police Department to keep quiet about what she knew. Even after she received a subpoena to appear before the Warren Commission, the same friends urged that she not go to Washington. She recalled, "They seemed to feel that there might be some danger if I was to leave Dallas. They told me I wouldn't come back."

After Hill refused to go to Washington, Commission attorney Arlen Specter sent FBI agents to take her to make a deposition. She recalled that experience for this author:

The FBI took me to Parkland Hospital. I had no idea what I was doing there. They escorted me through a labyrinth of corridors and up to one of the top floors of Parkland. I didn't know where we were. They took me into this little room where I met Arlen Specter. He talked to me for a few minutes, trying to act real friendly, then this woman, a stenographer, came in and sat behind me.

He had told me that this interview would be confidential, then I looked around and this woman was taking notes. I reminded him that the discussion was to be private and he told the woman to put down her notebook, which she did. But when I looked around again she was writing. I got mad and told Specter, "You lied to me. I want this over." He asked me why I wouldn't come to Washington, and I said, "Because I want to stay alive." He asked why I would think that I was in danger and I replied, "Well, if they can kill the president, they can certainly get me!" He replied that they already had the man that did it and I told him, "No, you don't!"

He kept trying to get me to change my story, particularly regarding the number of shots. He said I had been told how many shots there were and I figured he was talking about what the Secret Service told me right after the assassination. His inflection and attitude was that I knew what I was supposed to be saying, why wouldn't I just say it. I asked him, "Look, do you want the truth or just what you want me to say?" He said he wanted the truth, so I said, "The truth is that I heard between four and six shots." I told him, "I'm not going to lie for you." So he starts talking off the record. He told me about my life, my family, and even mentioned that my marriage was in trouble. I said, "What's the point of interviewing me if you already know everything about me?" He got angrier and angrier and finally told me,

"Look, we can make you look as crazy as Marguerite Oswald and every-body knows how crazy she is. We could have you put in a mental institution if you don't cooperate with us." I knew he was trying to intimidate me. I kept asking to see that woman's notes, to see what she was putting down. I knew something was not right about this, because no one who is just taking a deposition gets that involved and angry, they just take your answers.

He finally gave me his word that the interview would not be published unless I approved what was written. But they never gave me the chance to read it or approve it. When I finally read my testimony as published by the Warren Commission, I knew it was a fabrication from the first line. After that ordeal at Parkland Hospital, they wrote that my deposition was taken at the US attorney's office in the Post Office Building.

Even Kennedy's own people were not immune to such pressures. In 1975 a CIA liaison told congressional investigators that two of Kennedy's aides, Kenneth O'Donnell and David Powers, initially said shots came from other than the Depository, but later changed their story after being warned by J. Edgar Hoover or one of his top aides that such testimony would only arouse public passions and could lead to an international incident. Both O'Donnell and Powers denied this story when it appeared in a Chicago newspaper column. But the story was confirmed in 1987 with the publication of former House speaker Thomas P. "Tip" O'Neill's book, *Man of the House*. He related:

> I was never one of those people who had doubts or suspicions about the War-ren Commission's report on the president's death. But five years after Jack died, I was having dinner with (former JFK aide) Kenny O'Donnell. . . . I was surprised to hear O'Donnell say that he was sure he had heard two shots from behind the fence. "That's not what you told the Warren Commission," I said. "You're right," he replied. "I told the FBI what I had heard, but they said it couldn't have happened that way and that I must have been imagining things. So I testified the way they wanted me to. I just didn't want to stir up any more pain and trouble for the family." Dave Powers was with us at dinner that night, and his recollection of the shots was the same as O'Donnell's. Kenny O'Donnell is no longer alive, but during the writing of this book I checked with Dave Powers. As they say in the news business, he stands by his story.

Considering the information presented in this section, it appears the sins of the Warren Commission went far beyond a few omissions and distortions. Little wonder that the vast majority of Americans today place little credence in the Commission's findings of a lone assassin and no conspiracy. Once again the charge of cover-up can be laid at the feet of the federal government.

During the April 30 Commission meeting J. Lee Rankin openly admitted that the June 1 date for closing the investigation was unreasonable.

A brief discussion was held regarding Jack Ruby, who had been found guilty and been sentenced to death. However, his attorneys were appealing the conviction on the grounds of his mental incompetence. When one member asked if Ruby would go to prison, Commissioner McCloy responded, "He goes to a mental institution. It is perfectly clear we cannot examine him at this stage." Rankin again referred to the problems arising from the contradictory medical evidence and suggested that some Commission members and a doctor should study the autopsy photographs "so that they could report to the commission that there is nothing inconsistent with the other findings." Warren added, "But without putting those pictures in our record. We don't want those in our record. . . . It would make it a morbid thing for all time to come."

The inaccessibility of Kennedy's autopsy X-rays and photographs have been a cornerstone of the criticism of the Warren Commission.

Before adjourning, commissioners agreed on the necessity of including a biography of Lee Harvey Oswald in their final report. It is significant to read Rankin's explanation at this time—five months before their final report—for including Oswald's background: "Some of it will be necessary to tell the story and to show why it is reasonable to assume that he did what the commission concludes that he did do."

On April 10, 1964, in a memo to Commission assistant counsel Albert Jenner regarding a chronology of Oswald's background by staffer John Hart Ely, Rankin wrote, "Our depositions and examinations of records and other data disclose that there are details in Mr. Ely's memoranda which will require material alteration and, in some instances, omission."

Despite the questions, contradictions, and gaps in the evidence at hand and with alterations and omissions, Oswald's guilt was already decided.

The Single-Bullet Theory

Nowhere was the manipulation of the facts more evident than the government's attempt to reconcile the ballistic and medical evidence by offering the idea that both President Kennedy and Governor Connally were struck by the same bullet.

On its face this concept is unpalatable. To believe the single-bullet theory, one must believe that a single rifle slug penetrated two men, causing seven wounds, shattering a rib and a wrist bone, then emerged almost totally unscathed to become the pristine Commission Exhibit 399.

Yet, to disbelieve the single-bullet theory means rejecting the Warren Commission's entire version of the assassination. Despite the testimony of many witnesses, the Warren Commission concluded that only three shots were fired during the assassination, based solely on three spent shells found on the sixth floor of the Texas School Book Depository.

Having concluded that only three shots were fired—the absolute maximum allowable for only one assassin within the time frame of the Zapruder film—commissioners set about determining the timing and effects of each shot.

In late 1963 and early 1964 there was no problem. Since the FBI early on had established an assassination time sequence by studying the Zapruder film and Zapruder's 8 mm camera, the Commission had a certain time frame to work within. This basis is now known to be questionable.

The original FBI and Secret Service reports made it clear that Kennedy was struck in the back by the first shot, Governor Connally hit by the second, and the president's head wound caused by the third. While this stretched the allowable time for such shooting to the limit—and despite the contradiction of Connally, who testified he was hit after the first shot—the Commission accepted this believable scenario for a time.

But then came the problem of James Tague, the man who was struck by a piece of cement while standing near the Triple Underpass. Initially both the FBI and the Warren Commission tried to ignore Tague. But after assistant US attorney Martha Jo Stroud in Dallas sent commissioners both an account of the Tague wounding and a Dallas news photograph of the bullet mark on the curb, the Commission was forced to action.

In early 1964—while the FBI was denying any curb shot in Dallas—Commission attorney Arlen Specter learned that JFK autopsy doctor James Humes had hypothesized that a single bullet could have caused the wounds to both Kennedy and Connally. Specter eagerly latched onto this concept, which neatly explained how the two men were wounded by the same shot.

However, it is now clear that the Warren Commission knew the single-bullet theory did not fit the facts. Page 193 of transcripts from the Commission's January 27, 1964, meeting revealed General Counsel Rankin's thoughts on the matter:

> It seems quite apparent now, since we have the picture of where the bullet entered in the back, that the bullet entered below the shoulder blade to the right of the backbone, which is below the place where the picture shows the bullet came out in the neck band of the shirt in front, and the bullet, according to the autopsy, didn't strike any bone at all, that particular bullet, and go through so that how it could turn and . . .

Rankin stops in midsentence, having reached the point where he too now realizes that for the single-bullet theory to work requires a rifle bullet without striking bone to course upward and turn in midair, then take a different trajectory, a physical impossibility.

Yet, despite this early recognition that the single-bullet theory was impossible, the Warren Commission Report offered this somewhat vague conclusion:

> Although it is not necessary to any essential findings of the commission to determine just which shot hit Governor Connally, there is very persuasive

evidence from the experts to indicate that the same bullet which pierced the President's throat also caused Governor Connally's wounds. However, Governor Connally's testimony and certain other factors have given rise to some difference of opinion as to this probability but there is no question in the mind of any member of the Commission that all the shots which caused the President's and Governor Connally's wounds were fired from the sixth floor window of the Texas School Book Depository. The shots which killed President Kennedy and wounded Governor Connally were fired by Lee Harvey Oswald."

What was essential was that Kennedy was never shot through the neck, as no exit wound from the throat was ever found.

Forensics expert Sherry Fiester said the single-bullet theory hinged on trajectory, the path of which "widely varied" in studies by the FBI and the House committee. She wrote in her 2012 book, *Enemy of the Truth: Myth, Forensics, and the Kennedy Assassination*, that aligning the trajectory of a bullet from the sixth floor of the Texas School Book Depository to Kennedy's two wounds and Connally's back wound is impossible and therefore "the Single-Bullet Theory remains a myth."

Douglas P. Horne, a staff member of the Assassination Records Review Board in the 1990s, noted, "The absurd single bullet theory of Arlen Specter [was]—a political invention rather than a scientific explanation—which has never convinced the American people, in spite of the best efforts of the HSCA's Michael Baden and Robert Blakey, and later Gerald Posner and Vince Bugliosi."

The presumption of Oswald's guilt was the first topic of a Commission meeting on June 4, 1964. The Commission had met on May 19, 1964, but records of that meeting were kept from the public on the grounds that it dealt only with "personal and medical files."

Also in May, Rankin had told Commission attorneys to "wrap up" their investigations and submit their area chapters by June 1 so that the final report could be issued by June 30. By June 1, however, only two attorneys had completed a draft and the deadline had to be moved back.

On June 17, it was announced that Commission hearings were completed. On June 30, it was announced that the final report would not be issued until after the Republican National Convention, set to begin July 13.

The Commission worked in secrecy, as evidenced by the minutes of an executive session conducted on June 23, 1964. These were withheld from the public by the National Archives with the following explanation: "Matters that are . . . specifically authorized under criteria established by an Executive Order [are] to be kept secret in the interest of national defense or foreign policy and are in fact properly classified pursuant to such Executive Order."

The immense pressure to hurry up the investigation and close down the Commission may have accounted for the fact that five of the senior attorneys—Francis Adams, William Coleman, Joseph Ball, Leon Hubert, and Albert Jenner—returned to their private practices and made virtually no contribution to the final report.

On July 9, 1964, commissioners Allen Dulles and John McCloy met with three psychiatrists who had been asked to develop a psychological profile on Oswald. During the seven-hour meeting, the psychiatrists went over complex psychological conjectures regarding Oswald's motives, but their interpretations of his thinking were severely limited due to the fact that first, they were operating under the assumption of Oswald's guilt, and second, the material studied was based on Commission and FBI reports, which undoubtedly were one-sided. Even though the psychiatrists spent hours detailing their theories, they also cautioned against putting too much confidence in their psychological speculation since they had not had the opportunity to interview Oswald personally.

Yet in its final report the Warren Commission did use the psychiatrists' opinions to underscore the case against Oswald as a lonely and troubled man. And the public did not laugh them off. After all, the Warren Commission represented some of the most prestigious men in the nation.

Dulles suspected the truth of the matter when, during a discussion of whether to present the psychological material in the final report, he opened this dialogue with Jenner:

DULLES: But nobody reads. Don't believe people read in this country. There will be a few professors who will read the record . . .
JENNER: And a few newspaper reporters who will read parts of it.
DULLES: The public will read very little.

In its final report, the Warren Commission made no specific reference to the psychiatric panel. Yet portions of the report presented ideas that originated with the doctors. In the report, after fully detailing Oswald's difficulty with human relationships, his discontent with the world, his search for personal truth and a place in history, his censure of certain aspects of American life, and his professed commitment to Marxism, commissioners wrote, "Out of these and many other factors which may have molded the character of Lee Harvey Oswald there emerged a man capable of assassinating President Kennedy."

With the Commission investigation winding down and most of the senior attorneys gone, the job of writing the Warren Commission Report fell to assistant counsel Norman Redlich and staff member Alfred Goldberg. Redlich was a law professor at New York University School of Law and Dr. Goldberg (a PhD) was a historian for the US Air Force Historical Division.

When Goldberg told Warren it was impossible to complete the report by mid-July, the deadline again was moved back, this time to August 1. Through August, Goldberg and Redlich continued to rewrite the report's chapters—some as many as twenty times—and the deadline was moved back into September. It was in this time period that Commission member Gerald Ford ordered the wording changed from "Kennedy was shot in the back" to "a shot through the throat."

The Commission, well aware of the ever-nearing November presidential election, reportedly received intense pressure from Johnson aide McGeorge Bundy to hurry up and publish its findings.

On September 4, galley proofs of the final report draft were circulated among commissioners and staffers for last-minute comments. Two days later, a dissatisfied Liebeler submitted a twenty-six-page memorandum highly critical of the "Identity of the Assassin" chapter. It had to be revised again.

On September 7, commissioners Richard Russell, John Cooper, and Hale Boggs, still unsatisfied with the inevitable conclusion of Oswald's guilt, traveled to Dallas to reexamine Marina Oswald. Under questioning, she changed significant aspects of her story, prompting even more rewriting of the report.

The final Warren Commission session was on September 18, 1964, less than ten days before its final report would be issued to President Lyndon Johnson. According to the National Archives, no transcripts of this important final meeting exist. However, some descriptions of the meeting show that great concern was being voiced to Chief Counsel Rankin that material within the report conflicted with its summary and conclusions chapter.

On September 24, 1964, the Warren Commission's report was submitted to President Johnson by Chief Justice Warren with the introduction emphasizing its sponsorship:

> Dear Mr. President,
> Your Commission to investigate the assassination of President Kennedy on November 22, 1963, having completed its assignment in accordance with Executive Order No. 11130 of November 29, 1963, herewith submits its final report.

The report was signed by all seven commissioners, though Senator Russell refused to sign until the wording regarding the single-bullet theory was softened to indicate the idea was only a probability.

Russell's dissension and skepticism of the report's conclusions may have been the topic of the September 18 meeting for which the transcripts are missing. Russell told researcher Harold Weisberg that several of the commissioners voiced doubts about the Commission's conclusions at that meeting and he was "shaken" by the discovery that the record of these doubts was missing.

The Warren Commission Report was made public on September 28, 1964, with the news media voicing virtually unanimous praise and support for the document.

Upon receiving the report from Warren, President Johnson's only comment was, "It's heavy."

Today it is intriguing to note that Johnson refused to answer questions from his own commission. According to *Newsweek* of August 15, 1966, "A list of questions [concerning the assassination] for him was in fact prepared and submitted to John-son's confidant, Abe Fortas. Fortas returned a veto of the idea." Instead, both Johnson and his wife submitted unsworn statements.

Johnson's action prompted Commission attorney David Belin to comment in later years:

> If we could interrogate Mrs. Kennedy, whose husband has died before her eyes, there is no reason why President Johnson should not be examined in the same manner as every other witness [since] there was some speculation from abroad, however outlandish, that he might have had some indirect connection with the Dallas tragedy.

Two months after the Warren Commission Report was released with widespread publicity praising its thoroughness and conclusions, twenty-six volumes of Commission testimony and exhibits were quietly made public. It was only after years of diligent study that individual researchers finally were able to document the gross inconsistencies between these twenty-six volumes of material and the Commission's report. And by then they were largely ignored except by a few low-circulation periodicals. No one was in a position to receive new or clarified information regarding the assassination since—having completed its work on September 28—the Warren Commission had disbanded.

Researcher Sylvia Meagher, in *Accessories After the Fact*, produced a meticulous dissection of the Commission and its conclusions. She stated, "One of the most reprehensible actions of the Warren Commission is that it disbanded the moment it handed over its Report, leaving no individual or corporate entity to answer legitimate questions arising from demonstrable misstatements of fact in the Report."

After carefully researching both the activities and the conclusions of the Warren Commission, Meagher—who has never been successfully challenged in her assertions of the Commission's incompetence—wrote:

> Study has shown the Report to contain (1) statements of fact which are inaccurate and untrue, in the light of the official Exhibits and objective verification; (2) statements for which the citations fail to provide authentication; (3) misrepresentation of testimony: (4) omission of references to testimony inimical to findings in the Report; (5) suppression of findings favorable to Oswald; (6) incomplete investigation of suspicious circumstances which remain unexplained; (7) misleading statements resulting from inadequate attention to the contents of Exhibits; (8) failure to obtain testimony from crucial witnesses; and (9) assertions which are diametrically opposite to the logical inferences to be drawn from the relevant testimony or evidence.

After reviewing Warren Commission meeting transcripts in the mid-1970s, author Tad Szulc wrote:

If the investigation was as inadequate and incompetent as is suggested by the Commission's own internal documents, once Top Secret and now declassified, it IS [emphasis his] legitimate to question the specific conclusions of the report. The transcripts of the commission's executive sessions, staff memoranda . . . and other internal documents reveal the commissioners to be consumed by doubts and fears; troubled by their own ignorance; suspicious of the investigatory work performed for them by the FBI and the CIA; lacking clear direction; worried about a competing inquiry in Texas; and finally suffering from a stunning lack of confidence in their own ability to produce a report that would be credible to the American people, the world, and, for that matter, credible to themselves. . . . So many of [their] doubts apparently were not resolved that the impression emerges from the private discussions among the commissioners that, in the end, the Report was the only possible compromise they could produce—in terms of their knowledge and their conscience.

In the years following the release of the Warren Report, condemnation of its work and conclusions has only grown more widespread.

In 1976, the Senate Select Committee to Study Government Operations with Respect to Intelligence Activities, while claiming not to have found evidence of a conspiracy to kill Kennedy, nevertheless concluded:

The committee has . . . developed evidence which impeaches the process by which the intelligence agencies arrived at their own conclusions about the assassination, and by which they provided information to the Warren Commission. This evidence indicates that the investigation of the assassination was deficient and that facts which might have substantially affected the course of the investigation were not provided the Warren Commission. . . . Why senior officials of the FBI and the CIA permitted the investigation to go forward, in light of these deficiencies, and why they permitted the Warren Commission to reach its conclusions without all relevant information is still unclear. Certainly, concern with public reputation, problems of coordination between agencies, possible bureaucratic failure, and embarrassment and the extreme compartmentation of knowledge of sensitive operations may have contributed to these shortcomings. But the possibility exists that senior officials in both agencies made conscious decisions not to disclose potentially important information.

As has been demonstrated, in most cases, "potentially important information" meant any information that did not add to the evidence of Oswald's guilt.

The sins of the Warren Commission, the FBI, and the CIA go far beyond simple omission for face-saving purposes.

Senator Richard Schweiker, a member of the Senate Intelligence Committee's subcommittee that looked at the agencies' performance during the Warren Commission investigation, told news reporters in 1976 that both the CIA and the FBI deliberately lied to the Commission about significant assassination issues.

His charge was supported by former Texas attorney general Waggoner Carr, whose own investigation was usurped by the Warren Commission. Carr told the *Houston Chronicle* in 1975, "All of the records were in the hands of the two agencies [the FBI and CIA] and, if they so desired, any information or files could have been destroyed or laundered prior to the time the Commission could get them."

Schweiker added that lies from these agencies, coupled with the numerous deficiencies his panel saw, invalidated the Warren Commission's conclusions. He bluntly reported, "I think the Warren Commission has, in fact, collapsed like a house of cards. And I believe the Warren Commission was set up at the time to feed pabulum to the American people for reasons not yet known, and that one of the biggest cover-ups in the history of our country occurred at that time."

Widespread disbelief in the Warren Commission, though never publicly acknowledged, has carried forward right up until today. In January 2013, Robert F. Kennedy Jr., nephew of JFK and son of assassinated senator Robert Kennedy, told the Associated Press his father thought the Commission's work was a "shoddy piece of craftsmanship." He said his father "publicly supported the Warren Commission report but privately he was dismissive of it. . . . The evidence at this point I think is very, very convincing that it was not a lone gunman."

Today it can be clearly seen that the sins of the Commission included investigating from a preconceived idea, failing to substantiate evidence from the FBI, intimidating selected witnesses, stifling internal dissent, and misreporting its own information. These methods were actively employed to subvert a truthful investigation and to present flawed and inadequate conclusions to the unsuspecting public. In retrospect, it seems the Warren Commission provided a classic example of how not to conduct a meaningful investigation.

It appears the Commission slowly became aware of the massive power behind the assassination and simply could not—or would not—come to grips with it. Like subsequent inquiries into the Kennedy assassination, it released a slanted and timid version of the tragedy hoping to appease the public long enough that commissioners would not have to face the full ramifications of a truthful and incisive investigation. And their plan worked well.

For more than five decades much of the American public has been content with the palatable—but implausible—Warren Commission version of the assassination. Today, with firm evidence of a second assassin available and a continuing history of government deceit, a large number of citizens have reevaluated the official government assassination theory of a lone gunman. Today, national polls indicate the vast majority of Americans continue to doubt the basic tenets of the Warren Commission.

A 2004 FOX News poll conducted by Opinion Dynamics Corp. on the fortieth anniversary of the JFK assassination showed 74 percent of respondents believed there was a conspiracy and a cover-up involved. This poll reflected numbers similar to previous surveys conducted by Louis Harris and Associates in 1967, 1975, and 1981, when about two-thirds also felt the shooting was part of a larger conspiracy.

The Garrison Investigation

On the afternoon of November 22, 1963, two men sat drinking in the Katzenjammer Bar, located in New Orleans next door to 544 Camp Street, where a puzzling parade of anti-Castro Cubans and intelligence agents—including Lee Harvey Oswald—had been seen the previous summer.

One of the men was Guy Banister, the former FBI man who was running a private-investigation firm with intelligence connections out of an office at 544 Camp Street. The other man was one of his investigators, Jack Martin.

According to a police report prepared that day, the two men returned to Banister's office, where an argument erupted. Banister, his irritability inflamed by alcohol, accused Martin of stealing files, whereupon Martin reminded Banister that he had not forgotten some of the people he had seen in Banister's office that summer. Banister then beat Martin over the head with a heavy .357 Magnum pistol.

In the heat of the moment, Martin screamed out, "What are you going to do—kill me, like you all did Kennedy?"

A police ambulance was called and carried the bloodied Martin to Charity Hospital.

An angered Martin soon whispered to friends that Banister had often been in the company of a man named David Ferrie, who Martin claimed drove to Texas the day of Kennedy's assassination to serve as a getaway pilot for the assassins.

Martin's words soon reached the ears of New Orleans district attorney Jim Garrison, who arrested Ferrie upon his return to New Orleans, thus beginning an investigation into the JFK assassination that eventually turned into a worldwide cause célèbre.

Through Garrison's investigation much new assassination information became known to the public and the assassination was addressed for the first time in a courtroom—even though the defendant was acquitted.

Garrison claimed that the entire weight of the federal government was moved to block and ridicule his investigation, and indeed there were many strange aspects to this entire episode, including an attack by some in the national media before Garrison even had a chance to present his case.

A giant of a man, standing six-foot-six, Earling Carothers Garrison had shortened his name to simply "Jim" and was widely known to both friend and foe as the "Jolly Green Giant."

Born on November 20, 1921, in Knoxville, Iowa, Garrison grew up in New Orleans and enlisted in the US Army a year before Pearl Harbor. In 1942, he was commissioned a lieutenant in the field artillery.

After the war, Garrison followed a family tradition in law by enrolling in the Tulane University Law School. He eventually earned bachelor of laws and master of civil laws degrees.

Garrison then joined the FBI, serving briefly in Seattle and Tacoma, Washington. He wrote, "I was very impressed with the competence and efficiency of the Bureau. However, I was extremely bored as I rang doorbells to inquire about the loyalty and associations of applicants for employment in a defense plant. So I decided to return to the law profession."

He served as an assistant district attorney in New Orleans from 1954 to 1958, resigning with a scathing attack on mayor Victor H. Schiro. In 1961, Garrison decided to run for the district attorney's job, again blasting Schiro for corruption and failure to enforce the law. His attacks included incumbent district attorney Richard Dowling, whom he called "the great emancipator—he let everyone go free."

Not believing he had much of a chance, Garrison ran a meager campaign, composed mostly of some television talks. To many people's surprise, Garrison managed to defeat Dowling in a run-off election, and he took office as district attorney on March 3, 1962.

Although Garrison did begin to clean up some of the more disreputable gambling and prostitution dens of New Orleans, his critics noted that he did not share that same enthusiasm against the leaders of organized crime.

In 1962, Garrison was angered by the refusal of eight criminal-court judges to approve funds for investigating organized crime. He went so far as to publicly state that their refusal "raised interesting questions about racketeer influences." The judges sued him for defamation of character and won a $1,000 state court judgment. Garrison, however, fought this action all the way to the Supreme Court, which reversed the decision in a landmark case on the right to criticize public officials.

After hearing Jack Martin's remarks during the assassination weekend, Garrison attempted to locate David Ferrie. On Monday, November 25, Ferrie turned himself in.

Garrison, who had met the bizarre Ferrie once before, could hardly forget the man. Ferrie suffered from alopecia, a rare disease that causes total baldness. Garrison recalled, "The face grinning ferociously at me was like a ghoulish Halloween mask. The eyebrows plainly were greasepaint, one noticeably higher than the other. A scruffy, reddish homemade wig hung askew on his head as he fixed me with his eyes."

Ill at ease, Ferrie admitted his Friday trip to Texas, claiming he had wanted to go ice skating in Houston. However, he had no adequate answer for why he had chosen to drive through one of the worst thunderstorms in years and why, instead of skating, he had spent his time at the rink's pay phone. Ferrie also denied knowing Lee Harvey Oswald.

Garrison was unsatisfied with Ferrie's story. He ordered him and two friends held in jail for questioning by the FBI. He later told interviewer Eric Norden, "When we alerted the FBI, they expressed interest and asked us to turn the three men over to them for questioning. We did, but Ferrie was released soon afterward and most of [the FBI] report on him was classified top secret and secreted in the National Archives."

In his 1988 book, *On the Trail of the Assassins*, Garrison wrote:

> I was 43 years old and had been district attorney for a year and nine months when John Kennedy was killed. I was an old-fashioned patriot, a product of my family, my military experience, and my years in the legal profession. I could not imagine then that the government ever would deceive the citizens of this country. Accordingly, when the FBI released David Ferrie with surprising swiftness, implying that no evidence had been found connecting him with the assassination, I accepted it.

Over the next three years, Garrison's attention was centered on his job and family. Vaguely aware of contradictions in the assassination story, Garrison nevertheless chose to believe the official version. He wrote:

> By this time [1966] our military was deeply engaged in the war in Southeast Asia. Like most Americans, I took it for granted that our government had our troops over there to bring democracy to South Vietnam. Like most Americans, I also took for granted that our government had fully investigated President Kennedy's assassination and had found it to be indeed the result of a random act by a man acting alone. Certainly, it never crossed my mind that the murder of President Kennedy and the subsequent arrival of half a million members of the American military in Vietnam might be related.

Garrison's view began to change after a chance meeting with the powerful senator from Louisiana, Russell Long. Garrison said Long told him, "Those fellows on the Warren Commission were dead wrong. There's no way in the world that one man could have shot up John Kennedy that way."

It was a comment that was to put Garrison and his office back on the assassination investigation trail. First Garrison went back and studied the Warren Commission Report and volumes in detail. He was aghast, noting:

> Considering the lofty credentials of the commission members and the quality and size of the staff available to them, I had expected to find a thorough and professional investigation. I found nothing of the sort. The mass of information was disorganized and confused. The commission had provided no adequate index to its exhibits. . . . The number of promising leads that were never followed up offended my prosecutorial sensibility. And, perhaps worst of all, the conclusions in the report seemed to be based

on an appallingly selective reading of the evidence, ignoring credible testimony from literally dozens of witnesses.

Garrison, with his military background, was particularly shocked to read in the commission volumes where a Lieutenant Colonel Allison G. Folsom Jr. reported on a grade made by Oswald in a Russian examination. Garrison knew that the mere fact that Oswald had been tested in Russian indicated intelligence training.

Fired by growing suspicions, Garrison took another look at Oswald's activities while in New Orleans in the spring and summer of 1963. He began to discover the odd and mostly unexplained relationships between Oswald and anti-Castro Cubans, US intelligence agents including the FBI, and 544 Camp Street.

Quietly he began to assemble some of his most trusted assistants, whom he dubbed his "special team," and his investigation grew.

Garrison reinterviewed Jack Martin and found that Oswald had been part of that strange entourage of agents in and out of Banister's Camp Street office. He found that Banister and his associates were involved in activities far afield from normal New Orleans activity, honest or otherwise. There were tales of burglarized armories, missing weapons, raided ammunition caches, and gunrunning operations. Garrison wrote, "The Banister apparatus . . . was part of a supply line that ran along the Dallas–New Orleans–Miami corridor. These supplies consisted of arms and explosives for use against Castro's Cuba."

By 1966, Banister was dead—he reportedly suffered a heart attack in June 1964—and Garrison was looking for a living person to prosecute in the conspiracy he had begun to unravel.

One starting point was New Orleans attorney Dean Andrews, who told the Warren Commission that he had received a call from a "Clay Bertrand" the day after the assassination asking him to fly to Dallas and legally represent Lee Harvey Oswald. Andrews reiterated this story to Garrison and claimed that while he had "Clay Bertrand" as a client, he had never actually met the man.

As Garrison's investigators pried into the seamier areas of New Orleans nightlife, they began to piece together information from various sources that it was common knowledge in the homosexual underground that "Clay Bertrand" was the name used by none other than Clay Shaw, the respected director of the International Trade Mart in New Orleans.

Clay Shaw and Permindex

Clay Shaw, like Lee Harvey Oswald and Jack Ruby, was not merely some innocent with no connection to persons and/or organizations that may have played a role in President Kennedy's death.

Shaw had some of the most intriguing and unprobed connections of any person involved in the assassination case. Even when some of these connections were brought to the attention of the House Select Committee on Assassinations, the committee was either unable or unwilling to fully investigate them.

Shaw, a tall, distinguished man with silver hair and a polished manner, was born in Kentwood, Louisiana, on March 17, 1913. During the 1930s, Shaw was in New York City working as an executive for Western Union Telegraph Company and later as an advertising and public-relations consultant.

Once again, there is a military connection. In 1941, Shaw was with the US Army and, while his official biography states simply that he was an aide-de-camp to General Charles O. Thrasher, Shaw later admitted he was working for the Office of Strategic Services (OSS) as a liaison officer to the headquarters of Winston Churchill. It was here that Shaw may have become entangled in the murky world of intelligence.

Although there is precious little reliable information on exactly what Shaw's wartime experiences included, he did retire from the US Army in 1946 as a major; later he was made a colonel, with the Bronze Star, the Legion of Merit, France's Croix de Guerre, and Belgium's Order of the Crown.

After the war, Shaw returned to New Orleans, where he was known as a wealthy real-estate developer. He also became director of the International House, a "nonprofit association fostering the development of international trade, tourism and cultural exchange." Soon Shaw left this organization to found the International Trade Mart, which became quite profitable sponsoring permanent industrial expositions in the Caribbean.

According to several separate sources, including Garrison's files and an investigation by the US Labor Party, a short-lived political party that offered Lyndon LaRouche as a presidential candidate in 1976, Shaw's International Trade Mart was a subsidiary of a shadowy entity known as the Centro Mondiale Commerciale (World Trade Center), which was founded in Montreal, Canada, in the late 1950s, then moved to Rome in 1961.

The Trade Mart was connected with Centro Mondiale Commerciale (CMC) through yet another shadowy firm named Permindex (PERManent INDustrial EXpositions), also in the business of international expositions.

It is fascinating to note that in the 1962 edition of *Who's Who in the South and Southwest*, Shaw gave biographical information stating that he was on the board of directors of Permindex. However, in the 1963–1964 edition, the reference to Permindex was dropped.

In the late 1960s, both Permindex and its parent company, Centro Mondiale Commerciale, came under intense scrutiny by the Italian news media. It was discovered that on the board of CMC was Prince Gutierrez di Spadaforo, a wealthy aristocrat who had been undersecretary of agriculture under the dictator Benito Mussolini and whose daughter-in-law was related to Nazi minister of finance Hjalmar Schacht; Carlo D'Amelio, an attorney for the former Italian royal family; and Ferenc Nagy, former premier of Hungary and a leading anticommunist.

The Italian media reported that Nagy was president of Permindex and the board chairman and major stockholder was Major Louis Mortimer Bloomfield, a powerful Montreal lawyer who represented the Bronfmans, a Canadian family made wealthy by the liquor industry, as well as serving US intelligence services. Reportedly Bloomfield established Permindex in 1958 as part of the creation of worldwide trade centers connected with CMC.

According to a special report by investigative reporters David Goldman and Jeffrey Steinberg in 1981, Bloomfield was recruited into the British Special Operations Executive in 1938, during the war was given rank within the US Army, and eventually became part of the OSS intelligence system, including the FBI's Division Five, reportedly a small unit within the bureau dealing with counterespionage. According to this report, Bloomfield became quite close with J. Edgar Hoover.

Permindex began to draw attention in 1962, when French president Charles de Gaulle publicly accused the company of channeling funds to the outlawed Secret Army Organization (OAS), which had made several attempts on de Gaulle's life. De Gaulle identified several major and well-known international companies as investors in Permindex.

In tracing the money used to finance the assassination plots against de Gaulle, French intelligence discovered that some $200,000 in secret funds had been sent to Permindex accounts in the Banque de la Credit Internationale.

For years researchers have been intrigued by information Jim Garrison gathered early in his investigation: that in 1962 Guy Banister had dispatched an associate, Maurice Brooks Gatlin—the legal counsel to Banister's anticommunist League of the Caribbean—to Paris with a suitcase full of cash for the OAS, reportedly about $200,000.

As Garrison began to probe this area of interest, he discovered that Gatlin had been killed when he fell or was thrown from the sixth-floor window of a hotel in Panama.

To further complicate this maze of business, finance, European money, holdover Nazis, and intelligence agents, various investigators—including some from *Life* magazine—found that some of the banking connections from this secret empire reached to Mafia chief Meyer Lansky and his gambling operations in the Bahamas.

Whatever the truth behind Centro Mondiale Commerciale and its companion company, Permindex, the Italian government saw fit to expel both in 1962 for subversive activities connected to those in the much-publicized Propaganda-2 Masonic Lodge scandal of more recent years in Italy in which the lodge was accused of attempting to overthrow the Italian government and set up a fascist regime.

The news media in France, Italy, and Canada had a field day tying the two discredited firms to the CIA. And there is now evidence that Shaw indeed was connected to the CIA. Victor Marchetti, former executive assistant to the deputy director of the CIA and author of *The CIA and the Cult of Intelligence*, has revealed that in early 1969, he learned from CIA director Richard Helms that both Clay Shaw and David Ferrie had worked for the agency.

Marchetti said Helms repeatedly voiced concern over the prosecution of Shaw and even instructed top aides "to do all we can to help Shaw." Further, a CIA memo dated September 28, 1967, to the Justice Department, finally made public in 1977, revealed that Shaw had provided the agency with some thirty reports between 1949 and 1956.

It may also be pertinent that in May 1961, just after the disastrous Bay of Pigs Invasion, Shaw introduced CIA deputy director General Charles P. Cabell to the Foreign Policy Association of New Orleans.

By late 1966, Garrison had two suspects in mind in the murder of President Kennedy—the strange David Ferrie and the socially connected Clay Shaw.

David William Ferrie was a character straight out of some fiction novel, but he was frighteningly real. With his painted eyebrows and reddish wig, Ferrie looked like a clown. Yet he was an aggressive homosexual with an appetite for young boys. Ferrie considered himself a master hypnotist, a philosopher, a psychologist, a scientist, a cancer researcher, and a religious "bishop" in the Orthodox Old Catholic Church of North America.

Cashiered as a pilot for Eastern Airlines following publicity over a homosexual arrest, Ferrie continued his flying activities, which included work for both the CIA and reputed New Orleans mob boss Carlos Marcello.

Ferrie also was closely connected to anti-Castro Cubans. In 1961, Ferrie often was seen in the company of Sergio Archaca-Smith, New Orleans director of the virulently anti-Castro Cuban Democratic Revolutionary Front.

That same year, Ferrie was introduced to a meeting of the New Orleans Civic Club as one of the pilots involved in the ill-fated Bay of Pigs Invasion. There, Ferrie made a bitterly anti-Kennedy talk. He also made an anti-Kennedy talk to the New Orleans chapter of the Military Order of World Wars in which he said Kennedy "double-crossed" the invasion force by failing to authorize needed air support. Ferrie's speech was so vitriolic that several members of the audience walked out.

As Garrison continued his investigation, he found abundant evidence that Ferrie, who had been in contact with Oswald, also was connected to Clay Shaw.

Raymond Broshears, a longtime friend of Ferrie's, had seen Ferrie and Shaw together on several occasions. Furthermore, Broshears told Garrison how Ferrie once became intoxicated and detailed how he had driven to Houston the day of Kennedy's death to meet two members of the assassination team from Dallas. The pair was to have arrived in Houston in an airplane piloted by one of them, a Cuban exile known only as "Carlos." Ferrie was to have taken Carlos and his fellow assassin out of Houston. Ferrie told Broshears that something had gone wrong. The two men never showed up.

Whether or not the Broshears account of Ferrie's comments is accurate, Garrison soon found others who had known of the relationship between Ferrie and Shaw. Jules Ricco Kimble, a member of the Ku Klux Klan, told Garrison of being introduced to Shaw by Ferrie, as did a Ferrie acquaintance named David Logan. Nicholas Tadin, the head of the New Orleans musicians' union, told Garrison that he and his wife had sought out Ferrie for flying lessons when they saw Ferrie and Shaw together at New Orleans Airport.

As Garrison's investigation broadened to include trips to Dallas, Houston, and Miami by members of his team, the secrecy surrounding his probe began to crumble. On February 17, 1967, the dam broke when the *New Orleans States-Item* published a story on Garrison's activities with the headline: DA HERE LAUNCHES FULL JFK DEATH PLOT PROBE. The story noted that the district attorney's office had spent more than $8,000 in travel and "investigative expenses." Countering the charge that he was simply seeking publicity, Garrison later wrote, "We had operated as secretly as possible, assuming this was the most efficient and responsible way to handle such a potentially explosive situation. However, the voucher requests were public records, so they could not legally be concealed."

The local news story brought a deluge of media attention from across the nation. Reporters began arriving in New Orleans. The next day, Garrison was forced to come out in the open, announcing, "We have been investigating the role of the City of New Orleans in the assassination of President Kennedy, and we have made some progress—I think substantial progress. . . . What's more, there will be arrests."

Also arriving in the city were some odd characters who would add to the carnival atmosphere that was beginning to take shape. One was a self-styled Denver oilman who told Garrison he could "guarantee" him a federal judgeship if he would drop his investigation into the president's death. Garrison showed him the door.

Not long after this attempt at bribery a more sinister plan came to light. A professional criminal from Philadelphia named Edward Whalen came to Garrison and said he had been approached by David Ferrie with a proposal to kill Garrison for $25,000. When Whalen declined the offer, he said, Ferrie took him to Clay Shaw's apartment, where both men tried to persuade him to carry out the assassination of Garrison. This time Whalen not only was offered money but was told that if he did the job there would be top medical care and a college education for his daughter, who suffered from polio.

Ferrie even went so far as to claim he had helped set up the JFK assassination and told Whalen that Lee Oswald was a CIA agent who had been well taken care of until he made some mistakes that necessitated his death. Whalen believed Ferrie's story to be unfounded boasts, and he again declined the murder contract.

By the time Whalen revealed this plot to Garrison in September 1967, it was too late to verify it. On February 22, 1967, less than a week after the newspapers broke the story of Garrison's investigation, his chief suspect, David Ferrie, was found dead in his cluttered apartment.

His death was not entirely unexpected by Garrison. The day the newspaper story first ran, Ferrie had telephoned Garrison aide Lou Ivon to say, "You know what this news story does to me, don't you? I'm a dead man. From here on, believe me, I'm a dead man."

Ferrie's nude body had been discovered lying on a living-room sofa surrounded by prescription medicine bottles, several completely empty. One typed suicide note was found on a nearby table while a second was discovered on an upright piano. Three days later the New Orleans coroner ruled that Ferrie had died from "natural causes," specifically a ruptured blood vessel in the brain.

Unconvinced, Garrison checked the empty medicine bottles found near Ferrie's body and discovered one had contained a drug designed to greatly increase a person's metabolism.

It is known that Ferrie suffered from hypertension. A physician friend confirmed to Garrison that if someone suffering from hypertension took a whole bottle of this specific drug, it would cause death very quickly. Garrison later wrote, "I phoned immediately but was told that no blood samples or spinal fluid from Ferrie's autopsy had been retained. I was left with an empty bottle and a number of unanswered questions." Garrison also was left without the man he later described as "one of history's most important individuals."

And Ferrie was not the only person connected to the case to die. Banister reportedly died of a heart attack in June 1964, less than a month after his business partner, Hugh Ward—an investigator who had worked closely with Ferrie—died in a Mexico plane crash that also took the life of New Orleans mayor DeLesseps Morrison.

Yet another man closely connected to Ferrie was Eladio del Valle, a wealthy former Cuban congressman under Batista who had fled Cuba to become a well-known organizer of anti-Castro Cubans in Miami. Del Valle reportedly had paid Ferrie $1,500 a mission to make air raids against Cuba.

Three days before Ferrie's death, Garrison's investigators began trying to locate del Valle. Just twelve hours after Ferrie's death, del Valle's mutilated body was discovered in a Miami parking lot. Police reported that del Valle had been tortured and shot in the heart at point-blank range, and his skull split open with an ax. His murder has never been solved.

With Ferrie and del Valle dead, Garrison began to focus his attention on Clay Shaw. Fearing that Shaw might meet the same fate as Ferrie, Garrison moved rapidly. He and his "special team" had Shaw arrested on March 1, 1967.

Loud and long, Shaw protested his innocence, stating flatly, "I never heard of any plot and I never used any alias in my life."

The question of an alias came up as Shaw was being booked into jail. A police officer filling out forms asked Shaw if he had any aliases. Shaw calmly replied, "Clay Bertrand," thus confirming the information that Garrison had been receiving from various sources around New Orleans. The officer duly noted this alias on his form.

Between the time of his arrest and his trial, Shaw was allowed to go free after posting a $10,000 bail bond.

As Garrison's men searched Shaw's house they found several interesting items, such as two large hooks screwed into the ceiling of Shaw's bedroom along with five whips, several lengths of chain, and a black hood and cape. Shaw tried to shrug off this kinky collection as simply part of a Mardi Gras costume.

Harder to shrug off was Shaw's personal address book, which contained the names of important persons in Italy, Paris, and London.

But most intriguing was a listing for "Lee Odum, P.O. Box 19106, Dallas, Texas." What made this so intriguing was that the address "P.O. 19106" also appears in Lee Harvey Oswald's address book.

Garrison announced that "P.O. 19106" actually was a code for Jack Ruby's unlisted Dallas telephone number and noted that the number was in the address books of both Shaw and Oswald.

Interest in this issue dissipated rapidly following a May 17, 1967, story in the *Dallas Times Herald* revealing that Lee Odum was a real person living in Dallas.

Odum, then thirty-one, told the newspaper that he had traveled to New Orleans in 1966 to promote a bullfight and had been sent to Shaw as a businessman who might be interested in his scheme. He said he gave Shaw the P.O. box number, which had been rented in the name of a barbecue company he operated at the time.

This seemed to clear up the issue, except that the *Times Herald* noted that P.O. Box 19106 did not exist until 1965, when the post office substation involved was remodeled. Therefore, it remains to be explained why that particular box number appeared in Oswald's address book in 1963 and to what it truly pertained.

To further titillate Garrison's interest, he found on an unused page of Shaw's address book the words "Oct" and "Nov" and, following an indecipherable scribble, the name "Dallas."

After Shaw's arrest, the US government "awakened like an angry lion," according to Garrison.

Attorney general Ramsey Clark told news reporters that Shaw had been checked out and cleared of any responsibility in the Kennedy assassination. But since Shaw's name had never before come up in connection with the assassination, questions arose over who in the federal government had investigated Shaw and why. Quickly a Justice Department spokesman tried to backpedal for Clark by issuing this statement: "The attorney general has since determined that this [report of Shaw's investigation] was erroneous. Nothing arose indicating a need to investigate Mr. Shaw."

This explanation was further clouded when a Justice Department official tried to explain that the department had been aware that Clay Shaw and Clay Bertrand were the same man and that the FBI had investigated a Clay Bertrand.

Despite the federal government's protest that Garrison was on a "witch hunt," when his evidence was presented to a New Orleans grand jury, a true bill was returned. Clay Shaw was indicted on a charge that he "did willfully and unlawfully conspire with David W. Ferrie, herein named but not charged, and Lee Harvey Oswald, herein named but not charged, and others, not herein named, to murder John F. Kennedy."

To assure the public that he was doing only his sworn duty, Garrison even took the unprecedented step of having himself—the prosecutor—file for a preliminary hearing for Shaw. This hearing, usually the providence of the defense, took place on March 14, 1967, before three judges, who reviewed Garrison's evidence. After studying Garrison's case for three days, the three-judge panel upheld the indictment and ordered Shaw to a jury trial.

For the next year and a half, as the world waited for Garrison's case to be presented at Shaw's trial, the major US news media lambasted the events in New Orleans. Garrison later wrote:

> Some long-cherished illusions of mine about the great free press in our country underwent a painful reappraisal during this period. The restraint and respect for justice one might expect from the press to insure a fair trial not only to the individual charged but to the state itself did not exist. Nor did the diversity of opinion that I always thought was fundamental to the American press. As far as I could tell, the reports and editorials in *Newsweek, Time, The New York Times*, the *New York Post, The Saturday Evening Post*, and on and on were indistinguishable. All shared the basic view that I was a power-mad, irresponsible showman who was producing a slimy circus with the objective of getting elected to higher office, oblivious to any consequences.

Garrison also commented on further efforts to give Shaw every consideration:

> In this particular case, I've taken unusual steps to protect the rights of the defendant and assure him a fair trial. Before we introduced the testimony of our witnesses, we made them undergo independent verifying tests, including polygraph examination, truth serum, and hypnosis. We thought this would be hailed as an unprecedented step in jurisprudence. Instead, the press turned around and hinted that we had drugged our witnesses or given them posthypnotic suggestions to testify falsely.

This comment might have been aimed at James Phelan, a writer for the *Saturday Evening Post* who, after hearing Garrison's account of his evidence, reported that Garrison's key witness, Perry Russo, came up with his story of a Ferrie-Oswald-Shaw conspiracy only after being "drugged" and hypnotized by Garrison's people.

Phelan's account has been accepted by some researchers who failed to note that Russo told the press of the conspiracy meeting well before undergoing hypnosis. In fact, when Phelan appeared as a defense witness for Shaw, Russo soundly disputed his claims, though Russo's conviction that Shaw was the man at the meeting appeared to weaken.

Particularly galling to Garrison was an account by Hugh Aynesworth, then working for *Newsweek*, claiming Garrison had offered an unwilling witness $3,000 and an airline job to testify in the upcoming trial. The story added that the entire bribery attempt had been tape-recorded.

Aynesworth was a writer for the *Dallas Morning News* the day of the assassination and was at the scene of each important event. In 1988, Aynesworth wrote extensively for a special edition of the *Washington Times* commemorating the twenty-fifth anniversary of the assassination. While admitting "flaws" in the Warren Commission investigation, he nevertheless supported its conclusions by writing, "That report has been proven to have been considerably more honest, more objective and of far greater depth than any subsequent 'probe' or 'inquiry.'"

When asked to provide evidence of Garrison's bribery attempt, Aynesworth failed to present either a witness or the tape recording he had mentioned. Internal CIA documents later made public showed Aynesworth, then working as a reporter for the *Dallas Morning News,* offered his services to the agency prior to the assassination and later was considered "a Warren Commission man on the assassination." As late as 2012, Aynesworth was still being given much space in the *Dallas Morning News* to attack "conspiracy theorists."

During the Shaw trial, the media made much out of a visit to Las Vegas by Garrison, where reportedly he received a $5,000 credit line at the Sands Hotel. In 1979, a report to the House Select Committee on Assassinations even stated that Garrison met with mobster Johnny Roselli less than a month after Ferrie's death.

For his part, Garrison wrote to researcher John Judge, retorting, "I have never even seen John Roselli in my life; nor have I ever had a 'secret meeting' with any racketeer anywhere."

An NBC program stated that one of Garrison's witnesses had lied under oath, but when requested to present their evidence to a New Orleans grand jury, news executives declined. In that same NBC program, newsman Frank McGee claimed two of Garrison's star witnesses had failed their polygraph tests. Garrison publicly offered to resign if the network could substantiate this charge. Again, no proof was forthcoming.

CBS interviewed Garrison, but as he later reported, "When the CBS program was shown across the nation, my half hour had been reduced to approximately 30 seconds. This gave me just about enough time to be a discordant bleep in the network's massive four-hour tribute to the Warren Commission."

Shortly before Clay Shaw's trial, Garrison believed he may have been the object of a setup to implicate him with a known homosexual and a former client. He escaped arrest and was shocked to learn that one of his "special team" members, a former FBI man, may have been responsible for the bizarre episode. However, before Garrison could question the man, he hurriedly left New Orleans, taking many of the district attorney's files with him. Garrison also claimed that someone had "bugged" the telephones of his office, his home, and even his staff.

The anti-Garrison media blitz coupled with the strange incidents surrounding his investigation prompted Garrison to claim that "a tremendous amount of federal power" had been arrayed against him in an effort to block his investigation of Kennedy's death.

He voiced his concern over a fair trial when he told interviewer Eric Norden, "I'm beginning to worry about the cumulative effect of this propaganda blitzkrieg on potential jurors for the trial of Clay Shaw. I don't know how long they can withstand the drumbeat obligato of charges exonerating the defendant and convicting the prosecutor."

Garrison claimed this concerted effort to stop his investigation proved two things: "First, that we were correct when we uncovered the involvement of the CIA in the assassination; second, that there is something very wrong today with our government in Washington, D.C., inasmuch as it is willing to use massive economic power to conceal the truth from the people."

But Garrison was not without supporters. A group of New Orleans businessmen, going under the name "Truth or Consequences," gave Garrison both moral and financial backing.

Surprising solidarity came from Boston's Cardinal Richard Cushing, father confessor to the Kennedy family, who commented, "I think they [the investigation in New Orleans] should follow it through. . . . I never believed the assassination was the work of one man."

Another odd show of support for Garrison came years later from a most unlikely source. Shortly before his disappearance, Teamster boss Jimmy Hoffa stated, "Jim Garrison's a smart man . . . goddamned smart attorney. . . . Anybody thinks he's a kook is a kook themselves."

There is some evidence that Robert Kennedy also took Garrison's probe seriously. He indicated to his friend Arthur M. Schlesinger Jr. that he believed Garrison might be onto something. But once when his staff began to tell him about Garrison's findings, he turned away, saying, "Well, I don't think I want to know."

By January 29, 1969, the day the Clay Shaw trial finally got under way, Garrison's case was already foundering. His chief suspect, Ferrie, was dead and others had fled New Orleans and were safe in other states that refused to honor Garrison's legal extradition requests.

Governor John Connally, himself a victim in Dallas, refused to extradite Cuban leader Sergio Archaca-Smith, while California governor Ronald Reagan declined to allow extradition for one Edgar Eugene Bradley. Garrison, in a mistake that would cost him further credibility, apparently had mistaken Bradley for Mafia man Eugene Hale Brading, who was arrested in Dealey Plaza shortly after the assassination.

But Garrison's major "missing witness" was Gordon Novel, then a young electronics expert who eventually became embroiled in some of this nation's most controversial cases. Novel first approached Garrison in early 1967 with information about David Ferrie and Cuban exile activities, but soon Garrison came to believe that Novel was a CIA "plant." Some researchers also identified Novel as the "umbrella man" in Dealey Plaza but his claim to have been in New York City at the time and the fact that he lived until his seventy-fourth year belied that notion.

After Garrison subpoenaed Novel, he fled to Ohio, where governor James Rhodes, despite a personal call from Louisiana governor John McKeithen, refused to allow extradition. Likewise, the governor of Nebraska declined to honor an extradition order for Sandra Moffett, a former girlfriend of Perry Russo's who was present at the gathering of Ferrie, Shaw, and Oswald in September 1963.

A note left behind in his New Orleans apartment, which was later authenticated as being written by Novel, mentioned his work for Double Check Corporation, a

CIA "front" located in Miami. The letter stated, "Our connection and activity of that period [with Double Check] involves individuals presently . . . about to be indicted as conspirators in Mr. Garrison's investigation."

In 1974 Novel, who later in life claimed to have worked with the CIA, though never as an employee, met with President Nixon's special counsel Charles Colson and discussed developing a special degaussing machine that would erase Nixon's incriminating White House tapes from afar. Novel also cropped up as an electronics expert in the case of automobile magnate John DeLorean and again as an imaging expert in the court trial of Waco's Branch Davidians. Novel died in October 2012.

Despite the media attacks and missing witnesses, Garrison gamely moved ahead with his prosecution of Clay Shaw. His goals were twofold: (1) convince the jury that a conspiracy was behind President Kennedy's death, and (2) prove that Clay Shaw was a part of that conspiracy. Garrison achieved the first goal but failed on the second.

After a string of witnesses from Dallas—including the Bill Newmans and railroad man James L. Simmons and others not called before the Warren Commission—told of shots to Kennedy's front and medical experts pointed out the shortcomings of the president's autopsy, the jury became convinced of Garrison's charge that a conspiracy had existed. This conviction solidified when the jury viewed the Zapruder film of the assassination—made available for the first time thanks to Garrison's subpoena power. After the trial, the polled jury agreed that Garrison had convinced them that Kennedy had died as the result of a conspiracy.

However, the evidence of Shaw's involvement proved less convincing. Despite several credible people who testified they had seen David Ferrie and Lee Oswald with a man matching Clay Shaw's description, including several prominent residents of Clinton, Louisiana, many jurors remained skeptical.

Insurance salesman Perry Russo repeated his 1967 statements that he was present when Shaw and Ferrie talked about assassinating Kennedy. Russo said that Shaw was introduced to him as Clem Bertrand. He said Ferrie and the man he identified as Shaw talked of triangulation of gunfire and the need to have alibis at the time of the assassination.

Defense attorneys countered that Russo had been given a truth serum drug to help his recall and reiterated the charge that Garrison had implanted the entire Ferrie-Shaw story while Russo was under the drug's influence.

One particularly compelling witness was Vernon Bundy, who testified he had seen Clay Shaw meet with Lee Harvey Oswald at a seawall on Lake Pontchartrain, near New Orleans, in June 1963. Bundy said he knew the man speaking with Oswald was Shaw because he noticed the man had a slight limp. A puzzled Shaw was asked to walk down the center aisle of the courtroom and everyone, including an amazed Garrison, noticed for the first time a nearly imperceptible limp.

Another credible witness was postman James Hardiman, who testified that during 1966 he had delivered letters addressed to "Clay Bertrand" to a forwarding address for Clay Shaw. Hardiman said none of the letters were returned.

Then came Charles Spiesel, a New York accountant who had suddenly shown up in New Orleans to tell Garrison that he had met David Ferrie on a visit and that they had been joined by Clay Shaw. Appearing to be a credible witness, he had been belatedly added to Garrison's witness list.

Once Spiesel was on the stand, Garrison cringed at the man's cross-examination. The man rambled on about how he had been hypnotized on several occasions by various unidentified people and how he regularly fingerprinted his daughter upon her return from Louisiana State University to make sure she was really his daughter.

Garrison's case also was not helped by several statements Spiesel made prior to the Shaw trial, including the claims that Shaw had met with Ruby and Oswald in the Jack Tar Capital House in Baton Rouge on September 3, 1963, and handed them money, and that the man who killed President Kennedy had fired a .45-caliber pistol, then fled through the Dallas drainage system to another part of town. None of these claims were substantiated.

More harm came in the testimony of attorney Dean Andrews, who, while under a perjury charge by Garrison, changed his story of being called by a man named Clay Bertrand and asked to defend Oswald just after the assassination. On the stand, Andrews said the name "Clay Bertrand" was simply a "figment of [his] imagination" and that he had never known Clay Shaw. Andrews's statements strongly affected the jury, although later Garrison convicted Andrews of perjury based on this testimony.

And when assistant district attorney James L. Alcock tried to discredit Andrews's testimony, it appeared he was impeaching the core of Garrison's allegation that Shaw and Bertrand were one and the same.

So the crux of the case came down to whether Clay Shaw, the respected director of the International Trade Mart, and Clay (or Clem) Bertrand, the man overheard plotting against Kennedy, were the same man.

Garrison's strongest piece of evidence was Shaw's jail card, which showed he used the alias Clay Bertrand. Yet Criminal District Court judge Edward Aloysius Haggerty refused to allow the jail card to be introduced as evidence, arguing that Shaw had not been allowed to have a lawyer with him during the booking procedure.

Garrison's hole card became New Orleans policeman Aloysius J. Habighorst, the jailer who filled out Shaw's admission form, and who was expected to testify that Shaw had told him his alias was Clay Bertrand. However, before Habighorst could take the stand, Judge Haggerty ordered the jury removed from the courtroom. He told stunned prosecutors that he was not allowing Habighorst's testimony to be admitted because again no attorney had been present and his alias story appeared to violate Shaw's rights.

Judge Haggerty then said, "Even if [Shaw] did [admit the alias], it is not admissible. If Officer Habighorst is telling the truth—and I seriously doubt it . . ." This remark brought Assistant District Attorney Alcock to his feet, saying, "Are you passing on the credibility of a state witness in front of the press and the whole world?" To this Judge Haggerty responded, "It's outside the presence of the jury. I do not care.

The whole world can hear that I do not believe Officer Habighorst. I do not believe Officer Habighorst."

Alcock moved to have a mistrial declared, but Judge Haggerty denied this, ordering the trial to proceed without the crucial testimony of Officer Habighorst.

With the judge's statements, Garrison's case, already severely weakened by dead, incredible, and unobtainable witnesses, collapsed.

Clay Shaw took the stand in his own defense, claiming that he never knew Ferrie, Oswald, or Ruby and that he had not participated in a plot to kill Kennedy. Garrison's team was unable to provide any motivation for Shaw's involvement in such a scheme.

Just past midnight on March 1, 1969—two years to the day that Shaw had first been arrested—the jury filed into Judge Haggerty's courtroom to announce Clay Shaw's acquittal after less than an hour of deliberation.

Two days later, on March 3, Garrison filed perjury charges against Shaw for maintaining that he never met David Ferrie. Garrison later wrote:

> We had more witnesses to prove this flagrant case of perjury than I had ever encountered as district attorney. . . . Given my personal choice, I would much rather have let the matter rest once and for all. . . . However, the choice was not mine. My decision had been made automatically when— contrary to the numerous statements in our files—Shaw had taken the witness stand and, in his grand and courtly manner, made a mockery of the law against lying under oath.

But again Garrison had not counted on the federal government.

According to federal law at the time, "A court of the United States may not grant an injunction to stay proceedings in a State Court except as expressly authorized by an Act of Congress, or where necessary in aid of its jurisdiction, or to protect or effectuate its judgments."

Garrison wrote:

> Fortunately for Shaw, the federal judicial system shut its eyes to that federal law. The United States District Court DID [*sic*] enjoined me from prosecuting Shaw for committing perjury, and the federal appellate structure firmly backed up the District Court's ruling all the way. When the assassination of a dead president has been ratified by a live national government, details such as the law very quickly become irrelevant.

Clay Shaw, his finances depleted after years of defending himself and despondent over the revelations of his homosexual connections, retired to his New Orleans home, where he died on August 14, 1974.

Even Shaw's death did not pass without question. Neighbors saw some men carrying what appeared to be a body completely covered by a sheet on a stretcher into a carriage house belonging to Shaw. They called the coroner's office, which dispatched investigators. The coroner's investigators found Shaw's home empty and, after a day of searching, learned that Shaw had just been buried in his hometown of Kentwood. A death certificate signed by a Dr. Hugh Betson stated death was caused by lung cancer.

New Orleans coroner Dr. Frank Minyard, concerned over the circumstances of Shaw's death and the rapidity of burial, initially said he would seek a court order to exhume Shaw's body. However, word reached the news media, which immediately editorialized against such a move, hinting that the exhumation was just another attack by Garrison, and Minyard dropped the whole matter.

Despite his courtroom loss and the tidal wave of negative publicity—the *New York Times* called the case "one of the most disgraceful chapters in the history of American jurisprudence" while the *New Orleans States-Item* demanded Garrison's resignation—the scrappy district attorney nevertheless handily won reelection later that year.

But his troubles with the federal government were not over. On June 30, 1971, Garrison was arrested at his home by Internal Revenue Service agents who charged him with accepting illegal payoffs from pinball-machine operators. After two years of more bad publicity, he was finally brought to trial. Several pinball-machine operators told of making payoffs, but none of them could directly implicate Garrison.

Finally, a former Garrison investigator and Army buddy, Pershing Gervais, took the stand and told how Garrison had accepted $150,000 in payoffs. He even produced a tape recording reportedly made of the district attorney discussing the matter. But on cross-examination, Gervais admitted that he had told a television reporter that the Justice Department had forced him to lie and incriminate Garrison. Gervais had admitted the case against Garrison was "a total, complete political frame-up, absolutely." Furthermore, a speech expert testified that the incriminating tape had been created by splicing together several innocuous comments Garrison had made.

Garrison and two codefendants were quickly found not guilty, but enough damage had been done. Busy defending himself in court, Garrison failed to mount an effective campaign in 1973 and was defeated for district attorney by 2,000 votes.

Furthermore, the federal government came at him again, this time alleging income tax evasion in connection with the discredited pinball payoffs. Again Garrison was found not guilty, but by this time the national audience had largely turned its back on the "controversial" lawman in New Orleans.

Even today many assassination researchers believe Garrison was far afield of truth about Kennedy's death. Many agree with House Select Committee on Assassinations chief counsel Robert Blakey, who bluntly wrote, "In short, the Garrison case was a fraud."

Blakey, who claims organized crime killed Kennedy, apparently fails to see any suspicious connection in that David Ferrie was with New Orleans mob boss Carlos Marcello in court on the morning of the assassination; that Ferrie was the Civil Air

Patrol leader of Lee Harvey Oswald; and that Ferrie and Clay Shaw both worked for the CIA and were connected to anti-Castro Cubans.

It should also be pointed out that critics of Blakey's work on the House committee noted a cozy relationship between Blakey and government agencies, such as the FBI and CIA.

Buried at the end of the "Principal Sources" section in his book, *The Plot to Kill the President*, Blakey gives evidence of pre-censorship as well as his relationship with certain government agencies by writing:

> Pursuant to agreement with the House Select Committee on Assassinations, the Central Intelligence Agency and the Federal Bureau of Investigation reviewed this book in manuscript form to determine that classified information it contained had been properly released for publication and that no informant was identified. Neither the CIA nor the FBI warrants the factual material or endorses the views expressed.

Another Garrison detractor, author David E. Scheim, who also espouses the Mafia-did-it theory, cited the charges against Garrison made by NBC, *Newsweek,* the *New York Times*, and the *Saturday Evening Post* apparently without considering that few of their accusations were ever proven.

Citing Garrison's failure to loudly identify Jack Ruby as Mafia-connected, Scheim wrote, "Although Garrison made extravagant charges against an assortment of Cuban exiles, CIA agents, Minutemen, White Russians, and Nazis, he conspicuously avoided any reference to one prime assassination suspect: the Mafia."

Indeed, Garrison's failure to acknowledge Carlos Marcello and the mob's activities in New Orleans has caused many raised eyebrows among researchers otherwise kindly disposed toward the former DA.

Scheim claims Garrison's former investigator Gervais, was a Marcello associate and when Garrison cleaned up Bourbon Street nightspots, he "selectively avoided the clubs controlled by Marcello." The author also expressed the belief that Garrison's acquittal in the 1971 payoff case was the result of more bribes.

Scheim goes beyond Blakey by stating that Garrison's activities in New Orleans had a sinister design, writing: "The purpose of the Garrison assassination probe [was that] Jim Garrison conducted a fraudulent probe of the Kennedy assassination, which deflected attention from Carlos Marcello and disrupted serious investigation of the case."

Stung by such suspicions, Garrison wrote, "While I lay no pretense to being the epitome of virtue, with regard to connections with organized crime, I think you can safely place me as having approximately the same such connections as Mother Teresa and Pope Paul. What has been occurring here, quite obviously, is the CIA's disinformation machinery has been hard at work for a long time."

Further, Garrison once told this author that while elements within the mob undoubtedly played a role in Kennedy's assassination, they were certainly aided by elements within the US government. He said he wanted the architects of the assassination, not just the mechanics.

To the charge that he was simply grandstanding, hoping for higher office, Garrison has stated, "A politically ambitious man would hardly be likely to challenge the massed power of the federal government and criticize so many honorable figures and distinguished agencies. Actually, this charge is an argument in favor of my investigation: Would such a slimy type, eager to profiteer on the assassination, jeopardize his political ambitions if he didn't have an ironclad case?"

While charge and countercharge, claim and counterclaim, surrounded Garrison, he continued to serve as an elected appeals court judge in New Orleans. Until his death from cancer in 1992, Garrison continued to speak out for a truth he claimed was denied five decades ago.

Garrison believed President Kennedy was killed for one primary reason—he was working for reconciliation with Soviet Russia and Castro's Cuba. Garrison wrote:

> To anyone with a grain of intelligence, it should be apparent that John Kennedy was eliminated by forces desiring the continuation of the Cold War—an artificial conflict draining the assets of and greatly changing, for the worst, the character of our nation. The clandestine arm for those Cold War forces was the Central Intelligence Agency—the destructive talents of which run the gambit [*sic*] from deception to murder.

He has even identified those "forces," stating:

> On the operative level of the conspiracy, you find anti-Castro Cuban exiles who never forgave Kennedy for failing to send in U.S. air cover at the Bay of Pigs. . . . They believed sincerely that Kennedy had sold them out to the communists. On a higher, control level, you find a number of people of ultra-right persuasion—not simply conservatives, mind you, but people who could be described as neo-Nazi including a small clique that had defected from the Minutemen because it had considered the group "too liberal." These elements had their canteens ready and their guns loaded; they lacked only a target. [After the secret agreements of the Cuban Missile Crisis] Kennedy . . . began to crack down on CIA operations against Cuba. As a result, on July 31, 1963, the FBI raided the headquarters of the group of Cuban exiles and Minutemen training north of Lake Pontchartrain and confiscated all their guns and ammunition—despite the fact that the operation had the sanction of the CIA. This action may have sealed Kennedy's fate. . . . The link between the "command" level and the Cuban exiles was an amorphous group called the Free Cuba Committee [recall that this name was tied to Lee Harvey Oswald the night of the assassination by Dallas County district attorney Henry Wade, who was then corrected by none other than Jack Ruby], which with CIA sanction had been training north

of Lake Pontchartrain for an assassination attempt on Fidel Castro. . . .
Our information indicates that it was shortly after this setback [the July
31, 1963, FBI raid] that the group switched direction and decided to assassinate John Kennedy instead of Fidel Castro.

This synopsis was voiced by Garrison in 1967, before there was any public knowledge of Operation Mongoose. Theologian James W. Douglass came to the same
conclusion in his 2008 book, *JFK and the Unspeakable*, writing:

JFK and RFK were targeted because they refused to comply with the national security demands imposed upon them from the Bay of Pigs to the
Cuban Missile Crisis and Vietnam. Two and a half years into his presidency, enlightened by the Missile Crisis and emboldened by the hope of
peace, JFK had reached a point where he began to transcend the ruling
assumptions of national security. He was inspired to seek peace with such
enemies of the state as Nikita Khrushchev and Fidel Castro.

While this assessment may be debated for years to come, it nevertheless remains
true that Garrison's investigation in New Orleans did turn up much previously unknown evidence—another argument against his employment by the mob to deflect
the truth.

Even the House committee's Blakey, who termed Garrison's investigation a
"fraud," conceded, "Garrison might have been on the right track, at least up until
Ferrie's untimely death . . . for evidence of an association between Ferrie and Oswald, presented at the Clay Shaw trial, was found by the committee to be credible."

The House Select Committee on Assassinations

By the mid-1970s, national polls indicated that very few Americans still believed the
Warren Commission's lone-assassin theory, despite assurances of the Establishment
media and government spokesmen. According to one Gallup poll, 81 percent of
the American public believed President Kennedy's death resulted from a conspiracy,
while 70 percent believed the same regarding the death of Dr. Martin Luther King.

These nagging doubts prompted congressman Henry Gonzalez of Texas to introduce a House resolution in February 1975 calling for a select committee to study
not only the death of John F. Kennedy, but also the deaths of Robert Kennedy and
Martin Luther King, and the 1972 shooting of Alabama governor George Wallace.

In remarks to fellow congressmen, Gonzalez said, "I have introduced this resolution after much consideration. It has not been a decision I have made hastily. . . .
There are questions to be resolved. I was at Dallas the day that President Kennedy
was killed and I suspended judgment on the questions that arose then and shortly

thereafter until Watergate, August 1972, revealed possibilities heretofore considered not possible."

In an article published by St. Mary's School of Law two months later, Gonzalez added, "There are a few who have offered criticism of my efforts. . . . The attitude of these people is to 'let sleeping dogs lie.' . . . I say that this investigation is a need and has its proper place in our list of priorities. What future do we have as a nation if we let valid questions about these assassinations go unresolved and uninvestigated except by private individuals?"

Gonzalez's House Resolution 204 was joined by a similar resolution, sponsored by lame-duck representative Thomas N. Downing of Virginia. In remarks to fellow congressmen on March 18, 1976, Downing complained of foot-dragging:

> In the past few weeks, certain events have transpired in this House which concern me deeply and which lead me to believe either I don't understand the House half as well as I thought I did, or that the House is undergoing a deep and fundamental transformation as a result of those tragic events which we collectively label "Watergate." Until now, it has seemed to me that, although Congress might not have dealt with all problems wisely, it has not been its policy simply and doggedly to refuse to look at a serious national problem, no matter how difficult, no matter how distressing. Yet, I fear that is precisely what it is doing today. It is simply and doggedly refusing to look at the problem of who executed our former President, John F. Kennedy, and why he was executed. I do not exaggerate. I have chosen my words carefully, and I mean precisely what I say. . . . However, we not only have failed to make any progress toward establishment of such an investigating committee, we also have not even been able to get a hearing on the merits before the Rules Committee. . . . I have been told informally that "the Leadership" is against reopening the Warren Commission's findings, and that is that. . . . Why would there be reluctance on the part of the Leadership and the committee? Have they been told by the Intelligence Community, which, incidentally, possibly acted as sole investigators for the Warren Commission, what really did happen to our young President, and why? Do they know who was behind the killing? Is it too horrible for the American people to face? . . . Someone apparently does not want us to see the evil, hear the evil and certainly does not want us to talk about it. . . . After all, if a President is eliminated, not by a "lone nut," but for political reasons, isn't the whole fabric of our form of government in direct danger if we cover up the political motivations and go on as if nothing happened?

Despite these passionate appeals for a reinvestigation into the assassinations, action stalled in the House for more than a year. The Rules Committee simply refused to even consider the idea.

Finally in mid-1976, the Black Caucus, at the instigation of Dr. King's wife,

Coretta, put pressure on the House leadership, and the Gonzalez and Downing bills were merged into House Resolution 1540 and passed in September 1976. However, the committee would expire at the end of the congressional term on January 3, 1977.

Trouble began immediately. House tradition dictated that the author of a resolution creating a select committee be named chair. Downing, who had not sought reelection in 1976, would soon retire and Gonzalez, a highly individualistic Mexican-American, was not liked by House power brokers.

Despite Downing's lame-duck status, he was named chairman of the House Select Committee on Assassinations by Speaker Thomas P. "Tip" O'Neill, a decision that did not please Gonzalez, who began to serve as cochairman.

Early on, Downing wanted Washington attorney Bernard Fensterwald to serve as the committee's chief counsel and director. Fensterwald, who had formed a clearinghouse of assassination material called the Committee to Investigate Assassinations, was an early critic of the Warren Commission and thoroughly familiar with most aspects of the John F. Kennedy case.

Gonzalez objected and Fensterwald withdrew from consideration, but not before an article appeared in the *Washington Star* under the headline ASSASSINATION INQUIRY STUMBLING—IS FENSTERWALD A CIA PLANT? Later it was learned that information for this attack came from Gonzalez's office.

In October 1976, Downing and Gonzalez settled on a former Philadelphia prosecutor, Richard A. Sprague, as the committee's chief counsel. Initially, Sprague seemed like an excellent choice. He had a record of sixty-nine convictions out of seventy homicide cases, and was well regarded as a tough and independent prosecutor. He had received national attention by his prosecution of United Mine Workers president Tony Boyle for the murder of UMW reformer Joseph Yablonski.

Sprague stated he planned to break his investigation into two separate areas: one for John Kennedy and one for Dr. King. He said these assassination inquiries would be treated as homicide investigations. This was a novel approach to the Kennedy assassination since, until that time, all investigation and deliberation had been conducted in secret by the government.

Bypassing the FBI and the CIA, Sprague hired professional investigators and criminal lawyers from New York City. He made it clear that his investigation would not hesitate to look into FBI and CIA involvement and that he would use subpoena power and lie-detector tests to get to the truth. Aware of the CIA connections to the Kennedy assassination, Sprague let it be known he planned to subpoena both agency files and personnel.

Sprague also contacted many of the responsible Kennedy assassination researchers, including district attorney Jim Garrison in New Orleans, and privately told them he planned to use them as committee consultants. He was also truthful in projecting the costs of such a massive investigation, saying he needed a staff of at least two hundred and an initial budget of $6.5 million to start work.

Sprague's openness about both his needs and his goals prompted immediate outrage among congressmen who had never wanted the committee in the first place.

Many of these lambasted Sprague for his statements about using lie detectors, voice stress analyzers, and hidden tape recorders to learn the truth. Soon Sprague was too busy fending off media attacks to get his investigation rolling.

Other developments began to raise doubts in the minds of many assassination researchers, whose hopes had grown since the committee was created. To begin with, Sprague early on stated, "I have not, as of this date, read the Warren Commission Report or testimony. But I have never read any books by the critics, either."

This unfamiliarity with the assassination was reflected in Sprague's selection of the prosecutors and lawmen as investigators and staff for the committee. Many were aggressive and able but they did not understand the full ramifications of the case. Many had ties back to the FBI or CIA and none of them had the time to properly study the convoluted assassination issues.

In recent years it was learned that the CIA had a man inside the committee. The CIA grudgingly acknowledged that George Joannides, a thirty-year veteran of the agency, was paying out $51,000 a month to the Cuban Student Directorate, an anti-Castro organization whose members publicized Lee Oswald's pro-Castro activities both before and after the assassination. It also was learned that Joannides served as the CIA's principal coordinator with the committee but did not disclose his role in the anti-Castro events of 1963.

In 2009 reporter Scott Shane of the *New York Times* wrote, "That concealment has fueled suspicion that Mr. Joannides's real assignment was to limit what the House committee could learn about CIA activities." In 2013, the agency still was withholding nearly three hundred documents pertaining to the anti-Cuban activities of the early 1960s, claiming release could cause "extreme grave damage" to national security.

Documents released in 2007 following a Freedom of Information Act lawsuit showed that Joannides had received the Career Intelligence Medal, one of the CIA's highest honors, in July 1981, less than three years after he stonewalled the House committee regarding agency activities. A Justice Department official denied that the medal had any relation to Joannides's work with the committee but failed to provide any substantiation.

Despite Sprague's wooing of the research community, those with detailed knowledge of the cases, with few exceptions, were excluded from the House committee's staff.

Then there was the question of Sprague's close friendship with his former boss Arlen Specter, the Warren Commission staffer who created the "single bullet" theory of the assassination. Sprague was pushed to protest, "I did not talk to Arlen before I took this thing."

Sprague incensed Gonzalez immediately by renting a plush apartment in Washington's Watergate complex, then leaving for a vacation in Acapulco without informing the committee's founder.

With his absence and presumptuous pronouncements, Sprague was making enemies everywhere. Representative Robert E. Bauman of Maryland charged that Sprague "virtually assumed the role of chairman of the committee."

As 1976 drew to a close and Sprague found himself under attack by the media, including the *New York Times*, the committee's reconstitution in January suddenly began to appear precarious.

Sprague was baffled at the hostility directed at him. He told committee staffers, "You know, I don't understand it. I've never been in a situation like this before where I am getting criticized for things I might do. It's nonsense, but I don't know why it's happening."

His proposed budget was targeted for attack, but Sprague held his ground, saying, "Several people around here who are familiar with the bureaucratic game told me to first present a smaller budget. They assured me that I could always go back later and plead for more. That's the way they do things in Washington, I was told. Well, I won't play that game."

The press attacks caused second thoughts in Congress. A resolution reconstituting the Assassinations Committee by a unanimous-consent voice vote on January 4, 1977, failed. It would take weeks of maneuvering before the committee could officially be reconstituted. By this time, Downing had retired and Gonzalez had been named chairman.

Suddenly the outside media attacks on Sprague were joined by an unexpected source—committee chairman Gonzalez. According to people familiar with this situation, Gonzalez, already angered at not being named chairman until after Downing retired and at Sprague's early activities or lack of them, was further incensed that Sprague would not allow him to run the committee the way he saw fit.

And there was the continuing problem of funding. Sprague had been told he had $150,000 a month for expenses until the committee was reconstituted in January 1977. Later he found out that amount actually was only $84,000, which caused a cost overrun for which Gonzalez was taken to task by the House Rules Committee—the same committee that had stalled the Assassinations Committee in the first place. Gonzalez claimed Sprague had spent money without his knowledge or consent.

Gonzalez ordered Sprague to take a "number of steps," including giving written assurance that he would stay within the financial constraints of the committee's funding and firing recently hired staff members. Sprague's refusal to bow to Gonzalez's demands prompted the hot-tempered Texas representative to order Sprague to return all Gonzalez letterhead material.

Staff investigator Gaeton Fonzi noted, "Since all congressional committees use the postal franking privileges of its chairman, and every expense voucher, travel order, and most directives and requests are made under the chairman's signature, what Gonzalez was doing, in effect, was virtually stopping the operation of the committee."

Next Gonzalez further blocked the committee's work by asking the attorney general to deny staffers' access to FBI files and by cutting off their long-distance phone calls. Sprague reportedly remarked to coworkers, "Gonzalez went berserk."

Finally, in a hand-delivered letter, Gonzalez charged Sprague with being "engaged in a course of conduct that is wholly intolerable for any employee of the House" and ordered him to vacate his office that same day. However, within a few hours the other eleven members of the committee had written their own letter, instructing Sprague to ignore Gonzalez. This infighting continued, with Gonzalez telling reporters that Sprague was a "rattlesnake."

It appears that both Gonzalez and Sprague may have been the objects of secret personal smear campaigns—with Sprague being told Gonzalez was trying to subvert the committee's work while Gonzalez was being told that Sprague was a CIA plant on the committee.

Early in March 1977, Gonzalez resigned from the Assassinations Committee claiming that Sprague had refused to cut costs and had tried to undermine his authority as chairman. Back home in San Antonio, Gonzalez told a reporter he had been forced out of the investigation by "vast and powerful forces, including the country's most sophisticated criminal element." Gonzalez told reporters, "I am like a guy who's been slugged before he's got a chance to fight. . . . It was an exercise in futility. The fix was in."

While the life of the committee had been extended for two more months in January, it was due to expire at the end of March 1977. Near that time, a new chairman was named—Representative Louis Stokes, a low-key black Democrat from Ohio. With the more acceptable Stokes in charge, the Assassinations Committee was revived by House Resolution 433, which passed on March 30, 1977, reconstituting the committee until January 3, 1979, and assigning it a pared-down budget of $2.5 million.

Just before the House vote to continue the committee, Sprague was called to Stokes's office. Despite having been promised support by Stokes and other committee members, Sprague could see the writing on the wall. He told them, "Gentlemen, it's clear it's in everyone's best interest if I resign." Sprague's resignation prompted several committee members to state publicly that the chief counsel had been the victim of a McCarthy-like witch hunt and character assassination.

Although the committee had existed for six months, the constant bickering and lack of funds prevented any meaningful work. Throughout its brief life, its focus so far had been not on assassinations, but on sheer survival.

Earlier in March, Fonzi—still on the job—had tried to contact the last-known close friend of Lee Harvey Oswald, George DeMohrenschildt, who was staying in Manalapan, Florida. Soon after arriving home and learning of Fonzi's visit, DeMohrenschildt was found fatally shot. His death was ruled a suicide. Fonzi later wrote, "The manner in which the Assassination Committee reacted to the death of George DeMohrenschildt revealed that the Committee—six months after it was formed—was still totally incapable of functioning as an investigative body. It reflected six months of political reality and how successful its opponents had been in keeping it distracted and off-balance."

Representative Gonzalez stated simply, "Strong organized forces have combined to stop the inquiry at any cost."

In June 1977, a new chief counsel was selected—G. Robert Blakey, a respected academician with impressive credentials but with no real desire to probe the assassinations.

Blakey at the Helm

No investigation can be better than its leadership, and with its new chief counsel and director, the House Select Committee on Assassinations was no exception.

G. Robert Blakey, a professor of law and director of the Notre Dame Institute on Organized Crime, spent four years in the organized-crime and racketeering section of the Kennedy Justice Department; was chief counsel to the Senate Subcommittee on Criminal Laws and Procedures; was principal consultant to president Lyndon Johnson's Commission on Law Enforcement and Administration of Justice; and was a consultant to the publications *Time, Life,* and *Look.*

Upon becoming chief counsel and director for the House Select Committee on Assassinations, Blakey firmly took control of the panel and its investigation. He oversaw every aspect of the committee's work, selecting witnesses, deciding which leads to follow and which to ignore, picking the expert panels, hiring and firing staff members, and setting the committee's agenda.

It quickly became obvious that the Assassinations Committee was changing directions in key areas. Where Sprague had opted for openness in the committee's inquiry, Blakey advocated secrecy. In fact, in his first statement to the news media, Blakey announced, "The purpose of this news conference is to announce there will be no more news conferences."

Blakey also announced that the committee would not look at any new evidence in the Kennedy and King assassinations, but would concentrate on evaluating the old evidence the federal government had accumulated.

His turnaround prompted assassination researchers to take a closer look at the new chief counsel, with some disturbing results.

Having worked for both President Johnson and President Nixon, Blakey had close contact with other ranking government officials involved in the Kennedy assassination case, among them:

Nicholas Katzenbach: the deputy attorney general who in 1964 put strong pressure on the Warren Commission to quickly endorse the premise that Lee Harvey Oswald acted alone.

Leon Jaworski: the Watergate special prosecutor who served as a special counsel to the Warren Commission charged with determining whether Oswald had any ties to US intelligence. (Jaworski found none, but some years later it was discovered that a foundation of which Jaworski was a trustee secretly used CIA funds.)

Lewis F. Powell: the attorney named by the American Bar Association as an observer to the Warren Commission to protect Oswald's rights, but who spent much of his time trying to have Commission critic Mark Lane disbarred.

Although considered an expert in the "war against crime," Blakey apparently had a strange connection with a reputed big-time gambler. In 1975, when *Penthouse* magazine was sued for referring to California's La Costa Resort and Spa as a playground for gangsters, it was Blakey who sold his expertise and provided an affidavit condemning the magazine's charges of mob ownership while conceding ignorance of the truth of the charges. Any questions concerning this odd support of a resort built by Teamster pension-fund money were referred to Blakey's own attorney, Louis Nizer.

Furthermore, Blakey was recommended as chief counsel by Committee member representative Christopher Dodd, the former law partner of former FBI director L. Patrick Gray, who was indicted during the Watergate scandals.

While these connections don't prove compromise on Blakey's part, they do cast a shadow over his credentials as an uncompromising crime-buster. They also raised concerns in many minds about Blakey's motives.

But is there any evidence that the Assassinations Committee's findings were undermined?

Apparently so. The main weapon Blakey used to stop a meaningful investigation was a nondisclosure agreement. Signing this agreement, which was instituted within one week of Blakey's arrival, was mandatory for continued employment with the committee. Even independent researchers who attempted to share assassination information with the panel were made to sign it.

The agreement bound the signer not to reveal that he or she even worked for the committee or to reveal anything learned while serving with the committee; gave the committee the power to take legal action against the signer in the event of disclosures, even long after the committee ended; and made the signer agree that all legal fees would be paid should the signer lose such a court suit.

Many persons who have seen this agreement, including attorneys, claim it violates the US Constitution and therefore is illegal. However, it stopped most of the committee's personnel and hired consultants from discussing the workings of the HSCA.

Evidence of the weak legal standing of this agreement may be found in that Gaeton Fonzi has written scathing articles against the committee and its operation, in apparent violation of this agreement, yet there has been no prosecution.

The agreement also effectively muzzled many of the assassination researchers. Blakey invited ten prominent critics of the Warren Commission to Washington to exchange assassination information. All were required to sign the nondisclosure agreement, and all presented their information. Blakey reciprocated with nothing of value. After their departure, Blakey instructed the committee staff to have no further contact with these researchers without his personal and specific authorization. He explained such secrecy was necessary to protect the reputations of people involved in the investigation—the "innocent associates"—and that he wanted the committee to "remain immune from the fever of assassination demonology."

Even more disquieting to researchers was Blakey's accommodating attitude toward the FBI and the CIA—the two agencies that over the years have become suspects themselves in many people's minds. Earlier, Sprague had put both agencies on notice that subpoenas might be issued for access to assassination material withheld from previous investigations, such as pre-assassination CIA activity in Mexico City and the connections between Ruby and Oswald and the FBI.

Under Blakey, committee investigators had to sign a CIA secrecy oath before examining any classified files, thus giving the agency the authority to "clear" any information, including investigators' notes.

A January 25, 1978, committee report stated:

> All staff members on the Committee have received or are in the process of receiving "Top Secret" security clearances. The FBI, as an accommodation to the Committee, conducts the background investigations for these security clearances. The CIA then reviews the background investigations done by the FBI. After consultation with the FBI and CIA, the full Committee makes the determination regarding an individual's security clearance.

In other words, both intelligence agencies had direct control over who participated in the committee's investigation. This situation did nothing to ease the minds of researchers who already were convinced of intelligence involvement in the Kennedy assassination.

Several people were fired from the committee staff for failing to receive a security clearance, including one person whom Blakey reportedly told, "The CIA would be more comfortable if you were gone." It has never been explained how this clearance review was made to conform with the CIA charter prohibition against domestic activities.

In a TV interview, original counsel Sprague stated he had refused to yield to CIA and FBI demands for security clearances, as such agreements would have given these agencies authority to decide what the committee could disclose. Sprague argued, "What's the point of getting material in the first place, if they are going to control who sees it and what we can do with it?"

Blakey showed no such insight. In fact, in an article by writer Jerry Policoff, Blakey is quoted as saying, "I've worked with the CIA for twenty years. Would they lie to me?"

And there is evidence that Blakey's trust in the agency went beyond simple naïveté. After it was discovered that the CIA held a 201 file on Lee Harvey Oswald—evidence that he worked for the agency, according to several former CIA agents—Blakey retrieved the file from CIA headquarters. According to the House committee, the folder was virtually empty. Agency officials explained that the file was actually just a "personality" file that had contained a few news clippings on Oswald after being opened on December 9, 1960.

Yet researchers today have a copy of a CIA "Memorandum for the Record" dated April 27, 1979, which states:

> On 27 April, 1979, Mr. G. Robert Blakey, chief counsel and staff director of the House Select Committee on Assassinations (HSCA), visited CIA Headquarters. . . . Mr. Blakey examined only that material held [Blanked out]. He apparently did not go elsewhere within the Agency, [Blanked out] to examine their holdings. . . . Comment: Files reviewed by HSCA staff members fill nine four-drawer safes. The files include the Lee Harvey Oswald 201, which fills two four-drawer safes. Oswald's 201 file was not completely reviewed by HSCA staff members.

Despite not reviewing all of the CIA's held material—including Oswald's 201 file—the House committee confidently concluded, "The Secret Service, Federal Bureau of Investigation, and Central Intelligence Agency were not involved in the assassination of President Kennedy."

In 1978, the CIA agent assigned as liaison to the HSCA reportedly was fired from the agency after rifling the safe containing the Kennedy autopsy photos and X-rays. The agent claimed he had an innocent explanation but would not give it to the press. "There's other things that are involved," he told the *Washington Post*'s George Lardner, "that are detrimental to other things."

Such activities forced some investigators to resign from the committee, citing control by intelligence agencies and their feeling that the investigation had become too narrow in focus.

Other staff members—including twenty-four investigators—were discharged on grounds that the committee had no money. Yet in February 1978, Blakey returned $425,000 to Congress, saying the funds were not needed.

Whether or not the charges that Blakey sidetracked any meaningful investigation are true, the seeds of doubt were sown. This is reflected in a magazine article by Jerry Policoff and William Scott Malone, who wrote in 1978, "So poisoned has the atmosphere become from months of bitterness that whatever conclusions the Committee comes up with will be suspect."

According to assassination researchers who followed the HSCA closely, Blakey forced out or fired some of the most able investigators, severely restricted areas of investigation, handpicked scientific experts who mostly denied any hint of conspiracy, and then locked committee investigative material away for fifty years.

Although there has been no definitive evidence to demonstrate that this was his agenda, if Blakey had wanted to restrict and misdirect the investigations of the House Select Committee on Assassinations, he could not have done a better job.

With Blakey's arrival, aspects of the HSCA investigation changed dramatically. Under Sprague, committee investigators had been running down promising leads in Dallas, Miami, New Orleans, and Memphis. Under Blakey, these field investigations—far from the oversight of Washington power—were severely restricted. The focus of the Kennedy probe moved away from looking at intelligence and anti-Castro Cuban involvement and began scrutinizing the organized-crime aspects.

Somewhere along the way, the committee dropped any investigation into the Robert F. Kennedy assassination and the shooting of Alabama governor Wallace, despite the abundance of evidence raising serious questions about the official versions of both those events.

By October 1977, a Scripps-Howard article stated, "The Committee's investigation of the assassination of President John F. Kennedy has been scaled down and the panel's professional staff apparently has been spending virtually all its time exploring new leads in the King case."

On March 13, 1978, the HSCA received House approval for $2.5 million in funding to last until January 3, 1979. The final vote of 204 to 175 was achieved despite objections from some Republican representatives who claimed the committee had accomplished little in its year and a half of existence.

Scaled down and with a restricted agenda, the committee nevertheless went to work. According to Blakey, the committee spent a total of $5.5 million during its thirty-month investigation. In an introduction to the committee's report, Blakey wrote, "[This] may sound like a lot, but it should be contrasted with the fact that the Warren Commission spent the equivalent in 1977 dollars of over $10 million in ten months."

Blakey admitted that early on the HSCA experienced "some rough sailing" and that the period of "rigorous fact-finding" lasted only six months—from January to July 1978. However, this fact-finding was "intense and wide ranging," wrote Blakey. He claimed that committee members and staffers made trips to Mexico, Canada, Portugal, England, and Cuba. There were a total of 562 trips to 1,463 points for more than 4,758 days of field investigation. More than 4,924 interviews were conducted and 335 witnesses heard, some in public hearings and some in executive session.

Beginning in late July 1978, the HSCA conducted a series of public hearings that lasted until September 28, 1978. There was a parade of technical and scientific experts, but no one cross-examined them. No one asked the obvious follow-up or embarrassing question. And the testimony of each witness seemed designed to further cement the idea that Lee Harvey Oswald was the lone assassin of Kennedy.

Some witnesses, such as Louie Steven Witt—who claimed to have been the "umbrella man" in Dealey Plaza—gave an implausible story that went unchallenged.

Dr. James Humes, the leader of the Kennedy autopsy team, was never asked why he waited fifteen years to become convinced that a bullet entered near the top of Kennedy's head well above where the other two autopsy doctors still placed it. Humes also could have given more details about the military authorities present at the autopsy who directed the doctors in their inadequate work, but he was never asked in public. Humes later quipped, "They had their chance and they blew it."

Many of the researchers watching the televised hearings felt the testimony was orchestrated and that it followed carefully selected lines of interrogation. This perception prompted a group of researchers who had formed an Assassination Information Bureau to comment:

> [There was] no one to remind the on-looking press and the nation that Blakey's case against Oswald looks as good as it does primarily because no one with equal staff, budget and time has had the opportunity to take it in hand, pull open its seams and show the world what it is really made of. Blakey and the Committee may at the moment enjoy a certain sense of victory, but their decision to shut down the other side's chances at rebuttal and rejoinder will eventually work against the credibility of their results. Another one-sided trial of an undefended Oswald is not what the people paid $6 million to see.

The committee also failed to mention the amount of medical evidence that is still missing.

And—more ominously—some material given to the committee also turned up missing. FOX News commentator Bill O'Reilly in 1963 was a news reporter for WFAA-TV in Dallas. He recalled:

> A guy who was [in Dealey Plaza] at the time watching the motorcade. His son found [a bullet]. I can't remember his name. . . . But he wanted to remain anonymous. . . . He gave me this little cylinder. He said that his son had found it on the ground that day. . . . It was definitely a slug. And the guy said he definitely dug it out of there. . . . It was something I came across and held. And then when the Committee started, I handed it over to Gaeton [Fonzi], . . . and I don't think anything ever came of it. It was a pistol slug, I'm pretty sure. But again, I'm not positive. . . . But again I am no ballistics expert so it could have been a rifle slug.

Fonzi recalled getting the slug from O'Reilly. He said, "I wound up with the slug just prior to going with the Committee. I gave the slug to the chief investigator, Cliff Fenton, with the Committee and never heard any more of it. I kept asking Cliff whether he turned it over for analysis or what he did with it. I kept getting noncommittal answers."

Asked about the slug in 1982, Fenton said, "I don't know nothing about that. The best thing I can tell you is to talk to Rep. Stokes. I don't make any comment on the Assassinations Committee. . . . You got to forgive me for that but that's the way I am."

As the committee closed its public hearings and moved toward presenting its final report in the late fall of 1978, it was apparent that its findings in regard to the JFK assassination would parallel those of the Warren Commission—that Kennedy had been killed by two bullets fired by Lee Harvey Oswald from the sixth floor of the Texas School Book Depository and that Oswald had acted alone.

But then Blakey—who had carefully restricted the JFK assassination investigation to simply a reevaluation of previous evidence—was hoisted on his own petard.

Two separate scientific studies of a Dallas police radio recording revealed evidence that more than one gunman fired on Kennedy in Dallas.

The Dallas Police Radio Recording

Even before asking for more funding in March 1978, the House Select Committee on Assassinations already had uncovered a bombshell in the JFK investigation.

Sophisticated scientific acoustical studies of a Dallas police radio recording indicated that more than one assassin was involved in Kennedy's death. This evidence, which prompted immediate controversy, destroyed the Warren Commission's theory of a lone gunman and forced the Assassinations Committee to completely reverse its findings at the last moment.

The episode began with an event very familiar to serious assassination researchers—an eight-minute "gap" in Dallas police radio broadcasts during the assassination gunfire.

Apparently a Dallas policeman—a motorcycle officer by the sound of a nearby motorcycle engine—opened his microphone about two minutes before the shooting started and left it open for about eight minutes.

In late 1976, Gary Mack, today curator of the Sixth Floor Museum in Dallas, obtained a copy of the Dallas police radio recording in the belief that the open microphone had been in Dealey Plaza. He began studying it for sounds of gunfire. He reasoned that if the microphone was indeed open in Dealey Plaza, it must have picked up the sounds of the shots.

By September 1977, he had enhanced the quality of the tape and concluded that the recording indicated as many as seven shots.

Mack obtained a copy of the tape closer to the original. He explained, "Finding the precise location of the shots, then, was easy and [after filtering out much of the motorcycle engine noise] we heard the first shot . . . a very loud, sharp crack immediately following some conversation between two policemen."

The existence of the police recording became known to the Assassinations Committee, which then obtained what was thought to be the original recording from a retired Dallas police lieutenant.

This original recording—termed a Dictabelt—was turned over to the acoustics firm of Bolt, Beranek & Newman Inc. for sophisticated scientific tests. Dr. James Barger, the firm's chief scientist, converted the sounds on the tape into digitized waveforms to produce a visual picture. The study also looked into "sequence of impulses," which could differentiate sharp, loud noises such as gunshots from subsequent echoes.

Barger determined there were at least six such impulses and asked for further tests, including an on-site test in Dealey Plaza.

By summer 1978, Blakey was aware that the acoustical scientists supported Mack's contention that the tape showed gunfire from more than one location. In fact, during their public testimony, the acoustical scientists stated that there were as many as nine sounds on the Dallas recording that could not be ruled out as gunshots.

But after the Dealey Plaza testing from two locations, they could confirm only four shots—at least one from the Grassy Knoll.

Additionally, the tape showed that one shot came only 1.6 seconds behind another. Since the FBI had carefully determined that it required at least 2.3 seconds to cock and fire the Carcano rifle twice, this was further evidence of more than one assassin.

Blakey shocked committee members with this information, and staff members began to reconsider their conclusions—but not until after the police tape was turned over to yet another team of acoustical scientists for a second opinion. Blakey wrote, "It was deemed judicious to seek an independent review of Barger's analysis before proceeding with the acoustical reconstruction."

The tape was then studied by Professor Mark Weiss of Queen's College of the City University of New York and his associate, Ernest Aschkenasy. Weiss and Aschkenasy agreed with Barger's findings and also encouraged on-site testing. The idea was to create computerized graphic pictures of the sound patterns of rifle shots in Dealey Plaza and to match them against the patterns discovered in the police recording.

Beginning at dawn on Sunday, August 20, 1978, three Dallas police sharpshooters fired a total of fifty-six live bullets into three piles of sandbags located along the motorcade route on Elm Street. Rifles were fired from two locations—the southeast comer of the sixth floor of the Texas School Book Depository and from behind the wooden picket fence on the Grassy Knoll.

Interestingly, a .38-caliber pistol also was fired from the knoll, leading many researchers to speculate that the committee must have received information leading them to believe a pistol may have been used in the assassination. However, at the time no one could explain why the pistol was test fired. Dallas police commented they were unaware of the committee's desire to test fire the pistol until the day before the tests.

It also should be noted that two of the three piles of sandbags were located in the middle lane of Elm Street, exactly where films show the presidential limousine. However, one pile—apparently representing one of the early shots—was located in the far left lane. Asked why it was in this location, Dallas police sharpshooter Jerry Compton, positioned in the Depository, said he could not get a line of sight on the bags when it was in the center lane due to intervening tree branches.

Less than a year before these tests, a film crew had worked in Dealey Plaza producing a network movie titled *The Trial of Lee Harvey Oswald*. The tree that prevented a line of sight between the sixth-floor Depository window and the location of the first shot had been pruned back to its 1963 size, based on photographs taken the day of the assassination. Compton's inability to fire at the center lane because of the obstructing tree supported researchers who had long claimed that a gunman on the Depository's sixth floor would have no unobstructed line of sight to this location.

As the police marksmen fired their weapons, a line of microphones was moved along the motorcade route recording 432 impulses or "acoustical fingerprints."

Later, matching up the tape sounds with the test sounds, two of the six possible shots were ruled out as having been fired from the Depository or the knoll—leaving the possibility that shots came from other locations.

This still left four sounds that did match.

After refining their acoustical tests, Weiss and Aschkenasy concluded, "With a certainty factor of 95 percent or better, there was a shot fired at the presidential limousine from the Grassy Knoll."

Barger agreed with this assessment and added that sound from the knoll was preceded by an N-wave, or supersonic shock wave, proving that the sound was that of a rifle bullet, which is a supersonic missile.

The House committee studied photographs taken on November 22, 1963, as well as Dallas police assignments and concluded that the microphone that recorded the shots was on the motorcycle of Patrolman H. B. McLain.

McLain testified his was the first motorcycle to the left of Vice President Johnson's car. He acknowledged that his motorcycle was in the correct location to record the shots, based on the acoustical studies, and that his microphone often got stuck in the "on" position.

However, a week after the committee was disbanded, McLain suddenly reversed his position, claiming it could not have been his microphone that relayed the sounds. Stating that he had accompanied the presidential limousine to Parkland Hospital, McLain told news reporters, "That wasn't my motorcycle. There would have been a siren on that Channel 1 all the way to the hospital. Everybody had their sirens on . . . you would have heard that on Channel 1." McLain said he came to this conclusion belatedly because when he testified to the committee, he had not listened to the police recording. To complicate matters, an assassination photograph showed McLain had lagged behind and was still in Dealey Plaza after the presidential limousine raced off.

But McLain's criticism of these findings was just the beginning of a controversy over the acoustical studies and their conclusions. Not long after the committee issued its report citing at least four shots at Kennedy, the FBI publicly disputed the acoustical studies. In news stories carried nationwide, the bureau stated that the findings of the acoustical scientists and the committee were "invalid." This announcement prompted Blakey to term the FBI report "a sophomoric analysis . . . superficial, shoddy and shot full of holes."

And the controversy continued.

At the request of the Justice Department—parent agency of the FBI—the National Science Foundation authorized a $23,360 study of the acoustical evidence by a National Academy of Sciences panel headed by Harvard University physics professor Norman S. Ramsey.

The Ramsey panel, as it came to be called, decided on the basis of apparent sounds from police Channel 2 (the motorcade security channel) being found on Channel 1 (the regular police channel) that such "cross talk" meant the police recordings were unreliable. Ramsey's Committee on Ballistic Acoustics concluded, "The acoustic analyses do not demonstrate that there was a Grassy Knoll shot . . . [and] do not support a conclusion that there was a second gunman."

However, in the months following the Ramsey panel's announcement, its findings were called into question by researcher Gary Mack, the originator of the recording study, who pointed out that Ramsey had based his studies on problems involving the automatic gain control (AGC), a system to equalize the volume of a radio receiver. Dallas police Channel 1 had no AGC circuitry at that time, Mack pointed out. Two members of Ramsey's panel admitted that if there was no AGC in the Dallas police radios, their analysis of the tapes would have to be redone.

Well into the mid-1980s the controversy over the acoustical tests continued, with one expert challenging another expert and one technical argument being resolved only to find yet another waiting. A 2001 peer-reviewed article in *Science and Justice*, a quarterly publication of Britain's Forensic Science Society, claimed the Ramsey panel study was seriously flawed. The author of the article, D. B. Thomas, a government scientist and JFK assassination researcher, said his study proved there was a shot from the Grassy Knoll in addition to three shots from the Depository. HSCA chief counsel Blakey said Thomas's work proved a shot from a second gunman on the knoll. "We thought there was a 95 percent chance it was a shot. He puts it at 96.3 percent. Either way, that's beyond a reasonable doubt," Blakey commented.

Keep in mind that there is now evidence to suggest that the Dallas police recordings may have been edited or otherwise altered while in the hands of federal authorities in the days following the assassination. If the tapes were altered, then the entire acoustical controversy has to go back to square one.

Despite the continuing controversy, the acoustical evidence prompted a complete turnabout in the official version of the JFK assassination.

The House Select Committee on Assassinations issued a preliminary report on December 30, 1978.

Out of time and money, but faced with the acoustical test results, it could conclude only that President John F. Kennedy "was probably assassinated as a result of a conspiracy" but that the committee was "unable to identify the other gunman or the extent of the conspiracy."

Under Blakey, the committee had gone right to the finish trying to find Oswald the lone assassin. Then at the eleventh hour, they were forced to conclude that at least two assassins were involved.

Conspiracy advocates were greatly pleased with this substantiation of more than one gunman in the Kennedy murder. Others were not so impressed.

Warren Commission attorney David Belin argued, "Congress is just plain wrong. There was no second gunman firing from the Grassy Knoll. I've seen lots of expert testimony where people differ." Oswald's mother, Marguerite, commented, "The select committee has done its work, tried hard, they are men of integrity, but they made the same mistake as the Warren Commission. My late son, Lee Harvey Oswald, was framed for the murder of President Kennedy."

So the controversy over President Kennedy's assassination, far from being settled by the House committee, continued anew. Only this time, researchers and critics of the Warren Commission had gained new ammunition through information gained by the committee, and they were now supported in their conspiracy theories by a governmental body.

Even after the committee had concluded its work, controversy about its operation continued. Five months later, Robert Groden, who had served as staff photographic consultant to the HSCA, told the news media the committee had pulled its punches:

> The direction of the entire House Assassinations Committee rested on one piece of evidence from the beginning—the autopsy photographs. And, from the beginning until the introduction of the acoustical evidence, the autopsy panel assumed the autopsy evidence was genuine. I was not allowed to study the autopsy photographs until December [1978—less than a month before the committee disbanded] and when I did study them, I found at least two were phonies, which can be proved to any reasonable person.

Groden's charge has now been substantiated by autopsy photographer Floyd Rebe and by several of the Dallas doctors who worked to save President Kennedy's life. Interviewed by the *Baltimore Sun* in 1979, the Dallas physicians unanimously agreed that the photograph the House Committee made public was not remotely like the wounds they saw in 1963.

Veteran newsman Seth Kantor, who, because of his years working in both Dallas and Fort Worth prior to and during the assassination, may be one of the most knowledgeable media persons on that event, told this author the entire House committee episode was "strange and unusual":

> The Committee tried to play to Congress . . . by not touching certain bases because certain congressmen didn't want it. . . . The original chairman [Downing] was about to retire . . . the committee was loaded with second-echelon House members, not leadership quality and with not much clout. . . . When Blakey came in, he wiped out the leadership of the [committee's] staff and the new people that came in had to start from square one. The investigators sent to Dallas had no working knowledge of the case. . . .

My biggest grievance with the committee is that they did not investigate the Dallas police force. Blakey said he had no mandate to investigate the Dallas police. More than half the life of the committee was frittered away.

Many researchers' view of the committee's work was summed up by Groden, who wrote:

In the end, the Committee consumed millions of dollars and accomplished little. The Select Committee never did the simple things required to get to the truth. Reluctantly, the committee identified the existence of a "conspiracy" in the Kennedy and King assassinations. But the admission of "conspiracy" was a small breakthrough—the public had suspected it for years. The real truth about who was behind the conspiracies was left undisturbed.

Having totally reversed the government's view of the JFK assassination by stating publicly that a conspiracy "probably" resulted in Kennedy's death and that at least two gunmen fired at the president, chief counsel Blakey, writing in an introduction to the committee's report, noted, "Realizing that there would be an opportunity for others to fill in the details—that there might be indictments and trials as a result of future investigation—we decided to present an understated case. We chose a cautious approach."

An understated case? Consider these points as determined by the committee:

- A conspiracy involving at least two gunmen resulted in President Kennedy's death.
- Jack Ruby's killing of Oswald was not spontaneous and Ruby likely entered the Dallas police station basement with assistance.
- The Dallas police withheld from the Warren Commission relevant information about Ruby's entry to the Oswald slaying scene.
- The Secret Service was deficient in performing its duties in connection with the assassination.
- The FBI performed with varying degrees of competency and failed to investigate adequately the possibility of conspiracy.
- The CIA was deficient in its collection and sharing of assassination information.
- The Warren Commission failed to investigate the idea of conspiracy adequately, partly because of the failure of government agencies to provide the Commission with relevant information.
- Investigation of conspiracy by the Secret Service was terminated prematurely by President Johnson's order that the FBI assume investigative responsibility.
- Since the military 201 file on Oswald was destroyed before the committee could view it, the question of Oswald's affiliation with military intelligence could not be fully resolved.

All of these startling conclusions—and this was the "understated case."

The committee ended by recommending that the Justice Department pick up where it left off and attempt to unravel the conspiracy that led to the deaths of John F. Kennedy and Martin Luther King. The only action on the part of Justice was the Ramsey panel, which called into question the acoustical evidence of multiple gunmen. The panel's conclusions were themselves called into question in a peer-reviewed scientific paper published in 2001.

An internal Justice Department memo made public only in 1988 revealed what researchers had suspected all along—despite the findings and requests by the House committee, Justice officials had let the whole thing drop.

It should be noted that in 1999, the King family won a wrongful death civil case in which they claimed King had been the victim of an assassination conspiracy involving the Memphis police as well as federal agencies. This jury verdict affirmed the innocence of James Earl Ray and awarded the King family their sought sum of $100, evidence they were not pursuing financial gain. This groundbreaking story received scant coverage in the corporate mass media.

The Oliver Stone Film *JFK*

Public awareness of the Kennedy assassination conundrum was expanded worldwide in 1991 with the release of the $40 million film *JFK*, directed by the already controversial director Oliver Stone.

To understand the movie, one must consider the words of its director. Stone told this author, "I am not making a documentary. I am making a movie." The film was a Herculean effort, distilling more than a thousand hours of film containing JFK assassination facts and information into slightly more than three hours.

Despite being lambasted as "absurd" and "untrue" by the corporate mass media even prior to its release, the film galvanized both sides of the conspiracy argument. Researchers who had been claiming a conspiracy in Kennedy's death saw vindication in the movie while lone-assassin advocates held the film up as an exercise in presenting unsupported theories.

The film was based on two primary sources—former New Orleans district attorney Jim Garrison's book *On the Trail of the Assassins*, his account of the Clay Shaw prosecution, and the 1989 edition of this book, *Crossfire: The Plot That Killed Kennedy*.

But Stone was not content to simply use the writings of others. He also organized an entire research team coordinated by Harvard and Yale graduate Jane Rusconi, who studied more than two hundred books on the subject. Rusconi's team also reinterviewed some of the same people and reviewed the same documents as this author. Interestingly enough, she and her team came to the same conclusions espoused by both Garrison and this author.

Despite a slow start, the film eventually built a huge international audience, which must have created concern within the circles of those who wished the troublesome and unanswered questions about the assassination would simply go away. The response of the mass media was mixed, with news commentators calling it fictionalized trash while movie reviewers gave it high marks.

Preemptive Attacks

Harsh criticism of the film began months even before it was first screened, with the leaking of a first draft. The script went through almost a dozen drafts before being finalized. But this did not slow the media attack dogs. The film was excoriated by the *Chicago Tribune*, the *Washington Post*, and *Time* magazine. But at least those critics had actually viewed the picture. National Public Radio's Cokie Roberts, daughter of Warren Commission member Hale Boggs, refused to even view it.

Others were more open-minded. In 2010 Stephen Rosenfeld, senior editorial writer for the *Washington Post*, noted, "That the assassination probably encompassed more than a lone gunman now seems beyond cavil [quibbling about]."

If there was more than one gunman, it follows that there was a conspiracy of some sort and it follows that the Warren Commission was incorrect. It should follow also that journalists writing about the Kennedy assassination should be more interested in what actually did happen than in dismissing every Warren Commission critic as a paranoid. Yet, from the start, the media has consistently promoted the thesis that Rosenfeld now says is wrong beyond cavil.

The experience of Pat Dowell, film critic for the *Washingtonian*, provided an example of the break between film critics and corporate bosses. Her review for the January 1992 issue was rejected by her editor, John Limpert, who said he didn't want a positive review for a film he felt was "preposterous." Dowell resigned in protest.

In his review for the *Chicago Sun-Times*, Roger Ebert named *JFK* as Best Picture of the Year, writing, "The achievement of the film is not that it answers the mystery of the Kennedy assassination, because it does not, or even that it vindicates Garrison, who is seen here as a man often whistling in the dark. Its achievement is that it tries to marshal the anger which ever since 1963 has been gnawing away on some dark shelf of the national psyche."

While the film went to great lengths to reenact the assassination scenes as authentically as possible—at the last moment some old Harley-Davidson motorcycles were located to re-create the motorcade's police escort—the script prompted complaints of fictionalization by using composite characters and condensing events and dialogue.

For example, in the film Garrison travels to Washington meet with a mysterious "Mr. X," who gives him insider information regarding the assassination. This character largely represented Colonel Fletcher Prouty, who indeed told these things to Garrison but only long after the Clay Shaw trial. In truth, at the time of the trial Garrison went to Washington to meet with Army intelligence agent Richard Case Nagell. To say Nagell said all this would have been untruthful, just as saying Prouty met Garrison at the time of the trial would have been equally untruthful. So both men were turned into "Mr. X," who nevertheless spoke the truth.

One unreported event during the film's shooting in Dallas indicated that Providence was watching over Stone's production. One day when filming of the motorcade paused, a couple dozen extras who had been standing in the middle of Houston Street moved to the Texas School Book Depository curb to get out of the hot Texas sun. High above them, technicians were mounting a camera on the seventh floor of the building. The Sixth Floor Museum had refused to allow Stone to film from the actual sixth-floor window, most probably because it would have shown that there is no clear line of sight to Elm Street due to evergreen trees in the way. Suddenly a huge glass windowpane came loose and fell down toward the crowd of extras standing on the curb below. Fortunately, a gust of wind caught the pane at the last moment, causing it to slide sideways, crashing into the center of Houston Street, just vacated by the crowd. The pile of shattered glass was quickly swept up and filming continued. Many people on the set, including some of the endangered extras, did not even realize that disaster had been averted.

Despite acceptance by both film critics and most of the public, the debunking efforts continued well into the next decade. Former Los Angeles prosecutor Vincent Bugliosi, in his 2007 1,600-page opus on the assassination, wrote the film was "virtually a continuous lie." He claimed, "*JFK*, the movie about Garrison's prosecution of [Clay] Shaw, has caused far more damage to the truth about the case than perhaps any single event other than Ruby's killing of Oswald, which the American people widely view as an act by Ruby to 'silence' Oswald."

Bugliosi voiced concern that more Americans would believe the CIA-LBJ-Pentagon plot by Stone than the Warren Commission's lone-assassin theory. Bugliosi even argued with himself over the merits of denigrating the film, explaining, "Serious non-fiction books don't stoop to the discussion of wild fairy tales, which the movie *JFK* is." He nevertheless stooped to trash the film for several more pages, referring to Stone's sources as "kooks and nuts."

The prosecutor of Charles Manson made it quite clear in his tome that he felt "the various conspiracy theories [in the JFK assassination] are utterly vapid and bankrupt. . . . Oswald, a lone nut, killed Kennedy and was thereafter killed by another lone nut, Ruby. Two small men who wanted to become big, and succeeded."

Bugliosi, whose book should have been titled *Reclaiming the Warren Commission*, offered the same tortured logic as that discredited commission. He wrote that after all the years, there was *no credible evidence* (emphasis his) of any conspiracy, without justifying his interpretation of "credible." It would appear that anyone who agreed with his views was credible, while those who differed were not credible.

His work is a classic example of the debate method termed "appeal from authority," in which fallacious arguments are presented from a real or imagined authoritarian source. For example, he stated there is no evidence of Oswald's being "seen getting in a car after the shooting in Dealey Plaza" despite noting that two motorists, Roy Cooper and Marvin C. Robinson, supported deputy Roger Craig's claim of seeing Oswald leave the book depository in a Nash Rambler station wagon. Yet Bugliosi confidently wrote, "In any case, we can be certain he [Craig] was wrong because we already know where Oswald was at the time."

He also offered the old argument that a conspiracy could not be kept secret. Here, Bugliosi fails to mention that numerous people, from organized-crime bosses to intelligence operatives, have indeed spoken out over the years about a conspiracy or that more than 25,000 government employees were able to keep the atomic bomb Manhattan Project a secret until one was detonated over Hiroshima, Japan.

Historian and education consultant Grover B. Proctor Jr., widely acknowledged as an expert on the assassination of President Kennedy, said, "If Stone's film, based on the cumulative efforts of many researchers, shows a distrust of and bias against the government's involvement and the media's cover-up, there is some justification." He explained:

> Stone has been quoted widely about his attempt in this film to "fictionalize" the assassination, and to create a new mythology of the event. It is a poor, if technically accurate, choice of words. Those most closely wedded to the official version have leapt on this and said, "See? Didn't we tell you? There is no truth here and he admits it." However, what he has done is more subtle and literarily permissible than this simplistic response. In "fictionalizing" the story, Stone has collapsed long, laborious facts, witness lists, and theories into one speech or one character, a time-honored device dating to Shakespeare and beyond.

Proctor summed up the feelings of many on both sides of the conspiracy argument when he concluded, "The Great Debate over the film will rage on for a while, and each side will continue to vilify the integrity, accomplishments, and motivations of the other. But when the smoke has cleared, the questions posed by the film will still be on the table for resolution—not a bad end for a blockbuster Hollywood venture."

Noting that Stone's film made public a possibility that most Americans had been afraid to face—that the assassination was the result of a coup by the US military-industrial-intelligence complex—Proctor added, "The chilling thing is that the solution presented by *JFK* may also be very close to exactly what happened."

The Assassinations Records Review Board

Whether perceived as ground truth or Hollywood fiction, the film *JFK* produced enough renewed public interest in the assassination that Congress was spurred into action. The public outcry over the film and sealed assassination records resulted in the passage of the President John F. Kennedy Assassination Records Collection Act, signed by president George H. W. Bush on October 26, 1992. The act, designed to restore government credibility, called for the creation of a temporary Assassinations Records Review Board (ARRB). This independent agency reviewed and later released to the National Archives nearly 5 million pages of once-secret JFK assassination records.

The board began its work in 1994 and finished in the fall of 1998, although the further declassification of government records continued afterward. The ARRB was to be composed of five citizens with a background in history, archives, and the law who were not government employees. They and their staff held high-level security clearances and were able to seek out heretofore classified documents within government agencies. Board members were to have been named within ninety days of passage of the act but there was an eighteen-month delay due to the transition between the Bush and Clinton administrations.

In the executive summary of the ARRB's final report, this creation of the Establishment nevertheless described the JFK assassination as an "inexplicable act" shrouded in "secrecy and mystery." The avowed intention of the ARRB was to penetrate this mystery but it failed to produce a solution to the case.

Board member Kermit Hall explained:

> The Review Board is a unique and, in many ways, unprecedented institution in American history. . . . Never before has a group of private citizens been given the opportunity to bring some order to the record of one great historical event. The Board, we should remember, is not charged with answering the question of who murdered President Kennedy. It is not running an investigation; it is, instead, seeking to disclose documents in an age of open secrets, an age in which we have come to embrace the idea that openness is to be preferred and that accountability is the touchstone for public confidence in government.

Hall prophetically stated when the ARRB closed shop, it could take ten years before its work could be adequately analyzed and evaluated.

Despite the conclusion of conspiracy by the House committee and the massive amount of documents the board uncovered, Minnesota federal district judge Jack Tunheim, who headed the ARRB, continued to support the Warren Commission by stating that after viewing the available evidence, he had not seen any direct proof to change the verdict that Lee Harvey Oswald committed the act alone.

While most board members have remained coy about their opinions and conclusions based on their ARRB work, at least one staff member dissented from Tunheim's Warren Commission support.

Douglas Horne's Discoveries

Douglas P. Horne, the chief analyst for military records for ARRB, wrote more extensively about discrepancies and outright confabulation in the medical evidence, fakery in the Zapruder film, and the deliberate destruction of Secret Service records in his 2009 book set, *Inside the Assassination Records Review Board.*

Horne, who wrote that his work with the ARRB did not begin with the idea of publishing a book, pulled no punches in his five volumes. In his overly detailed description and analysis of his experience on the board, he wrote, "Let me make it clear here and now that I consider the assassination of President Kennedy to have been *an action of the state* [emphasis his]: the national security establishment made a decision late in 1962 or early in 1963 to fire the President, and it was a broad consensus."

A former Navy navigator, Horne got to the crux of the case by detailing the tainting of the physical evidence, both by suppression and by fabrication. He noted:

> Once the researcher is convinced that the President was killed by multiple shooters in a crossfire—and through this, understands that he was killed by a conspiracy—the precise details of how that shooting occurred become irrelevant. Of equal or greater importance than understanding that President Kennedy was killed by a crossfire, is understanding that the Federal government covered up the facts of his death, in the most brazen and outrageous manipulation of physical evidence in any murder case in American history.

He added that the mere fact that no one in government has admitted the truth of the assassination is the surest indication that the cover-up was sinister in nature. "If the cover-up had been a benign one, it would have been admitted to, and fully explained, long ago," he reasoned.

Based on the testimony of Bethesda Naval Hospital technicians and photographers, Horne was able to confirm the claims of author David Lifton that surgery was conducted on Kennedy's body prior to the official autopsy, the X-rays and autopsy photographs now in the National Archives are not the originals, and JFK's body arrived in circumstances different from the official account.

Kennedy's body left Dallas wrapped in a sheet inside a costly bronze coffin, yet arrived at Bethesda in a zippered body bag inside a plain military-style shipping coffin. Horne noted, "The shipping casket and body bag witnesses from Bethesda provide medico-legal proof that the body was intercepted in transit, that its chain-of-custody was broken, and that there was an opportunity to tamper with JFK's wounds in transit."

Based on initial reports, including notes made by LBJ's secretary aboard Air Force One, Kennedy's body was to have been sent to Walter Reed Army Medical Center rather than Bethesda. Horne explained:

> The original intent of the conspirators seems to have been to reunite the President's body with the empty Dallas casket at Walter Reed . . . and then take the Dallas casket, with the body inside it once again, to Bethesda. This plan was foiled by the President's widow, who refused a helicopter ride back to the White House, and instead insisted on remaining with the Dallas cas-

ket all the way to Bethesda Naval Hospital. This decision of hers, which no one could countermand, created major problems for those in charge of the cover-up who had been planning to quietly reintroduce JFK's body back into the Dallas casket at Walter Reed. It . . . created unwanted witnesses to multiple casket entries at Bethesda, and to the broken chain-of-custody for the body.

Horne also was able to confirm reports that the autopsy was controlled not by the medical personnel, but by military authorities crowded into the autopsy room. When the doctors started to examine Kennedy's throat wound, first thought to mark a tracheotomy and only later revealed as a bullet wound, according to witnesses, it was Admiral Calvin Galloway, Bethesda's commanding officer, who told them, "Leave it alone. Don't touch it. It's just a tracheotomy."

Horne found that the lead autopsist, Navy Commander Dr. James J. Humes, dissembled about a number of things including the time that Kennedy's body arrived at Bethesda. He said based on official reports, Humes's Warren Commission testimony that the body arrived at 7:35 p.m. was "intentionally misleading, deliberately off by an hour."

According to witness Paul O'Connor, Humes was "scared to death" during the autopsy. Horne said this was "no wonder" as "Humes had been involved in obstruction of justice, in a grisly charade forced upon him by his military superiors in order to create a dishonest photographic and x-ray record, and was about to reveal the questionable results of his handiwork to a morgue packed with over 35 visitors, many of them of Flag rank."

Bethesda technician James Jenkins described the JFK autopsy as a "circus" and said that Humes was being carefully directed through the procedure by Dr. George Burkley, the president's personal physician, through Admiral Galloway. Jenkins added, "People need to understand that this was a cover-up. For what reason, I can only speculate, but certainly the evidence—presented by Humes to the public—was not the evidence we found at the autopsy."

Horne also demonstrated that Dr. Burkley was untruthful in several statements he made to both the Warren Commission and the later House committee. "If he were alive today, he would be subject to prosecution for perjury," noted Horne.

The Zapruder Film: Fundamental or Fraud?

Over the years, many serious researchers have questioned the authenticity of the famous Abraham Zapruder film. Horne dealt extensively with the famous Zapruder film in his volumes because, he wrote, assessing the legitimacy of the film could lead to a better understanding of what really happened.

Like most Americans, Horne had initially accepted the film as legitimate evidence in the assassination. But in June 1997, he said the ARRB staff "became aware of evidence that pointed toward the possible creation of a modified version of the

Zapruder film the weekend of the assassination at Kodak's main industrial plant in Rochester, New York."

Horne wrote, "Throughout that summer, I became painfully aware that asking Kodak to perform an authenticity study of the Zapruder film for the ARRB (and the fact that Kodak agreed to do so on a pro bono basis, free of charge!) constituted a potential conflict of interest of major proportions."

Because of both time and financial considerations, Kodak was allowed to continue with the authenticity study, conducted by Rollie Zavada, a former Kodak employee called out of retirement. However, his report was presented only five days before the ARRB ceased operation, leaving no time for questions or further study. Furthermore, while the Zavada study listed some characteristics indicating the film was an original, it also carried technical language and exhibits that some, including Horne, felt cast doubt on the film's authenticity.

Confusion over how and where the Zapruder film was processed began immediately. Originally taken by Secret Service agent in charge Forrest Sorrels and reporter Harry McCormack to WFAA television station for processing, they found the station was not equipped to develop 8 mm color film. So the film was taken to the Eastman Kodak Company plant that was already processing the color transparencies of witness Phil Willis. Both Sorrels and Willis recalled that the Zapruder film was processed at the Kodak plant but a December 1963 FBI report from agent Robert Barrett quoted Zapruder as saying the processing took place at the Jamieson Film Company on Bryan Street.

A more serious question concerning the legitimacy of the Zapruder film stemmed from revelations out of the 1975 President's Commission on CIA Activities headed by then–vice president Nelson Rockefeller. In response to requests from the Commission, the CIA admitted that the agency's National Photographic Interpretation Center (NPIC) had performed a shot and timing analysis of the film, shot internegatives of the film, performed a print test, produced three print copies (the exact number of copies reported after the assassination weekend), and created four briefing board panels displaying twenty-eight enlargements of frames from the film. It is unclear exactly when all this involvement with the Zapruder film took place except that it was done before mid-December 1963 and apparently even took place prior to the film's being turned over to Time-Life on Monday, November 25, 1963. If this was the case, it was altered before anyone—at either Time-Life or the government—got to view it.

Such early covert handling of the Zapruder film led some assassination researchers to believe the government, in the form of the CIA's NPIC, may have doctored the film long before anyone in the public got to see it. Author Richard Trask commented, "The available records, unfortunately, give us scant information as to what in fact the CIA or NPIC did with the analyzing of the film."

Trask apparently was unfamiliar with Homer A. McMahon, who in 1963 was manager of NPIC's color lab, and his assistant Morgan Bennett Hunter, as neither was mentioned in his book. In 1997 this pair, located and interviewed by the ARRB, revealed that the Zapruder film indeed was worked on at NPIC the weekend of the assassination. McMahon also recalled that the film was flown from Dallas to a state-of-the-art CIA-funded Kodak lab in Rochester, New York, where it was actually developed rather than in Dallas. He remembered the film was brought to NPIC by a "Bill Smith" of the Secret Service from Rochester, although no such agent could later be found. Smith told McMahon he personally had obtained the film from the amateur who exposed it (apparently Abraham Zapruder), flew it to Rochester for developing, and then ferried it to the Washington Navy Yard for the NPIC work. Hunter later recalled a Secret Service agent being present along with a military captain named Sands. Smith ordered both Hunter and McMahon never to discuss their work with the film and to refer any queries to Captain Sands.

McMahon also told the ARRB that he and Hunter worked with the film Smith provided to produce blowups of approximately forty frames. He added that the film was never copied as a motion picture. Only selected frames were blown up to produce the briefing or presentation panels. McMahon added that although he conducted no official analysis, it was his opinion at the time that Kennedy was shot six to eight times from three separate locations. But he said Smith argued there were only three shots from behind and "you can't fight city hall."

In 2003, Kodak's Zavada wrote, "There is no detectable evidence of manipulation or image alteration on the '*Zapruder in-camera* original' and all supporting evidence precludes any forgery thereto. The film that exists at NARA [the National Archives and Records Administration] was received from Time/Life, has all the characteristics of an original film per my report."

But the issue of alterations remains unsettled. Recall that the Dallas surveyors, Robert West and Chester Breneman, said they conducted their survey of Dealey Plaza on the morning of November 25, 1963, with the use of eight-by-ten-inch color photo prints of the Zapruder film frames. While it has been truthfully argued that it would be difficult, if not impossible, to retouch a tiny 8 mm movie frame, it would be simple to blow up each frame to eight-by-ten-inch size, perform some retouching, and reshoot the frames individually. When run as a moving film, especially if reshot with the original camera, it would be most difficult to detect alterations.

The evidence indicates that the Zapruder film manipulated at NPIC was not even the real film. "If McMahon was correct that he had viewed the original, 16mm-wide, unslit double 8 movie film the weekend of the assassination, and if it was really developed in Rochester at a CIA lab run by Kodak (as he was unambiguously told it was), then the extant film . . . is not a camera original film, but a simulated 'original' created with an optical printer at the CIA's secret film lab in Rochester," explained Horne.

In 2009 Peter Janney, author of the revealing book on JFK confidante Mary Pinchot Meyer, *Mary's Mosaic,* interviewed at length Dino Brugioni, former head of NPIC's Information Branch. Brugioni recalled participating in the NPIC production of assassination briefing boards using an original Zapruder film on November 23, 1963, the day after the assassination. These boards reportedly were ordered by the

Secret Service but delivered to CIA director John McCone. On December 9, 1963, based on analysis of the boards, McCone told Robert Kennedy "two people were involved in the shooting." McCone attempted to show this evidence to President Johnson but was brushed off. In the 1990s, the CIA finally turned over some of the briefing boards to the ARRB.

Brugioni identified "Captain Sands" as Navy Captain Pierre Sands, who served as deputy director of NPIC, and described the CIA-backed Kodak lab in Rochester, known as the "Hawkeye Plant," as a facility that "had everything" including an optical printer, a film printer used for making optical effects through the use of special lenses and a projector to transfer images to film stock, and, in fact, "had the capability to do almost anything."

Additional proof of government manipulation of the Zapruder film prior to its purchase by Time-Life on November 25, 1963, came from Hollywood special effects experts.

Hollywood Takes a Look

In 2008, Sydney Wilkinson, with more than twenty years' experience in the Hollywood postproduction industry, became intrigued by the Zapruder film. She was surprised to learn there had never been a nongovernmental scientific imaging study of its authenticity. After contacting the National Archives and Records Administration and being given authorization by Dallas's Sixth Floor Museum, which holds the Zapruder copyright, she obtained a certified third-generation 35-millimeter "forensic version" (untouched) duplicate negative of the film.

This was scanned directly to a 6K DPX digital form using a Northlight scanner, today considered state-of-the-art technology in feature-film postproduction. The digital file exactly replicates the film's image and reveals all information in each frame via 6144 by 4668 pixels. In comparison, home HD TV is only 1920 by 1080 pixels.

Wilkinson was stunned by what she found in the blown-up frames. "When I viewed the frames following the head shot, I felt the hair stand up on the back of my neck," she recalled. "In the frames that weren't blurry—frames 317, 321, 323, and others—a solid black 'patch' on the rear of his head jumped out at me. It was clearly artificial." Some believe this patch was painted on to mask the massive exit wound in the right rear portion of his head indicating a shot from the front.

More than two dozen film industry professionals—special-effects artists, film editors, imaging specialists, and technical engineers, including restoration and preservation professionals at major studios—evaluated the Zapruder frames and all perceived the painted patch on the rear of his head. "They are convinced this black patch was artificial and not a natural shadow on the back of JFK's head," said Wilkinson.

Ned Price, a film restoration expert at a major studio, exclaimed, "Oh, that's horrible, that's just terrible! That's such a bad fake." Paul R. Rutan Jr., president and chief technician of a Hollywood film restoration company, noted, "We are not looking at opticals [original images]; we are looking at artwork." Their observations were confirmed by others but most did not want their names involved, such as the film expert who commented, "I am as convinced as I can be that frame 317 is a man-made special effect placed there to deceive."

Leo Zahn, a director and cinematographer with thirty years' experience including extensive work with the standard 8 mm format of the 1960s and '70s, explained:

> In Frame 317, the shadow on the backside of JFK's head looks like an artifact not created by sunlight striking an object. This shadow with razor-sharp edges and almost d-max (maximum film density) looks more like a patch. . . . For comparison I have pulled Frame 295 (1.5 seconds before Frame 317) where JFK's head is in similar position to the sun, and here the shadow on the backside of his head looks the way it should on Kodachrome film.

The ARRB's Douglas Horne noted:

> The considered opinions of [these] professionals, who together have spent over five decades restoring and working with films of the 1940s, 1950s, and 1960s (when visual effects were done optically—not digitally) in that one moment [have] superseded the statements of all those in the JFK research community who have insisted for two decades now that the Zapruder film could not have been altered, because the technology did not exist to do so.

But the evidence of alteration aside, other problems remain with the historic film. Trask, Horne, and most assassination researchers agree that contrary to the popular opinion that the Zapruder film represents photographic historic truth, just like any other photo, it merely captures a brief period of time and is actually subjective, open to the viewer's interpretation. "The fact [is] that the different possible interpretations of the Zapruder film—even if we assume that the extant film is the authentic camera original film—are almost endless, and are not getting simpler with the passage of years," noted Horne.

So now, along with fake government documents and phony autopsy X-rays and photographs, the public must understand that even the Zapruder film, long heralded as the ultimate truth of the assassination, cannot be accepted at face value.

Jack Tunheim, by 2012 a Minnesota federal district judge, said all but a few of the JFK assassination documents are now public. "Is there a cache of records someplace? I don't think so. We looked as far and as wide as we possibly could," proclaimed Tunheim to a Minnesota news station. "It would have been a violation of law to not turn over records to us for our decision making. I just don't think there was much left."

Tunheim said that after many years of seeing all the available evidence—from Oswald's rifle and bullets, to Kennedy's autopsy photos, to FBI and CIA documents—he has not seen any direct evidence of any kind to change the verdict, which is that Lee Harvey Oswald acted alone.

However, researchers claim many thousands of records, especially CIA documents, are still being withheld.

Researcher and historian William E. Kelly Jr., one of the founders of the Coalition on Political Assassinations, in an open letter to Judge Tunheim in 2012, wrote:

It was with deep regret and some indignation that I read your comments regarding the JFK Assassination records that remain withheld, their numbers and the lack of any other cache of records someplace. . . . In fact, all the evidence isn't "out there" and there are many thousands of records, especially CIA documents that are still being withheld, so many in fact that the National Archives and Records Administration (NARA) can't count them or say exactly how many.

Kelly said the National Archives estimates that 1 percent of the known records still remain classified, which would mean there are still an estimated 50,000 still-secret records. Not a few, there are so many they can't even tell you how many documents are still sealed or how many pages are being withheld, and they're not going to count them until they are required to do so. Kelly said:

Just among the CIA records alone, there are over 1,000 documents identified by the ARRB that are currently locked in a sealed vault at the Archives II facility in College Park, Maryland, and are scheduled to be released to the public in 2017, but are expected to remain sealed indefinitely at the request of the CIA. According to some reports, the CIA has already identified the documents that they intend to ask the president to postpone beyond 2017.

Some assassination records were destroyed even after the ARRB was formed to obtain them. Page 149 of the ARRB's final report dryly noted:

Congress passed the JFK Act in [October] 1992. One month later, the Secret Service began its compliance efforts. However, in January 1995, the Secret Service destroyed Presidential protection survey reports for some of President Kennedy's trips in the fall of 1963. The Review Board learned of the destruction approximately one week after the Secret Service destroyed them, when the Board was drafting its request for additional information. The Board believed that the Secret Service files on the President's travels in the weeks preceding his murder would be relevant.

The website *JFK Facts*, moderated by former *Washington Post* reporter Jefferson Morley, described the JFK assassination as "the key political and historical issue of our time." The site noted:

> The JFK Records Act, passed unanimously in 1992, is no longer being enforced. Since the Assassinations Records Review Board (ARRB) dissolved in 1998, its recommendations have gone unheeded, especially the one requesting that the historical and archival associations that recommended them continue to conduct oversight of the law. Congress has failed to hold any oversight hearings on the JFK Act in over 15 years and shows no inclination to do so.

Far from closed, the JFK assassination case continues to raise even more questions. *JFK Facts* asked:

> If JFK was killed by a deranged lone nut, why are so many records from 1963 considered so significant in 2012? Why were records destroyed? Who ordered their destruction? Where are the Air Force One tapes? Why can't they be found? Why are so many CIA documents about undercover officers with pre-assassination knowledge of Lee Harvey Oswald classified for reasons of national security? Why doesn't Congress oversee the JFK Records Act? Why don't they hold public hearings on these issues and get answers to these questions?

Such questions prompted former-Minnesota-governor-turned–TV personality Jesse Ventura to reason, "If the government were telling the truth, there would be no reason to lock up anything from the people of this country. Clearly they are not, because here we are 50 years later, and they are still withholding documents from us."

Researcher William Kelly concluded, "Today, the American government is afraid of its people, afraid to enforce its own laws and afraid to allow its citizens to know the complete truth about the assassination of President Kennedy. Such complete truth must involve the term 'coup d'état.'"

A Question of Oswald

One of the most intriguing yet misunderstood issues surrounding the JFK assassination involves questions about the identity of Lee Harvey Oswald. This issue can be broken into two segments—one is the evidence pointing to someone impersonating Oswald in the weeks prior to the assassination, and the second concerns the identity of the man Jack Ruby killed.

This whole question of Oswald doppelgangers—or lookalikes—is admittedly bizarre. However, the evidence suggesting such duplication is considerable.

Questions about Oswald's identity did not suddenly surface years after the assassination, as many people believe. Recall that J. Edgar Hoover expressed concern over Oswald's identity as far back as June 3, 1960, when he warned the State Department against an Oswald impostor.

Despite assurances by government agencies at the time of the assassination that they were unaware of Oswald or his background, there is now evidence that people within the government were checking frequently on the ex-Marine long before the assassination.

On March 31, 1961, the deputy chief of the Passport Office wrote to the Consular Section of the State Department regarding Oswald, stating:

> This file contains information first, which indicates that mail from the mother of this boy is not being delivered to him and second, that it has been stated that there is an impostor using Oswald's identification data and that no doubt the Soviets would love to get hold of his valid passport, it is my opinion that the passport should be delivered to him only on a personal basis and after the Embassy is assured to its complete satisfaction that he is returning to the United States.

Another State Department communication, this time to the US embassy in Moscow, on July 11, 1961, stated, "The Embassy's careful attention to the involved case of Mr. Oswald is appreciated. It is assumed that there is no doubt that the person who has been in communication with the Embassy is the person who was issued a passport in the name of Lee Harvey Oswald."

Contrary to the public announcements, government officials were keenly aware of Oswald. Only two weeks before the assassination, someone signing for the State Department checked out Oswald's file from military records.

The New Orleans FBI office apparently kept close tabs on Oswald while he was in that city and then shipped its file on him to Dallas in the fall of 1963, where agent James Hosty tried to reach Oswald. At the same time, a military intelligence unit in Texas was receiving information on Oswald for its files.

An Impostor

After the assassination, literally hundreds of people claimed to have seen Oswald in the days preceding the tragedy. This outpouring of sightings is normal in a case of this magnitude. While this phenomenon is to be expected, many reputable people encountered a Lee Harvey Oswald at a time when Oswald was reported elsewhere and whose stories cannot be easily dismissed.

However, the Warren Commission found it easy enough to dismiss these people. The Commission's rationale was simple: if someone saw Oswald at a time when the

Commission had determined him to be elsewhere, then the observer was mistaken in his identification.

One such encounter with a bogus Oswald is especially intriguing since it occurred long before Oswald reportedly arrived back in the United States from his sojourn in Russia. Oscar Deslatte, manager of a Ford dealership in New Orleans, contacted the FBI immediately after the assassination. He told the bureau that a man identifying himself as "Joseph Moore" had tried to buy ten trucks on January 10, 1961. He said the man was accompanied by a Cuban and had said he wanted Deslatte to "give a good price because we're doing this for the good of the country." At this time the CIA and its Cuban allies were preparing for the April 17 Bay of Pigs Invasion of Cuba.

Deslatte said "Moore" asked that the name "Oswald" be placed on the purchase estimate sheet. The man said "Oswald" would be paying for the trucks on behalf of an anti-Castro Cuban organization.

In 1979, the FBI released a copy of Deslatte's estimate sheet and it showed the anti-Castro organization involved was "Friends of Democratic Cuba," which just happened to have been the anti-Castro group that included in its membership ex-FBI agent Guy Banister. Banister, of course, was the fervent anti-Castro agent who was connected to Oswald in the summer of 1963 at 544 Camp Street.

Another story involves testimony heard by the Senate Intelligence Committee from a former immigration inspector in New Orleans. While keeping the man's identity secret, the committee reported:

> He is absolutely certain that he interviewed Lee Harvey Oswald in a New
> Orleans jail cell sometime shortly before April 1, 1963. Although the in-
> spector is not now certain whether Oswald was using that particular name
> at that time, he is certain that Oswald was claiming to be a Cuban alien.
> He quickly ascertained that Oswald was not a Cuban alien, at which point
> he left Oswald in his jail cell.

According to the Warren Commission, Oswald did not arrive in New Orleans until the end of April, nearly a month after the inspector's meeting with the jailed "Oswald."

During his time in New Orleans, Oswald was seen in many and varying situations. He was handing out pro-Castro literature on New Orleans streets, while at the same time approaching anti-Castro Cuban leaders with proposals to help train their followers.

Some of the people who encountered Oswald in New Orleans described him as a clean and well-kept, courteous young man, while others said he was dirty and disheveled and a swearing hard drinker. It is difficult to believe these people were talking about the same individual.

As the assassination drew closer, the strange reports of second Oswalds began to increase.

On September 25, 1963, Mrs. Lee Dannelly, an official with the Selective Service system in Austin, Texas, reported that a young man came to her office for help. He said his name was Harvey Oswald and that he wished to get his military discharge with "other than honorable conditions" changed to an honorable discharge. The man said he was living in Fort Worth. Dannelly said she could find no such person in her files and she told the man to check with Selective Service in Fort Worth. She next saw Oswald on television after the assassination and promptly reported her experience. Oswald did have a dishonorable discharge and he had lived in Fort Worth, but on September 25, he was on his way to Mexico City, according to the Warren Commission.

After the assassination, some residents of Irving said they recalled Oswald there. Leonard Hutchinson of Hutch's Market came forward to say that he had been asked to cash a check for Oswald earlier in November. He said on one occasion this man, accompanied by a young woman, spoke in some foreign language. Hutchinson said he recognized both Oswald and Marina when their photographs were broadcast over television after the assassination. Near Hutchinson's store was a barbershop where a man identified as Oswald went for haircuts. The barber also said he saw the same man entering Hutchinson's store. Despite all this, the Warren Commission concluded, "Oswald is not known to have received a check for this amount from any source. . . . Examination of Hutchinson's testimony indicates a more likely explanation is that Oswald was not in his store at all."

Next is the well-documented story of Oswald's wild car ride weeks before the assassination. Albert G. Bogard, a salesman for Downtown Lincoln-Mercury, just west of the Triple Underpass in Dealey Plaza, told the Warren Commission that before the assassination—"the ninth day of November, I think it was, to be exact"—a man came into the dealership and introduced himself as "Lee Oswald" and indicated he wanted to purchase a Lincoln Continental. Bogard told the Commission:

> I show him a car on the showroom floor, and take him for a ride out Stemmons Expressway and back, and he was driving at 60 to 70 miles an hour and came back to the showroom. And, I made some figures and he told me he wasn't ready to buy, that he would be in a couple or three weeks, that he had some money coming in. And when he finally started to leave I got his name and wrote it on the back of one of my business cards, and never heard from the man any more.

Bogard said on the day of the assassination, he heard Oswald had been arrested and threw away the business card with Oswald's name on it, saying, "He won't be a prospect anymore because he is going to jail." His story was supported by two other dealership employees, Eugene Wilson and Frank Pizzo.

However, the Warren Commission concluded:

> Several persons who knew Oswald have testified that he was unable to drive, although Mrs. Paine, who was giving Oswald driving lessons, stated

that Oswald was showing some improvement by November. Moreover, Oswald's whereabouts on November 9, as testified to by Marina Oswald and Ruth Paine, would have made it impossible for him to have visited the automobile showrooms as Mr. Bogard claims.

In a 1977 *Dallas Morning News* story, Wilson said the FBI and the Warren Commission dismissed the story of Oswald's drive because they had it occurring on November 9.

Wilson told the newspaper the man was Oswald and that he did know how to drive and that the incident actually occurred on November 2, a more plausible date. He also said he recalled that when Oswald was turned down for a credit purchase, he said, "Maybe I'm going to have to go back to Russia to buy a car." Wilson said he could pinpoint the date because later the day of Oswald's drive, he used the same car to carry his wife and some friends home after a meeting of the Lone Star Bulldog Club. Wilson said the next day at a Dallas dog show he won some ribbons that carried the date.

The Warren Commission indeed published a copy of an unsigned application for a Texas driver's license in the name of Lee Harvey Oswald.

If the car buyer was Oswald, he was expecting to come into money at the exact time of the assassination. If it wasn't Oswald, it was an impostor.

Recall the incident involving C. A. Hamblen, the night manager of Western Union in Dallas, who told of Oswald collecting money orders during the early part of November. Another Western Union employee, Aubrey Lee Lewis, said he recalled a man resembling Oswald as a "feminine, very slender-built fellow" who was involved with a small money order to the Dallas YMCA and was accompanied by a "man of Spanish descent." The man used a "little Navy ID release card" and a library card for identification.

This story of Oswald receiving money just before the assassination caused a minor uproar within both the Warren Commission and Western Union. Western Union's officials were quick to remind employees that they were not to discuss customers or their money orders or amounts. It is apparent that the Western Union employees were under pressure not to tell more about the money order incidents.

A check by Western Union failed to turn up any money orders in the name of Lee Harvey Oswald. But if it was not the Marine Oswald using a Navy ID and library card to receive money orders, then who was it? The Warren Commission apparently was unable to find out.

It is interesting to note the Western Union workers mentioned someone they believed to be Oswald sending money orders to the Dallas YMCA.

According to the Warren Commission, "Oswald did not contact his wife immediately when he returned to Dallas [supposedly from a trip to Mexico City in late September 1963]. . . . He spent the night at the [Dallas] YMCA, where he registered as a serviceman in order to avoid paying the membership fee."

YMCA records showed an Oswald staying there on October 3 and 4. The records also indicated that Oswald lived at the YMCA between October 15 and 19, 1962.

The Dallas YMCA also had a member who frequented its health-club facilities quite often during this time—Jack Ruby.

Dallas police saw a man resembling Oswald handing out pro-Castro literature on downtown streets in the months preceding the assassination. Was it really Oswald? The Warren Commission had Oswald leafleting in New Orleans at the time.

Then there are the strange incidents involving Oswald or someone resembling Oswald using a foreign-made rifle in the weeks preceding the assassination. On November 1, a "rude and impertinent" man bought rifle ammunition in Morgan's Gunshop in nearby Fort Worth. Three people recalled this incident after the assassination and claimed the man was Oswald. The Warren Commission, however, determined that Oswald was elsewhere at the time.

Dial Duwayne Ryder, the service manager at the Irving Sports Shop, recalled working on a rifle but it was not an Italian weapon. He even gave the FBI an undated check stub for $6 that bore the name "Oswald." The stub indicated that work done on the rifle was "drilling and tapping and boresighting." Ryder said the work was probably done during the first two weeks of November.

However, since there was a $1.50 charge for boresighting and the drilling and tapping was $1.50 per hole, it indicated to Ryder that three holes were drilled in the rifle for a telescopic sight.

The Carcano identified as Oswald's rifle had only two holes for the sight and the telescopic sight came already fixed to the rifle. Furthermore, neither Ryder nor his boss could readily identify pictures of Oswald as the man ordering the work. Thus it would appear that someone using Oswald's name ordered work on a weapon that was not the Oswald rifle.

The Warren Commission, never willing to admit the possibility that someone might have been fabricating evidence against Oswald, hinted that Ryder had made up the story about working on the rifle.

Again in early November, shooters at the Sports Drome Rifle Range recalled a young man who was there sighting in a foreign-made rifle. One of these shooters, Malcolm Price, helped adjust the rifle sight for the man shooting and another, Garland Slack, argued with the man on another occasion because the man was shooting at Slack's target. Both Dr. Homer Wood and his son, Sterling Wood, recalled the man and both were shocked to see his photograph on television in the days following the assassination. They remained convinced the man was Lee Harvey Oswald.

However, the Warren Commission noted that these witnesses were not consistent in their descriptions of the rifle-range gunman or of the rifle and scope. In addition, some of the gun-range witnesses said Oswald was accompanied by a man in a late-model car. Since Oswald reportedly could not drive and did not know anyone with a late-model car, the Commission concluded, "Although the testimony of these witnesses was partially corroborated by other witnesses, there was other evidence which prevented the Commission from reaching the conclusion that Lee Harvey Oswald was the person these witnesses saw."

Furthermore, Price remembered helping "Oswald" sight his rifle on September 28, 1963, a time when Oswald reportedly was in Mexico City.

In October 1963, Mrs. Lovell Penn heard shooting on her property just outside Dallas. Accosting three men shooting a rifle in a field, Penn ordered them to leave. After they left, she found a 6.5 mm Mannlicher-Carcano rifle shell near where the men had been target shooting. After the assassination, she turned the shell casing over to the FBI and told them that one of the men looked like Oswald while another was "Latin, perhaps Cuban." However, the FBI reported that laboratory tests showed the shell had not been fired from the Oswald rifle.

The reports of Oswald accompanied by Cubans came from many different sources. Recall the incident of three anti-Castro Cubans—one by the name of Leon Oswald—visiting Silvia Odio shortly before the assassination.

Someone was posing as Oswald in the days preceding the assassination, carefully laying out a pattern of an irritating young man who was in possession of and practicing with a foreign-made rifle.

But the Warren Commission stated, "In most instances, investigation has disclosed that there is no substantial basis for believing that the person reported by the various witnesses was Oswald."

Of course, if the man in question was not Oswald, it means that someone was laying a trail of evidence to the real Oswald. This gives great credence to Oswald's cry to news reporters in the Dallas police station: "I'm just a patsy!"

But the question of Oswald's identity leads to even stranger areas.

Was Oswald Really Oswald?

Was the Oswald killed in Dallas the same Oswald born in New Orleans in 1939? Bizarre as this may sound, there is considerable evidence to suggest that the man killed by Ruby was not the original Lee Harvey Oswald.

The first major publicity over this issue came in 1977 with the publication of *The Oswald File* by British author and attorney Michael Eddowes. Eddowes, who acknowledged to this author his connections with British intelligence dating back to World War II, theorized, "Lee Harvey Oswald was captured by the Soviets after traveling to Russia in 1959 and a look-alike substitute was returned to the United States in his place."

Eddowes said that after studying the issue of Oswald's identity, he became "100 percent convinced" that President Kennedy was killed by a Soviet KGB agent impersonating the real Oswald. The British attorney noted the following discrepancies to support his theory:

- A mastoidectomy scar that was noted on Oswald's Marine Corps medical records was not mentioned in Oswald's autopsy report.
- Oswald's Marine records showed a vaccination scar on his arm, along with other scars. No vaccination scar was noted in Oswald's autopsy report and

the location of scars differed from those in his military records.

- In Warren Commission documents, including Marine and passport application papers, at least eleven give Oswald's height as five-foot-eleven, while at least thirteen documents—all produced after Oswald's return from Russia—give his height as five-foot-nine.
- During Oswald's twenty-month disappearance in Russia, US government agencies—including the FBI and the State Department—expressed suspicions regarding Oswald's identity.
- When Marina met Oswald at a dance in Minsk, she believed him to be a native Russian with a Baltic area accent. Since there is no doubt that the man she met in Russia was the man killed in Dallas, it should be understood that Marina knew only the one Oswald. But this fact does not eliminate the possibility that a substitution took place prior to their meeting.

There are a number of other intriguing hints that point toward substitution.

Just weeks before leaving Russia for home, Oswald wrote his mother and asked her to send him pictures of her and himself. Some researchers wonder if he needed such photos so he would know which woman to greet at the airport.

Jeanne DeMohrenschildt claimed that Oswald's knowledge of Russia extended beyond just its language. Recall that native Russians thought he spoke the language better than they did. She said her husband, George, and Oswald would have lengthy discussions about Russian literature, including such authors as Tolstoy and Dostoevsky—an incredible feat for a high-school dropout whose Russian was self-taught.

She said Oswald even subscribed to a Soviet satirical journal titled *The Crocodile* and had a large collection of photographs he claimed to have taken in several different areas of Russia. Officially, Oswald never ventured outside Moscow and Minsk.

Gary Mack has reported that three language experts at Southern Methodist University in Dallas studied tape recordings made of Oswald. They were not told the identity of the man whose voice they heard. All agreed that the English words spoken seemed acquired later in life—that English was not the native tongue of the man on the tape.

This startling conclusion was supported by Mrs. DeMohrenschildt, who told this author she was more amazed by Oswald's English than his Russian. She said he spoke in deliberate and precise terms, rarely ever using slang or curse words. She said, "Everybody always talks about how good his Russian was. I was always surprised at the English coming from this boy who was brought up in the South. I wondered, 'Where did he learn such proper English—certainly not from his mother.'"

A particularly intriguing hint at impersonation came in the fall of 1963, when a letter was sent to the Russian embassy in Washington. It was signed by Lee Harvey Oswald, who was writing about his alleged travel to Mexico City. The second sentence of the letter—the Warren Commission published both his handwritten draft and the typed letter—reads, "I was unable to remain in Mexico indefinitely [*sic*] because of my mexican [*sic*] visa restrictions which was [*sic*] for 15 days only. I could not take a chance on requesting a new visa *unless I used my real name* [emphasis added], so I returned to the United States."

Since his passport and visa forms—as well as the November 9, 1963, embassy letter—were in the name of Lee Harvey Oswald, researchers are left to wonder about the meaning of having to use "my real name."

In 2003, researcher John Armstrong published a lengthy and heavily documented book advancing the theory that a second Oswald, rather than a Soviet agent, had been groomed at a young age by US intelligence with an eye toward sending him into Russia as a spy. Armstrong titled his book *Harvey & Lee: How the CIA Framed Oswald*. Meticulously footnoted and running to more than 1,000 pages, his book today is both costly and hard to obtain. His evidence, however, is compelling.

Under Armstrong's theory, in the late 1950s a young man in New York City from a family with an Eastern European background who could speak Russian fluently was to be sent as a spy to Russia. But he would not go under his real name, so his background was merged with that of a patriotic American youth named Lee Harvey Oswald. A switch was made when both Lee and the New Yorker Armstrong identifies as Harvey were in military service. This identity switch very probably was accomplished with the knowledge and assistance of Lee Oswald.

Harvey went to Russia and eventually became the Oswald arrested in Dallas. He was the only Oswald known to his wife, Marina, and to his New Orleans coworker Judyth Vary Baker.

The real Lee Oswald was seen working with anti-Castro Cubans at a time when Harvey was in Russia and most probably was eliminated by the time of the assassination or shortly thereafter. Fantastic as this may sound, it fits all the known evidence and goes far in explaining the scramble by US intelligence agencies to cover up the truth of the legend that is Lee Harvey Oswald.

Some examples of Armstrong's findings include:

- Statements by New Orleans resident Ed Voebel, who claimed to have befriended Oswald while both were attending Beauregard Junior High School in that city, at a time in 1954 when both his mother and brother said Oswald was attending Stripling Junior High in Fort Worth.
- Frank Kudlaty, former assistant principal of Stripling, recalled that the day after the assassination, he was ordered to retrieve Oswald's records from the school and hand them over to FBI agents. Neither Oswald's records nor any mention of Kudlaty has been found in the National Archives.
- FBI records show information was developed that an Oswald lived with his father and two uncles, who were Hungarian communists, at 77th and 2nd Avenue in New York City. Oswald, whose father died before he was born, grew up in Fort Worth.
- In Warren Commission Exhibit 1384 are New York school records showing Oswald attended 171 days at Public School No. 44. Yet, New York City attendance officer James Brennan reported Oswald was excessively absent

from PS No. 44, more than forty-six days. Armstrong concluded, "These contradictory records appear to reflect the activities of two different people—both named 'Lee Harvey Oswald.' The short, malnourished Oswald truanted [often] and was remanded to the Youth House, while the tall, well-built Oswald attended PS No. 44 regularly."

- In December 1963 as requested, Administrative Judge Florence Kelley of the Family Court of the State of New York personally handed over Oswald's New York school (Case File 23979) and psychiatric records to FBI special agent in charge John Malone with the condition he give the files directly to the Warren Commission. Later, the original documents turned up missing and only photographic copies were available prompting Armstrong to conclude, "Whenever original records are destroyed and only copies or photographs remain, it is probable that the original documents were altered and then photographed."
- Palmer E. McBride told the FBI he had worked with Oswald in 1957–1958 at the Pfisterer Dental Lab in New Orleans. Military records showed Oswald was serving in the Marines in Japan at this time.
- Although records show five-year-old Oswald had his tonsils removed in 1945, military records noted he was treated for tonsillitis while in the Marines.
- The husky, older Oswald photographed and tape recorded in Mexico City in 1963 obviously was not the Oswald arrested in Dallas.
- Deputy sheriff Roger Craig claimed he witnessed Oswald getting into a station wagon moments after the assassination. His account was supported by passing motorists Roy Cooper and Marvin Robinson. Yet, officially, Oswald was boarding a city bus driven by Cecil McWatters.

Based on indisputable evidence of impersonation if not a physical switch, author Eddowes went into a Texas court on January 10, 1979, and asked that Oswald's grave be opened. He had the support of the Dallas County Medical Examiner's Office, which was convinced there was enough question about the identity of the body to warrant an exhumation.

The Oswald Exhumation

Soon after Eddowes asked to have Oswald's body exhumed, political fights sprang up between conflicting jurisdictions. Oswald had been killed in Dallas County, but his body was buried in Rose Hill Cemetery, which is in nearby Tarrant County. While the Dallas County Medical Examiner's Office had authorized an exhumation, Tarrant County officials balked.

On June 1, 1979, Texas district judge James Wright denied Eddowes's exhumation request. Dallas County assistant medical examiner Dr. Linda Norton told news reporters, "I feel it would be in the public interest to conduct the exhumation.

However, there are apparent legal disagreements . . . and political forces who do not want this body dug up."

Norton said her efforts to exhume the body were being thwarted by Tarrant County district attorney Tim Curry, an elected official. The case dragged on.

Eddowes was not the first to seek an exhumation of Oswald's body. A Warren Commission document declassified only in 1975 revealed that CIA officials were suspicious of Oswald's true identity as early as 1964. In a Commission memorandum dated March 13, 1964, staff member W. David Slawson wrote about a letter from FBI director J. Edgar Hoover on February 26, 1964. In this memo, Slawson quoted Hoover as writing, "The CIA is interested in the scar on Oswald's left wrist. . . . The FBI is reluctant to exhume Oswald's body as requested by the CIA." In this same memo, Slawson expressed his own questions about what may have happened to Oswald in Russia:

> This whole aspect of Oswald's life and especially our attempt to authenticate it are highly secret at this point. . . . [Slawson mentions the reported suicide attempt by Oswald cutting his wrist shortly after arriving in Russia.] Therefore, if the suicide incident is a fabrication, the time spent by Oswald recovering from the suicide [attempt] in a Moscow hospital could have been spent by him in Russian secret police custody, being coached, brainwashed, etc.

Funeral director Paul Groody, who buried Oswald in 1963, told this author that Secret Service agents came to him three weeks after Oswald's burial asking questions about marks on the body. Groody said, "They told me, 'We don't know who we have in that grave.'"

Furthermore, Oswald's own mother asked for an exhumation in 1967, expressing questions as to the identity of the body in her son's grave. Marguerite Oswald told local news reporters that she did not believe her son had scars on his body as described by the Warren Commission.

Mrs. Oswald previously had told the Warren Commission how her son had seemed changed after arriving back in Fort Worth from Russia. She said she noticed he was losing his hair and that Oswald told her he was going bald "because of the cold weather in Texas." She also noted, "And Lee was very, very thin when I saw him."

Oswald's brother Robert also noted changes in Oswald when he arrived back in the United States. He told the Warren Commission:

> His appearance had changed to the extent that he had lost a considerable amount of hair; his hair had become very kinky in comparison with his naturally curly hair prior to his departure to Russia. . . . He appeared the first couple of days upon his return . . . to be rather tense and anxious. I also noted that his complexion had changed somewhat to the extent that he had always been very fair complected—his complexion was rather ruddy at

this time—you might say it appeared like an artificial suntan that you get out of a bottle, but very slight—in other words, a tint of brown to a tint of yellow. . . . He appeared to have picked up something of an accent.

Oswald's half-brother, John Edward Pic, was even more pointed in his comments to the Warren Commission concerning Lee's appearance after returning from Russia:

> I would have never recognized him, sir. . . . He was much thinner than I remembered him. He didn't have as much hair. . . . His face features were somewhat different, being his eyes were set back maybe, you know like in these Army pictures, they looked different than I remembered him. His face was rounder . . . when he went in the Marine Corps [Oswald had] a bull neck. This I didn't notice at all. I looked for this, I didn't notice it at all, sir.

Pic went on to tell how he became angered when Oswald introduced him to a visitor as his half-brother. He said Oswald had never previously mentioned that Pic was only a half-brother.

Shown a photo reportedly taken of young Oswald in 1953 at the Bronx Zoo, Pic told Warren Commission attorney Albert Jenner, "Sir, from that picture, I could not recognize that that is Lee Harvey Oswald." Jenner queried, "He doesn't look like you recall Lee looked in 1952 and 1953 when you saw him in New York City?" Pic replied, "No, sir."

In August 1979, Dallas County medical examiner Dr. Charles Petty formally called for an exhumation and asked his counterpart in Tarrant County to order it. However, this request, along with Eddowes's offer to pay the premium on a $100,000 indemnification bond to allow the exhumation to proceed, was rejected by District Attorney Curry.

Then in February 1980, Dr. Petty reversed himself and said he would not order an exhumation. Meanwhile, the court found that Eddowes, being a British citizen, lacked any legal standing in a Texas court.

By the summer of 1980, Eddowes was joined in his exhumation efforts by Marina Oswald, who provided the necessary legal standing.

As the foot-dragging of Tarrant County officials to an Oswald exhumation began to ease, another roadblock was thrown in the way of an exhumation—this time by Oswald's brother Robert. On August 15, 1980, Robert Oswald won an injunction against the exhumation, saying it would cause his family anguish. This was considered very odd by assassination researchers because if the exhumation showed the man in the grave was not Oswald, it would have exonerated his brother as a presidential assassin. If the exhumation proved the body was Oswald, nothing would have changed. So what harm could be done?

The case dragged on for more months. Finally, on August 20, 1981, Marina filed suit to have the grave opened. And on October 4, 1981—nine months after Marguerite Oswald died from cancer in a Fort Worth hospital and was quietly buried alongside her son Lee—the exhumation of the Oswald grave took place. Opposition to the exhumation had suddenly vanished. Robert Oswald said he could not afford to fight the issue further in court.

The body was taken from Rose Hill Cemetery in the early morning hours and driven to Baylor Medical Center in Dallas for study. A team of four forensic pathologists compared the teeth of the corpse brought from the Oswald grave with Oswald's Marine Corps dental records.

Almost four hours after the study began, the results were in. Dr. Norton, who headed the exhumation study, stated, "Beyond any doubt, and I mean any doubt, the individual buried under the name Lee Harvey Oswald in Rose Hill Cemetery is in fact Lee Harvey Oswald."

Within hours, local newspapers carried the headlines:

—DOCTORS IDENTIFY BODY AS OSWALD,

—AUTOPSY PROVES BODY IS OSWALD'S and

—OSWALD ISSUE FINALLY AT REST

While some discrepancies were found between the corpse's teeth and Oswald's military dental records, the doctors were satisfied that enough similarities remained to warrant their conclusion. Also, a hole was discovered behind the left ear, which corresponded to Oswald's known mastoid operation.

The issue appeared to be settled. But, as with so much else in the Kennedy assassination, this was not to be.

A few weeks after the Oswald exhumation, the two funeral home directors who prepared Oswald's body for burial in 1963 got together and talked. Paul Groody and Alan Baumgartner were troubled. They were not supposed to have been at the post-exhumation examination. But at the last minute, Marina Oswald had asked them to be present and identify rings on the corpse.

Entering the autopsy room in Dallas, both men confirmed that the rings were on the corpse in the same location they had placed them in 1963. However, as the forensic examination continued, both Groody and Baumgartner noticed that the skull of the corpse under examination was in one piece—completely intact.

Weeks later, after discussing the matter between themselves, the funeral home directors discussed the situation with Texas assassination researchers and gave startling information—the body that was exhumed in 1981 was not the same body they buried in 1963.

What confirmed this idea in their minds was the absence of signs of a craniotomy, a normal autopsy procedure. A craniotomy involves drawing the skin off the human skull and cutting off the top of the skull with a bone saw, usually in a V-shaped cut. This allows forensic pathologists to view the brain. There can be no question that this procedure was performed on Oswald's body since the weight of his brain was recorded in the autopsy report. Furthermore, both funeral home directors recalled the craniotomy in preparing the body for burial. Groody said, "I put the skull back together and sewed up his scalp."

Yet both men have said they noticed no sign of the craniotomy on the skull they viewed during the 1981 exhumation study. If there was no craniotomy performed on the skull in Oswald's grave, it is proof that the body is not the same one buried there in 1963.

There are other indications that some manipulation may have taken place with the body. To begin with, Marina Oswald told news reporters that she received a telephone call around Easter 1964 from government officials asking her to sign papers authorizing the installation of an electronic alarm system at the Oswald grave. She said a "respectful" man in a gray suit came to her home shortly after the call and had her sign some papers. She told United Press International, "I signed lots of papers and they were never translated or explained to me. I didn't even speak English. I just did what I was told."

Prior to the exhumation, Marina was nearly convinced that Oswald's body had been removed from the grave, most probably after the signing of the papers in 1964.

As far as is known, no electronic alarm system was ever installed at the Oswald grave.

Prior to the exhumation, mortician Groody told reporters how carefully Oswald had been embalmed. He also described how the body was placed in an airtight coffin that was placed inside an airtight cement vault. Groody said that upon exhumation Oswald's body should look exactly as it had the day he was buried.

However, when workers exhumed the grave, they found the cement vault in pieces and the seal on the coffin broken. Water and air had gotten into the coffin and Oswald's body had deteriorated to skeletal remains.

While the rupture of seals on both the vault and the coffin is not an impossible occurrence, several morticians interviewed by this author said such an event is highly unusual. It could be explained by movement of the earth, although north-central Texas is regarded as a very stable area. The broken seals also could be explained by someone having opened the grave prior to the 1981 exhumation.

A logical time for such a pre-exhumation grave opening would have been earlier in 1981, when Marguerite Oswald was buried next to Oswald's grave. The presence of earthmoving equipment and a canopy covering both graves provided an opportunity for covertly opening Oswald's adjacent grave.

So, the question has been asked: Was a substitution made for the body in Oswald's grave?

The answer may be found in a four-hour videotape made of the 1981 exhumation study. The tape was commissioned by Marina Oswald and Eddowes and was produced by Hampton Hall, the son of a Texas politician.

Once the craniotomy question became known to Marina, a friend and neighbor was asked to view the tape. The neighbor, along with his personal physician, viewed the videotape and reported that there was no sign or mention of a craniotomy. This added further suspicions about the exhumation.

Finally, in 1984—four years after the exhumation—a detailed report on the exhumation findings was published in the *Journal of Forensic Sciences*. The report claimed, "A previous autopsy saw cut in the usual fashion was present on the calvarium with an anterior inverted V-notch in the right frontal region. The calvarium was maintained in continuity with the remainder of the skull by virtue of decomposed mummified tissue. The previously sawed calvarium was not separated nor was it easily dislodged."

In other words, decomposed, jelly-like skin had coated the Oswald skull, which made it appear to be in one piece.

Researchers were skeptical of this information and turned to Marina for confirmation of the craniotomy by viewing the videotape of the exhumation. Oddly enough, photographer Hall refused to give up the tape, claiming that so much time had elapsed that ownership of the tape had reverted to him.

In February 1984, Marina was forced to go to court to retrieve the videotape she had commissioned. By the summer of 1986, an out-of-court settlement resulted in a promise to return the tape. Apparently, the tape still has not been returned.

The issue should have been a simple one: view the tapes and photos of the exhumation and resolve whether the craniotomy marks were visible on the Oswald skull. But with the tapes still not available even by 2013, this issue remains in controversy, like so much else in the JFK assassination case.

Researchers remain intrigued. If the body exhumed in 1981 was indeed that of Oswald—as confirmed by the forensic pathologists and his Marine dental X-rays—but the exhumed corpse was not that of the man buried in 1963—as claimed by the two morticians—then it is possible that an impostor Oswald was killed in Dallas and his body—or at least the head—exchanged for Oswald's sometime prior to the exhumation.

And who might have the power and authority to accomplish such a momentous task? The idea that the Soviets, Castro agents, or mobsters could switch bodies is ludicrous. Only the federal government of the United States, with its access to the military and such devices as the Federal Witness Protection Program, could accomplish something of that magnitude.

The impersonation of Oswald would appear to be an issue that could be resolved easily by a truthful government investigation. Instead, it is another area of the assassination full of omissions, inconsistencies, and possible deceit.

In the end, the issue of Oswald's impersonation may be a moot point, since persuasive evidence suggests that the Oswald in Dallas—whether lone nut, American agent, communist operative, genuine, or substitute—did not kill President Kennedy.

Convenient Deaths

In the three-year period that followed the murders of President Kennedy and Lee Harvey Oswald, eighteen material witnesses died—six by gunfire, three in motor accidents, two by suicide, one from a cut throat, one from a karate chop to the neck, and five from natural causes.

An actuary, engaged by the *London Sunday Times*, concluded that on November 22, 1963, the odds against these witnesses being dead by February 1967 were one hundred thousand trillion to one.

The above comment on the deaths of assassination witnesses was published in a tabloid companion piece to the movie *Executive Action*, released in 1973. By that time, part of the mythology of the Kennedy assassination included the questionable deaths of people who were connected with it.

By the mid-1960s, people in Dallas already were whispering about the number of people who died under strange or questionable circumstances. Well into the 1980s, witnesses and others were hesitant to come forward with information because of the stories of strange and sudden death that seemed to visit some people with information about the assassination.

Finally, in the late 1970s, the House Select Committee on Assassinations felt compelled to look into the matter. But aside from attempting to discredit the *London Sunday Times* actuarial study, the committee was unable to come to any conclusions regarding the growing number of deaths. The committee said it could not make a valid actuarial study due to the broad number and types of people that had to be included in such a study.

In response to a letter from the committee, *London Sunday Times* legal manager Anthony Whitaker backpedaled on the publication's original statements by writing, "Our piece about the odds against the deaths of the Kennedy witnesses was, I regret to say, based on a careless journalistic mistake and should not have been published. This was realized by the *Sunday Times* editorial staff after the first edition—the one which goes to the United States . . . —had gone out, and later editions were amended."

Whitaker said there was no question of the actuary having gotten his answer wrong: it was simply that they asked him the wrong question. "He was asked what were the odds against 15 named people out of the population of the United States dying within a short period of time to which he replied—correctly—that they were very high. However, if one asks what are the odds against 15 of those included in the Warren Commission Index dying within a given period, the answer is, of course, that they are much lower. Our mistake was to treat the reply to the former question as if it dealt with the latter," he explained.

This settled the matter for the House committee, which apparently made little or no attempt to seriously study the number of deaths that followed the JFK assassination. Jacqueline Hess, the committee's chief of research for the JFK investigation, reported, "Our final conclusion on the issue is that the available evidence does not establish anything about the nature of these deaths which would indicate that the deaths were in some manner, either direct or peripheral, caused by the assassination of President Kennedy or by any aspect of the subsequent investigation."

But the controversy continued well into 2013. Blogger Richard Charnin, who holds a master's degree in applied mathematics and is a former numerical control engineer for Grumman Aerospace Corporation, has provided a detailed analysis of this issue. Charnin argued that the US population is not relevant—the number of JFK-related witnesses is. Charnin also pointed out that Whitaker neglected to provide unnatural-death mortality statistics.

Utilizing a comprehensive spreadsheet database of suspicious unnatural witness deaths, probability calculations, and Warren Commission, Garrison/Shaw trial, and HSCA witnesses, Charnin stated:

> The identity of the actuary has never been revealed. The *Sunday Times* editor did not provide details on the methodology. In fact, he claimed that the problem was misstated, implying that the actuary's probability calculation was wrong. [My] analysis will show that the actuary's calculation was essentially correct. It will show that the editor's 1977 response to the House Select Committee on Assassinations was misleading and incomplete. And that HSCA statistical expert Jacqueline Hess's claim that the actuary's calculation was "invalid" due to the "impossibility" of defining the "universe" of material witnesses was disinformation. The number of JFK-related witnesses is a finite 1,400 plus [as provided by Michael Benson's 1993 book *Who's Who in the JFK Assassination*]. The dismissal of the actuary's odds was just a continuation of the cover-up.

Former Los Angeles prosecutor Vincent Bugliosi also argued against the significance of the JFK witness deaths, citing Robert M. Musen, vice president and senior actuary at Metropolitan Life Insurance Company. Musen had calculated the odds of 15 people out of 2,479 in the Warren Commission Index dying within a three-year period, assuming a median age of 40, to be 98.16 percent.

Bugliosi failed to note that fewer than five hundred witnesses actually testified to the Commission and that several names included in the index, such as George Washington and other presidents, were not witnesses and, in fact, had no connection to the assassination. Furthermore, Musen failed to consider unnatural deaths. "Even assuming 2,479 names," explained Charnin, "approximately four unnatural and 70 natural deaths from the list would be expected over a three year period. . . . The odds that at least 15 of 2,479 would die unnaturally within 3 years is one in 46,000. The odds of 18 dying unnaturally is 1 in 3.6 million."

Charnin said his analysis countered the "feeble attempts to rebut and obfuscate the actuary's 100,000 trillion to 1 odds" by showing at least 33 of 1,400 JFK assassination-related witnesses died unnaturally in the three years following the assassination. "The probability of this occurrence is 1 in 137 TRILLION TRILLION! Only two or three would normally be expected," he said.

An objective look at both the number and the causes of death balanced against the importance of the person's connection to the case plus the timing with concurrent investigations still causes raised eyebrows among researchers.

This section has been titled "Convenient Deaths" because these deaths certainly would have been convenient for anyone not wishing the truth of the JFK assassination to become public.

Government apologists, in particular the CIA, have gone to some lengths to discredit the idea of mysterious deaths plaguing assassination witnesses. A 1967 memo from CIA headquarters to station chiefs advised, "The [Warren] Commission staff questioned 418 witnesses—the FBI interviewed far more people, conducting 25,000 interviews and reinterviews—and in such a large group, a certain number of deaths are to be expected."

However, the means of eliminating unwanted witnesses certainly existed, both then and now. Testifying before the Church Committee about CIA improprieties in 1975, CIA technicians revealed a variety of TWEP technology—"Termination With Extreme Prejudice"—that cannot be detected in a postmortem examination.

One letter from an agency consultant to a CIA officer listed circumstances under which people could be killed but made to look like natural death, accident, or suicide. The letter went on to show that undetected murders do not necessarily have to be the result of sophisticated technology. It stated, "There are two techniques which I believe should be mentioned since they require no special equipment besides a strong arm and the will to do such a job. These would be either to smother the victim with a pillow or to strangle him with a wide piece of cloth such as a bath towel. In such cases, there are no specific anatomic changes to indicate the cause of death."

While it is obvious that the CIA—and hence the mob through operatives who work for both—has the capability of killing, it is less well known that the agency has developed drugs to induce cancer. Jack Ruby claimed to have been given such a drug just as he was granted a new trial.

As far back as 1952, a CIA memo reported on the cancer-causing effects of beryllium: "This is certainly the most toxic inorganic element and it produces a peculiar fibrotic tumor at the site of local application. The amount necessary to produce these tumors is a few micrograms."

Local law-enforcement officers and coroners are not equipped, either by training or by inclination, to detect deaths induced by such sophisticated means. They look for signs of a struggle, evidence of a break-in, bruises, or marks on the victim. With no evidence to the contrary, many deaths are ruled suicide or accident. Others are ruled due to natural causes, such as heart attack.

The possibility of convenient deaths leads one into a well of paranoia, yet this long list cannot be summarily dismissed.

Consider the question: When does coincidence end and conspiracy begin?

It is especially interesting to note how the deaths are grouped.

Early Deaths

Early deaths included Mary Richardson, wife of the New Orleans minister to whom Judyth Vary Baker revealed knowledge of the New Orleans cancer lab; Jack Zangretti, who expressed foreknowledge of Oswald's shooting; and Gary Underhill, a CIA officer who claimed the agency was involved.

Early in 1964, as the Warren Commission investigation was getting under way, there was a rash of deaths of people who may have known of an Oswald-Ruby connection. These included former Ruby employees Betty McDonald and Teresa Norton; Hank Killam, husband of a Ruby employee, and Teresa Norton; Dallas reporters Bill Hunter and Jim Koethe, both of whom had been in Ruby's apartment the weekend of the assassination. Dead in New Orleans were former FBI agent Guy Banister and his private investigator Hugh Ward, who was killed in a plane crash along with New Orleans mayor DeLesseps Morrison. Eddie Benavides, brother to J. D. Tippit shooting witness Domingo Benavides, was shot in the head, apparently mistaken for his brother.

About the time the Warren Commission Report was released in the fall of 1964, Mary Pinchot Meyer, a JFK confidante and former wife to CIA chief Cord Meyer, was murdered and C. D. Jackson, the *Life* magazine senior vice president who locked away the Zapruder film, died. Shortly after Jackson's death, *Life* writer Paul Mandel, who tried to explain Kennedy's throat wound by saying he turned rearward to wave, also died.

Deaths in 1965 included Ruby's first lawyer, Tom Howard; Guy Banister's pilot Maurice Gatlin; and Rose Cheramie, who reported the assassination in advance. Also dead were Mona B. Saenz, a Texas employment clerk who had interviewed Oswald; David Goldstein, who had helped the FBI trace Oswald's pistol; and columnist Dorothy Kilgallen and her close friend Mrs. Earl Smith, who may have kept Kilgallen's JFK notes, which subsequently disappeared. In December 1965 William Whaley, the cabdriver who reportedly drove Oswald to Oak Cliff, became the only Dallas cabdriver killed on duty.

The deaths of those potential witnesses continued in 1966, including Ruby trial judge Joe Brown, Oswald's landlady Earlene Roberts, and Ruby dancers Marilyn Delilah Walle and Karen "Little Lynn" Carlin. Also dead were Albert Bogard, who told of Oswald test driving a new car prior to the assassination; captain Frank Martin, the Dallas police official who said there was a lot more to be said in the assassination; and Lee Bowers Jr., who told of seeing men behind the wooden picket fence at the time of the shooting.

Deaths in late 1966 included the reported suicide of William Pitzer, who photographed the JFK autopsy; Jimmy Levens, a Fort Worth nightclub owner who hired Ruby employees; James Worrell Jr., who saw someone flee the rear of the Texas School Book Depository; Clarence Oliver, a district attorney investigator who worked the Ruby case; and Hank Suydam, the *Life* magazine official in charge of JFK stories.

In 1967, as New Orleans district attorney Jim Garrison began his JFK investigation, Jack Ruby died, along with Navy photographer Leonard Pullin and Harold Russell, who witnessed the escape of Officer Tippit's killer. There were also the deaths of key Garrison witnesses David Ferrie, who died from a blow to the neck ruled accidental; former Ferrie roommate Eladio Del Valle; and cancer researcher Dr. Mary Sherman.

New Orleans–connected deaths continued into 1968 with that of New Orleans coroner Dr. Nicholas Chetta, who had ruled on Ferrie's death, and Philip Geraci, who spoke of an Oswald–Clay Shaw connection.

In early 1969, deaths included Henry Delaune, the brother-in-law to coroner Chetta; E. R. "Buddy" Walthers, the deputy sheriff who saw the bullet in the grass in Dealey Plaza; and the Reverend Clyde Johnson, who was scheduled to testify in the Shaw trial. Also dead were Charles Mentensana, who had filmed a rifle being brought out of the Depository; John Crawford, a close friend to both Jack Ruby and witness Wesley Frazier; and Mary Bledsoe, an Oswald neighbor who also knew David Ferrie.

In 1970, Dallas underworld figure George McGann, who was married to the "babushka lady" Beverly Oliver, was murdered. That year also witnessed the deaths of Abraham Zapruder and Dallas County sheriff Bill Decker. In 1971, a fiery explosion at work killed Roscoe White, identified by his son as the Grassy Knoll gunman. Also dying by mid-1971 was Darrell Garner, arrested for shooting Tippit witness Warren Reynolds; Clayton Fowler, Ruby's chief defense attorney; CIA deputy director General Charles Cabell; and mobsters James Plumeri and Salvatore Granello, tied to CIA assassination plots.

Strange Deaths Continue

Between 1972 and the end of 1976, during the time of the Church Committee investigations into CIA improprieties, there again was a spurt of deaths among JFK assassination figures. These included House Majority Leader and Warren Commissioner Hale Boggs; FBI director J. Edger Hoover, along with his assistant Clyde Tolson; Chief Justice Earl Warren; Garrison suspect Clay Shaw; Dallas mayor Earle Cabell; CIA officer William Harvey; and General Earl Wheeler, a liaison between JFK and the CIA. Murder victims included Dave Yaras, a close friend to both Jimmy Hoffa and Jack Ruby, and mafia bosses Sam Giancana and John Roselli, both scheduled to testify to the Church Committee. Also dying during this time were Ruby-connected gunrunner Thomas E. Davis; Ruby business partner Ralph Paul; Connally's physician Dr. Charles Gregory; Dallas motorcycle officer James Chaney; and J. A. Milteer, the Miami right-winger who predicted JFK's death and the capture of a scapegoat.

The year 1977 produced a bumper crop of candidates for listing under convenient deaths connected to the JFK assassination—including the deaths of six top FBI officials, all of whom were scheduled to testify before the House Select Committee on Assassinations.

Topping this list was former number-three man in the FBI William C. Sullivan, who had already had a preliminary meeting with investigators for the House committee. Sullivan was shot with a high-powered rifle near his New Hampshire home by a man who claimed to have mistaken him for a deer. The man was charged with a misdemeanor—"shooting a human being by accident"—and released into the custody of his father, a state policeman. There was no further investigation of Sullivan's death.

Louis Nicholas was a special assistant to J. Edgar Hoover as well as Hoover's liaison with the Warren Commission. Alan H. Belmont also was a special assistant to Hoover. James Cadigan was a document expert with access to many classified assassination documents, while J. M. English headed the FBI laboratory where Oswald's rifle and pistol were tested. Donald Kaylor was the FBI fingerprint expert who examined prints found at the assassination scene. None of these six bureau officials lived to tell what they knew to the House committee.

During the House committee investigation into the JFK assassination, the news media reported the deaths of other key assassination witnesses, such as George DeMohrenschildt and former Cuban president Carlos Prio Socarras, who died within weeks of each other in 1977, just as they, too, were being sought by the House committee.

The ranks of both organized crime and US intelligence agencies were thinned by deaths beginning in 1975, the time of the Senate Intelligence Hearings, and 1978, the closing months of the House committee.

Charles Nicoletti, a mobster connected with the CIA-Mafia assassination plots, was murdered in Chicago, while William Pawley, a former diplomat connected with both organized-crime and CIA figures, reportedly committed suicide. Other deaths during this time included Lou Staples, a Dallas radio talk show host who told friends he would break the assassination case; Air Force One chief steward Joseph C. Ayres; and U-2 pilot Francis G. Powers.

Adding to rumors that "hit teams" may have been at work, a *Time* magazine article reported that federal agents had initiated a nationwide investigation into more than twenty gangland assassinations constituting what agents believed was an "open underworld challenge to governmental infiltration of Mafia activities."

A *New York News* story concerning this official fear of roving assassination squads specifically mentioned the death of Sam Giancana, killed one day before he was to testify about mob-CIA connections and despite being under government protection.

The shooting death of Mary Pinchot Meyer may provide insights into the machinations of top government officials. She was the former wife of Cord Meyer, since 1962 the head of the CIA's Directorate of Plans Covert Action Staff. The scion of a wealthy, socially prominent, and politically connected family, a WWII combat hero and honors graduate of Yale, Cord Meyer was probably the closest rival to JFK in position, intelligence, and opportunity. This story of wealth and prominence mixed with intrigue and murder was made public in the brilliant 2012 book *Mary's Mosaic* by Peter Janney, who was friends with Mary's children and was the son of CIA official Wistar Janney.

In early 1945, while attending Yale Law School, Meyer met and wed a beautiful socialite named Mary Pinchot. Their marriage became a partnership of idealistic equals as they crusaded for world peace. Cord Meyer caught the attention of United Nations higher-ups by writing a paper advocating a federation of nations and on

May 2, he became an aide to Harold Stassen, who helped establish the United Nations.

With his new bride, Meyer accompanied Stassen to a conference on the United Nations later that month. Mary was reporting for United Press International. There she became reacquainted with John F. Kennedy, who was reporting on the conference for the *Chicago Herald-American*. But when Kennedy attempted to interview Cord, he was snubbed. Reportedly this was a rebuke he never forgot, later ignoring Cord's request for an ambassadorship.

Later that same month, Cord Meyer's outlook on life changed when his fraternal twin brother, Quintin, was killed in action on Okinawa. He slowly became more and more distant from Mary. His focus turned inward and he became a chain-smoker and alcoholic. In 1951, he left the United World Federalists, which he had helped fund, and joined the CIA at the invitation of Allen Dulles.

According to author Janney:

> Somewhere in the bowels of the Washington E Street offices of the newly formed CIA, Cord Meyer transformed all his poetic, insightful visionary and wisdom into perfecting schemes and strategies for America's greater power and control, the often subtle but effective attempts at world domination—no matter what the cost. [He was a] Cold Warrior by day, increasingly frustrated and intoxicated at night.

The Meyer marriage broke up in 1956 and, following the death of her son Michael, who was hit by a car, Mary moved to Massachusetts, where she socialized in the same circles as JFK. Kennedy reportedly was unhappy with Jackie and wanted out of this marriage but knew it would be political suicide. He began to visit Mary at her rented home, which was within an hour of the Kennedy compound. Their relationship grew and matured. Janney wrote, "She was one of the few women he really respected, maybe the only one."

This liaison continued through 1963, with Mary introducing Jack to a broader view of the world, the benefits of peace, and even drugs such as LSD and marijuana. Communicating with Harvard psychologist and drug culture guru Timothy Leary, Mary devised a plan to give careful amounts of LSD to ranking government officials so as to reprogram them to build a more peaceful society.

Theologian James W. Douglass wrote, "Although Kennedy was a Cold Warrior who had taken the world to the very brink of nuclear war, there was a more peaceful element in his character from which God could create something new. What was the seed of his transformation? . . . What was the seed of his change from the president of a national security state into a leader with a more universal humanity, which . . . would then mark him out for assassination?" Janney came to believe the seed was his relationship with Mary Meyer, an intellectual, self-assured woman who bridled at playing the meek Washington socialite.

Following the JFK assassination and despite warnings from her friends, Mary could not stop talking about it in the capital's social circles, raising questions and pointing out inconsistencies in the official version.

On October 12, 1964, she was shot in the head while walking on the C&O Chesapeake Canal towpath near her home. When the shot failed to kill her, a second shot angled just beneath her right shoulder blade severed her aorta, killing her instantly. The precision of the shots indicated the work of a professional assassin. However, police found an unfortunate black man, Raymond Crump Jr., drunk and sleeping in the area and charged him with the crime. Despite oddities in the evidence and testimony (one key witness was found to have a fraudulent identity and disappeared), it seemed Crump's guilt was a foregone conclusion.

However, a determined young attorney named Dovey J. Roundtree fought a tenacious defense, fully detailed in *Mary's Mosaic*. Roundtree was able to show there was no hard evidence to link Crump to the murder and that he likely was set up to take the blame. Crump was found not guilty and released.

Before the news of Mary's murder even was made public, a small group of people gathered at her Georgetown home, apparently searching for her diary, in which she had made copious notes. Cord Meyer and another ranking CIA official were there along with James J. Angleton, head of the CIA's counterintelligence division, and his wife, Cicely, a close friend of Mary's. Also present were Tony Bradlee, Mary's sister and the wife of *Washington Post* editor Ben Bradlee. There were conflicting accounts as to whether the group had broken into her home. Later it was revealed that Angleton admitted he had found the diary and related papers and burned them.

All this interconnection between members of Washington's elite must be noted when taking into account the deathbed confession of CIA operative and Watergate burglar E. Howard Hunt.

Following Hunt's death in 2007, his sons St. John Hunt and David Hunt said their father had told them who was involved in the conspiracy to assassinate JFK. Topping Hunt's list was Lyndon B. Johnson, followed by CIA officers Cord Meyer, William Harvey, and David Atlee Phillips. He also named CIA operative David Morales and a "French gunman on the Grassy Knoll," thought by his son St. John to be Lucien Sarti.

Could these names have been found in Mary Meyer's diary? Regardless, her murder may well have played an intricate part in the higher levels of the conspiracy to kill Kennedy. After all, his relationship with Mary Meyer may have been the catalyst for Kennedy to attempt to construct a more peaceful and just world. This could not have set well with the war machine that America had become. As Mary once described Kennedy to Timothy Leary, "They couldn't control him anymore."

Near the end of his life, Cord Meyer himself may have indicated some intimate knowledge of the assassination. According to author C. David Heymann, once when Meyer was asked who killed Mary, he bitterly replied, "The same sons of bitches that killed John F. Kennedy."

PART IV

CONCLUSIONS

Since November 22, 1963, a massive amount of information has become available concerning the assassination of president John F. Kennedy. Some of it was made public immediately, but most of this information leaked out only after many years had passed. Much has proven erroneous, incomplete, and misleading in light of later developments.

What does the information available today tell us about Kennedy's assassination? What conclusions may be drawn from the existing record? Based on all currently available information, most researchers have concluded:

1. Lee Harvey Oswald was involved in intelligence activities. He was—or at least he believed he was—working on behalf of the United States.

2. It is entirely possible that Lee Harvey Oswald did not fire a gun on November 22, 1963, thus making him innocent in the deaths of both President Kennedy and police officer J. D. Tippit.

3. If Lee Harvey Oswald did participate in the assassination—and much evidence indicates he did not—he certainly did not act alone.

4. An abundance of evidence indicates that Lee Harvey Oswald was framed for the assassination of President Kennedy. The evidence for someone posing as Oswald in the months leading up to the assassination is more than compelling.

5. This framing of Oswald coupled with evidence of attempts to cover up vital evidence in the case proves the existence of a conspiracy to kill Kennedy.

6. Because this cover-up went far beyond simple face-saving and was conducted at the federal level, it is apparent that persons within the US government were both involved in and aware of such a conspiracy. If there had been a legitimate reason for such activities, it would have been revealed long before now.

7. The two most powerful men in the federal government in 1963—next to the president and his brother—were vice president Lyndon B. Johnson and his

close friend FBI director J. Edgar Hoover. Both men were facing the end of their careers if Kennedy was reelected in 1964. Johnson may have even faced prison time due to his involvement in the TFX, Bobby Baker, and Billie Sol Estes scandals.

8. Both Johnson and Hoover could have been convicted—if not for orchestrating the assassination itself—certainly for participating in the demonstrable cover-up that took place in its aftermath. Under the law, both men were accessories after the fact and subject to criminal penalties.

Even if Oswald—real or impersonator—was recruited as a Soviet agent, he was playing double, acting under orders from persons he believed to be in US intelligence. Despite his pro-Castro posturing, his contacts with Guy Banister and David Ferrie in New Orleans and George DeMohrenschildt in Dallas and assorted FBI agents proved that in the months just prior to the assassination, Oswald was in contact with persons connected to US intelligence.

Once it is understood that Oswald was—or believed he was—working as an intelligence operative, assassination evidence takes on a new perspective.

It is apparent to many researchers that while Oswald most probably did obtain a rifle and a pistol and may have made some sort of trip to Mexico, he likely was following orders from persons he considered to be his intelligence superiors.

Thus, many of Oswald's activities in the weeks prior to the assassination were carefully calculated to both incriminate him and link him with foreign governments.

While it is probable that Oswald was in some way connected with persons involved in a plot against Kennedy, he may have felt secure in the belief that he was reporting on that plot to the US government—most likely through the FBI.

While it cannot be stated with absolute assurance that Oswald never fired a weapon on November 22, 1963, there is an abundance of supporting evidence that he did not. The Dallas police paraffin test showed no gunpowder on Oswald's hands or cheek, evidence that he had not fired a rifle, particularly the loose-bolted Italian Carcano. Oswald maintained he was in the Depository lunchroom at the time of the shooting and accurately named two coworkers who indeed ate in the lunchroom that day. Testimony of other employees indicates that Oswald was seen on lower floors both minutes before and after the assassination.

All this, together with the fact that less than ninety seconds after the shots were fired Depository superintendent Roy Truly and Dallas policeman Marion Baker encountered a calm and collected Oswald standing in a downstairs lunchroom with a soft drink in his hand, tends to support Oswald's alibi.

Whoever fired from the Depository did not act alone. This fact was supported in 1979 by the House Select Committee on Assassinations' scientific study of acoustical material indicating that at least one shot came from the Grassy Knoll. These acoustical studies are supported by many witnesses as well as the photographic enlargement of Mary Moorman's snapshot depicting the "badgeman" figure.

Today it is obvious to many researchers that multiple gunmen were shooting at

Kennedy and that the three shots fired in Dealey Plaza were actually three volleys fired simultaneously—probably coordinated by radio.

The presence of Secret Service agents in Dealey Plaza at a time when all official agents were accounted for elsewhere is a particularly pertinent piece of evidence. Either these men were bogus agents carrying identification good enough to fool Dallas policemen or they were real agents carrying out some undocumented and unexplained activity.

The medical and ballistic evidence, most of which can be called into question, bears all the earmarks of tampering and indicates Kennedy was struck by at least three shots—one in the back below the shoulder blades, which did not penetrate his body, one in the throat, and one in the head (although there is some evidence to suggest that two shots may have struck his head almost simultaneously).

Most probably, at least two shots struck Governor Connally—one penetrating his chest and lung while a separate bullet shattered his right wrist and entered his left thigh.

At least one shot definitely missed the limousine altogether, striking the curb near the Triple Underpass, slightly wounding bystander James Tague. Furthermore, there is evidence of three additional shots—one bullet struck the grass on the south side of Elm Street, another hit in the street near the presidential limousine, and yet another struck the Stemmons Freeway sign.

This count would mean at least six shots were fired in Dealey Plaza—perhaps as many as nine. It is significant to note that acoustical experts testified before the House Select Committee on Assassinations that they had discovered as many as nine sound signals that they could not rule out as gunshots, but only four were confirmed since only two sites for comparison tests were used.

It is apparent to most researchers that the assassination was the result of a well-executed military-style ambush utilizing multiple gunmen firing from hidden positions—perhaps using fragmenting or "sabot" bullets and even silencers.

To attempt to pinpoint each gunman's location and calculate the number and effect of each shot is an exercise in futility since actions were taken immediately to eliminate evidence and confuse investigators. Even the Zapruder film is now under question as evidence.

Since there would have been efforts to eliminate any evidence of foreknowledge of the assassination, it is not surprising that the proof of the framing of Oswald is meager and largely circumstantial. However, it should be noted that circumstances cannot be altered and thus may prove to be better evidence than physical evidence, which can be falsified or planted.

What is obvious and demonstrable is the cover-up perpetrated after the assassination.

Herein lies the real key to understanding the truth of Kennedy's death.

While anyone could have engineered the assassination—Castro agents, KGB assassins, mob hit men, anti-Castro Cuban exiles, dissident CIA or FBI agents, even the infamous "lone nut"—who had the power to subvert and misdirect any meaningful investigation after the assassination had occurred? Only ranking officials of the federal government of the United States.

Consider that in the wake of the assassination there has been:

—A continuing and consistent pattern of suppression of evidence, destruction of evidence, and intimidation of witnesses on the part of federal authorities, especially the FBI and the Warren Commission.

—A continued unwillingness by the Justice Department—of which the FBI is a part—to pursue and prosecute assassination leads, even after being urged to do so by Congress.

—Revelations concerning the presence of Secret Service agents encountered in Dealey Plaza at the time of the shooting, when no agents were present according to official records.

—The questionable activities of the CIA in providing false evidence to the Warren Commission while suppressing other vital evidence, such as the existence of assassination plots involving the agency and organized-crime members.

—The disconcerting pattern of communications blackouts occurring at the time of the assassination that involved the Texas School Book Depository, the Dallas police radio channel dedicated to presidential security, the missing code book in the airplane carrying Kennedy's cabinet, and the virtual shutdown of the Washington, DC, telephone system at a time when most Americans were only just becoming aware that something had happened in Dallas.

—The fact that elements of the 49th Armored Division were in the air returning from exercises in Germany on the day of the assassination, available to quell any disturbance caused by the event.

—The revelation that Kennedy's autopsy was performed by inexperienced Navy doctors who were ordered by higher authorities present not to follow established autopsy procedures, such as examining the president's clothing and probing his wounds. It was this flawed autopsy that has been most responsible for the continuing controversy over the medical evidence.

—An effort on the part of federal authorities to lock assassination evidence away from the public. President Johnson ordered evidence locked up until the year 2039, while the House Select Committee on Assassinations sealed up its evidence for fifty years. Even the Assassinations Records Review Board of the 1990s, while regaining many records, was not able to secure all government documents.

The loss of the Oswald note while in the hands of the FBI, the premature elimination of military and Secret Service files, and the immediate cleansing of the presidential limousine plainly constitute destruction of evidence.

Evidence altered while in the hands of federal authorities includes the autopsy X-rays and photographs, the General Edwin Walker home photograph, the location of Kennedy's back wound, the nature of Kennedy's throat wound, the Dallas police evidence sheet, the location of book boxes in the "sniper's nest," and the testimony of FBI official James Cadigan along with that of several key witnesses, such as Phil Willis, Jean Hill, Roger Craig, Julia Ann Mercer, and the reenactment surveyors.

Instances of suppressed evidence include Kennedy's missing brain, missing bullets, the actual results of spectrographic and neutron activation tests, Oswald's photographic and optical equipment (including the Minox camera), Oswald's paraffin test, the third Oswald backyard photograph, the incidents involving Silvia Odio and Yuri Nosenko, and a variety of crucial assassination witnesses, including Bill and Gayle Newman, Charles Brehm, James Simmons, J. C. Price, Beverly Oliver, Ed Hoffman, Dallas policeman James Chaney, and many others.

The intimidation of witnesses runs the full gamut from simple pressure to alter portions of their testimony to strange and unnatural deaths.

Witnesses Charles Givens, James Tague, Phil Willis, Kennedy aides Kenneth O'Donnell and David Powers, and former senator Ralph Yarborough were pressured to alter their statements, while others—including Ed Hoffman, A. J. Millican, Sandy Speaker, Acquilla Clemons, and Richard Carr—were threatened into silence.

All of these examples of official misconduct go far beyond any innocent attempt to avoid tarnishing an agency's reputation. Many of these incidents were obvious attempts to misdirect an impartial investigation and to incriminate Oswald. Persons who conduct such activity in connection with a murder case are legally considered accomplices and subject to the same punishments as the perpetrators.

The government had a strong ally in perpetrating a cover-up in the Kennedy assassination—a national news media that seemed incapable of looking past official pronouncements.

Assassination Coverage

From the moment the Kennedy assassination occurred, coverage of the tragedy involved government manipulation of a news media that appeared only too willing to be manipulated.

The Establishment media allowed themselves to be set up by official leaks and pronouncements about the assassination to the point where later official findings had to be accepted and defended.

In the days following the assassination, Dallas-area newspapers were filled with factual, if contradictory, information—Dallas County district attorney Henry Wade voiced suspicion of a plot, various people told of seeing Oswald and Ruby together prior to Kennedy's death, and information concerning more than three shots fired from more than one location was published. Outside Texas, however, wire-service reporting was limited to the official version of a lone assassin firing three shots.

Information on Oswald's procommunist background was leaked by the FBI and transmitted nationwide. Immediately media speculation was turned from whether Oswald acted alone to speculation on his motives.

Despite the occasional insertion of the word "alleged" before the word "assassin," the entire thrust of news coverage was aimed at Oswald's guilt. The *New York Times* proclaimed: EVIDENCE AGAINST OSWALD DESCRIBED AS CONCLUSIVE, while the *New York Post* simply headlined: ASSASSIN NAMED.

Even the Dallas–Fort Worth papers were not immune to this rush to judgment. The day after the assassination, the *Dallas Morning News* told readers: PRO-COMMUNIST CHARGED WITH ACT. And the nearby *Fort Worth Star-Telegram* carried a front-page headline erroneously stating: PARAFFIN TESTS OF OSWALD SHOW HE HAD FIRED GUN.

After Oswald's death, with no one except his mother to contradict them, the media began going further in their presumption of his guilt. A *New York Times* headline stated: PRESIDENT'S ASSASSIN SHOT. A *Time* magazine article combining Oswald's obituary and biography was titled: THE MAN WHO KILLED KENNEDY.

The presumption of Oswald's guilt was cemented by the February 21, 1964, edition of *Life*, which carried one of the infamous backyard photos on its cover with the caption, "Lee Oswald with the weapons he used to kill President Kennedy and Officer Tippit." This issue was in the hands of the public nearly eight months before the Warren Commission emerged from behind closed doors and proclaimed Oswald the lone assassin.

Later, *Life* devoted much of its October 2, 1964, issue to coverage of the just-released Warren Report. Rather than assigning a staff member to evaluate the report, *Life* editors chose Representative Gerald Ford, himself a Commission member, to review his own work.

In that same issue, a still frame from the Zapruder film depicting Kennedy's rearward fall at that moment of the head shot was substituted with an earlier frame that gave no indication of the direction his head moved.

One *Life* editor, Ed Kearns, was later asked about the changes. He told assassination researcher Vincent Salandria, "I am at a loss to explain the discrepancies between the three versions of *Life* which you cite. I've heard of breaking a [printing] plate to correct an error. I've never heard of doing it twice for a single issue, much less a single story. Nobody here seems to remember who worked on the early Kennedy story."

On September 27, 1964, the Warren Report was released to near-unanimous praise from the national news media, the primary source of public information. The *New York Times* even went to the expense of publishing the entire report as a supplement to its September 28 edition. The paper then published both a hardcover and paperback edition of the report in collaboration with Bantam Books and the Book of the Month Club.

Two months later, the *Times* again sought to lead the public's understanding of the assassination by helping publish *The Witnesses*, consisting of "highlights" of Warren Commission testimony. After studying this publication, assassination researcher Jerry Policoff wrote:

The selection and editing of testimony for this volume showed a clear understanding of that evidence which supported the Warren Commission findings and that which did not. Testimony which fit into the latter category was edited out in a manner which could hardly have been accidental. . . . In short, a volume purporting to be an objective condensation of relevant testimony compiled by America's "newspaper of record" was little more than deliberately slanted propaganda in support of the Warren Commission Report.

Respected researcher Sylvia Meagher complained, "*The Witnesses*, therefore, was one of the most biased offerings ever to masquerade as objective information. In publishing this paperback, *The Times* engaged in uncritical partisanship, the antithesis of responsible journalism."

By 1966, so much controversy had been generated by researchers critical of the Warren Report that Richard Billings, then *Life's* associate editor in charge of investigative reporting, was ordered to look more closely at certain aspects of the assassination, particularly the "single-bullet" theory.

After analyzing the Zapruder film, Billings's staff concluded that the one-bullet theory was untenable and, in its November 25, 1966, issue, *Life* called for a new investigation.

However, another part of Time-Life Corporation, *Time* magazine, in its November 25, 1966, issue editorialized against the "phantasmagoria" of Warren Commission critics and concluded, "There seems little valid excuse for so dramatic a development as another full-scale inquiry."

Asked about these conflicting editorial postures, Hedley Donovan, editor in chief of both *Time* and *Life*, responded, "We would like to see our magazines arrive at consistent positions on major issues, and I am sure in due course we will on this one."

This reconciliation occurred two months later when Billings said he was told by a superior, "It is not *Life's* function to investigate the Kennedy assassination." Similar admonitions have been echoed in newsrooms throughout America over the intervening years. Billings's investigation was terminated and the November 25 article, which was to have been the first of a series, became the last.

The one television network that continually backed the Warren Commission version of the assassination was CBS, where newsman Dan Rather served as one of the anchors on assassination reports since 1967. Rather was one of the only news reporters who managed to see the Zapruder film in the days following the assassination and falsely reported at the fatal head shot his head "went forward with considerable violence."

In a 1967 assassination documentary, CBS conducted a series of tests designed to prove that Oswald could have fired his rifle in the time established by the Warren Commission. When these tests essentially failed to support this contention, narrator Walter Cronkite nevertheless reported, "It seems reasonable to say that an expert could fire that rifle in five seconds. It seems equally reasonable to say that Oswald, under normal circumstances, would take longer. But these were not normal circumstances. Oswald was shooting at a president."

Cronkite's mistake was the same as that of the Warren Commission and later the House Select Committee on Assassinations—a presumption of Oswald's guilt guided his interpretation.

Of course, a presumption of Oswald's innocence would have led investigators into a confrontation with government agencies, the military, big business, and powerful politicians.

Therefore, the major news media have been content to let sleeping assassination conspiracies lie, compounding this timidity by characterizing anyone who dared look hard at the case as a "buff," "fantasist," "theorist," or "sensationalist." In the Dallas area, for instance, diligent reporters were warned off the assassination story by superiors despite a continuing spate of new developments and information.

Early on there was some excuse for this pathetic media track record. News reporters in the early 1960s were used to getting their information from official sources and did not suspect that these same sources might lie to them. Questioning the word of J. Edgar Hoover was tantamount to blasphemy.

When news reporters from all over the world descended on Dallas, they were at the mercy of local and federal authorities. They didn't know the city or its leaders and they didn't know how to talk to its residents. So the bulk of reporters waited in the police station for the next official pronouncement.

Oswald's brother Robert noticed and commented in his book, *Lee*:

> It seemed to me that the police, who should be conducting a careful investigation to discover just what had happened and how deeply Lee might be involved, had instead surrendered to the mob of reporters, photographers and television cameramen. I knew that these men from the newspapers, magazines and television networks were workingmen, just like I was, and I could not blame them for carrying out their assignments. But I could and did blame the Dallas Police Department for its failure to retain any control over the situation. The most casual remark by any of the investigators or police officers was broadcast to the world immediately, without any effort being made to determine whether it was somebody's wild speculation, a theory that deserved further investigation or a fact supported by reliable evidence.

Independent investigating was virtually nonexistent. The few reporters who dared investigate moved on quickly to another topic after realizing the power arranged against them.

Author Leonard Sanders was a young reporter in the Dallas area at the time. He told this author that he discontinued investigating the assassination after becoming convinced that his telephone was tapped and his movements monitored.

In the late 1970s, *Dallas Morning News* investigative reporter Earl Golz was actually ordered not to write about the Kennedy assassination again. This order was later ignored in the wake of revelations made public by the House Select Committee on Assassinations. This author once was told not to write any more about the Kennedy assassination as it was "upsetting people at the Petroleum Club," a private club for persons connected to the oil industry.

In this type of atmosphere, it is no wonder that the public remains confused about the facts of Kennedy's death.

As researcher Jerry Policoff wrote, "The Kennedy Assassination cover-up has survived so long only because the press, confronted with the choice of believing what it was told or examining the facts independently, chose the former."

Sensing a power shift at the highest levels of government and commerce, the major news media—like other official segments of American society—simply failed to function properly in response to the assassination of President Kennedy.

The normal police function was subordinated to pressure from the federal government. The usual legal precautions to protect against wrongful conviction, such as a presumption of innocence until proven guilty, cross-examination of evidence and witnesses, and the securing of defense counsel for the accused, were bypassed in the case of Lee Harvey Oswald.

The possibility of wrongdoing at the top of this nation's political structure panicked otherwise honest leadership in local, state, and federal government. Major business leaders, sensing the enormity of what had happened, kept their peace.

Never had the old saying "Who will watch the watchers?" carried more meaning.

What essentially began as a plot by a few fearful and greedy men grew into a full-scale palace revolt—a national coup d'état aided by the business, banking, industrial, media, and defense communities that played no active role in the plot. The results of this revolt were accepted by the "status quo"—the Establishment—after the fact.

The seventeenth-century courtier Sir John Harington, inventor of the flush toilet, summed it up when he wrote the oft-repeated epigram:

> *Treason doth never prosper: what's the reason?*
> *Why, if it prosper, none dare call it treason.*

A Likely Scenario

Since so much information concerning the plot to kill Kennedy has been destroyed, altered, or masked by false leads, it remains impossible to state with authority details of the plan. Even those involved were probably not informed of every aspect of the plot.

However, there is enough information available today to begin to construct a likely scenario of what happened.

Because of his family's great wealth, John F. Kennedy was incorruptible by bribes and when his father suffered a stroke, all control over him was lost. By 1963, it had become quite clear that Kennedy was determined to be his own man. Speaking to the United Auto Workers on May 8, 1962, Kennedy proclaimed:

> I know there are some people who . . . believe that the President of the United States should be honorary chairman of a great fraternal organization and confine himself to ceremonial functions. . . . But that is not what the Constitution says. And I did not run for President of the United States to fulfill that office in that way. . . . I believe it is the business of the President to concern himself with the general welfare.

He also was the only president since Franklin Roosevelt who was an intellectual. Kennedy had a rich sense of history and a global outlook. With Mary Meyer, he had gained an idealistic vision of making the world more peaceful and less corrupt. In other words, he really believed he was president and he set out to shake up the status quo of Big Banking, Big Oil, Big Military-Industrial Complex with its powerful intelligence community, and Big Organized Crime, which had gained deep inroads into American life since Prohibition.

There is also the argument that Kennedy was opposed to Israel's development of nuclear weapons and was demanding inspections of Israel's Dimona nuclear plant, a position that alienated powerful Zionists.

The new directions being taken by the young president provoked serious talk against him within many groups—organized crime, the anti-Castro Cubans, the CIA, business and banking, the oil industry, and even the military. There were many connections among all these groups—particularly in Operation Mongoose, the secret war against Castro. Once word of this pervasive anti-Kennedy feeling reached the ears of certain members of the southwestern oil and business communities, secret meetings were held where money was raised. Tacit approval was given by the ruling financiers of Wall Street, where Council on Foreign Relations members led by David Rockefeller had railed against Kennedy's economic policies. A consensus was reached that Kennedy was a threat and had to go.

From this point on, there would be no further contact between the individuals who initiated the plot and those who carried it out. Consequently, there is little likelihood that the originators of the plot will ever be identified or brought to justice. However, the broad outlines of the plot can be discerned by diligent study of all available assassination information.

There remain numerous ties among all of these powerful factions. It is now well documented that the mob and the CIA worked together on many types of operations, including assassination. The various US intelligence services were closely interwoven, and in some cases, such as the National Security Agency, were superior to the FBI and CIA.

Therefore, when Kennedy and his brother attorney general Robert Kennedy began to wage war on organized crime, to the mob and the industries it controlled and the banks that handled their money this quickly became a matter of self-defense, the strongest motivation for killing.

Officials of the FBI and CIA likewise feared the Kennedys, who had come to realize how dangerously out of control these agencies had become. The anti-Castro Cubans felt betrayed by Kennedy because of his orders stopping US military assistance to the Bay of Pigs invaders and were quite willing to support an assassination.

However, no matter how violent or powerful these crime-intelligence-industrial cliques might have been, they never would have moved against this nation's chief executive without the approval of—or at the very least the neutralization of—the US military and its greatest political supporter, vice president Lyndon Baines Johnson, former chairman of the powerful Senate Armed Services Committee.

Already angered by Kennedy's liberal domestic policies, the Bay of Pigs fiasco, and his signing of the Nuclear Test Ban Treaty with the Soviet Union, top military brass undoubtedly were incensed in late 1963 when Kennedy let it be known that he planned to withdraw all US military personnel from Vietnam by the end of 1965. The military leadership turned against him.

The stage was set. General Charles Cabell, the CIA deputy director Kennedy fired after the Bay of Pigs, was back in the Pentagon, and his brother, Earle Cabell, was mayor of Dallas.

It was widely rumored that Vice President Johnson—long associated with dirty politics, gamblers, and defense officials, and facing jail because of scandal—was to be dropped from the Democratic ticket in 1964. Texas oilmen, staunch friends of Johnson and the military-industrial complex, were dismayed that Kennedy was talking about doing away with the lucrative oil-depletion allowance.

International bankers were shocked when Kennedy ordered the Treasury Department to print its own money, rather than distributing interest-bearing Federal Reserve notes. Soldiers, mobsters, and conniving businessmen feared their apple cart was about to be upset by this youthful president.

So the decision was made at the highest level of the American business-banking-politics-military-crime power structure that should anything happen to Kennedy, it would be viewed as a blessing for the nation, and certainly for them.

And simply voting him out of office wouldn't suffice. After all, what was to stop someone from carrying on his policies? Two more Kennedys—Robert and Edward—were waiting in the wings for their turn at the presidency. A Kennedy "dynasty" was in place.

Therefore, the decision was made to eliminate John F. Kennedy by means of a public execution for the same reason criminals are publicly executed—to serve as a deterrent to anyone considering following in his footsteps.

Unlike the Roman senator Brutus who participated in the stabbing of Caesar, the men at the top of this consensus didn't even have to risk getting their hands bloody.

Colonel L. Fletcher Prouty—a former Pentagon-CIA liaison officer and long-time assassination researcher—explained that most assassinations are set in motion not so much by a specific plan to kill as by efforts to remove or relax the protection around a target.

Prouty noted:

> No one has to direct an assassination—it happens. The active role is played secretly by permitting it to happen. That was why President Kennedy was killed. He was not murdered by some lone gunman or by some limited conspiracy, but by the breakdown of the protective system that should have made an assassination impossible. . . . Once insiders knew that he would not be protected, it was easy to pick the day and the place. . . . All the conspirators had to do was let the right "mechanics" [professional assassins] know where Kennedy would be and when and, most importantly, that the usual precautions would not have been made and that escape would be facilitated. This is the greatest single clue to the assassination—Who had the power to call off or reduce the usual security precautions that are always in effect whenever a president travels? Castro did not kill Kennedy, nor did the CIA. The power source that arranged that murder was on the inside. It had the means to reduce normal security and permit the choice of a hazardous route. It also had the continuing power to cover that crime for . . . years.

Operational orders most probably originated with ranking members of the government elite, men such as Allen Dulles and Cord Meyer, and military officers like Generals Charles Cabell and Curtis LeMay and Johnson's military aide, Colonel Howard Burris. Actual planning was tasked to men knowledgeable in the ways of state assassins, such as the CIA's William Harvey, David Atlee Phillips, and General Edward Lansdale of Operation Mongoose, that nexus of the military, mobsters, CIA operatives, and anti-Castro Cubans. Organized-crime chieftains such as Carlos Marcello and his associates Santos Trafficante and Sam Giancana were contacted. They already were involved with the CIA and provided personnel and logistics.

But these mob bosses were smart. They realized the consequences if their role in Kennedy's death should ever become known. Therefore, they insisted that elements within the government be involved. Several separate assassination plots were initiated.

A world-class assassin was recruited—perhaps Michael Victor Mertz, the shadowy Frenchman with both crime and intelligence connections, or even an unknown but competent shooter like John Christian.

Slowly, as the true assassination plot began to come together, word must have reached the ears of J. Edgar Hoover, a power unto himself with plenty of cause to hate the Kennedy brothers. Hoover was in contact with his close friend Lyndon Johnson and with Texas oilmen such as H. L. Hunt and Clint Murchinson of Dallas. His agents and informers were in daily contact with mob figures.

Operatives from both intelligence and the mob were recruited. Many were like the CIA's David Morales, Watergate burglar Frank Sturgis, and David Ferrie in that they had connections to criminal circles as well as to US intelligence and anti-Castro Cubans. It was a military-style operation in that overall knowledge of the plot was kept on a strict need-to-know basis. Many people on the lower end of the conspiracy truthfully could say they didn't know exactly what happened.

To distract public attention from the real conspirators a scapegoat—or patsy—was needed. Enter Lee Harvey Oswald, a patriotic young man who followed the tradition of his father and brothers by voluntarily joining the US military where apparently he was recruited into US intelligence, first through the Office of Naval Intelligence and then on to the CIA. Whether the Dallas Oswald was a Soviet agent or a US agent posing as a procommunist, he was the perfect patsy for the assassination. As an intelligence agent, he would have followed orders and easily could have been manipulated into incriminating himself as the assassin. Furthermore, his position as a spy would have prevented the Russians from proclaiming the truth of the assassination to their world, since they could hardly be expected to admit their knowledge of Oswald.

Once the idea of conspiracy is acknowledged, questions of who fired a gun, from what location, and how many times become irrelevant. Much more important are the questions of who benefited from the assassination and had the ability to cover up the truth.

It appears there may have been two serious slip-ups for the conspirators. First, it appears unlikely that as many as three shots were intended. More likely the assassination was to have been constructed so that it would appear that Kennedy was killed by one lucky shot from the Depository. The conspirators, of course, would have been prepared to fire another volley if necessary. Second, it is equally likely that their scapegoat, Oswald, was to have been killed by a conspirator during return fire by Kennedy's security men. However, there was no return fire and Oswald managed to slip away from the Depository.

When the shooting started, confusion was rampant. No one except the conspirators knew what was happening, and the Dallas police radio channel used for the presidential motorcade security was blocked for more than eight minutes due to an open microphone.

The true assassins simply strolled away, after dumping their rifles into nearby car trunks or passing them to confederates. One weapon may have been hidden down a water drain pipe on the Grassy Knoll, as a section of the pipe collapsed many years later. It had been cut open but not welded when replaced and the city claimed no knowledge of this activity.

Oswald may well have been exactly where he said he was during the shooting—safely out of sight in the downstairs lunchroom of the Depository. Perhaps he had been told to wait for a telephone call at that time. He may have strayed by briefly stepping up a short flight of stairs and peeking out the front door of the Depository where he was captured in the Altgens photograph.

Oswald left the Depository and made his way to his South Oak Cliff rooming house, where he retrieved his pistol to defend himself. His landlady said that within minutes of his arrival, he hurried from his room after a Dallas police car stopped out front and beeped its horn twice. It now seems likely that it was Dallas patrolman J. D. Tippit who picked up Oswald around the corner from his rooming house and drove him to the Texas Theater, which explained why he was unseen en route.

The slaying of Tippit may have played some part in this scheme to have Oswald killed, perhaps to eliminate co-conspirator Tippit or simply to anger Dallas police and cause itchy trigger fingers.

Regardless, Tippit was killed by someone other than Oswald. Whoever shot Tippit meant to kill him, not simply escape a policeman. The HSCA determined that one shot was fired point-blank into his head, a coup de grâce.

Oswald, who was given every opportunity to flee through a rear exit of the Texas Theater, instead was captured alive, creating a bad situation for the conspirators. Oswald could not be permitted to stand trial and possibly reveal his true connections.

Jack Ruby—the mob's "bag man" in Dallas and the man who apparently handled funds for the local activities of the assassination conspirators—received his orders to kill Oswald from organized-crime leaders eager to protect the secret of their contract, and there were no alternatives for a mob directive.

The key to understanding the Oswald slaying is not that Ruby somehow knew when Oswald was to be transported from the police station, but rather that the Oswald transfer was delayed until Ruby was in position—thanks to mob influence in the Dallas Police Department, one of the nation's most corrupt at that time. The House Select Committee on Assassinations concluded that Ruby most likely entered the police basement down a back stairway with the assistance of one or more policemen.

One shot and Oswald was dead. A cover-up began immediately, leaving only his mother to question the official version of the assassination.

While this scenario can be disputed, it nevertheless represents the only narrative that conforms to all of the known facts.

———

Lyndon B. Johnson was sworn in as president within two hours of the assassination.

His first act as president was to violate the laws of his own state by ordering the removal of Kennedy's body from Parkland Hospital over the objections of the Dallas County medical examiner who was required by law to conduct an inquest. By that evening, Johnson was exerting undue influence over the Dallas investigation both directly and through his aides.

Within two weeks, Johnson had coerced a reluctant chief justice Earl Warren into heading a special presidential commission charged with finding Oswald alone guilty of the deed. The creation of the Warren Commission effectively blocked several other assassination investigations in both Texas and Washington.

The Warren Commission, composed of captains of both intelligence and corporate business—with representative Gerald Ford spying on behalf of Hoover's FBI—paid precious little attention to anything that did not tend to prove the "lone-nut assassin" theory. The Commission had no staff of independent investigators. It relied almost entirely on the FBI and CIA for information. Both agencies, along with the Secret Service, today have been officially chastised for concealing evidence from the two government investigations.

Government investigators found a virtual smorgasbord of assassination evidence available in Dallas and New Orleans. By carefully selecting data that fit the official version of a lone gunman, they were able to present a believable—if untruthful—account of Kennedy's death.

Meanwhile, a documented campaign of intimidation of witnesses began in Dallas. Some were simply told to keep quiet while others died under unusual circumstances. While some of this suppression might be blamed on mob thugs, many people in Dallas have claimed that it was FBI agents who warned them not to talk about the assassination—an odd admonition since officially it was the work of just one troubled man. This theory was presented despite embarrassing evidence indicating Oswald was an informant for the FBI.

There is now abundant evidence that Hoover's FBI destroyed critical evidence in this case, suppressed other evidence, and intimidated witnesses. The FBI solely directed the verdict that Oswald acted alone.

There was never a real cover-up of the assassination, only official pronouncements for the major mass media and lots of red herrings for diligent investigators.

As long as the US government backed by a supportive Establishment and corporate media refuses to seek and reveal the truth of what happened on November 22, 1963, it will be up to individual Americans to cull through the mounds of Kennedy assassination material and find the elusive truth for themselves.

Who done it? Powerful men in leadership positions within the major corporate-military-defense-intelligence communities and the bankers who fund them, along with associated organized-crime bosses, reached a consensus that Kennedy was a danger to the status quo and had to be eliminated. Their faithful agents manipulated Mafia-Cuban-CIA pawns to kill the chief.

President Kennedy was killed in a military-style ambush orchestrated by elements within the US government that included the military with the active assistance of organized crime.

Pressure from the top thwarted any truthful investigation.

It was an American coup d'état.

This is no theory, which is informed speculation based on supposition. If something is provable, it is no longer a theory. The information presented within this book substantiates the fact that in 1963 US government policies were changed through an act of violence.

Even today there is still pressure from the top of the American power structure to keep the lid on this sordid affair. Many officials who continue to obscure the Kennedy case played no part in the assassination conspiracy. They simply do not want to alert the American public to the corruption found in the interconnections between government, big business, the military, intelligence, and the mob. It might prove bad for business.

What then is the legacy of president John F. Kennedy? The fact is that we will never know. His presidency always will be remembered, not for what he did, but for what he might have done.

But it may be worth considering what kind of America we might have today if President Kennedy had lived. Imagine the United States if there had been no divisive Vietnam War, with its attendant demonstrations, riots, deaths, and loss of faith in government. There may not have been the scandals of Watergate, other political assassinations, or the Iran-Contra Pentagon-CIA attempt at a "secret government." No 9/11 attacks with the ensuing wars in Iraq and Afghanistan. No American "Reich" with military operations spanning the globe. Détente with communist Russia and China might have come years earlier, saving hundreds of millions of wasted defense dollars—dollars that could have been put to use caring for the needy and cleaning up the environment. Picture a nation where no organized-crime syndicate gained control over such divergent areas of national life as drugs, gambling, labor unions, politicians, and even toxic waste disposal.

Is it possible to consider that we might have had a nation where peace and prosperity were achieved without the need for a massive military buildup, or that we might have experienced a kinder and gentler nation all along?

John F. Kennedy was no superman. Today there seems to be a movement to focus attention on the "morality" of his private life. But history will eventually record that Kennedy truly believed he had the best interests of his nation at heart. He wanted to lead America forward into a peaceful and prosperous future.

Kennedy was in the mold of Mikhail Gorbachev, complete with his own American brand of *glasnost*, or openness with the public. But he was premature. America—at least the backstage rulers of America—was not ready for such innovation.

The emperor has no clothes on—or in this case, American business and political emperors wear bloodstained clothing—but no one of any prominence wants to be the first to say so.

Members of Kennedy's inner circle also came to understand what had really happened. But this knowledge came too late. The proof had been taken up and they realized the extent of the power arrayed against them. Some kept their peace, some soon retired from government, and others left the country.

No one was closer to President Kennedy and his work than his secretary Evelyn Lincoln. She was at his elbow constantly, yet no one in America can recall seeing a nationwide interview with her. This is probably because, as she wrote in a 1994 letter, "it is my belief that there was a conspiracy. . . . These five conspirators, in my opinion, were Lyndon B. Johnson, J. Edgar Hoover, the Mafia, the CIA and the Cubans in Florida."

Robert Kennedy also came to understand the tremendous power behind the events in Dallas. On June 3, 1968, just two days before his own assassination, the younger Kennedy told close friends, "I now fully realize that only the powers of the presidency will reveal the secrets of my brother's death."

He obviously had come to realize that the truth of John Kennedy's death could come only after Robert Kennedy gained control over the FBI, CIA, Secret Service, and the Pentagon—all of which had become powers unto themselves.

Surely no one believes it was sheer coincidence that the younger Kennedy was gunned down the very night he received the 1968 California Democratic nomination for president, which most probably would have clinched his national nomination.

While it may be too late for justice for John F. Kennedy, it is never too late for the truth. Camelot was killed from within, by men whose fear and ambition overpowered their faith in and loyalty to the US Constitution and the people it was designed to protect.

After assimilating the information in this book, the thoughtful reader can now perceive the truth of the Kennedy assassination. An apt precedent may be found in William Shakespeare's immortal *Julius Caesar*, where Roman leaders—"all honorable men"—plotted to kill Caesar out of fear that they were losing total power in their country. Brutus defended his participation by explaining, "Not that I loved Caesar less, but that I loved Rome more." Or to paraphrase the American officer in Vietnam who defended the destruction of a village there, "In order to save the country, they had to destroy it."

Until the public forces politicians, academics, and the corporate mass media to confront the reality of Kennedy's death and the power behind it, the wars, near-wars, the wasteful military buildup, foreign adventurism, death, squandered millions, trampled human rights, moral decline, environmental pollution, and the savaging of the US Constitution will continue.

The path to a confrontation with the evil that has gained a hold on America lies within each individual citizen—in our minds and, perhaps more important, in our hearts.

One can still hear the sad spirit of John F. Kennedy echoing from Dealey Plaza: Et tu, Lyndon?

SOURCES AND NOTES

In a work such as this, extensive footnoting within the text can often impede the flow of ideas, reducing comprehension.

There are further problems in the case of the JFK assassination. Too often official government reports do not accurately reflect the actual evidence or statements of witnesses.

Major statements in this work or ones that contradict the official version of the assassination are attributed in this section. Usually only one reference is given, though multiple sources may be found in most instances.

Any statements without attribution or a source listing indicate historical fact or issues that are undisputed among the majority of credible assassination researchers.

Accounts of witnesses sometimes represent a synthesis of their words from more than one source. It should be pointed out that just because a statement is attributed to some source does not make that statement true. People's accounts can result from mistakes as well as lies due to fear and intimidation.

WC Report refers to the Warren Commission Report, while its attendant hearings and exhibits are referred to by volume and page—for example, XXII.644. Similarly, the House Select Committee on Assassinations volumes will appear as HSCA VIII.64.

It is significant to add that while all assassination works—including this book—must rely heavily on official government reports and publications, such reports can often be called into question. Therefore, the burden of separating fact from fiction must unfortunately fall on the reader. This sad fact necessitates access to the broadest amount of information, often going far beyond official sources.

A comprehensive bibliography of sources for *Crossfire* may be found at the JimMarrs.com website.

PART I: THE KILL ZONE

Dallas—The Stage Is Set

The Thirty-fifth President

2   JFK's affair with suspected Nazi agent: John H. Davis, *The Kennedys: Dynasty and Disaster 1848–1983*, New York, McGraw-Hill, 1984, pp. 111–112.

3   Joe Kennedy quote: Ibid., p. 135.

3   Evelyn Lincoln on blackmail: www.viewzone.com/lbj/lbj2.html.

4   Talk to ministers in Houston: David Wallechinsky and Irving Wallace, *The People's Almanac*, Garden City, New York, Doubleday & Company, 1975, p. 313.

4   Slim margin of 1960 election: Ibid., p. 314.

4   Comparison to Eisenhower: Wallechinsky and Wallace, p. 316.

5   Yarborough: author's interview, summer 1986.

5   Kennedy's sunshine comment: *Report of the Select Committee on Assassinations of the US House of Representatives; Findings in the Assassination of President John F. Kennedy in Dallas, Tex., November 22, 1963, p. 38.*

Dealey Plaza—November 22, 1963

The Motorcade

8   Organization of motorcade: WC Report, pp. 43–46.

8   Yarborough's comments: author's interview, summer 1986. Press car moved: author's interview with Dallas researcher Mary Ferrell, 1986. Her husband, Buck, had loaned his station wagon for press use in the motorcade.

9   Amazed at crowd: Bob Hollingsworth, "Rapid Bang of Gun Changes History's Course," *Dallas Times Herald*, Nov. 23, 1963.

10 Truly: III.220.

10 Lawson: IV.351.

10 Kellerman: H.73–74.

11 Mrs. Connally: IV.147.

11 Greer: 11.117.

11 Connally: IV. 133.

11 Connally's cry: WC Report, p. 50.

11 Mrs. Kennedy: Ibid., p. 49.

12 Mrs. Kennedy on brains in hand: XVIII.730.

12 Dr. Marion Jenkins: Richard B. Trask, *Pictures of the Pain: Photography and the Assassination of President Kennedy*, Danvers, Mass., Yeoman Press, 1994, p. 71.

12 Decker: "President Dead, Connally Shot," *Dallas Times Herald*, Nov. 22, 1963.

12 Ellis: HSCA XII.23.

13 Landis: XVIII.758.

13 Bennett: XXIV.542.

13 Hill: 11.138–141.

14 Powers: VII.473.

14 Mrs. Cabell: VII.486–487.

15 Yarborough: author's interview, summer 1986.

15 11.2 mph limousine speed: WC Report, p. 49.

15 Atkins: "JFK Assassination Film No One Wanted to See," *Midnight*, March 1, 1977, pp. 21–22.

The Crowd

16 Hathaway, Lawrence, and Owens: XXIV.211, 214, and 220.

16 Mercer: XIX.483.

18 Smith: XIX.516.

18 West: author's interview, April 1978.

18 Rowland: II.165–190.

19 Walther: Anthony Summers, *Conspiracy*, New York, McGraw-Hill, 1980, p. 74.

20 Earl Golz, "Was Oswald in the Window?" *Dallas Morning News*, Nov. 28, 1978.

20 Carr: interview with researcher Gary Shaw, April, 1975; HSCA XIII.8–9.

20 Henderson: XXIV.524.

21 Bronson film: Earl Golz, "JFK Film May Reveal Two Gunmen," *Dallas Morning News*, Nov. 26, 1978.

21 Prisoners: Earl Golz, "Witnesses Overlooked in JFK Probe," *Dallas Morning News*, Dec. 19, 1978; http://derosaworld.typepad.com/derosaworld/2009/11/30-days-of-jfk-assassination-facts-windows-and-witnesses.html.

22 Similas: Harold Weisberg, "Photographic Whitewash," pp. 223–235; J. Gary Shaw with Larry R. Harris, Coverup, p. 51.

22 Fischer: VI.195.

22 Edwards: VI.204.

22 Betzner: XIX.467–468.

23 Willis: VII.493–497; Jim Marrs, "JFK Killing Witness Not Surprised Tests Indicated 2nd Gunman," *Fort Worth Star-Telegram*, Dec. 22, 1978; author's interview, October 1978.

24 Linda Willis: Author's interview, October 1978.

25 Brennan: XXIV.203.

25 Brennan again questioned by WC: III.211.

25 Speaker: author's interview, July 1987.

26 Euins: WC Exhibit 367.

26 Terry: author's interview, 1978.

26 Truly: III.220.

26 Campbell: XXII.638.

26 Mrs. Reid: III.273.

26 Arce: VI.365.

27 Baker: VII.508–509.

27 Woodward: Mary E. Woodward, "Witness from the News Describes Assassination," *Dallas Morning News*, Nov. 23, 1963.

27 Calvery and Westbrook: XXII.638 and 679.

28 Millican: XIX.486.

28 Speaker: author's interview, July 1987.

28 Mrs. Chism: XIX.472.

Two Suspicious Men

29 Robert Cutler: *The Flight of CE-399: Evidence of Conspiracy*, Beverly, Mass., Cutler Designs, 1970.

31 Witt: HSCA IV.432–433.

32 Kounas: XXII.659.

32 Altgens: VII.517–518.

33 Altgens mistaken: WCR, p. 112.

34 Brehm: Mark Lane and Emile de Antonio's film of assassination witnesses, *Rush to Judgment*, 1966.

34 Nix: Ibid.

The Babushka Lady

35 Oliver: "Area Woman to Testify in JFK Slaying Probe," *Lubbock Avalanche-Journal*, April 10, 1977; Interview with researcher J. Gary Shaw 1970; author's interviews, 1988–2011.

37 Hill: VI.207; author's interviews, 1986–1991.

38 Newman: XIX.490; author's interview, April 1988.

38 Merriman Smith: http://mcadams.posc.mu.edu/gk_name.htm.

38 Price: XIX.492; Lane, *Rush to Judgment*, p. 33.

39 FBI statements: CE 1381.

The Texas School Book Depository

40 Oswald's job: WC Report, pp. 737–738.

40 Truly: III.237.

40 Frazier: II.225–228.

41 Oswald's denial: WC Report, p. 604.

41 Dougherty: VI.376.

The Distracting Seizure

42 Belknap: Jerry D. Rose, "The Epileptic Seizure," Penn Jones's *The Continuing Inquiry*, Feb. 22, 1984, pp. 8–22.

43 Rike: author's interviews, 1978, 2002, 2008.

43 Geneva L. Hine: VI.695.

44 Wilson: XXII.685.

44 Dorman: XXII.644.

44 Garner: XXII.648.

44 Adams: VI.388.

44 Styles: XXII.676.

44 Frazier: 11.234.

The Man in the Doorway

45 Oswald Innocent Campaign: www.oswald-innocent.com.

45 Lovelady: VI.338–339; "Time Gives Back Identity," *Dallas Times Herald*, Nov. 21, 1971.

46 Shelley: VI.329.

46 Sarah Stanton: XXII, p. 675.

46 1971 reenactment: Trask, p. 324.

47 Shelley says no more work: WC Report, p. 182.

47 Ralph Cinque: www.oswald-innocent.com/wrap.html.

47 Curry's quote: "'Not Sure' on Oswald, Author Curry Indicates," *Dallas Morning News*, Nov. 6, 1969.

48 Oswald on first floor: WC Report, p. 600.

48   Williams: III.175.
48   Norman: III.191.
48   Jarman: III.205.
50   Arnold: XXII.635; Summers, p. 108; *Dallas Morning News*, Nov. 26, 1978.

The Oswald Encounter
52   Baker: III.246.
53   Reid: III.273.
53   Oswald tells of Coca-Cola: WC Report, p. 600.
54   Bookhout and Hosty report: WC Report, p. 613.
54   Bookhout reports Coca-Cola: WC Report, p. 619.
54   Mooneyham: XXIV.531.
55   Report dismisses Adams: WC Report, p. 154.
55   Garner 2011 interview: http://mysite. verizon.net/restu5kb/id1.html.
56   Stroud's letter: Ibid.
56   Molina: VI.371.

The Triple Underpass
57   Foster: VI.251.
58   White: VI.255.

Smoke on the Grassy Knoll
58   Holland: VI.243; Lane, *Rush to Judgment* film.
59   Simmons, Dodd, etc.: Ibid.
61   Brown: VI.233.
61   Skelton: XIX.496.
61   Miller: XIX.485.

The Third Wounded Man
62   Tague: VI.553; author's interviews, 1977, 1988, 2002.
62   Haygood: VI.297.
63   Walthers: XIX.518.
64   Stroud: Sylvia Meager, *Accessories After the Fact: The Warren Commission, the Authorities, and the Report*, New York, Bobbs-Merrill, 1967; Vintage, 1976, pp. 6–7.

The Grassy Knoll
The Zapruder Film
66   Zapruder: VII.571.

67   Timing of shot: WC Report, p. 105.
67   Kennedy turned to wave: Paul Mandel, "End of Nagging Rumors: The Six Critical Seconds," *Life*, December 6, 1963.
69   Film compromised: David S. Lifton, *Best Evidence: Disguise and Deception in the Assassination of John F. Kennedy*, New York, Macmillan Publishing Co., 1980, footnote, p. 557.
72   Newman: XXII.842; Author's interview, April 1988.
72   Journalism major: Cheryl McKinnon, "My Last Look at Mr. President," *San Diego Star News*, Nov. 20, 1983. Hudson: VII.559.
73   Hudson: VII.559.

The Black Dog Man
75   Hargis: VI.294.
75   Weitzman: VII.106.
76   Smith: VII.535.
76   Smith smells gunpowder: Summers, p. 62.
77   Bowers: VI.287; Lane's *Rush to Judgment*.
79   Arnold: "SS 'Imposters' Spotted by JFK Witnesses," *Dallas Morning News*, August 27, 1978; author's interview, summer 1985.

The Badge Man
81   Attempts to study "Badgeman": author's interview with Jack White and Gary Mack, 1984; Turner documentary.

A Grassy Knoll Witness
83   Hoffman: author's interview, summer, 1985; FBI Airtel and memorandum, June 28, 1967, and April 5, 1977. (These FBI documents were obtained Dec. 2, 1985, after a FOIA request was filed with the bureau by researcher J. Gary Shaw.)
87   M. Duke Lane: http://mcadams.posc. mu.edu/FreeWayman.htm.

PART II: MEANS, MOTIVES, AND OPPORTUNITIES

Lee Harvey Oswald— Assassin or Patsy?

A Mother in History

90 Marguerite Oswald's reaction to HSCA: "Panel's Finding Pleases Mother of Lee Oswald," *Fort Worth Star-Telegram*, Dec. 31, 1978.

90 Marguerite Oswald background: WC Report, pp. 669–681; author's interviews, 1974–1979.

92 Complaints on son's death: "Mother of Oswald Blames Officers," *Fort Worth Star-Telegram*, Dec. 2, 1963.

92 FBI shows her picture: 1.152–153.

93 Marguerite Oswald on Watergate: "Marguerite Oswald Not Bitter After 10-Year Infamy," *Fort Worth Star-Telegram*, Nov. 18, 1973.

95 Marguerite on payment: author's interview, 1974.

95 Lee's bed: E. Graham Ward, *Transcripts I: An Interview with Marguerite Oswald*, Boston, Houghton Mifflin Company, 1973, p. 35.

96 No potential assassin: WC Report, p. 379.

96 Dr. Hartogs on Oswald: Gerald Posner, *Case Closed: Lee Harvey Oswald and the Assassination of JFK*, New York Random House, 1993, p. 12.

96 Hartogs to WC: VIII, pp. 216–219.

97 Lee's favorite TV show: Robert L. Oswald, *Lee: A Portrait of Lee Harvey Oswald*, p. 47.

97 Lee's Marxism: Ibid., pp. 71–72.

97 Oswald's introduction to communism: Don Delillo, *Libra*, New York, Penguin Books, 1988, p. 12.

97 Robert Oswald: www.reference.com/browse/lee+harvey+oswald.

Oswald's Library Card

99 Ferrie asks about card: Summers, p. 497.

99 Secret Service questions Ferrie: Jim Garrison, *Heritage of Stone*, New York, Berkley Medallion Books, 1975, p. 103.

99 False affadavit: WC Report, p. 680.

100 Oswald on communism: Ibid., p. 384.

100 Oswald's military service: Ibid., pp. 681–689.

Semper Fidelis

100 Sherman Cooley: Henry Hurt, *Reasonable Doubt*, New York, Holt, Rinehart, and Winston, 1985, p. 99.

100 Nelson Delgado: Lane, pp. 388–389.

101 Oswald's absences: Edward J. Epstein, *Legend: The Secret World of Lee Harvey Oswald*, New York, McGraw-Hill, 1978, p. 65.

Oswald Overseas

102 Race Car: Ibid., pp. 53–55.

102 Secrets interest: Ibid., p. 68.

102 Slawson and Coleman report: www.aarclibrary.org/publib/jfk/wc/wcmemos/pdf/Oswald_Foreign_2_Soviet.pdf.

102 Oswald and "Queen Bee": Epstein, pp. 71–72.

102 Bucknell: Interview with Mark Lane, April 1978; "The Assassination of President John F. Kennedy—How the CIA Set Up Oswald," *Hustler*, October 1978, p. 50.

103 Hemming: Summers, p. 172.

103 Wilcott: "Couple Talks About Bad Days in CIA," *San Francisco Chronicle*, Sept. 12, 1978; HSCA Report, pp. 198–199.

103 Oswald's VD: IX.603; VII.313; XIX.601.

103 Executive session: Transcript of Warren Commission proceedings, Jan. 27, 1964. (This transcript was classified "top secret" and made public only in 1974 after suit was filed by a private researcher.)

104 Bagshaw and Connor: Summers, p. 155.

104 John Wayne: Epstein, p. 76.

104 Rodriguez: Ibid., p. 78.

105 Rhodes: Ibid., pp. 81–82.

106 Dejanovich: Ibid., p. 82.

Oswaldskovich the Marine

106 Oswaldskovich: WC Report, p. 686.
106 Thornley: Kerry Thornley, "Oswald," pp. 23–32.
106 Officer's reaction: Ibid., p. 21.
106 Thornley's comment: WC Report, p. 389.
107 Botelho: Lane, op. cit., p. 94.
107 Bucknell: Ibid., p. 94.
108 Botelho on assignment: James W. Douglass, *JFK and the Unspeakable*, Maryknoll, N.Y., Orbis Books, 2008, p. 40.
108 Oswald's letter and trip: WC Report, pp. 689–690.

Russians

109 Powers deployed: Wallechinsky and Wallace, p. 650.

Oswald and the U-2

110 Oswald's letter: XVI.871.
110 Ofstein: X.203.
110 Defectors: Summers, p. 176.

Robert E. Webster—Another Oswald?

111 Webster: Summers, pp. 177–178.
111 Marchetti: Ibid., p. 174.
112 Otepka: Bernard Fensterwald with Michael Ewing, *Coincidence or Conspiracy?*, p. 231.

A Phony Defection

113 Sweden: Summers, p. 557, Note 38.
113 Shirokova: WC Report, pp. 690–691.
113 Attempted defection: Ibid., pp. 392–393.
114 McVickar: XVIII.155.
114 Johnson: FBI Memorandum from A. Rosen to Mr. Belmont, Nov. 23, 1964.
115 "Historic Diary": WC Report, p. 258.
116 Rankin: Warren Commission Executive Session transcript, Jan. 27, 1964.

Comrade Oswald

116 MVD funds: WC Report, p. 272.
116 Life in Russia: WC Report, pp. 697–

712; author's interview with Jeanne DeMohrenschildt, 1978.
117 Hoover warning: Summers, p. 409.
118 Marguerite Oswald: author's interviews, 1974–1979.

A Whirlwind Romance

119 Didenko: Priscilla Johnson McMillan, *Marina and Lee*, p. 205.
120 CIA concerns: Addendum to CIA document, Nov. 25, 1963; Epstein, p. 138; Summers, p. 192.
120 New identity: Epstein, p. 139.
121 Relationship cooled: WC Report, p. 395.
122 Raikin: Summers, p. 217.
123 Marina Oswald: Myrna Blyth and Jane Farrell, "Marina Oswald—Twenty-Five Years Later," *Ladies' Home Journal*, November 1988.

A Soviet Defector's Story

124 Nosenko: Epstein, pp. 3–50, 257–274; Summers, pp. 194–202; "How the CIA Tried to Break Defector in Oswald Case," *Washington Star*, Sept. 16, 1978; Edward Jay Epstein, "The War of the Moles: Russian Spies Inside the CIA and the FBI," *New York*, Feb. 27, 1978, and March 6, 1978; G. Robert Blakey and Richard N. Billings, *The Plot to Kill the President*, New York, New York Times Books, 1981, pp. 118–134.

Cubans

Disaster at the Bay of Pigs

130 Nixon pushes Cushman: Peter Wyden, *Bay of Pigs: The Untold Story*, pp. 29–30.
130 Hunt and Barker: Ibid., p. 33.
131 US force barred: *New York Times*, April 12, 1961.
131 "Minimum" scale: Wyden, p. 170.
132 *Barbara* fired upon: http://cuban-exile.com/doc_026–050/doc0041.html.
132 Robert Davis: Wyden, p. 300.
132 "Orphan" quote: Ibid., p. 305.
133 JM/WAVE: Blakey and Billings, p. 159.

133 RFK "stops" Mafia dealings: *New York Times*, March 10, 1965.
135 Daniel: Summers, pp. 431–434; Blakey and Billings, p. 144.
135 Attwood: Summers, p. 453.
137 Mobile visit: WC Report, p. 728.
137 Martello and Austin: Summers, p. 301.

544 Camp Street

138 CRC at 544 Camp Street: Blakey and Billings, p. 165.
139 Banister "agent": Summers, p. 324; Henry Hurt, *Reasonable Doubt*, pp. 291–292.
139 Rodriquez: Summers, p. 318.

Oswald and the Exiles

140 Veciana: Ibid., pp. 353–392, 508–513; Hurt, pp. 327–337.
141 Phillips character: www.spartacus.schoolnet.co.uk/JFKphillips.htm.
141 Echevarria: Blakey and Billings, pp. 170–171; Hurt, p. 327.
141 Odio: WC Report, pp. 321–325; Hurt, pp. 372–374; Summers, pp. 411–418.
143 Oswald not at Odio home: WC Report, p. 324.
143 Hall: WC Report, p. 301; Silvia Meagher, *Accessories After the Fact: The Warren Commission, the Authorities, and the Report*, New York, Vintage, 1976, p. 387.

Oswald's Girlfriend

144 Oswald quote: Judyth Vary Baker, *Me & Lee: How I Came to Know, Love and Lose Lee Harvey Oswald*, Walterville, Ore., TrineDay, 2010, p. 317.
144 Gave up following the players: Ibid.
145 Charles Le Blanc: XXIII.701.
146 Clinton incident: Jim Garrison, *On the Trail of the Assassins*, New York, Sheridan Square Press, 1988, pp. 105–108; Hurt, p. 280; Summers, pp. 333–337.
146 Ochsner on expendable: Baker, p. 470.
147 Eyes opened to corruption: Baker, p. 553.
148 The 1972 false Judyth Baker: Edward T. Haslam, *Dr. Mary's Monkey*, Walterville, Ore., TrineDay, 2007, pp. 286–288.

148 Morgan: *Washington Post*, May 2, 1976.
148 Martino: Summers, p. 451.
149 Oswald on policy toward Cuba: WC Report, p. 609.
149 A provocation: Bill Moyers, "The CIA's Secret Army," *CBS Reports*, June 10, 1977.
149 Johnson stopped investigations: John Armstrong, *Harvey & Lee: How the CIA Framed Oswald*, Arlington, Texas, Quasar Ltd., 2003, p. 916.

Mobsters

Lucky Goes to War

153 Lansky: Dennis Eisenberg, Uri Dan, and Eli Landau, *Meyer Lansky: Mogul of the Mob*, p. 184.

Carlos Marcello

155 Becker: Summers, pp. 287–288; Blakey and Billings, pp. 244–245; Davis, pp. 379–380.
156 Michael Wacks: Hillel Levin, "How the Outfit Killed JFK," *Playboy*, Nov. 22, 2011.
157 Dorfman: Blakey and Billings, pp. 193, 206.

Santos Trafficante and Cuba

158 Lansky and Trafficante: Howard Kohn, "The Hughes-Nixon-Lansky Connection: The Secret Alliances of the CIA from WWII to Watergate," *Rolling Stone*, May 20, 1976; Blakey and Billings, pp. 227–229.
159 Bradlee: Moldea, p. 149.
160 Aleman: Blakey and Billings, p. 246; Davis, p. 490; Summers, p. 284.

The War on Hoffa

161 Hoffa threat: Levin, p. 148; Fensterwald, pp. 351–352; Blakey and Billings, p. 202; Summers, p. 282.
162 Valachi evaluated: Blakey and Billings, p. 200.
163 Mob eliminated or crippled: Davis, *The Kennedys*, p. 484.

Momo and His Girlfriends

164 Hoover with Cohn and Costello: http://bitterqueen.typepad.com/friends_of_ours/frank-costello.

164 Exner: Judith Exner as told to Ovid Demaris, *My Story*, pp. 86–89, 100–105; Kitty Kelly, "The Dark Side of Camelot," *People*, Feb. 29, 1988.

165 Lawrence Houston: Evan Thomas, *Robert Kennedy: His Life*, New York, Simon & Schuster, 2000, p. 171.

167 Blakey: author's telephone interview, June 1981.

Agents

168 Truman: Victor Marchetti and John D. Marks, *The CIA and the Cult of Intelligence*, p. 304; David Wise and Thomas B. Ross, *The Invisible Government*, New York, Bantam Books, 1965, p. 101.

169 Innocuous words: Marchetti and Marks, pp. 33–34.

170 Dulles and United Fruit: David Wallechinsky and Irving Wallace, *The People's Almanac #2*, p. 309.

170 Allen and John Foster Dulles: Wise and Ross, p. 104.

The Manchurian Candidates

171 LSD and MK-ULTRA: John D. Marks, *The Search for the "Manchurian Candidate,"* pp. 53–67.

172 Edward Gillin: http://cliffordshack-article-archive-storage.blogspot.com/2012/01/cia-lsd-lho.html.

CIA-Mafia Death Plots

173 Dr. Rolando Cubela: Epstein, pp. 231–233.

New Orleans

174 Ferrie statement missing: Fensterwald, p. 297.

174 Marchetti: Robert Sam Anson, *"They've Killed the President!" The Search for the Murderers of John F. Kennedy*, New York, Bantam Books, 1975, p. 122.

174 Martin: HSCA IX.104.

174 Delphine Roberts: Summers, pp. 324–325.

The Saga of Tosh Plumlee

175 Tosh in Florida and Dallas: author's interviews, 1991–2004.

Was Oswald a Spy?

180 Rose: Earl Golz, "Oswald Camera Disappeared During FBI Investigation," *Dallas Morning News*, June 15, 1978.

181 Lohn: Ibid.

181 Minox photos released: Earl Golz, "Oswald Pictures Released by FBI," *Dallas Morning News*, Aug. 7, 1978.

181 CIA document: HSCA IV.210; "Paper Shows Oswald Eyed," *Fort Worth Star-Telegram*, Oct. 1, 1976.

181 Oswald as CIA agent: CIA "201" document: HSCA Report, pp. 200–205.

181 Harry Dean: "JFK Exclusive: Oswald was U.S. Agent!" *Argosy*, October 1976; www.spartacus.schoolnet.co.uk/JFK-deanH.htm.

182 Agents knew of Oswald: Jefferson Morley, "What Can We Do About JFK's Murder?" *The Atlantic*, Nov. 21, 2012.

183 Cox's box top: XXIV.345.

184 Incredible cable: Mark Lane, "CIA Conspired to Kill Kennedy," *LA Free Press*, Special Report Number One, 1978, p. 5.

185 Azcue: Anthony Summers, *Conspiracy*, New York, McGraw-Hill, 1980, p. 374.

185 Duran: Summers, pp. 376–377.

185 Phillips: Ibid., p. 384.

185 No accurate manner: Appendix to the HSCA Report, the "Lopez Report," p. 8.

A Message from Oswald

186 Oswald note: Penn Jones Jr., *The Continuing Inquiry*, Feb. 22, 1977; "Alleged Oswald Letter Checked for Its Authenticity by FBI Agents," *Dallas Morning News*, Feb. 6, 1977.

187 McNally: HSCA IV.357–359.

187 William Gaudet: Summers, pp. 363–365.

189 Osborne/Bowen: Fensterwald, pp. 232–235; Summers, pp. 369–370.

DeMohrenschildt and the Agency

189 Gary Taylor: IX.100.

189 Letters to LBJ: http://ciajfk.com/Doris.html.

189 Reports to CIA: "Oswald Friend Labeled CIA Informant in Memo," *Dallas Times Herald*, July 27, 1978.

190 J. Walton Moore: HSCA XII.53–54; author's interviews with Jeanne DeMohrenschildt, 1978–1979.

190 CIA mail opening: *Associated Press*, "Letters Reveal CIA Opened Mail to Oswald," *Fort Worth Star-Telegram*, Sept. 12, 1978.

191 Plausible account: Robert Morrow, *Betrayal: A Reconstruction of Certain Clandestine Events from the Bay of Pigs to the Assassination of John F. Kennedy*, Chicago, Henry Regnery Co., 1976.

191 FBI ammo document: http://jfk.hood.edu/Collection/Weisberg%20Subject%20Index%20Files/N%20Disk/Neutron%20Activatin%20Analyses%200226%20Appeal%20FBI%20Releases/Item%2005.pdf.

191 Underhill: Robert J. Groden and Harrison Edward Livingstone, *High Treason*, Baltimore, Conservatory Press, 1989, p. 124.

The French Connection to the Assassination

193 Alderson: researcher J. Gary Shaw's interview, Oct. 6, 1977; Hurt, p. 418.

194 Helms: "Senate Intelligence Committee Report on Foreign Assassinations," p. 142.

196 Davis in Algiers: Seth Kantor, *Who Was Jack Ruby?*, New York, Everest House, 1978, p. 16.

196 Eldon Moyers: author's interview, spring 1986.

197 Virgil Bailey: interview with researcher Gary Shaw, spring 1980; Hurt, p. 416.

197 Steve Rivele: "A New Theory: 3 French Gangsters Killed JFK, New Book Alleges," *Dallas Morning News*, Oct. 26, 1988; Turner documentary.

198 Conein: Henrik Kreuger, *The Great Heroin Coup: Drugs, Intelligence & International Fascism*, Cambridge, Mass., South End Press, 1980, pp. 133–135.

198 A tremendous power: Richard D. Starnes, "Starnegazing," *Reading Eagle*, Oct. 10, 1963, p. 20.

198 Watson: "Senate Intelligence Committee Report," Vol. 6, 1976, p. 4.

G-Men

The Top G-Man

201 3,000 citizens: www.vdare.com/articles/why-no-ashcroft-raids.

202 Sullivan on communists: William C. Sullivan with Bill Brown, *The Bureau: My Thirty Years in Hoover's FBI*, New York, W. W. Norton, 1979, p. 266.

203 Mafia monograph: Ibid., p. 121.

203 Sullivan on lack of mob prosecution: Ibid., pp. 117–118.

203 Don Fulsome: http://crimemagazine.com/j-edgar-hoover-blackmailed-mafia.

203 Wicker: Pat Watters and Stephen Gillers, eds., *Investigating the FBI*, Garden City, N.Y., Doubleday & Company, 1973, p. 14.

205 FBI alumni: Sullivan, p. 115.

205 FBI and Dallas police: Earl Golz, "Hoover's Vendetta Targeted Dallas Police, Memos Reveal," *Dallas Morning News*, Dec. 30, 1980.

206 FBI growth: Richard Gid Powers, *Secrecy and Power: The Life of J. Edgar Hoover*, New York, Free Press, 1988, p. 218.

206 Arvad: Davis, p. 111; Powers, p. 359.

206 Hoover and JFK: Sullivan, p. 50.

207 Files destroyed: Powers, p. 266.

207 Hoover and Johnson: Sullivan, p. 60.

208 Retirement waived: Powers, p. 396; Note: Hoover's retention as FBI director was assured by Executive Order 11154.

208 Relationship changed: Sullivan, pp. 60–61.

209 Tolson quote: Ibid., p. 48.

Did Oswald Work for the FBI?

211 Quigley: WC Report, pp. 436–437; IV.431–432.

211 Pena: CBS Reports Inquiry, *The American Assassins*, Part Two, Nov. 26, 1975.

212 Walter: "Never Before Published Documents Prove: FBI Had Five-Day Warning," *LA Free Press*, Special Report Number One, 1978, p. 10.

213 Alba: Summers, pp. 312–313; Hurt, pp. 296–298.

214 Coffee company employees: Jim Garrison, *A Heritage of Stone*, New York, G. P. Putnam's Sons, 1970, pp. 128–130.

214 Garrison: Ibid., p. 131.

214 Oswald as agent: Warren Commission transcripts, meeting of Jan. 22, 1964; meeting of Jan. 27, 1964.

217 Hosty note destroyed: "Senate Intelligence Committee Report on the Kennedy Assassination," p. 95; Davis, pp. 550, 560; Summers, pp. 394–396.

218 Marina: WC I.79.

Cuban Grand Central Station

220 Maurice B. Gatlin: http://education-forum.ipbhost.com/index.php?showtopic=14855.

221 Delphine Roberts: Summers, pp. 322–326.

221 Roberts's daughter: Ibid., p. 296.

221 Chief Curry: IV.195.

221 Police turn over evidence: "FBI to Receive Slaying Evidence," *Dallas Times Herald*, Nov. 26, 1963; Transfer to federal control: "FBI Takes Over All Evidence Police Collected on Oswald," *Dallas Morning News*, Nov. 27, 1963.

222 Cadigan: VII.434–435.

223 Hundley and Powers: Ovid Demaris, *The Director*, New York, Harper's Magazine Press, 1975, p. 175.

The Secret Service

225 O'Donnell: William Manchester, *The Death of a President*, New York, Penguin Books, 1977, p. 37.

225 Bolden: Fensterwald, pp. 560–562; Groden and Livingston, pp. 136–137;

Shaw with Harris, p. 22; author's interview, 2010.

226 Luncheon site decision: Jerry Bruno and Jeff Greenfield, *The Advance Man*, New York, William Morrow and Company, 1971, p. 90.

227 O'Donnell: Ibid., p. 92.

227 Angry at Connally: Ibid., p. 94.

227 Incomplete information: Jesse E. Curry, *Retired Dallas Police Chief Jesse Curry Reveals His Personal JFK Assassination File*, Dallas, Texas, American Poster and Publishing Co., 1969, p. 17.

228 Greer: 11.117.

A Few Drinks at the Cellar

230 Rowley: WC Report, p. 451.

231 Kirkwood and Hill: "Remembering the Cellar," Startime Section, *Fort Worth Star-Telegram*, May 25, 1984, p. 14; author's interviews with Pat Kirkwood, 1978 and 1984.

232 Johnson on Youngblood: VIII.562.

232 Agents waved off: www.jfklancer.com/LNE/limo.html.

233 Johnson's elaboration: Lyndon B. Johnson, *The Vantage Point*, New York, Holt, Rinehart and Winston, 1974.

233 Yarborough: author's interview, summer 1986.

233 Secret Service deficiencies: HSCA Report, p. 237.

Rednecks and Oilmen

235 Sorenson on civil rights: Davis, p. 410.

A Bullet for the General

237 Edwin Walker: author's interview, November 1964.

237 Weissman: V.509.

238 Stovall and Rose: XXII.583.

238 Marina: XI.294.

240 William Duff: www.maryferrell.org/mffweb/archive/viewer/showDoc.do?docId=11711&relPageId=4.

240 Walker's name in Oswald's notebook: WC Report, p. 663.

241 Paine: III.87.

241 Meagher: Meagher, p. 287.
242 Bullets don't match: George Michael Evica, *And We Are All Mortal*, West Hartford, University of Hartford, 1978, p. 75.
242 Compelling evidence: Meagher, p. 62.
243 Russell's opposition: James Hepburn, *Farewell America*, Vaduz, Liechtenstein, Frontier Publishing Company, 1968, p. 71.
243 King as instrument: Sullivan, p. 135.
243 Hoover gathered material: Ibid., p. 50.
244 Coretta Scott King: www.trutv.com/ conspiracy/assassinations/james-earl -ray/3.html.
244 Dangerous enemy: Davis, p. 427.

The Miami Prophet

244 Milteer: Davis, p. 513; Shaw with Harris, pp. 169–170; Hurt, pp. 410–411; Summers, pp. 429–430, 606–607.
245 Kennedy and steel industry: Wallechinsky and Wallace, *The People's Almanac*, p. 246.

Nixon and the JFK Assassination

247 Nixon's flight from Dallas: http:// mtracy9.tripod.com/kennedy.html.
248 Marcello cash to Nixon: Dan R. Moldea, *The Hoffa Wars*, New York and London, Paddington Press, 1978, p. 108.
249 Rubenstein FBI memo: author's interview with Ford, 1977; Shaw with Harris, p. 54; Groden and Livingstone, p. 254.
250 Nixon FBI interview: Warren Commission Exhibit 1973.
251 Nixon's version: Jules Witcover, *Saturday Evening Post*, Feb. 25, 1967.
251 Marina's statements: WC Report, p. 188.
251 Nixon-Haldeman: June 23, 1972, White House Transcript, meeting between President Richard Nixon and H. R. Haldeman.
252 Watergate figures: Fensterwald, p. 550.
252 Justice official: Moldea, p. 352.

A Killing on Wall Street

253 Wall Street: *Book of the Year, 1964*, Chicago, Encyclopedia Britannica, 1964, p. 847;

Lincoln Lawrence, *Were We Controlled?*, New York, University Books Inc., 1967, p. 146; Theodore H. White, *The Assassination of the President*, Year Book Special Report, Chicago, 1964 World Book Encyclopedia, 1964, p. 64; "Stocks Take Record Rise," *Dallas Morning News*, Nov. 27, 1963.
254 "United States Note": author's interview with the librarian of the Comptroller of the Currency, winter 1988; "The Spotlight," Oct. 31, 1988, p. 2.

Kennedy and Oilmen

257 Curington: "JFK Assassins Got $$ From Kennedy-Hating Billionaire," *National Enquirer*, June 14, 1977.

Oswald's Friends

258 DeMohrenschildt: IX.179.
259 CIA reports filed: "Oswald Friend Labeled CIA Informant in Memo," *Dallas Times Herald*, July 27, 1978.
259 Mrs. DeMohrenschildt: author's interviews, 1978 and 1983.
260 Oswald's Russian: IX.226.
261 DeMohrenschildt liked Oswald: IX.227.
262 Oswald shoots at leaves: author's interviews with Jeanne DeMohrenschildt, 1978.
263 Browder with Ruby: David E. Scheim, *Contract on America*, Silver Spring, Md., Argyle Press, 1983, p. 201.
263 Herb Atkin: www.spartacus.schoolnet. co.uk/JFKdemohrenschildt.htm.
264 FBI letter: IX.167.
264 DeMohrenschildt on FBI letter: IX.167.
265 Mendoza: author's interview with Mrs. DeMohrenschildt, 1978.
267 Thomas Merton: Douglass, p. xv.
268 Tension with Establishment: Donald Gibson, *Battling Wall Street*, New York, Sheridan Square Press, 1994, p. 5.
268 Two influential groups: Gibson, p. 55.

All the Way With LBJ

269 LBJ and Rayburn: J. Evetts Haley, *A Texan Looks at Lyndon: A Study in Illegitimate*

Power, Canyon, Texas, Palo Duro Press, 1964, p. 14.

271 Correction made: Clyde Wantland, *Texas Argus*, San Antonio, April 1962.

271 Salas: "Man Admits Fixing LBJ's '48 Election," *Fort Worth Star-Telegram*, July 31, 1977.

271 IRS files burned: Haley, p. 92.

272 Diane Bishop: author's interview, July 1990.

273 Envelopes with cash: Robert A. Caro, *Atlantic Monthly*, October 1981.

273 Halfen: Scheim, p. 169.

273 LBJ pardon for Hoffa: Bobby Baker with Larry L. King, *Wheeling and Dealing: Confessions of a Capitol Hill Operator*, New York, W. W. Norton & Company, 1978, p. 17.

274 Oilmen threatened: Haley, p. 238.

275 LBJ dumped: "Nixon Predicts JFK May Drop Johnson," *Dallas Morning News*, Nov. 22, 1963.

275 LBJ's treatment: Sam Houston Johnson, *My Brother Lyndon*, New York, Cowles, 1969, p. 108.

275 Wagenvoord: www.spartacus.schoolnet.co.uk/JFKwagenvoord.htm.

275 Marshall: "Suicide Changed to Murder in Billie Sol Estes Case," *Fort Worth Star-Telegram*, August 14, 1985; "Estes Claims LBJ Had Slush Fund, Sources Say," *Dallas Morning News*, March 24, 1984; "Estes Cited Electric Chair in Refusal to Discuss Deaths," *Dallas Times Herald*, March 26, 1984; Haley, pp. 134–135.

276 LBJ to Kilduff: Jack Bell, *The Johnson Treatment: How Lyndon B. Johnson Took Over the Presidency and Made It His Own*, New York, Harper & Row, 1965, p. 12.

276 Gearhart: Manchester, pp. 62–63.

277 O'Donnell: Ibid., p. 235.

277 LBJ to Galbraith: Ibid., p. 472.

277 LBJ's master plan: Bell, p. 22.

277 Connally's clothing: Shaw with Harris, p. 78.

278 Goodwin: "Was Lyndon Johnson Unstable?" *Time*, Sept. 5, 1988.

278 Sam Houston Johnson: Richard Starnes, "LBJ's Long-Distance Tantrum Over

Boozy Brother Is Told," *El Paso Herald Post*, Nov. 19, 1969.

278 Madeleine Brown: author's interviews, 1988 and 1989.

279 Watson quotes LBJ: Senate Intelligence Committee Final Report, Vol. 6, 1976, p. 182.

Soldiers

The Military-Industrial Complex

282 NSAM 55 and 57: L. Fletcher Prouty, *The Secret Team: The CIA and Its Allies in Control of the United States and the World*, Englewood Cliffs, N.J., Prentice-Hall, 1973, pp. 114–116, 116–119.

283 Kennedy on America's fallibility: Speech at the University of Washington, Seattle, Nov. 16, 1961.

JFK and Vietnam

284 Hilsman: Michael Maclear, *The Ten Thousand Day War—Vietnam: 1945–1975*, New York, Avon Books, 1981, p. 60.

286 NSAM 273: Peter Dale Scott, Paul L. Hoch, and Russell Stetler, *The Assassinations: Dallas and Beyond: A Guide to Cover-ups and Investigations*, New York, Random House, Vintage Press, 1976, pp. 406–442.

286 JFK's order rescinded: Kenneth P. O'Donnell, David Powers, and Joe McCarthy, *Johnny, We Hardly Knew Ye: Memories of John Fitzgerald Kennedy*, New York, Pocket Books, 1973, p. 18.

287 Hosty and agent: IV.461.

287 Powell: Warren Commission Document 354; Shaw with Harris, p. 194.

288 Revill: Ibid., p. 194; V.57.

288 Jones: HSCA Report, pp. 221–222.

288 Oswald and military intelligence: HSCA Report, p. 224.

The Man Who Was to Kill Oswald

289 Nagell: William Turner, "The Garrison Commission on the Assassination of President Kennedy," *Ramparts*, January 1968, pp. 56–58; Richard Russell with

Dave Navard, "The Man Who Had a Contract to Kill Lee Harvey Oswald Before the Assassination of President John F. Kennedy," *Gallery*, March 1981, pp. 37–38, 88–95; Garrison, *On the Trail of the Assassins*, pp. 182–186.

Lone Gunmen on the Grassy Knoll

293 Loy Factor's story: Robin Ramsey, *Who Shot JFK?* Sparkford, Somerset, J. H. Haynes, 2007, pp. 94–95.
294 Fingerprints on the sixth floor: HSCA Vol. XI, p. 213.
296 Joseph West and exhumation: Editors, "Judge Refuses to Grant Request to Exhume JFK," *Houston Chronicle*, July 8, 1992, p. 15.
297 Allan Eaglesham on headstamps: www. manuscriptservice.com/Headstamp.
297 John Christian: author's interview, June 2010.
298 Christian's taxes: author's interview with attorney Sheila Grace Neal, March 2013.
299 Roscoe White: 1990 Press Kit, JFK Assassination Center, Dallas, Texas; Ricky Don White, *Mandarin: The Grassy Knoll Gunman*, unpublished manuscript; author's interviews with Ricky White, 1990, 2006, 2010.

PART III: AFTERMATH

Dallas

303 Fritz: IV.205.
304 Biffle: Kent Biffle, "Reporter Recalls the Day Camelot Died in Dallas," *Dallas Morning News*, April 5, 1981.
305 Cabluck: author's interview, 1976 and 1986.
305 Hartman: author's interview, summer 1986.
306 Pocketed bullet: Jesse E. Curry, *Retired Dallas Police Chief Jesse Curry Reveals His Personal JFK Assassination File*, Dallas, Texas, American Poster and Printing Company, 1969, p. 46.
306 Bullet hole in sign: *In Retrospect of the*

John F. Kennedy Assassination, Asahi Broadcasting Network, Japan, Aug. 4, 2004.
306 Lester: Associated Press, Jan. 5, 1978.
306 Luster: "Man Claims He Found Live Bullet Buried Under Top of Grassy Knoll," *Dallas Morning News*, Dec. 23, 1978.
307 Morgan: author's interview, spring 1989.
307 Robert DePugh: author's interview with radio host Stan Major, May 1992.
307 Harper: James H. Fetzer, *Murder in Dealey Plaza*, Chicago, Catfeet Press, 2000, p. 41.
308 Carr: Shaw with Harris, p. 13.
309 Speaker: author's interviews, July 1987.

Mysterious Secret Service Men

309 Smith: Summers, p. 81.
310 Summers: Jack Anderson TV documentary, *Who Murdered JFK?* aired Nov. 2, 1988.
310 Holland: Lane, p. 34.
310 Weitzman: VII.107.
311 Harkness: VI.312.
311 Sorrels: "SS 'Imposters' Spotted by JFK Witnesses," *Dallas Morning News*, Aug. 27, 1978.
312 Oswald and agent: WC Report, p. 629.
312 Hill: author's interviews, 1986 and 1989.
314 Curry: Summers, p. 51.
314 Adams: VI.393.
315 Lopez: FBI report File No. DL 89–43, dated Dec. 1, 1963.
315 Willis and Ruby: author's interview, October 1978.
315 Wanda Walker: author's interview, April 1986.
316 Ruby at Parkland: Kantor, pp. 192–194. Roy Stamps: author's interview, April 1986.

The Black Car Chase

316 Tilson: "Ex-Officer Suspects He Chased '2nd Gun,'" *Dallas Morning News*, August 20, 1978.

The Account of Roger Craig

318 Craig: Roger Craig, *When They Kill*

a President, unpublished manuscript, 1971, p. 7; XIX.524.

320 Craig not in office: WC Report, p. 160.

The Three Tramps

322 Biffle: "Reporter Recalls the Day Camelot Died in Dallas," *Dallas Morning News,* April 5, 1981.
324 White: author's interview, spring 1980–1982.
324 Cook: author's telephone interview, spring 1982.
325 Harrelson's confession: "Events Turn Sour . . . ," *Dallas Morning News,* March 20, 1981; "Is Kennedy's Assassin Sitting in Texas Jail?" *News Tribune,* Fort Worth, Texas, June 11, 1982.
325 Matthews: KDFW-TV (Channel 4, Dallas) interview with Harrelson, aired Feb. 14, 1982.
326 The Company: "Story of Spies, Stolen Arms and Drugs," *San Francisco Chronicle,* April 28, 1982.
326 Trial testimony: "Chagra Says Harrelson Told Him He also Killed JFK," *Fort Worth Star-Telegram,* Nov. 2, 1982.

The Mafia Man in Dealey Plaza

327 Braden: Summers, pp. 476–477; Hurt, pp. 123–124; Fensterwald, pp. 287–289.
329 Lawrence: Sheldon Inkol, "Jack Lawrence Responds," *Third Decade,* Vol. 8, No. 6, Sept. 1992.
330 Holt on confusion: www.thedailybeast.com/newsweek/1991/12/23/bottom-line-how-crazy-is-it.html.

The Shooting of J. D. Tippit

331 Tippit unknown: Meagher, p. 253.
331 Markham: III.311.
331 Whaley: 11.261.
332 Scoggins: III.335.
332 Clemons: Lane, p. 194.
332 Wright: George and Patricia Nash, *New Leader,* October 12, 1964, pp. 6–9.
333 Poe: XXIV.415.

334 Kinsley: Notes of interview by *Dallas Morning News* reporter Earl Golz, spring 1979.
335 Alterations to pistol: WC Report, p. 558.
335 Howard: author's interview, 1987.
335 Oswald's jacket: WC Report, p. 176.
336 Benavides: VI.453.
336 Roberts: VI.439.
336 Davis: III.347.
336 Scoggins: III.328.
336 Westbrook: WC Report, p. 175.
337 Roberts: VI.443–444.
339 Bowles: interview with Gary Mack, winter 1981; Gary Mack, "NAS Panel Stuck On Channel 1, Report Delayed," *Continuing Inquiry,* March 22, 1982, p. 5; Gary Mack, "J.D. Tippit: The 'Missing' Broadcasts," *Coverups,* September 1984, p. 2.
339 Coup de grace: HSCA Report, pp. 59–60.

The Arrest of Oswald

340 McDonald: "Officer Recalls Oswald Capture," *Dallas Morning News,* Nov. 24, 1963.
341 Gibson: VII.72.
341 Brewer: VII.6.
341 Applin: VII.91; "Man Believes He Saw Ruby at Scene of Oswald's Arrest," *Dallas Morning News,* March 11, 1979.
342 Burroughs: author's interview, summer 1987.
343 Davis: author's interview, fall 1988.
344 Haire: author's interview, summer 1987.
344 Rose: VII.228; Nigel Turner documentary.
345 January: Shaw with Harris, p. 111.
345 Robert Vinson: Douglass, pp. 298–301.
346 Hoover: "Hoover Called Oswald 'A Nut' FBI Files Show," *Fort Worth Star-Telegram,* Dec. 7, 1977.
346 Preliminary reports of conspiracy: "Wade Calls Killing a 'Dastardly Act,'" *Dallas Morning News,* Nov. 23, 1963.
346 Wade to say no conspiracy: Edward Oxford, "Destiny in Dallas," *American History Illustrated,* November 1988, p. 24.

The FBI Takes Control

347 Curry: IV.195.
349 Cadigan: VII.435.
350 Quote changed: VII.434.

Two Hospitals

352 Stamps: author's interview, April 1986.
352 Kennedy shot from front: Charles A. Crenshaw, MD, with J. Gary Shaw, D. Bradley Kizzia, JD, Gary Aguiklar, MD, and Cyril Wecht, MD, *Trauma Room One,* New York, Paraview Press, 2001, p. 9.
353 Lyndon Johnson's call: Crenshaw, p. 133.
353 Crenshaw perplexed: Ibid., p. 14.
354 Dr. Earl Rose: www.twincities.com/ci_20524461/dallas-medical-examiner-barred-from-conducting-jfk-autopsy.
355 Fuller: "7 Shared Emergency Room with JFK," *Dallas Morning News,* Nov. 22, 1973.
355 Tomlinson: VI.133–134.
356 Commission Exhibit 399 not from JFK stretcher: WC Report, p. 81.

Jack Ruby at Parkland

356 Ruby meeting: Kantor, pp. 192–194.
357 Tice: XV.389.
358 Connally bullet: John Connally and Mickey Herskowitz, *In History's Shadow: An American Odyssey,* New York, Hyperion Books, 1993, p. 18.
359 Burkley: XXII.96.
359 Finck: Garrison, pp. 246–249.
361 Sibert-O'Neill Report: Edward Jay Epstein, "Inquest," pp. 166–170.
362 Ford and Morningstar: Mike Feinsilber, "Ford Says He Edited Report on JFK's Death for "Clarity," Associated Press, July 3, 1997.

The Switching of Bodies

364 O'Connor: David Lifton, *Best Evidence,* pp. 598–599.
364 Custer: Ibid., p. 620.
364 Custer and Riebe: Jeanne King, "Kennedy Autopsy Photos Doctored, Technicians Say," Reuters, May 29, 1992.
366 Brazen manipulation: Douglas P. Horne, *Inside the Assassination Records Review Board: The US Government's Final Attempt to Reconcile the Conflicting Medical Evidence in the Assassination of JFK,* Vol. IV, self-published, 2009, p. 987.
366 Bone fragment: Josiah Thompson, *Six Seconds in Dallas: A Micro-study of the Kennedy Assassination,* New York, Bernard Geis Associates, 1967; (rev.) New York, Berkley Publishing Corp., 1976, p. 65.
367 Burkley on conspiracy: Hurt, p. 49.
368 Pitzer and Marvin: www.spartacus.schoolnet.co.uk/JFKpitzerW.htm; author's interview with Daniel Marvin, August 2006.
369 Specter: Groden and Livingston, p. 74.
369 Wecht: HSCA 1.358.
370 Key to understanding: Groden and Livingston, p. 7.

Jack Ruby

371 A terrible conspiracy: taped interview with Bob Huffaker of KRLD News, Dallas, following hearing for a new trial, Sept. 9, 1965.
371 The true facts of what occurred: Turner documentary.
371 Young Ruby: WC Report, pp. 779–786.
372 Ruby and union: V.200; Kantor, pp. 99–100.
373 Guthrie: Kantor, pp. 105–106.
375 Brown: author's interviews, 1988 and 1989.
375 Ester Mash: author's interview, spring 1988.

Jack Ruby—Gangster

375 Ruby's associates are discussed in the HSCA Report and volumes; Kantor; Fensterwald; Blakey and Billings; Summers; Scheim, op. cit.
378 Abadie: Commission Exhibits 1750 and 1753; Scheim, p. 105.
378 Breen-Curry: Scheim, p. 82.

Jack Ruby—Gunrunner and FBI Informant

379 Thompson: Ibid., p. 201.
379 Browder: William Scott Malone, "The Secret Life of Jack Ruby," *New Times*, January 23, 1978, pp. 47–48.
379 Weston: "Ruby-Oswald Link Cited by Witness," *Fort Worth Star-Telegram*, July 18, 1976.
380 WC on McWillie: WC Report, p. 370.
380 Ruby lied repeatedly: Blakey and Billings, pp. 293–294.
380 McWillie: Malone, pp. 50–51; Fensterwald, pp. 285–286; Kantor, pp. 131–132; Blakey and Billings, p. 293.
381 McKeown: Kantor, p. 137; Scheim, pp. 202–203; Fensterwald, pp. 364–366.
382 Perrin: Scheim, p. 206.
382 Wilson: Kantor, p. 132.
383 Hemming: author's interview, January 1991.
383 Flynn: Ibid., p. 128; Malone, p. 49; Fensterwald, p. 260; Blakey and Billings, pp. 295–296.
384 No ulterior motive: Ibid., p. 296.
384 Ruby buys bugging devices: Malone, p. 49.
385 Willens: Kantor, p. 127.
385 Ruby and Roselli: Malone, p. 51.

The Woman Who Foresaw the Assassination

386 Cheramie: HSCA X.199–205; Douglass, pp. 244–246.

Did Ruby and Oswald Know Each Other?

387 No evidence: WC Report, p. 650.
387 Griffin-Hubert: Blakey and Billings, p. 82.
387 Ruby-Oswald connections: HSCA Report, p. 148.
387 Oswald-Ruby not loners: Ibid., p. 180.
387 Walker: author's interview, fall 1964.
388 Alexander: "Any Oswald-Rubenstein Tie in Dallas Sought by Police," *Dallas Morning News*, Nov. 26, 1963.
388 Brown: author's interviews, spring and fall 1988.
388 Cummings: "Oswald-Ferrie Link Made by Ex-Cabbie," *Fort Worth Star-Telegram*, March 10, 1967.
388 Crowe: "Magician Says Oswald Was Patron in Ruby Night Club," *Dallas Morning News*, Nov. 25, 1963; Kent Biffle, "Memory Expert Interests Agents," *Dallas Morning News*, Nov. 26, 1963.
389 Oliver: Turner television documentary; author's interview, 1991.
389 Carlin: XV.620.
389 Kay: "FBI Eyes on Ruby Strippers in JFK Case," *Dallas Times Herald*, May 22, 1975.
389 Meserole: author's interviews, spring and summer 1988.
389 Weston: "Ruby-Oswald Link Cited by Witness," *Fort Worth Star-Telegram*, July 18, 1976; "JFK Murder Hatched in Ruby's Club—Oswald Was There," *Midnight*, November 15, 1976.
391 Billet: Ibid.
392 C. B. Caldera: author's interview, July 1990.
392 Mash: author's interviews, summer and fall 1988.
393 Jarnagin: author's interview, summer 1988; XXVI.254–257.
394 Plot papers: "'JFK assassination plot' papers found in Dallas safe," *The Guardian*, Feb. 18, 2008.
394 Box of documents: "Papers Link Ruby, Oswald," *Dallas Morning News*, March 28, 1976.
396 Gleam of recognition: Curry, p. 133.
396 Ruby's phone contacts: Blakey and Billings, pp. 302–305.
397 Tax liens: WC Report, p. 705.
397 Tax connection: Blakey and Billings, p. 308.
397 Ruby's business: Blakey and Billings, p. 309.

The Shooting of Lee Harvey Oswald

398 Ruby's note to Tonahill: Blakey and Billings, p. 333.
398 This silly story: Melvin Belli with Maurice Carroll, *Dallas Justice*, New York, David McKay, 1964, p. 39.
398 Ruby: V.191.
400 Sightings: HSCA Report, p. 158.

Jack Ruby's Warnings

400 Authorities warned: WC Report, p. 209.
400 Grammer: Turner documentary.
401 Richey-Smith-Walker: WC Report, pp. 352–353.
401 Rushing: XII.75–79; Shaw with Harris, p. 21.
401 Pitts: WC Report, p. 353; Kantor, pp. 59–60.
401 Carlin: XIX.306.
402 Senator's call: Kantor, p. 217.
402 Howard: Commission Exhibit 2002, p. 73.
402 Leavelle: author's interview, fall 1988.
402 Alleyway: HSCA Report, p. 157.
403 Some premeditation: Ibid.
403 Ruby: V.206.
403 Roselli: Malone, p. 51.
404 Graves: Edward Oxford, "Destiny in Dallas," *American History Illustrated*, November 1988, p. 47.
405 I stayed in my office: Curry, p. 127.
405 Curry: Ibid., p. 130.
405 Archer: Turner documentary.
406 Alexander: Kantor, p. 114.
406 Kilgallen possibility: Lee Israel, *Kilgallen*, New York, Dell Publishing Co., 1979, p. 358.
407 Crawford: Ibid., p. 361.
407 Lane: Ibid., p. 378.
407 Story isn't going to die: Ibid., p. 388.
407 Dorothy's death: Ibid., p. 395.
407 Carter called Henry Wade: Noel Tyman, *Bloody Treason: On Solving History's Greatest Murder Mystery: The Assassination of John F. Kennedy*, Rancho Santa Fe, CA, Laurel Publishing, 1997, pp. 792–793.
408 Tonahill: Kantor, p. 4.
408 Ruby: V.203–213.
410 Hoover: WC Report, p. 815.

The Sudden Death of Jack Ruby

411 Stevenson: Kantor, p. 167. Ruby letter: Penn Jones, *The Continuing Inquiry*, Nov. 22, 1978, and Dec. 22, 1978.
412 Second letter: copy in files of researcher J. Gary Shaw.
413 Dr. Julian Mardock: author's interview,

fall 1989. Maddox: unpublished interview with *Dallas Morning News* reporter Earl Golz, winter 1982.
414 Tilson: unpublished interview with reporter Earl Golz, summer 1978.
414 West: www.csj.org/infoserv_profile/west_louis.htm.
414 Bruce McCarty: author's interview, spring 1988.

The Evidence

415 Witnesses: Shaw with Harris, pp. 8–9.
416 Palm print mess: WC Report, p. 566.
416 Day: IV.265.
417 Craig: Roger Craig, p. 18.
418 Weitzman: XXIV.228.
418 Wade: XXIV.831.
419 Boone: III.294.
419 Substitution of rifles: Meagher, p. 100.
420 Pistol bought in Fort Worth: WC Report, p. 606.
420 Simmons: III.443.
421 Warren Commission on serial number: WC Report, p. 81.
421 Serial number: XXV.808.

An Incriminating Palm Print

422 Latona: IV.24.
422 "FBI team": "Body of JFK Assassin Is Under Guard in FW," *Fort Worth Press*, Nov. 25, 1963.
423 Groody: author's interviews, 1979 and 1988.
423 Harrison: telephone interview with researcher Gary Mack, 1978.
423 Wade: "Oswald's Prints Revealed on Rifle Killing Kennedy," *Dallas Times Herald*, Nov. 25, 1963.
423 Drain: Hurt, p. 109.
423 Question over palm print: FBI memo, Rosen to Belmont, Aug. 28, 1964 (FBI 105–82555 4814).
424 Day: XXVI.829.
424 Wecht: HSCA VII.200.
425 No significant differences: Hurt, p. 80.
425 Hoover: HSCA 1.558.
425 Guinn: Hurt, p. 83.
426 Western Cartridge: XXVI.62.

426 Fithian: HSCA 1.557.

427 *Times* article on Guinn: Lane, pp. 152–153.

427 Grossly flawed analysis: Sherry P. Fiester, *Enemy of the Truth: Myth, Forensics, and the Kennedy Assassination*, Southlake, TX, JFK Lancer Publications, 2012, p. 166.

427 Bag touching blanket: Curry, pp. 88–89.

429 Stroughton on limousine: Trask, p. 42.

429 Connally's clothing: Penn Jones Jr., *Forgive My Grief II*, Midlothian, Midlothian Mirror, 1967, pp. 77–79.

Questionable Backyard Photos

430 Oswald to Fritz: WC Report, p. 608.

431 Committee: HSCA 11.358–359.

431 Hester: "Dallas Man Claims FBI Had Oswald Film," *Fort Worth Star-Telegram*, Sept. 20, 1978; author's interview with Patricia Hester, spring 1986.

432 Pickard: Summers, p. 95.

432 Thompson: Ibid., p. 96.

432 White: author's interviews, 1978 and spring 1988.

433 Blakey: HSCA 11.319.

Reenactment Problems

433 Breneman: author's interview, spring 1978; "Surveyor: More Than 1 Man Shot Kennedy," *Fort Worth Star-Telegram*, April 14, 1978.

433 Robert West: author's interview, April 16, 1978.

The Warren Commission

436 Hoover: Senate Intelligence Committee Report on the Kennedy Assassination, p. 33.

436 Media leaks: "FBI Data Seen Spiking Reports of Conspiracy," *Dallas Morning News*, Dec. 4, 1963.

436 Katzanbach memo: HSCA III.567.

437 Commission heads off inquiries: "President Names Board to Probe JFK's Slaying," *Dallas Morning News*, Nov. 30, 1963.

438 Gallup poll: "52% Believe 'Group' Tied to JFK Slaying," *Dallas Morning News*, Dec. 6, 1963.

The Reluctant Chairman

439 Nixon badgered Eisenhower: Jack Harrison Pollack, *Earl Warren: The Judge Who Changed America*, Englewood Cliffs, NJ, Prentice-Hall, 1979, p. 6.

440 Warren: Ibid., p. 228.

440 Johnson treatment: Ibid., pp. 228–229.

440 Eisenberg: Fensterwald, p. 73.

444 Sacred right: Mark Lane, "A Lawyer's Brief; Is Oswald Innocent?" *National Guardian*, December 1963.

444 WC transcripts: Tad Szulc, "The Warren Commission in Its Own Words," *New Republic*, Sept. 27, 1975.

445 No more memorandums: Edward Jay Epstein, *Inquest: The Warren Commission and the Establishment of Truth*, New York, Bantam Books, 1966, p. 119.

446 Rankin on Oswald: Szulc, p. 11.

Conflicts in the Testimony

453 Bowers: Lane, *Rush to Judgment* documentary.

453 Powell: Warren Commission Document 1542 in files of researcher J. Gary Shaw.

454 Holland: Thompson, *Six Seconds, rev. ed.*, p. 146; Holland's comment to Lane is from *Rush to Judgment* documentary.

454 Fischer: "Witnesses Overlooked in JFK Probe," *Dallas Morning News*, Dec. 19, 1978.

454 Belin changed testimony: Craig, p. 27.

454 Mercer: Shaw, p. 26; Garrison, p. 218.

454 Willis: "JFK Killing Witness Not Surprised Tests Indicate 2nd Gunman," *Fort Worth Star-Telegram*, Dec. 22, 1978.

455 Pipes: Ibid.

455 Breneman: author's interview, fall 1978.

455 Yarborough: Shaw, p. 186; author's interview, summer 1986.

456 Hill: author's interviews, summer 1986 and spring 1988.

457 Dave Powers and Kenneth O'Donnell: O'Neill, p. 178.

The Single-Bullet Theory

459 Persuasive evidence: WC Report, p. 19. A myth: Fiester, p. 332.Political invention: Horne, p. 1205.

463 David Belin: Fred T. Newcomb and Perry Adams, *Murder from Within: Lyndon Johnson's Plot Against President Kennedy*, Bloomington, IN, AuthorHouse, 2011, p. 246.

463 Reprehensible actions: Meagher, p. xxiv. Warren Report deficiencies: Ibid., p. xxviii.

464 Questioning legitimate: Szulc, p. 9.

464 Senate Intelligence Committee: Report of Senate Select Committee to Study Government Operations with Respect to Intelligence Activities Report, 1976, pp. 6–7.

465 Schweiker: "Warren Report Held Unbelievable," *Fort Worth Star-Telegram*, June 24, 1976.

465 Robert F. Kennedy Jr.: Jamie Stengle, "RFK Children Speak About Assassination in Dallas," Associated Press, January 11, 2013.

465 FOX poll: www.foxnews.com/story /0,2933,102511,00.html#ixzz2 ChbOMefx.

The Garrison Investigation

466 Martin: Garrison, pp. 29–32.

467 Impressed with FBI: Ibid., p. 10.

467 Ferrie: Ibid., p. 6.

468 Ferrie released: Eric Norden interview, *Playboy*, October 1967, p. 74.

468 43 years old: Garrison, p. 11.

468 Military engaged: Ibid., p. 12.

468 Lofty credentials: Ibid., pp. 14–15.

469 Banister apparatus: Ibid., p. 40.

Clay Shaw and Permindex

469 Shaw background: *Who's Who in the South and Southwest*, 8th ed., Chicago, Marquis—Who's Who, 1963, p. 755.

470 Permindex: Garrison, pp. 87–90; Konstandinos Kalimtgis, David Goldman and Jeffery Steinberg, *Dope, Inc.: Britain's Opium War Against the US*, New York, New Benjamin Franklin House Publishing Co., 1978, pp. 301–320 and 321–329; "Permindex: Britain's International Assassination Bureau," *Executive Intelligence Review*, Nov. 14, 1981, pp. 5–23.

471 Shaw and CIA: Garrison, p. 90.

473 Operated secretly: Ibid., p. 130.

473 I'm a dead man: Ibid., p. 138.

476 Free press reappraised: Ibid., p. 161.

476 Unusual steps: Norden, p. 62.

477 Roselli meeting denied: Garrison letter to John Judge, Feb. 25, 1986; Garrison reiterated this denial to author in fall 1989.

477 CBS interview: Garrison, p. 172.

477 Propaganda blitzkrieg: Norden, p. 62.

478 Cardinal Cushing: Fensterwald, p. 461.

478 Hoffa: Ibid., p. 464.

478 Robert Kennedy: Arthur M. Schlesinger Jr., *Robert Kennedy and His Times*, New York, Ballantine Books, 1979, p. 665.

478 Novel note: Fensterwald, p. 456; Garrison, p. 181.

479 Jurors agree on conspiracy: Ibid., p. 251.

480 Holecard: "Garrison Seeks High Court Help," *Fort Worth Star-Telegram*, Feb. 20, 1969.

481 Garrison charges perjury: Garrison, pp. 252–253.

481 Federal judicial system: Ibid., p. 253.

481 Shaw's death: Ibid., p. 274.

482 Garrison acquitted: "Jury Acquits DA Garrison in Bribe Case," *Fort Worth Star-Telegram*, Sept. 28, 1973.

482 Garrison case a fraud: Blakey and Billings, p. 46.

483 Blakey and agencies: Ibid., p. 401.

483 Extravagant charges: Schiem, p. 57.

483 Garrison's purpose: Ibid., p. 59.

483 CIA disinformation: Garrison letter to researcher John P. Judge, Feb. 25, 1986.

483 Aided by government: author's interview, fall 1989.

484 Ambitious man: Norden, p. 68.

484 Garrison's outline of assassination: Norden, pp. 74 and 156–159.

485 Emboldened by hope for peace: Douglass, p. 374.

485 Garrison on right track: Blakey and Billings, p. 170.

The House Select Committee on Assassinations

485 Gonzalez: "Proceedings and Debates of the 94th Congress, First Session," *Congressional Record*, Vol. 121, No. 24, Washington, 1975.

486 Criticism: Rep. Henry B. Gonzalez, "Assassinations and Lingering Doubts," *Witan*, Vol. 2, No. 8, St. Mary's of Texas School of Law, 1975, pp. 7–8.

486 Downing: Remarks to US House of Representatives, March 18, 1976.

487 Fensterwald: "Assassination Inquiry Stumbling—Is Fensterwald a CIA Plant?" *Washington Star*, Oct. 4, 1976.

488 Joannides's real assignment: Scott Shane, "CIA Is Still Cagey About Oswald Mystery," *New York Times*, Oct. 16, 2009.

488 Sprague and Specter: Groden and Livingston, p. 315.

489 Robert Bauman: Groden and Livingston, p. 317.

489 Sprague vs. Gonzalez: Ibid., p. 317.

489 Proposed budget: Gaeton Fonzi, *The Last Investigation*, New York, Thunder's Mouth Press, 1993, p. 200.

489 Won't play that game: Fonzi, p. 179.

489 Gonzalez stops committee: Ibid., p. 181.

489 Gonzalez went berserk: http://cuban-exile.com/doc_001–025/doc0019b.html.

490 Gonzalez: Fonzi, p. 201.

490 Vast and powerful forces: Ibid., p. 184.

490 The fix is in: Groden and Livingston, p. 318.

490 Key witness death: http://cuban-exile.com/doc_001–025/doc0019b.html.

Blakey at the Helm

491 No more news conferences: "JFK-King Panel Seeks Seclusion," *Fort Worth Star-Telegram*, June 21, 1977.

491 Blakey's contacts: Jerry Policoff and William Scott Malone, "A Great Show, A Lousy Investigation," *New Times*, Sept. 4, 1978, p. 6.

492 Secrecy agreement: author is grateful to researcher Richard E. Sprague for providing a copy of his secrecy agreement with the HSCA.

493 Blakey: Report of the Select Committee on Assassinations, *The Final Assassinations Report*, New York, Bantam Books, 1979, p. xxxii.

493 Sprague: Policoff and Malone, p. 8.

493 Blakey: Jerry Policoff, "Investigations That Were Bound to Fail," *Gallery*, Special Report, July 1979, pp. 62–66.

494 Policoff and Malone, p. 12.

495 Blakey: "The Final Assassinations Report," pp. xxxvi–xxxvii.

496 AIB comment: "The JFK Hearings: A Preliminary Critique," *Clandestine America*, newsletter of the Assassination Information Bureau, Vol. 2, No. 4, p. 1.

496 O'Reilly: Notes from interview with *Dallas Morning News* reporter Earl Golz, January 1982.

496 Fonzi: Ibid., 203.

496 Fenton: Ibid.

The Dallas Police Radio Recording

497 Mack: "7 Shots Believed Fired at Kennedy," *Fort Worth Star-Telegram*, Sept. 1, 1977.

499 McLain: "Officer Says JFK Tape Not His," *Fort Worth Star-Telegram*, Jan. 5, 1979.

500 Ramsey: "Study to Belittle Assassination Data," *Dallas Morning News*, July 9, 1981.

500 HSCA reactions: "House Panel Claims Plots Likely in JFK, King Slayings," *Fort Worth Star-Telegram*, Dec. 31, 1978.

501 Groden: "JFK Panel Photo Expert Alleges Cover-Up," *Fort Worth Star-Telegram*, May 16, 1979.

501 Medical testimony: Harrison E. Livingstone, "Parkland Doctors' Testimony

Shows Autopsy Photos Forged," *Baltimore Chronicle*, July 30, 1979 (reprinted in Penn Jones's *The Continuing Inquiry*, Oct. 22, 1980, pp. 5–6); "Dispute on JFK Assassination Evidence Persists," *Boston Sunday Globe*, June 21, 1981.

501 Kantor: author's interview, October 1978.

502 Groden: author's interview, summer 1986.

502 Blakey: "The Final Assassinations Report," p. XXXVIII.

503 Justice Department memo: "Papers Reveal Justice Ended Kennedy, King Death Probes," *Dallas Times Herald*, Sept. 4, 1988.

The Oliver Stone Film *JFK*

503 Stone distilled: Dr. Grover Proctor, "Oliver Stone's *JFK*: A Historical Analysis," *Saginaw News*, Dec. 21, 1991.

Preemptive Attacks

504 Cokie Roberts: Sam Smith, "Why They Hate Oliver Stone," *Progressive Review*, February 1992.

504 Stephen Rosenfeld: www.zoominfo.com/#!search/profile/person?personId=1880014&targetid=profile.

505 *JFK* caused more damage: Vincent Bugliosi, *Reclaiming History*, New York, W. W. Norton & Company, 2007, p. 1355.

505 Serious books: Ibid., p. 1356.

505 Vapid and bankrupt: Ibid., p. 1437.

505 Cooper and Robinson: Ibid., p. 890.

506 Dr. Grover B. Proctor Jr.: www.groverproctor.us/jfk/jfk91c.html.

The Assassinations Records Review Board

507 Kermit Hall: http://jfkcountercoup2.blogspot.com/2012/08/kermit-l-hall-on-jfk-assassination.html.

Douglas Horne's Discoveries

508 Action of the state: Horne, p. 1800.

508 A crossfire: Ibid., p. 987.

508 Body tampering: Ibid., p. 996.

509 Galloway: Ibid., p. 1020.

509 Humes misleading: Ibid., p. 1000.

509 Humes scared: Ibid., p. 1026.

509 Jenkins: Ibid., pp. 1047 and 1049.

509 Burkley and perjury: Ibid., p. 1052.

The Zapruder Film: Fundamental or Fraud?

509 Zavada study: Horne, p. 1188.

510 CIA and NPIC: Trask, p. 107.

510 McMahon and Hunter: Fetzer, pp. 311–324.

511 Zavada: http://home.earthlink.net/~joejd/jfk/zaphoax/zavada-hoax-comments-r1.pdf.

511 Endless interpretations: Horne, p. 1213.

511 A simulated original: Ibid., p. 1226.

511 Dino Brugioni: Ibid., pp. 1230–1234.

511 McCone on two shooters: http://jfkcountercoup.blogspot.com.

Hollywood Takes a Look

512 Black patch artificial: Author's interviews with Sydney Wilkinson, November 2009.

512 Ned Price: Horne, p. 1361.

512 Paul Rutan: Ibid.

513 Leo Zahn: correspondence with author.

513 Considered opinions: Horne, p. 1361.

513 No cache of records: http://minnesota.cbslocal.com/2012/12/04/ventura-supporting-author-who-says-oswald-didnt-shoot-jfk.

514 Bill Kelly: http://jfkcountercoup.blogspot.com/2012/12/open-letter-to-judge-john-tunheim.html.

514 50,000 documents: http://jfkcountercoup.blogspot.com/2012/10/playing-politics-with-history-still.html.

515 JFK Facts: http://jfkfacts.org/assassination/news/jfk-remains-in-the-shade-during-sunshine-week.

A Question of Oswald

516 Passport Office message: HSCA III.573.

516 July 11, 1961, message: XVIII.374.

516 Military records: http://jfk.hood.edu/Collection/Weisberg%20Subject%20

Index%20Files/S%20Disk/Scott%20
Peter%20Dale/Item%2002.pdf.

An Impostor

517 Deslatte: Summers, pp. 407–408.
517 Intelligence Committee: Fensterwald, pp. 404–405.
518 Dannelly: Fensterwald, pp. 393–394.
518 Hutchinson: WC Report, pp. 308–309.
518 Bogard: X.353.
518 WC conclusion: WC Report, p. 321.
518 Wilson: "Salesman Insists FBI Discounted Facts on Oswald," *Dallas Morning News*, May 8, 1977.
519 Hamblen: WC Report, pp. 309–310; Summers, p. 402; XI.312.
520 Morgan's Gunshop: XXIV.704.
520 Ryder: WC Report, pp. 315–316; XXIV.328–329.
520 Sports Drome Rifle Range: WC Report, pp. 318–319.
520 WC conclusion: Ibid., p. 319.
521 Penn: Summers, pp. 405–406.
521 No substantial basis: WC Report, p. 318.

Was Oswald Really Oswald?

521 Discrepancies: Michael Eddowes, *The Oswald File*, New York, Clarkson N. Potter, 1977.
522 Jeanne DeMohrenschildt on literature: author's interviews, 1978.
522 Language experts: author's interviews with Gary Mack, 1984.
522 Oswald's letter: XVI.33; (handwritten draft) XVI.443.
523 Ed Voebel: Armstrong, p. 915.
523 Frank Kudlaty: Ibid., p. 914.
523 Two different people: Ibid., pp. 62–63.
524 Missing school records: Ibid.
524 Palmer McBride: Ibid.
524 Roy Cooper and Marvin Robinson: http://spot.acorn.net/jfkplace/09/fp.back_issues/17th_issue/rambler_witness.html.

The Oswald Exhumation

524 Norton: "Oswald Grave Now Battle Site," *Fort Worth Star-Telegram*, Oct. 19, 1979.
525 Slawson: "Author Not the First to Ask Exhumation," *Fort Worth Star-Telegram*, Jan. 11, 1979.
525 Groody: author's interview, November 1988.
525 Marguerite Oswald: "Oswald's Mother Asks Exhumation," *Fort Worth Star-Telegram*, Nov. 17, 1967.
525 Robert Oswald: I.330–331.
526 Pic: XI.55–56.
526 Pic fails to recognize Lee: XI.65.
527 Groody: author's interview, 1988.
527 Saw cut: Linda E. Norton, James A. Cottone, Irvin M. Sopher, and Vincent J. M. DiMaio, "The Exhumation and Identification of Lee Harvey Oswald," *Journal of Forensic Sciences*, Vol. 29, No. 1, January 1984, p. 25.

Convenient Deaths

530 Whitaker: HSCA IV.464–465.
530 Hess: HSCA IV.467.
532 CIA memo: CIA memo to "Chiefs, Certain Stations and Bases" titled "Countering Criticism of the Warren Report, April 1, 1967," Document No. 1035–960.
532 Disguised murders: Philip H. Melanson, "High Tech Mysterious Deaths," *Critique*, Vol. 4, No. 3, 4, Fall/Winter 1984–1985, p. 214.
532 Beryllium: Ibid., p. 215.

Strange Deaths Continue

534 Sullivan: Jeff Goldberg and Harvey Yazijian, "The Death of 'Crazy Billy' Sullivan," *New Times*, July 24, 1978, pp. 4–8.
535 FBI deaths: "Ex-Agent 6th to Die in Six-month Span," *Fort Worth Star-Telegram*, Nov. 10, 1977.
536 Frustrated Cold Warrior: Peter Janney, *Mary's Mosaic: The CIA Conspiracy to Murder John F. Kennedy, Mary Pinchot Meyer, and Their Vision for World Peace*,

New York, Skyhorse Publishing, 2012, p. 181.

536 Only woman JFK respected: Janney, p. 207.

536 What seed changed JFK: Douglass, pp. 277–278.

537 St. John Hunt: author's interview, Nov. 22, 2010.

537 Same sons of bitches: David C. Heymann, *The Georgetown Ladies' Social Club*, New York, Atria Books, 2003, p. 168.

PART IV: CONCLUSIONS

Assassination Coverage

544 Kearns: Jerry Policoff, "The Media and the Murder of John Kennedy," *New Times*, Aug. 8, 1975, p. 31.

544 Unaided assassin: "Ruby Murder Trial Postponed," *Dallas Times Herald*, Dec. 3, 1963.

545 Slanted propaganda: Policoff, p. 30.

545 Biased offerings: Meagher, p. 459.

545 Donovan: Policoff, pp. 35–36.

546 Mob of reporters: Robert Oswald with Myrick and Barbara Land, *Lee: A Portrait of Lee Harvey Oswald*, New York, Coward-McCann, 1967, p. 23.

547 Press choices: Policoff, p. 36.

A Likely Scenario

548 Concerned with general welfare: http://news.google.com/newspapers?nid=1338&dat=19620510&id=xzJYAAAAIBAJ&sjid=SPcDAAAAIBAJ&pg=2728,2462469.

550 No one has to direct an assassination: L. Fletcher Prouty, "An Introduction to the Assassination Business," *Gallery*, September 1975, pp. 86–87.

554 Evelyn Lincoln: letter in author's files.

555 RFK quote: Davis, p. 603.

CROSSFIRE: THE PLOT THAT KILLED KENNEDY

NAME AND SUBJECT INDEX

Compiled by Jim Marrs and Maritha Gan,
with special thanks to
Stan Szerszen

Abadie, William,
  on Ruby's racket connections, 378
Abrams, Gus W., 323, 326
Accardo, Anthony (Chicago gangster),
  163–164, 373
Acoustical Studies, 61, 80–83, 339, 497–503,
  540–541
Adams, Francis W. H. (WC assistant
  counsel), 461, 449
Adams, Victoria (witness), 44, 55–56, 314
Agnew, Spiro, 253
Alba, Adrian Thomas (New Orleans garage
  operator), 213
Alcock, James L. (New Orleans assistant
  district attorney), 480–481
Alderson, Lawrence M., 192–193
Aleman, Jose, 160
Alexander, Lucia, 5
Alexander, William (Dallas assistant district
  attorney), 388, 406, 448
Alik (Oswald's name in Russian), 119
Allman, Pierce (journalist), 312
Alpha 66 (anti-Castro Cubans),
  connection with Oswald, 140–142, 178,
  238, 290
Alsop, Joseph (journalist), 68, 437
Altgens, James W. (Associated Press
  photographer and witness), 32–34,
  45–47, 51, 57, 551

Alyea, Tom (newsman), 417
Anastasia, Albert, 156
Anderson, Jack (journalist), 296, 377, 385,
  403
Andrews, Dean (New Orleans attorney),
  469, 480
"Angel" or "Angelo." *See* Odio, Silvia
Angel, Shari (Ruby stripper), 390, 394. *See
  also* Messrole, Bobbie Louise
Anglcton, James Jesus (CIA chief of
  counterintelligence), 182, 537
  and Nosenko (Soviet defector), 124–127
Angola State Prison, 145
Anti-Castro movement, 30, 89, 98–99, 103,
  122, 128–129, 132, 135–144, 147–150,
  159, 174, 175, 178, 182, 187, 188, 191,
  196, 211, 217, 220, 221, 235, 237, 239,
  240, 251, 252, 257, 260, 268, 290, 381,
  382, 399, 466, 469, 472, 474, 483, 484,
  488, 495, 517, 521, 523, 541, 548–551.
  See also Cuba
Applin, George J. (Texas Theater witness),
  Ruby in theater, 341–342
Arbenz, Jacobo, 129, 170
Arce, Danny G. (witness), 26
Archaca-Smith, Sergio, 138, 472, 478
Archer, Don Ray, 405
Armstrong, Andrew (Ruby club employee),
  398

Armstrong, John (author, *Harvey & Lee: How the CIA Framed Oswald*, 2003), 523–524

Arnold, Carolyn (witness). *See aka* Johnston, Carolyn

Arnold, Gordon (witness), 16, 79–80, 82, 310

ARRB, Assassination Records Review Board, 47, 71, 126, 134, 278, 362, 365, 460, 506–512, 514, 515, 542

ARTICHOKE (CIA behavior-modification program). *See* BLUEBIRD

Arvad, Inga, 206–207. *See* "Inga binga"

Aschkenasy, Ernest, 498–499

Assassination,
  evidence, 278–279, 297, 348–349, 350, 366, 417–450, 542, 553

Assassination theories,
  French connection, 192–199
  Garrison investigation, 466–485
  "one gunman" or more, 497–503
  Russian link, 123–127
  Single-bullet theory, 252, 316, 356, 362, 369, 424–425, 441, 443, 453, 455, 458–466
  Triple Underpass theory, 57–63
  "umbrella man," 29–35, 323, 478, 495

Atkins, Thomas (White House photographer and filmmaker of *The Last Two Days*, 1963, witness), 15, 16

Attwood, William, 135

Auchincloss, Mrs. Hugh D. (*aka* Mrs. Janet Bouvier, Jacqueline Kennedy's mother),
  on being DeMohrenschildt's friend, 264

Austin, Emory (witness), 331

Austin, Horace, 137

Autopsy of Kennedy, 351–356

Aynesworth, Hugh (Dallas journalist),
  on Garrison bribe, 506
  on Oswald's Diary, 87

Ayers, Bradley E. (CIA officer), 182

Azcue, Eusebio, 185

"Babushka lady" (witness), 16, 35–37, 147, 167, 174, 302, 325, 389, 394, 534, 543.
  See also Oliver, Beverly

Baden, Michael, 460

"Badge man,"
  evidence of uniformed officer on Grassy Knoll, 80–83

Bagshaw, Thomas (former Marine), 104

Bailey, Virgil (immigration officer ordered to pick up Frenchman), 197

Baker, Bobby. *See* Baker, Robert Gene

Baker, Judyth Vary (author, *Me and Lee*, 2010), 82, 143–148, 295, 414, 523, 532

Baker, T. L. (Dallas police lieutenant.), 321

Baker, Marrion L. (motorcycle police officer), 13, 52–56, 540

Baker, Mrs. Donald (witness), 27. *See also* Rachley, Virgie

Baker, Robert (Husband to Judyth Vary Baker), 147

Baker, Robert "Barney," 375, 396

Baker, Robert Gene "Bobby" (trusted friend of LBJ), 273–275, 540

Baker, William, 428

Ball, Joseph A. (WC attorney), 41, 44, 58, 78–79, 252, 311, 331, 342, 408, 449, 461

Banister, Guy (New Orleans investigator and former FBI agent),
  background of, 139, 220–221, 471, 540
  Banister apparatus, 469
  beats Jack Martin, 466
  connections, 174, 188, 191, 220
  death of, 139, 469, 474, 533
  with Maurice Brooks Gatlin, 220, 471, 533
  on Oswald, 174, 188, 191, 220–221
  also mentioned on pgs. 98, 144, 146, 175, 239, 517

Barbee, Emmett, 230

Barger, James Dr., 339, 497–499

Barka, Mehdi Ben, 194

Barker, Bernard L. (Watergate burglar), 130, 138

Barker, Ma, 204

Barnes, Tracy (CIA officer), 129, 175

Barr, Candy, 376

Barrett, Robert (FBI agent), 510

Bass, Jettie, 325

Batista, Fulgencio, 127, 128, 136, 138, 158, 159, 174, 379, 474

Bauman, Robert E., 489

Baumgartner, Alan (funeral director), 527

Baxter, Charles Dr. (Parkland witness), 535

Bay of Pigs Invasion, 4, 7, 30, 109, 129, 131–134, 138–139, 142, 159, 173–175, 190, 220, 238, 251–252, 282, 284, 318, 441, 472, 484–485, 517, 549

Beavers, William R. Dr., 410

Beck, Dave (Teamsters official), 157

Becker, Edward,
on Marcello threat, 155

Beers, Jack (Dallas news photographer), 416

Behn, Gerald (Secret Service agent, White House detail), 225

Belin, David (WC attorney),
intimidation of witness, 449, 454
with Lawyers for Nixon, 252
on LBJ, 463
"Rosetta Stone" to the JFK assassination, 330
on TSBD crime scene rearranged, 416
also mentioned on pgs. 19, 336, 501

Belknap, Jerry Boyd (TSBD seizure victim), 42–43

Bell, Jack (press reporter, the *New York Times*, November 23, 1963), 276–277

Belli, Melvin (author, *Dallas Justice*, 1964), 398, 406

Belmont, Alan H., 535

Benavides, Domingo (Tippit witness),
on Oswald's jacket, 336
Tippit shooting time, 338
also mentioned on pgs. 332–333, 533

Benavides, Eddie (brother to Domingo)
death of, 533

Bennett, Glen (Secret Service agent), 13

Bertrand, Clay (alias of Clay Shaw), 469, 474–475, 479–480

Bertrand, Clem (alias of Clay Shaw), 479–480

Betson, Hugh Dr., 482

Betzner, Hugh W. (witness), 22–23, 74

Bewley, Paul (Fort Worth Police officer), 272

Bielaski, Alexander Bruce, 200

Biffle, Kent (Dallas journalist), 304, 322, 388

Billet, Myron Thomas, 391

Billings, Richard (associate editor, *Life* magazine), 545

Binion, Benny "Cowboy," 325, 373

Bird, Christopher, 111

Bishop, Diane, 272

Bishop, Maurice (*possible aka* David Atlee Phillips), 140–142, 147, 188

Bissell, Richard M. Jr., 129–130

"Black dog man" (figure seen on Grassy Knoll), 74–75

Black, Hugo (Supreme Court Justice), 437

Blackwell, Tom (photo section)

Blakey, G. Robert (chief counsel and director for House Select Committee on assassinations, author, *The Plot to Kill the President*, 1981),
background of, 491
Backyard photographs, 433
association with CIA, 483, 493
"a cautious approach," 502
connection to Mob, 159, 167, 325, 492
on Garrison prosecution, 482–483, 485
and HSCA, 491, 494–495, 497, 501–502
on RFK's Organized Crime and Racketeering staff, 166–167
returns money to congress, 494
on "rigorous fact finding," 495
on Ruby eliminating Oswald, 398
on Ruby's Mob-connected trips, 380
on Santos Trafficante, 158, 380
on secrecy, 491–493
also mentioned on pgs. 155, 164, 460, 498, 499, 500

Blanch, Antonio Veciana (founder of Alpha 66), 140, 142, 147

Bloomfield, Louis Mortimer, 470–471

Bludworth, David (DeMohrenschildt), 266

BLUEBIRD, CIA behavior-modification program (*see also* ARTICHOKE), 171

Bocognoni (possible French hit-man of 3 hit-man team who is said to have assassinated JFK), 197–198

Bogard, Albert G. (car salesman), 518–519, 533

Boggs, Hale (Warren Commission Member, father of Cokie Roberts)
death, 441, 534
as WC critic, 441, 445
as WC member, 441, 462, 504
also mentioned on pgs. 216, 448, 451

Bolden, Abraham (Secret Service agent), 225–226

Bonanno, Joseph (gangster), 156, 164, 296

Bonanno, Salvatore "Bill" (son of Joseph), 296

Bonaparte, Charles J., 200

Bonnie and Clyde, 204, 273

Bonventre, John, 156

Bookbinder, George, 111

Bookhout, James W. (FBI), 53–54

Boone, Eugene L. (Dallas Deputy Sheriff), 418–419

Booth, John Wilkes, 224

Boster, Eugene (White House Soviet Affairs Officer), 118

Boswell, J. Thornton Dr. (chief of pathology at Bethesda Naval Hospital), 368, 371

Botelho, James Judge (Oswald roommate), on Oswald as American intelligence agent, 107–108, 180

Bothun, Richard O. "Dick," (the *Dallas Morning News*, November 23, 1963-photo section)

Boudreaux, Mrs. Anne, 452

Bouvier, Jackie. *See* Kennedy, Jacqueline

Bouvier, John V. "Jack," 258

Bouvier, Mrs. Janet (*aka* Mrs. Hugh D. Auchincloss), on being DeMohrenschildt's friend, 258

Bowen, John Howard (*aka* John Bowen), 189

Bowers, Lee Jr. (Railroad supervisor, witness),
sees men with radios, 77–79, 84
sees three men in RR car, 322, 533
Warren Commission, 453

Bowie, Jim (assistant DA), 408

Bowles, J. C. (Dallas radio room supervisor), 339

Bowley, T. F. (Tippit witness), 338

Bowron, Diana (Parkland nurse), 354

Boyle, Tony, 487

Braden, Jim (Mafia courier), 167, 327–329

Brading, Eugene Hale. *See* Braden, Jim

Bradlee, Benjamin (journalist), 537

Bradlee, Tony (sister of Mary Meyer), 537

Bradley, Edgar Eugene, 478

Brandt, Willy, 170

Branyon, John D., 214

Breen, James, 378

Brehm, Charles (witness), 16, 34, 35, 37, 63, 313, 452, 543

Breneman, Chester (Dallas surveyor), 433–435, 455, 511

Brennan, Howard Leslie (witness), 25, 26, 28, 309

Brennan, James (NYC attendance officer), 523

Brewer, Johnny (Oak Cliff shoe store manager), 340–342

Bright, H. R. "Bum" (Dallas Cowboys owner), 237

Bringuier, Carlos (head of the New Orleans Cuban Student Directorate), 137–139, 141, 145, 191, 220, 237

Bronson, Charles L. (witness), 21

Brooks, Jerry Milton (The *Dallas Morning News*, November 23, 1963), 220

Broshears, Raymond, 472

Browder, Edward (gun runner), 263, 379

Brown, Arnold (FBI special agent), 210

Brown, Earle V. (Dallas police officer), 61, 84

Brown, George (Brown & Root Construction), 261, 270

Brown, Herman (Brown & Root Construction), 261, 270

Brown, Joe B. Judge (Ruby's trial), 406, 533

Brown, Madeleine Duncan (LBJ's mistress, author, *Texas in the Morning*, 1977),
first meeting with Ruby, 375
LBJ's foreknowledge, 278
Ruby's early mention of Oswald, 388
also mentioned on pgs. 16, 394

Brown, Morgan, 328

Brown, Mrs. G. Stanley, 115

Brown, Pat, 248

Brugioni, Dino, 511–512

Bruneau, Emile, 137

Bruno, Jerry (White House aide), 226–227

Brutus (*Julius Caesar*, Shakespeare), 549, 555

Buccilli, Paul, 391

Buchanan, James P., 270

Bucknell, David (Marine buddy of Oswald), 102–103, 107–108

Bugliosi, Vincent (LA prosecutor, author, *Reclaiming History*, 2007), 460, 505–506, 531

Bundy, McGeorge, 462

Bundy, Vernon, 479

Burkley, George G. Dr. (JFK's physician),
on conspiracy, 362, 367, 509
on Jackie's request for Bethesda, 359
also mentioned on pg., 452

Burris, Howard Col. (LBJ's military aide), 550

Burroughs, W. H. "Butch" (Texas Theatre employee),
on double entries, 342–343
also mentioned on pgs. 340, 453

Butler, Ed (New Orleans broadcaster), 138

Butler, George Lt. (Dallas police officer),
suspicions of, 373–374
also mentioned on pg., 452

Butler, Ron (FBI agent), 300–301

Cabell, Charles P. (Air Force Gen., brother of Dallas mayor Earle Cabell),
   as Deputy Director of the CIA during the Bay of Pigs,
   brands JFK a "traitor," 7
   death of, 534
   fired by JFK, 7, 133
   introduced by Clay Shaw, 472
   also mentioned on pg., 131, 375, 549, 550
Cabell, Earle (Dallas mayor),
   death of, 534
   also mentioned on pgs. 7, 405, 549
Cabell, Mrs. Earle,
   smelled gunpowder, 7, 14
Cabluck, Harry (news photographer), 305
Cadigan, James C (FBI fingerprint expert), 222, 349–350, 535, 543
Caldera, C. B. (Neely St. neighbor to Oswald), 392, 394
Callahan, Mike (Dallas Deputy Constable), 394
Calloway, Ted (witness), 331
Calvery, Mrs. Gloria (witness), 27, 46
Campbell, Don J. (advertising, *Dallas Morning News*), 315
Campbell, Judy (*aka* Judith Exner), 164
Campbell, Ochus V. (Texas Book Depository vice president), 26–27
Campisi, Joseph (alleged Dallas gangster), 376–377
CAP. S*ee* Civil Air Patrol
Capone, Al (gangster), 371, 377
Caracci, Frank, 376
Carlin, Karen Bennett "Little Lynn,"
   death of, 533
   money order from Ruby, 389, 400–401
Carlos (Cuban exile mentioned by David Ferry), 472
Caro, Robert (author), 273
Carolla, Sam (gangster), 154–155
Carr, Richard Randolph (witness),
   threats on, 20, 308–309, 543
   also mentioned on pgs. 223, 453
Carr, Waggoner (Texas attorney general), 215, 252, 437, 445, 448, 465
Carrico, Charles J. Dr. (Parkland physician), 352, 368
Carswell, Daniel, 323
Carter, Amon Jr., 91–92, 323
Carter, Amon Sr., 377
Carter, Clifton C. (LBJ aide), 149, 273, 277, 294, 346, 348, 407, 429

Carter, George (police reporter, the *Dallas Times Herald*), 196, 215
Carter, John, 387
Carter, Tom, 209
Cary, Goerge L, 190
Cascio, Nick, 325
Cash, Ben (Dallas Deputy Constable), 394–395
Castro, Fidel,
   assassination plots against, 133, 140–142, 146, 158–159, 165, 171, 173, 174, 181, 196, 220, 485
   Bay of Pigs Invasion, 129–133
   on JFK assassination, 135, 147–149, 412, 550
   and organized crime, 159, 248, 377, 379, 381, 383
   personal biography, 127–129
   also mentioned on pgs. 4, 135, 138, 175, 240, 263, 284, 287, 290, 291, 322, 377, 382, 548
Castro, Juanita, 128
Catena, Gerardo, 156
Cellar (nightspot in Fort Worth), 272, 298, 401
   Secret Service drinking, 229–234
Cellini, Dino, 158, 377
Cellini, Eddie, 158
Central Intelligence Agency. *See* CIA
Chagra, Jimmy, 326
Chagra, Joe, 326
Chamberlain, Neville, 31
Chaney, Alton, 178–179
Chaney, James M. (motorcycle officer), 12, 452, 534, 543
Charles, Clemard, 263
Chavez, Frank, 376
Cheasty, John Cye, 157
Cheek, Bertha, 387
Cheramie, Rose (*aka* Melba Christine Marcades)
   foresees assassination, 386–389
   also mentioned on pgs. 394, 533
Chetta, Nicholas (New Orleans coroner), 534
Chism, John A. (witness), 28–29
Chism, Mrs. John A. (witness), 28
Chrisman, Fred Lee, 323
Christian, John, 297–298, 302, 550
Chotiner, Murray, 247–248
Church Committee Investigation, 178, 532, 534

Churchill, Winston, 470
CIA (Central Intelligence Agency),
  and anti-Castro Cubans, 138–140
  and the Bay of Pigs 129–138
  CIA-backed Cuban Revolutionary
    Council, 98, 129, 138–140, 142, 187,
    211, 220
  Document No., 632–769, 192–193
  history of, 167–171
  Item 450, 70–71
  and Mafia death plots, 173–174
  and mind control experiments, 171–173
  and Nosenko (Soviet defector), 124–126
  Oswald as Agent, 36, 101–103, 122, 141
  Zapruder film, 68–71
  ZR/RIFLE project, 147, 194–198
Cinque, Ralph C., 45, 47
Civello, Joseph (gangster), 155–156, 376,
  380
Civil Air Patrol, CAP
  and Oswald, 97, 98, 139, 156, 174, 220,
    328, 482
Claasen, Fred, 148
Clark, Ed (attorney to LBJ), 269, 294
Clark, Kyle G., 211
Clark, Max, 260
Clark, Ramsey, 367, 475
Clark, William Kemp Dr. (Parkland director
    of neurological surgery),
  description of head wound, 367–368
  description of neck wound, 367
  pronounces JFK dead, 352
Claude, Alfred, 214
Claunch, Max, 242–243
Claverie, Marguerite (Marguerite Oswald's
    maiden name), 90, 94
Clemons, Acquilla (Tippit witness), 309,
  332, 543
Cleveland, Grover, 224
Clifton, Chester Gen.,
  orders Walter Reed autopsy, 358
Coalition on Political Assassinations
  (COPA), 514
Coffee, Melvin,
  accompanied Ferrie to Houston, 214
Cohen, Mickey (gangster), 155, 248, 376
Cohn, Roy, 164
"Coke" (Oswald Coca-Cola issue), 52–54
Colby, William (CIA official), 171, 281
Coleman William T. Jr. (WC attorney), 102,
  450, 461
Coleman, Kay. See aka Kay, Kathy

Coleman, Walter Kirk, 242
Collom, Mark (co-author, The Man on the
    Sixth Floor, 1995), 293
Colson, Charles, 198, 479
Compton, Jerry, 499
Condon, Richard, 171
Condon, Robert L., 207
Conein, Lucien "Black Luigi," 195, 198, 285
Conforto, Janet Adams "Jada," 389–390
Connally, John B. Jr. (Texas Governor),
  on assassination, 8–15
  on knowing Ruby, 272
  Connally's clothing, 429
  Democratic Party rift, 6–7
  at Parkland Hospital, 352–355, 367
  in motorcade, 8, 11–12
  "single-bullet" theory, 356–358, 455,
    458–466
  spectrographic analysis, 424–425
  testimony to Warren Commission, 11
  also mentioned on pgs. 5, 14, 23, 26, 59,
    62, 63, 65, 67, 226–229, 236, 271, 274,
    346, 377, 393, 394, 450, 453, 478, 541
Connally, Mrs. John B. Jr. "Nellie,"
  in motorcade, 8, 10–12, 15
Connor, Pete (former Marine), 104
Conservatives in Dallas politics, 1
Conspiracy theories. See Assassination
  theories
Cook, Chuck (Dallas newsman), 324
Cooke, Leon R., 372, 375
Cooley, Sherman (former Marine),
  on Oswald as "Shitbird," 100
Coolidge, Calvin, 214
Cooper, John Sherman (WC member), 441,
  450, 451, 462
Cooper, Roy, 505, 524
Cooper, William, 229
COPA, Coalition on Political
  Assassinations, 514
Costello, Frank (gangster), 154–156, 164,
  273
Couch, Malcolm O. (TV cameraman), 315
Cox, Archibald, 437, 440
Crafard, Larry (Ruby employee), 389
Craig, Roger Dean (deputy sheriff and
    witness),
  actions on Nov. 19, 308, 318–321
  also mentioned on pgs. 417, 418, 453,
    454, 505, 506, 524, 543
Crawford, Joan, 250, 407
Crawford, John, 534

Cronkite, Walter, 279, 545–546

Crow, Jim, 439

Crowe, William D. Jr. (*aka* Bill DeMar, Ruby entertainer),
tells of Oswald in club, 388

Crump, Raymond Jr. (accused of murdering of Mary Meyer), 537

Cuba,
Anti-Castro movement in United States, 138–143
Banister and anti-Castro Cubans, 98
Bay of Pigs, 127–129
CIA-backed Cuban Revolutionary Council, 98, 129, 136–138, 140, 142, 187, 211, 220
and CIA-Mafia death plots, 173–174
Fidel Castro, 127–128
history of, 127
and Jack Ruby, 379–385
and organized crime, 158–160
Shaw's "umbrella man" theory, 30

Cubela, Rolando, 173–174

Cummings, Raymond, 388

Curington, John W. (aide to H. L. Hunt), 257

Curry, Eileen, 378

Curry, Jesse (Dallas police chief),
after assassination, 221, 306, 351–352
on fake Secret Service agents, 314
on JFK's security, 227
and man in doorway, 46
in motorcade, 8, 12
on Oswald's death, 525–526
on Oswald's innocence, 47
on Rifle substitution, 419
photo of Roger Craig, 321
on Ruby/Oswald connection, 396
on taking of evidence, 239, 347–348
also mentioned on pgs. 56, 88, 181, 205, 227, 295, 526

Curry, Tim (Tarrant County DA), 525

Cushing, Richard Cardinal, 478

Cushman, Robert E. Jr., 130

Custer, Jerrol F. (Bethesda x-ray technician), 364, 365

Cutler, Robert (researcher),
"umbrella man" theory, 29–30

Czolgosz, Leon F. (lone assassin of President William McKinley in 1901), 241

D'Amelio, Carlo, 470

Daley, Richard, 163

Dalitz, Morris "Moe," 164

Dallas,
Kennedy's trip, 5–7
Police Radio Recording, 497–503
Political climate, 1

The *Dallas Morning News,*
day of assassination, 6–7
and Robert Groden, 21

Dallas Times Herald
Day of assassination, 6, 329

Dallek, Robert (professor of History), 82

Damaris, Ovid, 163

Daniel, Jack (witness), 351–352

Daniel, Jean (journalist),
Castro's reaction to assassination, 135

Dannelly, Mrs. Lee (Selective Service official), 518

Darby, Nathan (Austin Police Dept.), 294

David, Christian (French gangster), 194–198

David, Dennis, 368

Davis, 195, 381

Davis, Avery (witness), 315

Davis, Barbara (witness), 336

Davis, Jack, 343

Davis, John H. (Kennedy relative and author, *The Kennedys*, 1984), 163, 173, 244

Davis, Robert (CIA station chief), 132

Davis, Thomas Eli III,
with Jack Ruby, 195–196
also mentioned on pgs. 381, 534

Davison, Captain, 122

Davison, Natasha, 122

Day, John Carl Lt. (Dallas Police crime lab), 416, 417, 419, 422–424

De Brueys, Warren (FBI special agent), 137, 180, 211–212

de Gaulle, Charles, 194, 471

DeLorean, John, 479

De Menil, Jean, 260

Dealey, George Bannerman, 9

Dealey Plaza (site of first Masonic Lodge in Dallas), 9–10, 13–16

Dean, Harry J., 181

Dean, John (Nixon aide), 252

Dean, Patrick T. (Dallas police officer), 356

Decker, J. E. "Bill" (Dallas County Sheriff),
  death of, 534
  in motorcade, 8, 12, 351
  also mentioned on pgs. 18, 61, 87, 88,
    318, 319, 321, 408, 414
Dejanovich, Owen (Marine with Oswald),
  106
del Valle, Eladio (associated with Ferrie),
  474
Delaune, Henry, 534
Delgado, Nelson (former Marine), 100, 106,
  136
Delillo, Don (author, Libra, 1988), 97
Deloach, Cartha D. (FBI official), 208, 250,
  442
DeLorean, John, 479
DeLucia, Felice. See aka Ricca, Paul
DeMar, Bill. See aka Crowe, William D. Jr.
DeMohrenschildt, George S. (aka Philip
  Harbin, last known close contact of
  Lee Oswald),
  background, 258–268
  on Backyard photograph, 266–267
  discusses, Russian literature with Oswald,
    522
  relationship with CIA, 189–192
  also mentioned on pgs. 16, 180, 264–267,
    535, 540
DeMohrenschildt, Jeanne,
  on Oswald's language, 522
  on Oswald in Russia, 260–262
  also mentioned on pgs. 16, 117, 522, 535
The Depository. See Texas School Book
  Depository (TSBD)
DeSimone, Frank, 156
Deslatte, Oscar, 517
DePugh, Robert, 307
Dewey, Thomas E., 152, 153, 207, 247, 438
di Spadaforo, Gutierrez, 470
Diallo, Syedou, 135
Diamond, Legs, 152
Didenko, Nikolai, 119
Diehl, Harold Dr., 143
Diem, 198, 284, 285, 286
Dillard, Tom C. (news photographer), 55, 64
Dirksen, Everett, 437
Dodd, Christopher, 492
Dodd, Richard C. (witness), 59–60, 452
Donahue, Howard (ballistics expert), 234
Donovan, Hedley, 545
Donovan, William "Wild Bill," 168
Dorfman, Allen, 248

Dorfman, Paul J., 157, 392
Dorfman, Rose, 157
Dorman, Mrs. Elsie, 44
Dostoevski, Fyodor Mikhailovich, 522
Dougherty, Jack E. (TSBD employee), 41,
  428
Douglas, Helen, 247
Douglass, James W. (author, JFK and the
  Unspeakable, 2008), 267, 345, 485, 536
Dowell, Pat (film critic, the Washingtonian),
  504
Dowling, Mary (Dobbs House waitress),
  452
Dowling, Richard, 467
Downing, Thomas N. (Representative),
  and formation of HSCA, 486, 487, 489,
    501
Doyle, Harold, 323, 326
Drain, Vincent "Vince" (FBI special agent),
  Drain's conflicting report, 222, 428
  Oswald's palm print, 422–423
  takes assassination evidence, 422
Duff, William McEwan (Gen. Walker
  employee), 240
Dukel, Lawrence Alan. See aka Mack, Gary
Dulles, Allen W. (CIA Director fired by
  Kennedy and WC member),
  Bay of Pigs invasion, 128–138
  as CIA director, 169–171
  destroy WC record, 216–217
  mind control, 128–130
  "nobody reads," 216, 461
  on Oswald as agent, 216–217, 447–449
  on psychological profile, 460–462
  also mentioned on pgs. 68, 347, 441, 445,
    450, 536, 550
Dulles, John Foster,
  CIA and United Fruit, 170–171
Duran, Silvia Tirado de,
  arrest of, 140, 183–185
Duvalier, Francois "Papa Doc" (Haitian
  president), 263–264
Dyson, W. F. (Dallas police officer), 370

Eaglesham, Allan, 297
Eames, Mrs. Doris (neighbor of Oswald in
  New Orleans), 99
Eastland, James O., 437
Ebert, Robert (journalist, Chicago Sun-
  Times), 504
Echevarria, Homer S. (Cuban militant), 141
Echeverria, Louis, 170

Eddowes, Michael (British author),
    impersonation and exhumation of
    Oswald, 521–528
Edwards, Robert E. (witness), 22
Egeter, Betty, 182
Ehrlichman, John, 252
Eisenberg, Melvin A. (WC attorney),
    349–350, 440
Eisenhower, Dwight "Ike,"
    authorizes covert action against Cuba,
    129–131
    with Khrushchev, 109
    "military-industrial complex," 280–281
    also mentioned on pgs. 3, 4, 228, 235,
    247, 248, 256, 289, 439, 445
Ekdahl, Edwin A., 91, 95
Ellis, Starvis, 12
Ellsberg, Daniel, 111
Ellsworth, Frank, 314
Ely, John Hart, 458
English, J. M., 535
Epstein, Edward Jay (author), 102, 120,
    125, 173, 190, 266, 441
Estes, Billie Sol (LBJ associate), 275, 294,
    504
Euins, Amos Lee (TSBD witness), 25–26
Evans, Courtney, 208
Evica, George Michael (researcher), 242
Exchange Stabilization Fund, 169, 255
Executive Order #11110 (EO-11110),
    254–255
Exner, Judith (aka Judy Campbell),
    with Jack Kennedy, 164–165

Factor, Lawrence Lloyd "Loy," 293
Fain, John W. (FBI agent), 209–210
Fall, Albert B., 256
Farris, Tom (FBI agent), 300–301
FBI. See also Federal Bureau of
    Investigations,
    Commission Document 1245, 42
    history of, 199–201
    and Julia Ann Mercer, 16–17, 454
    manipulation of assassination
    investigation, 221–223, 422–423,
    428
    search for Oswald in 1959, 117–118
    and Tague testimony, 62–63
    and witness Ed Hoffman, 83–87
    also mentioned on pgs. 199–234
Fedora (KGB Defector Code Name),
    124

Fedorenko, Nikolai T., 126
Fenley, Bob (reporter Dallas Times Herald),
    215
Fenner, Nancy (FBI receptionist), 217
Fensterwald, Bernard (researcher), 487
Fenton, Cliff, 496
Ferrie, David W.,
    with Judyth Baker, 144–148
    background and death, 472–474,
    533–534
    544 Camp Street, 138–139
    connections, 239–240, 328, 466, 471
    Ferrie as CIA agent, 174–175, 540, 550
    Garrison investigation, 214, 466–468,
    472–485
    Oswald's library card, 98–101
    in Ruby's club, 36, 388–389
    also mentioned on pgs. 155, 156, 167,
    188, 191, 220, 268
Fetzer, James H. PhD., 45
Fiester, Sherry (author, Enemy of the Truth:
    Myth, Forensics, and the Kennedy
    Assassination, 2012), 427, 460
Files, James (aka James Sutton), 179,
    294–297
Finck, Pierre (Army Lt. Colonel, Bethesda
    Naval Hospital coroner), 359–360
Fischer, Ronald B. (witness), 22, 454
Fisher, Dr. Russell, 367
Fithian, Floyd J., 426
FitzGerald, Desmond, 173
Fitzsimmons, Frank, 157
Fleming, Ian, 136, 179
Florer, Larry,
    arrested in Dal-Tex bldg., 327
Flynn, Charles W. (FBI agent), 219,
    383–384
Flynn, William J., 200
Folsom, Allison G. Jr., 469
Fonzi, Gaeton (HSCA investigator), 489,
    490–492, 496
Ford, Gerald R. "Jerry" (WC member),
    as FBI informant, 442, 552
    Jack Ruby interview, 408
    also mentioned on pgs. 82, 157, 253, 362,
    450, 451, 462, 544
Ford, Trowbridge (researcher), 249
Fortas, Abe, 437, 441, 463
Foster, J. W. (Dallas police officer),
    and Triple Underpass, 57–60, 88, 306
    on bullet in grass, 304
Fowler, Clayton, 534

Frankfurter, Felix, 450
Frazier, Wesley (Oswald companion),
    on assassination, 44–46
    curtain rod story, 41
    paper sack, 427–428
    also mentioned on pgs. 40, 534
French Connection,
    to Kennedy assassination, 192–199
Freyss, Pierre, 258
Fritz, Will (Dallas homicide captain),
    arrival at TSBD, 303–304, 417
    with Lt. Francis Fruge, 385–386
    interview with Oswald, 47
    Left out of motorcade, 227
    on Mauser rifle, 419–420
    Oswald denies backyard photos, 430
    order to move Oswald, 402
    Roger Craig in Fritz' office, 320–321
    Testimony to Warren Commission, 53
    also mentioned on pgs. 219, 319, 347,
        348, 358
Fruge, Francis Lt. (LA State Police),
    385–386
Fuller, Mrs. Ross (mother of injured child),
    355
Fuller, Ronald (injured child at Parkland),
    355

Galbraith, John Kenneth, 277
Galloway, Calvin (Admiral), 509
Gambino, Carlo (gangster), 156
Gandy, Helen, 207
Garfield, James A., xv, 224
Garner, Darrell W., 534
Garner, Mrs. Jesse (Oswald's landlady in
    New Orleans), 99
Garner, Dorothy Ann (witness), 44,
    55–56
Garrison, Earling Carothers "Jim" (New
    Orleans district attorney). See also
    Garrison Investigation
    conspiracy theory of, 70, 139, 174,
        466–487
    on Gerald Ford and CIA, 442
    A Heritage of Stone, 214
    on NASA, 214
    also mentioned on pgs. 17, 98, 146–147,
        240, 260, 328, 388, 454, 503–505, 531,
        533–534
Garrison Investigation, 466–487
Gatlin, Maurice Brooks (Banister
    employee), 220, 471, 533

"Gator" (possible CIA field operative),
    177–178
Gaudet, William George (CIA employee),
    187–188, 384
Gearhart, Ira D. (warrant officer, codenamed
    "Bag man" or "Football," presidential
    launch code carrier), 276
Gedney, John Forester, 323, 326
Gehlen, Reinhard, 259
Genna Brothers, 163
Genovese, Vito (gangster), 152, 156, 162,
    273
Gervais, Pershing, 482–483
Giancana, Angeline, 164
Giancana, Sam "Momo" (Momo Salvatore
    Guingano),
    background of, 163–166
    death of, 534–535
    Jack Ruby connections, 373–374, 377
    at Ruby's club, 391
    also mentioned on pgs. 133, 157, 160,
        381, 385, 396, 550
Gibson, Donald (professor/author, Battling
    Wall Street: The Kennedy Presidency,
    1994), 268
Gibson, John, 341
Gibson, Lois, 323
Gill, C. Wray (New Orleans attorney), 99
Gillin, Edward (New Orleans assistant
    district attorney), 172
Givens, Charles (TSBD witness), 543
Glover, Everett, 262
Goering, Hermann, 206
Goldberg, Alfred Dr., 461
Goldman, David, 471
Goldstein, David, 533
Goldwater, Barry (senator), 77, 135
Golovachev, P. Y. (Hero of the Soviet Union
    General, father of Pavel), 116
Golovachev, Pavel (friend of Oswald in
    Russia), 116
Golz, Earl (Dallas newsman), 20–21, 181,
    187, 334–335, 395, 546
Gonzalez, Reinaldo, 141–142
Gonzalez, Henry (Congressman),
    Connally's clothing, 277, 429
    HSCA, 429, 485–491
Goodrich, Herbert F., 450
Goodwin, Richard, 278
Google, Barney, 371
Gorbachev, Mikhail, 554
Gossett, B. D., 319

Gottlieb, Sidney Dr., 171–172
Grammer, Billy R., 400
Granady, Octavious, 163
Granello, Salvatore, 159, 534
Grant, Eva (Jack Ruby's sister), 295, 357, 371, 367
Grassy Knoll,
  and Gordon Arnold, 79–80, 82
  and Lee Bowers (RR man), 77–79, 82
  defined, 66
  and Ed Hoffman, 83–88
  Holland's eyewitness report, 82–83
  Julie Ann Mercer, 16–17
  and one-gunman theory, 293–302
  shots heard from, 13, 15, 18, 20, 22, 23, 39, 75
  smoke smelled and seen on, 15, 58–61
  also mentioned on pgs. xvi, 10, 17, 27–31, 34, 35, 37, 38, 44, 46, 62, 68, 69, 72–74, 81, 88, 179, 192, 197, 303, 305, 309, 310, 312–314, 316, 318, 319, 329, 415, 452, 456, 498–501, 534, 537, 540, 551
Graves, L. C. (Dallas detective), 404
Gray, L. Patrick, 492
Green, Hollis de Lois, 325
Greer, William (Secret Service agent),
  applies brakes, 11, 228
  Wm. Cooper alleges possible shooter, 229
  in motorcade, 8, 10
  Parkland Hospital, 351–352
Gregory, Charles Dr. (Connally's physician), 534
Gregory, Dick,
  on Tramp picture, 323
  on Zapruder film release, 70
Griffin, Burt (WC attorney), 385, 387, 396, 408, 450, 454
Griffin, Will Hayden (Dallas FBI agent), 212
Grinnan, Joseph, 237
Groden, Robert (researcher),
  autopsy photos altered, 369–370, 501–502
  on Charles Bronson film, 21
  on Zapruder film release, 70
Gromyko, Andrei, 129
Groody, Paul (funeral director),
  FBI placed Oswald's dead hand on rifle, 422–423
  Secret Service questions Oswald's identity, 525
  new questions on Oswald body, 527–528

Gruber, Al (Ruby associate), 376
Guerini, Meme, 197
Guevara, Ernesto "Che" 128
Guingano, Momo Salvatore, 173
Guinn, Vincent P. Dr. (WC expert), 425–427
Guiteau, Charles, xv
Gurfein, Murray, 153
Guthrie, Steve (Dallas County sheriff), 373–374

Habighorst, Aloysius J. (New Orleans jailer), 480–481
Haffenden, Charles Radcliffe, 153
Haggerty, Edward Aloysius (New Orleans judge), 480–481
Haig, Alexander, 252
Haire, Bernard J. (Oswald arrest witness), 344
Haldeman, H. R., 251–252
Haley, J. Evetts, 271, 274, 411
Halfen, Jack, 273
Hall, Hampton, 528–529
Hall, Kermit (ARRB board member), 507
Hall, Tammany, 150
Hamblen, C. A., 215, 219
Hamilton, Charles A., 411
Hanson, Lars, 229
Hardie, Julius (witness), 17
Hardiman, James (New Orleans mailman), 479
Hargis, Bobby W. (police officer),
  in motorcade, 13
  splattered with blood, 13–14, 75
Harkness, D. V. (Dallas police sergeant), 42, 311, 322
Harper, Billy (recovered skull fragment), 307
Harrelson, Charles Voyde (convicted Texas hit man), 36, 323–326, 377
Harrelson, Jo Ann (Charles Harrelson's wife), 324
Harrelson, Woody, 36, 324
Harris, Larry (researcher), 339
Harrison, John F. (Dallas Police reservist and JFK assassination researcher), 294
Harrison, Richard E. "Dick" (FBI special agent), 423
Hartman, Edna (witness), 305
Hartman, Wayne (witness), 305

Hartogs, Renatus Dr. (psychiatrist who examined Oswald as an 11 year old boy), 96

Harvey, William (CIA official), 147, 173, 175, 196, 534, 537, 550

Haslam, Edward T. (author, *Dr. Mary's Monkey*, 2007), 147–148

Hathaway, Phillip B. (witness), 16

Haygood, Clyde A., 62–63

Hearst, Patty, 414

Helms, Richard (CIA Deputy Director), ZR/RIFLE, 195
  DeMorenschildt reports, 189–190, 259
  also mentioned on pgs. 124, 171–172, 174, 182, 195, 471

Hemming, Gerry Patrick, 103, 136, 180, 383

Henderson, Ruby (witness), 20

A Heritage of Stone (book), 214–215

Hernandez (man with Oswald and Robert McKeown), 382

Hess, Jacqueline, 530

Hester, Patricia (Dallas photo developer), 431

Hester, Robert (Dallas photo developer), 431

Heymann, C. David (author, *The Georgetown Ladies' Social Club*, 2004), 537

Hickey, George W. Jr. (Secret Service agent), 84, 234

Hidell, Alek James (Oswald alias *aka* Alek and A. J.),
  as president of Fair Play for Cuba Committee, 137, 211
  false ID in name of, 262, 344
  in military intelligence files, 288, 292
  Dallas Police and FBI letter, 219
  rifle ordered by, 262, 419–420
  also mentioned on pgs. 298, 334, 349

Hill, Clinton J. "Clint" (Secret Service agent assigned to Mrs. Kennedy), 12–13, 15, 228, 352, 368

Hill, Gerald (Dallas police sergeant), 333, 340

Hill, Jean (witness),
  in Dealey Plaza, 15, 37–38, 312–313
  sees Jack Ruby in Dealey Plaza, 316
  and Secret Service agents, 58, 223, 313
  Warren Commission treatment, 453, 456, 543
  also mentioned on pgs. xvi, 62, 82

Hill, Jimmy, 231

Hilsman, Roger, 284

Himmler, Heinrich, 201

Hine, Geneva L. (witness), 52
  on electricity going off at TSBD, 43–44

Hiss, Alger, 247

Hitler, Adolf, 206

Hoffa, James Riddle "Jimmy,"
  on background, 160–162
  Paul J. Dorfman, 157
  Nixon pardons, 162, 249
  and organized crime, 158–160, 248
  payoffs to LBJ, 273
  also mentioned on pgs. 247, 375, 376, 377, 478, 534

Hoffman, Virgil Edward "Ed" (witness),
  background and testimony, 83–88
  warned by FBI, 223, 309, 543
  also mentioned on pgs. xvi, 234, 304

Hoffman, Robert (Dallas policeman, relative of Ed Hoffman), 85

Holland, Sam M. (witness), 58–60, 82–83, 310, 318, 452, 454

Hollingsworth, Bob (*Times Herald* reporter), 9

Holt, Chauncey (*aka* Charles Frederick Rogers), 323, 330

Holt, Gloria Jeanne (witness), 57

Hood, Bill, 182

Hoover, Annie M. Scheitlin, 201

Hoover, Dickerson N., 201

Hoover, J. Edgar (Director of the FBI),
  on Inga Arvad, 2, 3, 206
  background of, 200–201
  bullets strike on curb, 64
  comparison of Walker bullet, 242
  FBI involvement, 209, 213–214, 216, 218, 222–223, 279, 346, 349, 436, 445, 449, 457, 540, 552–554
  Hoover's reluctance to pursue Mafia, 203–206, 550
  Hoover reports assassination to RFK, 166, 346
  KGB defector "Fedora," 124
  as LBJ's neighbor, 207–208, 223–224, 276
  Louis Mortimer Bloomfield, 470–471
  Martin L. King, 207, 243–244
  Mannlicher-Carcano, 421–422
  Masters of Deceit (book), 202
  Oswald as FBI informant, 214–215, 448–450
  Oswald imposter, 116–118, 209, 516, 525

"printing error" (reversing Zapruder frames), 69
Ruby as FBI informant, 219, 383
Ruby's polygraph exam, 410
Spectrography tests, 242, 425–426
also mentioned on pgs. 39, 124, 145, 154, 163–165, 196, 199, 236, 251, 291, 441–442, 534–535, 540, 546
Horne, Douglas P. (author, *Inside the Records and Review Board*, 2009),
ARRB, 365, 507
on autopsy, 365–366, 507–509
on single bullet theory, 460
on Zapruder tampering, 507–513
Hosty, James P. Jr. (FBI agent),
Oswald interview, 53–54
destruction of Oswald note, 214, 217–218, 223, 237, 287
Oswald known to FBI, 205, 214
on omission of Oswald connection with Hosty, 214, 314, 451
with Army Intelligence officer, 287, 516
also mentioned on pgs. 125, 219
House Select Committee on Assassination (HSCA),
on Altgens photo, 46
on ammunition used at assassination, 28, 61, 242, 306, 420, 424–425
acoustical studies, 61, 339, 500, 541
Bronson film, 21
conclusions of, 186, 192, 199, 234, 316, 387, 402, 450, 482
conspiracy theory, 91, 326
on Edward Browder, 263
and G. Robert Blakey (chief counsel and director), 166, 483, 491–497
on gunman issue, 460–491
history of, 31, 485–491
investigation scaled down, 495
Kennedy's assassination, 156
and Kennedy's wounds, 24–25, 360, 366, 368, 369
on Lovelady in doorway, 46
and Milteer's assassination plot, 245
and Moorman photograph, 80–82, 540
non-disclosure agreement, 492–494
on Oswald murder, 265, 398–400
on Soviet government, 114–115, 121, 126
on Tippit murder, 552
on "umbrella man," 29–31
also mentioned on pgs. 28, 36, 43, 55, 74, 80, 98, 103, 111, 113, 115, 119, 139,

140, 155, 160, 164, 182, 187, 190, 196, 212, 213, 218, 226, 265, 266, 272, 288, 289, 314, 318, 324, 328, 352, 357, 377, 378, 380, 381, 383, 384, 386, 387, 396, 398, 400, 413, 426, 531
Houston, Lawrence, 133, 165
Howard, Larry (researcher), 335
Howard, Tom, 195, 398, 402, 406, 553
Howe, Kenneth, 218
HSCA. *See* House Select Committee on Assassinations
HT-Lingual (CIA mail intercept program), 190
Hubert, Leon D. (WC assistant counsel), 21, 385, 387, 396, 408, 450, 461
Hudkins, Alonzo (newsman), 448, 452
Hudson, Emmett J. (witness), 73–75, 82
Hughes, Howard, 160, 248
Hughes, Robert J. (witness), 20–21
Hughes, Sarah T. (Federal Judge), 276, 358
Hull, Cordell, 220
Humes, James J. (Navy Commander, autopsy doctor), 359–362, 365–367, 495–496, 509
Humphrey, Hubert H., 3, 276
Hundley, William, 223
Hunt, David (brother to St. John), 537
Hunt, E. Howard (CIA officer),
with Carlos Bringuier, 137–138
Cuban Revolutionary Council, 129–130, 138
deathbed confession, 147, 537
identified as Tramp, 323
Oswald note, 187
Watergate involvement, 251–252, 537
Hunt, H. L. (Dallas oilman),
Gambling, 272
George Butler, 374
Hunt note, 186–187
Jim Braden, 327
John W. Curington, 257
Madeleine Brown, 375
W. C. Kirkwood, 377
also mentioned on pgs. 240, 375, 550
Hunt, Lamar, 327
"Hunt, Mr." (addressee of L. H. Oswald note), 186–187
Hunt, Nelson Bunker, 187, 237
Hunt, St. John (son of E. Howard Hunt), 537
Hunter, Bill (Deputy Constable), 533
Hunter, Morgan Bennett, 510–511

Hurt, Henry (author, *Reasonable Doubt*, 1985), 100, 362, 367, 423, 426
Hussein, King, 170
Hutchinson, Leonard E., 215, 518
Hutton, Bill (deputy constable), 75
Huxley, Aldous, 136
Hyer, Judge Julian C., 54

Ickes, Harold, 256
Ida, Joseph, 156
"Inga binga." *See aka* Arvad, Inga
Iran-Contra, 7, 175–178, 256, 554
Israel, Lee, 406–407
Ivanov, Boris Col. (Chief of the Soviet Committee for State Security), 126
Ivon, Lou (Garrison aide), 473

JFK (movie, 1991), 503–505
J. M. P. (initials of police officer Poe inscribed on cartridges at Tippet murder scene), 333–304
Jacks, Hurchel D. (Texas State trooper), 8
Jackson, Andrew, 224
Jackson, C. D. (publisher, *Life* magazine) on Zapruder film, 68, 533
Jackson State Mental Hospital, 145
Jacob, Stella Mae (witness), 57
"Jada" (Ruby dancer), 389
James, Billy V., 311
Janney, Peter (author, *Mary's Mosaic*, 2012), 511, 535–536
Janney, Winstar (CIA, father of Peter Janney), 535
Janos, James George. *See aka* Ventura, Jesse
January, Wayne (Red Bird Airport manager), 345
Japanese Communists, and Oswald, 102
Jarman, James E. Jr. (TSBD witness), 20, 48–50
Jarnagin, Carroll (Fort Worth attorney who overheard Ruby/Oswald plotting), 393–394
Jaworski, Leon (WD Special Council), 252, 408, 437, 491
Jefferson, Thomas, 224
Jenkins, James, 509
Jenkins, Marion, Dr. (Parkland Hospital), 12
Jenkins, Walter (LBJ aide), 189, 436
Jenner, Albert E. (WC attorney), 252, 264, 458, 461, 526
Joannides, George (CIA), 488

"John" (Dallas jail prisoner who received letter from Jack Ruby), 411
John Birch Society, 1, 181, 220, 225, 237
Johnsen, Richard (Secret Service agent), 356
Johnson, Blaney Mack, 379
Johnson, Clemon E. (witness), 60
Johnson, Clyde (Reverend), 534
Johnson, Josefa (LBJ's sister), 294
Johnson, Lady Bird. *See* Johnson, Mrs. Lyndon
Johnson, Lyndon B.,
    1960 election, 3–5
    on assassination plot, 7, 22, 268–269
    as suspect, 81, 278, 438, 537, 539–540, 549, 554
    background, 269–274
    blunts investigation, 149, 234, 277, 279, 346, 350, 353, 456, 542, 552
    Brown & Root Construction, 270–271
    cancels Vietnam withdrawal, 279, 284–289
    Connally's clothing, 277, 429
    Dallas Trade Mart, 226–227
    death of Henry Marshall, 275, 294
    Earl Warren, 93, 438–440
    General Dynamics TFX case, 91, 540
    neighbor of Hoover, 207–209, 224, 276, 550
    Jack Ruby on letter and death of, 371, 411–412
    knowledge of conspiracy, 436
    in motorcade, 8, 14
    Murder Inc., 173
    Nixon on, 250–252
    Parkland Hospital, 276, 353
    reaction to assassination, 276, 279
    SS Agent Rufus Youngblood, 232–233
    Sam Rayburn, 270–271, 274
    Soviet view of, 125–126, 408
    sworn in as President, 276–277, 357–365, 552
    Texas Democrats, 3–6
    to be dropped from Democratic ticket, 250, 275
    Warren Commission, 93, 436–466
    W. C. and Pat Kirkwood, 272, 377
    also mentioned on pgs. 23, 80, 135, 141, 189, 198, 235, 236, 255, 258, 261, 375, 409, 436, 491, 512, 549
Johnson, Mrs. Lyndon "Lady Bird," 8, 82, 233, 269
Johnson, Mrs. A. C., 40

Johnson, Priscilla (*aka* Priscilla Johnson
    McMillan, journalist and author,
    Marina and Lee, 1980), 114–115
Johnson, Sam Ealy, 269
Johnson, Sam Houston (LBJ's brother), 274,
    278
Johnston, Carolyn (*aka* Carolyn Arnold,
    witness), 51
"Jolly Green Giant" (nickname of Jim
    Garrison), 466
Jones, Penn Jr. (researcher), 31, 186, 187,
    237, 240, 287, 316, 374, 411
Jones, Milton, 452
Jones, Paul Roland, 373–374
Jones, Robert E. Lt. Col. (military
    intelligence officer), 288–289
Jonsson, Erik (Dallas mayor), 205
Judge, John (researcher), 477
Junta Revolucionaria (Cuban Revolutionary
    Junta or JURE), 142

Kaack, Milton R. (FBI agent), 210
Kantor, Seth (Dallas journalist/author, *Who
    Was Jack Ruby?* 1978),
    George Senator, 402
    Jack Ruby in Las Vegas, 397
    HSCA, 357, 501
    Ruby at Parkland, 316, 356–357
    Ruby's suicide attempt, 411
    Testimony to Warren Commission,
        356–357
    Thomas Eli Davis, 195–196
    also mentioned on pgs. 385, 406, 408
Karamessines, Tom, 182
Kastel, Phil, 154
Katzenbach, Nicholas D. (deputy attorney
    general),
    Bill Moyers' memo, 154
    also mentioned on pgs. 437, 440, 441,
        491
Kaufman, Stanley M. (Ruby's attorney), 21
Kavner, Richard, 376
Kay, Kathy (*aka* Kathy Coleman, Ruby
    stripper), 390, 399
Kaylor, Donald, 535
Kearns, Ed, 544
Kefauver, Estes, 3, 152, 154
Kellerman, Roy (Secret Service agent),
    in motorcade, 8, 10, 11, 228
    Testimony to Warren Commission, 228
    also mentioned on pgs. 229, 352
Kelly, Clarence, 186

Kelly, Thomas J. (Secret Service inspector),
    363
Kelly, William E. Jr. (COPA), 514–515
Kendall, Don, 250
Kennedy, Caroline, 398
Kennedy, Edward,
    with Frank Sinatra, 164
    also mentioned on pg., 549
Kennedy, Jacqueline,
    Bethesda Naval Hospital, 277, 359,
        364–365
    connection to DeMohrenschildt, 264
    in motorcade, 5, 8, 10–12, 27, 67, 73
    request for Agent Clint Hill, 13, 228
    Parkland Hospital, 352–353
    "They Shot Jack," 72
    Warren Commission, 10, 369, 446, 463
    also mentioned on pgs. 5, 75, 258, 264,
        295, 398, 402, 536
Kennedy, John F.,
    1960 Presidential election, 5–7, 164, 166,
        274
    1962 Kennedy Act, 256
    ARRB, 507–515
    assassination, 8–16, 23, 26–28, 30, 45–46,
        48, 59, 60–63, 65, 142, 148–149, 162,
        174, 181, 188, 190, 192, 212, 219,
        244–245, 268–269, 293, 295–299, 312,
        325, 389–395, 443
    autopsy of, 351–370, 415–416, 420,
        424–425, 458–462, 479, 541
    background of, 1–8
    Bay of Pigs invasion, 4, 109, 129–140,
        143
    Charles Harrelson, 324–326
    CIA/Mafia plots, 140, 147, 160–161,
        166–167, 173–174, 192, 198, 212, 268,
        289–292, 322
    French Connection, 192–198
    Garrison trial, 472–485
    HSCA, 24, 55, 90, 485–503
    Hoover's hatred of, 206–209, 223, 244,
        279
    "Inga binga" (Inga Arvad), 206–207
    on integration, 234–236, 243–244
    Judith Exner, 164–165
    a likely scenario, 547–557
    Mary Meyer, 535–537
    McClellan Committee, 157–158
    and military, 280–284, 287–292
    modified defense intelligence operations,
        281–283

Kennedy, John F., (*continued*)
  monetary reform (EO 11110), 163, 254–256
  motorcade running late, 43, 51
  nuclear test ban treaty, 283
  oil depletion allowance, 7, 256–257, 274, 549
  and oilmen, 235, 237, 240, 246, 256–258, 267, 272, 279, 283
  Parkland Hospital, 42–43, 276, 351–358
  Tosh Plumlee, 175
  Pricilla Johnson McMillan, 115
  *Portrait of a President,*1967, 136
  Profiles in Courage, 1956, 136
  and right-wing extremists, 157, 244–245, 253
  Secret Service protection, 134, 225–234
  Soviet Involvement, 125–127, 282, 283, 378–380, 521
  and Vietnam, 198, 282, 284–287
  Why England Slept, 1940, 2
  Zupruder film, 29, 66–75
  also mentioned on pgs. xiii, xv, xvi, xvii, xviii, 17, 19, 20, 31, 32, 34, 36, 37, 57, 66, 80, 81, 83, 86, 87, 89, 91, 93, 98, 115, 117, 118, 123, 147, 155, 171, 175, 186, 204, 243, 244, 247, 248, 249, 250, 252, 260, 265, 271, 275, 276, 277, 278, 305, 306, 315, 317, 318, 320, 329, 345, 346, 347, 351, 375, 376, 383, 385, 386, 406, 408, 409, 412, 414, 427, 430, 436, 437, 439, 441, 444, 452, 453, 455, 457, 465, 466, 468, 469, 504, 505, 506, 527, 529, 530, 539, 540, 542, 543, 544, 546
Kennedy, Joseph Jr. (JFK's older brother), 2–3
Kennedy, Joseph P. (JFK's father),
  US ambassador to Great Britain, 2–3, 31
  bootlegging, 151, 163, 267
Kennedy, Regis, 36
Kennedy, Robert F. (author, *The Enemy Within*, 1960),
  Antitrust Division, 247
  Carlos Marcello, 155–156
  attempts on Castro, 173
  denies LBJ's swearing in order, 277
  on Garrison investigation, 468–485
  on Hoffa and Dorfman, 375, 396
  on Hoover's retirement, 233–224
  Hoover's surveillance of, 207–209
  Hoover informs RFK, 166, 346
  JFK's brain taken by, 543, 369

  institutionalized Gen. Walker, 236–242
  with McClellan Committee, 157–158
  and organized crime, 157, 160–167, 202–203, 548–549
  RFK assassination probe dropped by HSCA, 495
  also mentioned on pgs. xvii, 133, 135, 172, 244, 267, 275, 276, 282, 393, 412, 437, 448, 456, 465, 512, 549, 554, 555
Kennedy, Robert F. Jr., 465
Kenney, Edward C. (Admiral), 360
Kerner, Otto (US attorney from Chicago), 154
Kerr, Robert, 260, 264
Khrushchev, Nikita (Soviet Premier),
  Cuban Missile Crisis, 4, 134, 282–283
  also mentioned on pgs. xvii, 109, 126, 485
Kilduff, Malcolm (assistant press secretary), 276
Kilgallen, Dorothy (journalist),
  Connection to JFK case, 406
  death of, 407, 533
Killam, Hank, 533
Killam, Wanda, 387
Kimble, Jules Ricco, 472
King, Henry (Judge), 540
King, Martin Luther Jr.,
  COINTELPRO, 145, 243–244
  Hoover comments, 207, 243
  also mentioned on pgs. xvii, 204, 208, 235, 244, 267, 485, 487, 491, 495, 502, 503
King, Coretta Scott, 244, 486–487
  on winning suit against the government, 503
Kinser, John, 294
Kinsley, Eddie, 334–335
Kirkwood, Pat, 230–231, 325, 377–378, 380
  the Cellar, 272, 298, 401
Kirkwood, W. C. (father of Pat),
  Four Deuces Club, 272, 325, 380
  Oilmen gamblers, 272, 377
KKK. *See* Ku Klux Klan
Kleberg, Richard M., 269
Kleindienst, Richard, 248
Klihr, Charles, 239
Knox, Frank, 153
Koch, Graham R. E., 397
Koethe, Jim (journalist), 533
Kohn, Howard (journalist), 158–159, 248
Korth, Fred (Navy Secretary), 91, 274
Kostikov, Valery Vladimirovich, 125, 149

Kounas, Dolores (witness), 32
Ku Klux Klan "KKK," 1, 374, 472
Krulak, Victor H. (Marine lieutenant general and special assistant for counterinsurgency activities of the Joint Chiefs of Staff), 322
Kutler, Stanley (professor of history), 82

Labriola, Paul "Needle Nose," 374
Ladner, Mrs. Judy, 317
"Lady Bird." See Johnson, Mrs. Lyndon
LaGuardia, Fiorello, 154
Landis, Paul E. Jr. (Secret Service agent, motorcade), 13
Lansdale, Edward (Gen. and Assistant Sec. of Defense for Special Operations), 133, 322, 550
Lane, M. Duke (writer), 87
Lane, Mark (New York attorney and author, *Rush to Judgment*, 1992)
    Dorothy Kilgillen, 407
    Oswald's Marine pals, 102, 107
    also mentioned on pgs. 184, 444, 454, 492
Lansky, Jake (Meyer's brother), 154, 323, 328, 275, 379, 471
Lansky, Meyer (gangster),
    Luciano & Naval Intelligence, 152–153
    Organized crime in Cuba, 158–159
    Prohibition, 163
    with Lewis McWillie, 377
    with Richard Nixon, 248
    also mentioned on pgs. 154, 323, 328, 375, 379, 471
Lanza, Joseph "Socks," 153
The Last Two Days (film by Thomas Atkins, 1963), 17
Latona, Sebastian, 422
Lawrence, Jack (arrested car salesman), 329–330
Lawrence, John (witness), 16
Lawson, Winston G. (Secret Service agent), 8, 10–12, 226–227, 351–352
Leary, Timothy, 536, 537
Leavelle, Jim (Dallas detective), 402, 404
Le Blanc, Charles, 145
Lechuga, Carlos, 135
Lee, O. H. (Oswald alias), 337, 393–394
Lee, V. T. (Oswald alias), 136
LeGon, Christiana, 259
LeGon, Jeanne Fromenke (Mrs. DeMohrenschildt), 259

LeGon, Robert, 259
LeGon, Sergio, 259
LeMay, Curtis (Gen.), 550
Lemnitzer, Lyman Gen. (Chairman of the Joint Chief of Staff), Operation Northwoods, 134
"Leopoldo." See Odio, Silvia
Lesar, James H. (researcher), 198
Lester, Richard, 306
Levens, Jimmy, 533
Levy, Michael, 259
Lewallen, James, 214
Lewis, Aubrey Lee, 519
Lewis, C. L. "Lummie" (Dallas deputy sheriff), 319, 327
Lewis, David, 144
Lewis, Anna (Mrs. David), 144
Liebeler, Wesley J. (WC attorney)
    Abraham Zapruder, 68–69
    Emmett Hudson, 73–74
    Marina Oswald, 238–239
    Orest Pena, 212
    Rankin memo, 445–446, 462
    Joe Smith, 76
    also mentioned on pg., 27, 64
Limpert, John (editor, the *Washingtonian*), 504
Lifton, David (author, *Best Evidence*, 1992), on Zapruder film, 70–71
    also mentioned on pgs. 364–365, 508
Lincoln, Abraham, 204, 224, 231, 254, 256
Lincoln, Evelyn (JFK's secretary), 554
Lindbergh, Charles, 205
"Little Lynn." See Carlin, Karen Bennett
Lodge, Henry Cabot, 3
Logan, David, 472
Lohn, Kurt, 181
Lombardozzi, Carmine, 156
Long, Russell (Senator), 376, 468
Lopez, Lucy, 315
Louis, Joe, 157
Love, Robie (Dallas constable), 394
Lovelady, Billy N. (witness), on steps of TSBD, 45–47, 49, 55
LSD (lysergic acid diethylamide, hallucinogenic drug given to JFK), 130, 171–172, 536
Lucania, Salvatore, 151
Lucchese, Tommy, 159

Luciano, Charles "Lucky,"
    background, 151–152
    Navel intelligence, 153
    also mentioned on pgs. 158
Lumpkin, G. L. (Dallas deputy police chief)
    in motorcade, 8

Maas, Peter, 202
Mabra, W. W. (Dallas County bailiff), 18
MacDonald, Betty Mooney, 333
Macedo, Joseph D., 105
Mack, Gary (aka Lawrence Alan Dukel,
    curator of the 6th Floor Museum)
    Badge man, 81–82
    Dallas police radio tape, 339, 497, 500
    English not native language of Oswald,
        522
    Inside the Target Car (2008 documentary),
        82
    Richard E. Harrison, 423
    Tom Alyea, 417
    also mentioned on pgs. 394
Maddox, Al (Dallas deputy sheriff),
    413–414
Mafia. See Organized crime
Magaddino, Anthony, 156
Magliocco, Joseph, 156
Maheu, Robert, 159, 165, 220
Major, Stan, 307
Majuri, Frank, 156
Makarios, Archbishop, 172
Malcolm X, 267
Malone, John F., 250, 524
Malone, William Scott, 494
Manchester, John (Clinton town marshal),
    146
Manchester, William (author), 277
Mandal, Paul (Life writer), 69, 533
Mann, James Robert,
    Mann Act of 1910, 200
Mannlicher-Carcano rifle,
    as curtain rods, 41, 427
    and incriminating palm print, 422–424,
        429
    metal shims to correct sight, 420
    multiple serial numbers, 421
    substitution of, 419, 426
    also mentioned on pgs. 47, 65, 122, 189,
        191, 198, 434, 498, 520, 521, 540
Mansfield, Mike (senator), 285
Manson, Charles, 505
Marachini, Dante, 214

Maranzano, Salvatore, 151
Marcades, Melba Christine (aka Rose
    Cheramie), 386–387, 389, 394, 533
Marcello, Carlos (Mafia Boss),
    and organized crime, 154–158
    brother with Charles Harrelson, 326
    David Ferrie, 98–99, 328, 472, 482
    Jack Halfen and LBJ, 273
    Jim Garrison, 483
    meeting with Hoffa, 159–160
    "take the stone out of my shoes," 155
    also mentioned on pgs. 36, 144, 161, 174,
        197, 247–248, 376, 396, 550
Marchetti, Victor, 169, 174, 182, 471
Marina and Lee, 1977 (Priscilla Johnson),
    115
US Marines,
    and Oswald, 90–91, 97, 99–108, 189, 302,
        421, 524
Markham, Helen (Tippit witness),
    on Oswald's jacket, 336
    on Tippit shooting, 331–332
    also mentioned on pg, 338
Marks, John (author, The Search for the
    Manchurian Candidate, 1991), 172
Marshall, Henry, 275, 294
Martello, Francis (New Orleans Police
    lieutenant), 137
Martin, B. J. (police officer), 13–14
Martin, Frank, 533
Martin, Jack (Banister investigator), 174,
    179, 220, 466, 469
Martin, Jim (Dallas attorney), 402
Martin, John (man who photographed Gen.
    Walker and Oswald on same roll of
    film), 239
Martin, John (Union President who shot
    Jack Ruby's friend, attorney Leon
    Cooke), 372
Martino, John, 148
Marvin, Daniel (Special Forces), 368
"Mary" (woman who possessed a box of
    letters of Oswald), 395
Mash, Ester Ann (Ruby waitress), xvi,
    372–394
Mason, Bill, 271
Masseria, Giuseppe, 151
Masters of Deceit, 1959 (Hoover), 202
Mathews, Quin (TV newsman), 325
Matthews, Russell Douglas,
    and Santos Trafficante, 325
    friend to Charles Harrelson, 36, 325

friend to Ruby, 325
Joseph Campisi, 376–377
Lewis McWillie, 325, 380–381
significance of, 167
Maximo, Jefe, 128
Maynard, Harry, 212–213
Mazo, Earl, 159
McCarthy, Joseph, 204, 206, 490
McCarty, Bruce (medical technician),
Studied Ruby's cancer cells, 414
McClellan, Barr (author, *Blood, Money &
Power*, 2002), 269
McClellan, John L.,
on McClellan Committee, 157, 160–162
McClelland, Robert, 368
McClelland, Scott (son of Barr McClellan),
269
McCloy, John J. (Warren Commission
member),
background, 443
"Not a Banana Republic," 441
on FBI, SS culpability, 444
on Ruby's institutionalization, 458
WC dependence on FBI, 449
on Zapruder film, 68
also mentioned on pgs. 252, 446, 448,
451, 461
McCone, John, 149, 512
McCormack, Harry (reporter), 68, 276, 510
McDonald, Betty, 533
McDonald, Hugh M. (LA County Sheriff's
detective), 299
McDonald, M. N. (Dallas police officer),
340–342
McGann, George (gangster, married
Beverly Oliver), 36, 167, 325, 534
McGarvey, Patrick (CIA agent), 182
McGee, Frank (TV newsman), 477
McGee, H. L. (Dallas detective), 402
McGrath, J. Howard (US attorney general),
153–154
McGuire, Dennis, 43
McGuire, Phyllis, 164–165
McKeithen, John, 478
McKeown, Robert Ray (gun runner),
138–139, 381–382
McKinley, William, 224
McKinnon, Cheryl (witness), 72–73
McLain, H. B. (Dallas police officer),
499
McMahon, Patrick (PT-109 crew), 2
McMahon, Homer A., 510–511

McMillan, Priscilla Johnson. *See* Johnson,
Priscilla
McNally, Joseph P., 187
McNamara, Robert, 281, 283, 286
McNeil, Robert, 312
McVickar, John, 114–115
McWillie, Lewis J. "Chilly,"
and organized crime, 377–385
as gangland killer, 167, 396–397
background and guns from Ruby, 377,
380
friend to Ruby and Kirkwoods, 272, 325
guns and Cuba, 377
"idol" of Ruby, 159, 377, 380, 383
Meagher, Sylvia (researcher and author,
Accessories After the Fact, 1992),
chastises the *New York Times*, 545
substitution of rifles, 419
also mentioned on pgs. 241–242,
331–332
Mecom, John, 260
Medina, Juan, 292
Medvedev, Alexander, 119
Mendoza, Dr. Charles, 265
Menninger, Bonar (author, *Mortal Error*,
1992), 234
Mentensana, Charles, 534
Mercer, Julia Ann (witness),
Dealey Plaza experience, 16–17
testimony altered by FBI, 454
also mentioned on pgs. 314–315, 387,
543
Meredith, James, 236–237
Merton, Thomas (Catholic priest),
267
Mertz, Irma Rio, 193
Mertz, John, 193
Mertz, Michael Victor (*aka* Michel Roux;
see also Jean Soutre),
on French connection to the
assassination, 194–197
Mertz, Sara, 193
Meserole, Bobbie Louise. *See aka* Angel,
Shari
Meyer, Cord (CIA), 147, 533, 535–537, 550
Meyer, Mary Pinchot (Mrs. Cord Meyer
and JFK's mistress), 511, 533, 535–548
Meyer, Michael (son of Mary Meyer killed
at age 9), 536
Meyer, Quintin (twin to Cord Meyer killed
in action in WWII), 536
Meyers, Edward, 328

Meyers, Lawrence (friend of Jack Ruby), 328
Meyers, Nina Palmquist, 438
Military, relations with Kennedy, 280–289
Miller, Austin L. (witness), 61, 87
Miller, Giles,
    Ruby "directed" to Dallas, 373
Millican, A. J. (witness), 28, 32, 309, 543
Milteer, Joseph A.,
    foreknowledge of assassination plot, 226, 244–245, 253
    death of, 534
Minacore, Calogero, 154
Mind Control (Manchurian Candidate), 171–173
Minyard, Frank, 482
Mitchell, John, 252
MK-ULTRA (CIA behavior-modification program), 171–172, 414
Mobsters. *See* Organized crime
Moffett, Sandra, 478
Mohrenskuld (original family name of DeMohrenschildt), 258
Moldea, Dan E. (author, *The Hoffa Wars*, 1992), 157, 159, 252, 376
Molina, Joe R. (witness), 56–57
Montranga, Charles, 154
Mooney, Luke (Dallas Deputy sheriff), 417
Mooneyham, Mrs. Lillian (District Court clerk), 52–53
Moore, Elmer W. (Secret Service agent), 363, 408
Moore, G. Walter. *See also* Moore, J. Walton
Moore, J. Walton (CIA man in Dallas), *aka* G. Walter Moore as named by the WC possibly to misdirect people from the CIA, 190, 260
Moore, Joseph, 517
Moorman, Mary Ann (witness),
    "Badge man" photograph, 37–38, 80–81
    also mentioned on pgs. 62, 312–314
Morales, Dan (Texas attorney general), 302
Morales, David (CIA), 147, 537, 550
Morgan, Dean, 307
Morgan, J. P., 268
Morgan, Robert, 148
Morgan, William (Captain), 383
Morley, Jefferson (editor, the *Washington Post* and the *Atlantic*), 182, 515
Morningstar, Robert, 362
Morrison, Delesseps, 474, 533

Morrow, Robert D. (author, *Betrayal*, 1964), 191
Morton, Fred (US district attorney), 292
Mosby, Aline, 97, 115
Mossadegh, Mohammed Dr., 170
Mother Theresa, 483
Motorcade, 8–16
Moyers, Bill, 149, 278, 312, 436
Moyers, Eldon, 196
Muchmore, Mrs. Maria "Mary" (witness), 34
Murchinson, Clint, 259–260, 272, 377, 550
Murphy, Thomas J. (witness), 59–60
Murret, Charles "Dutz" (Oswald's uncle), 96, 137, 156
Murret, Lillian, 96
Mussolini, Benito, 152, 421, 470

Nagy, Ferenc, 470
Nagell, Richard Case, 197–199, 332
Naman, Rita, 120
Neal, Sheila Grace (attorney), 298
Neill, Sam, 382
Nelson, Sharon (witness), 57
Newman, William E. "Bill" and family (Gayle, Children ages 2 & 4 witnesses), 38, 72, 452, 543
Newman, Mrs. William E. "Gayle," xvi, 72, 452, 543
Newman, Jean (witness), 29
Newman, John M. (Military historian), 183
Newman, Mort, 374
Newman, Sam, 139
Newnam, John (employee of the *Dallas Morning News*), 315, 398
Nhu, Ngo Dinh, 285
Nichols, Louis, 535
Nicoletti, Charles "Chuckie" (gangster), 295–296, 535
Nicoli, Michel, 198
Nikolaevna, Marina (Marina Oswald), 119–120
Nikolai (possible name of Marina Oswald's father), 120
Nitti, Frank, 163
Nix, Orville O. (witness), 15, 34–35, 228, 453
Nixon, Richard M.,
    on background, 247
    action against Castro, 130
    in Dallas 1963, 247–249, 328, 407
    fearful of Earl Warren, 439–440

and Kennedy assassination, 246–253
Mafia money to, 152
Mob help in 1960 election, 161–163
Oswald's attempted murer on, 122, 241
secrets from Hoover, 203, 207
as visitor to Cuba, 159
also mentioned on pgs. 3, 4, 36, 130, 198, 253, 274, 442, 491
Nizer, Louis, 492
Noble, Herbert, 373
Norden, Eric, 467–468
Norman, Harold, 20, 48–50
Norton, Linda Dr. (Dallas County assistant medical examiner), 524–525, 527
Norton, Teresa, 533
Nosenko, Yuri (soviet defector), 123–126, 268, 290, 543
Novel, Gordon, 478, 479
Noyes, Peter (author, *Legacy of Doubt*, 2010), 328
NPIC, CIA's National Photo Interpretation Center, 510–512

O'Connor, Paul K. (Bethesda witness), 364, 509
O'Donnell, Kenneth P. (witness), 15, 225, 227, 232, 277, 286, 353, 457, 543
O'Neal, Vernon, 534
O'Neill, Francis X. Jr., 361–364, 367, 453
O'Neill, Thomas P. "Tip" (Speaker of the House), 457, 487
O'Reilly, Bill (WFAA-TV, Dallas), 496
"Oaxaca," 291
Ochsner, Alton Dr., 143, 144, 146, 148
Odio, Annie, 141–142
Odio, Silvia ("Angel" and "Leopaldo"), 141–143, 290, 446, 521, 543
Odum, Bradwell D. (FBI Agent), 92
Odum, Lee, 475
Ofstein, Dennis, 110, 262
Oglesby, Carl (author), 248
Oliver, Beverly (author, *Nightmare in Dallas*, 1994, witness),
  "the babushka lady," 35–37
  Ferrie in Ruby's club, 36, 174
  film taken, 35–37, 543
  introduced to Lee Oswald, 389
  married to George McGann, 35, 36, 167, 534
  also mentioned on pgs. 16, 394
Oliver, Clarence, 533
Oliver, Revilo Pendleton, 452

Olney, Warren III, 445
Olsen, Harry, 399
Olson, Culbert, 438
Oltmans, Willems, 265
Operation Brilab, 156
Operation Mongoose, 133, 173, 322, 485, 548, 550
Operation Northwoods (1962 false flag gov't proposals), 123
Operation Underworld, 153
Organized Crime,
  and Jim Braden, 167, 327–329
  and Carlos Marcello, 98–99, 144, 154–156
  and CIA-Mafia death plots, 173–174
  and Cuba, 173–174
  and Sam Giancana, 157–160
  and Hoffa, 158–159
  and Kennedy assassination, 157–167
  Lansky in Cuba, 158–159
  and Lewis McWillie, 325–385
  and Lucky Luciano, 152–153
  and Prohibition, 163
  and Jack Ruby, 379–385
  Scheim and Mafia-did-it theory, 483
Orwell, George, 106
Osborne, Albert. *See* Bowen, John Howard
Oser, Alvin, 360
Oswald (name used to purchase trucks for Cubans), 517
  man who ordered work on rifle at Dallas gun shop, 520–521
Oswald, Harvey, 518
Oswald, Harvey Lee, 211, 288
Oswald Innocent Campaign, 45–47
Oswald, June Lee, 121, 262, 264
Oswald, Lee, 183, 213, 226, 266, 382
Oswald, Lee Harvey,
  aka A. J. (or Alek James) Hidell, 211, 219, 262, 288, 334, 349–350, 420
  Alpha 66 (anti-Castro Cubans), 140–142, 178, 238, 290
  arrest of, 330–333, 340–347
  approached by Marrion L. Baker, 52
  on background, 89–111, 450–458, 461
  backyard photographs, 266, 299–302, 429–433
  on Judyth Vary Baker, 143–149
  Belorussian connection, 111
  and bulging shell cases, 333–335
  at Depository, 13, 16–17, 19, 25, 27, 39, 40, 45

Oswald, Lee Harvey, (*continued*)
CIA 201 file on, 182–183, 268, 445, 473, 483, 493–494, 551
and Civil Air Patrol (CAP), 97–98, 139, 156, 174, 220, 328
and "coke" issue, 51–54, 540
Roger Dean Craig, 308, 320–321
Curtain Rod Story, 41, 428
Dallas test drive, 518–519
George DeMohrenshildt, 189–192, 258, 266, 289–292, 490
encounter with Secret Service, 312, 314
evidence against, 415, 461–464
exhumation, 446, 524–529
with David Ferrie, 36, 98–99, 143–149, 156, 174, 389, 467, 472–473, 479–480, 485
on James Files, 294–295
and FBI, 39, 199–224, 447–452, 542, 553
fingerprints in TSBD, 294, 416, 423
William George Gaudet, 187–188, 384
Hosty notation, 214–215, 217–218, 223, 237, 287, 314, 451
"I Led Three Lives," 97
identity prior to assassination, 515–524
and Japanese Communists, 102
LBJ on Oswald, 278–279, 411–412
legal rights denied, 332
"Lee Oswald of the CIA," 82, 183, 389
man in TSBD doorway, 33–34, 45–57
and Mannlicher-Carcano rifle, 191, 213, 238, 242, 262, 288, 419–421, 425–427, 429, 543, 545
in Marines, 100–108
in Mexico City, 125, 141–143, 147, 183–185, 187–189, 289–292, 328, 518, 521–522
Minox Camera, 180–181, 431
mind control, 172–174
mismatched bullets, 417–418
in New Orleans, 136–141, 174–175, 220–221
on Richard Nixon, 250–251
note to Mr. Hunt, 186–187
Oswald doppelganger, 111–112, 185, 342–343, 345, 446, 515–524, 540
Oswald's library card, 98–100
Oswald's jackets, 335–337
"P.O. 19106," 475
palm print, 422–424
paper bag, 427–428
paraffin test on, 421–422, 540, 543

Tosh Plumlee, 175–179
in police line-up, 332
pubic hair, 451
revoked citizenship, 114–115
roll call at TSBD, 304
Russian language test, 104, 260, 469, 522
with Ruby, 36, 174, 315, 387–398, 484, 493, 543
in Russia, 101, 108–127, 185, 190, 522
on use of a sabot, 306–307
shooting of, 398–410
as spy, 102, 172, 179–183, 447–451, 539
Gen. Edwin Walker, 223, 236–242, 262, 387–388
Roscoe White, 299–303
and U-2 program, 101–117, 123, 134, 283
also mentioned on pgs. xv, xvi, xvii, 65, 68, 83, 86, 93, 157, 162, 166, 194, 196, 198, 227, 245, 249, 257, 272, 287, 289, 293, 304, 308, 325, 327, 338, 339, 348, 353, 356, 357, 367, 370, 371, 374, 375, 378, 383, 387, 388, 413, 414, 415, 417, 434, 436, 437, 438, 442, 443, 453, 454, 460, 466, 478, 481, 488, 491, 492, 496, 497, 500, 502, 505, 506, 507, 514, 515, 533, 534, 535, 541, 544, 547, 551, 552
Oswald, Lee Henry, 181, 182
Oswald, Leon (*aka* Lee Harvey Oswald), 142
Oswald, Marguerite Claverie (Oswald's mother),
1961 visit to Washington, 118–119
1967 request for exhumation, 525
background of, 90–97
begs for legal counsel, 443–444
CIA opens mail, 190
death of, 94, 527–528
destroys backyard photograph, 238–239, 430
questions changes in Oswald appearance, 525–526
reaction to HSCA, 501
shown photo of Ruby on Nov. 17, 92–93, 314, 387
also mentioned on pgs. xvi, 209, 397, 451–452, 457
Oswald, Marina (Marina Nikolaevna Prusakova, Oswald's wife),
on altered photograph, 238–239
Amsterdam "boardinghouse," 121

on backyard photographs, 266, 430
changes testimony, 251, 267, 431, 462
destroyed backyard photograph, 238–239
exhumation alarm, 528
exhumation tape, 528–529
FBI intimidation, 218–219
files exhumation suit, 526–527
with H.L. Hunt, 257
on "Hunter of fascists" photo, 266
Nixon allegation, 250–251
meeting Lee Harvey Oswald, 119–123,
    262, 522
on Oswald's jacket, 335–337
on Gen. Walker shooting, 238–242
tells Robert Webster's story, 111–112
also mentioned on pgs. xvi, 31, 40, 41, 94,
    101, 115, 136, 209, 210, 215, 260, 261,
    262, 263, 321, 446, 449, 518, 519, 523
Oswald, Robert,
blames Dallas Police, 546
fights exhumation, 526–527
notes changes in Oswald, 525–526
on Oswald's camera, 431
on Lee being right handed, 421
also mention on pgs. 90, 91, 95, 97, 99,
    110, 122, 133, 209, 251, 523, 551
Oswald, Robert E. (Oswald's father), 91, 92
Otepka, Otto, 112
Oufkir (Moroccan General), 205
Owens, Ernest Jay (witness), 16
Oxford, Edward, 404

P. S. (initials of anonymous letter sent to
    JFK researcher Penn Jones, Jr.), 186
Paine, Michael,
Minox camera, 180–181
also mentioned on pgs. 40, 238, 240, 262
Paine, Ruth,
gives Oswald driving lessons, 518
meets Marina, 262–263
Minox camera, 180–181, 431
obtains TSBD job for Oswald, 40–41
on Oswald FBI note, 218, 240–241
station wagon, 320–321
also mentioned on pgs. 215, 238, 430
Palmer, A. Mitchell (attorney general),
    200–204
Palmer, Henry, 146
Paradis, Jerry, 98
Parr, George, 271
Partin, Edward, 161–162, 248
Patrick, Lenny, 377

Patterson, Robert K., 389
Paul, Ralph, 534
Pawley, William, 535
Pearson, Drew (journalist), 230
Pecora, Nofio J., 377, 396
Pena, Orest, 211–212
Penn, Mrs. Lovell,
    tells of target practice near her home, 521
Peoples, Clint (Texas Ranger), 275
Perez, Leander, 240
Permindex, 469–471
Perrin, Robert, 382
Perry, Malcolm Dr. (Parkland) 363, 368
Peterman, Mrs. Viola, 452
Petty, Dr. Charles (Dallas County medical
    examiner), 360, 526
Phelan, James, 476
Philbrick, Herbert, 97, 100
Phillips, David Atlee (CIA officer),
    on James Files, 295
    Bay of Pigs invasion, 129
    "Maurice Bishop," 141, 147
    on destruction of Oswald tapes, 185–187
    on Mary Meyer, 537, 550
Pic, Edward John Jr. (Marguerite Oswald's
    first husband), 91
Pic, John Edward (Oswald's half brother),
    notes changes in Oswald appearance, 526
    also mentioned on pgs. 91, 95
Pickard, John (Major), 432
Pigano, Sylvia, 161
Pipes, Mrs. Linda (Phil Willis' daughter),
    455
Pironti, Sauveur (possible French hit-man
    of 3 hit-man team who is said to have
    assassinated JFK), 197–198
Pitts, Mrs. Elnora, 401
Pitzer, William Lt. Cmdr. (Bethesda
    technician), 368, 453, 533
Pizzo, Frank, 518
Plumlee, William Robert "Tosh," 175–179,
    377, 385
Plumeri, James, 159, 534
Poe, J. M. (police officer),
    initials lacking, 333–334
    marks Tippit shell casings, 333
Police Radio Recording, 338–339, 497–500
Policoff, Jerry, 554, 547
Politburo, 126
Pollack, Jack Harrison (Biography of Earl
    Warren), 439–440
Portrait of a President, 1967 (Kennedy), 136

Posner, Gerald (author, *Case Closed*, 2003), 96, 460
Potter, Nolan H. (witness), 60
Powell, James (military intelligence agent),
　TSBD photo by, 55
　caught in TSBD, 287
Powell, John L. (Johnny)
　witness in TSBD, 21
Powell, Lewis F., 492
Powell, Mrs. Nancy, 453
Powers, Daniel Patrick, 101
Powers, David F. (Presidential aide, witness), 14, 223, 457, 543
Powers, Francis Gary (CIA pilot, author, *Operation Overflight*, 1970), 109–110, 535
Powers, Richard Gid, 209
Presidential election of 1960, 2–4
Preston, Billy (Dallas Deputy Constable), 394–395
Price, Jesse C. (witness), 38–39, 87, 543
Price, Malcolm, 520–521
Price, Ned (film restoration expert), 512
Prio (*see also* Socarras, Carlos Prio),
　suicide of, 535
　with Robert McKeown, 138–139, 158, 381
Proctor, Dr, Grover B. Jr. (historian), 506
Project Paperclip, 171
Profaci, Joseph, 156
Prohibition and organized crime, 150–152
Prouty, L. Fletcher Col.,
　4th Army stand down, 287
　assassination as inside job, 504, 549–550
　also mentioned on pgs. 295, 322
Provenzano, Anthony "Tony Pro," 162, 248, 376
Prusakov, Ilya Vasilyevich, 120
Prusakova, Marina Nikolaevna (Marina Oswald), 119
Pullin, Leonard, 533

Q J/WIN (cryptonym of an assassin employed by CIA), 195–197
Quigley, John (FBI agent),
　report on Oswald, 137, 211–212
　also mentioned on pgs. 217

Rachley, Virgie (witness), 27. *See also* Baker, Mrs. Donald
Rademacher, John, 296–297
Ragsdale, Jerome, 375

Raigorodsky, Paul, 261
Raikin, Spas T., 122
Ramsey, Norman S. (Harvard physics professor), 339, 500–503
Ramsey, Robin (author, *Who Shot JFK?*, 2007), 293
Rand, Henry, 111
Randle, Mrs. Linnie Mae, 40, 427
Rankin, J. Lee (WC General Counsel)
　edits Nixon White House tapes, 252
　hurries WC, 446, 460
　Oswald at Monterey Military Language School, 103
　on Oswald FBI informant rumor, 215–217, 446–447, 449–450
　possibilities for training in Russia, 116
　questions legitimacy of Oswald palm print, 423
　questions medical evidence, 450, 458–459
　on Ruby as FBI informant, 383
　on Ruby's Mob connections, 408–410
　Warren Commission as "A Rankin operation," 445
　also mentioned on pgs. 64, 348, 443, 448, 451, 462
Rasofsky, Barney, 371
Rather, Dan (author, *The Camera Never Blinks*, 1987), 70, 545
　on Zapruder film, 69–70
Rawlston, Col. *See aka* Roselli, Johnny
Ray, James Earl, 244, 503
Rayburn, Sam, 256, 296–270, 272, 274, 377
Ready, John D., 232
Reagan, Ronald (US President), 255, 478
Rebozo, Charles G. "Bebe," 247, 152
Record, Tony (news photographer), 399
Redlich, Norman, 461
Reedy, George (LBJ aide), 277
Reich, Maximillian Col., 287
Reid, Mrs. Robert A. (witness), 26, 53
Reily Coffee Company, 136, 139, 144–145, 213–214, 221
Reily, William, 136
Reuther, Walter, 237
Revill, Lt. Jack (Dallas Police),
　on FBI foreknowledge of Oswald, 205
　with military intelligence agent, 288
　with Jack Ruby, 401
Reynolds, O. C., 179
Reynolds, Warren (witness), 240, 333, 534
Rhodes, Charles R., 105
Rhodes, James (Ohio Governor), 478

Ricca, Paul "The Waiter" (*aka* Felice DeLucia), 163

Rich, Nancy Perrin (Ruby employee), 382

Richey, Bonnie (witness), 57

Richey, Warren, 411

Riebe, Floyd (Autopsy photographer), 364–365, 369

Right-wing extremists, enemies of Kennedy, 235–279

Rike, Aubrey (ambulance driver for seizure victim), 42–43, 354

Rivele, Steve J. (researcher), 197–198

Roberts, Cokie (NPR commentator), 504

Roberts, Delphine (Banister's secretary), 139, 174–175, 179, 221

Roberts, Earlene (Oswald's landlady), 336–337, 387, 533

Roberts, Emory (Secret Service special-agent-in-charge), 232

Roberts, Ray (congressman), 14

Robertson, Rip, 175

Robinson, Marvin C., 321, 453, 505, 524

Rockefeller, David, 548

Rockefeller, Nelson, 510

Rodriguez, Ernesto, 139

Rodriguez, Miguel (Technical sergeant), 104

Rogers, Charles Frederick (*aka* Chauncey Holt), 323

Rogers, Lillian, 66

Rogers, William P. (US attorney general), 161

Rojas, Emanuel, 175–177

Roman, Jane, 182

Roosevelt, Franklin D. (US President), 269–271, 438, 548

Roosevelt, Kermit, 170, 256

Roosevelt, Theodore (US President), 200, 206

Rose, Earl Dr. (Dallas Medical Examiner), 354, 413

Rose, Guy F. (Dallas detective), 180, 238, 344

Rose, Jerry D. (researcher), 42

Roselli, Johnny (*aka* Col. Rawlston), 130–133
    CIA-Mob assassination plots, 154, 158, 160, 165, 196, 295, 377
    death of, 534
    with Jack Ruby, 295, 377, 391–392
    meeting with Garrison, 477
    on Ruby ordered to kill Oswald, 403

William Harvey, 196
    also mentioned on pg., 381

Rosenberg, Ethel, 97

Rosenberg, Julius, 97

Rosenfeld, Stephen (senior editorial writer, the *Washington Post*), 504

Ross, Barney, 371

Ross, Thomas B., 170

Rostow, Eugene (Yale law professor), 437

Rothman, Norman "Rough-house," 379–380

Rothstein, Arnold "The Brain," 151

Roundtree, Dovey J. (attorney for Raymond Crump), 537

Rousselot, John, 181

Roux, Michel (French assassin deported from US) *aka* Jean Soutre and Michael Mertz,
    on French connection to the assassination, 192, 194, 197

Rowan, Dan (comedian), 165

Rowland, Arnold L. (witness), 18, 19, 51, 319, 321

Rowland, Mrs. "Barbara" (witness), 18, 19, 51, 319

Rowley, James J. (Secret Service chief), 230–231

Rubenstein, Earl (*see also* Ruby, Earl, brother of Jack Ruby), 373

Rubenstein, Fannie (mother of Jack Ruby), 372

Rubenstein, Hyman (brother of Jack Ruby), 373–374

Rubenstein, Jack (*aka* Jack Ruby), 144, 249, 371–373, 381, 387

Rubenstein, Jacob (birth name of Jack Ruby), 371

Rubenstein, Sam (brother of Jack Ruby), 373

Ruby, Earl, 373, 413

Ruby, Jack,
    accuses LBJ, 412
    background, 370–385
    as "bag man," 552
    entry to basement, 356, 374, 402–405, 502, 552
    and the Cellar, 13, 230–231
    Rose Cheramie, 386
    on Conspiracy quote, 371
    and Cuba, 380–390
    at *Dallas Morning News*, 315–316, 387–388, 398

Ruby, Jack, (*continued*)
  at Dallas YMCA, 520
  in Dealey Plaza, 22, 43, 315, 317
  death of, 410–415
  Thomas Eli Davis, 195–196
  Paul Dorfman, 157
  as FBI informant, 219, 379–385, 493
  James Files, 295
  financial problems, 397
  Gambling connections, 148, 156, 272,
    375–379
  Gangsters, 324–325, 327–328, 333,
    375–379, 483
  Gun runner, 139, 379–385
  held incommunicado, 406
  recognized by Jean Hill, 38, 314
  motive from Tom Howard, 398
  in Hunts office, 327–328
  injection of cancer cells, 414, 532
  Dorothy Kilgallen, 406–407
  letter from jail, 411–412
  meeting with Kathy Kay and Harry
    Olsen, 400
  Lewis McWillie, 159, 167, 272, 380–381,
    383
  and Julia Ann Mercer, 17, 387, 454
  Lawrence Meyers, 328
  mind control, 172, 414
  at midnight news conference, 399–400
  money order to Karen Carlin, 389, 401
  working for Nixon in 1947, 249
  and Beverly Oliver, 36–37, 302, 389
  link with Oswald, 387–396, 543
  and Marguerite Oswald, 92–93, 314,
    387
  at Parkland Hospital after assassination,
    316, 356–358, 398
  reaction to shooting, 405–406
  shooting of Lee Harvey Oswald,
    398–402
  stalking Oswald, 398–402
  Clay Shaw, 469–472
  in Texas Theater, 342
  corrects Henry Wade, 399, 484–485
  Gen. Edwin Walker, 239–240, 387–388
  with Warren Commission, 408–431,
    457–458
  Dr. "Jolly" West, 414
  Roscoe White, 298–300
  in Willis photo, 24, 37, 315
  also mentioned on pgs. xvi, xvii, 99, 147,
    149, 162, 191, 192, 293, 312, 342, 452,
      453, 454, 458, 469, 480, 481, 505, 515,
      521, 533, 534
Ruby, Sam (brother of Jack Ruby, *aka* Sam
    Rubenstein), 384
Rusconi, Jane, 503
Rushing, Ray, 401, 460
Rusk, Dean, 118, 132, 437
Russell, Richard "Dick" (author, *The Man
    Who Knew Too Much*, 1992), 263,
    289–292
Russell, Harold (Tippit witness), 533
Russell, Richard B. (Warren Commission
    member),
  background of, 443
  on commission dilemma, 449
  critical of FBI, 217, 443, 445, 446
  on J. Edgar Hoover, 448
  on Marina Oswald, 122, 462
  opposition to JFK's legislation, 243
  also mentioned on pgs. 451, 462
Russia, 109–127
  history of Communism, 109–110
  and Nosenko (Soviet defector), 124–128
  Oswald in, 91–93, 97, 103, 106, 108–109
  Robert Webster, 111–112
  also mentioned on pgs. 4, 7, 66, 134, 136,
    138, 179–180, 182, 188–191, 199,
    209–210, 219, 241, 258, 261, 268, 288,
    291, 346–347, 411–412, 445, 447,
    449–450, 484, 517, 519, 521–523,
    525–526, 554
Russo, Perry,
  mind alteration by Garrison, 476
  with Shaw and Ferrie, 479
Rutan, Paul R., Jr., 512
"Ruth Ann" (co-conspirator with Loy
    Factor), 293
Rybka, Henry J. (WFAA/ABC affiliate
    cameraman),
  film of Secret Service being waived off
    Kennedy Limo, 232
Ryder, Dial Duwayne, 520

Sabin, Albert, 143
Saenz, Mona B., 533
Saia, Frank "Tickie," 376
Salandria, Vincent, 544
Salas, Luis, 271
Salk, Jonas, 143
Sample, Glen (co-author, *The Man on the
    Sixth Floor*, 1995), 293
Sanders, Barefoot (US attorney.), 451

Sanders, Leonard (author), 546
Sands, Pierre (Military Captain, Deputy
    Director of the NPIC), 511–512
Santiago, Filipe Vidal, 238
Sapp, Charles, 245
Sarti, Lucien (possible French hit-man of
    3 hit-man team who is said to have
    assassinated JFK),
    as "badge man," 81–82, 197–198, 537
Save the Rosenbergs (pamphlet given to
    Oswald), 97
Saxon, James J., 255, 444
Scelso, John (aka John Whitten), 182
Schacht, Hjalmar, 470
Scheim, David E. (author), 248, 263
    and Mafia theory, 483
Schiro, Victor H., 467
Schlesinger, Arthur M. Jr., 478
Schmidt, Larrie, 237
School Book Depository. See Texas School
    Book Depository (TSBD)
Schorre, Al, 300
Schultz, Dutch, 152
Schweiker, Richard (senator), 213, 465
Scofield, Frank L., 271
Scoggins, William (witness), 331–332, 336
Secret Service,
    drinking in the Cellar, 229–234
    history of, 224–229
    and Kennedy assassination, 199–210
    motorcade cars, 8–10
Senator, George (Ruby's business partner),
    376, 401–402
Senseney, Charles, 30
Sergio (CIA field operative), 176–177
Sergio (worker on the Manhattan atomic
    bomb project brother of Jeanne
    Fromenke LeGon), 259
Shah of Iran, 256
Shane, Scott (reporter, the New York Times),
    488
Shaneyfelt, Lyndal L. (FBI photographic
    expert), 488
Shanklin, J. Gordon (Dallas FBI chief),
    211, 217–218, 260, 295, 427
Shaw, Clay (New Orleans Trade Mart
    director),
    background, 469
    with CIA, 191, 471, 483
    as Clay Bertrand, 469, 474, 480
    in Clinton, LA, 145–146
    with David Ferrie, 473–474

Dean Andrews, 480–481
    death of, 479
    Garrison consideration toward, 476
    imperceptible limp, 479
    introduced Gen. Charles B. Cabell, 472
    introduced to Oswald, 240
    Permindex, 469–472
    P.O. Box 19106 in address book, 475
    also mentioned on pgs. 70, 144, 191, 308,
        359, 477, 478, 485, 503, 504, 531, 534
Shaw, J. Gary (researcher),
    on Beverly Oliver, 35–36
    on Charles Harrelson, 326
    discovers contradictory FBI document,
        428
    "umbrella man" theory, 30
    also mentioned on pgs. 197, 238, 243
Shaw, Dr. Robert, 367
Sheets, Richard, 266
Shelley, William H. (Texas School Book
    Depository manager), 46–47, 50, 55
Shelton, Zechariah "Zack" (FBI agent), 296
Sheridan, Walter, 161
Sherman, Dr. Mary, 533
Shevchenko, Arkady N., 126
Shirokova, Rima, 113
Sibert, James W. (FBI agent), 361–364, 367,
    453
Siegel, Benjamin "Bugsy," 152, 159, 375
Simian Immunodeficiency Virus (SV), 43
Similas, Norman (Canadian journalist and
    witness), 22
Simmons, James L. (witness), 452, 479, 543
    and Triple Underpass, 59–60
Simmons, Ronald, 420
Simson, Edward Dr., 172
Sinstra, Frank (singer), 3, 164–165
Single-bullet theory, 458–466
Sirhan, Sirhan, 414, 172
Sitzman, Marilyn (witness), 66–68
Skelton, Royce G. (witness),
    bullet strike in street, 61, 87
Slack, Garland,
    rifle range incident, 520
Slawson, W. David, 102, 450, 525
Smith, "Bill" (Secret Service), 511
Smith, Mrs. Earl, 533
Smith, Joe M. (Dallas police officer and
    witness),
    encounters Secret Service, 76, 83, 309,
        310, 314
Smith, John, 401

Smith, L. C. (Deputy), 18

Smith, Merriman (UPI reporter, noted for using the words *Grassy Knoll* for the first time), 38

"Mr. Smith," 298

Smith, Sergio Archaca. *See* Archaca

Smith, Walter Bedell, 68, 170

Smithwick, Sam, 271

Snyder, Richard E., 110, 114, 118

Socarras, Carlos Prio (Cuban President), 138, 158, 381, 535

Somersett, William (Miami police informant), 244–245

Sorensen, Theodore, 235

Sorrels, Forrest V. (Dallas Secret Service agent), 8, 12, 34, 68, 226, 311, 314, 351, 510

Soutre, Jean (French assassin deported from US) *aka* Michel Roux and Michael Mertz,
    on French connection to the assassination, 193–197

"Sparky" (nickname of Jack Ruby), 371

Speaker, Sandy (witness),
    on Brennan's treatment by Feds, 25
    corroborates Millican, 28
    Millican threats, 309
    also mentioned on pg, 543

Specter, Arlen (Warren Commission attorney),
    attempts to confuse Tomlinson, 354–355
    and CREEP, 252
    interviews Jean Hill, 456–457
    photos and x-rays withheld from the WC, 369
    single-bullet theory "architect," 354–355, 459, 460, 488
    also mentioned on pgs. 408, 449

Spectrographic test, 242, 424–425

Speed (nickname of J. Edgar Hoover), 201

Spiesel, Charles, 480

Sprague, Richard (assassination researcher), 249

Sprague, Richard A. (First Chief Counsel of the HSCA),
    possibilities of subpoenas, 487, 493
also mentioned on pgs. 488–490, 495

Stamps, Roy (radio newsman), 316, 352, 357

Stanton, Sarah D. (witness), 46

Staples, Lou (Dallas talk show host), 535

Starnes, Richard (reporter *Scripps-Howard*), 163

Stassen, Harold, 536

Steadman, Martin, 367

Steinberg, Jeffrey, 471

Stern, Samuel A (WC attorney), 44, 211, 450

Stevenson, Adali, 3, 7, 132, 135

Stevenson, Coke, 271

Stevenson, Jess (Deputy Sheriff), 411

Stiles, John R., 442

Stilwell, Richard, 282

Stimson, Dr. Paul G., 297

Stokes, Louis (HSCA chairman), 490, 496

Stone, Harlan Fiske, 204

Stone, Oliver (director, *JFK*, 1991), 385, 503–506

Storey, Dean, 437

Storey, Robert G., 408

Stovall, R. S. (Dallas detective),
    on mutilated photograph, 238
    searched Paine house, 180

Stover, John, 364

Stringer, John T., 453

Stroud, Martha Jo (assistant US attorney), 56, 64, 459

Stroughton, Cecil, 429

Stuckey, William, 138

Studebaker, R. L. (Dallas Police photographer), 416

Sturgis, Frank, 138, 159, 323, 379, 381, 550

Styles, Sandra (witness), 44, 55–56

Sullivan, Jack, 273

Sullivan, William C. (FBI official, author, *The Bureau*, 1979),
    on Communist Party, 202
    on FBI training, 205
    Hoover gathers damaging material on JFK, MLK, 207–209
    Hoover's reluctance to pursue Mafia, 203
    Lyndon Johnson and Hoover, 207–209
    Oswald note, 218
    shooting death of, 534
    also mentioned on pg., 206, 243

Summers, Anthony (researcher),
    on backyard photos faked, 432
    on defectors, 110–112
    on Delphine Roberts, 221
    on Oswald at Walker talk, 240
    on Secret Service Agents in Dealey Plaza, 309–310, 314
    on Silvia Duran, 185
    on Silvia Odio, 142
    on Spas T. Raikin, 122

on U-2, 110
on William Attwood, 135
on William Gaudet, 188
also mentioned on pgs. 76, 148
Summers, Malcolm (witness), xvi, 310
Surgue, Thomas (historian), 82
Surrey, Robert Allan, 237, 239, 242
Suydam, Hank, 533
Sweatt, Allan (Dallas deputy sheriff), 216, 448
Szulc, Tad (author), 463–464

Tadin, Nicholas, 472
Tague, James Thomas "Jim" (witness), xvi, 62–65, 303, 453, 459, 541, 543
Tannenbaum, Harold, 396
Tannenbaum, Robert (HSCA attorney), 36
Tatro, Edgar F., 428
Tatum, Jack Ray (witness), 338–339
Taylor, Claudia Alta, 269
Taylor, Gary (son-in-law of George DeMohrenschildt, interviewed by the WC), 189–190
Taylor, Maxwell General, 286
Terry, L. R. (witness), 26
Teuter, Werner, 412
Texas School Book Depository (TSBD), 39–49, 415
on electricity going off at TSBD, 43–44
The Sixth Floor Museum, 71, 81, 394, 497, 505, 512
The Men Who Killed Kennedy (1988 documentary produced by Nigel Turner), 81
Thomas, D. B. (Gov't scientist), 500
Thompson, J. Walter, 249
Thompson, Josiah (author), 356, 362, 366, 454
Thompson, Malcolm, 432
Thompson, Mrs. Mary, 379
Thornberry, Homer (US Dist. Judge, El Paso), 292
Thornley, Kerry, 106–107
Thrasher, Gen. Charles O., 470
Tice, Mrs. Wilma (Parkland witness), Ruby at Parkland, 357
Tilson, Tom G. Jr. (Dallas police officer), chases Ruby look-alike, 316–318
also mentioned on pg., 414
Tilson, Judy, 317
Tippit, Jefferson Davis "J. D." (Dallas police officer shot in Oak Cliff),

covered Tom Tilson beat, 316
known by Ruby, 409
possible role of Tippit, 191, 552
shooting of, 330–340
also mentioned on pgs. xvii, 69, 238, 240, 309, 343, 345, 430, 448, 449, 452, 533, 534, 539, 544, 552
Tippit, Mrs., 69
Tito, Marshal, 189
Todd, James, 325
Toland, W. S., 300
Tolson, Clyde (companion of Hoover), 201, 203, 207, 209, 534
Tolstoy, Lev Nikolayevich "Leo," 522
Tomlinson, Darrell C., finds slug at Parkland, 354–356
Tonahill, Joe H., 398, 406, 408
Tourine, Charlie "The Blade," 381
Tower, John, 6
Towner, Jim (photographer), 30
Trafficante, Santos Sr., 155, 158
Trafficante, Santos Jr., and organized crime in Cuba, 156–160
with William Harvey, 196–197
with Russell D. Matthews, 36, 377
with Louis J. McWillie, 325, 377–379, 381, 383, 385
with Richard Nixon, 252
with Tosh Plumlee
with Norman "Roughhouse" Rothman, 379–380
with Jack Ruby, 379–383, 385
with Irwin S. Wiener, 377, 396
also mentioned on pgs. 161, 550
Trask, Richard B. (archivist/author, Pictures of the Pain, 1994), 24, 46, 510, 513
"Tricky Dick," 247. See also Nixon, Richard
Triple Underpass theory, 57, 58
True, Tammi (Mrs. Nancy Powell), 453
Truly, Mildred (Mrs. Roy Truly), 309
Truly, Roy (Depository superintendent)
intimidation of, 309
Limousine hits curb, 10, 26–27
Oswald encounter, 13, 52–53
with Marrion Baker, 27, 52–53, 56, 540
testimony to Warren Commission, 52–53, 56, 540
also mentioned on pgs. 41, 55

Truman, Harry S. (US President),
    1951 attack on, 225
    on CIA, 168–169
    fellow Mason Earl Warren, 438
    National Security Council, 281
    also mentioned on pgs. 207, 228
TSBD, Texas School Book Depository
TSS (CIA's Technical Services Staff), 171
Tunheim, Jack (Minneapolis district judge
    and ARRB head), 507, 513–514
Turner, Nigel (producer, *The Men Who Killed
    Kennedy* documentary, 1988), 81
Tyler, John, 224

U-2 program, 101–103, 109–110, 117, 123,
    134, 283, 535
"Umbrella man," theories of, 29–32
"Uncle Corn Pone" (derisive name for LBJ
    by Kennedy staffers), 275
Underhill, Gary (Intelligence operative)
    reported suicide, 191–192
Union of Soviet Socialist Republics (USSR).
    See Russia

Valachi, Joseph (gangster), 162, 203
Vallee, Thomas Arthur, 225, 323
Vandergriff, Tom, 91
Veciana. *See* Blanch, Antonio Veciana
Ventura, Jesse (MN Governor, actor,
    wrestler, author, *aka* James George
    Janos), 515
Vernon, Robert G., 297
Vietnam and Kennedy administration,
    284–289
Vinson, Chief Justice Fred, 439
Vinson, Robert G (Air Force Sgt. and a
    member of NORAD), 345–346
Vlassov, General Andrei Andreïevitch (Nazi
    backed anti-Communist leader), 259
Voorhis, Jerry, 247
Voshinin, Igor, 261

Wade, Henry (Dallas district attorney),
    corrected by Ruby, 399, 484
    documents linking Ruby and Oswald,
        394–395
    first mention of fingerprints, 423
    knew Jack Ruby, 375
    open-and-shut case, 415
    on Oswald as FBI informant, 215, 448
    more than one person involved, 346, 543
    rifle as Mauser, 418

skirts conspiracy, 346, 407–408
    also mentioned on pgs. 149, 348, 401
Wagenvoord, James (executive editor, *Life*
    magazine), 275
Waldo, Thayer (journalist), 452
Walker, Gen. Edwin A.,
    assassination attempt on, 122, 236–243,
        262, 388
    Lee Harvey Oswald, 181, 236–243, 262,
        388
    retained by CIA, 237–238
    Ruby/Oswald link, 387
    also mentioned on pgs. xvi, 7, 543
Walker, Ira, 401
Walker, Wanda (*Dallas Morning News*
    employee), 315, 398
Wall Street and Kennedy assassination,
    253–255
"Wallace" (*aka* Jack Ruby), 293
Wallace, George (Governor of Alabama),
    7, 243, 485, 495
Wallace, Irving, 109
Wallace, Malcolm "Mac," 293–294
Walle, Marilyn "Delilah," 533
Wallechinsky, David, 109
Walsh, Edmund A., 206
Walter, William S., 212–213
Walther, Mrs. Carolyn (witness), 19–20
Walthers, Eddy R. "Buddy" (Sheriff deputy),
    20, 63, 303, 304, 306, 319, 534
Wantland, Clyde, 271
Ward, Hugh, 474, 533
Wardlaw, T. T., 321
Warner, Roger C., 389
Warren Commission (WC),
    Bowers testimony, 77–78
    Document 205, 18
    formation of, 436–438
    Foster testimony, 57–58
    and Kantor testimony, 316, 356–357
    on Oswald murder, 398–410
    on Oswald palm print on Mannlicher-
        Carcano rifle, 415, 422–429
    on Oswald and Russian language, 104
    on Oswald/Ruby link, 387–396
    on Oswald's stay in Russia, 108–127
    on shell cases evidence, 333–335
    and single-bullet theory, 459–488
    testimony conflicts, 451–458
    on General Walker's assailant,
        236–245
    Willis testimony, 23–24

Warren, Earl (Chief Justice),
  as Chairman WC, 438–440
  death of, 534
  reluctance to chair commission, 438–440, 552
  Jack Ruby interview, 408–412
  as Presidential candidate, 247
  WC blocks other investigations, 552
  WC minutes voicing doubts missing, 462
  also mentioned on pgs. 93, 216, 247
Watson, Marvin, 198, 279
Wayne, John, 104
WC, *See* Warren Commission
Webster, Robert E. (American defector to Russia), 111–112
Wecht, Cyril H. Dr. (coroner),
  intolerable autopsy, 369
  also mentioned on pg., 424
Weigman, Dave (witness), 60
Weinberg, Jim, 374
Weiner, Irwin S., 396
Weisberg, Harold (researcher), 362, 425, 443, 462
Weiss, Mark, 498–499
Weiss, Victor Dr., 386
Weissman, Bernard (wrote anti-JFK ad for Dallas newspaper), 237, 409
Weitzman, Seymour (witness), 75–76, 82, 310–311, 418–419
West, Aase Jean (*aka* Jean West), 328
West, Joseph H. (Dallas PI), 296–297
West, Louis Joyon, Dr. "Jolly" (Professor and Director of UCLA's Neuropsychiatric Institute), 414
West, Robert H. (witness and Dallas Co. Surveyor), 18, 434–435, 455, 511
Westbrook, Karen (witness), 27
Westbrook, W. R. Capt. (Dallas Police), 336–337
Weston, Walter "Wally" (Ruby club emcee), 379, 390–391, 394
Wetli, Charles Dr. (chief medical examiner, Dade County), 296
Whalen, Edward, 473
Whaley, William (cab driver), 331, 336, 533
Wheeler, Earl, 534
Whitaker, Anthony, 530–531
White, J. C. (police officer)
  and Triple Underpass, 58
White, Jack (researcher)
  on Zapruder film, 71
  "badge man" photo, 81

Joseph Milteer, 245
  Harrelson as tramp, 324–325
  on backyard photos, 432–433
White, Geneva (Mrs. Roscoe), 299, 303, 430
White, Ricky Don (son of Roscoe White), 299–303
White, Roscoe Anthony (possible shooter), 299–303, 430, 534
Whitman, Walt, 101
Whitmayer, George Lt. Col., 8
Whitten, John (*aka* John Scelso), 182
WI/ROGUE (cryptonym of CIA employed assassin), 194–195
Wicker, Tom (journalist), 203
Wickersham, George W., 200
Wiener, Irwin S., 377
Wilcott, James (CIA finance officer), 103, 212
Wilkins, George, 104
Wilkinson, Sydney (film post-production expert), 512
Willens, Howard P. (WC staff), 385
Williams, Bonnie Ray (witness), 48–49
Williams, Edward Bennett (Hoffa attorney), 157
Willis, Bill (Ruby musician), 390, 394
Willis, Linda (witness), 23, 24
Willis, Phillip L. (witness),
  background, 23
  "black dog man," 74–75
  Dal-Tex arrest, 327
  single bullet theory, 24, 455
  photographs assassination, 23–24
  photographs Ruby in front of TSBD, 23–24, 315
  on the WC, 453–455, 543
  also mentioned on pgs. xvi, 37, 510
Willis, Rosemary (witness), 23–24
Wilson, Clifford, 265
Wilson, Eugene, 518–519
Wilson, John, 382
Wilson, Steven F. (witness), 44
Wilson, Woodrow, 150, 200
Winborn, Walter L (witness), 60
Wirtz, Alvin, 270
Wise, David, 170
Wise, Wes (witness), 315
Witcover, Jules, 250–251
Witherspoon, Ronnie, 311
Witt, Louis Steven ("umbrella man"), 31–32, 495
Wood, Homer Dr., 520

Wood, John (federal judge), 324–326
Wood, Sterling, 520
Woods, James (FBI agent), 260
Woodward, Mary E. (witness), 27
Worrell, James R. Jr. (witness), 308, 533
Wright, Frank (Tippit witness), 332
Wright, James C. Jr. (Texas District Judge), 524
Wright, Mrs. O. P. (Parkland nurse), 356
Wright, O. P. (Parkland security chief), 356
Wrone, David R., 45, 47

Yablonski, Joseph, 487
Yaras, Dave, 534
Yaras, Sam, 155
Yarborough, Ralph (Senator),
    1963 Texas political scene, 6–8
    denies Youngblood story, 232–234
    location in motorcade, 6, 15
    proximity to JFK, 6
    sluggish SS response, 232
    smelled gun powder, 14, 80
    suggests JFK visit, 5
    treatment by the WC, 455–456, 543
Youngblood, Rufus W. (Secret Service agent),
    reactions to shots, 232
    also mentioned on pg., 8

Zahn, Leo (director and cinematographer expert), 513

Zapruder, Abraham. See also Zapruder film,
    background, 66
    death of, 534
    government compensates Zapruder $16 mil, 71
    Life pays $150,000, 69
    sale to Life magazine, 68–69
    on shots from behind, 67–68
    also mentioned on pgs. xv, 72, 81, 296, 306, 455
Zapruder film (Z film),
    alleged driver as gunman, 228–229
    called into question, 70–71, 509–515
    CIA manipulation of, 71, 434, 508, 541, 549
    frames transposed by Life, 306, 435
    frames transposed by WC, 69
    Garrison obtains, 70, 479
    at NPIC, 511
    Dan Rather's description, 69–70
    umbrella man, 29
    also mentioned on pgs. 15, 23, 24, 25, 66–67, 87, 339, 459, 545
Zavada, Rollie, 510–511
Zoppi, Tony (Dallas Morning News columnist), 398
ZR/RIFLE project (CIA Executive Action program for assassinations), 147, 194–196, 198

Lighten up your emotional, physical, and mental load with simple exercises and rituals.

CLEAN SWEEP

Banishing Everything You Don't Need to Make Room for What You Want

DENNY SARGENT